Everyman, I will go with thee,
and be thy guide

Immanuel Kant

CRITIQUE OF
PURE REASON

A revised and expanded translation
based on Meiklejohn

Edited by
VASILIS POLITIS
Trinity College, University of Dublin

EVERYMAN
J. M. DENT · LONDON
CHARLES E. TUTTLE
VERMONT

Introduction and Chronology © J. M. Dent, 1993

First published in Everyman's Library in 1934
Reissued in 1991
This edition first published in Everyman's Library in 1993

Reprinted 1994, 1996

J. M. Dent
Orion Publishing Group
Orion House
5 Upper St Martin's Lane
London WC2H 9EA
and
Charles E. Tuttle Co. Inc.
28 South Main Street,
Rutland, Vermont 05701, USA

Printed in Great Britain by
The Guernsey Press Co. Ltd, Guernsey, C.I.

British Library Cataloguing-in-Publication Data is available upon request.

ISBN 0 460 87358 X

CONTENTS

Note on the Author and Editor   xiii
Chronology of Kant's Life and Times   xiv
Philosophical Events   xxvi
Introduction by Vasilis Politis   xxvii
Note on the Text and Translation   liii

PREFACE TO THE FIRST EDITION   3
PREFACE TO THE SECOND EDITION   11

INTRODUCTION

I. THE DIFFERENCE BETWEEN PURE AND EMPIRICAL
KNOWLEDGE   30
II. COMMON HUMAN UNDERSTANDING IS ALWAYS IN POSSESSION OF
CERTAIN KNOWLEDGE *A PRIORI*   31
III. PHILOSOPHY STANDS IN NEED OF A SCIENCE WHICH SHALL
DETERMINE THE POSSIBILITY, PRINCIPLES, AND EXTENT OF
HUMAN KNOWLEDGE *A PRIORI*   33
IV. THE DIFFERENCE BETWEEN ANALYTICAL AND SYNTHETICAL
JUDGMENTS   35
V. IN ALL THEORETICAL SCIENCES OF REASON, SYNTHETICAL *A
PRIORI* JUDGMENTS ARE CONTAINED AS PRINCIPLES   37
VI. THE GENERAL PROBLEM OF PURE REASON   39
VII. IDEA AND DIVISION OF A SPECIAL SCIENCE, UNDER THE NAME OF
A *CRITIQUE OF PURE REASON*   42

TRANSCENDENTAL DOCTRINE OF ELEMENTS

PART I: TRANSCENDENTAL AESTHETIC
1 Introductory   48

SECTION I: SPACE

  2   Metaphysical Exposition of the Concept of Space   49
  3   Transcendental Exposition of the Concept of Space   51
  4   Conclusions from the foregoing Concepts   52

SECTION II: TIME

  5   Metaphysical Exposition of the Concept of Time   54
  6   Transcendental Exposition of the Concept of Time   55
  7   Conclusions from the above Concepts   56
  8   Elucidation   58
  9   General Remarks on the Transcendental Aesthetic   61
  10 Conclusion of the Transcendental Aesthetic   68

PART II: TRANSCENDENTAL LOGIC

INTRODUCTION: IDEA OF A TRANSCENDENTAL LOGIC

  I   Logic in general   69
  II Transcendental Logic   71
  III The Division of General Logic into Analytic and Dialectic   73
  IV The Division of Transcendental Logic into Transcendental
        Analytic and Dialectic   75

TRANSCENDENTAL LOGIC: FIRST DIVISION

TRANSCENDENTAL ANALYTIC   76

BOOK I: ANALYTIC OF CONCEPTS   77

CHAPTER I: The Clue to the Discovery of all Pure Concepts of the
    Understanding   77
SECTION I: The Logical Use of the Understanding in general   78
SECTION II: The Logical Function of the Understanding in
                    Judgments   79
SECTION III: The Pure Concepts of the Understanding, or
                    Categories   83

CHAPTER II: The Deduction of the Pure Concepts of the
                    Understanding   91
SECTION I: The Principles of any Transcendental Deduction   91
    Transition to the Transcendental Deduction of the Categories   95

SECTION II: TRANSCENDENTAL DEDUCTION OF THE PURE CONCEPTS
                    OF THE UNDERSTANDING   98
    The Possibility of a Connection in general   98
    The Original Synthetical Unity of Apperception   99

The Principle of the Synthetical Unity of Apperception is the highest
    Principle of all employment of the Understanding 101
What Objective Unity of Self-consciousness is 103
The Logical Form of all Judgments consists in the Objective Unity of
    Apperception of the Concepts which they contain 104
All Sensible Intuitions are subject to the Categories, as Conditions
    under which alone the Manifold of Intuitions can be united in
    one Consciousness 105
Observation 105
A Category has no use in Knowledge other than its Application
    to Objects of Experience 107
The Application of the Categories to Objects of the Senses in
    general 109
Transcendental Deduction of the universally possible employment
    in Experience of the Pure Concepts of the Understanding 114
Result of this Deduction of the Concepts of the Understanding 117
Short view of the above Deduction 118

[FIRST EDITION]

DEDUCTION OF THE PURE CONCEPTS OF THE UNDERSTANDING

SECTION II: *A PRIORI* FOUNDATIONS OF THE POSSIBILITY OF
                    EXPERIENCE 120

Preliminary Remark 121
1 The Synthesis of Apprehension in Intuition 122
2 The Synthesis of Reproduction in the Imagination 122
3 The Synthesis of Recognition in a Concept 124
4 Preliminary Explanation of the Possibility of the Categories, as *a
    priori* Knowledge 128

SECTION III: THE RELATION OF THE UNDERSTANDING TO OBJECTS IN
                    GENERAL, AND THE POSSIBILITY OF KNOWING THEM *A
                    PRIORI* 130

SUMMARY PRESENTATION OF THE CORRECTNESS OF THE DEDUCTION OF
THE PURE CONCEPTS OF THE UNDERSTANDING, AND OF ITS BEING
THE ONLY POSSIBLE DEDUCTION 137

BOOK II: ANALYTIC OF PRINCIPLES 139

INTRODUCTION: The Transcendental Faculty of Judgment in
    general 140

TRANSCENDENTAL DOCTRINE OF JUDGMENT OR ANALYTIC OF
PRINCIPLES 142

CHAPTER I: The Schematism of the Pure Concepts of the
Understanding 142

CHAPTER II: System of all Principles of the Pure Understanding 148

SYSTEM OF THE PRINCIPLES OF THE PURE UNDERSTANDING

SECTION I: The Supreme Principle of all Analytical Judgments 149

SECTION II: The Supreme Principle of all Synthetical Judgments 151

SECTION III: Systematic Representation of all Synthetical Principles of
the Pure Understanding 153
1 Axioms of Intuition 156
2 Anticipations of Perception 159
3 Analogies of Experience 165
A: First Analogy. Principle of the Permanence of Substance 168
B: Second Analogy. Principle of the Succession in Time according
to the Law of Causality 172
C: Third Analogy. Principle of Co-existence, according to the Law
of Reciprocity or Community 185
4 The Postulates of Empirical Thought 190
Refutation of Idealism 194
General Remark on the System of Principles 201

CHAPTER III: The Ground of the Distinction of all Objects in general
into Phenomena and Noumena 205

APPENDIX The Amphiboly of the Concepts of Reflection arising from
the Confusion of the Transcendental with the Empirical
Use of the Understanding 216
Remark on the Amphiboly of the Concepts of
Reflection 220

TRANSCENDENTAL LOGIC – SECOND DIVISION

TRANSCENDENTAL DIALECTIC – INTRODUCTION

I. Transcendental Illusion 233
II. Pure Reason as the Seat of Transcendental Illusion 236
A. REASON IN GENERAL 236

B. The Logical Use of Reason 238
C. The Pure Use of Reason 239

TRANSCENDENTAL DIALECTIC: BOOK I

The Concepts of Pure Reason 243
Section I: Ideas in general 244
Section II: Transcendental Ideas 248
Section III: System of Transcendental Ideas 255

TRANSCENDENTAL DIALECTIC: BOOK II

The Dialectical Inferences of Pure Reason 258

Chapter I: The Paralogisms of Pure Reason 259
Refutation of the Proof of Mendelssohn for the Permanence of the
    Soul 266
Conclusion of the Solution of the Psychological Paralogism 272
General Remark on the Transition from Rational Psychology to
    Cosmology 273

[FIRST EDITION]

FIRST PARALOGISM: SUBSTANTIALITY 276
Criticism of the first Paralogism of Pure Psychology 276

SECOND PARALOGISM: SIMPLICITY 277
Criticism of the Second Paralogism of Transcendental
    Psychology 278

THIRD PARALOGISM: PERSONALITY 283
Criticism of the Third Paralogism of Transcendental Psychology 283

FOURTH PARALOGISM: IDEALITY (WITH REGARD TO
    EXTERNAL RELATION) 286
Criticism of the Fourth Paralogism of Transcendental
    Psychology 286

CONSIDERATION OF PURE PSYCHOLOGY AS A WHOLE, IN
    VIEW OF THESE PARALOGISMS 293

CHAPTER II: The Antinomy of Pure Reason 307

SECTION I: System of Cosmological Ideas   308

SECTION II: Antithetic of Pure Reason   315
   First Conflict of the Transcendental Ideas   317
   Second Conflict of the Transcendental Ideas   322
Third Conflict of the Transcendental Ideas   329
Fourth Conflict of the Transcendental Ideas   334

SECTION III: The Interest of Reason in these Conflicts   341

SECTION IV: The Absolute Necessity of being able to Resolve the
   Transcendental Problems of Pure Reason   348

SECTION V: Sceptical Exposition of the Cosmological Questions
   presented in the four Transcendental Ideas   353

SECTION VI: Transcendental Idealism as the Key to the Solution of
   Cosmological Dialectic   355

SECTION VII: Critical Solution of the Cosmological Conflict of Reason
   with itself   359

SECTION VIII: Regulative Principle of Pure Reason in Relation to the
   Cosmological Ideas   364

SECTION IX: The Empirical Use of the Regulative Principle of Reason
   with regard to all the Cosmological Ideas   368
I   Solution of the Cosmological Idea of the Totality of the
        Composition of Appearances in the Universe   369
II   Solution of the Cosmological Idea of the Totality of the Division of
        a Whole given in Intuition   372
     Concluding Remark on the Solution of the Transcendental
        Mathematical Ideas – and Preliminary Observation to the
        Solution of the Transcendental Dynamical Ideas   374
III Solution of the Cosmological Idea of the Totality of the Derivation
        of World Events from their Causes   376
     Possibility of Causality through Freedom in Harmony with the
        Universal Law of Natural Necessity   379
     Exposition of the Cosmological Idea of Freedom in its Connection
        with Universal Natural Necessity   381
IV   Solution of the Cosmological Idea of the Totality of the
        Dependence of Appearances as regards their Existence in
        general   390
     Concluding Remarks on the whole Antinomy of Pure
        Reason   393

CHAPTER III: The Ideal of Pure Reason 394

SECTION I: The Ideal in general 394

SECTION II: The Transcendental Ideal 396

SECTION III: The Arguments of Speculative Reason in Proof of the
Existence of a Supreme Being 402

SECTION IV: The Impossibility of an Ontological Proof of the
Existence of God 407

SECTION V: The Impossibility of a Cosmological Proof of the Existence
of God 412
Detection and Explanation of the Dialectical Illusion in all
Transcendental Proofs of the Existence of a Necessary Being 418

SECTION VI: The Impossibility of a Physico-Theological Proof of the
Existence of God 422

SECTION VII: Critique of all Theology based upon Speculative
Principles of Reason 427

APPENDIX TO TRANSCENDENTAL DIALECTIC
The Regulative Employment of the Ideas of Pure Reason 433
The Ultimate Purpose of the Natural Dialectic of Human
Reason 448

TRANSCENDENTAL DOCTRINE OF METHOD 467

CHAPTER I: THE DISCIPLINE OF PURE REASON 468

SECTION I: The Discipline of Pure Reason in its Dogmatic Use 470

SECTION II: The Discipline of Pure Reason in its Polemical Use 483

SECTION III: The Discipline of Pure Reason in Regard to
Hypotheses 499

SECTION IV: The Discipline of Pure Reason in Regard to its
Proofs 506

CHAPTER II: THE CANON OF PURE REASON 513

SECTION I: The Ultimate End of the Pure Use of Reason 514

SECTION II: The Ideal of the Highest Good as a Determining Ground
of the Ultimate End of Pure Reason 517

SECTION III: Opinion, Knowledge, and Belief   526

CHAPTER III: THE ARCHITECTONIC OF PURE REASON   532

CHAPTER IV: THE HISTORY OF PURE REASON   542

Suggestions for Further Reading   547
Index   551

NOTE ON THE AUTHOR AND EDITOR

IMMANUEL KANT was born on 22 April 1724 in Königsberg, East Prussia. His father was a saddler and his mother of similar background. He spent virtually all his life in Königsberg, except for the years 1747–54, when he was employed as domestic tutor in provincial households. In 1740 he went to the university in Königsberg where he studied mainly physics and philosophy. In 1755 he was awarded the doctoral degree in philosophy, after which he became a *Privatdozent* (lecturer) at the university. In 1770 he was appointed to the chair of logic and metaphysics, and went on to establish his reputation as one of the greatest modern philosophers. He was twice elected vice-chancellor of the university. Kant gave his last lecture on 23 June 1796. He died on 12 February 1804.

The *Critique of Pure Reason* was soon recognized as one of the most important works in philosophy, introducing a new and highly original approach to the foundations and limits of knowledge. Kant, who was fifty-seven when the *Critique* was first published in 1781, had already written several works, both scientific and philosophical, but the decade of the seventies was entirely dedicated to the preparation of the *Critique*. This is the heart of his mature philosophy and the basis of the two later critiques, the *Critique of Practical Reason* (1788), on the nature of morality, and the *Critique of Judgment*, on the nature of aesthetics and teleology as well as an attempt to unify the previous critiques.

VASILIS POLITIS is lecturer in Ancient and German Philosophy at Trinity College, Dublin. He is a graduate of St John's College and St Anne's College, Oxford, and he has written on Aristotle's ethics.

CHRONOLOGY OF KANT'S LIFE

Year	Age	Life
1724		22 April Immanuel Kant is born in Königsberg
1732–40	8–16	Attends secondary school, mainly studying Latin and theology

CHRONOLOGY OF HIS TIMES

Year	Artistic Events	Historical Events
1725	Pope's edition of Shakespeare Academy of Science founded at St Petersburg	Treaty of Vienna between Austria and Spain Treaty of Herrenhausen between Prussia, England and France
1726	Pope's translation of Homer's *Odyssey* Swift, *Gulliver's Travels*	Treaty of Wusterhausen between Prussia and Austria
1727	German Society founded by Gottshed in Leipzig	War between England and Spain
1728	Pope, *Dunciad*	Foreign Ministry established in Prussia Treaty of Berlin between Prussia and Holy Roman Emperor
1729	J. S. Bach, *St Matthew Passion*	Treaty of Seville between England and Spain
1730	Gottshed, *Critical Art of Poetry for the Germans* Senate House, Cambridge, built by J. Gibbs	Frederick, Crown Prince of Prussia, tries to flee to England but is imprisoned by his father, Frederick William I
1731		Treaty of Vienna between England, Holland, Spain and Austria Maritime Powers guarantee Pragmatic Sanction
1732	Pope, *Essay on Man* (1732–4)	Empire except Saxony, Bavaria and Palatinate guarantees Pragmatic Sanction
1733	Bach, *B-minor Mass*	Conscription introduced in Prussia

Year   *Age*   *Life*

1737   13   Mother dies

1740–47   16–23   Studies mainly physics and philosophy at the
                       university of Königsberg

1746   22   Father dies
                       Kant's first work, *Thoughts on the True Estimation of
                       Living Forces*
1747–54   23–30   Employed as domestic tutor in provincial households

Year	Artistic Events	Historical Events
1734	Voltaire, *Lettres sur les Anglais* Bach, *Christmas Oratorio*	Holy Roman Empire declares war on France
1736		Austria and Russia at war with Turkey
1737	Göttingen University founded by George II	
1737–49	J. Gibbs builds Radcliffe Library, Oxford	
1739	Voltaire, *La Pucelle* (published 1755)	England declares war on Spain
1740	Richardson, *Pamela*	Frederick William I of Prussia dies, succeeded by Frederick II Frederick II abolishes torture and introduces liberty of press and worship
1741	Handel, *Messiah*	Frederick II defeats Austrians and conquers Silesia Treaty between Prussia and France against Austria
1742		Anglo-Prussian alliance
1743	Erlangen University founded	
1744	Hogarth, *Marriage à la Mode*	France declares war on England Alliance between Prussia and France Prussia acquires East Friesland Frederick II invades Saxony and enters Bohemia
1745		Prussia defeats Austria Prussia recognizes Pragmatic Sanction
1746		Austro-Russian alliance against Prussia
1747	Frauenkirche, Dresden, completed by Baehr	Prusso-Swedish alliance
1748	Richardson, *Clarissa* Montesquieu, *Esprit des lois* Gellert, *Fables*	
1749	H. Fielding, *Tom Jones* Bach, *Art of the Fugue*	

Year	Age	Life
1754	30	Returns to Königsberg
1755	31	*Universal Natural History and Theory of the Heavens.* Awarded doctorate for the work *On Fire.* Awarded postdoctoral degree for *Exposition of the First Principles of Metaphysical Knowledge.* Begins lecturing at the university of Königsberg
1756	32	Writes on the earthquake in Lisbon
1758	34	Unsuccessful application for professorship in Königsberg
1759	35	Essay on optimism
1762	38	*False Subtlety of the Four Syllogistic Figures. The One Possible Basis for a Demonstration of the Existence of God.* Begins reading Rousseau. Herder attends Kant's lectures

Year	Artistic Events	Historical Events
1750	Frederick II, *Oeuvres du Philosophe de Sanssouci* Rousseau, *Discours sur les arts et les sciences*	
1751	Linné, *Philosophia Botanica* Thomas Gray, *Elegy Written in a Country Churchyard* The French *Encyclopédie*, edited by Diderot and d'Alembert (1751–72)	England accedes to Austro-Russian alliance against Prussia
1752	Hume, *Political Discourses*	
1753	British Museum founded	
1754	Rousseau, *L'inégalité parmi les hommes* Hume, *English History* (–1762)	Anglo-French war in North America
1755	Lessing, *Miss Sara Sampson* Hume, *Natural History of Religion* Samuel Johnson, *Dictionary of the English Language*	Earthquake at Lisbon End of British alliance with Austria
1756	Holberg, *Le Christianisme dévoilé*	Treaty of Westminster between England and Prussia England declares war on France Frederick II invades Saxony Outbreak of Seven Years' War
1757	*Nibelungenlied*, edited by Bodmer Diderot, *Le Fils Naturel*	Holy Roman Empire, Russia, Poland and Sweden at war with Prussia
1759	Voltaire, *Candide* Lessing, Nicolai and Mendelssohn, *Letters concerning modern literature* Bavarian Academy of Science founded	
1761	Rousseau, *Julie ou la Nouvelle Héloïse*	
1762	Rousseau, *Émile, Contrat Social* Wieland's translation of Shakespeare (1762–6)	

Year	Age	Life
1763	39	*Attempt to Introduce the Concept of Negative Quantities into Philosophy*
1764	40	*Observation on the Feeling of the Beautiful and Sublime. An Inquiry into the Distinctness of the Principles of Natural Theology and Morals*
1766	42	*Dreams of a Spirit-Seer.* Takes up assistant-librarianship in the royal palace
1768	44	*Differentiation of Regions in Space*
1769	45	Declines offer of professorship at the university of Erlangen
1770	46	Declines offer of professorship at the university of Jena. Appointed professor of Logic and Metaphysics at the university of Königsberg. Inaugural dissertation, *On the Forms and Principles of the Sensible and Intelligible World*
1772	47	21 February Letter to M. Herz containing an initial indication of the main idea of the *Critique of Pure Reason.* Gives up librarianship
1778	54	Appointed member of the senate of the university

Year	Artistic Events	Historical Events
1762–63		End of Seven Years' War Prussia cedes Silesia
1763	Voltaire, *Treatise on Tolerance*	
1764	Winckelmann, *History of Ancient Art*	Treaty of Prussia and Russia to control Poland
1766	Goldsmith, *Vicar of Wakefield* Lessing, *Laocoön*	
1767	Lessing, *Minna of Barnhelm* Wieland, *Agathon* M. Mendelssohn, *Phaidon* Sterne, *Tristram Shandy*	
1768	Sterne, *Sentimental Journey*	War between Russia and Turkey (1768–74)
1769	Lessing, *Hamburgische Dramaturgie*	Frederick II meets Josef II of Austria (1769 and 1770)
1772	Lessing, *Emilia Galotti*	First partition of Poland between Prussia and Russia
1773	Goethe, *Göetz von Berlichingen* Herder, *Ven Deutscher Art und Kunst, Über Shakespeare* Klopstock, *Messiah* Bürger, *Leonore*	Boston Tea Party
1774	Goethe, *Sorrows of Werther*	
1776	Klinger, *Storm and Stress* Lenz, *Soldiers* E. Gibbon, *Decline and Fall of the Roman Empire* (1776–88)	American Declaration of Independence
1777		First constitution of USA
1778	Herder's collection of folk-songs F. Burney, *Evelina*	Prussia declares war on Austria on behalf of Bavaria Relief Act for Roman Catholics in England

Year	Age	Life
1781	57	*Critique of Pure Reason* published in May
1783	59	*Prolegomenal to Any Future Metaphysics.* Buys own house
1784	60	*Idea for a Universal History from a Cosmopolitan point of View.* Essay on 'What is Enlightenment?'
1785	61	*Groundwork of the Metaphysics of Morals.* Review against Herder's *Ideas for a Philosophy of the History of Mankind*
1786	62	*Metaphysical Foundations of Natural Science.* Appointed vice-chancellor of the university. Appointed member of the Berlin Academy of Sciences. Essay on *What Does it Mean to Orient Oneself in Thought?*
1787	63	*Critique of Pure Reason,* second edition
1788	64	*Critique of Practical Reason.* Re-appointed vice-chancellor
1790	65	*Critique of Judgment.* Fichte seeks Kant's acquaintance
1793	69	*Religion within the Limits of Reason Alone*

Year	Artistic Events	Historical Events
1779	Lessing, *Nathan the Wise* Goethe, *Iphigenia*	
1780	Frederick II, *De la littérature allemande* Wieland, *Oberon*	Russia and Holland declare armed neutrality between England and USA
1781	Schiller, *The Robbers* Rousseau, *Confessions* J. H. Voss's German translation of Homer's *Odyssey*	Prussia joins League of Armed Neutrality
1783	Schiller, *Fiesco*	Peace of Versailles between England, France, Spain and USA England officially recognizes USA
1784	Schiller, *Cabal and Love*	
1785	Mozart, *Marriage of Figaro*	Commercial treaty between Prussia and USA
1786		Frederick II dies, succeeded by Frederick William II
1787	Schiller, *Don Carlos* Mozart, *Don Giovanni*	
1787–92		Russia and Austria at war against Turkey
1789	Goethe, *Tasso* Blake, *Songs of Innocence*	Fall of the Bastille Declaration of Rights of Man
1790	E. Burke, *Reflections on the French Revolution* Goethe, *Faust, A Fragment*	
1791	J. Boswell, *Life of Johnson* Mozart, *The Magic Flute* T. Paine, *Rights of Man*	
1792		Prussia and Austria at war with France French Republic proclaimed
1793		Reign of Terror begins

Year	Age	Life
1794	70	Appointed member of the St Petersburg Academy of Sciences
1795	71	*Perpetual Peace*
1796	72	23 June Kant's last lecture
1797	73	*Metaphysics of Morals*
1798	74	*Anthropology from a Pragmatic Point of View*
1799	75	Writes against the philosophy of Fichte
1804	79	12 February Kant dies

Year	Artistic Events	Historical Events
1794	Schiller, *Letters concerning the aesthetic education of mankind* Beginning of friendship with Goethe	
1795		Napoleon Bonaparte made commander of the French army
1796	Goethe, *Wilhelm Meister's Apprenticeship* Haydn, *Emperor Quartet*	Bonaparte defeats Austrians Treaty between Prussia and France
1797	Hölderlin, *Hyperion*	Frederick William II dies, succeeded by Frederick William III
1798	Wordsworth and Coleridge, *Lyrical Ballads*	
1799	Schiller, *Wallenstein* Schleiermacher, *Sermons concerning Religion*	
1800	Beethoven, *First Symphony*	
1801		Peace between France and Austria
1802		Peace between Britain and France Russia and France agree on redistribution of Germany
1803		Russia and Turkey make peace with France Reconstruction of Germany (*Reichsdeputationshauptshluss*)
1804	Schiller, *William Tell*	Napoleon becomes Emperor

PHILOSOPHICAL EVENTS

1561 Francis Bacon (–1626)
1564 Galileo Galilei (–1642)
1588 Thomas Hobbes (–1679)
1596 René Descartes (–1650)
1597 Bacon, *Essays*
1632 Baruch Spinoza (–1677)
     John Locke (–1704)
1641 Descartes, *Meditations*
1642 Isaac Newton (–1727)
1651 Hobbes, *Leviathan*
1646 Gottfried W. Leibniz (–1716)
1668 Giambattista Vico (–1744)
1677 Spinoza, *Ethics*
1685 George Berkeley (–1753)
     Leibniz, *Discourse on Metaphysics*
1687 Newton, *Principia*
1690 Locke, *An Essay Concerning Human Understanding*
1704 Leibniz, *New Essays on Human Understanding* (critique of
     Locke's *Essay*)
1710 Berkeley, *A Treatise Concerning the Principles of Human
     Knowledge*
     Thomas Reid (–1796)
1711 David Hume (–1776)
1712 Jean-Jacques Rousseau (–1778)
1714 Leibniz, *Monadology*
1739 Hume, *A Treatise on Human Nature*
1744 Johann Gottfried Herder (–1803)
1748 Jeremy Bentham (–1832)
1762 Rousseau, *The Social Contract, Émile*
     Johann Gottlieb Fichte (–1814)
1770 G. W. F. Hegel (–1831)
1784 Herder, *Ideas towards a Philosophy of History of Mankind*
1788 Arthur Schopenhauer (–1860)
1806 John Stuart Mill (–1873)
1807 Hegel, *Phenomenology of Spirit*

INTRODUCTION

1. Kant and his Predecessors

How can we know what things are truly like? By means of the senses and experience alone? Or by means of pure reason, reason employed independently of sense-experience? This, very simply stated, is the dispute between empiricism and rationalism. The dispute, in one form or another, is as old as philosophy. Plato thought that if we want to know what it is for a person to be just or for something to be beautiful, and in general if we want to know the unchanging nature of something, we must investigate the issue by means of reason alone, untainted by the senses. Against this view are those he mockingly calls 'lovers of sounds and spectacles', empiricists of his day (see *Republic* 475–76 and *Phaedo* 65–66).

Kant's philosophy was a lifelong struggle between empiricism and rationalism. This was not a mere academic dispute, it involved his whole person, and the determination that went into it is impressive. At the time Kant was writing the *Critique of Pure Reason* Goethe was casting Faust, one of his most elemental creations, as torn irreconcilably between the life of reason, confined to the study and the desk, and the life of experience, conducted out in the open. There is something elemental in Kant's struggle, but with the difference that Kant never left the study or felt the urge to do so. There was room enough in his imagination. It is curious that Kant, who appears to have had no great desire to travel and who is known for never having been beyond the remoter provinces of his native Prussia, was a keen and sensitive reader of the accounts of travellers, and a student of geography and anthropology, subjects in which he became a gifted and popular lecturer. But Kant set his eyes on reconciling the pulls of reason and experience. His lasting philosophical achievement is to have attempted, perhaps even successfully, to reconcile empiricism and rationalism. The *Critique of Pure Reason*, in which he undertook the attempt, is for that reason alone a landmark in the history of philosophy.

With Plato and Aristotle there is no serious worry about whether we could know what things are truly like; the question for them is what role reason and experience play in such knowledge. But with modern philosophy, certainly since Descartes, scepticism about knowledge had become a worry, perhaps the main worry (see Descartes' *Meditations*). How do we know what the world is truly or objectively like, as opposed to how it appears to us? How do we know that the world answers to our concepts of it? While scepticism goes back to Hellenistic or post-Aristotelian philosophy, the sixteenth century saw its revival, encouraged by the rediscovery of ancient sceptical writings. But Descartes took scepticism further and questioned the very existence of an objective world, a world to be distinguished from how the world appears to us. He did so in the hope of discovering something solid and indubitable to hold on to in order to show that the world does answer to our view of it, at least to our best view of it. Descartes' sceptical journey is thus only provisional and is meant to lead to unshakable objective certainty.

This is a journey of pure reason and it invokes a twofold use of reason. First we must use reason to examine our concepts and to purify them. Descartes calls such purified concepts 'clear and distinct ideas'. Perhaps nothing in the world corresponds to our concept of a tomato, but this concept is complex, so perhaps something corresponds to the concepts that make it up. Perhaps nothing corresponds to our concept of the colour red; perhaps things are not really coloured at all. But what about the concept of something round and in general of something extended and shaped, together with its properties as defined by geometry. Could the physical world fail to exhibit geometrical properties? Descartes uses reason to purify concepts along these lines and he concludes that, if we can know what things are truly like, all we can know about them is that they are extended and capable of motion, so geometry and mechanics will make up the proper science of things.

Should we fail to know even that, we will, Descartes argues, still know that there are extensionless minds that think, like the mind of Descartes. One must exist, at least as an extensionless mind, in order to be thinking. But such knowledge is by itself small consolation if what we want is knowledge of what things are truly like, for it does not tell us whether our thoughts or concepts are true of anything. Perhaps there is no world for even our best concepts to be true of. How, then, are we to know whether there is a world answering to our best and most purified concepts? Here we must use reason to become certain of God's existence. Only God could guarantee that there is a world agreeing with our best concepts, while God, being not deceitful but perfectly good, can also be relied on to exercise his capacity and to create such a world.

Descartes' world is a good example of the impoverished and colourless world that one is left with if one is only prepared to use reason alone to discover what things are truly like. But does Descartes' journey of pure reason succeed? It has to rely on God, so it has to rely on the belief that something really exists corresponding to our concept of God. But, remember, only God could guarantee the correspondence between our concepts and things that really exist. So we could never know whether God exists since we would need to assume his existence in order to show that he exists. Reason has let us down where we most needed it: in our desire to know whether our best concepts of the world are indeed true of the world, or, in Kant's words, whether they are *objectively valid*.

Kant's critical philosophy is in fundamental and conscious disagreement with Cartesian dualism, i.e. the separation that Descartes creates between an external and material world, whose defining characteristic is extension, and an inner and immaterial world – the mind – which is extensionless and whose defining characteristic is thinking. Kant argues that there is just one world, the world that we experience, and that we who experience it and think about it are just one of its ingredients – the familiar persons in experience rather than immaterial minds. Cartesian dualism separates how the world appears to us in experience from the very world that appears to us in experience. It turns how the world appears to us in experience into peculiar kinds of entities, appearances, whose existence is not tied to the existence of a world. Conversely, it turns the world into an entity distinct from and independent of how the world appears to us in experience. Kant's *Critique* is an extended effort to overcome this dualism. The world and how the world appears to us in experience are not two distinct and independent kinds of entities; rather they are aspects of a single thing, a world capable of being experienced. It follows that to understand the notions of appearance and reality, we must understand both notions in relation to each other. So, on the one hand, Kant argues that a world is necessarily capable of appearing to us in experience; on the other hand, he argues that we can describe such things as appearances only if the latter are of a world and not if they are cut off from a world. This last claim is perhaps the most important claim in the *Critique*, namely that we can describe what we experience only if our experience is objective, is experience valid of a world.

Descartes' dualism is one important target of the *Critique*. An equally important target is the idealism of Hume and Berkeley. Idealism grows directly out of dualism. Having separated the mind and its ideas from the world, dualism still holds onto the notion of a world separate from the mind and its ideas. It does so in the trust that we may know, by the use of reason alone, that there exists such a world and what it is like. Hume does not have such trust in reason. He argues, plausibly and perhaps rightly, that once we have separated ideas from the world, we can have access only to our ideas (see Hume's *Treatise*). What a world separate from our ideas is like or whether it exists at all is not something we could possibly know. Hume is ready to accept the result: all we have access to in experience and thought is our ideas, the contents of our minds. The notion of a world separate from our mind and its ideas is one that we should give up as being of no interest or use. So all that exists, according to idealism, is minds and their ideas. Hume, notably, went as far as claiming that only ideas exist and that the mind itself can be understood simply in terms of ideas. But he was concerned that this might be going too far, and one wonders whether he appreciated the full implication of his claim. Idealism without minds ceases to be idealism proper and turns into phenomenalism, a related but importantly different position.

Idealism, we have seen, grows naturally out of dualism. But dualism and idealism share a fundamental assumption. They both assume that the distinction between the world and how the world appears to us is a distinction between two distinct and independent kinds of entities, ideas or appearances as distinct from the so-called external world. The disagreement between dualism and idealism should not make us overlook the underlying agreement, and this is precisely Kant's target. In arguing that the world and how the world appears to us in experience are not two distinct things but two sides of one thing, Kant is arguing against dualism and idealism at once. This is a striking and brilliant move. We might be inclined to think that dualism and idealism are all there is to choose between here: either we can know something about the external world and can reach beyond our ideas (dualism), or we cannot know anything about an external world and can have access only to our ideas (idealism). Kant asks us to refuse the choice. The choice is forced on us by the underlying assumption of a separation between appearance and reality, and this separation, Kant argues, is mistaken. This is well-worth emphasizing. It means that Kant does not so much intend to respond to the challenge of Descartes' extreme scepticism by answering the question: 'Can we have access to anything beyond the contents of our minds?' either in the affirmative, as did Descartes, or in the negative, as did Hume and Berkeley. Rather Kant thinks the question is ill-conceived. This is indeed a characteristic of his critical approach in general: to be critical of the question before you set off in search of an answer.

In Kant's view the question should be: 'Are we properly entitled to draw a distinction between the world and how the world appears to us?' But while claiming that two things are distinct certainly entails drawing a distinction between them, drawing a distinction between two things need not amount to claiming that they are distinct. We need only think of the distinction between the face and its expression, its look. Kant often reminds us that in drawing a distinction between the world and how the world appears to us, he does not mean a world separate from appearances, 'a world *in itself*' as he calls it, nor does he mean appearances existing in a mind separate from the world. The notion of 'things in themselves' occupies an important position in Kant's moral philosophy, and in the *Critique* he wants to leave room for and even to prepare for this later positive use of the notion. But in the *Critique* itself, where he is concerned not with practical but with theoretical philosophy, no positive use is made of the notion, and he is emphatic that here it is empty of all content. Moreover, he thinks the belief in a separate mind, a Cartesian self or ego, is sheer illusion.

Why is it important for Kant to defend the notion of objectivity, of a world to be distinguished from, though not distinct from, how the world appears to us? We must ask what the view is which maintains, against Kant, that the notion of a world is to be understood entirely in terms of how things appear to us, in purely phenomenal terms. This view, phenomenalism, does not, or need not necessarily, separate appearance and reality, so it can agree with Kant that the world is capable of appearing to us in experience. But, according to phenomenalism, to talk of a world capable of appearing to us in experience is simply to talk of how things appear to our senses. To describe the world that we experience in this way is to use only certain kinds of concepts, concepts which leave no conceivable room for doubting whether they are applicable to the world that we experience. Kant calls such concepts 'empirical concepts', and phenomenalism is certainly an extreme form of empiricism. Kant's target here is again Hume, but now the precise target is Hume's phenomenalism rather than his idealism. Such empirical or phenomenal concepts will include above all those of perceptual qualities peculiar to each sense, i.e. of the things that we cannot perceive by more than one sense: colours and shapes by sight, sounds by hearing, texture and heat or cold by touch, etc. Since it is plausible to think that these are the only concepts that leave no conceivable room for doubt as to whether they apply to the world that we experience, every description of the world will, according to phenomenalism, take the form 'At this moment I am seeing what appears to be something red', 'At this moment I am hearing what appears to be something shrill', 'At this moment I am feeling what appears to be something hard and cold', etc.

It is important to distinguish between phenomenalism and idealism. Kant argues against phenomenalism that we need to distinguish between appearance and reality, but he does not conceive of the distinction as a distinction between mind and matter, as it is conceived in idealism. Idealism and phenomenalism agree in limiting knowledge to appearance. Idealism is an answer to the question 'What are the basic things that exist?' It is in this sense an ontological position, as when the Pre-Socratics asked whether all that exists is basically water, air, or whatever. The basic things that exist are either minds and matter (dualism) or only minds (idealism). Phenomenalism, by contrast, provides an idiom for describing anything that exists ('At this moment I am seeing what appears to be something red', etc.). It is an answer to the question 'What is it for something to exist?' To exist is to be describable in phenomenal terms. Phenomenalism is in this sense a definitional or metaphysical position. Idealism entails phenomenalism and is therefore a suitable way of supporting phenomenalism. In this way the idealism of Berkeley and Hume supports their phenomenalism, though aspects of Hume also suggest an attempt to adopt phenomenalism without idealism. In our century advocates of phenomenalism have generally wanted to divorce phenomenalism from idealism and indeed from any ontology. The distinction between phenomenalism and idealism (or a precursor to idealism) is classically drawn in Plato's *Theaetetus* (151–87), a dialogue whose central question is precisely 'What is knowledge?' Like Kant, Plato is anxious to refute phenomenalism. Plato's refutation in fact anticipates Kant's, arguing that phenomenalism cannot account for the fact that experience is undergone by a single person or mind and not by a collection of unconnected senses, and, further, that phenomenalism cannot account for the notion of judgment (184–7).

Is phenomenalism an unduly restrictive idiom for describing the world that we experience? Kant thought it was. Phenomenalism appears to leave out certain concepts that figure prominently and pervasively in our description of the world, in particular the concept of a substance. The *something* that we experience according to phenomenalism (as in 'At this moment I am seeing what appears to be something red') is an object only in a highly attenuated sense, barely distinguishable from how it appears to be perceptually qualified. Phenomenal objects are quite peculiar. They cannot possess perceptual qualities perceived by different senses. If I am experiencing a green, hard, cold apple, I am, according to phenomenalism, really experiencing three things that just happen to be experienced together, and that are perhaps commonly experienced together. Moreover, phenomenal objects cannot change their perceptual quality without ceasing to be the same object. If what I am seeing changes from being red to being a blue colour patch, I can no longer be said to be seeing the same colour patch since, within phenomenalism, the colour patch is specified simply in terms of how things appear to my senses, that is to say in terms of its colour. Further, it makes no sense to apply the notion of *numerical* identity to phenomenal objects, and in particular it makes no sense to say that numerically the same object is perceived from different perspectives by different observers. To say that you and I are perceiving the same colour patch from different perspectives is simply to say that it appears to us that things are *qualitatively* the same, say red, when we face in a certain direction. Finally, it makes no sense to say of phenomenal objects that they persist in time, for to talk of objects persisting in time requires the notion of numerical identity (as in 'The person I met yesterday was you, not your qualitatively identical twin'), and this is a notion we are not entitled to here. In sum, phenomenalism asserts that in describing what we experience we are merely reporting how things, phenomenal objects, appear to our senses.

Contrast substances. The unity of a substance is not undermined by its possessing perceptual properties perceived by different senses. The one apple is both green and hard. The identity of a substance is not undermined by its changes in its perceptual properties. The one tomato changes from being green to being red in ripening. The notion of numerical identity is essential for understanding the notion of a substance: the numerically same substance can be perceived from different perspectives by different observers and can persist in time. In sum, by describing what we experience in terms of substances, we are not reporting how things, phenomenal objects, appear to our senses; we are rather judging how things, substances, are. This notion of *judgment* is central to Kant's criticism of phenomenalism.

The question is whether phenomenalism can account for or even allow talk of substances. According to Hume, phenomenalism can allow this only if our talk of substances is radically revised or re-interpreted. Kant agrees. To describe the world that we experience in terms of substances is not to describe it merely in terms of how things appear to us in experience, for there is room for doubting whether our concept of a substance is valid of the world that we experience. One may raise this doubt by arguing, as Hume does, that in saying that we experience substances what we are really doing is imposing an order on phenomenal objects, without, however, having any justification for imposing such an order. Phenomenalism is thus a revisionist position which either completely jettisons our talk of substances or which re-interprets this talk in terms of an idiom in which the notion of a substance does not figure fundamentally.

Kant is not prepared for such revision. The concept of a substance is, he thinks, both objectively valid and primitive; it is neither to be given up nor to be re-interpreted in purely phenomenal terms. His insistence on the need to distinguish between the world and how the world appears to us is a consequence of the distinction, which he develops against the background of Hume and phenomenalism, between concepts that are indisputably valid of the world that we experience because they can readily be defined merely in terms of how things appear to us in experience, and disputable concepts which cannot be shown to be objectively valid in this way. Kant calls the latter *a priori* concepts, which is a way of saying that they cannot be shown to be objectively valid by appeal to experience. In setting out to defend the objective validity of these disputed concepts, Kant is arguing for a distinction between how the world appears to us, to be described in purely phenomenal terms, and the world that appears to us, to be described in terms of substances. Kant, then, is faced with the challenge of showing how concepts which cannot be defined merely in terms of how things appear to us in experience can nonetheless be valid of the world that we experience. The *Critique* is a sustained attempt to meet this challenge. 'How is synthetic *a priori* knowledge possible?' Kant asks at the outset, as the central and guiding question of the inquiry. The question means 'How is it possible to show that *a priori* concepts, i.e. concepts that cannot be defined merely in terms of how things appear to us in experience, are nonetheless synthetic, i.e. valid of objects that we experience?'

2. *Kant's Development*

How did Kant come to ask the central question of the *Critique*, 'How is synthetic *a priori* knowledge possible?' Kant was fifty-seven when the *Critique* was published in May 1781. He had already written a number of larger works, though of lesser importance compared to the *Critique of Pure Reason* or the critiques that followed it (*Critique of Practical Reason*, 1788; *Critique of Judgment*, 1790). He had, however, written hardly anything during the preceding decade, the silent years of the seventies. He had been grappling with what he saw to be crucially important and which proved more intractable than he had expected. We gather from his letters that this was precisely the question of how concepts, such as those of substance or causality, which cannot be defined simply in terms of how things appear to us in experience, are nevertheless applicable to the world that we experience. In the early seventies Kant was confident that the answer was within immediate reach, but in fact it took several years before he was satisfied that he had provided the solution.

Kant was appointed professor at the university of Königsberg as late as 1770, and his new position would have helped him pursue the central question at his own pace. He was very much a self-made man, and resolution, perseverance and independence of mind and character were traits he valued particularly. He saw himself in the light of a Stoic ideal, modified by a tendency to melancholy but also by a good portion of wit. He had come from an artisan family of saddle-makers, whose means were moderate or humble. Later he remembered his mother as an example of simple piety and quiet goodwill. During his formative years he was encouraged by the vicar F. A. Schultz, who recommended him for the Gymnasium and supervised his education there, consisting mainly in Latin and the

Latin authors, for whom Kant retained a special affection, especially
the poets whom he would quote from memory. Later, while a
student at the university of Königsberg, which was not in general a
centre of intellectual activity, the highly gifted but prematurely-
deceased teacher M. Knutzen introduced Kant to the philosophy of
Leibniz and above all to Newtonian science. It was during this
period that Kant contributed a work on physical force and its
measurement. After he completed his studies in 1746 at the age of
twenty-two, there followed seven years of service as domestic tutor
in various provincial households, first at a vicar's, then at a major's,
finally at a count's. Such a career meant that you were accomplished
but penniless, and some of the most able minds, such as Hegel or
the poet Hölderlin, had later to suffer similar precarious years.
Kant, however, appears to have come through the experience
surprisingly well and even to have found room for his mainly
scientific research. He remained popular and at ease with the
professional classes throughout his life, and preferred to spend his
spare time in such company, mainly by way of dining followed by
hours of conversation. It was only relatively late in life that Kant
became gradually more withdrawn, as we know him from contemporary descriptions and portraits, clearly under the strain of devel-
oping his mature philosophy. Kant returned to Königsberg in 1754
to teach at the university as Privatdozent. The title meant above all
an inordinate workload, sometimes up to thirty lectures a week,
and it meant that the lecturer depended on the number and
generosity of his students, whom, therefore, he had very good
reason to attract. Kant taught mathematics and physics, every area
of philosophy, as well as geography and anthropology. He remained
in a similar position until 1770.

In 1755 Kant published two major works, on science and on the
fundamental principles of science, in particular the principle that
there is a reason or cause for everything that exists or happens, the
principle of sufficient reason (*Universal Natural History and Theory
of the Heavens* and *New Exposition of the First Principles of
Metaphysical Knowledge*). In the *Natural History* Kant proposed a
theory of evolutionary cosmology, arguing that the system of
heavenly bodies could have developed from an unformed nebula.
The theory is an original contribution, later defended by P. S.
Laplace. The *First Principles* shows Kant's growing preoccupation
with philosophical issues at the root of science. Science does not
merely describe how things appear to us in experience, it assumes

that things are subject to explanation. Kant defends the assumption as self-evident, indeed as analytic, that is to say as true by virtue of the concepts it employs, so that to deny it is self-contradictory. The defence is in line with Leibniz's view that fundamental truths can be defended on conceptual grounds alone. Leibniz argued that the principle of sufficient reason is true by virtue of the concept of the proposition or judgment, i.e. by virtue of the concept of asserting that something is the case. We must, Leibniz points out, have a reason for thinking that a proposition is true rather than false, i.e. for asserting rather than denying that something is the case (an epistemic reason or *ratio cognoscendi*); and to this reason there will, Leibniz thought, correspond a reason in nature for why something is the case, why something exists or happens (a cause or *ratio essendi*).

In the 1750s, then, Kant follows Leibniz, whose work he knew mainly through the lesser thinker C. Wolff. There is still no trace of Kant's later critical or sceptical challenge, where he insists that to defend a principle as true by virtue of the concepts it employs (as analytic) is not yet to show that it has any application to reality, for one has not yet shown that the concepts it employs apply to reality, i.e. that they are objectively valid. For example, it is analytically true that all bachelors are unmarried men, but the objective validity of this truth depends not on its being analytic but on the fact that the concept of an unmarried man is readily and indisputably applicable to objects. By contrast, Kant came to appreciate that it is possible to dispute the objective validity of concepts such as those of substance, of reasons, and in general of judgment as to how things or substances are, as opposed to reporting how things or phenomenal objects appear to one. Such disputed concepts stand in need of defence beyond mere analysis of them and expression of the analysis in analytic truths. We may recall Leibniz's move from there being a reason for thinking that something is the case (an epistemic reason) to there being a cause for something being the case (a reason in reality, i.e. a cause), the move Leibniz relies on in arguing that the principle of sufficient reason is objectively valid. Kant is questioning this central move, he is asking why we should think that there is anything in reality corresponding to our practice of demanding that people should have a reason for asserting what they assert.

Leibniz was not oblivious to the problem of moving from knowledge of concepts (analytic knowledge) to knowledge of objects (synthetic knowledge). He addressed the problem by arguing that, fundamentally, there is no distinction between knowing concepts and knowing objects. The distinction, which is central to Kant's critical philosophy, Leibniz thinks is a symptom of our occupying a limited perspective on reality, the perspective of space and time in sense-experience. In aspiring to a properly scientific description of reality, we must abstract from this perspective and describe things *sub specie aeterni*, as if from a godlike position. Leibniz's rejection of the distinction between knowledge of concepts and knowledge of objects is a consequence of his view that to be true is to be provable, which means in particular that for a predicate to be true of a subject is for the concept of the predicate to be contained in the concept of the subject, so that analysis of the subject-concept will reveal the predicate-concept as part of it. For example, if it is true that all human beings are mortal, this must, according to Leibniz, be true by virtue of the concept of a human being, analysis of which would reveal mortality as part of the concept. Such analysis may not be available from our limited perspective, but Leibniz trusts it is available from a godlike position. We might say that according to Leibniz all truth is analytic, but it would be better to avoid the terms analytic and synthetic to characterise Leibniz's position. For Kant, analytic truth is trivial truth – truth merely by virtue of the concepts we happen to employ as speakers of this or that language. A concept is the meaning of a word, and to analyse concepts is to analyse such meanings. This is clearly not what Leibniz means by a concept, which is for him rather the minimal account of something, the account that captures the core of the nature of that thing. Analysing concepts means gaining a properly scientific account of things.

Leibniz's account of truth is more plausible when we consider universal propositions, such as 'All men are mortal', especially if we think that such truths are based not on enumeration ('Bill is mortal', 'Jane is mortal', ...) but on scientific knowledge of the nature of things, in this case human beings. The account is much less plausible when we consider singular propositions, such as 'The current US president will be elected for a second term'. One could not establish such a proposition by appeal to the concept or to the nature of human beings in general, and it is not clear whether there is such a thing as the concept or nature of the president in particular, that is to say of individuals as opposed to species. This is a crucial objection to Leibniz's view, for it is arguable that only singular propositions refer to anything existing while universal propositions are merely hypothetical ('If human beings exist, they are mortal'). So it is only if Leibniz's account of truth holds for singular propositions that it can provide an account of things that really exist.

Leibniz's answer is to argue that in making a concept progressively more determinate and specific, as when we move from the concept of animal to that of mammal to that of human being, we will eventually obtain a concept of a single individual substance, say the US president. A full specification of a concept will, therefore, be a full account of an object, so that knowledge of concepts and knowledge of objects will eventually coincide. One may think of the concept of H_2O, which applies to a single thing, the one aggregate – water, which happens to be dispersed over many seas, lakes, pools, jugs, etc. Leibniz calls concepts applicable to just one individual thing or substance 'complete individual concepts', and he goes on to apply his view of truth to them: 'God, seeing the individual concept of Alexander, sees in it at the same time the foundation of and reason for all the predicates which can truly be asserted of him'(*Discourse on Metaphysics*, section 8).

Leibniz's view presupposes that it is not essential for our referring to objects that we should do so by identifying them within a spatio-temporal framework in experience. Indeed, this empirical way of referring to objects must, if Leibniz's view is correct, be only a symptom of our not having adopted a properly scientific description of things. For however determinate and specific one makes the concept of an object of the senses, say of a raindrop as perceived, the concept may apply to an indefinite number of objects (raindrops at different places or times), and an individual raindrop will have various properties that could not be specified in the concept of a raindrop, namely those properties that it has by virtue of being in space and time (say its being ready to turn into snow). Thus Leibniz is denying two mutually dependent theses that are central to Kant's critical philosophy: (1) a full specification of a concept could not suffice for a full account of an object; and (2) we can refer to objects only by identifying them within a spatio-temporal framework in sense-experience. Kant began to develop these theses in the sixties and in doing so he turned away from the Leibnizian legacy. If there is a godlike perspective, only God is fit to occupy it, while we must remain firmly rooted to earth.

In the course of the sixties Kant wrote a number of important works, part of whose thrust is to develop and consolidate the distinction between concept and object and the corresponding distinction between analytic and synthetic knowledge. This productive period of reorientation ends with the inaugural dissertation of 1770, Kant's defence of his new academic position. Here he argues that our capacity to know things must be divided into two capacities: sensibility, the capacity of referring to objects by experiencing them within a spatio-temporal framework; and understanding, the capacity to bring objects under general concepts, in particular concepts that cannot be defined simply in terms of how things appear to us in experience. The dissertation is an initial statement of Kant's qualified empiricism, directed against Leibniz's rationalism as well as against extreme empiricism or phenomenalism. It is not clear how well Kant knew Hume in 1770. The qualified empiricism may rather have been influenced by, and been a response to, the empiricism of C. A. Crucius. The trouble with the inaugural dissertation is that it fails to connect the two fundamental capacities for knowledge, sensibility and understanding, to show how they are co-operatively involved in knowledge. Moreover, Kant's refusal to take empiricism the whole way is dogmatic. As J. H. Lambert complained to Kant in a letter of October 1770, Kant has failed to defend the central claim that concepts of the understanding, concepts which cannot be defined simply in terms of how things appear to us in experience, are applicable to anything, in particular to the world that we experience. Why should one not take empiricism the whole way and argue that our knowledge of objects is confined to experiencing and describing things simply in terms of how they appear to us in experience, i.e. in purely phenomenal terms? By early 1772 Kant had fully taken in the complaint. He writes to Marcus Herz that Hume has awakened him from dogmatism and has challenged him to argue for the central claim, the mitigation of empiricism. Kant worked in silence on the challenge for the next nine years.

3. The Critical Method

The *Critique of Pure Reason* is above all an answer to the question 'How is synthetic *a priori* knowledge possible?' The aim in raising this question is to determine in what way or ways we can establish whether a concept is objectively valid, whether it is applicable to anything, so that we can use the concept to describe things and in that sense know things ('synthetic' here means 'applicable to objects' or simply 'of objects'). Kant's distinctive answer is clear and striking. There are, Kant thinks, two ways of establishing that a concept is objectively valid: an empirical and a transcendental way (cf. A95). One uncontroversial way is by defining the concept in terms of what we experience, in particular in terms of how things appear to us in experience. The concept of something red, say, is defined in this way. Identifying objects in sense-experience is a way, in fact Kant thinks it is the only way, of referring to objects. It follows that defining a concept in terms of how things appear to us in sense-experience is a way of ensuring that the concept will refer to and be applicable to things that we experience. Kant calls this way of establishing the objective validity of concepts 'empirical', and so far he is following standard empiricism, for example that of Hume.

How could there be another way of determining whether a concept is objectively valid? One might suggest, in a rationalist spirit, that we may refer to objects in some way other than by experiencing them or being able to experience them. In that case we would describe them by using concepts that have no application to what we refer to in experience and which for that reason could not be defined in terms of what we experience. But Kant is emphatic that experience is our only way of referring to objects, so he denies that a concept that has no application to what we experience could have any other application. As he puts it epigrammatically, concepts without intuitions (i.e. without sense-impressions) are empty, they have no application to anything (A52/B76; the precise quote is 'Thoughts [i.e. concepts] without content [i.e. intuitions] are empty').

It is here that we encounter Kant's distinctive suggestion: a concept can apply to what we experience even if it cannot be defined in terms of what we experience; it may do so by being a necessary condition for the possibility of experiencing things and of using concepts to describe what we experience. Kant calls this way of establishing objective validity of concepts 'the *a priori* or *transcendental* way'. 'Transcendental' means 'concerning the necessary conditions for the possibility of experiencing things and of describing what we experience' (cf. A13/B26). This is Kant's distinctive method and his break with unqualified empiricism.

The method is *a priori* or independent of experience in the sense that it does not defend the empirical validity of concepts by defining them in terms of what we experience. Kant argues, it would seem rightly, that a concept that is a necessary condition for experiencing things could not be defined by appeal to what we experience. What we experience could always have been different from what we experience it to be; it is contingent rather than necessary states of affairs that we experience. But concepts that are necessary conditions for experiencing things constitute necessary features of anything that we experience. It follows that such concepts could not be defined by appeal to what we experience. The method, however, is not *a priori* in the sense of applying concepts to things that we could not refer to in experience. Such application Kant thinks is impossible.

Kant sums up the method in the dictum 'intuitions [i.e. sense-impressions] without concepts are blind' (A52/B76). This does not mean that sense-impressions require concepts. Animals have sense-impressions, they experience things, and in that sense they are clearly not blind. But animals lack concepts, they do not use language to describe what they experience, and it is only in this sense that they are 'blind'. The dictum means rather that if we are to be able to describe what we experience, which is what concepts are for, it is not enough to use concepts that can be defined in terms of how things impress our senses. By 'experiencing things' Kant always means 'experiencing things that one can go on to describe', and by 'knowledge' (as in 'How is synthetic *a priori* knowledge possible?') he means the ability to refer to things and to describe them.

Kant's transcendental method raises three major questions. (1) What results does he claim for the method, i.e. what are the concepts thought to be necessary for experiencing things? (2) How is the method supposed to work, i.e. how does one argue that a certain concept is necessary for experiencing things? (3) Why does he associate the method with a certain kind of idealism (though not the idealism of Hume and Berkeley, which separates appearance and reality), and what does this idealism consist in? Kant, we should note, refers to his distinctive position as 'transcendental idealism', though he is also at pains to distance himself from the idealism of Hume and Berkeley.

Following the dissertation of 1770, the *Critique* divides our capacity for knowledge into two co-operative capacities: sensibility, which is the capacity to refer to things in sense-experience, and understanding, which is the capacity for using concepts to describe these things. Kant's procedure is first to treat of each capacity separately (he does that in the 'Aesthetic' and the 'Analytic of Concepts'), then to connect the two capacities and to show how they must co-operate (the 'Analytic of Principles'). The 'Aesthetic' argues that we can refer to things in sense-experience only if these things are in space and time, so the concepts of space and time constitute necessary conditions for the possibility of experiencing things. The 'Analytic of Concepts' argues for the central claim that if we are to be able to describe what we experience, we must do so by judging how things or substances are; we cannot describe what we experience merely by reporting how things or phenomenal objects appear to the senses. The 'Analytic of Principles' connects understanding and sensibility by asking under what conditions substances can be met with in experience, that is to say in space and time. Here the main claim is that we can experience substances in space and time, in particular we can distinguish between experiencing substances in space and time and experiencing events (i.e. what happens to substances) in space and time, only if we assume that events are subject to the principle of causality, the principle that there is a cause for everything that happens (cf. the 'Second Analogy').

The 'Aesthetic' expounds rather than argues for the fundamental claim that (1) 'we can refer to things only in sense-experience'. Kant is content to emphasize the distinction between knowledge of concepts and knowledge of objects, the distinction inseparably tied to (1). He does not address Leibniz's challenge and argue for the distinction, and it is perhaps difficult to see how there could be room for argument here. The claim that (2) 'we can refer to things in sense-experience only if things are in space and time' is perhaps Kant's least controversial claim. But the 'Aesthetic' goes further and claims that (3) 'we can refer to things in sense-experience if and only if things are in space and time'. A physicist might accept (2) but deny (3), arguing that there might be entities in space and time, say certain sub-atomic particles, which one could not even in principle directly experience, as opposed to experiencing their traces, however powerful one's senses or magnifying equipment might be. Kant would have to reply either that such alleged entities are really theoretical constructions or that they are really properties of entities, which could in principle be directly experienced, e.g. he might argue that electrons are not really entities but rather charges of atoms.

There remains the bold, and most puzzling, claim of the 'Aesthetic', perhaps of the *Critique*: (4) 'for something to be in space and time is for that thing to be capable of being experienced by us'. While Berkeley's idealism claimed that to exist is to be perceived, Kant is claiming that to exist is to be capable of being perceived. We must emphasise that (4) is a stronger claim than (3): one may agree that something exists if and only if it can be experienced, without thinking that the concept of something existing should be defined in terms of the concept of our capacity to experience things. There is no trace of idealism in (3), but there is an unmistakable element of idealism in (4), in so far as the existence of things is defined relatively to us. We must also emphasise that the transcendental method, the method of asking under what conditions we can experience things, is exemplified in (3) and does not require that one should go as far as (4). Kant sometimes states (4) in the provocative but literally nonsensical way that space and time are nothing outside us and exist only in us.

Kant sums up his distinctive idealism by the metaphor of mind imposing order on nature, a view he compares to Copernicus' revolution in astronomy. Just as Copernicus realised that we can better explain the motion of the heavenly bodies by assuming that it is we on earth that revolve around the sun rather than the sun that revolves around us, so Kant thinks we must explain our knowledge of things by assuming that at least part of this knowledge is not something we derive from things but rather something we ourselves supply and impose on them in order to be able to experience them. More soberly expressed, Kantian idealism is the claim that concepts which are necessary for our experiencing things could not state how things are in abstraction from us and our capacity to experience them, so such concepts are applicable to things only by virtue of our capacity to experience those things.

Kant's approach has enjoyed prominent influence recently, in particular in the work of P. Strawson and the debate Strawson's work has engendered about transcendental arguments. The resurgence of a transcendental approach has above all been a reaction to logical positivism, which maintains that *a priori* knowledge cannot be synthetic (knowledge of how things are) but can only be analytic or trivial (knowledge of concepts or the meaning of words). Logical positivism has also tended to go together with phenomenalism. But the recent followers of a transcendental approach have been anxious to divorce the approach from Kant's idealism. Equally influential, in particular in the more recent work of H. Putnam, has been Kant's view that our notion of the world is to be understood as the notion of a world that we are capable of experiencing and knowing, the view associated in Kant with the criticism of the separation of appearance and reality. Putnam calls this view 'internal realism', though it should also be noted that he wants to divorce the view from the Kantian transcendental approach. However, Putnam readily adopts a version of Kant's idealism, and he goes as far as saying that 'objects themselves are as much made as discovered' (*Reason, Truth and History*, p. 54).

Why did Kant associate the transcendental method with a distinctive kind of idealism? There are two reasons, though especially the second reason is not explicit but rather a fundamental assumption Kant never thought of questioning. First, Kant thinks that if space and time are not defined in terms of our capacity to experience things but in terms of things themselves, then the problem arises as to how we can know these things. Kant wants to argue that this problem is ill-conceived, rather than answer it in its own terms, either those of Cartesian dualism or those of Humean or Berkeleyan idealism (see also section 1). If space and time are defined independently of our capacity to experience things, then, Kant thinks, we must adopt a representationalist account of what it is to experience things – according to which, to experience something is for something external to cause a representation in one's mind. But in that case all we could have direct access to in experience would be our mental representations (ideas, appearances), and then the problem arises as to how we could know things (cf. e.g. A372–3). Kant rejects the representationalist account of experiencing because it assumes a separation of appearance and reality: reality is one kind of entity, matter, while appearance is a different kind of entity, the mind and its content. Kant argues that in order to avoid the separation of appearance and reality, we need to conceive of space and time as essentially tied to our capacity to experience things, and he provides such a conception by defining space and time in terms of our capacity to experience things.

This source of Kant's idealism explains why space and time are defined in terms of our capacity to experience things, i.e. in terms of our sensibility. It does not explain why concepts of the understanding, concepts that cannot be defined in purely phenomenal terms, are defined analogously in terms of our capacity to describe things, i.e. in terms of our understanding. Why does Kant not adopt the weaker position, which is not idealist, namely that concepts such as those of substance and causality state how things are, even in abstraction from us, but at the same time we can describe what we experience if and only if what we experience is like that? The reason lies in Kant's very separation of our capacity to know things (to refer to and describe things) into two capacities, sensibility and understanding. The separation implies that we can understand what an object is by relying on sensibility alone, the capacity to experience objects, without relying on understanding, the capacity to describe objects. An object of sensibility is a sense-impression, or rather the content of a sense-impression; it is a purely phenomenal object. The conditions for describing what we experience state, to use Kant's terminology, how phenomenal objects must be synthesized or processed if we are to be able to describe what we experience. So these conditions depend on a notion of an object being already available. Such objects of sensibility could not be substances or be subject to causality, for then we would be relying on understanding in characterising them. They are, to be precise, purely phenomenal objects.

The separation of sensibility and understanding is arguably the Achilles heel of the *Critique*. It is one thing to argue that in our capacity to know things we must distinguish two aspects. It is quite a different thing to assume that our capacity to know things consists of two capacities, which can be treated separately. Kant's separation of sensibility and understanding shows him to be a victim of phenomenalism even while arguing that phenomenal objects are not enough. At the same time, the understanding of the transcendental method as a transcendental inquiry into *phenomena* in particular has enjoyed considerable influence, above all in the work of Husserl, and it has given the name to phenomenology, a philosophical movement prominent in the early twentieth century. Husserl, however, is also anxious to dissociate phenomenology from Kant's psychological idiom of mental faculties or capacities.

How, then, does Kant argue that we could not describe what we experience in purely phenomenal terms, i.e. merely by reporting how things or phenomenal objects appear to our senses, but must in describing what we experience judge how things or substances are? The argument occurs in the 'Analytic of Concepts', in particular in the 'Transcendental Deduction of the Pure Concepts of the Understanding' ('deduction' means simply 'defence' or 'defence of objective validity'). This is the very heart of the *Critique* and a high point in philosophical argument. Kant argues as follows against a purely phenomenal description. Suppose one adopted a purely phenomenal description. This means that every time one experienced something, one would or could describe what one experienced just by reporting 'At this moment I see (hear, touch, ...) what appears to be something red (shrill, hard, ...)'. Now to describe what one experiences one must have the notion of oneself as the person or subject experiencing things ('At this moment *I* experience ... '); in particular one must have a notion of oneself as experiencing different things at different times (cf. B132-3, perhaps the single most famous passage of the *Critique*). Kant calls this the notion of self-consciousness, which he also calls *apperception*, and its unity. But how, Kant asks, could one have a notion of oneself as experiencing different things at different times if all one did in describing what one experienced was report one's momentary and fleeting sense-impressions? Kant objects that in that case 'I should have as many coloured and diverse a self as I have representations [sense-impressions] of which I am conscious to myself' (B134). So Kant objects against phenomenalism that it avails, and must avail, itself of a notion which, however, it is unable to explain in its own terms, the notion of self-consciousness and its unity.

Kant goes on to argue that if in describing what one experiences one judges how things or substances are, then one can have a notion of oneself as experiencing different things at different times (cf. B142). In this way he turns the criticism of phenomenalism into a positive proposal. The line of argument is as follows. If in experiencing things one judges how things or substances are, then one conceives of what one experiences as a single unitary world – a world that can be experienced from different perspectives and at different times (see also section 1 on substances). It is precisely the conception of what one experiences as being a world capable of being experienced from different perspectives and at different times that provides one with a notion of oneself as experiencing different things at different times, namely as a subject capable of occupying different perspectives at different times. And it is precisely because with a purely phenomenal description the notion of a single unitary world is lacking and what one experiences is just a series of momentary and fleeting sense-impressions, that a purely phenomenal description cannot provide one with a notion of oneself as experiencing different things at different times. The argument is brilliant, if it works.

Kant's argument assumes that in experiencing things one must have a notion of oneself as experiencing things; it assumes that experience is self-conscious. Is Kant entitled to the assumption? Arguably he is, in so far as he is considering under what conditions one can describe what one experiences. It is precisely in describing what one experiences that one exhibits self-consciousness ('At this moment *I* experience what appears to be . . .', or alternatively '*I* judge on the basis of experience that . . .'). We may say that self-consciousness is essentially tied to language and concepts. This also indicates what Kant does *not* mean by self-consciousness. He does not mean merely consciousness of oneself, though he does mean consciousness of oneself as experiencing things, that is to say consciousness of the fact that one is experiencing things. Some animals may be conscious of themselves and may be able to recognise themselves. A chimpanzee might, by looking in a mirror, realise that something was stuck on top of its head. But animals, not using language or concepts, are not conscious of themselves as experiencing things; they are not conscious of the fact that they experience things. Nor does Kant mean by self-conscious consciousness of a Cartesian self or ego, the mind conceived as an immaterial entity. For he denies that there is any such thing.

4. *The Limitations of Reason*

In the 'Analytic' Kant argued that even where knowledge of things is not based on experience, we must still have recourse to experience, for we can have knowledge of things not based on experience only by asking under what conditions we could experience things. The essential recourse to the possibility of experiencing things imposes a strict limitation on reason. It means that knowledge of things that we could not refer to in experience is impossible. In the 'Dialectic' Kant draws out the implications of the limitation. His approach is to ask why we should be inclined to claim knowledge of non-empirical entities, i.e. those we could not refer to in sense-experience, be it God, the universe conceived as a whole, or the human mind or soul conceived as an immaterial entity. He offers a diagnosis of the inclination, which at the same time shows why it is illegitimate. But Kant also thinks the inclination is natural and unavoidable, and the diagnosis must also do justice to this.

For Kant, the inclination to use reason alone, divorced from experience, in order to know things, must be illegitimate and a source of illusory knowledge. But the 'Dialectic' is particularly important in the influence it had on Kant's more immediate successors, in particular on Schelling, Fichte and Hegel. They saw, in Kant's diagnosis of how we are naturally and unavoidably inclined to use reason independently of experience, not the diagnosis of illusion but rather that of true knowledge of reality, conceived as the reflection of the dialectic or movement of reason towards absolute knowledge. Absolute idealism exercised a lasting influence on British philosophy and to a lesser extent also on American philosophy, in particular on T. H. Green, F. H. Bradley and J. Royce.

In considering the notion of God, we may be inclined to argue that the universe as a whole must have a cause, or simply that everything must have a first cause, which we identify with God (the cosmological argument for God's existence). Kant objects that in the cosmological argument we are losing sight of why the concept of a cause is objectively valid, namely because it enables us to describe what we experience ('The Impossibility of a Cosmological Proof of the Existence of God'). Since a first cause or indeed the universe conceived as a whole is not something we could refer to in experience, the concept of a cause is not used legitimately here. It is naturally but wrongly extended from where it can be argued to be objectively valid to where we could not show that it applies to anything.

The cosmological argument at least starts from what we refer to in experience. By contrast, the ontological argument attempts to establish God's existence from the concept of God alone: the concept of God is the concept of the most perfect being; but the concept of God would not be the concept of a most perfect being if it were not the concept of something existing; therefore, God must exist. Kant agrees that to say of a certain kind of thing that it is a perfect kind of thing is to characterize it and to say something about the concept of that thing. But, Kant objects, to say that a certain kind of thing exists is not to characterize it or to say anything about the concept of it. So assuming that God does not exist is compatible with conceiving of God as the most perfect being ('The Impossibility of an Ontological Proof of the Existence of God'). Kant is exploiting his distinction between concept and object here. But this is not a distinction one would want to uphold in defending the ontological argument, so Kant may appear to be begging the question.

In considering the notion of the universe, we may be inclined to argue that the regress of causes from a given event must be either infinite or finite, so that the universe as a whole must be either finitely or infinitely extended in space and time. Kant objects along similar lines that the universe conceived as a whole is not something we could refer to in experience, hence the concept of a cause is not used legitimately here ('The Antinomy of Pure Reason'). We could not in experience refer to the universe conceived as a whole because, according to Kant, we could never have conclusive experiential evidence that beyond a certain point in space or time there is nothing. Kant thinks we ought to regulate our scientific inquiries by looking for ever remoter existences in space and time. Even if we keep finding nothing, we cannot deny that there might be something there. Kant concludes that we can have no grounds for asserting either that the universe is finite or that it is infinite. In a surprising move, Kant uses this conclusion as support for his own transcendental idealism, the view that concepts such as space, time, substance and causality are applicable to things only by virtue of our capacity to experience things. He argues that if in particular the concept of causality were applicable to things even in abstraction from our capacity to experience them, then we would have conclusive grounds for asserting both that the universe is infinite and that it is finite. This is Kant's indirect argument for transcendental idealism, namely that the denial of transcendental idealism leads to a contradiction or antinomy.

The heart of the 'Dialectic' is perhaps the 'Paralogisms of Pure Reason', where Kant argues against the Cartesian conception of the mind as an immaterial object. Kant, we recall, argued that in describing what one experiences, one must have a notion of oneself as the subject of experience ('*I* judge on the basis of experience that . . .'). In the 'Paralogisms' he uses this notion of self-consciousness to offer a diagnosis of the mistake in conceiving of the mind as an immaterial object. He argues that the Cartesian conception of the mind as an immaterial object confuses the notion of oneself as a condition for the possibility of describing what one experiences with a notion of oneself as an object. Two questions arise in assessing Kant's diagnosis. First, is Kant faithful to Descartes in associating Descartes' notion of the mind with his own notion of self-consciousness, with the notion of oneself as the condition for the possibility of describing or judging what one experiences? Descartes' notion of the mind is introduced through the 'cogito' in the 'cogito, ergo sum'. So whether Kant is faithful to Descartes depends on what Descartes meant by 'cogitare', in particular whether he meant 'to judge' as opposed to merely 'to experience'. Arguably, but controversially, Descartes did mean precisely 'to judge'. If so, Kant is being faithful to Descartes.

Secondly, how does Kant use the general diagnosis (confusing a condition for experiencing objects with an object) to explain why Descartes conceives of the mind as an immaterial object? The diagnosis explains why Descartes conceives the mind as an object: he mistook the condition of experiencing objects for an object. Kant responds that in avoiding the mistake one may rather conceive of the mind as an aspect of an object, namely of a person, of people we encounter in experience. Further, the notion of oneself as the condition for being able to describe what one experiences is not a notion of something material. That is to say, in pointing out that to be able to describe what one experiences, one needs a notion of oneself as the subject of experience, the question of whether this subject is material or immaterial simply does not arise. But if one confuses the notion of oneself as a condition for experiencing objects with the notion of an object, then one will conclude that this object, oneself, is positively immaterial. Kant responds that in avoiding the mistake one may grant that with regard to the notion of oneself as a condition for the possibility of describing what one experiences the question of materiality does not arise; but at the same time one may point out that the notion of oneself as an object is a notion of a person, the kind of thing we encounter in dealing with people in experience, which is clearly not a notion of something immaterial. We must remember that for Kant the notion of an object is essentially the notion of something one could encounter in experience. Kant's criticism of the Cartesian notion of the mind is a high point in the *Critique*, comparable to what is best in the 'Analytic'.

Limiting reason is not just an end in itself; it is Kant's way of making room for morality and thus preparing for his moral philosophy (*Groundwork of the Metaphysics of Morals*, 1785; *Critique of Practical Reason*, 1788). 'I had to deny knowledge in order to make room for faith' (BXXXI). Faith refers to religion, but it refers primarily to morality, and Kant thinks that religion must derive its content and legitimacy from morality. Kant's moral philosophy is above all a way of articulating the view that for an action to be moral is for the action to be performed from moral motivation. The notion of moral motivation is at the heart of Kant's moral philosophy; it is what supplies the key to the very content of morality, which Kant identifies with the requirements of duty. Kant thinks that for one's motive for performing an action to be moral it must be precisely because the action is what duty requires. Any other motive will undermine, or at least it will fail to affect, the morality of the action, whether it is one's concern to live happily or to earn immortality for oneself, e.g. by doing God's will.

Central to Kant's moral philosophy is the notion of freedom, and in limiting knowledge in order to make room for morality, Kant's primary concern is to reconcile freedom with the principle of causality. Kant's conception of freedom is basically incompatibilist: freedom cannot be made compatible with causality by thinking that to act freely it is sufficient that one should act as one desires, whether the desire is caused or not. Indeed, Kant thinks that all our desires are caused and therefore not free, and he concludes, in accordance with the incompatibilist assumption, that all our actions that are the expression of our desires are not free. Kant thinks that to act freely we must set aside our desires and act out of the understanding of what duty requires, so it is only in acting morally that we are acting freely. Kant's incompatibilist conception of freedom implies that if the principle of causality were true without qualification, then there would be no room for freedom or morality. But it is precisely by thinking that the principle of causality is true without qualification that we are inclined to use the principle to argue for the existence of God or the nature of the universe as a whole. Kant's transcendental idealism allows him to deny that the principle of causality is true without qualification. According to transcendental idealism, the principle of causality can be applied to things only by virtue of our capacity to experience them, so it is not true of things considered in abstraction from our capacity to experience them. In Kant's words, the principle of causality is not true of things *in themselves*. Now the concern to act morally is not a concern to experience things; it is, in Kant's words, a practical and not a theoretical concern. We may, therefore, when our concern is to act morally, set aside the principle of causality and consider ourselves under the aspect of freedom.

VASILIS POLITIS

The Editor gratefully acknowledges the assistance of David Berman of Trinity College, University of Dublin, who was Consultant Editor for this edition.

NOTE ON THE TEXT AND TRANSLATION

The *Critique of Pure Reason* was first published in 1781 and was revised for a second edition in 1787. In addition to a new preface, the principal changes in the B-edition are: a new version of 'The Transcendental Deduction of the Pure Concepts of the Understanding' (see B126–169); the addition of the 'Refutation of Idealism' (B274–79); and a new version of 'The Paralogisms of Rational Psychology' (B406–32). Kant expresses his own view of the changes at the conclusion of the Preface to the B-edition.

The present translation is in part a revised version of J. M. D. Meiklejohn's translation, which is of the B-edition. Here my aim has been to avoid errors and inaccuracies as well as to bring terminology up to date. I have offered my own translation of what Kant did not include in the B-edition: the Transcendental Deduction as in the A-edition (A95–130) and the Paralogisms as in the A-edition (A348–406). These sections are now regarded as an essential part of the full text of the *Critique*.

The standard way of referring to any particular page in the *Critique* is displayed in this edition at the foot of each page and refers to the A- and B-edition respectively.

BACO DE VERULAMIO

INSTAURATIO MAGNA PRAEFATIO

DE NOBIS IPSIS SILEMUS: DE RE AUTEM, QUAE AGITUR, PETIMUS: UT HOMINES EAM NON OPINIONEM, SED OPUS ESSE COGITENT; AC PRO CERTO HABEANT, NON SECTAE NOS ALICUJUS, AUT PLACITI, SED UTILITATIS ET AMPLITUDINIS HUMANAE FUNDAMENTA MOLIRI. DEINDE UT SUIS COMMODIS AEQUI — IN COMMUNE CONSULANT — ET IPSI IN PARTEM VENIANT. PRAETEREA UT BENE SPERENT, NEQUE INSTAURATIONEM NOSTRAM UT QUIDDAM INFINITUM ET ULTRA MORTALE FINGANT, ET ANIMO CONCIPIANT: QUUM REVERA SIT INFINITI ERRORIS FINIS ET TERMINUS LEGITIMUS.[1]

---

[1] 'Bacon of Verulam. Instauratio magna. Preface. Of myself I say nothing; but with regard to the issue in hand, I urge you to believe that it is not a mere opinion, but a needful task. Also, I urge you to have no doubt that we are establishing the foundations not of a school or doctrine, but of human welfare and dignity. In this way people may themselves and for their own good join in consultation. Besides which I ask and hope that you will accept our *Instauratio*, not as something infinite and beyond mere mortals, but as the rightful terminus of limitless error.'

PREFACE TO THE FIRST EDITION

Human reason, in one sphere of its cognition, is called upon to consider questions, which it cannot decline, as they are presented by its own nature, but which it cannot answer, as they transcend every faculty of human reason.

It falls into this difficulty without any fault of its own. It begins with principles, which cannot be dispensed with in the field of experience, and the truth and sufficiency of which are, at the same time, insured by experience. With these principles it rises, in obedience to the laws of its own nature, to ever higher and more remote conditions. But it quickly discovers that, in this way, its labours must remain ever incomplete, because new questions never cease to present themselves; and thus it finds itself compelled to have recourse to principles which transcend the region of experience, while they are regarded by common sense without distrust. It thus falls into confusion and contradictions, from which it conjectures the presence of latent errors, which, however, it is unable to discover, because the principles it employs, transcending the limits of experience, cannot be tested by that criterion. The arena of these endless contests is called *metaphysics*.

Time was, when she was the *queen* of all the sciences; and, if we take the will for the deed, she certainly deserves, so far as regards the high importance of her object-matter, this title of honour. Now, it is the fashion of the time to heap contempt and scorn upon her; and the matron mourns, forlorn and forsaken, like Hecuba:

> Modo maxima rerum,
> Tot generis, natisque potens . . .
> Nunc trahor exul, inops.
> OVID, *Metamorphoses*

At first, her government, under the administration of the *dogmatists*, was an absolute *despotism*. But, as the legislative continued to show traces of the ancient barbaric rule, her empire gradually broke up, and intestine wars introduced the reign of *anarchy*; while the *sceptics*, like nomadic tribes, who hate a permanent habitation and settled mode of living, attacked from time to time those who had organized themselves into civil communities. But their number was, very happily, small; and thus they could not entirely put a stop to the exertions of those who persisted in raising new edifices, although on no settled or uniform plan. In recent times the hope dawned upon us of seeing those disputes settled, and the legitimacy of her claims established by a kind of *physiology* of the human understanding – that of the celebrated Locke. But it was found that – although it was affirmed that this so-called queen could not refer her descent to any higher source than that of common experience, a circumstance which necessarily brought suspicion on her claims – as this *genealogy* was incorrect, she persisted in the advancement of her claims to sovereignty. Thus metaphysics necessarily fell back into the antiquated and rotten constitution of *dogmatism*, and again became obnoxious to the contempt from which efforts had been made to save it. At present, as all methods, according to the general persuasion, have been tried in vain, there reigns nought but weariness and complete *indifferentism* – the mother of chaos and night in the scientific world, but at the same time the source of, or at least the prelude to, the re-creation and reinstallation of a science, when it has fallen into confusion, obscurity, and disuse from ill-directed effort.

For it is in reality vain to profess *indifference* in regard to such inquiries, the object of which cannot be indifferent to humanity. Besides, these pretended *indifferentists*, however much they may try to disguise themselves by the assumption of a popular style and by changes in the language of the schools, unavoidably fall into metaphysical declarations and propositions, which they profess to regard with so much contempt. At the same time, this indifference, which has arisen in the world of science, and which relates to that kind of knowledge which we should wish to see destroyed the last, is a phenomenon that well deserves our attention and reflection. It is plainly not the effect of the levity, but of the matured *judgment*[1]

[1] We very often hear complaints of the shallowness of the present age, and of the decay of profound science. But I do not think that those which rest upon a secure foundation, such as Mathematics, Physical Science, etc., in the least deserve this reproach, but that they rather maintain their ancient fame, and in the latter case, indeed, far surpass it. The same would be the case with the other kinds of cognition, if their principles were but firmly established. In the absence of this security, indifference, doubt, and finally, severe criticism are rather signs of a habit of thorough thought. Our age is the age of criticism, to which

of the age, which refuses to be any longer entertained with illusory knowledge. It is, in fact, a call to reason, again to undertake the most laborious of all tasks – that of self-examination, and to establish a tribunal, which may secure it in its well-grounded claims, while it pronounces against all baseless assumptions and pretensions, not in an arbitrary manner, but according to its own eternal and unchangeable laws. This tribunal is nothing less than the *Critique of Pure Reason.*

I do not mean by this a criticism of books and systems, but a critical inquiry into the faculty of reason, with reference to the knowledge to which it strives to attain *independently of all experience*; in other words, the solution of the question regarding the possibility or impossibility of metaphysics, and the determination of the origin, as well as of the extent and limits of this science. All this must be done on the basis of principles.

This path – the only one now remaining – has been entered upon by me; and I flatter myself that I have, in this way, discovered the cause of – and consequently the mode of removing – all the errors which have hitherto set reason at variance with itself, in the sphere of non-empirical thought. I have not returned an evasive answer to the questions of reason, by alleging the inability and limitation of the faculties of the mind; I have, on the contrary, examined them completely in the light of principles, and, after having discovered the cause of the doubts and contradictions into which reason fell, have solved them to its perfect satisfaction. It is true, these questions have not been solved as dogmatism, in its vain fancies and desires, had expected; for it can only be satisfied by the exercise of magical arts, and of these I have no knowledge. But then neither was this the intention of the natural constitution of reason; and it was the duty of philosophy to destroy the illusions which had their origin in misconceptions, whatever darling hopes and valued expectations may be ruined by its explanations. My chief aim in this work has been completeness; and I make bold to say, that there is not a single metaphysical problem that does not find its solution, or at least the key to its solution, here. Pure reason is a perfect unity; and therefore, if the principle presented by it prove to be insufficient

---

everything must be subjected. The sacredness of religion, and the authority of legislation, are by many regarded as grounds of exemption from the examination of this tribunal. But, if they are exempted, they become the subjects of just suspicion, and cannot lay claim to sincere respect, which reason accords only to that which has stood the test of a free and public examination.

for the solution of even a single one of those questions to which the very nature of reason gives birth, we must reject it, as we could not be perfectly certain of its sufficiency in the case of the others.

While I say this, I think I see upon the countenance of the reader signs of dissatisfaction mingle with contempt, when he hears declarations which sound so boastful and extravagant; and yet they are beyond comparison more moderate than those advanced by the commonest author of the commonest philosophical programme, in which the dogmatist professes to demonstrate the simple nature of the soul, or the necessity of a first beginning of the world. Such a dogmatist promises to extend human knowledge beyond the limits of possible experience; while I humbly confess that this is completely beyond my power. Instead of any such attempt, I confine myself to the examination of reason alone and its pure thought; and I do not need to seek far to attain complete knowledge of these, because they have their seat in my own mind. Besides, common logic presents me with a complete and systematic catalogue of all the simple operations of reason; and it is my task to answer the question how far reason can go, without the material presented and the aid furnished by experience.

So much for the completeness and exhaustiveness necessary in the execution of the present task. The aims set before us are not arbitrarily proposed, but are imposed upon us by the nature of knowledge itself, this being the subject-matter of our critical inquiry.

The above remarks relate to the *matter* of our critical inquiry. As regards the *form*, there are two indispensable conditions, which any one who undertakes so difficult a task as that of a critique of pure reason, is bound to fulfil. These conditions are *certitude* and *clearness*.

As regards *certitude*, I have fully convinced myself that, in this sphere of thought, *opinion* is perfectly inadmissible, and that everything which bears the least semblance of an hypothesis must be excluded, as of no value in such discussions. For it is a necessary condition of all knowledge that is to be established upon *a priori* grounds, that it shall be held to be absolutely necessary; much more is this the case with an attempt to determine all pure *a priori* knowledge, and to furnish the standard – and consequently an example – of all apodeictic (philosophical) certitude. Whether I have succeeded in what I professed to do, it is for the reader to determine; it is the author's business merely to adduce grounds and reasons, without determining what influence these ought to have on the mind of his judges. But, lest anything he may have said may become the innocent cause of doubt in their minds, or tend to weaken the effect which his arguments might otherwise produce – he may be allowed to point out those passages which may occasion mistrust or difficulty, although these do not concern the main purpose of the present work. He does this solely with the view of removing from the mind of the reader any doubts which might affect his judgment of the work as a whole, and in regard to its ultimate aim.

I know no investigations more necessary for a full insight into the nature of the faculty which we call *understanding*, and at the same time for the determination of the rules and limits of its use, than those undertaken in the second chapter of the Transcendental Analytic, under the title of *Deduction of the Pure Concepts of the Understanding*; and they have also cost me by far the greatest labour – labour which, I hope, will not remain uncompensated. The view there taken, which goes somewhat deeply into the subject, has two sides. The one relates to the objects of the pure understanding, and is intended to demonstrate and to render comprehensible the objective validity of its *a priori* concepts; and it forms for this reason an essential part of the *Critique*. The other considers the pure understanding itself, its possibility and its powers of cognition – that is, from a subjective point of view; and, although this exposition is of great importance, it does not belong essentially to the main purpose of the work, because the question is, What and how much can reason and understanding, apart from experience, know? and not, How is the *faculty of thought* itself possible? As the latter is an inquiry into the cause of a given effect, and has thus in it some semblance of an hypothesis (although, as I shall show on another occasion, this is really not the fact), it would seem that, in the present instance, I had allowed myself to enounce a mere *opinion*, and that the reader must therefore be at liberty to hold a different *opinion*. But I beg to remind him, that, if my subjective deduction does not produce in his mind the conviction of its certitude at which I aimed, the objective deduction, with which alone the present work is properly concerned, is in every respect satisfactory.

As regards *clearness*, the reader has a right to demand, in the first place, *discursive* or logical clearness, that is, on the basis of concepts, and, secondly, *intuitive* or aesthetic clearness, by means of intuitions, that is, by examples or other modes of illustration *in concreto*. I have done what I could for the first kind of intelligibility. This was essential to my purpose; and it thus became the accidental cause of my inability to do complete justice to the second requirement. I have been almost always at a loss, during the progress of this work, how to settle this question. Examples and illustrations always appeared to me necessary, and, in the first sketch of the *Critique*, naturally fell into their proper places. But I very soon became aware of the magnitude of my task, and the numerous problems with which I should be engaged; and, as I perceived that this critical investigation would, even if delivered in the driest *scholastic* manner, be far from being brief, I found it unadvisable to enlarge it still more with examples and explanations, which are necessary only from a *popular* point of view. I was induced to take this course from the consideration also, that the present work is not intended for popular use, that those devoted to science do not require such helps, although they are always acceptable, and that they would have materially interfered with my present purpose. Abbé Terrasson remarks with great justice, that if we estimate the size of a work, not from the number of its pages, but from the time which we require to make ourselves master of it, it may be said of many a book – *that it would be much shorter, if it were not so short*. On the other hand, as regards the comprehensibility of a system of speculative cognition, connected under a single principle, we may say with equal justice – many a book would have been much clearer, if it had not been intended to be so very clear. For explanations and examples, and other helps to intelligibility, aid us in the comprehension of *parts*, but they distract the attention, dissipate the mental power of the reader, and stand in the way of his forming a clear conception of the *whole*; as he cannot attain soon enough to a survey of the system, and the colouring and embellishments bestowed upon it prevent his observing its articulation or organization – which is the most important consideration with him, when he comes to judge of its unity and stability.

The reader must naturally have a strong inducement to co-operate with the present author, if he has formed the intention of erecting a complete and solid edifice of metaphysical science, according to the plan now laid before him. Metaphysics, as here represented, is the only science which admits of completion – and with little labour, if it is united, in a short time; so that nothing will be left to future generations except the task of illustrating and applying it *didactically*. For this science is nothing more than the *inventory* of all that is given us by *pure reason*, systematically arranged. Nothing can escape our notice; for what reason produces from itself cannot lie concealed, but must be brought to the light by reason itself, so soon as we have discovered the common principle of the ideas we seek. The perfect unity of this kind of knowledge, which are based upon pure concepts, and uninfluenced by any empirical element, or any *peculiar* intuition leading to determinate experience, renders this completeness not only practicable, but also necessary.

Tecum habita, et noris quam sit tibi curta supellex.

PERSIUS

Such a system of pure speculative reason I hope to be able to publish under the title of *Metaphysics of Nature*. The content of this work (which will not be half so long) will be very much richer than that of the present *Critique*, which has to discover the sources of pure reason and expose the conditions of its possibility, and at the same time to clear and level a fit foundation for the scientific edifice. In the present work, I look for the patient hearing and the impartiality of a *judge*; in the other, for the goodwill and assistance of a *co-labourer*. For, however complete the list of *principles* for this system may be in the *Critique*, the correctness of the system requires that no *derived* concepts should be absent. These cannot be presented *a priori*, but must be gradually discovered; and, while the *synthesis* of concepts has been fully exhausted in the *Critique*, it is necessary that, in the proposed work, the same should be the case with their *analysis*. But this will be rather an amusement than a labour.

PREFACE TO THE SECOND EDITION

Whether the treatment of that portion of our knowledge which lies within the province of reason, advances with that undeviating certainty which characterizes the progress of *science*, we shall be at no loss to determine. If we find those who are engaged in metaphysical pursuits unable to come to an understanding as to the method which they ought to follow; if we find them, after the most elaborate preparations, invariably brought to a stand before the goal is reached, and compelled to retrace their steps and strike into fresh paths, we may then feel quite sure that they are far from having attained to the certainty of scientific progress, and may rather be said to be merely groping about in the dark. In these circumstances we shall render an important service to reason if we succeed in simply indicating the path along which it must travel, in order to arrive at any results – even if it should be found necessary to abandon many of those aims which, without reflection, have been proposed for its attainment.

That *Logic* has advanced in this sure course, even from the earliest times, is apparent from that fact that, since Aristotle, it has been unable to advance a step, and thus to all appearance has reached its completion. For, if some of the moderns have thought to enlarge its domain by introducing *psychological* discussions on the mental faculties, such as imagination and wit, *metaphysical* discussions on the origin of knowledge and the different kinds of certitude, according to the difference of the objects (Idealism, Scepticism, and so on), or *anthropological* discussions on prejudices, their causes and remedies: this attempt, on the part of these authors, only shows their ignorance of the peculiar nature of logical science. We do not enlarge, but disfigure the sciences when we lose sight of their respective limits, and allow them to run into one another. Now logic is enclosed within limits which admit of perfectly clear definition; it is a science which has for its object nothing but the exposition and proof of the *formal* laws of all thought, whether it be *a priori* or empirical, whatever be its origin or its object, and whatever the difficulties – natural or accidental – which it encounters in the human mind.

The early success of logic must be attributed exclusively to the narrowness of its field, in which abstraction may, or rather must, be made of all the objects of knowledge with their characteristic distinctions, and in which the understanding has only to deal with itself and with its own form. It is, obviously, a much more difficult task for reason to strike into the sure path of science, where it has to deal not simply with itself, but with objects external to itself. Hence, logic is properly only a *propaedeutic* – forms, as it were, the vestibule of the sciences; and while it is necessary to enable us to form a correct judgment with regard to the various branches of knowledge, still the acquisition of real, substantive knowledge is to be sought only in the sciences properly so called, that is, in the objective sciences.

Now these sciences, in so far as they are, at least partly, the province of reason, must contain elements of *a priori* knowledge, and this knowledge may stand in a two-fold relation to its object. Either the knowledge may *determine* the object and its concept (which must be supplied from elsewhere), or it may make it real. The former is *theoretical*, the latter *practical*, rational knowlege. In both, the *pure* or *a priori* element must be treated first, and must be carefully distinguished from that which is supplied from other sources. Any other method can only lead to irremediable confusion.

Mathematics and *physics* are the two theoretical sciences which have to determine their objects *a priori*. The former is purely *a priori*, the latter is partially so, but is also dependent on other sources of knowledge than reason.

In the earliest times of which history affords us any record, *mathematics* had already entered on the sure course of science, among that wonderful nation, the Greeks. Still it is not to be supposed that it was as easy for this science to strike into, or rather to construct for itself, that royal road, as it was for logic, in which reason has only to deal with itself. On the contrary, I believe that it must have remained long – chiefly among the Egyptians – in the stage of blind groping after its true aims and destination, and that it was revolutionized by the happy idea of one man, who struck out and determined for all time the path which this science must follow, and which admits of an indefinite advancement. The history of this intellectual revolution – much more important in its results than the discovery of the passage round the celebrated Cape of Good

Hope – and of its author, has not been preserved. But Diogenes Laertius, in naming the supposed discoverer of some of the simplest elements of geometrical demonstration – elements which, according to the ordinary opinion, do not even require to be proved – makes it apparent that the change introduced by the first indication of this new path, must have seemed of the utmost importance to the mathematicians of that age, and it has thus been secured against the chance of oblivion. A new light must have flashed on the mind of the first man (*Thales*, or whatever may have been his name) who demonstrated the properties of the *isosceles* triangle. For he found that it was not sufficient to meditate on the figure, as it lay before his eyes, or on the concept of it, as it existed in his mind, and thus endeavour to get at the knowledge of its properties, but that it was necessary to produce these properties, as it were, by a positive *a priori* construction; and that, in order to arrive with certainty at *a priori* knowledge, he must not attribute to the object any other properties than those which necessarily followed from that which he had himself, in accordance with his concept, placed in the object.

A much longer period elapsed before *physics* entered on the highway of science. For it is only about a century and a half since the wise BACON gave a new direction to physical studies, or rather – as others were already on the right track – imparted fresh vigour to the pursuit of this new direction. Here, too, as in the case of mathematics, we find evidence of a rapid intellectual revolution. In the remarks which follow I shall confine myself to the *empirical* side of natural science.

When Galilei experimented with balls of a definite weight on the inclined plane, when Torricelli caused the air to sustain a weight which he had calculated beforehand to be equal to that of a definite column of water, or when Stahl, at a later period, converted metals into lime, and reconverted lime into metal, by the addition and subtraction of certain elements,[1] a light broke upon all natural philosophers. They learned that reason only perceives that which it produces after its own design; that it must not be content to follow, as it were, in the leading-strings of nature, but must proceed in advance with principles of judgment according to unvarying laws, and compel nature to reply to its questions. For accidental observations, made according to no preconceived plan, cannot be united

---

[1] I do not here follow with exactness the history of the experimental method, of which, indeed, the first steps are involved in some obscurity.

under a necessary law. But it is this that reason seeks for and requires. It is only the principles of reason which can give to concordant phenomena the validity of laws, and it is only when experiment is directed by these rational principles that it can have any real utility. Reason must approach nature with the view, indeed, of receiving information from it, not, however, in the character of a pupil, who listens to all that his master chooses to tell him, but in that of a judge, who compels the witnesses to reply to those questions which he himself thinks fit to propose. To this single idea must the revolution be ascribed, by which, after groping in the dark for so many centuries, natural science was at length conducted into the path of certain progress.

We come now to *metaphysics*, a purely speculative science, which occupies a completely isolated position, and is entirely independent of the teachings of experience. It deals with mere concepts – not, like mathematics, with concepts applied to intuition – and in it, reason is the pupil of itself alone. It is the oldest of the sciences, and would still survive, even if all the rest were swallowed up in the abyss of an all-destroying barbarism. But it has not yet had the good fortune to attain to the sure scientific method. This will be apparent, if we apply the tests which we proposed at the outset. We find that reason perpetually comes to a stand, when it attempts to gain *a priori* the perception even of those laws which the most common experience confirms. We find it compelled to retrace its steps in innumerable instances, and to abandon the path on which it had entered, because this does not lead to the desired result. We find, too, that those who are engaged in metaphysical pursuits are far from being able to agree among themselves, but that, on the contrary, this science appears to furnish an arena specially adapted for the display of skill or the exercise of strength in mock contests – a field in which no combatant ever yet succeeded in gaining an inch of ground, in which, at least, no victory was ever yet crowned with permanent possession.

This leads us to inquire why it is that, in metaphysics, the sure path of science has not hitherto been found. Shall we suppose that it is impossible to discover it? Why then should nature have visited our reason with restless aspirations after it, as if it were one of our weightiest concerns? Nay, more, how little cause should we have to place confidence in our reason, if it abandons us in a matter about which, most of all, we desire to know the truth – and not only so, but even allures us to the pursuit of vain phantoms, only to betray us in the end? Or, if the path has only hitherto been missed, what indications do we possess to guide us in a renewed investigation, and to enable us to hope for greater success than has fallen to the lot of our predecessors?

It appears to me that the examples of mathematics and natural philosophy, which, as we have seen, were brought into their present condition by a sudden revolution, are sufficiently remarkable to fix our attention on the essential circumstances of the change which has proved so advantageous to them, and to induce us to make the experiment of imitating them, so far as the analogy which, as species of rational knowledge, they bear to metaphysics may permit. It has hitherto been assumed that our knowledge must conform to the objects; but all attempts to ascertain anything about these objects *a priori*, by means of concepts, and thus to extend the range of our knowledge, have been rendered abortive by this assumption. Let us then make the experiment whether we may not be more successful in metaphysics, if we assume that the objects must conform to our knowledge. This appears, at all events, to accord better with the *possibility* of our gaining the end we have in view, that is to say, of arriving at the knowledge of objects *a priori*, of determining something with respect to these objects, before they are given to us. We here propose to do just what COPERNICUS did in attempting to explain the celestial movements. When he found that he could make no progress by assuming that all the heavenly bodies revolved round the spectator, he reversed the process, and tried the experiment of assuming that the spectator revolved, while the stars remained at rest. We may make the same experiment with regard to the intuition of objects. If the intuition must conform to the nature of the objects, I do not see how we can know anything about that nature *a priori*. If, on the other hand, the object (*qua* subject of the senses) conforms to the nature of our faculty of intuition, I can then easily conceive the possibility of such an *a priori* knowledge. Now as I cannot rest in the mere intuitions, but – if they are to become knowledge – must refer them, as *representations*, to something, as *object*, and must determine the latter by means of the former, here again there are two courses open to me. *Either*, first, I may assume that the concepts, by which I effect this determination, conform to the object – and in this case I am reduced to the same perplexity as before with regard to how I can know something *a priori*; *or* secondly, I may assume that the objects, or, which is the same thing, that *experience*, in which alone objects, as given, are known, conform to my conceptions – and then I am at no loss how to proceed. For experience itself is a mode of knowledge which requires understanding. Before objects are given to me, that is, *a priori*, I must presuppose in myself laws of the understanding which are expressed in concepts *a priori*. To these concepts, then, all the objects of experience must necessarily conform. Now there are objects which reason *thinks*, and that necessarily, but which cannot be given in experience, or, at least, cannot be given *so* as reason thinks them. The attempt to think these objects will hereafter furnish an excellent test of the new method of thought which we have adopted, and which is based on the principle that we only know in things *a priori* that which we ourselves place in them.[1]

This attempt succeeds as well as we could desire, and promises to metaphysics, in its first part – that is, where it is occupied with concepts *a priori*, of which the corresponding objects may be given in experience – the certain course of science. For by this new method we are enabled perfectly to explain the possibility of *a priori* knowledge, and, what is more, to demonstrate satisfactorily the laws which lie *a priori* at the foundation of nature, as the sum of the objects of experience – neither of which was possible according to the procedure hitherto followed. But from this deduction of the faculty of *a priori* knowledge in the first part of metaphysics, we derive a surprising result, and one which, to all appearance, militates against the great end of metaphysics, as treated in the second part. For we come to the conclusion that our faculty of knowledge is unable to transcend the limits of possible experience ; and yet this is precisely the most essential object of this science. The estimate of our rational knowledge *a priori* at which we arrive is that it has only to do with appearances, and that things in themselves, while real in themselves are nothing to us. Here we are enabled to put the justice

---

[1] This method, accordingly, which we have borrowed from the natural philosopher, consists in seeking for the elements of pure reason in that *which admits of confirmation or refutation by experiment*. Now the propositions of pure reason, especially when they transcend the limits of possible experience, do not admit of our making any experiment with their *objects*, as in natural science. Hence, with regard to those *concepts* and *principles* which we assume *a priori*, our only course will be to view them from two different sides. We must regard one and the same concept, *on the one hand*, in relation to experience as an object of the senses and of the understanding, or *on the other hand*, in relation to reason, isolated and transcending the limits of experience, as an object of mere thought. Now if we find that, when we regard things from this double point of view, the result is in harmony with the principle of pure reason, but that, when we regard them from a single point of view, reason is involved in self-contradiction, then the experiment will establish the correctness of this distinction.

of this estimate to the test. For that which of necessity impels us to transcend the limits of experience and of all appearances, is the *unconditioned*, which reason absolutely requires in things as they are in themselves, in order to complete the series of conditions. Now, if it appears that when, on the other hand, we assume that our knowledge conforms to its objects as things in themselves, *the unconditioned cannot be thought without contradiction*, and that when, on the other hand, we assume that our representation of things as they are given to us does not conform to these things as they are in themselves, but that these objects, as appearances, conform to our mode of representation, *the contradiction disappears*: we shall then be convinced of the truth of that which we began by assuming for the sake of experiment; we may look upon it as established that the unconditioned does not lie in things as we know them, or as they are given to us, but in things as they are in themselves, beyond the range of our knowledge.[1]

But, after we have thus denied the power of speculative reason to make any progress in the sphere of the supersensible, it still remains for our consideration whether data do not exist in *practical* knowledge, which may enable us to determine the transcendent concept of the unconditioned, to rise beyond the limits of all possible experience from a *practical* point of view, and thus to satisfy the great ends of metaphysics. Speculative reason has thus, at least, made room for such an extension of our knowledge; and, if it must leave this space vacant, still it does not rob us of the liberty to fill it up, if we can, by means of practical data – nay, it even challenges us to make the attempt.[2]

[1] This experiment of pure reason has a great similarity to that of the *chemists*, which they term the experiment of *reduction*, or, more usually, the *synthetic* process. The *analysis* of the metaphysician separates pure knowledge *a priori* into two heterogeneous elements, viz. the knowledge of things as appearances, and of things in themselves. *Dialectic* combines these again into harmony with the necessary rational idea of the unconditioned, and finds that this harmony never results except through the above distinction, which is, therefore, concluded to be just.

[2] So the central laws of the movements of the heavenly bodies established the truth of that which Copernicus, at first, assumed only as a hypothesis, and, at the same time, brought to light that invisible force (Newtonian attraction) which holds the universe together. The latter would have remained for ever undiscovered, if Copernicus had not ventured on the experiment – contrary to the senses, but still just – of looking for the observed movements not in the heavenly bodies, but in the spectator. In this Preface I treat the new metaphysical method as a hypothesis with the view of rendering apparent the first attempts at such a change of method, which are always hypothetical. But in the *Critique* itself it will be demonstrated, not hypothetically, but apodeictically, from the nature of our representations of space and time, and from the elementary concepts of the understanding.

This attempt to introduce a complete revolution in the procedure of metaphysics, after the *example* of the geometricians and natural philosophers, constitutes the aim of the *Critique of Pure Speculative Reason*. It is a treatise on the method to be followed, not a system of the science itself. But, at the same time, it marks out and defines both the external boundaries and the internal structure of this science. For pure speculative reason has this peculiarity, that, in choosing the various objects of thought, it is able to define the limits of its own faculties, and even to give a complete enumeration of the possible modes of proposing problems to itself, and thus to sketch out the entire system of metaphysics. For, on the one hand, in *a priori* knowledge, nothing must be attributed to the objects but what the thinking subject derives from itself; and, on the other hand, reason is, in regard to the principles of knowledge, a perfectly distinct, independent unity, in which, as in an organized body, every member exists for the sake of the others, and all for the sake of each, so that no principle can be viewed, with safety, in one relationship, unless it is, at the same time, viewed in relation to the total use of pure reason. Hence, too, metaphysics has this singular advantage – an advantage which falls to the lot of no other science which has to do with *objects* – that, if once it is conducted into the sure path of science, by means of this criticism, it can then take in the whole sphere of its knowledge, and can thus complete its work, and leave it for the use of posterity, as a capital which can never receive fresh accessions. For metaphysics has to deal only with principles and with the limitations of its own employment as determined by these principles. To this perfection it is, therefore, bound, as the fundamental science, to attain, and to it the maxim may justly be applied:

Nil actum reputans, si quid superesset agendum.

But, it will be asked, what kind of a treasure is this that we propose to bequeath to posterity! What is the real value of this system of metaphysics, purified by criticism, and thereby reduced to a permanent condition? A cursory view of the present work will lead to the supposition that its use is merely *negative*, that it only serves to warn us against venturing, with speculative reason, beyond the limits of experience. This is, in fact, its primary use. But this, at once, assumes a *positive* value, when we observe that the principles with which speculative reason endeavours to transcend its limits, lead inevitably, not to the *extension*, but to the *contraction* of the use of reason, inasmuch as they threaten to extend the limits of sensibility, which is their proper sphere, over the entire realm of thought, and thus to supplant the pure (practical) use of reason. So far, then, as this criticism is occupied in confining speculative reason within its proper bounds, it is only negative; but, inasmuch as it thereby, at the same time, removes an obstacle which impedes and even threatens to destroy the use of practical reason, it possesses a positive and very important value. In order to admit this, we have only to be convinced that there is an absolutely necessary use of pure reason — the moral use — in which it inevitably transcends the limits of sensibility, without the aid of speculation, requiring only to be insured against the effects of a speculation which would involve it in contradiction with itself. To deny the positive advantage of the service which this criticism renders us, would be as absurd as to maintain that the system of police is productive of no positive benefit, since its main business is to prevent the violence which citizen has to apprehend from citizen, so that each may pursue his vocation in peace and security. That space and time are only forms of sensible intuition, and hence are only conditions of the existence of things as appearances; that, moreoever, we have no concepts of the understanding, and, consequently, no elements for knowing things, except in so far as a corresponding intuition can be given to these concepts; that, accordingly, we can have no knowledge of an object, as a thing in itself, but only as an object of sensible intuition, that is, as appearance — all this is proved in the Analytical part of the *Critique*; and from this the limitation of all possible speculative knowledge to the mere objects of *experience*, follows as a necessary result. At the same time, it must be carefully borne in mind that, while we surrender the power of *knowledge*, we still reserve the power of *thinking* objects, as things in themselves.[1] For, otherwise, we should require to affirm the existence of an appearance without something that appears — which would be absurd. Now let us suppose, for a moment, that we had not

---

[1] In order to *know* an object, I must be able to prove its possibility, either from its reality as attested by experience, or *a priori*, by means of reason. But I can *think* what I please, provided only I do not contradict myself; that is, provided my concept is a possible thought, though I may be unable to answer for the existence of a corresponding object in the sum of possibilities. But something more is required before I can attribute to such a concept objective validity, that is real possibility — the other possibility being merely logical. We are not, however, confined to theoretical sources of knowledge for the means of satisfying this additional requirement, but may derive it from practical sources.

undertaken this criticism, and, accordingly, had not drawn the necessary distinction between things as objects of experience, and things as they are in themselves. The principle of causality, and, by consequence, the mechanism of nature as determined by causality, would then have absolute validity in relation to all things as efficient causes. I should then be unable to assert, with regard to one and the same being, e.g. the human soul, that its will is *free*, and yet, at the same time, subject to natural necessity, that is, not free, without falling into a palpable contradiction, for in both propositions I should take the soul in *the same signification*, as a thing in general, as a thing in itself – as, without previous criticism, I could not but take it. Suppose now, on the other hand, that we *have* undertaken this criticism, and have learnt that an object may be taken in *two senses*, first, as an appearance, secondly, as a thing in itself; and that, according to the deduction of the concepts of the understanding, the principle of causality has reference only to things in the first sense. We then see how it does not involve any contradiction to assert, on the one hand, that the will, in the sphere of appearances – in visible action, is necessarily obedient to the law of nature, and, in so far, *not free*; and, on the other hand, that, as belonging to a thing in itself, it is not subject to that law, and, accordingly, is *free*. Now, it is true that I cannot, by means of speculative reason, and still less by empirical observation, know my soul as a thing in itself, and consequently, cannot know freedom as the property of a being to which I ascribe effects in the world of sense. For, to do so, I must know this being as existing, and yet not in time, which – since I cannot support my concept by any intuition – is impossible. At the same time, while I cannot know, I can quite well *think* freedom, that is to say, my representation of it involves at least no contradiction, if we bear in mind the critical distinction of the two modes of representation (the sensible and the intellectual) and the consequent limitation of the concepts of the pure understanding, and of the principles which flow from them. Suppose now that morality necessarily presupposed freedom, in the strictest sense, as a property of our will; suppose that reason contained certain practical, original principles *a priori*, wihch were absolutely impossible without this presupposition; and suppose, at the same time, that speculative reason had proved that freedom was incapable of being thought at all. It would then follow that the moral presupposition must give way to the speculative affirmation, the opposite of which involves an obvious contradiction, and that freedom and, with it, morality must yield to the *mechanism of nature*; for the negation of morality involves no contradiction, except on the presupposition of freedom. Now morality does not require the speculative knowledge of freedom; it is enough that I can think it, that its concept involves no contradiction, that it does not interfere with the mechanism of nature. But even this requirement we could not satisfy, if we had not learnt the two-fold sense in which things may be taken; and it is only in this way that the doctrine of morality and the doctrine of nature are confined within their proper limits. For this result, then, we are indebted to a criticism which warns us of our unavoidable ignorance with regard to things in themselves, and establishes the necessary limitation of our theoretical knowledge to mere appearances.

The positive value of the critical principles of pure reason in relation to the concept of *God* and of the *simple nature* of the *soul*, admits of a similar exemplification; but on this point I shall not dwell. I cannot even make the assumption – as the practical interests of morality require – of God, Freedom, and Immortality, if I do not deprive speculative reason of its pretensions to transcendent insight. For to arrive at these, it must make use of principles which, in fact, extend only to the objects of possible experience, and which cannot be applied to objects beyond this sphere without converting them into appearances, and thus rendering the *practical extension* of pure reason impossible. I must, therefore, abolish *knowledge*, to make room for *faith*. The dogmatism of metaphysics, that is, the presumption that it is possible to advance in metaphysics without previous criticism, is the true source of the unbelief (always dogmatic) which militates against morality.

Thus, while it may be no very difficult task to bequeath a legacy to posterity, in the shape of a system of metaphysics constructed in accordance with the *Critique of Pure Reason*, still the value of such a bequest is not to be depreciated. It will render an important service to reason, by substituting the certainty of scientific method for that random groping after results without the guidance of principles, which has hitherto characterized the pursuit of metaphysical studies. It will render an important service to the inquiring mind of youth, by leading the student to apply his powers to the cultivation of genuine science, instead of wasting them, as at present, on speculations which can never lead to any result, or on the idle attempt to invent new ideas and opinions. But, above all, it will confer an inestimable benefit on morality and religion, by showing that all the objections urged against them may be silenced for ever by the *Socratic* method, that is to say, by proving the ignorance of the objector. For, as the world has never been, and, no doubt, never will be, without a system of metaphysics of one kind or another, it is the highest and weightiest concern of philosophy to render it powerless for harm, by closing up the sources of error.

This important change in the field of the sciences, this loss of its fancied possessions, to which speculative reason must submit, does not prove in any way detrimental to the general interests of humanity. The advantages which the world has derived from the teachings of pure reason are not at all impaired. The loss falls, in its whole extent, on the *monopoly of the schools*, but does not in the slightest degree touch the *interests of mankind*. I appeal to the most obstinate dogmatist, whether the proof of the continued existence of the soul after death, derived from the simplicity of its substance; of the freedom of the will in opposition to the general mechanism of nature, drawn from the subtle but impotent distinction of subjective and objective practical necessity; or of the existence of God, deduced from the concept of an *ens realissimum* – the contingency of the changeable, and the necessity of a prime mover – has ever been able to pass beyond the limits of the schools, to penetrate the public mind, or to exercise the slightest influence on its convictions. It must be admitted that this has not been the case, and that, owing to the unfitness of the common understanding for such subtle speculations, it can never be expected to take place. On the contrary, it is plain that *the hope of a future life* arises from the feeling, which exists in the breast of every man, that the temporal is inadequate to meet and satisfy the demands of his nature. In like manner, it cannot be doubted that the clear exhibition of duties in opposition to all the claims of inclination, gives rise to the consciousness of *freedom*, and that the glorious order, beauty, and providential care, everywhere displayed in nature, gives rise to the belief in a wise and great Author of the Universe. Such is the genesis of these general convictions of mankind, so far as they depend on rational grounds; and this public property not only remains undisturbed, but is even raised to greater importance, by the doctrine that the schools have no right to arrogate to themselves a more profound insight into a matter of general human concernment, than that to which the great mass of men, ever held by us in the highest estimation, can without difficulty attain, and that the schools should therefore confine themselves to the elaboration of these universally comprehensible, and, from a moral point of view, amply satisfactory proofs. The change, therefore, affects only the arrogant pretensions of the schools, which would gladly retain, in their own exclusive possession, the key to the truths which they impart to the public.

Quod mecum nescit, solus vult scire videri.

At the same time it does not deprive the speculative philosopher of his just title to be the sole depositor of a science which benefits the public without its knowledge – I mean, the *Critique of Pure Reason.* This can never become popular, and, indeed, has no occasion to be so ; for fine-spun arguments in favour of useful truths make just as little impression on the public mind as the equally subtle objections brought against these truths. On the other hand, since both inevitably force themselves on every man who rises to the height of speculation, it becomes the manifest duty of the schools to enter upon a thorough investigation of the rights of speculative reason, and thus to prevent the scandal which metaphysical controversies are sure, sooner or later, to cause even to the masses. It is only by criticism that metaphysicians (and, as such, theologians too) can be saved from these controversies and from the consequent perversion of their doctrines. Criticism alone can strike a blow at the root of Materialism, Fatalism, Atheism, Free-thinking, Fanaticism, and Superstition, which are universally injurious – as well as of Idealism and Scepticism, which are dangerous to the schools, but can scarcely pass over to the public. If governments think proper to interfere with the affairs of the learned, it would be more consistent with a wise regard for the interests of science, as well as for those of society, to favour a criticism of this kind, by which alone the labours of reason can be established on a firm basis, than to support the ridiculous despotism of the schools, which raise a loud cry of danger to the public over the destruction of cobwebs, of which the public has never taken any notice, and the loss of which, therefore, it can never feel.

This critical science is not opposed to the *dogmatic procedure* of reason in pure knowledge; for pure knowledge must always be dogmatic, that is, must rest on strict demonstration from sure principles *a priori* – but to *dogmatism,* that is, to the presumption that it is possible to make any progress with pure knowledge, derived from (philosophical) concepts, according to the principles which reason has long been in the habit of employing – without first inquiring in what way and by what right reason has come into the possession of these principles. Dogmatism is thus the dogmatic procedure of pure reason *without previous criticism of its own powers*, and in opposing this procedure, we must not be supposed to lend any countenance to that loquacious shallowness which arrogates to itself the name of popularity, nor yet to scepticism, which makes short work with the whole science of metaphysics. On the contrary, our criticism is the necessary preparation for a thoroughly scientific system of metaphysics, which must perform its task entirely *a priori*, to the complete satisfaction of speculative reason, and must, therefore, be treated, not popularly, but academically. In carrying out the plan which the *Critique* prescribes, that is, in the future system of metaphysics, we must have recourse to the strict method of the celebrated Wolff, the greatest of all dogmatic philosophers. He was the first to point out the necessity of establishing fixed principles, of clearly defining our concepts, and of subjecting our demonstrations to the most severe scrutiny, instead of rashly jumping at conclusions. The example which he set, served to awaken that spirit of profound and thorough investigation which is not yet extinct in Germany. He would have been peculiarly well fitted to give a truly scientific character to metaphysical studies, had it occurred to him to prepare the field by a criticism of the *organ*, that is, of pure reason itself. That he failed to perceive the necessity of such a procedure, must be ascribed to the dogmatic mode of thought which characterized his age, and on this point the philosophers of his time, as well as of all previous times, have nothing to reproach each other with. Those who reject at once the method of Wolff, and of the *Critique of Pure Reason*, can have no other aim but to shake off the fetters of *science*, to change labour into sport, certainty into opinion, and philosophy into philodoxy.

In this *second edition*, I have endeavoured, as far as possible, to remove the difficulties and obscurity, which, without fault of mine perhaps, have given rise to many misconceptions even among acute thinkers. In the propositions themselves, and in the demonstrations by which they are supported, as well as in the form and the entire plan of the work, I have found nothing to alter; which must be attributed partly to the long examination to which I had subjected the whole before offering it to the public, and partly to the nature of the case. For pure speculative reason is an organic structure in which there is nothing isolated or independent, but every single part is essential to all the rest; and hence, the slightest imperfection, whether defect or positive error, could not fail to betray itself in use. I venture, further, to hope, that this system will maintain the same unalterable character for the future. I am led to entertain this confidence, not by vanity, but by the evidence which the equality of the result affords, when we proceed, first, from the simplest elements up to the complete whole of pure reason, and then, backwards from the whole to each individual part. We find that the attempt to make the slightest alteration, in any part, leads inevitably to contradictions, not merely in this system, but in human reason itself. At the same time, there is still much room for improvement in the *exposition* of the doctrines contained in this work. In the present edition, I have endeavoured to remove misapprehensions of the Aesthetic, especially with regard to the conception of Time; to clear away the obscurity which has been found in the deduction of the concepts of the understanding; to supply the supposed want of sufficient evidence in the demonstration of the principles of the pure understanding; and, lastly, to obviate the misunderstanding of the paralogisms which immediately precede the Rational Psychology. Beyond this point – the end of the second Main Division of the Transcendental Dialectic – I have not extended my alterations,[1]

---

[1] The only addition, properly so called – and that only in the method of proof – which I have made in the present edition, consists of a new refutation of psychological *idealism*, and a strict demonstration – the only one possible, as I believe – of the objective reality of external intuition. However harmless idealism may be considered – although in reality it is not so – in regard to the essential ends of metaphysics, it must still remain an embarrassment to philosophy and to the general human reason to be obliged to assume, as an article of mere faith, the existence of things external to ourselves (from which, yet, we derive the whole material of knowlewdge even for the internal sense), and not to be able to oppose a satisfactory proof to any one who may call it in question. As there is some obscurity of expression in the demonstration as it stands in the text, I propose to alter the passage in question as follows: 'But this permanent cannot be an intuition in me. For all the determining grounds of my existence which can be found in me, are representations, and, as such, do themselves require a permanent, distinct from them, which may determine my existence in relation to their changes, that is, my existence in time, wherein they change.' It may, probably, be urged in opposition to this proof, that, after all, I am only conscious immediately of that which is in me, that is, of my *representation* of external things, and that, consquently, it must always remain uncertain whether anything corresponding to this representation does or does not exist externally to me. But I am conscious, through internal *experience*, of my *existence in time* (consequently, also, of the determinability of the former in the latter), and that is more than the simple consciousness of my representation. It is, in fact, the same as the *empirical consciousness of my existence*, which can only be determined in relation to something, which, while connected with my existence, is *external to me*. This consciousness of my existence in time is, therefore,

partly from want of time, and partly because I am not aware that any portion of the remainder has given rise to misconceptions among intelligent and impartial critics, whom I do not here mention with that praise which is their due, but who will find that their suggestions have been attended to in the work itself.

In attempting to render the exposition of my views as intelligible as possible, I have been compelled to leave out or abridge various passages which were not essential to the completeness of the work, but which many readers might consider useful in other respects, and might be unwilling to miss. This trifling loss, which could not be avoided without swelling the book beyond due limits, may be supplied, at the pleasure of the reader, by a comparison with the first edition, and will, I hope, be more than compensated for by the greater clearness of the exposition as it now stands.

I have observed, with pleasure and thankfulness, in the pages of

identical with the consciousness of a relation to something external to me, and it is, therefore, experience, not fiction, sense, not imagination, which inseparably connects the external with my internal sense. For the external sense is, in itself, the relation of intuition to something real, external to me ; and the reality of this something, as opposed to the mere imagination of it, rests solely on its inseparable connection with internal experience as the condition of its possibility. If with the *intellectual consciousness* of my existence, in the representation : *I am*, which accompanies all my judgments, and all the operations of my understanding, I could, at the same time, connect a determination of my existence by *intellectual intuition*, then the consciousness of a relation to something external to me would not be necessary. But the internal intuition in which alone my existence can be determined, though preceded by that purely intellectual consciousness, is itself sensible and attached to the condition of time. Hence this determination of my existence, and consequently my internal experience itself, must depend on something permanent which is not in me, which can be, therefore, only in something external to me, to which I must look upon myself as being related. Thus the reality of the external sense is necessarily connected with that of the internal, in order to the possibility of experience in general ; that is, I am just as certainly conscious that there are things external to me related to my sense, as I am that I myself exist, as determined in time. But in order to ascertain to what given intuitions objects, external to me, really correspond, in other words, what intuitions belong to the external sense and not to imagination, I must have recourse, in every particular case, to those rules according to which experience in general (even internal experience) is distinguished from imagination, and which are always based on the proposition that there really is an external experience. We may add the remark, that the representation of something *permanent* in existence, is not the same thing as the *permanent representation* ; for a representation may be very variable and changing – as all our representations, even that of matter, are – and yet refer to something permanent, which must, therefore, be distinct from all my representations and external to me, the existence of which is necessarily included in the determination of my own existence, and with it constitutes *one* experience – an experience which would not even be possible internally, if it were not also at the same time, in part, external. To the question *How ?* we are no more able to reply, than we are, in general, to think the stationary in time, the co-existence of which with the variable, produces the conception of change.

various reviews and treatises, that the spirit of profound and thorough investigation is not extinct in Germany, though it may have been overborne and silenced for a time by the fashionable tone of a licence in thinking, which gives itself the airs of genius – and that the difficulties which beset the paths of criticism have not prevented energetic and acute thinkers from making themselves masters of the science of pure reason to which these paths conduct – a science which is not popular, but academic in its character, and which alone can hope for a lasting existence or possess an abiding value. To these deserving men, who so happily combine thoroughness of view with a talent for lucid exposition – a talent which I myself am not conscious of possessing – I leave the task of removing any obscurity which may still adhere to the statement of my doctrines. For, in this case, the danger is not that of being refuted, but of being misunderstood. For my own part, I must henceforward abstain from controversy, although I shall carefully attend to all my suggestions, whether from friends or adversaries, which may be of use in the future elaboration of the system of the Propaedeutic. As, during these labours, I have advanced pretty far in years – this month I reach my sixty-fourth year – it will be necessary for me to economize time, if I am to carry out my plan of elaborating the metaphysics of nature as well as of morals, in confirmation of the correctness of the principles established in this *Critique of Pure Reason*, both speculative and practical; and I must, therefore, leave the task of clearing up the obscurities of the present work – inevitable, perhaps, at the outset – as well as the defence of the whole, to those deserving men who have made my system their own. A philosophical system cannot come forward armed at all points like a mathematical treatise, and hence it may be quite possible to take objection to particular passages, while the organic structure of the system, considered as a unity, has no danger to apprehend. But few possess the ability, and still fewer the inclination, to take a comprehensive view of a new system. By confining the view to particular passages, taking these out of their connection and comparing them with one another, it is easy to pick out apparent contradictions, especially in a work written with any freedom of style. These contradictions place the work in an unfavourable light in the eyes of those who rely on the judgment of others, but are easily reconciled by those who have mastered the idea of the whole. If a theory possesses stability in itself, the action and reaction which seemed at first to threaten its existence, serve only, in the course of time, to smooth down any superficial roughness or inequality; and – if men of insight, impartiality, and truly popular gifts, turn their attention to it – to secure to it, in a short time, the requisite elegance also.

KÖNIGSBERG,
April 1787

INTRODUCTION

I: THE DIFFERENCE BETWEEN PURE AND
EMPIRICAL KNOWLEDGE

That all our knowledge begins with experience there can be no doubt. For how is it possible that the faculty of knowledge should be awakened into exercise otherwise than by means of objects which affect our senses, and partly of themselves produce representations, partly rouse our powers of understanding into activity, to compare, to connect, or to separate these, and so to convert the raw material of our sense impressions into a knowledge of objects, which is called experience? In respect of time, therefore, no knowledge of ours is antecedent to experience, but begins with it.

But, though all our knowledge begins with experience, it by no means follows, that all arises out of experience. For, on the contrary, it is quite possible that our empirical knowledge is a compound of that which we receive through impressions, and that which the faculty of knowledge supplies from itself (sensible impressions giving merely the *occasion*), an addition which we cannot distinguish from the original element given by sense, till long practice has made us attentive to, and skilful in separating it. It is, therefore, a question which requires close investigation, and is not to be answered at first sight – whether there exists a knowledge altogether independent of experience, and even of all sense impressions. Knowledge of this kind is called *a priori*, in contradistinction to empirical knowledge, which has its sources *a posteriori*, that is, in experience.

But the expression, '*a priori*', is not as yet definite enough, adequately to indicate the whole meaning of the question above started. For, in speaking of knowledge which has its sources in experience, we are wont to say, that this or that may be known *a priori*, because we do not derive this knowledge immediately from experience, but from a general rule, which, however, we have itself borrowed from experience. Thus, if a man undermined his house, we say, 'he might know *a priori* that it would have fallen'; that is, he needed not to have waited for the experience that it did actually fall. But still, *a priori*, he could not know even this much. For, that bodies are heavy, and, consequently, that they fall when their supports are taken away, must have been known to him previously, by means of experience.

By the term 'knowledge *a priori*', therefore, we shall in the sequel understand, not such as is independent of this or that kind of experience, but such as is absolutely so of *all* experience. Opposed to this is empirical knowledge, or that which is possible only *a posteriori*, that is, through experience. Knowledge *a priori* is either pure or impure. Pure knowledge *a priori* is that with which no empirical element is mixed up. For example, the proposition, 'Every change has a cause', is a proposition *a priori*, but impure, because change is a concept which can only be derived from experience.

II: COMMON HUMAN UNDERSTANDING IS ALWAYS IN POSSESSION OF CERTAIN KNOWLEDGE *A PRIORI*

The question now is as to a *criterion*, by which we may securely distinguish a pure from an empirical knowledge. Experience no doubt teaches us that this or that object is constituted in such and such a manner, but not that it could possibly exist otherwise. Now, in the first place, if we have a proposition which contains the idea of necessity in its very conception, it is a judgment *a priori*; if, moreoever, it is not derived from any other proposition, unless from one equally involving the idea of necessity, it is absolutely *a priori*. Secondly, an empirical judgment never exhibits strict and absolute, but only assumed and comparative universality (by induction); therefore, the most we can say is – so far as we have hitherto observed – there is no exception to this or that rule. If, on the other hand, a judgment carries with it strict and absolute universality, that is, admits of no possible exception, it is not derived from experience, but is valid absolutely *a priori*.

Empirical universality is, therefore, only an arbitrary extension of validity, from that which may be predicated of a proposition valid in most cases, to that which is asserted of a proposition which holds good in all; as, for example, in the affirmation, 'All bodies are heavy.' When, on the contrary, strict universality characterizes a judgment, it necessarily indicates another peculiar source of knowledge, namely, a faculty of knowledge *a priori*. Necessity and strict universality, therefore, are infallible tests for distinguishing pure from empirical knowledge, and are inseparably connected with each other. But as in the use of these criteria the empirical limitation is sometimes more easily detected than the contingency of the judgment, or the unlimited universality which we attach to a judgment is often a more convincing proof than its necessity, it may be advisable to use the criteria separately, each being by itself infallible.

Now, that in the sphere of human knowledge we have judgments which are necessary, and in the strictest sense universal, consequently pure *a priori*, it will be an easy matter to show. If we desire an example from the sciences, we need only take any proposition in mathematics. If we cast our eyes upon the commonest operations of the understanding, the proposition, 'Every change must have a cause', will amply serve our purpose. In the latter case, indeed, the concept of a cause so plainly involves the concept of a necessity of connection with an effect, and of a strict universality of the law, that the very notion of a cause would entirely disappear, were we to derive it, like Hume, from a frequent association of what happens with that which precedes, and the habit thence originating of connecting representations – the necessity inherent in the judgment being in that case merely subjective. Besides, without seeking for such examples of principles existing *a priori* in knowledge, we might easily show that such principles are the indispensable basis of the possibility of experience itself, and consequently prove their existence *a priori*. For whence could our experience itself acquire its certainty, if all the rules on which it depends were themselves empirical, and consequently contingent? No one, therefore, can admit the validity of the use of such rules as first principles. But, for the present, we may content ourselves with having established the fact, that we do possess and exercise a faculty of pure *a priori* knowledge; and, secondly, with having pointed out the proper tests of such knowledge, namely, universality and necessity.

Not only in judgments, however, but even in concepts, is an *a priori* origin manifest. For example, if we take away by degrees from our empirical concepts of a body all that can be referred to experience – colour, hardness or softness, weight, even impenetrability – the body will then vanish; but the space which it occupied still remains, and this it is utterly impossible to annihilate in thought. Again, if we take away, in like manner, from our empirical concept of any object, corporeal or incorporeal, all properties which mere experience has taught us to connect with it, still we cannot think away those through which we think it as substance, or adhering to substance, although our concept of substances is more determined than that of an object. Compelled, therefore, by that necessity with which the concept of substance forces itself upon us, we must confess that it has its seat in our faculty of knowledge *a priori*.

III: PHILOSOPHY STANDS IN NEED OF A SCIENCE WHICH SHALL DETERMINE THE POSSIBILITY, PRINCIPLES, AND EXTENT OF HUMAN KNOWLEDGE *A PRIORI*

Of far more importance than all that has been above said, is the consideration that certain of our knowledge rises completely above the sphere of all possible experience, and by means of concepts, to which there exists in the whole extent of experience no corresponding object, seem to extend the range of our judgments beyond its bounds. And just in this supersensible sphere, where experience affords us neither instruction nor guidance, lie the investigations of *reason*, which, on account of their importance, we consider far preferable to, and as having a far more elevated aim than, all that the understanding can achieve within the sphere of appearances. So high a value do we set upon these investigations, that even at the risk of error, we persist in following them out, and permit neither doubt nor disregard nor indifference to restrain us from the pursuit. These unavoidable problems of mere pure reason are GOD, FREEDOM, and IMMORTALITY. The science which, with all its preliminaries, has for its especial object the solution of these problems is named metaphysics – a science which is at the very outset dogmatical, that is, it confidently takes upon itself the execution of this task without any previous investigation of the ability or inability of reason for such an undertaking.

Now the safe ground of experience being thus abandoned, it seems nevertheless natural that we should hesitate to erect a building with the knowledge we possess, without knowing whence it comes, and on the strength of principles, the origin of which is undiscovered. Instead of thus trying to build without a foundation, it is rather to be expected that we should long ago have put the question, how can the understanding arrive at this *a priori* knowledge, and what is the extent, validity, and worth which it may possess? We say, this is natural enough, meaning by the word natural, that which is consistent with a just and reasonable way of thinking; but if we understand by the term, that which usually happens, nothing indeed could be more natural and more comprehensible than that this investigation should be left long unattempted. For one part of our pure knowledge, the science of mathematics, has been long firmly established, and thus leads us to form flattering expectations with regard to others, though these may be of quite a different nature. Besides, when we get beyond the bounds of experience, we are of course safe from opposition in that quarter; and the charm of widening the range of our knowledge is so great, that unless we are brought to a standstill by some evident contradiction, we hurry on undoubtingly in our course. This, however, may be avoided, if we are sufficiently cautious in the construction of our fictions, which are not the less fictions on that account.

Mathematical science affords us a brilliant example, how far, independently of all experience, we may carry our *a priori* knowledge. It is true that the mathematician occupies himself with objects and knowledge only in so far as they can be represented by means of intuition. But this circumstance is easily overlooked, because the said intuition can itself be given *a priori*, and therefore is hardly distinguished from a pure concept. Deceived by such a proof of the power of reason, we can perceive no limits to the extension of our knowledge. The light dove cleaving in free flight the thin air, whose resistance it feels, might imagine that her movements would be far more free and rapid in airless space. Just in the same way did Plato, abandoning the world of sense because of the narrow limits it sets to the understanding, venture upon the wings of ideas beyond it, into the void space of pure intellect. He did not reflect that he made no real progress by all his efforts; for he met with no resistance which might serve him for a support, as it were, whereon to rest, and on which he might apply his powers, in order to let the intellect acquire momentum for its progress. It is, indeed, the common fate of human reason in speculation, to finish the imposing edifice of thought as rapidly as possible, and then for the first time to begin to examine whether the foundation is a solid one or no. Arrived at this point, all sorts of excuses are sought after, in order to console us for its want of stability, or rather, indeed, to enable us to dispense altogether with so late and dangerous an investigation. But what frees us during the process of building from all apprehension or suspicion, and flatters us into the belief of its solidity, is this. A great part, perhaps the greatest part, of the business of our reason consists in the analysis of the concepts which we already possess of objects. By this means we gain a multitude of knowledge, which although really nothing more than elucidation or explanation of that which (though in a confused manner) was already thought in our concepts, are, at least in respect of their form, prized as new insight; whilst, so far as regards their matter or content, we have really made no addition to our concepts, but only taken them apart.

But as this process does furnish real *a priori* knowledge, which has a sure progress and useful results, reason, deceived by this, slips in, without being itself aware of it, assertions of a quite different kind; in which, to given concepts it adds others, *a priori* indeed, but entirely foreign to them, without our knowing how it arrives at these, and, indeed, without such a question ever suggesting itself. I shall therefore at once proceed to examine the difference between these two modes of knowledge.

IV: THE DIFFERENCE BETWEEN ANALYTICAL AND SYNTHETICAL JUDGMENTS

In all judgments wherein the relation of a suject to the predicate is thought (I mention affirmative judgments only here; the application to negative will be very easy), this relation is possible in two different ways. Either the predicate B belongs to the subject A, as somewhat which is contained (though covertly) in the concept A; or the predicate B lies completely outside the concept A, although it stands in connection with it. In the first instance, I term the judgment analytical, in the second, synthetical. Analytical judgments (affirmative) are therefore those in which the connection of the predicate with the subject is thought through identity; those in which this connection is thought without identity, are called synthetical judgments. The former may be called *explicative*, the latter *augmentative* judgments; because the former add in the predicate nothing to the concept of the subject, but only analyse it into its constituent concepts, which were thought already in the subject, although in a confused manner; the latter add to our concepts of the subject a predicate which was not contained in it, and which no analysis could ever have discovered therein. For example, when I say, 'All bodies are extended,' this is an analytical judgment. For I need not go beyond the concept of *body* in order to find extension connected with it, but merely analyse the concept, that is, become conscious of the manifold properties which I think in that concept, in order to discover this predicate in it: it is therefore an analytical judgment. On the other hand, when I say, 'All bodies are heavy', the predicate is something totally different from that which I think in the mere concept of a body. By the addition of such a predicate, therefore, it becomes a synthetical judgment.

Empirical judgments, as such, are always synthetical. For it would be absurd to think of grounding an analytical judgment on experience, because in forming such a judgment I need not go outside the sphere of my concepts, and therefore recourse to the testimony of experience is quite unnecessary. That 'bodies are extended' is not an empirical judgment, but a proposition which stands firm *a priori*. For before addressing myself to experience, I already have in my concept all the requisite conditions for the judgment, and I have only to extract the predicate from the concept, according to the principle of contradiction, and thereby at the same time become conscious of the necessity of the judgment, a necessity which I could never learn from experience. On the other hand, though at first I do not at all include the predicate of weight in my concept of body in general, that concept still indicates an object of experience, a part of the totality of experience, to which I can still add other parts ; and this I do when I recognize by observation that bodies are heavy. I can know beforehand by analysis the concept of body through the characteristics of extension, impenetrability, shape, etc., all of which are thought in this concept. But now I extend my knowledge, and looking back on experience from which I had derived this concept of body, I find weight at all times connected with the above characteristics, and therefore I synthetically add to my concepts this as a predicate, and say, 'All bodies are heavy.' Thus it is experience upon which rests the possibility of the synthesis of the predicate of weight with the concept of body, because both concepts, although the one is not contained in the other, still belong to one another (only contingently, however), as parts of a whole, namely, of experience, which is itself a synthesis of intuitions.

But to synthetical judgments *a priori*, such aid is entirely wanting. If I go out of and beyond the concept A, in order to apprehend another B as connected with it, what foundation have I to rest on, whereby to render the synthesis possible ? I have here no longer the advantage of looking out in the sphere of experience for what I want. Let us take, for example, the proposition, 'Everything that happens has a cause.' In the concept of *something that happens*, I indeed think an existence which a certain time antecedes, and from this I can derive analytical judgments. But the concept of a cause lies quite out of the above concept, and indicates something entirely different from 'that which happens,' and is consequently not contained in that concept. How then am I able to assert concerning the general concept – 'that which happens' – something entirely different from that concept, and to apprehend the concept of cause although not contained in it, yet as belonging to it, and even necessarily ? What is here the unknown=x, upon which the understanding rests when it believes it has found, out of the concept A a foreign predicate B, which it nevertheless considers to be connected with it ? It cannot be experience, because the principle adduced annexes the two representations, cause and effect, to the representation existence, not only with universality, which experience cannot give, but also with the expression of necessity, therefore completely *a priori* and from pure concepts. Upon such synthetical, that is augmentative propositions, depends the whole aim of our speculative knowledge *a priori*; for although analytical judgments are indeed highly important and necessary, they are so, only to arrive at that clearness of concepts which is requisite for a sure and extended synthesis, and this alone provides genuinely new acquisition of knowledge.

V: IN ALL THEORETICAL SCIENCES OF REASON, SYNTHETICAL *A PRIORI* JUDGMENTS ARE CONTAINED AS PRINCIPLES

1. Mathematical judgments are always synthetical. Hitherto this fact, though incontestably true and very important in its consequences, seems to have escaped the analysts of human reason, nay, to be in complete opposition to all their conjectures. For as it was found that mathematical conclusions all proceed according to the principle of contradiction (which the nature of every apodeictic certainty requires), people became persuaded that the fundamental principles of the science also were recognized and admitted in the same way. But this is erroneous; for although a synthetical proposition can certainly be discerned by means of the principle of contradiction, this is possible only when another synthetical proposition precedes, from which the latter is deduced, but never of itself.

Before all, be it observed, that mathematical propositions proper are always judgments *a priori*, and not empirical, because they carry with them necessity, which cannot be given by experience. If this be demurred to, it matters not; I will then limit my assertion to *pure* mathematics, the very concept of which implies that is consists of knowledge altogether non-empirical and *a priori*.

We might, indeed, at first suppose that the proposition $7+5=12$ is a merely analytical proposition, following (according to the principle of contradiction) from the concept of a sum of seven and five. But if we regard it more narrowly, we find that our concept of the sum of seven and five contains nothing more than the uniting of both sums into one, whereby it cannot at all be thought what this single number is which embraces both. The concept of twelve is by no means obtained by merely thinking the union of seven and five; and we may analyse our concept of such a possible sum as long as we will, still we shall never discover in it the notion of twelve. We must go beyond these concepts, and have recourse to an intuition which corresponds to one of the two – our five fingers, for example, or like Segner in his *Arithmetic* five points – and so by degrees, add the units contained in the five given in the intuition, to the concept of seven. For I first take the number 7, and, for the concept of 5 calling in the aid of the fingers of my hand as objects of intuition, I add the units, which I before took together to make up the number 5, gradually now by means of the material image my hand, to the number 7, and by this process, I at length see the number 12 arise. That 7 should be added to 5, I have certainly thought in my concept of a sum$=7+5$, but not that this sum was equal to 12. Arithmetical propositions are therefore always synthetical, of which we may become more clearly convinced by trying large numbers. For it will thus become quite evident, that turn and twist our concepts as we may, it is impossible, without having recourse to intuition, to arrive at the sum total or produce by means of the mere analysis of our concepts. Just as little is any principle of pure geometry analytical. 'A straight line between two points is the shortest', is a synthetical proposition. For my concept of *straight* contains no notion of *quantity*, but is merely *qualitative*. The concept of the *shortest* is therefore wholly an addition, and by no analysis can it be extracted from our concept of a straight line. Intuition must therefore here lend its aid, by means of which and thus only, our synthesis is possible.

Some few principles presupposed by geometricians are, indeed, really analytical, and depend on the principle of contradiction. They serve, however, like identical propositions, as links in the chain of method, not as principles – for example, $a=a$, the whole is equal to itself, or $(a+b)>a$, the whole is greater than its part. And yet even these principles themselves, though they derive their validity from mere concepts, are only admitted in mathematics because they can be presented in intuition. What causes us here commonly to believe that the predicate of such apodeictic judgments is already contained in our concept, and that the judgment is therefore analytical, is merely the equivocal nature of the expression. We must join in thought a certain predicate to a given concept, and this necessity cleaves already to the concept. But the question is, not what we must join in thought to the given concept, but what we really think therein, though only obscurely, and then it becomes manifest, that the predicate pertains to these concepts, necessarily indeed, yet not as thought in the concept itself, but by virtue of an intuition, which must be added to the concept.

2. Natural science (physics) contains in itself synthetical judgments *a priori*, as principles. I shall adduce two propositions. For instance, the proposition, 'In all changes of the material world, the quantity of matter remains unchanged'; or, that, 'In all communication of motion, action and reaction must always be equal.' In both of these, not only is the necessity, and therefore their origin *a priori* clear, but also that they are synthetical propositions. For in the concept of matter, I do not think its permanency, but merely its presence in space, which it fills. I therefore really go out of and beyond the concept of matter, in order to think on to it something *a priori*, which I did not think in it. The proposition is therefore not analytical, but synthetical, and nevertheless conceived *a priori*; and so it is with regard to the other propositions of the pure part of natural science.

3. As to metaphysics, even if we look upon it merely as an attempted science, yet, from the nature of human reason, an indispensable one, we find that it must contain synthetical *a priori* knowledge. It is not merely the duty of metaphysics to dissect, and thereby analytically to illustrate the concepts which we form *a priori* of things; but we seek to widen the range of our *a priori* knowledge. For this purpose, we must avail ourselves of such principles as add something to the original concept – something not identical with, nor contained in it, and by means of synthetical judgments *a priori*, leave behind us the limits of experience; for example, in the proposition, 'the world must have a beginning,' and such like. Thus metaphysics, at least in its intention, consists merely of synthetical propositions *a priori*.

VI: THE GENERAL PROBLEM OF PURE REASON

It is extremely advantageous to be able to bring a number of investigations under the formula of a single problem. For in this manner, we not only facilitate our own labour, inasmuch as we define it clearly to ourselves, but also render it more easy for others to decide whether we have done justice to our undertaking. The proper problem of pure reason, then, is contained in the question: 'How are synthetical *a priori* judgments possible?'

That metaphysics has hitherto remained in so vacillating a state of uncertainty and contradiction, is only to be attributed to the fact, that this great problem, and perhaps even the difference between analytical and synthetical judgments, did not sooner suggest itself to philosophers. Upon the solution of this problem, or upon sufficient proof of the impossibility of synthetical knowledge *a priori*, depends the existence or downfall of metaphysics. Among philosophers, David Hume came the nearest of all to this problem; yet it never acquired in his mind sufficient precision, nor did he regard the question in its universality. On the contrary, he stopped short at the synthetical proposition of the connection of an effect with its cause (*principium causalitatis*), insisting that such proposition was impossible *a priori*. According to his conclusions, then, all that we term metaphysics is a mere delusion, arising from the fancied insight of reason into that which is in truth borrowed from experience, and to which habit has given the appearance of necessity. Against this assertion, destructive to all pure philosophy, he would have been guarded, had he had our problem before his eyes in its universality. For he would then have perceived that, according to his own argument, there likewise could not be any pure mathematical science, which assuredly cannot exist without synthetical propositions *a priori* – an absurdity from which his good understanding must have saved him.

In the solution of the above problem is at the same time comprehended the possibility of the use of pure reason in the foundation and construction of all sciences which contain theoretical knowledge *a priori* of objects, that is to say, the answer to the following questions:

How is pure mathematics possible?

How is pure natural science possible?

Respecting these sciences, as they do certainly exist, it may with propriety be asked, *how* they are possible – for that they must be possible, is shown by the fact of their really existing.[1] But as to metaphysics, the poor progress it has hitherto made, and the fact

---

[1] As to the existence of pure natural science, or physics, perhaps many may still express doubts. But we have only to look at the different propositions which are commonly treated of at the commencement of proper (empirical) physical science – those, for example, relating to the permanence of the same quantity of matter, the *vis inertiae*, the equality of action and reaction, etc. – to be soon convinced that they form a science of pure physics (*physica pura*, or *rationalis*), which well deserves to be separately exposed as a special science, in its whole extent, whether that be great or confined.

that of no one system yet brought forward, as far as regards its true aim, can it be said that this science really exists, leaves any one at liberty to doubt with reason its very possibility.

Yet, in a certain sense, this kind of knowledge must unquestionably be looked upon as *given*; in other words, metaphysics must be considered as really existing, if not as a science, nevertheless as a natural disposition of the human mind (*metaphysica naturalis*). For human reason, without any instigations imputable to the mere vanity of great knowledge, unceasingly progresses, urged on by its own feeling of need, towards such questions as cannot be answered by any empirical application of reason, or principles derived therefrom; and so there has ever really existed in every man some system of metaphysics. It will always exist, so soon as reason awakes to the exercise of its power of speculation. And now the question arises: How is metaphysics, as a natural disposition, possible? In other words, how, from the nature of universal human reason, do those questions arise which pure reason proposes to itself, and which it is impelled by its own feeling of need to answer as well as it can?

But as in all the attempts hitherto made to answer the questions which reason is prompted by its very nature to propose to itself, for example, whether the world had a beginning, or has existed from eternity, it has always met with unavoidable contradictions, we must not rest satisfied with the mere natural disposition of the mind to metaphysics, that is, with the existence of the faculty of pure reason, whence, indeed, some sort of metaphysical system always arises; but it must be possible to arrive at certainty in regard to the question whether we know or do not know the things of which metaphysics treats. We must be able to arrive at a decision on the subjects of its questions, or on the ability or inability of reason to form any judgment respecting them; and therefore either to extend with confidence the bounds of our pure reason, or to set strictly defined and safe limits to its use. This last question, which arises out of the above universal problem, would properly run thus: How is metaphysics possible as a science?

Thus, the critique of reason leads at last, naturally and necessarily, to science; and, on the other hand, the dogmatical use of reason without criticism leads to groundless assertions, against which others equally specious can always be set, thus ending unavoidably in scepticism.

Besides, this science cannot be of great and formidable prolixity, because it has to do not with objects of reason, the variety of which is inexhaustible, but merely with reason itself and its problems; problems which arise out of its own bosom, and are not proposed to it by the nature of outward things, but by its own nature. And when once reason has previously become able completely to understand its own power in regard to objects which it meets with in experience, it will be easy to determine securely the extent and limits of its attempted application to objects beyond the confines of experience.

We may and must, therefore, regard the attempts hitherto made to establish metaphysical science dogmatically as non-existent. For the analysis, that is, mere dissection of concepts, contained in this or that, is not the aim of, but only a preparation for metaphysics proper, which has for its object the extension, by means of synthesis, of our *a priori* knowledge. And for this purpose, mere analysis is of course useless, because it only shows what is contained in these concepts, but not how we arrive, *a priori*, at them; and this it is its duty to show, in order to be able afterwards to determine their valid use in regard to all objects of experience, to all knowledge in general. But little self-denial, indeed, is needed to give up these pretensions, seeing the undeniable, and in the dogmatic mode of procedure, inevitable contradictions of reason with itself, have long since ruined the reputation of every system of metaphysics that has appeared up to this time. It will require more firmness to remain undeterred by difficulty from within, and opposition from without, from endeavouring, by a method quite opposed to all those hitherto followed, to further the growth and fruitfulness of a science indispensable to human reason – a science from which every branch it has borne may be cut away, but whose roots remain indestructible.

VII: IDEA AND DIVISION OF A SPECIAL SCIENCE, UNDER THE NAME OF A *CRITIQUE OF PURE REASON*

From all that has been said, there results the idea of a special science, which may be called the *Critique of Pure Reason*. For reason is the faculty which furnishes us with the principles of knowledge *a priori*. Hence, pure reason is the faculty which contains the principles of knowledge absolutely *a priori*. An Organon of pure reason would be a compendium of those principles according to which alone all pure knowledge *a priori* can be obtained. The exhaustive application of such an organon would afford us a system of pure reason. As this, however, is demanding a great deal, and it is yet doubtful whether any extension of our knowledge be here possible, or if so, in what cases ; we can regard a science of the mere criticism of pure reason, its sources and limits, as the *propaedeuctic* to a system of pure reason. Such a science must not be called a Doctrine, but only a Critique of Pure Reason ; and its use, in regard to speculation, would be only negative, not to enlarge the bounds of, but to purify our reason, and to shield it against error – which alone is no little gain. I apply the term *transcendental* to all knowledge which is not so much occupied with objects as with the mode of our knowledge of objects, so far as this mode of knowledge is possible *a priori*. A system of such concepts would be called *Transcendental Philosophy*. But this, again, is still beyond the bounds of our present essay. For as such a science must contain a complete exposition not only of our synthetical *a priori*, but of our analytical *a priori* knowledge, it is of too wide a range for our present purpose, because we do not require to carry our analysis any farther than is necessary to understand, in their full extent, the principles of synthesis *a priori*, with which alone we have to do. This investigation, which we cannot properly call a doctrine, but only a transcendental critique, because it aims not at the enlargement, but at the correction and guidance of our knowledge, and is to serve as a touchstone of the worth or worthlessness of all knowledge *a priori*, is the sole object of our present essay. Such a critique is consequently, as far as possible, a preparation for an organon ; and if this new organon should be found to fail, at least for a canon of pure reason, according to which the complete system of the philosophy of pure reason, whether it extend or limit the bounds of that reason, might one day be set forth both analytically and synthetically. For that this is possible, nay, that such a system is not of so great extent as to preclude the hope of its ever being completed, is evident. For we have not here to do with the nature of objects, which is infinite, but solely with the understanding, which judges of the nature of objects, and, again, with the understanding only in respect of its knowledge *a priori*. And the object of our investigations, as it is not to be sought outside, but altogether within ourselves, cannot remain concealed, and in all probability is limited enough to be completely surveyed and fairly estimated, according to its worth or worthlessness. Still less let the reader here expect a critique of books and systems of pure reason ; our present object is exclusively a critique of the faculty of pure reason itself. Only when we make this critique our foundation, do we possess a reliable touchstone for estimating the philosophical value of ancient and modern writings on this subject; and without this criterion, the incompetent historian or judge decides upon and corrects the groundless assertions of others with his own, which have themselves just as little foundation.

Transcendental philosophy is the idea of a science, for which the *Critique of Pure Reason* must sketch the whole plan architectonically, that is, from principles, with a full guarantee for the completeness and certainty of all the parts which enter into the building. It is the system of all the principles of pure reason. If this *Critique* itself does not assume the title of transcendental philosophy, it is only because, to be a complete system, it ought to contain a full analysis of all human knowledge *a priori*. Our critique must, indeed, lay before us a complete enumeration of all the fundamental concepts which constitute the said pure knowledge. But from the complete analysis of these concepts themselves, as also from a complete investigation of those derived from them, it abstains with reason; partly because it would be deviating from the end in view to occupy itself with this analysis, since this process is not attended with the difficulty and uncertainty to be found in the synthesis, to which our critique is entirely devoted, and partly because it would be inconsistent with the unity of our plan to burden this essay with the vindication of the completeness of such an analysis and deduction, with which, after all, we have at present nothing to do. This completeness of the analysis of these fundamental concepts, as well as of the deduction from the concepts *a priori* which may be given by the analysis, we can, however, easily attain, provided only that we are in possession of all these fundamental concepts, which are to serve as principles of the synthesis, and that in respect of this main purpose nothing is wanting.

To the *Critique of Pure Reason*, therefore, belongs all that constitutes transcendental philosophy; and it is the complete idea of transcendental philosophy, but still not that science itself; because it only proceeds so far with the analysis as is necessary for a complete assessment of our synthetical knowledge *a priori*.

The principal thing we must attend to, in the division of such a science, is: that no concepts must enter it which contain anything empirical; in other words, that the knowledge *a priori* must be completely pure. Hence, although the highest principles and fundamental concepts of morality are knowledge *a priori*, yet they do not belong to transcendental philosophy; because, though they certainly do not lay the concepts of pain, pleasure, desires, inclinations, etc. (which are all of empirical origin), at the foundation of its precepts, yet still into the concept of duty – as an obstacle to be overcome, or as an incitement which should not be made into a motive – these empirical concepts must necessarily enter, in the construction of a system of pure morality. Transcendental philosophy is consequently a philosophy of the pure and merely speculative reason. For all that is practical, so far as it contains motives, relates to feelings; and these belong to empirical sources of knowledge.

If we wish to divide this science from the universal point of view of a system in general, it ought to comprehend, first, a *Doctrine of the Elements*, and, secondly, a *Doctrine of the Method* of pure reason. Each of these main divisions will have its subdivisions, the separate reasons for which we cannot yet spell out. Only so much seems necessary, by way of introduction or anticipation, that there are two sources of human knowledge (which probably spring from a common, but to us unknown root), namely sensibility and understanding. By the former, objects are *given* to us, by the latter, they are *thought*. So far as the faculty of sensibility may contain representations *a priori*, which form the conditions under which objects are given, in so far it belongs to transcendental philosophy. The transcendental doctrine of sensibility must form the first part of our science of elements, because the conditions under which alone the objects of human knowledge are given, must precede those under which they are thought.

TRANSCENDENTAL DOCTRINE
OF ELEMENTS

PART I : TRANSCENDENTAL AESTHETIC

§ 1 : Introductory

In whatsoever mode, or by whatsoever means, our knowledge may relate to objects, it is at least quite clear, that the only manner in which it immediately relates to them, is by means of intuition, thought being only a means aiming at intuitions. But an intuition can take place only in so far as the object is given to us. This, again, is only possible, to man at least, on conditions that the object affect the mind in a certain manner. The capacity for receiving representations (receptivity) through the mode in which we are affected by objects, is called *sensibility*. By means of sensibility, therefore, objects are given to us, and it alone furnishes us with intuitions; by the understanding they are *thought*, and from it arise concepts. But all thought must directly, or indirectly, by means of certain signs, relate ultimately to intuitions; consequently, with us, to sensibility, because in no other way can an object be given to us.

The effect of an object upon the faculty of representation, so far as we are affected by the said object, is sensation. That sort of intuition which relates to an object by means of sensation, is called an empirical intuition. The undetermined object of an emipircal intuition, is called *appearance*. That which in appearance corresponds to the sensation, I term its *matter*; but that which effects that the manifold of appearance can be arranged under certain relations, I call its *form*. But that in which our sensations are merely arranged, and by which they are susceptible of assuming a certain form, cannot be itself sensation. It is, then, the matter of all appearances that is given to us *a posteriori*; the form must lie ready *a priori* for them in the mind, and consequently can be regarded separately from all sensation.

I call all representations *pure*, in the transcendental meaning of the word, wherein nothing is met with that belongs to sensation. And accordingly we find existing in the mind *a priori*, the pure form of sensible intuitions in general, in which all the manifold of appearances is arranged and viewed under certain relations. This pure form of sensibility I shall call pure intuition. Thus, if I take away from our representation of a body, all that the understanding thinks as belonging to it, as substance, force, divisibility, etc., and also whatever belongs to sensation, as impenetrability, hardness, colour, etc.; yet there is still something left us from this empirical intuition, namely, extension and shape. These belong to pure intuition, which exists *a priori* in the mind, as a mere form of sensibility, and without any real object of the senses or any sensation.

The science of all the principles of sensibility *a priori*, I call Transcendental Aesthetic.[1] There must, then, be such a science forming the first part of the transcendental doctrine of elements, in contradistinction to that part which contains the principles of pure thought, and which is called transcendental logic.

In the science of transcendental aesthetic accordingly, we shall first isolate sensibility, by separating from it all that is annexed to it by the concepts of understanding, so that nothing be left but empirical intuition. In the next place we shall take away from this intuition all that belongs to sensation, so that nothing may remain but pure intuition, and the mere form of appearances, which is all that the sensibility can afford *a priori*. From this investigation it will be found that there are two pure forms of sensible intuition, as principles of knowledge *a priori*, namely, space and time. To the consideration of these we shall now proceed.

SECTION I : SPACE

§2 : *Metaphysical Exposition of the Concept of Space*

By means of the external sense (a property of the mind), we represent to ourselves objects as outside us, and these all in space. Therein alone are their shape, dimensions, and relations to each other determined or determinable. The internal sense, by means of

---

[1] The Germans are the only people who at present use this word to indicate what others call the critique of taste. At the foundation of this term lies the disappointed hope, which the eminent analyst, Baumgarten, conceived, of subjecting the criticism of the beautiful to principles of reason, and so of elevating its rules into a science. But his endeavours were vain. For the said rules or criteria are, in respect to their chief sources, merely empirical, and consequently never can serve as determinate laws *a priori*, by which our judgment in matters of taste is to be directed. It is rather our judgment which forms the proper test as to the correctness of the principles. On this account it is advisable to give up the use of the term as designating the critique of taste, and to apply it solely to that doctrine, which is true science – the science of the laws of sensibility – and thus come nearer to the language and the sense of the ancients in their well-known division of the objects of cognition into αἰσθητὰ καὶ νοητά, or to share it with speculative philosophy, and employ it partly in a transcendental, partly in a psychological signification.

which the mind contemplates itself or its internal state, gives, indeed, no intuition of the soul as an object; yet there is nevertheless a determinate form, under which alone the contemplation of our internal state is possible, so that all which relates to the inward determinations of the mind is represented in relations of time. Of time we cannot have any external intuition, any more than we can have an internal intuition of space. What then are time and space? Are they real existences? Or, are they merely relations or determinations of things, such, however, as would equally belong to these things in themselves, though they should never become objects of intuition; or, are they such as belong only to the form of intuition, and consequently to the subjective constitution of the mind, without which these predicates of time and space could not be attached to any object? In order to become informed on these points, we shall first give an exposition of the concept of space. By exposition, I mean the clear, though not exhaustive, representation of that which belongs to a concept; and an exposition is metaphysical, when it contains that which represents the concept as given *a priori*.

1. Space is not an empirical concept which has been derived from outward experiences. For, in order that certain sensations may relate to something outside me (that is, to something which occupies a different part of space from that in which I am); in like manner, in order that I may represent them not merely as outside of and next to each other, but also in separate places, the representation of space must already exist as a foundation. Consequently, the representation of space cannot be borrowed from the relations of external phenomena through experience; but, on the contrary, this external experience is itself only possible through the said antecedent representation.

2. Space then is a necessary representation *a priori*, which serves for the foundation of all external intuitions. We never can imagine or make a representation to ourselves of the non-existence of space, though we may easily enough think that no objects are found in it. It must, therefore, be considered as the condition of the possibility of appearances, and by no means as a determination dependent on them, and is a representation *a priori*, which necessarily supplies the basis for external appearances.

3. Space is no discursive, or as we say, general concept of the relations of things, but a pure intuition. For in the first place, we can only represent to ourselves one space, and when we talk of divers spaces, we mean only parts of one and the same space.

Moreover, these parts cannot antecede this one all-embracing space, as the component parts from which the aggregate can be made up, but can be thought only as existing in it. Space is essentially one, and multiplicity in it; consequently the general concept of spaces depends solely upon limitations. Hence it follows that an *a priori* intuition (which is not empirical) lies at the root of all our concepts of space. Thus, moreover, the principles of geometry – for example, that 'in a triangle, two sides together are greater than the third' – are never derived from general concepts of line and triangle, but from intuition, and this *a priori*, with apodeictic certainty.

4. Space is represented as an infinite given quantity. Now every concept must indeed be considered as a representation which is contained in an infinite multitude of different possible representations (as their common characteristic), which therefore, comprises these under itself; but no concept, as such, can be so conceived, as if it contained within itself an infinite multitude of representations. Nevertheless, space is so conceived, for all parts of space, even to infinity, exist at once. Consequently, the original representation of space is an intuition *a priori*, and not a concept.

§ 3 : Transcendental Exposition of the Concept of Space

By a transcendental exposition, I mean the explanation of a concept, as a principle, whence can be discerned the possibility of other synthetical *a priori* knowledge. For this purpose, it is requisite, firstly, that such knowledge does really flow from the given concept; and, secondly, that the said knowledge is only possible under the presupposition of a given mode of explaining this concept.

Geometry is a science which determines the properties of space synthetically, and yet *a priori*. What, then, must be our representation of space, in order that such a knowledge of it may be possible ? It must be originally intuition, for from a mere concept, no propositions can be deduced which go beyond the concept, and yet this happens in geometry. (Introd. V.) But this intuition must be found in us *a priori*, that is, before any perception of objects, consequently must be pure, not empirical, intuition. For geometrical principles are always apodeictic, that is, united with the consciousness of their necessity, as: 'Space has only three dimensions.' But propositions of this kind cannot be empirical judgments, nor conclusions from them. (Introd. II.) Now, how can an external intuition anterior to objects themselves, and in which our concept of objects can be determined *a priori*, exist in the human mind? Obviously not otherwise than in so far as it has its seat in the subject only, as the *formal* capacity of the subject's being affected by objects, and thereby of obtaining immediate representation, that is, intuition; consequently, only as the *form of the external sense* in general.

Thus it is only by means of our explanation that the possibility of geometry, as a synthetical science *a priori*, becomes comprehensible. Every mode of explanation which does not show us this possibility, although in appearance it may be similar to ours, can with the utmost certainty be distinguished from it by these marks.

§ 4 : *Conclusions from the foregoing Concepts*

(*a*) Space does not represent any property of objects as things in themselves, nor does it represent them in their relations to each other; in other words, space does not represent to us any determination of objects such as attaches to the objects themselves, and would remain, even though all subjective conditions of intuition were abstracted. For neither absolute nor relative determinations of objects can be intuited prior to the existence of the things to which they belong, and therefore not *a priori*.

(*b*) Space is nothing else than the form of all appearances of the external sense, that is, the subjective condition of sensibility, under which alone external intuition is possible. Now, because the receptivity or capacity of the subject to be affected by objects necessarily antecedes all intuitions of these objects, it is easily understood how the form of all appearances can be given in the mind previous to all actual perceptions, therefore *a priori*, and how it, as a pure intuition, in which all objects must be determined, can contain principles of the relations of these objects prior to all experience.

It is therefore from the human point of view only that we can speak of space, extended objects, etc. If we depart from the subjective condition, under which alone we can obtain external intuition, or, in other words, by means of which we are affected by objects, the representation of space has no meaning whatsoever. This predicate [of space] is only applicable to things in so far as they appear to us, that is, are objects of sensibility. The constant form of this receptivity, which we call sensibility, is a necessary condition of all relations in which objects can be intuited as existing outside us, and when abstraction of these objects is made, is a pure intuition, to which we give the name of space. It is clear that we cannot make the special conditions of sensibility into conditions of the possibility of things, but only of the possibility of their existence as far as they are appearances. And so we may correctly say that space contains all which can appear to us externally, but not all things considered as things in themselves, be they intuited or not, or by whatsoever subject one will. As to the intuitions of other thinking beings, we cannot judge whether they are or are not bound by the same conditions which limit our own intuition, and which for us are universally valid. If we join the limitation of a judgment to the concept of the subject, then the judgment will possess unconditioned validity. For example, the proposition, 'All objects are beside each other in space,' is valid only under the limitation that these things are taken as objects of our sensible intuition. But if I join the condition to the concept, and say, 'All things, as external appearances, are beside each other in space,' then the rule is valid universally, and without any limitation. Our expositions, consequently teach the *reality* (i.e. the objective validity) of space in regard of all which can be presented to us externally as object, and at the same time also the *ideality* of space in regard to objects when they are considered by means of reason as things in themselves, that is, without reference to the constitution of our sensibility. We maintain, therefore, the *empirical reality* of space in regard to all possible external experience, although we must admit its *transcendental ideality*; in other words, that it is nothing, so soon as we withdraw the condition upon which the possibility of all experience depends, and look upon space as something that belongs to things in themselves.

But, with the exception of space, there is no representation, subjective and referring to something external to us, which could be called objective *a priori*. For there are no other subjective representations from which we can derive synthetical propositions *a priori*, as we can from the intuition of space. (See § 3.) Therefore, to speak accurately, no ideality whatever belongs to these, although they agree in this respect with the representation of space, that they belong merely to the subjective nature of the mode of sensible perception; such a mode, for example, as that of sight, of hearing, and of feeling, by means of the sensations of colour, sound, and heat, but which, because they are only sensations, and not intuitions, do not of themselves give us the cognition of any object, least of all, *a priori* knowledge. My purpose, in the above remark, is merely this: to guard any one against illustrating the asserted ideality of space by examples quite insufficient, for example, by colour, taste, etc.; for these must be contemplated not as properties of things, but only as changes in the subject, changes which may be different in different men. For, in such a case, that which is originally a mere appearance, a rose, for example, is taken by the empirical understanding for a thing in itself, though to every different eye, in respect of its colour, it may appear different. On the contrary, the transcendental concept of appearances in space is a critical admonition, that, in general, nothing which is intuited in space is a thing in itself, and that space is not a form which belongs as a property to things; but that objects are quite unknown to us in themselves, and what we call outward objects, are nothing else but mere representations of our sensibility, whose form is space, but whose real correlate, the thing in itself, is not known by means of these representations, nor ever can be, but respecting which, in experience, no inquiry is ever made.

SECTION II: TIME

§ 5: *Metaphysical Exposition of the Concept of Time*

1. TIME is not an empirical concept. For neither co-existence nor succession would be perceived by us, if the representation of time did not exist as a foundation *a priori*. Without this presupposition we could not represent to ourselves that things exist together at one and the same time, or at different times, that is, contemporaneously, or in succession.

2. Time is a necessary representation, lying at the foundation of all our intuitions. With regard to appearances in general, we cannot think away time from them, and represent them to ourselves as out of and unconnected with time, but we can quite well represent to ourselves time void of appearances. Time is therefore given *a priori*. In it alone is all reality of appearances possible. These may be all annihilated in thought, but time itself, as the universal condition of their possibility, cannot be so annulled.

3. On this necessity *a priori* is also founded the possibility of apodeictic principles of the relations of time, or axioms of time in general, such as: 'Time has only one dimension', 'Different times are not co-existent but successive' (as different spaces are not successive but co-existent). These principles cannot be derived from

experience, for it would give neither strict universality, nor apodeictic certainty. We should only be able to say, 'So common experience teaches us', but not it must be so. They are valid as rules, through which, in general, experience is possible; and they instruct us respecting experience, and not by means of it.

4. Time is not a discursive, or as it is called, general concept, but a pure form of sensible intuition. Different times are merely parts of one and the same time. But the representation which can only be given by a single object is an intuition. Besides, the proposition that different times cannot be co-existent, could not be derived from a general concept. For this proposition is synthetical, and therefore cannot spring out of concepts alone. It is therefore contained immediately in the intuition and representation of time.

5. The infinity of time signifies nothing more than that every determined quantity of time is possible only through limitations of one time lying at the foundation. Consequently, the original representation, time, must be given as unlimited. But as the determinate representation of the parts of time and of every quantity of an object can only be obtained by limitation, the *complete* representation of time must not be furnished by means of concepts, for these contain only partial representations. Concepts, on the contrary, must have immediate intuition for their basis.

§ 6: *Transcendental Exposition of the Concept of Time*

I may here refer to what is said above (§ 5, 3), where, for the sake of brevity, I have placed under the head of metaphysical exposition, that which is properly transcendental. Here I shall add that the concept of change, and with it the concept of motion, as change of place, is possible only through and in the representation of time; that if this representation were not an intuition (internal) *a priori*, no concept, of whatever kind, could render comprehensible the possibility of change, in other words, of a conjunction of contradictorily opposed predicates in one and the same object, for example, the presence of a thing in a place and the non-presence of the same thing in the same place. It is only in time that it is possible to meet with two contradictorily opposed determinations in one thing, that is, after each other. Thus our concept of time explains the possibility of so much synthetical knowledge *a priori*, as is exhibited in the general doctrine of motion, which is not a little fruitful.

§ 7 : *Conclusions from the above Concepts*

(*a*) Time is not something which subsists of itself, or which inheres in things as an objective determination, and therefore remains, when abstraction is made of the subjective conditions of the intuition of things. For in the former case, it would be something real, yet without presenting to any power of perception any real object. In the latter case, as an order or determination inherent in things themselves, it could not be antecedent to things, as their condition, nor discerned or intuited by means of synthetical propositions *a priori*. But all this is quite possible when we regard time as merely the subjective condition under which all our intuitions take place. For in that case, this form of the inward intuition can be represented prior to the objects, and consequently *a priori*.

(*b*) Time is nothing else than the form of the internal sense, that is, of the intuitions of ourselves and of our internal state. For time cannot be any determination of outward appearances. It has to do with neither shape nor position; on the contrary, it determines the relation of representations in our internal state. And precisely because this internal intuition presents to us no shape or form, we endeavour to supply this want by analogies, and represent the course of time by a line progressing to infinity, the content of which constitutes a series which is only of one dimension; and we conclude from the properties of this line as to all the properties of time, with this single exception, that the parts of the line are co-existent, whilst those of time are successive. From this it is clear also that the representation of time is itself an intuition, because all its relations can be expressed in an external intuition.

(*c*) Time is the formal condition *a priori* of all appearances whatsoever. Space, as the pure form of external intuition, is limited as a condition *a priori* to external appearances alone. On the other hand, because all representations, whether they have or have not external things for their objects, still in themselves, as determinations of the mind, belong to our internal state; and because this internal state is subject to the formal condition of the internal intuition, that is, to time, time is a condition *a priori* of all appearances whatsoever – the *immediate* condition of all internal, and thereby the *mediate* condition of all external appearances. If I can say *a priori*, 'All outward appearances are in space, and determined *a priori* according to the relations of space', I can also, from the principle of the internal sense, affirm universally, 'All appearances in general, that is, all objects of the senses, are in time, and stand necessarily in relations of time.'

If we abstract our internal intuition of ourselves, and all external intuitions, possible only by virtue of this internal intuition, and presented to us by our faculty of representation, and consequently take objects as they are in themselves, then time is nothing. It is only of objective validity in regard to appearances, because these are things which we regard as objects of our senses. It is no longer objective, if we make abstraction of the sensibility of our intuition, in other words, of that mode of representation which is peculiar to us, and speak of things in general. Time is therefore merely a subjective condition of our (human) intuition (which is always sensible, that is, so far as we are affected by objects), and in itself, independently of the mind or subject, is nothing. Nevertheless, in respect of all appearances, consequently of all things which come within the sphere of our experience, it is necessarily objective. We cannot say, 'All things are in time', because in this concept of things in general, we abstract and make no mention of any sort of intuition of things. But this is the proper condition under which time belongs to our representation of objects. If we add the condition to the concept, and say, 'All things, as appearances, that is, objects of sensible intuition, are in time', then the proposition has its sound objective validity and universality *a priori*.

What we have now set forth teaches, therefore, the empirical reality of time; that is, its objective validity in reference to all objects which can ever be presented to our senses. And as our intuition is always sensible, no object ever can be presented to us in experience, which does not come under the conditions of time. On the other hand, we deny to time all claim to absolute reality; that is, we deny that it, without having regard to the form of our sensible intuition, absolutely inheres in things as a condition of property. Such properties as belong to objects as things in themselves, never can be presented to us through the medium of the senses. Herein consists, therefore, the transcendental ideality of time, according to which, if we abstract the subjective conditions of sensible intuition, it is nothing, and cannot be reckoned as subsisting or inhering in objects as things in themselves, independently of its relation to our intuition. This ideality, like that of space, is not to be proved or illustrated by fallacious analogies with sensations, for this reason – that in such arguments or illustrations, we make the presupposition that the appearance, in which such and such predicates inhere, has objective reality, while in this case we can only find such an objective reality as is itself empirical, that is, regards the object as a mere appearance. In reference to this subject, see the remark in Section I (page 25).

§ 8 : Elucidation

Against this theory, which grants empirical reality to time, but denies to it absolute and transcendental reality, I have heard from intelligent men an objection so unanimously urged, that I conclude that it must naturally present itself to every reader to whom these considerations are novel. It runs thus: 'Changes are real (this the continual change in our own representations demonstrates, even if the existence of all external appearances, together with their changes, were denied). Now, changes are only possible in time, and therefore time must be something real.' But there is no difficulty in answering this. I grant the whole argument. Time, no doubt, is something real, that is, it is the real form of our internal intuition. It therefore has subjective reality, in reference to our internal experience, that is, I have really the representation of time, and of my determinations therein. Time, therefore, is not to be regarded as an object, but as the mode of representation of myself as an object. But if I could intuit myself, or be intuited by another being, without this condition of sensibility, then those very determinations which we now represent to ourselves as changes, would present to us a knowledge in which the representation of time, and consequently of change, would not appear. The empirical reality of time, therefore, remains, as the condition of all our experience. But absolute reality, according to what has been said above, cannot be granted it. Time is nothing but the form of our internal intuition.[1] If we take away from it the special condition of our sensibility, the concept of time also vanishes; and it inheres not in the objects themselves, but solely in the subject which intuits them.

But the reason why this objection is so unanimously brought against our doctrine of time, and that too by disputants who have nothing plausible to object against the doctrine of the ideality of space, is this – they have no hope of demonstrating apodeictically

---

[1] I can indeed say 'my representations follow one another, or are successive'; but this means only that we are conscious of them as in a succession, that is, according to the form of the internal sense. Time, therefore, is not a thing in itself, nor is it any objective determination pertaining to, or inherent in things.

the absolute reality of space, because their doctrine of idealism prevents them from doing so, according to which the reality of external objects is not capable of any strict proof while the reality of the object of our internal sense (that is, myself and my internal state) is clear immediately through consciousness. In their view the former – external objects in space – might be a mere illusion, but the latter – the object of my internal perception – is undeniably real. They do not, however, reflect that both, without questioning their reality as representations, are only appearances, which have always two aspects, the one, the object considered as a thing in itself, without regard to the mode of intuiting it, and the nature of which remains for this very reason problematical, the other, the form of our intuition of the object, which must be sought not in the object as a thing in itself, but in the subject to which it appears – which form of intuition nevertheless belongs really and necessarily to the object as appearance.

Time and space are, therefore, two sources of knowledge, from which, *a priori*, various synthetical knowledge can be drawn. Of this we find a striking example in the knowledge of space and its relations, which form the foundation of pure mathematics. They are the two pure forms of all intuitions, and thereby make synthetical propositions *a priori* possible. But these sources of knowledge, being merely conditions of our sensibility, do therefore, and as such, strictly determine their own range and purpose, in that they do not and cannot present objects as things in themselves, but are applicable to them solely in so far as they are considered as sensible appearances. The sphere of appearances is the only sphere of their validity, and if we venture out of this, no further objective use can be made of them. For the rest, this formal reality of time and space leaves the validity of our empirical knowledge unshaken; for our certainty in that respect is equally firm, whether these forms necessarily inhere in the things themselves, or only in our intuitions of them. On the other hand, those who maintain the absolute reality of time and space, whether as essentially subsisting, or only inhering, as modifications, in things, must find themselves at utter variance with the principles of experience itself. For, if they decide for the first view, and make space and time into substances, this being the side taken by mathematical natural philosophers, they must admit two self-subsisting nonentities, infinite and eternal, which exist (yet without there being anything real) for the purpose of containing in themselves everything that is real. If they adopt the second view of inherence, which is preferred by some metaphysical natural philosophers, and regard space and time as relations (contiguity in space or succession in time), abstracted from experience, though represented confusedly in this state of separation, they find themselves in that case necessitated to deny the validity of mathematical doctrines *a priori* in reference to real things (for example in space) – at all events their apodeictic certainty. For such certainty cannot be found in an *a posteriori* position; and the concepts *a priori* of space and time are, according to this opinion, mere creations of the imagination, having their source really in experience, inasmuch as, out of relations abstracted from experience, imagination has made up something which contains, indeed, general statements of these relations, yet of which no application can be made without the restrictions attached thereto by nature. The former of these parties gains this advantage, that they keep the sphere of appearances free for mathematical science. On the other hand, these very conditions (space and time) embarrass them greatly, when the understanding endeavours to pass the limits of that sphere. The latter has, indeed, this advantage, that the representations of space and time do not come in their way when they wish to judge of objects, not as appearances, but merely in their relation to the understanding. Devoid, however, of a true and objectively valid *a priori* intuition, they can neither furnish any basis for the possibility of mathematical knowledge *a priori*, nor bring the propositions of experience into necessary accordance with those of mathematics. In our theory of the true nature of these two original forms of the sensibility, both difficulties are surmounted.

In conclusion, that the Transcendental Aesthetic cannot contain any more than these two elements (space and time) is sufficiently obvious from the fact that all other concepts appertaining to sensibility, even that of motion, which unites in itself both elements, presuppose something empirical. Motion, for example, presupposes the perception of something movable. But space considered in itself contains nothing movable; consequently motion must be something which is found in space only through experience – in other words, is an empirical datum. In like manner, Transcendental Aesthetic cannot number the concept of change among its data *a priori*; for time itself does not change, but only something which is in time. To acquire the concept of change, therefore, the perception of some existing object and of the succession of its determinations, in one word, experience, is necessary.

§9 : General Remarks on the Transcendental Aesthetic

I. In order to prevent any misunderstanding, it will be requisite, in the first place, to recapitulate, as clearly as possible, what our opinion is with respect to the fundamental nature of our sensible knowledge in general. We have intended, then, to say, that all our intuition is nothing but the representation of appearances; that the things which we intuit are not in themselves the same as our representations of them in intuition, nor are their relations in themselves so constituted as they appear to us; and that if we take away the subject, or even only the subjective constitution of our senses in general, then not only the nature and relations of objects in space and time, but even space and time themselves disappear; and that these, as appearances, cannot exist in themselves, but only in us. What may be the nature of objects considered as things in themselves and without reference to the receptivity of our sensibility is quite unknown to us. We know nothing more than our own mode of perceiving them, which is peculiar to us, and which, though not of necessity pertaining to every being, does so to human beings. With this alone we have to do. Space and time are the pure forms thereof; sensation the matter. The former alone can we know *a priori*, that is, antecedent to all actual perception; and for this reason such knowledge is called pure intuition. The latter is that in our knowledge which is called knowledge *a posteriori*, that is, empirical intuition. The former appertain absolutely and necessarily to our sensibility, of whatsoever kind our sensations may be; the latter may be of very diversified character. Supposing that we should carry our empirical intuition even to the very highest degree of clearness, we should not thereby advance one step nearer to a appearances of the constitution of objects as things in themselves. For we could only, at best, arrive at a complete appearances of our own mode of intuition, that is, of our sensibility, and this always under the conditions originally attaching to the subject, namely, the conditions of space and time; while the question, 'What are objects considered as things in themselves?' remains unanswerable even after the most thorough knowledge of appearances.

To say, then, that all our sensibility is nothing but the confused representation of things containing exclusively that which belongs to them as things in themselves, and this under an accumulation of characteristic marks and partial representations which we cannot distinguish in consciousness, is a falsification of the concept of sensibility and of appearances, which renders our whole doctrine thereof empty and useless. The difference between a confused and a clear representation is merely logical and has nothing to do with content. No doubt the concept of *right*, as employed by a sound understanding, contains all that the most subtle investigation could unfold from it, although, in the ordinary practical use of the word, we are not conscious of the manifold representations comprised in the concept. But we cannot for this reason assert that the ordinary concept is a sensible one, containing a mere appearance, for *right* is not something that can appear to us; but the concept of it lies in the understanding, and represents a property (the moral property) of actions, which belongs to them in themselves. On the other hand, the representation in intuition of a body contains nothing which could belong to an object considered as a thing in itself, but merely the appearance of something, and the mode in which we are affected by that appearance; and this receptivity of our faculty of knowledge is called sensibility, and remains *toto caelo* different from the knowledge of an object in itself, even though we should examine the content of the appearance to the very bottom.

It follows that the Leibniz-Wolffian philosophy has assigned an entirely erroneous point of view to all investigations into the nature and origin of our knowledge and the intellectual as merely logical, whereas it is plainly transcendental and concerns not merely the clearness or obscurity, but the content and origin of both. For the faculty of sensibility not only does not present us with indistinct and confused knowledge of objects as things in themselves, but, in fact, gives us no knowledge of these at all. On the contrary, so soon as we abstract in thought our own subjective nature, the object represented, with the properties ascribed to it by sensible intuition, entirely disappears, because it was only this subjective nature that determined the form of the object as an appearance.

In appearances, we commonly, indeed, distinguish that which essentially belongs to the intuition of them, and is valid for the sensible faculty of every human being, from that which belongs to the same intuition accidentally, as valid not for the sensible faculty in general, but for a particular state or organization of this or that sense. Accordingly, we are accustomed to say that the former is knowledge which represents the object itself, whilst the latter presents only a particular appearance thereof. This distinction, however, is only empirical. If we stop here (as usual), and do not regard the empirical intuition as itself a mere appearance (as we ought to do), in which nothing that can appertain to a thing in itself is to be found, our transcendental distinction is lost, and we believe that we know objects as things in themselves, although in the whole range of the sensible world, investigate the nature of its objects as profoundly as we may, we have to do with nothing but appearances. Thus, we call the rainbow a mere appearance in a sunny shower, and the rain, the reality or thing in itself; and this is right enough, if we understand the latter concept in a merely physical sense, that is, as that which in universal experience, and under whatever conditions of the senses, is known in intuition to be so and so determined, and not otherwise. But if we consider this empirical datum generally, and inquire, without reference to its accordance with all our senses, whether there can be discovered in it anything which represents an object as a thing in itself (the raindrops of course are not such, for they are, as appearances, empirical objects), the question of the relation of the representation to the object is transcendental; and not only are the raindrops mere appearances, but even their circular form, nay, the space itself through which they fall, is nothing in itself, but both are mere modifications or fundamental dispositions of our sensible intuition, whilst the transcendental object remains for us utterly unknown.

The second important concern of our Aesthetic is, that it do not obtain favour merely as a plausible hypothesis, but possess as undoubted a character of certainty as can be demanded of any theory which is to serve for an organon. In order fully to convince the reader of this certainty, we shall select a case which will serve to make its validity apparent, and also to illustrate what has been said in §3.

Suppose, then, that space and time are in themselves objective, and conditions of the possibility of objects as things in themselves. In the first place, it is evident that both present us with very many apodeictic and synthetic propositions *a priori*, but especially space – and for this reason we shall prefer it for investigation at present. As the propositions of geometry are known synthetically *a priori*, and with apodeictic certainty, I inquire – whence do you obtain propositions of this kind, and on what basis does the understanding rest, in order to arrive at such absolutely necessary and universally valid truths?

There is no other way than through intuitions or concepts, as such; and these are given either *a priori* or *a posteriori*. The latter, namely, empirical concepts, together with the empirical intuition on which they are founded, cannot afford any synthetical proposition, except such as is itself also empirical, that is, a proposition of experience. But an empirical proposition cannot possess the qualities of necessity and absolute universality, which, nevertheless, are the characteristics of all geometrical propositions. As to the first and only means to arrive at such knowledge, namely, through mere concepts or intuitions *a priori*, it is quite clear that from mere concepts no synthetical knowledge, but only analytical knowledge, can be obtained. Take, for example, the proposition : 'Two straight lines cannot enclose a space, and with these alone no figure is possible', and try to deduce it from the proposition : 'It is possible to construct a figure with three straight lines', and endeavour in like manner, to deduce it from the mere concept of a straight line and the number three. All your endeavours are in vain, and you find yourself forced to have recourse to intuition, as, in fact, geometry always does. You therefore give yourself an object in intuition. But of what kind is this intuition ? Is it a pure *a priori*, or is it an empirical intuition ? If the latter, then neither an universally valid, much less an apodeictic proposition can arise from it, for experience never can give us any such proposition. You must therefore give yourself an object *a priori* in intuition, and upon that ground your synthetical proposition. Now if there did not exist within you a faculty of intuition *a priori*; if this subjective condition were not in respect to its form also the universal condition *a priori* under which alone the object of this external intuition is itself possible; if the object (that is, the triangle) were something in itself, without relation to you the subject; how could you affirm that that which lies necessarily in your subjective conditions in order to construct a triangle, must also necessarily belong to the triangle in itself ? For your concepts of three lines, you could not add anything new (that is, the figure); which therefore, must necessarily be found in the object, because the object is given before your knowledge, and not by means of it. If, therefore, space (and time also) were not a mere form of your intuition, which contains conditions *a priori*, under which alone things can become external objects for you, and without which subjective conditions the objects are in themselves nothing, you could not construct any synthetical proposition whatsoever regarding external objects. It is therefore not merely possible or probable, but induitably certain, that space and time, as the necessary conditions of all our external and internal experience, are merely subjective conditions of all appearances, and not things in themselves, presented to us in this particular manner. And for this reason, in respect to the form of appearances, much may be said *a priori*, whilst of the thing in itself, which may lie at the foundation of these appearances, it is impossible to say anything.

II. In confirmation of this theory of the ideality of the external as well as internal sense, consequently of all objects of sense, as mere appearances, we may especially remark, that all in our knowledge that belongs to intuition and contains nothing more than mere relations – the feelings of pain and pleasure, and the will, which are not knowledge, are excepted – the relations, to wit, of place in an intuition (extension), change of place (motion), and laws according to which this change is determined (moving forces). That, however, which is present in this or that place, or any operation going on, or result taking place in the things themselves, with the exception of change of place, is not given to us by intuition. Now by means of mere relations, a thing cannot be known in itself; and it may therefore be fairly concluded, that, as through the external sense nothing but mere representations of relations are given us, the said external sense in its representation can contain only the relation of the object to the subject, but not the essential nature of the object as a thing in itself.

The same is the case with the internal intuition, not only because, in the internal intuition, the representation of the external senses constitutes the material with which the mind is occupied; but because time, in which we place, and which itself antecedes the consciousness of, these representations in experience, and which, as the formal condition of the mode according to which objects are placed in the mind, lies at the foundation of them, contains relations of the successive, the co-existent, and of that which always must be co-existent with succession, the permanent. Now that which, as representation, can antecede every exercise of thought (of an object), is intuition; and when it contains nothing but relations, it is the form of the intuition, which, as it presents us with no representation, except in so far as something is placed in the mind, can be nothing else than the mode in which the mind is affected by its own activity, to wit, its presenting to itself representations, that is, it can be nothing but an internal sense in respect to its form. Everything that is represented through the medium of sense is so far always appearance; consequently, we must either refuse altogether to admit an internal sense, or the subject, which is the object of that sense, could only be represented by it as appearance, and not as it would judge of itself, if its intuition were pure spontaneous activity, that is, were intellectual. The difficulty here lies wholly in the question – How can the subject have an internal intuition of itself? – but this difficulty is common to every theory. The consciousness of oneself (apperception) is the simple representation of the *I*; and if by means of that representation alone, all the manifold representations in the subject were spontaneously given, then our internal intuition would be intellectual. This consciousness in man requires an internal perception of the manifold representations which are previously given in the subject; and the manner in which these representations are given in the mind without spontaneity, to be called sensibility. If the faculty of self-consciousness is to apprehend what lies in the mind, it must affect that, and can in this way alone produce an intuition of oneself. But the form of this intuition, which lies in the original constitution of the mind, determines, in the representation of time, the manner in which the manifold representations are to combine themselves in the mind; since the subject intuits itself, not as it would represent itself immediately and spontaneously, but according to the manner in which the mind is internally affected, consequently, as it appears, and not as it is.

III. When we say that the intuition of external objects, and also the self-intuition of the subject, represent both objects, and subject, in space and time, as they affect our senses, that is, as they appear – this is by no means equivalent to asserting that these objects are mere illusory appearances. For when we speak of things as appearances, the objects, nay, even the properties which we ascribe to them, are looked upon as really given; only that, in so far as this or that property depends upon the mode of intuition of the subject, in the relation of the given object to the subject, the object as appearance is to be distinguished from the object as a thing in itself. Thus I do not say that bodies seem or appear to be external to me, or that my soul seems merely to be given in my self-consciousness, although I maintain that the properties of space and time, in conformity to which I set both, as the condition of their existence, abide in my mode of intuition, and not in the objects in themselves. It would be my own fault, if out of that which I should reckon as appearance, I made mere illusory appearance.[1] But this will not

---

[1] The predicates of appearances can be affixed to the object itself in relation to our senses; for example, the red colour or the perfume to the rose. But illusory appearance never can be attributed as a predicate to an object, for this very reason, that it attributes to this object in itself that which belongs to it only in relation to our senses, or to the subject in general, e.g. the two handles which are formerly ascribed to Saturn. That which is never

happen, because of our principle of the ideality of all sensible intuitions. On the contrary, if we ascribe objective reality to these forms of representation, it becomes impossible to avoid changing everything into mere illusory appearance. For if we regard space and time as properties, which must be found in objects as things in themselves, if they are to be possible at all, and reflect on the absurdities in which we then find ourselves involved, inasmuch as we are compelled to admit the existence of two infinite things, which are nevertheless not substances, nor anything really inhering in substances, nay, to admit that they are the necessary conditions of the existence of all things, and moreover, that they must continue to exist, although all existing things were annihilated – we cannot blame the good Berkeley for degrading bodies to mere illusory appearances. Nay, even our own existence, which would in this case depend upon the self-existent reality of such a mere nonentity as time, would necessarily be changed with it into mere illusory appearance – an absurdity which no one has as yet been guilty of.

IV. In natural theology, where we think of an object – God – which never can be an object of intuition to us, and even to Himself can never be an object of sensible intuition, we carefully avoid attributing to His intuition the conditions of space and time – and all His cognition must be intuition, and not thought, which always includes limitation. But with what right can we do this if we make time and space forms of objects as things in themselves, and such, moreover, as would continue to exist as *a priori* conditions of the existence of things, even though the things themselves were annihilated? For as conditions of all existence in general, space and time must be conditions of the existence of God also. But if we do not thus make them objective forms of all things, there is no other way left than to make them subjective forms of our mode of intuition – external and internal – which is called sensible, because it is not primitive, that is, is not such as gives in itself the existence of the object of the intuition (a mode of intuition which, so far as we can

to be found in the object itself, but always in the relation of the object to the subject, and which moreover is inseparable from our representation of the object, we denominate appearance. Thus the predicates of space and time are rightly attributed to objects of the senses as such, and in this there is no illusion. On the contrary, if I ascribe redness to the rose as a thing in itself, or to Saturn his handles, or extension to all external objects, considered as things in themselves, without regarding the determinate relation of these objects to the subject, and without limiting my judgment to that relation – then, and then only, arises illusion.

judge, can belong only to the prime being), but is dependent on the existence of the object, is possible, therefore, only on condition that the representative faculty of the subject is affected by the object.

It is, moreover, not necessary that we should limit the mode of intuition in space and time to the sensible faculty of man. It may well be, that all finite thinking beings must necessarily in this respect agree with man (though as to this we cannot decide), but sensibility does not on account of this universality cease to be sensibility, for this very reason, that it is a derived (*intuitus derivativus*) and not an original (*intuitus originalis*), consequently not an intellectual intuition, and this intuition, as such, for reasons above mentioned, seems to belong solely to the prime being, but never to a being dependent, for its existence, as well as for its intuition (which its existence determines and limits relatively to given objects). This latter remark, however, must be taken only as an illustration, and not as any proof of the truth of our aesthetical theory.

§10 : *Conclusion of the Transcendental Aesthetic*

We have now completely before us one part of the solution of the general task of transcendental philosophy, namely, the question – How are synthetical propositions *a priori* possible ? That is to say, we have shown that we are in possession of pure *a priori* intuitions, namely, space and time, in which we find, when in a judgment *a priori* we pass out beyond the given concept, something which is not discoverable in that concept, but is certainly found *a priori* in the intuition which corresponds to the concept, and can be united synthetically with it. But the judgments which these pure intuitions enable us to make, never reach farther than to objects of the senses, and are valid only for objects of possible experience.

PART II : TRANSCENDENTAL LOGIC

INTRODUCTION : IDEA OF A TRANSCENDENTAL LOGIC

I: Logic in general

Our knowledge springs from two main sources in the mind, the first of which is the faculty or power of receiving representations (receptivity for impressions); the second is the power of knowing by means of these representations (spontaneity of concepts). Through the first an object is given to us; through the second, it is, in relation to the representation (which is a mere determination of the mind), thought. Intuition and concepts constitute, therefore, the elements of all our knowledge, so that neither concepts without an intuition in some way corresponding to them, nor intuition without concepts, can afford us any knowledge. Both are either pure or empirical. They are empirical, when sensation (which presupposes the actual presence of the object) is contained in them; and pure, when no sensation is mixed with the representation. Sensations we may call the matter of sensible knowledge. Pure intuition consequently contains merely the form under which something is intuited, and pure concept only the form of the thought of an object. Only pure intuitions and pure concepts are possible *a priori*; the empirical only *a posteriori*.

We apply the term *sensibility* to the receptivity of the mind for representations, in so far as it is in some way affected; and, on the other hand, we call the faculty of spontaneously producing representations, or the spontaneity of knowledge, *understanding*. Our nature is so constituted, that intuition with us never can be other than sensible, that is, it contains only the mode in which we are affected by objects. On the other hand, the faculty of thinking, the object of sensible intuition, is the understanding. Neither of these faculties has a preference over the other. Without the sensible faculty no object would be given to us, and without the understanding no object would be thought. Thoughts without content are empty; intuitions without concepts, blind. Hence it is as necessary for the mind to make its concepts sensible (that is, to join to them the object in intuition), as to make its intuitions intelligible (that is, to bring them under concepts). Neither of these faculties can exchange its proper function. Understanding cannot intuit, and the sensible faculty cannot think. In no other way than from the united operation of both, can knowledge arise. But no one ought, on this account, to overlook the difference of the elements contributed by each; we have rather great reason carefully to separate and distinguish them. We therefore distinguish the science of the laws of sensibility, that is, Aesthetic, from the science of the laws of the understanding, that is, Logic.

Now, logic in its turn may be considered as twofold – namely, as logic of the general, or of the special use of the understanding. The first contains the absolutely necessary laws of thought, without which no use whatever of the understanding is possible, and gives laws therefore to the understanding, without regard to the difference of objects on which it may be employed. The logic of the special use of the understanding contains the laws of correct thinking upon a special class of objects. The former may be called logic of elements – the latter, the organon of this or that science. The latter is for the most part employed in the schools, as a propaedeutic to the sciences, although, indeed, according to the course of human reason, it is the last thing we arrive at, when the science has been already matured, and needs only the finishing touches towards its correction and completion; for our knowledge of the objects of the science must already be tolerably extensive before we can indicate the laws by which a science of these objects can be established.

General logic is again either pure or applied. In the former, we abstract all the empirical conditions under which the understanding is exercised; for example, the influence of the senses, the play of the imagination, the laws of the memory, the force of habit of inclination, etc., consequently also, the sources of prejudice – in a word, we abstract all causes from which particular knowledge arises, because these causes regard the understanding under certain circumstances of its application, and, to the knowledge of them experience is required. Pure general logic has to do, therefore, merely with pure *a priori* principles, and is a canon of understanding and reason, but only in respect of the formal part of their use, be the content what it may, empirical or transcendental. General logic is called applied, when it is directed to the laws of the use of the understanding, under the subjective empirical conditions which psychology teaches us. It has therefore empirical principles, although, at the same time, it is in so far general, that it applies to the exercise of the understanding, without regard to the difference of objects. On this account, moreover, it is neither a canon of the understanding in general, nor an organon of a particular science, but merely a cathartic of the human understanding.

In general logic, therefore, that part which constitutes pure logic must be carefully distinguished from that which constitutes applied (though still general) logic. The former alone is properly science, although short and dry, as the methodical exposition of a doctrine of elements of the understanding ought to be. In this, therefore, logicians must always bear in mind two rules:

1. As general logic, it makes abstraction of all content of the knowledge of the understanding, and of the differences of objects, and has to do with nothing but the mere form of thought.

2. As pure logic, it has no empirical principles, and consequently draws nothing (contrary to the common persuasion) from psychology, which therefore has no influence on the canon of the understanding. It is a demonstrated doctrine, and everything in it must be certain, completely *a priori*.

What I call applied logic (contrary to the common acceptation of this term, according to which it should contain certain exercises for which pure logic gives the rules), is a representation of the understanding, and of the rules of its necessary employment *in concreto*, that is to say, under the accidental conditions of the subject, which may either hinder or promote this employment, and which are all given only empirically. Thus applied logic treats of attention, its impediments and consequences, of the origin of error, of the state of doubt, hesitation, conviction, etc., and to it is related pure general logic in the same way that pure morality, which contains only the necessary moral laws of a free will, is related to the doctrine of virtue, which considers these laws under all the impediments of feelings, inclinations, and passions to which men are more or less subjected, and which never can furnish us with a true and demonstrated science, because it, as well as applied logic, requires empirical and psychological principles.

II: Transcendental Logic

General logic, as we have seen, makes abstraction of all content of knowledge, that is, of all relation of knowledge to its object, and regards only the logical form in the relation of any knowledge to other knowledge, that is, the form of thought in general. But as we have both pure and empirical intuitions (as the Transcendental

Aesthetic proves), in like manner a distinction might be drawn between pure and empirical thought (of objects). In this case, there would exist a kind of logic, in which we should not make abstraction of all content of knowledge; for that logic which should comprise merely the laws of pure thought (of an object), would exclude all that knowledge which were of empirical content. This kind of logic would also examine the origin of our knowledge of objects, so far as that origin cannot be ascribed to the objects themselves; while, in the contrary, general logic has nothing to do with the origin of our knowledge, but contemplates our representations, be they given primitively *a priori* in ourselves, or be they only of empirical origin, solely according to the laws which the understanding observes in employing them in the process of thought, in relation to each other. Consequently, general logic treats of the form of the understanding only, which can be applied to representation, from whatever source they may have arisen.

And here I shall make a remark, which the reader must bear well in mind in the course of the following considerations, to wit, that not all knowledge *a priori* should be called transcendental, but only that knowledge through which we know that and how certain representations (intuitions or concepts) are applied or are possible only *a priori*; that is to say, the possibility of *a priori* knowledge and the *a priori* use of such knowledge. Therefore neither is space, nor any *a priori* geometrical determination of space, a transcendental representation, but only the knowledge that such a representation is not of empirical origin, and the possibility of its relating to objects of experience, although itself *a priori*, can be called transcendental. So also, the application of space to objects in general, would be transcendental; but if it be limited to objects of sense, it is empirical. Thus, the distinction of the transcendental and empirical belongs only to the critique of knowledge, and does not concern the relation of these to their object.

Accordingly, in the expectation that there may perhaps be concepts which relate *a priori* to objects, not as pure or sensible intuitions, but merely as acts of pure thought (which are therefore concepts, but neither of empirical nor aesthetical origin) – in this expectation, I say – we form to ourselves by anticipation, the idea of a science of pure understanding and rational knowledge, by means of which we may think objects entirely *a priori*. A science of this kind, which should determine the origin, the extent, and the objective validity of such knowledge, must be called *Transcendental*

Logic, because it concerns only the laws of understanding and reason, in so far as they relate *a priori* to objects, and does not, like general logic, concern both empirical and rational knowledge without distinction.

III : The Division of General Logic into Analytic and Dialectic

The old question with which people sought to push logicians into a corner, so that they must either have recourse to pitiful sophisms or confess their ignorance, and consequently the vanity of their whole art, is this – 'What is truth ?' The definition of the word *truth*, to wit, 'the accordance of concept with its object', is presupposed in the question ; but one desires to be told, in the answer to it, what is the universal and secure criterion of the truth of all knowledge.

To know what questions we may reasonably propose, is in itself a strong evidence of sagacity and intelligence. For if a question be in itself absurd and unsusceptible of a rational answer, it is attended with the danger – not to mention the shame that falls upon the person who proposes it – of seducing the unguarded listener into making absurd answers, and we are presented with the ridiculous spectacle of one (as the ancients said) 'milking the he-goat, and the other holding a sieve'.

If truth consists in the accordance of knowledge with its object, this object must be, *ipso facto*, distinguished from all others; for knowledge is false if it does not accord with the object to which it relates, although it contains something which may be true of other objects. Now a general criterion of truth would be that which is valid for any pieces of knowledge, without distinction of their objects. But it is evident that since, in the case of such a criterion, we make abstraction of all the content of knowledge (that is, of all relation to its object), and truth relates precisely to this content, it must be utterly absurd to ask for a mark of the truth of this content of knowledge ; and that, accordingly, a sufficient, and at the same time general, criterion of truth cannot possibly be found. As we have already termed the content of knowledge its *matter*, we shall say : 'Of the truth of our knowledge in respect of its matter, no general criterion can be demanded, because such a criterion is self-contradictory.'

On the other hand, with regard to our knowledge in respect of its mere form (excluding all content), it is equally manifest that logic, in so far as it exhibits the universal and necessary laws of the understanding, must in these very laws present us with criteria of truth. Whatever contradicts these rules is false, because thereby the understanding is made to contradict its own universal laws of thought; that is, to contradict itself. These criteria, however, apply solely to the form of truth, that is, of thought in general, and in so far they are perfectly correct, yet not sufficient. For although knowledge may be perfectly adequate as to logical form, that is, not self-contradictory, it is notwithstanding quite possible that it may not stand in agreement with its object. Consequently, the merely logical criterion of truth, namely the accordance of knowledge with the universal and formal laws of understanding and reason, is nothing more than the *conditio sine qua non*, or negative condition of all truth. Further than this logic cannot go, and the error which depends not on the future, but on the content of the knowledge, it has no test to discover.

General logic, then, resolves the whole formal business of understanding and reason into its elements, and exhibits them as principles of all logical judging of our knowledge. This part of logic may, therefore, be called *Analytic*, and is at least the negative test of truth, because all knowledge must first of all be estimated and tried according to these laws before we proceed to investigate them in respect of their content, in order to discover whether they contain positive truth in regard to their object. Because, however, the mere form of knowledge, however well it may accord with logical laws, is insufficient to supply us with material (objective) truth, no one, by means of logic alone, can venture to predicate anything of or decide concerning objects, unless he has obtained, independently of logic, well-grounded information about them, in order afterwards to examine, according to logical laws, into the use and connection, in a cohering whole, of that information, or, what is still better, merely to test it by them. Notwithstanding, there lies so seductive a charm in the possession of a specious art like this – an art which gives to all our knowledge the form of the understanding, although with respect to the content thereof we just be sadly empty and deficient – that general logic, which is merely a canon of judgment, has been employed as an organon for the actual production, or rather for the semblance of production of objective assertions, and has thus been grossly misapplied. Now general logic, in its assumed character of organon, is called *Dialectic*.

Different as is the signification in which the ancients used this term for a science or an art, we may safely infer, from their actual employment of it, that with them it was nothing else than a logic of illusion – a sophistical art for giving ignorance, nay, even intentional sophistries, the colouring of truth, in which the thoroughness of procedure which logic requires was imitated, and their topic employed to cloak the empty pretensions. Now it may be taken as a safe and useful warning, that general logic, considered as an organon, must always be a logic of illusion, that is, be dialectical, for, as it teaches us nothing whatever respecting the content of our knowledge, but merely the formal conditions of its accordance with the understanding, which do not relate to and is quite indifferent in respect of objects, any attempt to employ it as an instrument (organon) in order to extend and enlarge the range of our knowledge must end in mere prating; anyone being able to maintain or oppose, with some appearance of truth, any single assertion whatever.

Such instruction is quite unbecoming the dignity of philosophy. For these reasons we have chosen to denominate this part of logic *Dialectic*, in the sense of a critique of dialectical illusion, and we wish the term to be so understood in this place.

IV: The Division of Transcendental Logic into Transcendental Analytic and Dialectic

In transcendental logic we isolate the understanding (as in transcendental aesthetic the sensibility) and select from our knowledge merely that part of thought which has its origin in the understanding alone. The exercise of this pure knowledge, however, depends upon this as its condition, that objects to which it may be applied be given to us in intuition, for without intuition the whole of our knowledge is without objects, and is therefore quite empty. That part of transcendental logic, then, which treats of the elements of pure knowledge of the understanding, and of the principles without which no object at all can be thought, is transcendental analytic, and at the same time a logic of truth. For no knowledge can contradict it, without losing at the same time all content, that is, losing all reference to an object, and therefore all truth. But because we are very easily seduced into employing this pure knowledge and principles of the understanding by itself, and that even beyond the boundaries of experience, which yet is the only source whence we can obtain matter (objects) on which those pure concepts may be employed – understanding runs the risk of making, by means of empty sophisms, a material and objective use of the mere formal principles of the pure understanding, and of passing judgments on objects without distinction – objects which are not given to us, nay, perhaps cannot be given to us in any way. Now, as it ought properly to be only a canon for judging of the empirical use of the understanding, this kind of logic is misused when we seek to employ it as an organon of the universal and unlimited exercise of the understanding, and attempt with the pure understanding alone to judge synthetically, affirm, and determine respecting objects in general. In this case the exercise of the pure understanding becomes dialectical. The second part of our transcendental logic must therefore be a critique of dialectical illusion, and this critique we shall term Transcendental Dialectic – not meaning it as an art of producing dogmatically such illusion (an art which is unfortunately too current among the practitioners of metaphysical juggling), but as a critique of understanding and reason in regard to their hyperphysical use. This critique will expose the groundless nature of the pretensions of these two faculties, and invalidate their claims to the discovery and enlargement of our knowledge merely by means of transcendental principles, and show that the proper employment of these faculties is to test the judgments made by the pure understanding, and to guard it from sophistical delusion.

TRANSCENDENTAL LOGIC: FIRST DIVISION

TRANSCENDENTAL ANALYTIC

Transcendental analytic is the dissection of the whole of our *a priori* knowledge into the elements of the pure knowledge of the understanding. In order to effect our purpose, it is necessary (1) That the concepts be pure and not empirical; (2) That they belong not to intuition and sensibility, but to thought and understanding; (3) That they be elementary concepts, and as such, quite different from derived or compound concepts; (4) That our table of these elementary concepts be complete, and fill up the whole sphere of the pure understanding. Now this completeness of a science cannot be accepted with confidence on the guarantee of a mere estimate of its existence in an aggregate formed only by means of repeated experiments and attempts. The completeness which we require is possible only by means of an idea of the totality of the *a priori* knowledge of the understanding, and through the thereby determined division of the concepts which form the said whole; consequently, only by means of their connection in the system. Pure understanding distinguishes itself not merely from everything empirical, but also completely from all sensibility. It is a unity self-subsistent, self-sufficient, and not to be enlarged by any additions from without. Hence the sum of its knowledge constitutes a system to be determined by and comprised under an idea; and the completeness and articulation of this system can at the same time serve as a test of the correctness and genuineness of all the parts of knowledge that belong to it. The whole of this part of transcendental logic consists of two books of which the one contains the concepts, and the other the principles of pure understanding.

TRANSCENDENTAL ANALYTIC
BOOK I: ANALYTIC OF CONCEPTS

By the term 'Analytic of Concepts', I do not understand the analysis of these, or the usual process in philosophical investigations of dissecting the concepts which present themselves, according to their content, and so making them clear; but I mean the hitherto little attempted dissection of the faculty of understanding itself, in order to investigate the possibility of concepts *a priori*, by looking for them in the understanding alone, as their birthplace, and analysing the pure use of this faculty. For this is the proper duty of a transcendental philosophy; what remains is the logical treatment of the concepts in philosophy in general. We shall therefore follow up the pure concepts even to their germs and beginnings in the human understanding, in which they lie, until they are developed on occasions presented by experience, and, freed by the same understanding from the empirical conditions attaching to them, are set forth in their unalloyed purity.

ANALYTIC OF CONCEPTS
CHAPTER I: THE CLUE TO THE DISCOVERY OF ALL PURE
CONCEPTS OF THE UNDERSTANDING

When we call into play a faculty of knowledge, different concepts manifest themselves according to the different circumstances, and make known this faculty, and assemble themselves into a more or less extensive collection, according to the time or penetration that has been applied to the consideration of them. Where this process, conducted as it is mechanically, so to speak, will end, cannot be determined with certainty. Besides, the concepts which we discover in this haphazard manner present themselves by no means in order and systematic unity, but are at last coupled together only according to the quantity of their content, from the simpler to the more complex – series which are anything but systematic, though not altogether without a certain kind of method in their construction.

Transcendental philosophy has the advantage, and moreover the duty, of searching for its concepts according to a principle; because these concepts spring pure and unmixed out of the understanding as an absolute unity, and therefore must be connected with each other according to one concept or idea. A connection of this kind, however, furnishes us with a ready prepared rule, by which its proper place may be assigned to every pure concept of the understanding, and the completeness of the system of all be determined *a priori* – both of which would otherwise have been dependent on mere choice or chance.

TRANSCENDANTAL CLUE TO THE DISCOVERY OF ALL PURE CONCEPTS OF THE UNDERSTANDING

Section I: The Logical Use of the Understanding in general

The understanding was defined above only negatively, as a non-sensible faculty of knowledge. Now, independently of sensibility, we cannot possibly have any intuition; consequently, the understanding is no faculty of intuition. But besides intuition there is no other mode of knowledge, except through concepts; consequently, the knowledge of every, at least of every human, understanding is a knowledge through concepts – not intuitive, but discursive. All intuitions, as sensible, depend on affections; concepts, therefore, upon functions. By the word function I understand the unity of the act of arranging diverse representations under one common representation. Concepts, then, are based on the spontaneity of thought, as sensible intuitions are based on the receptivity of impressions. Now, the understanding cannot make any other use of these concepts than to judge by means of them. As no representation, except an intuition, relates immediately to its object, a concept never relates immediately to an object, but only to some other representation thereof, be that an intuition or itself a concept. A judgment, therefore, is the mediate knowledge of an object, consequently the representation of a representation of it. In every judgment there is a concept which applies to many other concepts, and which among these comprehends also a given representation, this last being immediately connected with an object. For example, in the judgment – 'All bodies are divisible', our concept of *divisibility* applies to various other concepts; among these, however, it is here particularly applied to the concept of body, and this concept of body relates to certain appearances which occur to us. These objects, therefore, are mediately represented by the concept of divisibility. All judgments, accordingly, are functions of unity in our representations, inasmuch as, instead of an immediate, a higher representation, which comprises this and various others, is used for our knowledge of the object, and thereby much possible knowledge is collected into one. But we can reduce all acts of the understanding to judgments, so that *understanding* may be represented as the *faculty of judging*. For it is, according to what has been said above, a faculty of thought. Now thought is knowledge by means of concepts. But concepts of a yet undetermined object. Thus the concept of *body* indicates something – for example, metal – which can be known by means of that concept. It is therefore a concept, for the reason alone that other representations are contained under it, by means of which it can relate to objects. It is therefore the predicate to a possible judgment; for example: 'Every metal is a body.' All the functions of the understanding therefore can be discovered, when we can completely exhibit the functions of unity in judgments. And that this may be effected very easily, the following section will show.

Section II: The Logical Function of the Understanding in Judgments

§ 9

If we abstract all the content of a judgment, and consider only the intellectual form thereof, we find that the function of thought in a judgment can be brought under four heads, of which each contains three momenta. These may be conveniently represented in the following table:

1
Quantity of judgments
Universal
Particular
Singular

2
Quality
Affirmative
Negative
Infinite

3
Relation
Categorical
Hypothetical
Disjunctive

4
Modality
Problematical
Assertorical
Apodeictical

As this division appears to differ in some, though not essential points, from the usual techniques of logicians, the following observations, for the prevention of otherwise possible misunderstanding, will not be without their use.

1. Logicians say, with justice, that in the use of judgments in syllogisms, singular judgments may be treated like universal ones. For, precisely because a singular judgment has no extension at all, its predicate cannot refer to a part of that which is contained in the concept of the subject and be excluded from the rest. The predicate is valid for the whole concept just as if it were a general concept, and had extent, to the whole of which the predicate applied. On the other hand, let us compare a singular with a general judgment, merely as knowledge, in regard to quantity. The singular judgment relates to the general one, as unity to infinity, and is therefore in itself essentially different. Thus, if we estimate a singular judgment (*judicium singulare*) not merely according to its intrinsic validity as a judgment, but also as a knowledge generally, according to its quantity in comparison with that of other knowledge, it is then entirely different from a general judgment (*judicium commune*), and in a complete table of the momenta of thought deserves a separate place – though, indeed, this would not be necessary in a logic limited merely to the consideration of the use of judgments in reference to each other.

2. In like manner, in transcendental logic, infinite judgments must be distinguished from affirmative judgments, although in general

logic they are rightly enough classed under affirmative. General logic abstracts all content of the predicate (though it be negative), and only considers whether the said predicate be affirmed or denied of the subject. But transcendental logic considers also the worth or content of this logical affirmation – an affirmation by means of a merely negative predicate – and inquires how much the sum total of our knowledge gains by this affirmation. For example, if I say of the soul, 'It is not mortal' – by this negative judgment I should at least ward off error. Now, by the proposition, 'The soul is not mortal', I have, in respect of the logical form, really affirmed inasmuch as I thereby place the soul in the unlimited sphere of immortal beings. Now, because of the whole sphere of possible existences, the mortal occupies one part, and the immortal the other, neither more or less is affirmed by the proposition, than that the soul is one among the infinite multitude of things which remain over, when I take away the whole mortal part. But by this proceeding we accomplish only this much, that the infinite sphere of all possible existences is in so far limited, that the mortal is excluded from it, and the soul is placed in the remaining part of the extension of this sphere. But this part remains, notwithstanding this exception, infinite, and more and more parts may be taken away from the whole sphere, without in the slightest degree thereby augmenting or affirmatively determining our concept of the soul. These judgments, therefore, infinite in respect of their logical extent, are, in respect of the content of their knowledge, merely limitative; and are consequently entitled to a place in our transcendental table of all the momenta of thought in judgments, because the function of the understanding exercised by them may perhaps be of importance in the field of its pure *a priori* knowledge.

3. All relations of thought in judgments are those (a) of the predicate to the subject; (b) of the ground to its consequence; (c) of the divided objects and all the members of the division of each other. In the first of these three classes, we consider only two concepts; in the second, two judgments; in the third, several judgments in relation to each other. The hypothetical proposition, 'If perfect justice exists, the obstinately wicked are punished', contains properly the relation to each other of two propositions, namely, 'Perfect justice exists', and 'The obstinately wicked are punished'. Whether these propositions are in themselves true, is a question not here decided. Nothing is thought by means of this judgment except a certain consequence. Finally, the disjunctive

judgment contains a relation of two or more propositions to each other – a relation not of consequence, but of logical opposition, in so far as the sphere of the one proposition excludes that of the other. But it contains at the same time a relation of community, in so far as all the propositions taken together fill up the sphere of knowledge. The disjunctive judgment contains, therefore, the relation of the parts of the whole sphere of such knowledge, since the sphere of each part is a complemental part of the sphere of the other, each contributing to form the sum total of the divided knowledge. Take, for example, the proposition, 'The world exists either through blind chance, or through internal necessity, or through an external cause'. Each of these propositions embraces a part of the sphere of our possible knowledge as to the existence of a world; all of them taken together, the whole sphere. To take the knowledge out of one of these spheres, is equivalent to placing it in one of the others; and, on the other hand, to place it in one sphere is equivalent to taking it out of the rest. There is, therefore, in a disjunctive judgment a certain community of pieces of knowledge, which consists in this, that they mutually exclude each other, yet thereby determine, as a whole, the true knowledge, inasmuch as, taken together, they make up the complete content of a particular given knowledge. And this is all that I find necessary, for the sake of what follows, to remark in this place.

4. The modality of judgments is a quite peculiar function, with this distinguishing characteristic, that it contributes nothing to the content of a judgment (for besides quantity, quality, and relation, there is nothing more that constitutes the content of a judgment), but concerns itself only with the value of the copula in relation to thought in general. Problematical judgments are those in which the affirmation or negation is accepted as merely possible (optional). In the assertorical, we regard the proposition as real (true); in the apodeictical, we look on it as *necessary*.[1] Thus the two judgments (*antecedens et consequens*), the relation of which constitutes a hypothetical judgment, likewise those (the members of the division) in whose reciprocity the disjunctive consists, are only problematical. In the example above given, the proposition, 'There exists perfect justice', is not stated assertorically, but as an optional judgment,

---

[1] Just as if thought were in the first instance a function of the *understanding*; in the second, of *judgment*; in the third, of *reason*. A remark which will be explained in the sequel.

which someone may choose to adopt, and the consequence alone is assertorical. Hence such judgments may be obviously false, and yet, taken problematically, be conditions of our knowledge of the truth. Thus the proposition, 'The world exists only by blind chance', is in the disjunctive judgment of problematical import only: that is to say, one may accept it for the moment, and it helps us (like the indication of the wrong road among all the roads that one can take) to find out the true proposition. The problematical proposition is, therefore, that which expresses only logical possibility (which is not objective); that is, it expresses a free choice to admit the validity of such a proposition – a merely arbitrary reception of it into the understanding. The assertorical speaks of logical reality or truth; as, for example, in a hypothetical syllogism, the *antecedens* presents itself in a problematical form in the *major*, in an assertorical form in the *minor*, and it shows that the proposition is in harmony with the laws of the understanding. The apodeictical proposition thinks the assertorical proposition as determined by these very laws of the understanding, consequently as affirming *a priori*, and in this manner it expresses logical necessity. Now because all is here gradually incorporated with the understanding – inasmuch as in the first place we judge problematically; then accept assertorically our judgment as true; lastly, affirm it as inseparably united with the understanding, that is, as necessary and apodeictical – we may safely reckon these three functions of modality as so many momenta of thought.

Section III : The Pure Concepts of the Understanding, or Categories

§ 10

General logic, as has been repeatedly said, makes abstraction of all content of knowledge, and expects to receive representations from some other quarter, in order, by means of analysis, to convert them into concepts. On the contrary, transcendental logic has lying before it *a priori* a manifold of sensibility, which transcendental aesthetic presents to it in order to give matter to the pure concepts of the understanding, without which transcendental logic would have no content, and be therefore utterly empty. Now space and time contain a manifold of pure *a priori* intuition, but are nevertheless the condition of the mind's receptivity, under which alone it can obtain representations of objects, and which, consequently, must always affect the concept of these objects. But the spontaneity of thought requires that this manifold be gone through after a certain manner, and connected, in order to form knowledge out of it. This process I call synthesis.

By the word *synthesis*, in its most general signification, I understand the process of joining different representations to each other, and of comprehending their multiplicity in one act of knowledge. This synthesis is pure when the manifold is not given empirically but *a priori* (as that in space and time). Our representations must be given previously to any analysis of them; and no concepts can arise, in respect of their content, analytically. But the synthesis of a manifold (be it given *a priori* or empirically) is the first requisite for the production of knowledge, which, in its beginning, indeed, may be crude and confused, and therefore in need of analysis – still, synthesis is that by which alone the elements of our knowledge are collected and united into a certain content, consequently it is the first thing on which we must fix our attention, if we wish to investigate the origin of our knowledge.

Synthesis, generally speaking, is, as we shall afterwards see, the mere operation of the imagination – a blind but indispensable function of the soul, without which we should have no knowledge whatever, but of the working of which we are seldom even conscious. But to bring this synthesis to concepts, is a function of the understanding, by means of which we attain to knowledge, in the proper meaning of the term.

Pure synthesis, represented generally, gives us the pure concept of the understanding. But by this pure synthesis, I mean that which rests upon a basis of *a priori* synthetical unity. Thus, our counting (and this is more observable in large numbers) is a synthesis according to concepts, because it takes place according to a common basis of unity (for example, the decade). By means of this concept, therefore, the unity in the synthesis of the manifold becomes necessary.

By means of analysis different representations are brought under one concept – an operation of which general logic treats. On the other hand, the duty of transcendental logic is to bring to concepts, not representations, but the pure synthesis of representations. The first thing which must be given to us in order to afford us *a priori* knowledge of all objects, is the manifold of pure intuition; the synthesis of this manifold by means of the imagination is the second; but this gives, as yet, no knowledge. The concepts which give unity to this pure synthesis, and which consist solely in the representation of this necessary synthetical unity, furnish the third requisite for the knowledge of an object, and these concepts are given by the understanding.

The same function which gives unity to the different representations in a judgment, give also unity to the mere synthesis of different representations in an intuition; and this unity we call the pure concept of the understanding. Thus, the same understanding, and by the same operations, whereby in concepts, by means of analytical unity, it produces the logical form of a judgment, introduces, by means of the synthetical unity of the manifold in intuition, a transcendental content into its representations, on which account they are called pure concepts of the understanding, and they apply *a priori* to objects, a result not within the power of general logic.

In this manner, there arise exactly so many pure concepts of the understanding, applying *a priori* to objects of intuition in general, as there are logical functions in all possible judgments. For there is no other function or faculty existing in the understanding besides those enumerated in that table. These concepts we shall, with Aristotle, call categories, our purpose being originally identical with his, notwithstanding the great difference in the execution.

1	**2**
Of Quantity	*Of Quality*
Unity	Reality
Plurality	Negation
Totality	Limitation

3
Of Relation
Of Inherence and Subsistence (*substantia et accidens*)
Of Causality and Dependence (cause and effect)
Of Community (reciprocity between agent and patient)

4
Of Modality
Possibility – Impossibility
Existence – Non-existence
Necessity – Contingence

This, then, is a catalogue of all the original pure concepts of the synthesis which the understanding contains *a priori*, and these concepts alone entitle it to be called a pure understanding; inasmuch as only by them it can render the manifold of intuition capable of, in other words think, an object of intuition. This division is made systematically from a common principle, namely, the faculty of judgment (which is just the same as the power of thought), and has not arisen rhapsodically from a search at haphazard after pure concepts, respecting the full number of which we never could be certain, inasmuch as we employ induction alone in our search, without considering that in this way we can never understand wherefore precisely these concepts, and none others, abide in the pure understanding. It was a design worthy of an acute thinker like Aristotle, to search for these fundamental concepts. Destitute, however, of any guiding principle, he picked them up just as they occurred to him, and at first hunted out ten, which he called *categories* (*predicaments*). Afterwards he believed that he had discovered five others, which were added under the name of *post predicaments*. But his catalogue still remained defective. Besides, there are to be found among them some of the modes of pure sensibility (*quando, ubi, situs,* also *prius, simul*), and likewise an empirical concept (*motus*) – which can by no means means belong to this genealogical register of the pure understanding. Moreover, there are derived concepts (*actio, passio*), enumerated among the original concepts, and of the latter, some are entirely wanting.

With regard to these, it is to be remarked, that the categories, as the true primitive concepts of the pure understanding, have also their pure deprived concepts, which, in a complete system of transcendental philosophy, must by no means be passed over; though in a merely critical essay we must be contented with the simple mention of the fact.

Let it be allowed me to call these pure, but derived concepts of the understanding, the *predicables* of the pure understanding, in contradiction to predicaments. If we are in possession of the original and primitive, the derived and subsidiary concepts can easily be added, and the genealogical tree of the understanding completely delineated. As my present aim is not to set forth a complete system, but merely the principles of one, I reserve this task for another time. It may be easily executed by any one who will refer to the ontological manuals, and subordinate to the category of causality, for example, the predicables of force, action, passion; to that of community, those of presence and resistance; to the categories of modality, those of origination, extinction, change; and so with the rest. The categories combined with the modes of pure sensibility, or with one another, afford a great number of derived *a priori* concepts; a complete enumeration of which would be a useful and not unpleasant, but in this place a perfectly dispensable occupation.

I purposely omit the definitions of the categories in this treatise. I shall analyse these concepts only so far as is necessary for the doctrine of method, which is to form a part of this critique. In a system of pure reason, definitions of them would be with justice demanded of me, but to give them here would only hide from our view the main aim of our investigation, at the same time raising doubts and objections, the consideration of which, without injustice to our main purpose, may be very well postponed till another opportunity. Meanwhile, it ought to be sufficiently clear, from the little we have already said on this subject, that the formation of a complete vocabulary of pure concepts, accompanied by all the requisite explanations, is not only a possible, but an easy undertaking. The compartments already exist; it is only necessary to fill them up; and a systematic topic like the present, indicates with perfect precision the proper place to which each concept belongs, while it readily points out any that have not yet been filled up.

§ *11*

Our table of the categories suggests considerations of some importance, which may perhaps have significant results in regard to the scientific form of all rational knowledge. For, that this table is useful in the theoretical part of philosophy, nay, indispensable for the sketching of the complete plan of a science, so far as that science rests upon concepts *a priori*, and for dividing it mathematically, according to fixed principles, is most manifest from the fact that it contains all the elementary concepts of the understanding, nay, even the form of a system of these in the understanding itself, and consequently indicates all the momenta, and also the internal arrangement of a projected speculative science, as I have elsewhere shown. Here follow some of these observations.

I. This table, which contains four classes of concepts of the understanding, may, in the first instance, be divided into two classes, the first of which relates to objects of intuition – pure as well as empirical; the second, to the existence of these objects, either in relation to one another, or to the understanding.

The former of these classes of categories I would entitle the *mathematical*, and the latter the *dynamical* categories. The former, as we see, has no correlates; these are only to be found in the second class. This difference must have a ground in the nature of the understanding.

II. The number of the categories in each class is always the same, namely, three – a fact which also demands some consideration, because in all other cases division *a priori* through concepts is necessarily dichotomy. It is to be added, that the third category in each triad always arises from the combination of the second with the first.

Thus totality is nothing else but plurality contemplated as unity; limitation is merely reality conjoined with negation; community is the causality of a substance, reciprocally determining, and determined by other substances; and finally, necessity is nothing but existence, which is given through possibility itself. Let it not be supposed, however, that the third category is merely a derived, and not a primitive concept of the pure understanding. For the conjunction of the first and the second, in order to produce the third concept, requires a particular act of the understanding, which is by no means identical with those which are exercised in the first and the second. Thus, the concept of a number (which belongs to the category of totality) is not always possible, where the concepts of multitude and unity exist (for example, in the representation of the infinite). Or, if I conjoin the concept of a cause with that of a substance, it does not follow that the concept of *influence*, that is, how one substance can be the cause of something in another substance, will be understood from that. Thus it is evident, that a particular act of the understanding is here necessary; and so in the other instances.

III. With respect to one category, namely, that of community, which is found in the third class, it is not so easy as with the others to detect its accordance with the form of the disjunctive judgment which corresponds to it in the table of the logical functions.

In order to assure ourselves of this accordance, we must observe: that in every disjunctive judgment, the sphere of the judgment (that is, the complex of all that is contained in it) is represented as a whole divided into parts; and, since one part cannot be contained in the other, they are thought as co-ordinated with, not subordinated to each other, so that they do not determine each other unilaterally, as in a linear series, but reciprocally, as in an aggregate (if one member of the division is posited, all the rest are excluded; and conversely).

Now a like connection is thought in a whole of things; for one thing is not subordinated, as effect, to another as cause of its existence, but, on the contrary, is co-ordinated contemporaneously and reciprocally, as a cause in relation to the determination of the others (for example, in a body – the parts of which mutually attract and repel each other). And this is an entirely different kind of cause and effect (of ground to consequence), for in such a relation the consequence does not in its turn determine the ground, and therefore does not constitute, with the latter, a whole – just as the Creator does not with the world make up a whole. The process of understanding by which it represents to itself the sphere of a divided concept, is employed also when we think of a thing as divisible; and, in the same manner as the members of the division in the former exclude one another, and yet are connected in one sphere, so the understanding represents to itself the parts of the latter, as having – each of them – an existence (as substances), independently of the others, and yet as united in one whole.

§ 12

In the transcendental philosophy of the ancients there exists one more chapter, which contains pure concepts of the understanding, and which, although not numbered among the categories, ought, according to them, as concepts *a priori*, to be valid of objects. But in this case they would augment the number of the categories; which cannot be. These are set forth in the proposition, so renowned among the schoolmen – '*Quodlibet ens est* UNUM, VERUM, BONUM.' Now, though the inferences from this principle were mere tautological propositions, and though it is allowed only by courtesy to retain a place in modern metaphysics, yet a thought which maintained itself for such a length of time, however empty it seems to be, deserves an investigation of its origin, and justifies the conjecture that it must be grounded in some law of the understanding, which, as is often the case, has only been erroneously interpreted. These pretended transcendental predicates are, in fact, nothing but logical requisites and criteria of all knowledge of objects, and they employ, as the basis for this knowledge, the categories of quantity, namely, unity, plurality, and totality. But these predicates, which must be taken as material, that is, as belonging to the possibility of things themselves, they employed merely in a formal signification, as belonging to the logical requisites of all knowledge, and yet most unguardedly changed these criteria of thought into properties of objects, as things in themselves. Now, in knowledge of an object, there is *unity* of knowledge, which may be called *qualitative unity*, so far as by this term we understand only the unity in our connection of the manifold; for example, unity of the theme in a play, a speech, or a story. Secondly, there is *truth* in respect of the deductions from it. The more true deductions we have from a given concept, the more criteria of its objective reality. This we might call the *qualitative plurality* of characteristic marks, which belong to a concept as to a common foundation, but are not thought as a quantity in it. Thirdly, there is *perfection* – which consists in this, that the plurality falls back upon the unity of the concept, and accords completely with that concept and with no other. This we may denominate *qualitative completeness*. Hence it is evident that these logical criteria of the possibility of knowledge are merely the three categories of quantity modified and transformed to suit an illegitimate manner of applying them. That is to say, the three categories, in which the unity in the production of the quantum must be homogeneous throughout, are transformed solely with a view to the connection of heterogeneous parts of knowledge in one act of consciousness, by means of the quality of the knowledge, which is the principle of that connection. Thus the criterion of the possibility of a concept (not of its object) is the definition of it, in which the unity of the concept, the truth of all that may be immediately deduced from it, and finally, the completeness of what has been thus deduced, constitute the requisites for the reproduction of the whole concept. Thus also, the criterion or test of an hypothesis is the intelligibility of the received principle of explanation, or its unity (without help from any subsidiary hypothesis) – the truth of our deductions from it (consistency with each other and with experience) – and lastly, the completeness of the principle of the explanation of these deductions, which refer to neither more nor less than what was admitted in the hypothesis, restoring analytically and *a posteriori*, what was thought synthetically and *a priori*. By the concept, therefore, of unity, truth, and perfection, we have made no addition to the transcendental table of categories, which is complete without them. We have, on the contrary, merely employed the objects of experience, as general logical laws of the consistency of knowledge with itself.

ANALYTIC OF CONCEPTS
CHAPTER II: THE DEDUCTION OF THE PURE CONCEPTS
OF THE UNDERSTANDING

Section I: The Principles of any Transcendental Deduction

§ 13

Teachers of jurisprudence, when speaking of rights and claims, distinguish in a case the question of right (*quid juris*) from the question of fact (*quid facti*), and while they demand proof of both, they give to the proof of the former, which goes to establish right or claim in law, the name of *Deduction*. Now we make use of a great number of empirical concepts, without opposition from any one; and consider ourselves, even without any attempt at deduction, justified in attaching to them a sense, and a supposed signification, because we have always experience at hand to demonstrate their objective reality. There exist also, however, usurped concepts, such as *fortune* or *fate*, which circulate with almost universal indulgence, and yet are occasionally challenged by the question, *quid juris*? In such cases, we have great difficulty in discovering any deduction for these terms, inasmuch as we cannot produce any manifest ground of right, either from experience or from reason, on which the claim to employ them can be founded.

Among the many concepts, which make up the very variegated web of human knowledge, some are destined for pure use *a priori*, independent of all experience; and their title to be so employed always requires a deduction, inasmuch as, to justify such use of them, proofs from experience are not sufficient; but it is necessary to know how these concepts can apply to objects without being derived from experience. I term, therefore, an explanation of the manner in which concepts can apply *a priori* to objects, the *transcendental deduction* of concepts, and I distinguish it from the *empirical* deduction, which indicates the mode in which a concept is obtained through experience and reflection thereon; consequently, does not concern itself with the right, but only with the fact of our obtaining concepts in such and such a manner. We have already seen that we are in possession of two perfectly different kinds of concepts, which nevertheless agree with each other in this, that they both apply to objects competely *a priori*. There are the concepts of space and time as forms of sensibility, and the categories as pure concepts of the understanding. To attempt an empirical deduction of either of these classes would be labour in vain, because the distinguishing characteristic of their nature consists in this, that they apply to their objects, without having borrowed anything from experience towards the representation of them. Consequently, if a deduction of these concepts is necessary, it must always be transcendental.

Meanwhile, with respect to these concepts, as with respect to all our knowledge, we certainly may discover in experience, if not the principle of their possibility, yet the occasioning causes of their production. It will be found that the impressions of sense give the first occasion for bringing into action the whole faculty of knowledge, and for the production of experience, which contains two very dissimilar elements, namely, a matter for knowledge, given by the senses, and a certain form for the arrangement of this matter, arising out of the inner fountain of pure intuition and thought; and these, on occasion given by sensible impressions, are called into exercise and produce concepts. Such an investigation into the first efforts of our faculty of knowledge to mount from particular perceptions to general concepts, is undoubtedly of great utility; and we have to thank the celebrated Locke, for having first opened the way for this inquiry. But a deduction of the pure *a priori* concepts of course never can be made in this way, seeing that, in regard to their future employment, which must be entirely independent of experience, they must have a far different certificate of birth from that of a descent from experience. This attempted physiological derivation, which cannot properly be called deduction, because it relates merely to a *quaestio facti*, I shall entitle an explanation of the *possession* of a pure knowledge. It is therefore manifest that there can only be a transcendental deduction of these concepts, and by no means an empirical one; also, that all attempts at an empirical deduction, in regard to pure *a priori* concepts, are vain, and can only be made by one who does not understand the altogether peculiar nature of this knowledge.

But although it is admitted that the only possible deduction of pure *a priori* knowledge is transcendental deduction, it is not, for that reason, perfectly manifest that such a deduction is absolutely necessary. We have already traced to their sources the concepts of space and time, by means of a transcendental deduction, and we have explained and determined their objective validity *a priori*. Geometry, nevertheless, advances steadily and securely in the province of pure *a priori* knowledge, without needing to ask from philosophy any certificate as to the pure and legitimate origin of its fundamental concept of space. But the use of the concept in this science extends only to the external world of sense, the pure form of the intuition of which is space; and in *this* world, therefore, all geometrical knowledge, because it is founded upon *a priori* intuition, possesses immediate evidence, and the objects of this knowledge are given *a priori* (as regards their form) in intuition by and through the knowledge itself. With the pure concepts of understanding, on the contrary, commences the absolute necessity of seeking a transcendental deduction, not only of these concepts themselves, but likewise of space, because, inasmuch as they make affirmations concerning objects not by means of the predicates of intuition and sensibility, but of pure thought *a priori*, they apply to objects without any of the conditions of sensibility. Besides, not being founded on experience, they are not presented with any object in *a priori* intuition upon which, antecedently to experience, they might base their synthesis. Hence results, not only doubt as to the objective validity and proper limits of their use, but that even our concept of space is rendered equivocal; inasmuch as we are very ready with the aid of the categories, to carry the use of this concept beyond the conditions of sensible intuition – and for this reason, we have already found a transcendental deduction of it needful. The reader, then, must be quite convinced of the absolute necessity of a transcendental deduction, before taking a single step in the field of pure reason; because otherwise he goes to work blindly, and after he has wandered about in all directions, returns to the state of utter ignorance from which he started. He ought, moreover, clearly to recognize beforehand, the unavoidable difficulties in his undertaking, so that he may not afterwards complain of the obscurity in which the subject itself is deeply involved, or become too soon impatient of the obstacles in his path; because we have a choice of only two things – either at once to give up all pretensions to knowledge beyond the limits of possible experience, or to bring this critical investigation to completion.

We have been able, with very little trouble, to make it comprehensible how the concepts of space and time, although *a priori* knowledge, must necessarily apply to external objects, and render a synthetical knowledge of these possible, independently of all experience. For inasmuch as only by means of such pure form of sensibility an object can appear to us, that is, be an object of empirical intuition, space and time are pure intuitions, which contain *a priori* the condition of the possibility of objects as appearances, and an *a priori* synthesis in these intuitions possesses objective validity.

On the other hand, the categories of the understanding do not represent the conditions under which objects are given to us in intuition; objects can consequently appear to us without necessarily connecting themselves with these, and consequently without any necessity binding on the understanding to contain *a priori* the conditions of these objects. Thus we find ourselves involved in a difficulty which did not present itself in the sphere of sensibility, that is to say, we cannot discover *how the subjective conditions of thought can have objective validity*, in other words, can become conditions of the possibility of all knowledge of objects; for appearances may certainly be given to us in intuition without any help from the functions of the understanding. Let us take, for example, the concept of *cause*, which indicates a peculiar kind of synthesis, namely, that with something, A, something entirely different, B, is connected according to a law. It is not *a priori* manifest why appearances should contain anything of this kind (we are of course debarred from appealing for proof to experience, for the objective validity of this concept must be demonstrated *a priori*), and it hence remains doubtful *a priori*, whether such a concept be not quite empty, and without any corresponding object among appearances. For that objects of sensible intuition must correspond to the formal conditions of sensibility existing *a priori* in the mind, is quite evident, from the fact that without these they could not be objects for us; but that they must also correspond to the conditions which understanding requires for the synthetical unity of thought, is an assertion, the grounds for which are not so easily to be discovered. For appearances might be so constituted as not to correspond to the conditions of the unity of thought; and all things might lie in such confusion, that, for example, nothing could be met with in the sphere of appearances to suggest a law of synthesis, and so correspond to the concept of cause and effect; so that this concept would be quite void, null, and without significance. Appearances would nevertheless continue to present objects to our intuition; for mere intuition does not in any respect stand in need of the functions of thought.

If we thought to free ourselves from the labour of these investigations by saying: "Experience is constantly offering us examples of orderliness in appearances, and in this way presents us with abundant opportunity of abstracting the concept of cause, and so at the same time of corroborating the objective validity of this concept', we should in this case be overlooking that fact, that the concept of cause cannot arise in this way at all; that, on the contrary, it must either have an *a priori* basis in the understanding, or be rejected as a mere chimera. For this concept demands that something, A, should be of such a nature, that something else, B, should follow from it necessarily, and according to an absolutely universal law. We may certainly collect from appearances a law, according to which this or that *usually* happens, but the element of necessity is not to be found in it. Hence it is evident that to the synthesis of cause and effect belongs a dignity, which is utterly wanting in any empirical synthesis; for it is no mere mechanical synthesis, by means of addition, but a dynamical one, that is to say, the effect is not to be thought as merely annexed to the cause, but as posited by and through the cause, and resulting from it. The strict universality of this law never can be a characteristic of empirical laws, which obtain through induction only a comparative universality, that is, an extended range of practical application. But the pure concepts of the understanding would entirely lose all their peculiar character, if we treated them merely as the productions of experience.

§ 14

Transition to the Transcendental Deduction of the Categories

There are only two possible ways in which synthetical representation and its objects can coincide with and relate necessarily to each other, and, as it were, meet together. Either the object alone makes the representation possible, or the representation alone makes the object possible. In the former case, the relation between them is only empirical, and an *a priori* representation is impossible. And this is the case with appearances, as regards that in them which is referable to mere sensation. In the latter case – although representation alone (for of its causality, by means of the will, we do not here speak) does not produce the object as to its existence, it must nevertheless be *a priori* determinative in regard to the object, if it is only by means of the representation that we can know anything as an object. Now there are only two conditions of the possibility of knowledge of objects; firstly, *intuition*, by means of which the object, though only as appearance, is given; secondly, concept, by means of which the object which corresponds to this intuition is thought. But it is evident from what has been said on aesthetic, that the first condition, under which alone objects can be intuited, must in fact exist, as a formal basis for them, *a priori* in the mind. With this formal condition of sensibility, therefore, all appearances necessarily correspond, because it is only through it that they can be appearances at all; that is, can be empirically intuited and given. Now the question is, whether there do not exist *a priori* in the mind, concepts of understanding also, as conditions under which alone something, if not intuited, is yet thought as object. If this question be answered in the affirmative, it follows that all empirical knowledge of objects is necessarily conformable to such concepts, since, if they are not presupposed, it is impossible that anything can be an object of experience. Now all experience contains, besides the intuition of the senses through which an object is given, *a concept* also of an object that is given in intuition. Accordingly, concepts of objects in general must lie as *a priori* conditions at the foundation of all empirical knowledge; and consequently, the objective validity of the categories, as *a priori* concepts, will rest upon *this*, that experience (as far as regards the form of thought) is possible only by their means. For in that case they apply necessarily and *a priori* to objects of experience, because only through them can an object of experience be thought.

The transcendental deduction of all *a priori* concepts has thus a principle according to which the whole inquiry must be directed: to show that these concepts are *a priori* conditions of the possibility of all experience. Concepts which afford us the objective foundation of the possibility of experience, are for that very reason necessary. But the unfolding of the experiences in which they are met with is not deduction, but only an illustration of them, because from experience they could never derive their necessity. Without their original relation to possible experience, in which all objects of knowledge present themselves, the relation of the categories to objects would be quite incomprehensible.

The celebrated Locke, for want of due reflection on these points, and because he met with pure concepts of the understanding in experience, sought also to derive them from experience, and yet proceeded so inconsequently as to attempt, with their aid, to arrive at knowledge which lies far beyond the limits of all experience. David Hume perceived that, to render this possible, it was necessary that the concepts should have an *a priori* origin. But as he could not explain how it was possible that concepts which are not connected with each other in the understanding, must nevertheless be thought as necessarily connected in the object – and it never occurred to him that the understanding itself might, perhaps, by means of these concepts, be the author of the experience in which its objects were presented to it – he was forced to derive these concepts from experience, that is, from a subjective necessity arising from repeated association of experiences erronously considered to be objective – in one word, from *habit*. But he proceeded with perfect consequence, and declared it to be impossible with such concepts and the principles arising from them, to overstep the limits of experience. The empirical derivation, however, which both of these philosophers attributed to these concepts, cannot possibly be reconciled with the fact that we do possess scientific *a priori* knowledge, namely, that of pure mathematics and of general physics, and hence is refuted by this fact.

The former of these two celebrated men opened a wide door to extravagance (for if reason is once allowed right on its side, it will not allow itself to be confined, by vague recommendations of moderation); the latter gave himself up entirely to scepticism having, as he believed, discovered that what passes for reason is nothing but a pervasive illusion of our knowledge faculty. We now intend to make a trial whether it be not possible safely to conduct reason between these two rocks, to assign her determinate limits, and yet leave open for her the entire sphere of her legitimate activity.

I shall merely premise an explanation of what the categories are. They are concepts of an object in general, by means of which its intuition is considered as determined in relation to one of the logical functions of judgment. The following will make this plain. The function of the categorical judgment is that of the relation of subject to predicate; for example, in the proposition: 'All bodies are divisible.' But in regard to the merely logical use of the understanding, it still remains undetermined to which of these two concepts belongs the function of subject, and to which that of predicate. For we could also say: 'Some divisible is a body.' But the category of substance, when the concept of a body is brought under it, determines that; and its empirical intuition in experience must be contemplated always as subject, and never as mere predicate. And so with all the other categories.

DEDUCTION OF THE PURE CONCEPTS OF THE UNDERSTANDING

SECTION II: TRANSCENDENTAL DEDUCTION OF THE PURE
CONCEPTS OF THE UNDERSTANDING

§ *15 : The Possibility of a Connection in general*

The manifold of representations can be given in an intuition which
is merely sensible – in other words, is nothing but receptivity; and
the form of this intuition can exist *a priori* in our faculty of
representation, without being anything else but the mode in which
the subject is affected. But the connection (*conjunctio*) of a manifold
never can be given us by the senses; it cannot therefore be contained
in the pure form of sensible intuition, for it is a spontaneous act of
the faculty of representation. And as we must, to distinguish it from
sensibility, entitle this faculty *understanding*, so all connection –
whether conscious or unconscious, be it of the manifold in intuition,
sensible or non-sensible, or of several concepts – is an act of the
understanding. To this act we shall give the general appellation of
synthesis, thereby to indicate, at the same time, that we cannot
represent anything as connected in the object without having
previously connected it ourselves. Of all mental notions, that of
connection is the only one which cannot be given through objects,
but can be originated only by the subject itself, because it is an act
of its purely spontaneous activity. The reader will easily enough
perceive that the possibility of connection must be grounded in the
very nature of this act, and that it must be equally valid for all
connection; and that analysis, which appears to be its contrary,
must, nevertheless, always presuppose it; for where the understanding has not previously connected, it cannot dissect or analyse,
because only as connected by it, must that which is to be analysed
have been given to our faculty of representation.

But the concept of connection includes, besides the concept of the
manifold and of the synthesis of it, also that of the unity of the
manifold. Connection is the representation of the synthetical unity
of the manifold.[1] The representation of unity, therefore, cannot
arise out of connection; much rather does that representation, by

---

[1] Whether the representations are in themselves identical, and consequently whether one
can be thought analytically by means of and through the other, is a question which we
need not at present consider. Our *consciousness* of the one, when we speak of the
manifold, is always distinguishable from our consciousness of the other; and it is only
respecting the synthesis of this (possible) consciousness that we here treat.

adding itself with the representation of the manifold, render the concept of connection possible. This unity, which *a priori* precedes all concepts of connection, is not the category of unity (§10); for all the categories are based upon logical functions of judgment, and in these functions we already have connection, and consenquently unity of given concepts. It is therefore evident that the category of unity presupposes connection. We must therefore look still higher for this unity (as qualitative, §12), in that, namely, which contains the ground of the unity of diverse concepts in judgments, the ground, consequently, of the possibility of the existence of the understanding, even in regard to its logical use.

§ 16

The Original Synthetical Unity of Apperception

The *I think* must be capable of accompanying all my representations, for otherwise something would be represented in me which could not be thought; in other words, the representation would either be impossible, or at least it would be nothing to me. That representation which can be given prior to all thought, is called intuition. All the manifold of intuition, has, therefore, a necessary relation to the *I think*, in the subject in which this manifold is found. But this representation, *I think*, is an act of *spontaneity*; that is to say, it cannot be regarded as belonging to sensibility. I call it pure apperception, in order to distinguish it from empirical apperception; or original apperception, because it is a self-consciousness which, by giving birth to the representation *I think*, must necessarily be capable of accompanying all our representations. It is in all acts of consciousness one and the same, and cannot be accompanied by any further representation. The unity of this apperception I call the transcendental unity of self-consciousness, in order to indicate the possibility of *a priori* knowledge arising from it. For the manifold representations which are given in an intuition would not all of them be my representations, if they did not all belong to one self-consciousness, that is, as my representations (although I am not conscious of them as such), they must conform to the condition under which alone they can exist together in a common self-consciousness, because otherwise they would not all without exception belong to me. From this original connection follow many important results.

This thorough-going identity of the apperception of the manifold given in intuition, contains a synthesis of representations, and is possible only by means of the consciousness of this synthesis. For the empirical consciousness which accompanies different representations is in itself fragmentary and disunited, and without relation to the identity of the subject. This relation, then, does not exist because I accompany every representation with consciousness, but because I join one representation to another, and am conscious of the synthesis of them. Consequently, only because I can connect a variety of given representations in one consciousness, it is possible that I can represent to myself the identity of consciousness in these representations; in other words, the analytical unity of apperception is possible only under the presupposition of a synthetical unity.[1] The thought, 'These representations given in intuition, belong all of them to me', is accordingly just the same as, 'I unite them in one self-consciousness, or can at least so unite them'; and although this thought is not itself the consciousness of the synthesis of representations, it presupposes the possibility of such a synthesis; that is to say, for the reason alone, that I can comprehend the variety of my representations in one consciousness, do I call them my representations, for otherwise I would have as many-coloured and various a self as are the representations of which I am conscious. Synthetical unity of the manifold in intuitions, as given *a priori*, is therefore the foundation of the identity of apperception itself, which antecedes *a priori* all determinate thought. But the connection of representations into a concept is not to be found in objects themselves, nor can it be, as it were, borrowed from them and taken up into the understanding by perception, but it is on the contrary an operation of the understanding itself, which is nothing more than the faculty of connecting *a priori*, and of bringing the

---

[1] All general concepts – as such – depend, for their existence, on the analytical unity of consciousness. For example, when I think of *red* in general, I thereby think to myself a property which (as a characteristic mark) can be discovered somewhere, or can be united with other representations; consequently, it is only by means of a presupposed possible synthetical unity that I can think to myself the analytical unity. A representation which is thought as common to *different* representations, is regarded as belonging to such as, besides this common representation, contain something *different*; consequently it must be previously thought in synthetical unity with other although only possible representations, before I can think in it the analytical unity of consciousness which makes it a *conceptus communis*. And thus the synthetical unity of apperception is the highest point with which we must connect every operation of the understanding, even the whole of logic, and after it our transcendental philosophy; indeed, this faculty is the understanding itself.

variety of given representations under the unity of apperception. This principle is the highest in all human knowledge.

This fundamental principle of the necessary unity of apperception is indeed an identical, and therefore analytical proposition; but it nevertheless explains the necessity for a synthesis of the manifold given in an intuition, without which the identity of self-consciousness cannot be thought. For the I, as a simple representation, presents us with no manifold; only in intuition, which is quite different from the representation I, can the manifold be given us, and by means of connection, it is thought in one self-consciousness. An understanding, in which all the manifold were given by means of consciousness itself, would be intuitive; our understanding can only think, and must look for its intuition to sense. I am, therefore, conscious of my identical self, in relation to all the variety of representations given to me in an intuition, because I call all of them my representations. In other words, I am conscious myself of a necessary *a priori* synthesis of my representations, which is called the original synthetical unity of apperception, under which rank all the representations presented to me, but that only by means of a synthesis.

§ 17

The Principle of the Synthetical Unity of Apperception is the highest Principle of all employment of the Understanding

The supreme principle of the possibility of all intuition in relation to sensibility was, according to our transcendental aesthetic, that all the manifold in intuition be subject to the formal conditions of space and time. The supreme principle of the possibility of it in relation to the understanding is: that all the manifold in intuition be subject to conditions of the originally synthetical unity of apperception.[1] To the former of these two principles are subject all the various representations of intuition, in so far as they are given to us; to the latter, in so far as they must be capable of connection

[1] Space and time, and all portions therof, are *intutions*; consequently are, with the manifold that they contain, single representations. (See the *Transcendental Aesthetic*.) Consequently, they are not pure concepts, by means of which the same consciousness is found in a great number of representations; but, on the contrary, they are many representations contained in one, the consciousness of which is, compound. The unity of consciousness is therefore *synthetical*, yet also primitive. This singularity of intuitions is important in what follows.

in one consciousness; for without this connection nothing can be thought or known, because the given representations would not have in common the act of the apperception *I think*; and therefore could not be comprehended in one self-consciousness.

Understanding is, to speak generally, *the faculty of concept.* This consists in the determinate relation of given representations to an object. But an object is that, in the concept of which the manifold in a given intuition is united. Now all union of representations requires unity of consciousness in the synthesis of them. Consequently, it is the unity of consciousness alone that constitutes the possibility of representations relating to an object, and therefore of their objective validity, and of their becoming knowledge, and consequently, the possibility of the existence of the understanding itself.

The first pure knowledge of understanding, then, upon which is founded all its other exercise, and which is at the same time perfectly independent of all conditions of mere sensible intuition, is the principle of the original synthetical unity of apperception. Thus the mere form of external sensible intuition, namely, space, affords us no knowledge; it merely contributes the manifold in *a priori* intuition to possible knowledge. But, in order to know something in space (for example, a line), I must draw it, and thus produce synthetically a determinate connection of the given manifold, so that the unity of this act is at the same time the unity of consciousness (in the concept of a line), and by this means alone is an object (a determinate space) known. The synthetical unity of consciousness is, therefore, an objective condition of all knowledge, which I do not merely require in order to know an object, but to which every intuition must necessarily be subject, in order to become an object for me; because in any other way, and without this synthesis, the manifold in intuition could not be united in one consciousness.

This proposition is, as already said, itself analytical, although it constitutes the synthetical unity, the condition of all thought; for it states nothing more than that all my representations in any given intuition must be subject to the condition which alone enables me to ascribe them, as my representation, to an identical self, and so to unite them synthetically in one apperception, by means of the general expression, *I think.*

But this principle is not to be regarded as a principle for every possible understanding, but only for that understanding by means of whose pure apperception in the thought *I am*, no manifold is given. The understanding which contained the manifold in intuition, through the act itself of its own self-consciousness, in other words, an understanding by the representation of which the objects of the representation should at the same time exist, would not require a special act of synthesis of the manifold as the condition of the unity of its consciousness, an act of which the human understanding, which thinks only and cannot intuit, has absolute need. But this principle is the first *principle* of all the operations of human understanding, so that we cannot form the least conception of any other possible understanding, either of one such as should be itself intuition, or possess a sensible intuition, but with forms different from those of space and time.

§ 18

What Objective Unity of Self-consciousness is

It is by means of the transcendental unity of apperception that all the manifold given in an intuition is united into a concept of an object. On this account it is called objective, and must be distinguished from the *subjective unity* of consciousness, which is a *determination of the internal sense*, by means of which the said manifold in intuition is given empirically to be so united. Whether I can be *empirically* conscious of the manifold as coexistent or as successive, depends upon circumstances, or empirical conditions. Hence the empirical unity of consciousness by means of asociation of representations, itself relates to appearances, and is wholly contingent. On the contrary, the pure form of intuition in time, merely as an intuition, which contains a given manifold, is subject to the original unity of consciousness, and that solely by means of the necessary relation of the manifold in intuition to the *I think*, consequently by means of the pure synthesis of the understanding, which lies *a priori* at the foundation of all empirical synthesis. The transcendental unity of apperception is alone objectively valid; the empirical which we do not consider in this essay, and which is merely a unity derived from the former under given conditions *in concreto*, possesses only subjective validity. One person connects the notion conveyed in a word with one thing, another with another thing; and the unity of consciousness in that which is empirical, is, in relation to that which is given by experience, not necessarily and universally valid.

§ 19

The Logical Form of all Judgments consists in the Objective Unity of Apperception of the Concepts which they contain

I could never satisfy myself with the definition which logicians give of a judgment. It is, according to them, the representation of a relation between two concepts. I shall not dwell here on the faultiness of this definition, in that it fits only categorical and not hypothetical or disjunctive judgments, these latter containing a relation not of concepts but of judgments – a mistake from which many troublesome results have followed.[1] It is more important for our present purpose to observe, that this definition does not determine in what the said relation consists.

But if I investigate more closely the relation of given knowledge in every judgment, and distinguish it, as belonging to the understanding, from the relation which is produced according to laws of the reproductive imagination (which has only subjective validity), I find that a judgment is nothing but the manner of bringing given knowledge under the objective unity of apperception. This is plain from our use of the copula *is* in judgments, in order to distinguish the objective unity of given representations from the subjective unity. For this word indicates the relation of these representations to the original apperception, and also their *necessary unity*, even although the judgment is empirical, therefore contingent, as in the judgment: 'All bodies are heavy.' I do not mean by this, that these representations do *necessarily* belong to each other in empirical intuition, but that by means of the *necessary unity* of apperception they belong to each other according to principles of the objective determination of all our representations, in so far as knowledge can arise from them, these principles being all derived from the main principle of the transcendental unity of apperception. In this way alone can there arise from this relation a *judgment*, that is, a relation which has objective validity, and is perfectly distinct from the relation of the very same representations which has only

[1] The lengthy doctrine of the four syllogistic figures concerns only categorical syllogisms; and although it is nothing more than an artifice by surreptitiously introducing immediate conclusions (*consequentiae immediatae*) among the premises of a pure syllogism, to give rise to an appearance of more modes of drawing a conclusion than that in the first figure, the artifice would not have had much success, had not its authors succeeded in bringing categorical judgments into exclusive respect, as those to which all others must be referred – a doctrine, however, which, according to §9, is false.

subjective validity – a relation, to wit, which is produced according to laws of association. According to these laws, I could only say: 'When I hold in my hand a body, I feel an impression of weight'; but I could not say: 'It, the body, is heavy'; for this is tantamount to saying that both these representations are connected in the object, that is, regardless of the condition of the subject, and do not merely stand together in my perception, however frequently the perceptive act may be repeated.

§ 20

All Sensible Intuitions are subject to the Categories, as Conditions under which alone the Manifold of Intuitions can be united in one Consciousness

The manifold given in a sensible intuition is necessarily subject to the original synthetical unity of apperception, because thereby alone is the *unity* of intuition possible (§17). But that act of the understanding, by which the manifold of given representations (whether intuitions or concepts) is brought under one apperception, is the logical function of judgments (§19). All the manifold, therefore, in so far as it is given in a single empirical intuition, is *determined* in relation to one of the logical functions of judgment, by means of which it is brought into one consciousness. Now the categories are nothing else than these functions of judgment, in so far as the manifold in a given intuition is determined in relation to them (§13). Consequently, the manifold in a given intuition is necessarily subject to the categories of the understanding.

§ 21

Observation

The manifold in an intuition, which I call mine, is represented by means of the synthesis of the understanding, as belonging to the necessary unity of self-consciousness, and this takes place by means of the category.[1] The category indicates accordingly, that the empirical consciousness of a given manifold in an intuition is subject

---

[1] The proof of this rests on the represented *unity of intuition*, by means of which an object is given, and which always includes in itself a synthesis of the manifold given in an intuition, and already contains the relation of this latter to unity of apperception.

to a pure self-consciousness *a priori*, in the same manner as an empirical intuition is subject to a pure sensible intuition, which is also *a priori*. In the above proposition, then, lies the beginning of a deduction of the pure concept of the understanding. Now, as the categories have their origin in the understanding alone, independently of sensibility, I must in my deduction make abstraction of the mode in which the manifold of an empirical intuition is given, in order to fix my attention exclusively on the unity which is brought by the understanding into the intuition by means of the category. In what follows (§26), it will be shown from the mode in which the empirical intuition is given in the faculty of sensibility, that the unity which belongs to it is no other than that which the category (according to §20) imposes on the manifold in a given intuition, and thus its *a priori* validity in regard to all objects of sense being established, the purpose of our deduction will be fully attained.

But there is one thing in the above demonstration, of which I could not make abstraction, namely, that the manifold to be intuited must be given prior to the synthesis of the understanding, and independently of it. How this takes place remains here undetermined. For if I consider an understanding which was itself intuitive (as, for example, a divine understanding which should not represent given objects, but by whose representation the objects themselves should be given or produced), the categories would possess no signification in relation to such a faculty of knowledge. They are merely rules for an understanding, whose whole power consists in thought, that is, in the act of submitting the synthesis of the manifold which is presented to it in intuition from a very different quarter, to the unity of apperception; a faculty, therefore, which knows nothing by itself, but only connects and arranges the material for knowledge, the intuition, namely, which must be presented to it by means of the object. But to provide reasons for this peculiar character of our understandings, that it produces unity of apperception *a priori* only by means of categories, and a certain kind and number thereof, is as impossible as to explain why there are precisely so many functions of judgment and no more, or why time and space are the only forms of our intuition.

§ 22

A Category has no use in Knowledge other than its Application to Objects of Experience

To think an object and to know an object are by no means the same thing. In knowledge there are two elements: firstly, the concept, whereby an object is thought (the category); and, secondly, the intuition, whereby the object is given. For supposing that to the concept a corresponding intuition could not be given, it would still be a thought as regards its form, but without any object, and no knowledge of anything would be possible by means of it, inasmuch as, so far as I could know, there would exist and could exist nothing to which my thought could be applied. Now all intuition possible to us is sensible; consequently, our thought of an object by means of a pure concept of the understanding, can become knowledge for us only in so far as this concept is applied to objects of the senses. Sensible intuition is either pure intuition (space and time) or empirical intuition – of that which is immediately represented in space and time by means of sensation as real. Through the determination of pure intuition we obtain *a priori* knowledge of objects, as in mathematics, but only as regards their form as appearances; whether there can exist things which must be intuited in this form is not thereby established. All mathematical concepts, therefore, are not by themselves knowledge, except in so far as we presuppose that there exist things which can only be represented conformably to the form of our pure sensible intuition. But things in space and time are given only in so far as they are perceptions (representations accompanied with sensation), therefore only by empirical representation. Consequently the pure concepts of the understanding, even when they are applied to intuitions *a priori* (as in mathematics), produce knowledge only in so far as the *a priori* (and therefore the concepts of the understanding by means of them) can be applied to empirical intuitions. Consequently the categories do not, even by means of pure intuition, afford us any knowledge of things; they can only do so in so far as they can be applied to empirical intuition. That is to say, the categories serve only to render empirical knowledge possible. But this is what we call experience. Consequently, in knowledge, their application to objects of experience is the only legitimate use of the categories.

§ 23

The foregoing proposition is of the utmost importance, for it determines the limits of the employment of the pure concepts of the understanding in regard to objects, just as transcendental aesthetic determined the limits of the employment of the pure form of our sensible intuition. Space and time, as conditions of the possibility of the presentation of objects to us, are valid no further than for objects of sense, consequently, only for experience. Beyond these limits they represent to us nothing, for they belong only to sense, and have no reality apart from it. The pure concepts of the understanding are free from this limitation, and extend to objects of intuition in general, be the intuition like or unlike to ours, provided only it be sensible, and not intellectual. But this extension of concepts beyond the range of our intuition is of no advantage; for they are then mere empty concepts of objects, as to the possibility or impossibility of the existence of which they furnish us with no means of discovery. They are mere forms of thought, without objective reality, because we have no intuition to which the synthetical unity of apperception, which alone make up the content of these forms, could be applied, for the purpose of determining an object. Our sensible and empirical intuition can alone give them significance and meaning.

If, then, we suppose an object of a non-sensible intuition to be given, we can in that case represent it by all those predicates which are implied in the presupposition that nothing *appertaining to sensible intuition belongs to it*; for example, that is is not extended, or in space; that its duration is not time; that in it no change (the effect of the determinations in time) is to be met with, and so on. But it is no proper knowledge if I merely indicate what the intuition of the object *is not*, without being able to say what is contained in it, for I have not shown the possibility of an object to which my pure concept of understanding could be applicable, because I have not been able to furnish any intuition corresponding to it, but am only able to say that our intuition is not valid for it. But the most important point is this, that to a *something* of this kind not one category can be found applicable. Take, for example, the concept of substance, that is, something that can exist as subject, but never as mere predicate; in regard to this concept I am quite ignorant whether there can really be anything to correspond to such a determination of thought, if empirical intuition did not afford me the occasion for its application. But of this more in the sequel.

§ 24

The Application of the Categories to Objects of the Senses in general

The pure concepts of the understanding apply to objects of intuition in general, through the understanding alone, whether the intuition be our own or some other, provided only it be sensible but are, for this very reason, mere forms of thought, by means of which alone no determined object can be known. The synthesis or connection of the manifold in these concepts relates, we have said, only to the unity of apperception, and is for this reason the ground of the possibility of *a priori* knowledge, in so far as this connection is dependent on the understanding. This synthesis is, therefore, not merely transcendental, but also purely intellectual. But because a certain form of sensible intuition exists in us *a priori* which is based on the receptivity of the faculty of representation (sensibility), the understanding, as spontaneity, is able to determine the internal sense by means of the manifold of given representations, conformably to the synthetical unity of apperception, and thus to think the synthetical unity of the apperception of the manifold of sensible intuition *a priori*, as the condition to which must necessarily be submitted all objects of human intuition. And in this manner the categories as mere forms of thought receive objective reality, that is, application to objects which are given to us in intuition, but that only as appearances, for it is only of appearances that we are capable of *a priori* intuition.

This synthesis of the manifold of sensible intuition, which is possible and necessary *a priori*, may be called figurative (*synthesis speciosa*), in contradistinction to that which is thought in the mere category in regard to the manifold of an intuition in general, and is called connection by the understanding (*synthesis intellectualis*). Both are transcendental, not merely because they themselves take place *a priori*, but also because they form the basis for the possibility of other knowledge *a priori*.

But the figurative synthesis, when it relates only to the originally synthetical unity of apperception, that is to the transcendental unity thought in the categories, must, to be distinguished from the purely intellectual connection, be entitled the *transcendental synthesis of imagination*. *Imagination* is the faculty of representing an object even without its presence in intuition. Now, as all our intuition is sensible, imagination, by reason of the subjective condition under which alone it can give a corresponding intuition to the concepts of the understanding, belongs to sensibility. But in so far as the synthesis of the imagination is an act of spontaneity, which is determinative, and not, like sense, merely determinable, and which is consequently able to determine sense *a priori*, according to its form, conformably to the unity of apperception, to that extent the imagination is a faculty of determining sensibility *a priori*, and its synthesis of intuitions according to the categories must be the transcendental synthesis of the imagination. It is an operation of the understanding on sensibility, and the first application of the understanding to objects of possible intuition, and at the same time, the basis for the exercise of the other functions of that faculty. As figurative, it is distinguished from the merely intellectual synthesis, which is produced by the understanding alone, without the aid of imagination. Now, in so far as imagination is spontaneity, I sometimes call it also the *productive* imagination, and distinguish it from the *reproductive imagination*, the synthesis of which is subject entirely to empirical laws, those of association, namely, and which, therefore, contributes nothing to the explanation of the possibility of *a priori* knowledge, and for this reason belongs not to transcendental philosophy, but to psychology.

*

This is the proper place for explaining the paradox, which must have struck every one in our exposition of the internal sense (§10), namely – how this sense represents us to our own consciousness, only as we appear to ourselves, not as we are in ourselves, because, to wit, we intuit ourselves only as we are inwardly affected. Now this appears to be contradictory, inasmuch as we thus stand in a passive relation to ourselves; and therefore in the systems of psychology, the internal sense is commonly held to be one with the faculty of apperception, while we, on the contrary, carefully distinguish them.

That which determines the internal sense is the understanding, and its original power of connecting the manifold of intuition, that is, of bringing this under an apperception (upon which rests the possibility of the understanding itself). Now, as the human understanding is not in itself a faculty of intuition, and is unable to exercise such a power, in order to connect, as it were, the manifold of its own intuition, the synthesis of understanding is, considered in isolation, nothing but the unity of action, of which, as being such, it is conscious, even apart from sensibility, by which, moreover, it is able to determine our internal sense in respect of the manifold which may be presented to it according to the form of sensible intuition. Thus, under the name of a transcendental synthesis of imagination, the understanding exercises an activity upon the passive subject, whose faculty it is; and so we are right in saying that the internal sense is affected thereby. Apperception and its synthetical unity are by no means one and the same with the internal sense. The former, as the source of all our synthetical connection, applies, under the name of the categories, to the manifold of intuition in general, prior to all sensible intuition of objects. The internal sense, on the contrary, contains merely the form of intuition, but without any synthetical connection of the manifold therein, and consequently does not contain any determined intuition, which is possible only through consciousness of the determination of the manifold by the transcendental act of the imagination (synthetical influence of the understanding on the internal sense), which I have named figurative synthesis.

This we can indeed always perceive in ourselves. We cannot think a line without *drawing* it in thought, nor a circle without *describing* it, nor represent the three dimensions of space without drawing three lines from the same point perpendicular to one another. We cannot even think time, unless, in drawing a straight line (which is to serve as the external figurative representation of time), we fix our attention on the act of the synthesis of the manifold, whereby we determine successively the internal sense, and thus attend also to the succession of this determination. Motion as an act of the subject (not as a determination of an object),[1] consequently the synthesis of the manifold in space, if we make abstraction of space and attend merely to the act by which we determine the internal sense according to its form, is that which produces the concept of succession. The understanding, therefore, does by no means *find* in the internal sense any such connection of the manifold, but *produces* it, in that it affects

[1] Motion of an *object* in space does not belong to a pure science, consequently not to geometry; because that a thing is movable cannot be known *a priori*, but only from experience. But motion, considered as the *description* of a space, is a pure act of the successive synthesis of the manifold in external intuition by means of productive imagination, and belongs not only to geometry, but even to transcendental philosophy.

this sense. At the same time, how [the] *I* who thinks is distinct from the *I* which intuits itself (other modes of intuition being conceivable as at least possible), and yet one and the same with this latter as the same subject; how, therefore, I am able to say: 'I, as an intelligence and *thinking* subject, know myself as an object *thought*, so far as I am, moreover, given to myself in intuition – only, like other appearances, not as I am in myself, and as considered by the understanding, but merely as I appear' – is a question that has in it neither more nor less difficulty than the question – 'How can I be an object to myself?' or this – 'How I can be an object of my own intuition and internal perceptions?' But that such must be the fact, if we admit that space is merely a pure form of the appearances of external sense, can be clearly proved by the consideration that we cannot represent time, which is not an object of external intuition, in any other way than under the image of a line, which we draw in thought, a mode of representation without which we could not know the unity of its dimension, and also that we are necessitated to take our determination of periods of time, of of points of time, for all our internal perceptions from the changes which we perceive in outward things. It follows that we must arrange the determinations of the internal sense, as appearances in time, exactly in the same manner as we arrange those of the external senses in space. And consequently, if we grant respecting this latter, that by means of them we know objects only in so far as we are affected externally, we must also confess, with regard to the internal sense, that by means of it we intuit ourselves only as we are internally affected by ourselves; in other words, as regards internal intuition, we know our own subject only as appearance, and not as it is in itself.[1]

§ 25

On the other hand, in the transcendental synthesis of the manifold representations, consequently in the synthetical unity of apperception, I am conscious of myself, not as I appear to myself, nor as I am in myself, but only that *I am*. This representation is a *thought*,

[1] I do not see why so much difficulty should be found in admitting that our internal sense is affected by ourselves. Every act of attention exemplifies it. In such an act the understanding determines the internal sense, conformably to the connection which it thinks, to internal intuition corresponding to the manifold in the synthesis of the understanding. How much the mind is usually affected thereby every one will be able to perceive in himself.

not an *intuition*. Now, as in order to know ourselves, in addition to the act of thinking, which subjects the manifold of every possible intuition to the unity of apperception, there is necessary a determinate mode of intuition, whereby this manifold is given; although my own existence is certainly not mere appearance (much less mere illusion), the determination of my existence[1] can only take place conformably to the form of the internal sense, according to the particular mode in which the manifold which I connect is given in internal intuition, and I have therefore no knowledge of myself as I am, but merely as I appear to myself. The consciousness of oneself is thus very far from a knowledge of oneself, in which I do not use the categories, whereby I think an object, by means of the connection of the manifold in one apperception. In the same way as I require, for knowledge of an object distinct from myself, not only the thought of an object in general (in the category), but also an intuition by which to determine that general concept, in the same way do I require, in order to the knowledge of myself, not only the consciousness of myself or the thought that I think myself, but in addition an intuition of the manifold in myself, by which to determine this thought. It is true that I exist as an intelligence which is conscious only of its faculty of connection, but subjected in relation to the manifold which this intelligence has to connect to a limitative condition called the internal sense. My intelligence (that is, I) can render that connection or synthesis perceptible only according to the relations of time, which are quite beyond the proper sphere of the concepts of the understanding, and consequently know itself in respect to an intuition (which cannot possibly by intellectual, nor given by the understanding), only as it appears to itself, and not as it would itself, if its intuition were intellectual.

[1] The *I think* expresses the act of determining my own existence. My existence is thus already given by the act of consciousness; but the mode in which I must determine my existence, is not thereby given. For this purpose intuition of oneself is required, and this intuition possesses a form given *a priori*, namely, time, which is sensible, and belongs to our receptivity of the determinable. Now, as I do not possess another intuition of myself which gives the *determining*, in the same manner as time gives the determinable, it is clear that I am unable to determine my own existence as that of a spontaneous being, but I am only able to represent to myself the spontaneity of my thought, that is, of my determination, and my existence remains ever determinable in a purely sensible manner, that is to say, like the existence of a appearance. But it is because of this spontaneity that I call myself an *intelligence*.

§ 26

Transcendental Deduction of the universally possible employment in Experience of the Pure Concepts of the Understanding

In the metaphysical deduction, the *a priori* origin of the categories was proved by their complete accordance with the general logical functions of thought; in the transcendental deduction was exhibited the possibility of the categories as *a priori* knowledge of objects of an intuition in general (§§20 and 21). At present we are about to explain the possibility of knowing, *a priori*, by means of the categories, all objects which can possibly be presented to our senses, not, indeed, according to the form of their intuition, but according to the laws of their connection, and thus, as it were, of prescribing laws to nature, and even of rendering nature possible. For if the categories were adequate to this task, it would not be evident to us why everything that is presented to our senses must be subject to those laws which have an *a priori* origin in the understanding itself.

I premise, that by the term *synthesis of apprehension* I understand the connection of the manifold in an empirical intuition, whereby perception, that is, empirical consciousness of the intuition (as appearance), is made possible.

We have *a priori* forms of the external and internal sensible intuition in the representations of space and time, and to these must the synthesis of apprehension of the manifold in a appearance be always comformable, because the synthesis itself can only take place according to these forms. But space and time are not merely forms of sensible intuition, but *intuitions* themselves (which contain a manifold), and therefore contain *a priori* the determination of the *unity* of this manifold.[1] (See the *Trans. Aesthetic.*) Therefore *unity of the synthesis* of the manifold without or within us, consequently also a connection to which all that is to be represented as determined

---

[1] Space represented as an *object* (as geometry really requires it to be) contains more than the mere form of the intuition; namely, a connection of the manifold given according to the form of sensibility into a representation that can be intuited; so that the *form of the intuition* gives us merely the manifold, but the *formal intuition* gives unity of representation. In the Aesthetic I regarded this unity as belonging entirely to sensibility, for the purpose of indicating that it antecedes all concepts, although it presupposes a synthesis which does not belong to sense, through which alone, however, all our concepts of space and time are possible. For as by means of this unity alone (the understanding determining the sensibility) space and time are given as intuitions, it follows that the unity of this intuition *a priori* belongs to space and time, and not to the concept of the understanding (§24).

in space or time must correspond, is given *a priori* along with (not in) these intuitions, as the condition of the synthesis of all apprehension of them. But this synthetical unity can be no other than that of the connection of the manifold of a given intuition in general, in a primitive act of consciousness, according to the categories, but applied to our sensible intuition. Consequently all synthesis, whereby alone is even perception possible, is subject to the categories. And, as experience is knowledge by means of connected perceptions, the categories are conditions of the possiblity of experience, and are therefore valid *a priori* for all objects of experience.

*

When, then, for example, I make the empirical intuition of a house by apprehension of the manifold contained therein into a perception, the *necessary unity* of space and of my external sensible intuition lies at the foundation of this act, and I, as it were, draw the form of the house conformably to this synthetical unity of the manifold in space. But this very synthetical unity remains, even when I abstract the form of space, and has its seat in the understanding, and is in fact the category of the synthesis of the homogeneous in an intuition; that is to say, the category of *quantity*, to which the aforesaid synthesis of apprehension, that is, the perception, must be completely conformable.[1]

To take another example, when I perceive the freezing of water, I apprehend two states (fluidity and solidity), which, as such, stand toward each other mutually in a relation of time. But in the time, which I place as an internal intuition, at the foundation of this appearance, I represent to myself synthetical *unity* of the manifold, without which the aforesaid relation could not be given in an intuition as *determined* (in regard to the succession of time). Now this synthetical unity, as the *a priori* condition under which I connect the manifold of an intuition, is, if I make abstraction of the permanent form of my internal intuition (that is to say, of time), the category of *cause*, by means of which, when applied to my sensibility, *I determine everything that occurs according to relations of time.* Consequently apprehension in such an event, and the event itself, as far as regards the possibility of its perception, stand under

---

[1] In this manner it is proved, that the synthesis of apprehension, which is empirical, must necessarily be conformable to the synthesis of apperception, which is intellectual, and contained *a priori* in the category. It is one and the same spontaneity which at one time, under the name of imagination, at another under that of understanding, produces connection in the manifold of intuition.

the concept of the relation of cause and effect: and so in all other cases.

*

Categories are concepts which prescribe laws *a priori* to appearances, consequently to nature as the complex of all appearances (*natura materialiter spectata*). And now the question arises – inasmuch as these categories are not derived from nature, and do not regulate themselves according to it as their model (for in that case they would be empirical) – how it is conceivable that nature must regulate itself according to them, in other words, how the categories can determine *a priori* the synthesis of the manifold of nature, and yet not derive their origin from it. The following is the solution of this enigma.

It is not in the least more difficult to conceive how the laws of the appearances of nature must harmonize with the understanding and with its *a priori* form – that is, its faculty of connecting the manifold – than it is to understand how the appearances themselves must correspond with the *a priori* form of our sensible intuition. For laws do not exist in the appearances any more than the appearances exist as things in themselves. Laws do not exist except by relation to the subject in which the appearances inhere, in so far as it possesses understanding, just as appearances have no existence except by relation to the same existing subject in so far as it has senses. To things as things in themselves, conformability to law must necessarily belong independently of an understanding to know them. But appearances are only representations of things which are utterly unknown in respect to what they are in themselves. But as merely representations, they stand under no law of connection except that which the connecting faculty prescribes. Now that which connects the manifold of sensible intuition is imagination, a mental act to which understanding contributes unity of intellectual synthesis, and sensibility, manifoldness of apprehension. Now as all possible perception depends on the synthesis of apprehension, and this empirical synthesis itself on the transcendental, consequently on the categories, is is evident that all possible perceptions, and therefore everything that can attain to empirical consciousness, that is, all appearances of nature, must, as regards their connection, be subject to the categories. And nature (considered merely as nature in general) is dependent on them as the original ground of its necessary conformability to law (as *natura formaliter spectata*). But the pure faculty (of the understanding) of prescribing laws *a priori* to appearances by means of mere categories, is not competent to enounce other or more laws than those on which a *nature* in general, as a conformability to law of appearances of space the time, depends. Particular laws, inasmuch as they concern empirically determined appearances, cannot be entirely deduced from pure laws, although they all stand under them. Experience must be superadded in order to know these particular laws; but in regard to experience in general, and everything that can be known as an object thereof, these *a priori* laws are our only rule and guide.

§ 27

Result of this Deduction of the Concepts of the Understanding

We cannot think any object except by means of the categories; we cannot know any object except by means of intuitions corresponding to these concepts. Now all our intuitions are sensible, and our knowledge, in so far as the object of it is given, is empirical. But empirical knowledge is experience; consequently no *a priori* knowledge is possible for us, except of objects of possible *experience*.[1]

But this knowledge, which is limited to objects of experience, is not for that reason derived entirely from experience, but – and this is asserted of the pure intuitions and the pure concepts of the understanding – there are, unquestionably, elements of knowledge, which exist in us *a priori*. Now there are only two ways in which a necessary harmony of experience with the concepts of its objects can be thought. Either experience makes these concepts possible, or the concepts make experience possible. The former of these statements will not hold good with respect to the categories (nor in regard to pure sensible intuition), for they are *a priori* concepts, and therefore independent of experience. The assertion of an empirical origin would attribute to them a sort of *generatio aequivoca*. Consequently, nothing remains but to adopt the second alternative

---

[1] Lest my readers should stumble at this assertion, and the conclusions that may be too rashly drawn from it, I must remind them that the categories in the *act of thought* are by no means limited by the conditions of our sensible intuition, but have an unbounded sphere of action. It is only the knowledge of the object of thought, the determining of the object, which requires intuition. In the absence of intuition, our thought of an object may still have true and useful consequences in regard to the exercise of reason by the subject. But as this exercise of reason is not always directed on the determination of the object, in other words, on knowledge thereof, but also on the determination of the subject and its volition, I do not intend to treat of it in this place.

(which presents us with a system, as it were, of the *Epigenesis* of pure reason), namely, that on the part of the understanding the categories do contain the grounds of the possibility of all experience. But with respect to the questions how they make experience possible, and what are the principles of the possibility thereof with which they present us in their application to appearances, the following section on the transcendental exercise of the faculty of judgment will inform the reader.

It is quite possible that someone may propose a species of *preformation-system* of pure reason – a middle way between the two – to wit, that the categories are neither self-thought and first *a priori* principles of knowledge, nor derived from experience, but are merely subjective aptitudes for thought implanted in us contemporaneously with our existence, which were so ordered and disposed by our Creator, that their exercise perfectly harmonizes with the laws of nature which regulate experience. Now, not to mention that with such an hypothesis it is impossible to say at what point we must stop in the employment of predetermined aptitudes, the fact that the categories would in this case entirely lose that character of *necessity* which is essentially involved in the very concept of them, is a conclusive objection to it. The concept of cause, for example, which expresses the necessity of an effect under a presupposed condition, would be false, if it rested only upon such an arbitrary subjective necessity of uniting certain empirical representations according to such a rule of relation. I could not then say – 'The effect is connected with its cause in the object (that is, necessarily)', but only, 'I am so constituted that I can think this representation as so connected, and not otherwise'. Now this is just what the sceptic wants. For in this case, all our knowledge, depending on the supposed objective validity of our judgment, is nothing but mere illusion; nor would there be wanting people who would deny any such subjective necessity in respect to themselves, though they must feel it. At all events, we could not dispute with any one on that which merely depends on the manner in which his subject is organized.

Short view of the above Deduction

The foregoing deduction is an exposition of the pure concepts of the understanding (and with them of all theoretical *a priori* knowledge), as principles of the possibility of experience, but of experience as the *determination* of all appearances in space and time *in general* — of experience, finally, from the principle of the *original* synthetical unity of apperception, as the form of the understanding in relation to time and space as original forms of sensibility.

*

I consider the division by paragraphs to be necessary only up to this point, because we had to treat of the elementary concepts. As we now proceed to the exposition of the employment of these, I shall not designate the chapters in this manner any further.

DEDUCTION OF THE PURE CONCEPTS OF THE UNDERSTANDING

SECTION II: *A PRIORI* FOUNDATIONS OF THE POSSIBILITY OF EXPERIENCE

It is utterly contradictory and impossible that a concept should be created entirely *a priori* and yet relate to objects, if that concept does neither itself belong to the concept of possible experience nor consist of elements in possible experience. The concept would in that case lack all content, for no intuition would correspond to it; and it is precisely intuitions in general, by means of which objects can be given to us, that make up the domain and the whole object of possible experience. An *a priori* concept which did not relate to possible experience would be only the logical form of a concept, it would not be a concept by means of which something is thought.

So, if pure *a priori* concepts exist, they can of course contain nothing empirical, yet at the same time they need to be nothing but *a priori* conditions for possible experience, this being the only basis for their objective validity.

If, therefore, one desires to know how pure concepts of the understanding are possible, one needs to examine what the *a priori* conditions are that render experience possible and serve as its basis, having once abstracted from everything empirical in appearances. A pure concept of the understanding is a concept that gives general and sufficient expression to this formal and objective condition of experience. Once one is already in possession of pure concepts of the understanding, one may well go on to invent objects that, whether impossible or in themselves possible, cannot be given in experience since either these concepts are connected in such a way that something is left out that belongs necessarily to the condition for possible experience (e.g. the concept of a spirit) or the pure concepts of the understanding are extended further than experience is capable of reaching (e.g. the concept of God). Although the elements for *a priori* knowledge, even of arbitrary and incoherent fictions, cannot be borrowed from experience (otherwise it would not be *a priori* knowledge), still they always need to contain the pure *a priori* conditions for possible experience and for the objects of possible experience; otherwise nothing would be thought by means of them and, moreover, they could not even arise in thinking due to lack of data.

Now these concepts, which contain *a priori* the pure thinking involved in all experiencing, are supplied by the categories, and we shall have provided a sufficient deduction of them and a justification of their objective validity if we can prove that only by their means is it possible to think an object. However, in view of the fact that such thoughts involve more than just the capacity to think, viz. the understanding, and that the understanding itself, by virtue of being a capacity for knowledge relating to objects, equally requires elucidation with regard to the possibility of this relation, we need to begin by considering the subjective sources that make up the *a priori* foundation for the possibility of experience, considering not the empirical but the transcendental nature of this foundation.

If each individual representation was an entire stranger to the rest and as it were isolated and separate from them, then no such thing as knowledge would ever arise, knowledge being a whole consisting of compared and connected representations. Since the intuition of the senses contains multiplicity, I attribute synopsis to the senses; but to a synopsis there always corresponds a synthesis, and receptivity can provide the possibility of knowledge only in conjunction with spontaneity. Spontaneity in turn carries with it a threefold synthesis, which is necessarily present in all knowledge: apprehension of representations as modifications of the mind in intuition; reproduction of representations in the imagination; and recognition of representations in a concept. These lead us to three subjective sources of knowledge, which provide the possibility of the understanding itself and, consequently, of all experience, experience being an empirical product of the understanding.

Preliminary Remark

The deduction of the categories involves so much difficulty and requires such deep penetration into the ultimate basis for the possibility of knowledge that, in order to avoid the lengthiness of a comprehensive theory yet without neglecting anything in such a necessary investigation, I have found it advisable to employ the following four numbers [sub-sections] more in order to prepare than to instruct the reader. In the third section, which follows these sections, I then go on to introduce the systematic exposition of these elements of the understanding. In the meantime, therefore, the reader must not be put off by the obscurity that is at first unavoidably part of a yet unexplored path, though I hope the obscurity will give way to full insight in the third section.

I. THE SYNTHESIS OF APPREHENSION IN INTUITION

Whatever the source of our representations may be, whether they are produced by the influence of external things or by inner causes, whether they arise *a priori* or empirically as appearances, still they belong, by virtue of being modifications of the mind, to inner sense, and as such all our knowledge is ultimately subject to time, the formal condition for inner sense, in which the representations must all be ordered, connected and brought in relation to each other. This serves as a general observation, which is fundamental to what follows.

Every intuition contains a manifold in it. But this manifold could not be represented as being such if the mind did not distinguish time in the sequence of impressions. For, since every representation is contained in a single moment of time, it can never be anything but abolute unity. In order to create unity of intuition out of the manifold (as in the representation of space) it is necessary to run through this multiplicity and to hold it together. I call this action the synthesis of apprehension because it is directed directly at intuition. Intuition supplies a manifold, but it can represent this manifold as being such, and as contained in a single representation, only through the synthesis.

This synthesis of apprehension must equally be carried out *a priori*, that is to say with regard to representations that are not empirical. For, without the synthesis we could not possess *a priori* the representations of space and time, since these can be created only through the synthesis of the manifold which sensibility presents us by virtue of being ultimate receptivity. Hence the pure synthesis of apprehension.

2. THE SYNTHESIS OF REPRODUCTION IN THE IMAGINATION

It is admittedly only an empirical law which says that representations that have often followed or accompanied each other finally become associated with each other, thus becoming connected in such a manner that, even in the absence of their object, the one representation brings about a transition of the mind to the other representation according to a fixed rule. However, this law of reproduction presupposes that appearances themselves are actually subject to such a rule and that there occurs an accompaniment or sequence in the manifold of the representations in conformity with certain rules. Otherwise our empirical imagination would never be presented with any task appropriate to its capacity and would consequently remain concealed within our minds as a dead capacity unknown to us. If cinnabar were one moment red, the next moment black, one moment light, the next moment heavy, if human beings one moment changed into one animal shape, the next moment into a different animal shape, if on the longest day the country were one moment covered with fruit, the next moment with ice and snow, then my empirical imagination would not even be able to think of the heavy cinnabar in connection with the representation of the colour red. Or again, if a word were one moment assigned to one thing, the next moment to a different thing, or if one and the same thing were one moment named in one way, the next moment in a different way, without any governance of a rule, a rule that appearances are subject to in their own right, then no empirical synthesis of reproduction could take place.

There must, therefore, be something which, by serving as the *a priori* basis for a necessary synthetic unity of appearances, makes possible the reproduction of appearances. We may soon discover what this is if we bear in mind that appearances are not things in themselves but the mere play of our representations, which ultimately amount to determinations of inner sense. Now, if we are able to demonstrate that even our most pure *a priori* intuitions can provide knowledge only in so far as they contain such a connection of the manifold as serves to make possible a pervasive synthesis of reproduction, we shall equally have provided a basis for this synthesis of the imagination prior to all experience. We would then have to assume a pure transcendental synthesis of the imagination which, since it is necessarily presupposed in the reproducibility of appearances, serves as the basis for the very possibility of experience. We would then have to assume a pure transcendental synthesis of the imagination which, since it is necessarily presupposed in the reproducibility of appearances, serves as the basis for the very possibility of experience. Now it is apparent that in drawing a line in thought, or in thinking the interval from noon one day to noon the next, or even in representing a particular number to myself, I must first of all necessarily apprehend the manifold representations one after another in my thoughts. But if in thinking I were to lose sight of the preceding representations (the first part of the line, the preceding parts of the time-interval, or the sequentially represented units) and were to move on to the next without reproducing the preceding ones, then a whole representation could never arise, including all the mentioned thoughts and even the most pure and elementary representations of space and time.

The synthesis of apprehension is, therefore, inseparably connected with the synthesis of reproduction. Since the former is the transcendental basis for the possibility of all knowledge (not only empirical knowledge but also pure *a priori* knowledge), the reproductive synthesis of the imagination belongs to the transcendental acts of the mind. We shall therefore also call this capacity the transcendental capacity of the imagination.

3. THE SYNTHESIS OF RECOGNITION IN A CONCEPT

If we were not conscious that what we are thinking at this moment is precisely what we were thinking a moment ago, all reproduction in the series of representations would be in vain. The representation in my present state would be new and would not belong to the act that was meant gradually to create it. The manifold of the representation would never form a whole, since it would be lacking in the unity that only consciousness can provide. If while counting I were to forget that the units that I am at this moment imagining were gradually added together by me, then I would not through this successive addition of units recognize the creation of a set, hence of a number. For the concept [of number] consists solely of the consciousness of the unity of a synthesis.

The word 'concept' might by itself have led us to this observation. For it is precisely the single consciousness that unites the manifold into a single representation, the manifold which has been gradually intuited and then reproduced. This consciousness may often be faint, so that we associate it directly with the creation of a representation only subsequently and not during the act itself. But, regardless of these differences, consciousness must always be present, even if it lacks manifest clarity, and without it concepts, hence knowledge of objects, are quite impossible.

At this point we need to explain what is meant by the expression 'an object of a representation'. It was said above that appearances themselves are nothing but sensible representations which in themselves we are not to regard as objects (apart from the capacity for representations). What, then, is meant by an object corresponding to our knowledge, hence also different from our knowledge? It is easily seen that this object can be conceived only as something X in general since we do not possess anything apart from our knowledge that we could set against this knowledge as corresponding to it.

However, we need to appreciate that the idea of the relation between all knowledge to its object involves some kind of constraint since the object is conceived as being that which prevents our knowledge from becoming haphazard or arbitrary and instead makes it *a priori* determined in a particular way. This is because our knowledge, on account of having to relate to an object, must necessarily agree with itself with regard to the object, that is to say it must possess such unity as serves to make up the concept of an object.

But it is clear that the unity which is made necessary by the object can be nothing but the formal unity of consciousness in the synthesis of the manifold of representations. For all that is available for us to deal with is the manifold of our representations, and the X that corresponds to the representations (i.e. the object), since it is meant to be something different from all our representations, is nothing prior to us. We may therefore say that we come to know the object precisely by creating synthetic unity in the manifold of intuition. But this synthetic unity is impossible unless the intuition is capable of being produced according to such a rule-governed function of synthesis as serves to make *a priori* necessary the reproduction of the manifold and serves to make *a priori* possible a concept in which the manifold is united. For example, we think of a triangle as an object by virtue of being conscious of having put together three straight lines according to a rule, a rule that will always allow us to represent such an intuition. Now, this unity of a rule determines everything manifold and limits it to conditions, conditions that are in turn made possible by the unity of apperception. The concept of this unity is the representation of the object X of which I am thinking by means of the mentioned predicates of a triangle.

All knowledge requires a concept, however imperfect or obscure. But a concept is always, as regards its form, something general serving as a rule. Thus the concept of a body serves, according to the unity of the manifold which is thought by means of it, as a rule for our knowledge of external appearances. But it can serve as a rule for intuitions only by virtue of serving to represent, when presented with appearances, the necessary reproduction of the manifold of appearances, hence to represent the synthetic unity in the consciousness of the appearances. Thus the concept of a body makes necessary, when we perceive something outside us, the representations of extension, impenetrability, shape, etc.

There is always a transcendental condition to be found at the basis of all necessity. Consequently the unity of consciousness must serve as the trascendental basis in the synthesis of the manifold of all our intuitions, hence also of the concepts of objects in general, and finally also of all objects of experience. Without such a basis it would be impossible to think that our intuitions have any object. For the object is nothing over and above that something, the concept of which expresses such a necessity of synthesis.

This original and transcendental condition is none other than transcendental apperception. The consciousness of oneself, according to the way our state is determined in inner perception, is merely empirical, it is always changeable and cannot afford any stable and persistent self in the midst of the flux of appearances. It is commonly called inner sense or empirical apperception. If something needs to be represented as being necessarily numerically identical, it cannot be thought of as such by means of empirical data. It needs to be a condition preceding all experience and serving to make experience possible, while experience serves to make valid such a transcendental presupposition.

There cannot be any knowledge within us nor can knowledge be connected and unified within itself without unity of consciousness preceding all empirical data and serving to make possible all representation of objects. This pure, original, and unchangeable consciousness I call 'transcendental apperception'. It is clear that it deserves the name since even the most pure and objective unity, the unity of *a priori* concepts (space and time), is possible only by virtue of intuitions being related to transcendental apperception. Thus the numerical unity of apperception provides the *a priori* basis for all concepts, just as the multiplicity in space and time provides the *a priori* basis for the intuitions of sensibility.

It is precisely the transcendental unity of apperception that produces, out of all the appearances capable of co-existing in a unitary experience, a connection of all representations according to rules. For this unity of consciousness would be impossible if the mind, in coming to know the manifold, could not become conscious of the identity of the function by means of which it synthetically connects the manifold into knowledge. Thus the original and necessary consciousness of the identity of oneself is at the same time a consciousness of an equally necessary unity in the synthesis of all appearances according to concepts, i.e. rules. The concepts not only serve to make appearances reproducible, they also, by doing so, serve to determine an object for their intuition, i.e. to determine the concept of something in which the appearances are necessarily connected. For the mind could not possibly *a priori* think to itself the identity of oneself in the multiplicity of its representations if it did not fix its attention on the identity of its act, an act that subjects all synthesis of apprehension (which is empirical) to a transcendental unity and only by doing so makes possible the interconnectedness of representations according to *a priori* rules.

We are now in a position to determine more adequately our concept of an object in general. All representations have, by virtue of being representations, their object, and the representations may in turn themselves be the object of other representations. Appearances are the only objects that can be directly given to us, and that which relates directly to an object here I call intuition. But appearances are not things in themselves, they are themselves only representations which in turn have their object, an object, therefore, which can no longer be intuited and that we may, therefore, call the non-empirical, i.e. the transcendental object X.

The pure concept of this transcendental object (which is really always one and the same (=X) in all knowledge) is precisely what is capable of providing all our empirical concepts with a relation to an object, i.e. with objective reality. Now this concept cannot contain any determinate intuition at all, hence it contains only such unity as is necessarily present in a manifold for knowledge in so far as the manifold relates to an object. But this relation is nothing but the unity of consciousness, hence also the necessary unity of the manifold by means of a common function of the mind which serves to connect the manifold into one representation. Since this unity must be considered *a priori* necessary (otherwise knowledge would be without an object), the relation of our empirical knowledge to a transcendental object, i.e. its objective reality, will rely on the transcendental law which says that all appearances, if objects are to be given to us by their means, must be subject to *a priori* rules for the synthetic unity of appearances, such rules being the only possible way of relating the appearances to one another in empirical intuition. That is to say, appearances must be subject in experience to the conditions of the necessary unity of apperception and they must equally be subject in intuition alone to the formal conditions of space and time. It is indeed only through these former conditions that all knowledge is made possible.

4. PRELIMINARY EXPLANATION OF THE POSSIBILITY OF THE CATEGORIES, AS *A PRIORI* KNOWLEDGE

Just as there exists only a single space and time in which all forms of appearance and all relation of existence and non-existence have their place, so equally there exists only a single [unitary] experience in which all perceptions are represented as part of a pervasive and orderly interconnected whole. In talking of different experiences, these make up a number of appearances by virtue of appearances belonging to the one and the same general experience. For it is precisely the form of experience that creates the pervasive and synthetic unity of perceptions, and this form of experience is nothing but the synthetic unity of appearances according to concepts.

Unity of synthesis, if it were merely according to empirical concepts, would be utterly contingent and, if the empirical concepts did not have a transcendental basis for unity, it would be possible that our soul would be filled with a chaos of appearances but without experience ever being capable of arising out of it. But then knowledge would equally lack every connection to objects, hence it would be mere thoughtless intuition, not knowledge. It would, in that case, be as good as nothing to us.

The *a priori* conditions of possible experience in general are at the same time conditions for the possibility of the objects of experience. Now, I am claiming that the categories stated earlier are nothing but the conditions for thought in possible experience, just as space and time contain the conditions of intuition in possible experience. It follows that the categories too are concepts that are fundamental for thinking of objects as corresponding to appearances, hence the categories *a priori* possess objective validity. This was precisely what we wanted to establish.

The possibility, indeed even the necessity, of these categories is based on the relation in which all sensibility, hence also all possible appearances, stand to original apperception. Here everything must conform to the conditions for the pervasive unity of self-consciousness, i.e. it must be subject to general functions of synthesis, namely the synthesis according to concepts, this being the only way in which apperception can obtain *a priori* its pervasive and necessary identity. Thus, for example, the concept of a cause is nothing but a synthesis (of that which follows in the time-series with other appearances) according to concepts, and without this kind of unity, whose rule is *a priori* and which makes appearances subject to it, there would be no pervasive, general and necessary unity of consciousness amidst the manifold of perceptions. In that case, however, the perceptions would not belong to experience either, hence they would lack any object and would be nothing but a blind play of representations. They would be less than a dream.

It follows that every attempt to derive the pure concepts of the understanding from experience and to attribute to them a merely empirical origin is utterly vain and useless. I need not, for example, point out that the concept of a cause carries with it the feature of necessity, which is not something experience can deliver. Experience instructs us that one appearance customarily follows upon another, but not that it must necessarily follow upon it, nor does it instruct us that an appearance, by virtue of being a condition, entitles us to infer, *a priori* and with complete universality, an effect. Let me ask instead: What is the basis for this law of nature and how is even such association possible? I mean the empirical rule of association which one surely needs to presuppose throughout if one says that every item in the series of events must be subject to rules in such a way that nothing ever occurs without something preceding it and upon which it universally follows. The basis for the possibility of associating the manifold, in so far as the basis lies in the object, is called the affinity of the manifold. I am asking, then: How do you propose to explain the pervasive affinity of appearances, on account of which they are necessarily subject to unchanging laws?

By my principles this is easily explicable. All possible appearances belong, by virtue of being representations, to one possible consciousness. But to self-consciousness belongs numerical identity, and does so by virtue of self-consciousness being a transcendental representation, inseparably and with *a priori* certainty. For nothing can become knowledge except by means of this original apperception. Since this identity must necessarily enter the synthesis of all the manifold of appearances if they are to become empirical knowledge, the appearances are subject to *a priori* conditions and the synthesis of them (the synthesis of apprehension) must throughout conform to these conditions. Now something is called a rule if it is a representation of a general condition according to which a particular manifold can be posited (regardless of how), and it is called a law if the manifold must be posited in this way. It follows that all appearances stand in a pervasive connectedness according to necessary laws, hence they stand in a transcendental affinity, empirical affinity being only a consequence of this.

It does indeed sound strange and absurd that nature should direct itself according to our subjective ground of apperception and that it should even depend on this for its orderliness. If, however, we bear in mind that nature is by itself nothing but the totality of appearances, hence not a thing in itself but merely so many representations of the mind, it is no wonder if we can discover nature only in the radical capacity of all our knowledge, namely in transcendental apperception, that is to say in the unity on account of which alone it can be called the object of all possible experience, i.e. nature. This is precisely the reason why we can know this unity *a priori*, hence can know it as being necessary, something we would not be able to do if nature were given in itself and independently of the ultimate sources of our thought. In that case I would not know where to derive the synthetic propositions of such a universal unity of nature from. One would have to derive them from the objects of nature themselves, but since this could only be done empirically, it would merely offer a contingent unity, which falls far short of the necessary connection that we have in mind when speaking of nature.

DEDUCTION OF THE PURE CONCEPTS OF THE UNDERSTANDING

SECTION III: THE RELATION OF THE UNDERSTANDING TO OBJECTS IN GENERAL, AND THE POSSIBILITY OF KNOWING THEM *A PRIORI*

What we have expounded separately and singly in the previous section we shall now present in a unified and interconnected manner. The possibility of experience in general as well as of the objects of experience is based on three subjective sources of knowledge: sense, imagination, and apperception. Each can be considered empirically, that is to say in its application to given appearances, but they are all equally elements or foundations *a priori* which serve to make possible the empirical employment itself. Sense represents appearances empirically in perception, imagination represents them in association (and reproduction), apperception represents them in empirical consciousness of the identity obtaining between these reproduced representations and the appearances that delivered them, hence represents them in recognition.

At the *a priori* basis of all perception lies pure intuition (and, with regard to pure intuition as representation, time, the form of inner intuition, serves as basis); at the *a priori* basis of association lies the pure synthesis of imagination; and at the basis of empirical consciousness lies pure apperception, that is to say the pervasive identity of oneself in all possible representations.

If, now, we desire to trace this inherent basis for the connection of representations back to the point at which they must all come together in order thereby to acquire in the first place the unity of knowledge in possible experience, we need to begin by considering pure apperception. Intuitions are nothing to us and do not in any way concern us unless they can be apprehended in consciousness, whether they enter it directly or indirectly, and only in this way is knowledge possible. We are *a priori* conscious of the pervasive identity of ourselves with regard to all representations that can ever become part of our knowledge, this identity serving as a necessary condition for the possibility of all representations. (For in me these represent something only by virtue of belonging, together with everything else, to a single consciousness, hence they must at least be capable of being connected in consciousness.) This principle is valid *a priori* and may be called the transcendental principle of the unity of all the manifold of our representations, hence also of all the manifold in intuition. Now the unity of the manifold in a subject is synthetic. It follows that pure apperception provides a principle for the synthetic unity of the manifold in all possible intuition.[1]

---

[1] This proposition is of great importance and deserves particular attention. All representations stand in a necessary relation to a possible empirical consciousness. Otherwise, if it were utterly impossible to become conscious of them, that would amount to saying that they did not exist at all. But all empirical consciousness stands in a necessary relation to a transcendental consciousness (prior to all specific experience), namely the consciousness of myself, this being the original apperception. It is therefore absolutely necessary that, in my knowledge, all consciousness should belong to one consciousness (of myself). Here, then, we have a synthetic unity of the manifold (consciousness), which is known *a priori* and precisely for this reason provides the basis for synthetic propositions *a priori*, propositions concerning pure thought, just as space and time provide the basis for

But this synthetic unity presupposes, or includes, a synthesis, and if the former is *a priori* necessary, the latter must also be an *a priori* synthesis. Thus the transcendental unity of apperception relates the pure synthesis of imagination, which is an *a priori* condition for the possibility of all connection of the manifold in unitary knowledge. But it is only the productive synthesis of the imagination that can take place *a priori* since the reproductive synthesis is based on empirical conditions. It follows that the principle of the necessary unity of the pure (productive) synthesis of the imagination in the face of apperception is the basis for the possibility of all knowledge and of experience in particular.

Now we say that the synthesis of the manifold in the imagination is transcendental if, regardless of what intuitions are involved, the synthesis is *a priori* directed at nothing other than the connection of the manifold, and the unity of the synthesis is called transcendental if it is represented as being *a priori* necessary in relation to the original unity of apperception. Since the latter lies at the basis of the possibility of all knowledge, the transcendental unity of the synthesis of the imagination is the pure form of all possible knowledge, and hence it is by means of it that all objects of possible experience must be represented *a priori*.

The understanding is the unity of apperception in relation to the synthesis of the imagination, and pure understanding is the very same unity in relation to the transcendental synthesis of the imagination. Thus the understanding possesses pure knowledge *a priori*, knowledge containing the necessary unity of the pure synthesis of the imagination with regard to all possible appearances. This is precisely the categories, that is to say the pure concepts of the understanding. This implies that the empirical capacity for knowledge in human beings necessarily contains an understanding relating to all objects of the senses, albeit only by means of intuition and, with regard to its synthesis, by means of imagination. All appearances, by virtue of being data for a possible experience, are,

propositions concerning the form of mere intuition. The synthetic proposition which says that all the different empirical consciousnesses must be connected into a single self-consciousness is the absolutely primary and synthetic principle of our thought at all. But we should not forget that it is the mere representation *I* that, in relation to all other representations (whose collective unity it makes possible), constitutes transcendental consciousness. This representation may be clear (empirical consciousness) or obscure; this is irrelevant here, indeed it is even irelevant whether it actually occurs. Rather, the possibility of the logical form of all knowledge is necessarily based on the relation to apperception as a capacity.

therefore, subject to the understanding. Since the relation of appearances to possible experience is equally necessary (otherwise appearances would not afford us any knowledge, hence would not concern us at all), it follows that pure understanding is, on account of the categories, a formal and synthetic principle of all experiences and that appearances stand in a necessary relation to the understanding.

Let us now consider the necessary connection which the understanding has with appearances on account of the categories and let us do so by beginning from below, i.e. from what is empirical. The first thing that is given to us is appearance, which, once it is connected with consciousness, is called perception. (Without being related to consciousness, or at least to possible consciousness, appearance could never become an object to us, hence it would be nothing to us, and since appearance does not in itself possess any objective reality and exists only through knowledge, it would be nothing at all.) But since every appearance contains a manifold, which implies that a variety of perceptions are by themselves scatered and isolated in the mind, they require connecting, and they cannot be provided this in sense itself. There is therefore present in us an active capacity for synthesis of the manifold, a capacity which we call imagination and whose direct action on perceptions I call apprehension.[1] For the imagination serves to bring the manifold of intuition onto an image, hence it must, prior to this, gather up impressions into its activity, that is to say it must apprehend them.

But it is also clear that even this apprehension of the manifold would not by itself produce an image or a connection in impressions unless a subjective basis existed for recalling a perception, which the mind has previously left behind in order to move on to the next, back to that second perception, in this way representing entire series of perceptions, i.e. unless there existed a reproductive capacity of imagination, which is indeed only empirical.

But if representations were reproduced any way whatever and just as they chanced to come together, then once again there would not arise any determinate connection among them, hence no knowledge would arise but merely an aggregate without any order. The reproduction of representations must, therefore, proceed

---

[1] No psychologist has so far had the idea that imagination is a necessary ingredient of perception itself. This is partly because this capacity has been confined to reproduction, partly because it was thought that the senses offer us not only impressions but also connect them, in this way creating images of objects. But this undoubtedly requires something more than receptivity for impressions, namely a function for synthesizing them.

according to a rule such that a representation becomes connected with this rather than that other representation in the imagination. This subjective and empirical basis for reproduction according to rules is called the association of representations.

But unless this unity of association also had an objective basis, which made it impossible for appearances to be apprehended by the imagination in any other way than under the condition of a possible synthetic unity of this apprehension, it would be equally accidental that appearances be fit to enter into an interconnected whole of human knowledge. For, whether or not we should then have the capacity to associate perceptions, it would be entirely undetermined and accidental whether they are also in themselves associable. If it turned out that they are not associable, a great deal of perception, even perhaps an entire sensibility, would be possible, in which my mind would contain a considerable empirical consciousness; but the consciousness would be fragmented and would not belong to my single consciousness. This is impossible. It is only because I ascribe all perceptions to one consciousness (to original apperception) that I can say of all perceptions that I am conscious of them. There must, therefore, exist an objective basis, i.e. a basis that we can discover *a priori* and prior to all empirical laws of the imagination which provides the possibility, indeed the necessity, of a law extending through all appearances, a basis that allows us to regard appearances as being throughout such data of the senses as are in themselves associable and subject to general rules for a pervasive connection in their reproduction. This objective basis for all association of appearances I call their affinity. This basis can only be located in the principle of the unity of apperception with regard to all the knowledge that belongs to me. According to this principle, all appearances must enter the mind apprehended in such a way that they accord with the unity of apperception, and this would be impossible without synthetic unity in their connection, a unity which is therefore also objectively necessary.

Thus the objective unity of all (empirical) consciousness in one consciousness (the original apperception) is the necessary condition of all possible perceptions, and the affinity of all appearances (whether near or remote) is a necessary consequence of a synthesis in the imagination which is based on *a priori* rules.

Thus the imagination too is a capacity for synthesis *a priori*, which is why we have called it the productive imagination, and since its sole purpose is the necessary unity in the synthesis of all the manifold of appearance this synthesis may be called the transcendental function of the imagination. So, although it may appear to be strange, it is nevertheless apparent from what we have said so far that the transcendental function of the imagination is the sole means of making possible even the affinity of appearances, hence to make association possible and, finally, in this way to make reproduction according to laws, that is to say experience itself, possible. For without this function no concepts of objects would converge into a unitary experience.

The permanent and abiding *I* (pure apperception) is the correlate of all our representations in so far as it is merely possible for one to become conscious of them, and all consciousness belongs to all-embracing pure apperception just as all sensible intuition belongs, as representation, to pure inner intuition, namely time. This apperception is precisely what needs to be added to pure imagination in order to make its function intellectual. For by itself alone the synthesis of the imagination, although it is exercised *a priori*, is always sensible, since it connects the manifold only as this appears in intuition; as, for example, with the shape of a triangle. But, by virtue of the relation of the manifold to the unity of apperception, concepts are created and they belong to the understanding; though again it is only by means of the imagination that the concepts can be brought in relation to sensible intuition.

We are thus in possession of pure imagination, which is a fundamental capacity of the human soul and which lies *a priori* at the basis of all knowledge. Through it we connect the manifold of intuition on the one hand with the condition of the necessary unity of pure apperception on the other. Both extremes, that is to say sensibility and understanding, must necessarily be tied together by means of this transcendental function of the imagination; otherwise sensibility would supply only appearances but no object of empirical knowledge, hence no experience. Genuine experience, which consists of the apprehension, association (reproduction) and finally recognition of appearances, contains, in the last and highest of the merely empirical elements of experience, certain concepts which make possible the formal unity of experience, consequently all objective validity (truth) of empirical knowledge. This basis for recognizing the manifold, in so far as it concerns merely the form of experience in general, is precisely the categories. Hence they provide the basis for all formal unity in the synthesis of the imagination and equally, by virtue of this unity, for all empirical employment of the imagination (in recognition, reproduction, association, apperception) right down to appearances. For it is only on account of these constituents of knowledge that appearances can belong to our consciousness, hence to ourselves, in the first place.

The order and regularity in appearances, which we call nature, are, then, something that we ourselves supply, nor would we encounter them if we, or the nature of our mind, had not originally supplied them. For this unity of nature must be necessary, i.e. it must be a particular *a priori* unity in the connection of appearances. But how would we be able *a priori* to undertake such a synthetic unity unless the original sources of knowledge in our mind contained a subjective basis for such an *a priori* unity and unless the subjective conditions were not at the same time objectively valid by virtue of being the basis for the possibility of knowing an object in experience in the first place?

We have so far offered various accounts of understanding: as a spontaneity of knowledge (in contrast to the receptivity of sensibility), as a capacity to think, as a capacity to employ concepts or judgments. Properly considered, the accounts amount to the same thing. We are now in a position to characterize the understanding as the capacity for rules. This characteristic is more fruitful and comes closer to grasping its nature. While sensibility provides us with forms of intuition, understanding provides us with rules. It is perpetually busy scrutinizing appearances with a view to discovering some rule or other in them. Rules, in so far as they are objective (hence necessarily dependent on the knowledge of an object) are called laws. It is true that we discover many laws through experience, but they are only particular determinations of even higher laws, the highest of which (all other laws being subject to them) deriving *a priori* from the understanding itself. They are not delivered by experience, rather they provide appearances with their orderliness, precisely in this way making experience possible. Thus the understanding is not merely a capacity to create rules by comparing appearances. Rather the understanding is itself the legislature facing nature, that is to say without understanding there would not be a nature at all, i.e. a synthetic unity of the manifold of appearances according to rules. For appearances cannot, as such, occur outside us, rather they exist only in our sensibility. Nature, by virtue of being the object of knowledge in a unitary experience, together with everything that it may contain, is possible only through the unity of apperception. But the unity of apperception is the transcendental basis for the necessary orderliness of all appear-

ances in a unitary experience. It is precisely this unity of apperception with regard to a manifold of representations (namely in order
to determine the manifold by a single representation) that constitutes a rule, and the capacity for such rules is the understanding.
Thus all appearances, in so far as they are possible experiences,
belong *a priori* in the understanding, and they obtain their formal
possibility from it; just as they, in so far as they are intuitions,
belong to sensibility and are made possible, with regard to their
form, through its means.

However exaggerated and absurd it sounds to say that the
understanding is itself the source of the laws of nature, hence of the
formal unity of nature, such a claim is nevertheless correct and
appropriate to the issue, namely experience. It is true that empirical
laws as such cannot in any way derive from pure understanding,
any more than the immeasurable multiplicity of appearances can be
adequately understood by appeal to the pure form of sensible
intuition. But all empirical laws are only specific determinations of
pure laws of the understanding, subject to which and according to
whose norm they are made possible in the first place and in the
same way too appearances assume a regulated form. Similarly all
appearances, regardless of the difference in their empirical form,
must always conform to the conditions of the pure form of
sensibility.

Pure understanding is thus, via the categories, the law for the
synthetic unity of all appearances, in this way making experience,
as regards its form, possible in the first place. We have now achieved
all that we needed to achieve in the transcendental deduction of the
categories, namely to render intelligible the relation of understanding to sensibility, and hence to all objects of experience, consequently to render intelligible the objective validity of the pure *a
priori* concepts of the understanding, hence to determine the origin
and truth of these concepts.

SUMMARY PRESENTATION OF THE CORRECTNESS OF THE
DEDUCTION OF THE PURE CONCEPTS OF THE UNDERSTANDING,
AND OF ITS BEING THE ONLY POSSIBLE DEDUCTION

If the objects with which our knowledge is concerned had been
things in themselves, we would not have been able to possess any *a
priori* concepts of them. For where would we get them from? If we
got them from the objects (even setting aside the question of how

the objects could become known to us), our concepts would be merely empirical, they would not be *a priori* concepts. Suppose, on the other hand, that we got them from ourselves. But the nature of an object distinct from our representations cannot be determined by something that is merely in us. That is to say, that which is merely in us cannot serve as a basis for settling why there should be something characterized by what is in our thoughts and why these representations should not rather be devoid of all content. By contrast, if all we are ever dealing with is appearances, it is not only possible, it is even necessary, that certain *a priori* concepts should precede all empirical knowledge of objects. For appearances constitute objects that are wholly in us, since a mere modification of our sensibility cannot exist outside us. Now this very idea – the idea that all appearances, hence all the objects that could occupy us, are all in me, i.e. are determinations of my identical self – is itself a way of asserting that a pervasive unity of appearances in one and the same apperception is necessary. But this very unity of possible consciousness constitutes the form of all knowledge of objects, on account of which the manifold is thought of as belonging to a single object. It follows that the way in which the manifold of sensible representation (intuition) belongs to one consciousness precedes, by virtue of being the intellectual form of the representation, all knowledge of the object and itself constitutes formal *a priori* knowledge of all objects in so far as objects are capable of being thought (the categories). The synthesis of representations through pure imagination and the unity of all representations in relation to the original apperception precede all empirical knowledge. Thus pure concepts of the understanding are *a priori* possible, and even necessary, for experience, precisely because our knowledge is concerned with nothing but appearances whose possibility, connection and unity (in the representation of an object) exist merely in us. Hence the pure concepts of the understanding precede all experience and need to make experience possible in the first place as regards its form. We have conducted our deduction of the categories on this basis, the only possible basis at all.

TRANSCENDENTAL ANALYTIC

BOOK II: ANALYTIC OF PRINCIPLES

General logic is constructed upon a plan which coincides exactly with the division of the higher faculties of knowledge. These are, *understanding, judgment, and reason*. This science, accordingly, treats in its analytic of *concepts, judgments, and inferences* in exact correspondence with the functions and order of those mental powers which we include generally under the generic denomination of understanding.

As this merely formal logic makes abstraction of all content of knowledge, whether pure or empirical, and occupies itself with the mere form of thought (discursive knowledge), it must contain in its analytic a canon for reason. For the form of reason has its law, which, without taking into consideration the particular nature of the knowledge about which it is employed, can be discovered *a priori*, by the simple analysis of the action of reason into its momenta.

Transcendental logic, limited as it is to a determinate content, that of pure *a priori* knowledge, to wit, cannot imitate general logic in this division. For it is evident that the *transcendental employment of reason* is not objectively valid, and therefore does not belong to the *logic of truth* (that is, to analytic), but as a *logic of illusion*, occupies a particular department in the scholastic system under the name of transcendental *dialectic*.

Understanding and judgment accordingly possess in transcendental logic a canon of objectively valid, and therefore true exercise, and are comprehended in the analytical department of that logic. But reason, in its endeavours to arrive by *a priori* means at some true statement concerning objects, and to extend knowledge beyond the bounds of possible experience, is altogether dialectic, and its illusory assertions cannot be constructed into a canon such as an analytic ought to contain.

Accordingly, the analytic of principles will be merely a canon for the *faculty of judgment*, for the instruction of this faculty in its application to appearances of the pure concepts of the understanding, which contain the necessary condition for the establishment of *a priori* laws. On this account, although the subject of the following chapters is the especial principles of *understanding*, I shall make use of the term '*doctrine of the faculty of judgment*', in order to define more particularly my present purpose.

INTRODUCTION : THE TRANSCENDENTAL FACULTY OF JUDGMENT IN GENERAL

If understanding in general be defined as the faculty of rules, the faculty of judgment may be termed the faculty of *subsumption* under these rules; that is, of distinguishing whether this or that does or does not stand under a given rule (*casus datae legis*). General logic contains no precepts for the faculty of judgment, nor can it contain any such. For as *it makes abstraction of all content of knowledge,* no duty is left for it, except that of exposing analytically the mere form of knowledge in concepts, judgments, and inferences, and of thereby establishing formal rules for all exercise of the understanding. Now if this logic wished to give some general direction how we should subsume under these rules, that is, how we should distinguish whether this or that did or did not stand under them, this again could not be done otherwise than by means of a rule. But this rule, precisely because it is a rule, requires for itself direction from the faculty of judgment. Thus, it is evident that the understanding is capable of being instructed by rules, but that judgment is a peculiar talent, which does not, and cannot require instruction, but only exercise. This faculty is therefore the specific quality of the so-called mother wit, the want of which no schooling can compenstate. For although instruction may furnish, and, as it were, engraft upon a limited understanding rules borrowed from other minds, yet the power of employing these rules correctly must belong to the apprentice himself; and no rule which we can prescribe to him with this purpose is, in the absence or deficiency of this gift of nature, secure from misuse.[1] A physician therefore, a judge or a statesman, may have in his head many admirable pathological, juridical, or political rules, in a degree that may enable him to be a profound teacher in his particular science, and yet in

---

[1]   Deficiency in judgment is properly that which is called stupidity ; and for such a failing we know no remedy. A dull or narrow-minded person, to whom nothing is wanting but a proper degree of understanding, may be improved by tuition, even so far as to deserve the epithet of *learned*. But as such persons frequently labour under a deficiency in the faculty of judgment, it is not uncommon to find men extremely learned who in the application of their science betray to a lamentable degree this irremediable want.

the application of these rules he may very possibly blunder – either because he is wanting in natural judgment (though not in understanding), and whilst he can comprehend the general *in abstracto*, cannot distinguish whether a particular case *in concreto* ought to rank under the former; or because his faculty of judgment has not been sufficiently exercised by examples and real practice. Indeed, the grand and only use of examples, is to sharpen the judgment. For as regards the correctness and precision of the insight of the understanding, examples are commonly injurious rather than otherwise, because, as *casus in terminis*, they seldom adequately fulfil the conditions of the rule. Besides, they often weaken the power of our understanding to apprehend rules in their universality, independently of particular circumstances of experience; and hence, accustom us to employ them more as formulae than as principles. Examples are thus the vehicle of judgment, which he who is naturally deficient in that faculty, cannot afford to dispense with.

But although general logic cannot give directions to the faculty of judgment, the case is very different as regards transcendental logic, insomuch that it appears to be the especial duty of the latter to secure and direct, by means of determinate rules, the faculty of judgment in the employment of the pure understanding. For, as a doctrine, that is, as an endeavour to enlarge the sphere of the understanding in regard to pure *a priori* knowledge, philosophy is worse than useless, since from all the attempts hitherto made, little or no ground has been gained. But, as a critique, in order to guard against the mistakes of the faculty of judgment (*lapsus judicii*) in the employment of the few pure concepts of the understanding which we possess, although its use is in this case purely negative, philosophy is called upon to apply all its acuteness and penetration.

But transcendental philosophy has this peculiarity, that besides indicating the rule, or rather the general condition for rules, which is given in the pure concept of the understanding, it can, at the same time, indicate *a priori* the case to which the rule must be applied. The cause of the superiority which, in this respect, transcendental philosophy possesses above all other sciences except mathematics, lies in this: it treats of concepts which must relate *a priori* to their objects, whose objective validity consequently cannot be demonstrated *a posteriori*, and is, at the same time, under the obligation of presenting in general but sufficient tests, the conditions under which objects can be given in harmony with those concepts;

otherwise they would be mere logical forms, without content, and not pure concepts of the understanding.

Our transcendental doctrine of the faculty of judgment will contain two chapters. The first will treat of the sensible condition under which alone pure concepts of the understanding can be employed – that is, of the *schematism* of the pure understanding. The second will treat of those synthetical judgments which are derived *a priori* from pure concepts of the understanding under those conditions, and which lie *a priori* at the foundation of all other knowledge, that is to say, it will treat of the principles of the pure understanding.

TRANSCENDENTAL DOCTRINE OF JUDGMENT
OR ANALYTIC OF PRINCIPLES

CHAPTER I : THE SCHEMATISM OF THE PURE CONCEPTS OF THE UNDERSTANDING

In all subsumptions of an object under a concept, the representation of the object must be homogeneous with the concept; in other words, the concept must contain that which is represented in the object to be subsumed under it. For this is the meaning of the expression: An object is contained under a concept. Thus the empirical concept of a *plate* is homogeneous with the pure geometrical concept of a *circle*, inasmuch as the roundness which is thought in the former is intuited in the latter.

But pure concepts of the understanding, when compared with empirical intuitions, or even with sensible intuitions in general, are quite heterogeneous, and never can be discovered in any intuition. How then is the *subsumption* of the latter under the former, and consequently the application of the categories to appearances, possible ? (For it is impossible to say, for example : causality can be intuited through the senses, and is contained in appearance.) This natural and important question forms the real cause of the necessity of a transcendental doctrine of the faculty of judgment, with the purpose, to wit, of showing how pure concepts of the understanding can be applied to appearances. In all other sciences, where the concepts by which the object is thought in general are not so different and heterogeneous from those which represent the object as it is given, *in concreto*, it is quite unnecessary to institute any special inquiries concerning the application of the former to the latter.

Now it is quite clear that there must be some third thing, which on the one hand is homogeneous with the category, and with the appearance on the other, and so makes the application of the former to the latter possible. This mediating representation must be pure (without any empirical content), and yet must on the one hand be *intellectual*, on the other sensible. Such a representation is the *transcendental schema*.

The concept of the understanding contains pure synthetical unity of the manifold in general. Time, as the formal condition of the manifold of the internal sense, consequently of the connection of all representations, contains *a priori* a manifold in pure intuition. Now a transcendental determination of time is so far homogeneous with the *category*, which constitutes its unity as it is universal, and rests upon a rule *a priori*. On the other hand, it is so far homogeneous with *appearance*, inasmuch as time is contained in every empirical representation of the manifold. Thus an application of the category to appearances becomes possible, by means of the transcendental determination of time, which, as the schema of the concepts of the understanding, mediates the subsumption of appearances under categories.

After what has been proved in our deduction of the categories, no one, it is to be hoped, can hesitate as to the proper decision of the question, whether the employment of these pure concepts of the understanding ought to be merely empirical or also transcendental; in other words, whether the categories, as conditions of a possible experience, relate *a priori* solely to appearances, or whether, as conditions of the possibility of things in general, their application can be extended to objects as things in themselves. For we have there seen that concepts are quite impossible, and utterly without signification, unless either to them, or at least to the elements of which they consist, an object be given; and that, consequently, they cannot possibly apply to objects as things in themselves without regard to the question whether and how these are given to us; and further, that the only manner in which objects can be given to us, is by means of the modification of our sensibility; and finally, that pure *a priori* concepts, in addition to the function of the understanding in the category, must contain *a priori* formal conditions of sensibility (of the internal sense, namely), which again contain the general condition under which alone the category can be applied to any object. This formal and pure condition of sensibility, to which the concept of the understanding is restricted in its employment, we shall name the *schema* of the concept of the understanding, and the procedure of the understanding with these schemata we shall call the *schematism* of the pure understanding.

The schema is, in itself, always a mere product of the imagination. But as the synthesis of imagination has for its aim no single intuition, but merely unity in the determination of sensibility, the schema is clearly distinguishable from the image. Thus, if I place five points one after another . . . . . this is an image of the number five. One the other hand, if I only think a number in general, which may be either five or a hundred, this thought is rather the representation of a method of representing in an image a sum (e.g. a thousand) in conformity with a concept, than the image itself, an image which I should find difficult to survey and compare with the concept. Now this representation of a general procedure of the imagination to present its image to a concept, I call the schema of this concept.

In truth, it is not images of objects, but schemata, which lie at the foundation of our pure sensible concepts. No image could ever be adequate to our concept of a triangle in general. For the generality of the concept it could never attain to, as this includes under itself all triangles, whether right-angled, acute-angled, etc., whilst the image would always be limited to a single part of this sphere. The schema of the triangle can exist nowhere else than in thought, and it indicates a rule of the synthesis of the imagination in regard to pure figures in space. Still less is an object of experience, or an image of the object, ever adequate to the empirical concept. On the contrary, the concept always relates immediately to the schema of the imagination, as a rule for the determination of our intuition, in conformity with a certain general concept. The concept of a dog indicates a rule, according to which my imagination can delineate the figure of a four-footed animal in general, without being limited to any particular individual form which experience presents to me, or indeed to any possible image that I can represent to myself *in concreto*. This schematism of our understanding in regard to appearances and their mere form, is an art, hidden in the depths of the human soul, whose true modes of action we shall only with difficulty discover and unveil. Thus much only can we say: The *image* is a product of the empirical faculty of the productive imagination – while the *schema* of sensible concepts (of figures in space, for example) is a product, and, as it were, a monogram of the pure imagination *a priori*, whereby and according to which images first become possible, which, however, can be connected with the concept only mediately by means of the schema which they indicate, and are in themselves never fully adequate to it. On the other hand, the schema of a pure concept of the understanding is something that cannot be reduced into any image – it is nothing else than the pure synthesis expressed by the category, conformably to a rule of unity according to concepts. It is a transcendental product of the imagination, a product which concerns the determination of the internal sense, according to conditions of its form (time) in respect to all representations, in so far as these representation must be connected *a priori* in one concept, conformably to the unity of apperception.

Without entering upon a dry and tedious analysis of the essential requisites of transcendental schemata of the pure concepts of the understanding, we shall rather proceed at once to give an explanation of them according to the order of the categories, and in connection therewith.

For the external sense the pure image of all quantities (*quantorum*) is space; the pure image of all objects of sense in general, is time. But the pure *schema* of *quantity* (*quantitatis*) as a concept of the understanding, is *number*, a representation which comprehends the successive addition of one to one (homogeneous quantities). Thus, number is nothing else than the unity of the synthesis of the manifold in a homogeneous intuition, by means of my generating time itself in my apprehension of intuition.

Reality, in the pure concept of the understanding, is that which corresponds to a sensation in general; that, consequently, the concept of which indicates a being (in time). Negation is that the concept of which represents a not-being (in time). The opposition of these two consists therefore in the difference of one and the same time, as a time filled or a time empty. Now as time is only the form of intuition, consequently of objects as appearances, that which in objects corresponds to sensation is the transcendental matter of all objects as things in themselves (thinghood, reality). Now every sensation has a degree of quantity by which it can fill time, that is to say, the internal sense in respect of the representation of an object, more or less, until it vanishes into nothing (=0=*negatio*). Thus there is a relation and connection between reality and negation, or rather a transition from the former to the latter, which makes every reality representable to us as a quantum; and the schema of a reality as the quantity of something in so far as it fills time, is exactly this continuous and uniform generation of the reality in time, as we descend in time from the sensation which has a certain degree, down to the vanishing thereof, or gradually ascend from negation to the quantity thereof.

The schema of substance is the permanence of the real in time; that is, the representation of it as a substratum of the empirical determination of time; a substratum which therefore remains, whilst all else changes. (Time passes not, but in it passes the existence of the changeable. To time, therefore, which is itself unchangeable and permanent, corresponds that which in the appearance is unchangeable in existence, that is, substance, and it is only by it that the succession and co-existence of appearances can be determined in regard to time.)

The schema of cause and of the causality of a thing is the real which, when posited, is always followed by something else. It consists, therefore, in the succession of the manifold, in so far as that succession is subject to a rule.

The schema of community (reciprocity), or the reciprocal causality of substances in respect of their accidents, is the co-existence of the determinations of the one with those of the other, according to a general rule.

The schema of possibility is the agreement of the synthesis of different representations with the conditions of time in general (as, for example, opposites cannot exist together at the same time in the same thing, but only after each other), and is therefore the determination of the representation of a thing at *any* time.

The schema of reality is existence at some determinate time.

The schema of necessity is the existence of an object at all time.

It is clear, from all this, that the schema of the category of quantity contains and represents the generation (synthesis) of time itself, in the successive apprehension of an object; the schema of quality the synthesis of sensation with the representation of time, or the filling up of time; the schema of relation the relation of perceptions to each other in all time (that is, according to a rule of the determination of time): and finally, the schema of modality and its categories, time itself, as the correlative of the determination of an object – whether it does belong to time, and how. The schemata, therefore, are nothing but *a priori determinations of time* according to rules, and these, in regard to all possible objects, following the arrangement of the categories, relate to *the series in time, the content in time, the order in time,* and finally, *to the totality in time in respect to all possible objects.*

Hence it is apparent that the schematism of the understanding, by means of the transcendental synthesis of the imagination, amounts to nothing else than the unity of the manifold of intuition in the internal sense, and thus indirectly to the unity of apperception, as a function corresponding to the internal sense (a receptivity). Thus, the schemata of the pure concepts of the understanding are the true and only conditions whereby our understanding receives an application to objects, and consequently receives *significance.* Finally, therefore, the categories are only capable of empirical use, inasmuch as they serve merely to subject appearances to the universal rules of synthesis, by means of an *a priori* necessary unity (on account of the necessary union of all consciousness in one original apperception); and so to render them susceptible of a complete connection in one experience. But within this whole of possible experience lie all our knowledge, and in the universal relation to this experience consists transcendental truth, which antecedes all empirical truth, and renders the latter possible.

It is, however, evident at first sight, that although the schemata of sensibility are the sole agents in realizing the categories, they do, nevertheless, also restrict them, that is, they limit the categories by conditions which lie beyond the sphere of understanding – namely, in sensibility. Hence the schema is properly only the phenomenon, or the sensible concept of an object in harmony with the category. (NUMERUS *est quantitas phaenomenon* – SENSATIO *realitas phaenomenon*; CONSTANS *et perdurabile rerum substantia phaenomenon* – AETERNITAS, NECESSITAS, *phaenomena, etc.*) Now, if we remove a restrictive condition, we thereby amplify, it appears, the formerly limited concept. In this way, the categories in their pure signification, free from all conditions of sensibility, ought to be valid of things *as they are,* and not, as the schemata represent them, merely as they appear, and consequently the categories must have a significance far more extended, and wholly independent of all schemata. In truth, there does always remain to the pure concepts of the understanding, after abstracting every sensible condition, a value and significance, which is, however, merely logical. But in this case, no object is given them, and therefore they have no meaning sufficient to afford us a concept of an object. The notion of substance, for example, if we leave out the sensible determination of permanence, would mean nothing more than a something which can be thought as subject, without the possibility of becoming a predicate to anything else. Of this representation I can make nothing, inasmuch as it does not indicate to me what determinations the thing possesses which must thus be valid as *primary* subject. Consequently, the categories, without schemata, are merely functions of the understanding for concepts, but do not represent any object. This significance they derive from sensibility, which at the same time realizes the understanding and restricts it.

CHAPTER II : SYSTEM OF ALL PRINCIPLES OF THE PURE UNDERSTANDING

In the foregoing chapter we have merely considered the general conditions under which alone the transcendental faculty of judgment is justified in using the pure concepts of the understanding for synthetical judgments. Our duty at present is to exhibit in systematic connection those judgments which the understanding really produces *a priori*. For this purpose, our table of the categories will certainly afford us the natural and safe guidance. For it is precisely the categories whose application to possible experience must constitute all pure *a priori* knowledge of the understanding; and the relation of which to sensibility will, on that very account, present us with a complete and systematic catalogue of all the transcendental principles of the use of the understanding.

Principles *a priori* are so called, not merely because they contain in themselves the grounds of other judgments, but also because they themselves are are not grounded in higher and more general knowledge. This peculiarity, however, does not raise them altogether above the need of a proof. For although there could be found no higher knowledge, and therefore no objective proof, and although such a principle rather serves as the foundation for all knowledge of the object, this by no means hinders us from drawing a proof from the subjective sources of the possibility of the knowledge of an object. Such a proof is necessary, moreoever, because without it the principle might be liable to the suspicion of being a mere gratuitous assertion.

In the second place, we shall limit our investigations to those principles which relate to the categories. For as to the principles of the Transcendental Aesthetic, according to which space and time are the conditions of the possibility of things as appearances, as also the restriction of these principles, namely, that they cannot be applied to objects as things in themselves – these, of course, do not fall within the scope of our present inquiry. In like manner, the principles of mathematical science form no part of this system, because they are all drawn from intuition, and not from the pure concept of the understanding. The possibility of these principles, however, will necessarily be considered here, inasmuch as they are synthetical judgments *a priori*, not indeed for the purpose of proving their accuracy and apodeictic certainty, which is unnecessary, but merely to render conceivable and deduce the possibility of such evident *a priori* knowledge.

But we shall have also to speak of the principle of analytical judgments, in opposition to synthetical judgments, which is the proper subject of our inquiries, because this very opposition will free the theory of the latter from all ambiguity, and place it clearly before our eyes in its true nature.

SYSTEM OF THE PRINCIPLES OF THE PURE UNDERSTANDING

Section I: The Supreme Principle of all Analytical Judgments

Whatever may be the content of our knowledge, and in whatever manner our knowledge may be related to its object, the universal, although only negative condition of all our judgments is that they do not contradict themselves; otherwise these judgments are in themselves (even without respect to the object) nothing. But although there may exist no contradiction in our judgment, it may nevertheless connect concepts in such a manner, that they do not correspond to the object, or without any grounds either *a priori* or *a posteriori* for justifying such a judgement, and thus, without being self-contradictory, a judgement may nevertheless be either false or groundless.

Now, the proposition: 'Nothing can have a predicate that contradicts it', is called the principle of contradiction, and is a universal but purely negative criterion of all truth. But it belongs to logic alone, because it is valid of knowledge, merely as knowledge, and without respect to their content, and declares that the contradiction entirely destroys and nullifies them. We can also, however, make a positive use of this principle, that is, not merely to banish falsehood and error (in so far as it rests upon contradiction), but also for the knowledge of truth. For *if the judgment is analytical*, be it affirmative or negative, its truth must always be recongnizable by means of the principle of contradiction. For the contrary of that which lies and is thought as concept in the knowledge of the object will be always properly negated, but the concept itself must always be affirmed of the object, inasmuch as the contrary thereof would contradict the object.

We must therefore hold the *principle of contradiction* to be the universal and fully sufficient *principle of all analytical knowledge*. But as a sufficient criterion of truth, it has no further utility or authority. For the fact that no knowledge can be at variance with this principle without nullifying itself, makes this principle the *sine qua non*, but not the determining ground of the truth of our knowledge. As our business at present is properly with the synthetical part of our knowledge only, we shall always be on our guard not to transgress this inviolable principle; but at the same time not to expect from it any direct assistance in the establishment of the truth of any synthetical proposition.

There exists, however, a formula of this celebrated principle – a principle merely formal and entirely without content – which contains a synthesis that has been inadvertently and quite unnecessarily mixed up with it. It is this: 'It is impossible for a thing to be and not to be at the same time.' Not to mention the superfluousness of the addition of the word *impossible* to indicate the apodeictic certainty, which ought to be self-evident from the proposition itself, the proposition is affected by the condition of time, and as it were says: 'A thing=A, which is something=B, cannot at the same time be *non-B*.' But both, B as well as *non-B*, may quite well exist in succession. For example, a man who is young cannot at the same time be old; but the same man can very well be at one time young, and at another not young, that is, old. Now the principle of contradiction as a merely logical proposition must not by any means limit its application merely to relations of time, and consequently a formula like the preceding is quite foreign to its true purpose. The misunderstanding arises in this way. We first of all separate a predicate of a thing from the concept of the thing, and afterwards connect with this predicate its opposite, and hence do not establish any contradiction with the subject, but only with its predicate, which has been conjoined with the subject synthetically – a contradiction, moreover, which obtains only when the first and second predicate are affirmed in the same time. If I say: 'A man who is ignorant is not learned', the condition 'at the same time' must be added, for he who is at one time ignorant, may at another be learned. But if I say: 'No ignorant man is a learned man', the proposition is analytical, because the characteristic *ignorance* is now a constituent part of the concept of the subject; and in this case the negative proposition is evident immediately from the proposition of contradiction, without the necessity of adding the condition 'at the same time'. This is the reason why I have altered the formula of this principle – an alteration which shows very clearly the nature of an analytical proposition.

SYSTEM OF THE PRINCIPLES OF THE PURE UNDERSTANDING

Section II: The Supreme Principle of all Synthetical Judgments

The explanation of the possibility of synthetical judgments is a task with which general logic has nothing to do; indeed it needs not even be acquainted with its name. But in transcendental logic it is the most important matter to be dealt with – indeed the only one, if the question is of the possibility of synthetical judgments *a priori*, the conditions and extent of their validity. For when this question is fully decided, it can reach its aim with perfect ease, the determination, to wit, of the extent and limits of the pure understanding.

In an analytical judgment I do not go beyond the given concept, in order to arrive at some decision respecting it. If the judgment is affirmative, I predicate of the concept only that which was already thought in it; if negative, I merely exclude from the concept its opposite. But in synthetical judgments, I must go beyond the given concept, in order to think, in relation with it, something quite different from that which was thought in it, a relation which is consequently never one either of identity or contradiction, and by means of which the truth or error of the judgment cannot be discerned merely from the judgment itself.

Granted, then, that we must go out beyond a given concept in order to compare it synthetically with another, a third thing is necessary, in which alone the synthesis of two concepts can originate. Now what is this *tertium quid*, that is to be the medium of all synthetical judgments? It is only a totality, in which all our representations are contained, the internal sense to wit, and its form *a priori*, time.

The synthesis of our representations rests upon the imagination; their synthetical unity (which is requisite judgment), upon the unity of apperception. In this, therefore, is to be sought the possibility of synthetical judgments, and as all three contain the sources of *a priori* representations

If knowledge is to have objective reality, that is, to relate to an object, and possess sense and meaning in respect to it, it is necessary that the object be given in some way or another. Without this, our concepts are empty, and we may indeed have thought by means of them, but by such thinking we have not, in fact, known anything, we have merely played with representation. To give an object, if this expression be understood in the sense of to present the object, not mediately but immediately in intuition, means nothing else than to apply the representation of it to experience, be that experience real or only possible. Space and time themselves, pure as these concepts are from all that is empirical, and certain as it is that they are represented fully *a priori* in the mind, would be completely without objective validity, and without sense and significance, if their necessary use in the objects of experience were not shown. Nay, the representation of them is a mere schema, that always relates to the reproductive imagination, which recalls the objects of experience without which they have no meaning. And so is it with all concepts without distinction.

The *possibility of experience* is, then, that which gives objective reality to all our *a priori* knowledge. Now experience depends upon the synthetical unity of appearances, that is, upon a synthesis according to concepts of the object of appearances in general, a synthesis without which experience never could become knowledge, but would be merely a rhapsody of perceptions, never fitting together into any context, according to rules of a thoroughly united (possible) consciousness, and therefore never subject to the transcendental and necessary unity of apperception. Experience has therefore for a foundation, *a priori* principles of its form, that is to say, general rules of unity in the synthesis of appearances, the objective reality of which rules, as necessary conditions – even of the possibility of experience – can always be shown in experience. But apart from this relation, *a priori* synthetical propositions are absolutely impossible, because they have no third term, that is, no pure object, in which the synthetical unity can exhibit the objective reality of its concepts.

Although, then, respecting space, or the forms which productive imagination describes therein, we do know much *a priori* in synthetical judgments, and are really in no need of experience for this purpose, such knowledge would nevertheless amount to nothing but an occupation with a mere chimera, were not space to be considered as the condition of the appearances which constitute the material of external experience. Hence those pure synthetical judgments do relate, though but mediately, to possible experience, or rather to the possibility of experience, and upon that alone is founded the objective validity of their synthesis.

While then, on the one hand, experience, as empirical synthesis, is the only possible mode of knowledge which gives reality to all other synthesis, on the other hand, this latter synthesis, as knowledge *a priori*, possesses truth, that is, agreement with its object, only in so far as it contains nothing more than what is necessary to the synthetical unity of experience.

Accordingly, the supreme principle of all synthetical judgments is: Every object is subject to the necessary conditions of the synthetical unity of the manifold of intuition in a possible experience.

A priori synthetical judgments are possible, when we apply the formal conditions of the *a priori* intuition, the synthesis of the imagination, and the necessary unity of that synthesis in a transcendental apperception, to possible knowledge of experience in general, and say: The conditions of the *possibility of experience* in general are at the same time conditions of the *possibility* of the objects of *experience*, and have, for that reason, objective validity in an *a priori* synthetical judgment.

SYSTEM OF THE PRINCIPLES OF THE PURE UNDERSTANDING

Section III: Systematic Representation of all Synthetical Principles of the Pure Understanding

That principles exist at all is to be ascribed solely to the pure understanding, which is not only the faculty of rules in regard to that which happens, but is even the source of principles according to which everything that can be presented to us as an object is necessarily subject to rules, because without such rules we never could attain knowledge of an object. Even the laws of nature, if they are contemplated as principles of the empirical use of the understanding, possess also a characteristic of necessity, and we may therefore at least expect them to be determined upon grounds which are valid *a priori* and antecedent to all experience. But all laws of nature without distinction, are subject to higher principles of the understanding, inasmuch as the former are merely applications of the latter to particular cases of experience. These higher principles alone therefore give the concept, which contains the necessary condition and, as it were, the exponent of a rule; experience, on the other hand, gives the case which comes under the rule.

There is no danger of our mistaking merely empirical principles for principles of the pure understanding, or conversely; for the character of necessity, according to concepts which distinguish the latter, and the absence of this in every empirical proposition, how extensively valid soever it may be, is a perfect safeguard against confounding them. There are, however, pure principles *a priori*, which nevertheless I should not ascribe to the pure understanding – for this reason, that they are not derived from pure concepts, but (although by the mediation of the understanding) from pure intuitions. But understanding is the faculty of concepts. Such principles mathematical science possesses, but their application to experience, consequently their objective validity, nay the possibility of such *a priori* synthetical knowledge (the deduction thereof) rests entirely upon the pure understanding.

On this account, I shall not reckon among my principles those of mathematics; though I shall include those upon the possibility and objective validity *a priori*, of principles of the mathematical science, which, consequently, are to be looked upon as the principle of these, and which proceed from concepts to intuition, and not from intuition to concepts.

In the application of the pure concepts of the understanding to possible experience, the employment of their synthesis is either *mathematical* or *dynamical*, for it is directed partly on the *intuition* alone, partly on the *existence* of appearance. But the *a priori* conditions of intuition are in relation to a possible experience absolutely necessary, those of the existence of objects of a possible empirical intuition are in themselves contingent. Hence the principles of the mathematical use of the categories will possess a character of absolute necessity, that is, will be apodeictic; those, on the other hand, of the dynamical use, the character of an *a priori* necessity indeed, but only under the condition of empiricial thought in an experience, therefore only mediately and indirectly. Consequently they will not possess that immediate certainty which is peculiar to the former, although their application to experience does not, for that reason, lose its certainty. But of this point we shall be better able to judge at the conclusion of this system of principles.

The table of the categories is naturally our guide to the table of principles, because these are nothing else than rules for the objective employment of the former. Accordingly, all principles of the pure understanding are:

1

AXIOMS of
Intuiton

2   3

ANTICIPATIONS   ANALOGIES
of Perception   of Experience

4

POSTULATES of
Empirical Thought
in general

These appellations I have chosen advisedly, in order that we might not lose sight of the distinctions in respect of the evidence and the employment of these principles. It will, however, soon appear that – a fact which concerns both the evidence of these principles, and the *a priori* determination of appearances – according to the categories of *Quantity* and *Quality* (if we attend merely to the form of these), the principles of these categories are distinguishable from those of the two others, inasmuch as the former are possessed of an intuitive, but the latter of a merely discursive, though in both instances a complete certitude. I shall therefore call the former *mathematical*, and the latter *dynamical* principles.[1] It

---

[1] All *combination* (*conjunctio*) is either *composition* (*compositio*) or *connection* (*nexus*). The former is the synthesis of a manifold, the parts of which do not necessarily belong to each other. For example, the two triangles into which a square is divided by a diagonal, do not necessarily belong to each other, and of this kind is the synthesis of the *homogeneous* in everything that can be *mathematically* considered. This synthesis can be divided into those of *aggregation* and *coalition*, the former of which is applied to *extensive*, the latter to *intensive* qualities. The second sort of combination (*nexus*) is the synthesis of a manifold,

must be observed, however, that by these terms I mean, just as little in the one case the principles of mathematics, as those of general (physical) dynamics in the other. I have here in view merely the principles of the pure understanding, in their application to the internal sense (without distinction of the representations given therein), by means of which the sciences of mathematics and dynamics become possible. Accordingly, I have named these principles rather with reference to their application, than their content; and I shall now proceed to consider them in the order in which they stand in the table.

I
AXIOMS OF INTUITION

The principle of these is: *All Intuitions are Extensive Quantities.*

PROOF

All appearances contain, as regards their form, an intuition in space and time, which lies *a priori* at the foundation of all without exception. Appearances, therefore, cannot be apprehended, that is, received into empirical consciousness otherwise than through the synthesis of a manifold, through which the representations of a determinate space or time are generated; that is to say, through the connection of the homogeneous, and the consciousness of the synthetical unity of this manifold (homogeneous). Now the consciousness of a homogeneous manifold in intuition, in so far as thereby the representation of an object is rendered possible, is the concept of a quantity (*quanti*). Consequently, even the perception of an object as appearance is possible only through the same synthetical unity of the manifold of the given sensible intuition, through which the unity of the connection of the homogeneous manifold in the concept of a *quantity* is thought; that is to say, all appearances are quantities, and *extensive* quantities, because as intuitions in space or time they must be represented by means of the same synthesis, through which space and time themselves are determined.

---

in so far as its parts do belong necessarily to each other; for example, the accident to a substance, or the effect to the cause. Consequently it is a synthesis of that which though *heterogeneous*, is represented as connected *a priori*. This combination – not an arbitrary one – I entitle *dynamical*, because it concerns the connection of the *existence* of the manifold. This, again, may be divided into the *physical* synthesis of the appearances among each other, and the *metaphysical* synthesis, or the connection of appearances *a priori* in the faculty of knowledge.

An extensive quantity I call that wherein the representation of the parts renders possible (and therefore necessarily antecedes) the representation of the whole. I cannot represent to myself any line, however small, without drawing it in thought, that is without generating from a point all its parts one after another, and in this way alone producing this intuition. Precisely the same is the case with every, even the smallest portion of time. I think therein only the successive progress from one moment to another, and hence, by means of the different portions of time and the addition of them, a determinate quantity of time is produced. As the pure intuition in all appearances is either time or space, so is every appearance in its character of intuition an extensive quantity, inasmuch as it can only be known in our apprehension by successive synthesis (from part to part). All appearances are, accordingly, to be considered as aggregates, that is, as a collection of previously given parts; which is not the case with every sort of quantities, but only with those which are represented and apprehended by us as extensive.

On this successive synthesis of the productive imagination, in the generation of figures, is founded the mathematics of extension, or geometry, with its axioms, which express the conditions of sensible intuition *a priori*, under which alone the schema of a pure concept of external intuition can exist; for example, 'between two points only one straight line is possible', 'two straight lines cannot enclose a space', etc. These are the axioms which properly relate only to quantities (*quanta*) as such.

But, as regards the quantity of a thing (*quantitas*), that is to say, the answer to the question: How large is this or that object? although, in respect to this question, we have various propositions synthetical and immediately certain (*indemonstrabilia*); we have, in the proper sense of the term, no axioms. For example, the propositions: 'If equals be added to equals, the sums are equals;' 'If equals be taken from equals, the remainders are equals;' are analytical, because I am immediately conscious of the identity of the production of the one quantity with the production of the other; whereas axioms must be *a priori* synthetical propositions. On the other hand, the self-evident propositions as to the relation of numbers, are certainly synthetical but not universal, like those of geometry, and for this reason cannot be called axioms, but numerical formulae. Thus $7+5=12$ is not an analytical proposition. For neither in the representation of seven, nor of five, nor of the connection of the two numbers, do I think the number twelve.

(Whether I think the number in the *addition* of both, is not at present the question; for in the case of an analytical proposition, the only point is, whether I really think the predicate in the representation of the subject.) But although the proposition is synthetical, it is nevertheless only a singular proposition. In so far as regard is here had merely to the synthesis of the homogeneous (the units), it cannot take place except in one manner, although our *use* of these numbers is afterwards general. If I say: 'A triangle can be constructed with three lines, any two of which taken together are greater than the third', I exercise merely the pure function of the productive imagination, which may draw the lines longer or shorter, and construct the angles at its pleasure. On the contrary, the number seven is possible only in one manner, and so is likewise the number twelve, which results from the synthesis of seven and five. Such propositions, then, cannot be termed axioms (for in that case we should have an infinity of these), but numerical formulae.

This transcendental principle of the mathematics of appearances greatly enlarges our *a priori* knowledge. For it is by this principle alone that pure mathematics is rendered applicable in all its precision to objects of experience, and without it the validity of this application would not be so self-evident; on the contrary, contradictions and confusions have often arisen on this very point. Appearances are not things in themselves. Empirical intuition is possible only through pure intuiton (of space and time); consequently, what geometry affirms of the latter, is indisputably valid of the former. All evasions, such as the statement that objects of sense do not conform to the rules of construction in space (for example, to the rule of the infinite divisibility of lines or angles) must fall to the ground. For, if these objections hold good, we deny to space, and with it to all mathematics, objective validity, and no longer know wherefore, and how far, mathematics can be applied to appearances. The synthesis of spaces and times as the essential form of all intuition, is that which renders possible the apprehension of appearance, and therefore every external experience, consequently all knowledge of the objects of experience; and whatever mathematics in its pure use proves of the former, must necessarily hold good of the latter. All objections are but the chicaneries of an ill-instructed reason, which erroneously thinks to liberate the objects of sense from the formal conditions of our sensibility, and represents these, although mere appearances, as things in themselves, presented as such to our understanding. But in this case, no *a priori* synthetical knowledge of them could be possible, consequently not through pure concepts of space, and the science which determines these concepts, that is to say, geometry, would itself be impossible.

2

ANTICIPATIONS OF PERCEPTION

The principle of these is: *In all Appearances the Real, that which is an Object of Sensation, has Intensive Quantity, that is, has a Degree.*

PROOF

Perception is empirical consciousness, that is to say, a consciousness which contains sensation. Appearances as objects of perception are not pure, that is, merely formal intuitions, like space and time, for they cannot be perceived in themselves. They contain, then, over and above the intuition, the materials for an object (through which is represented something existing in space or time), that is to say, they contain the real of sensation, as a representation merely subjective, which gives us merely the consciousness that the subject is affected, and which we refer to some object. Now a gradual transition from empirical consciousness to pure consciousness entirely evanishes, and there remains a merely formal consciousness (*a priori*) of the manifold in time and space; consequently there is possible a synthesis also of the production of the quantity of a sensation from its commencement, that is, from the pure intuition=o onwards, up to a certain quantity of the sensation. Now as sensation in itself is not an objective representation, and in it is to be found neither the intuition of space nor of time, it cannot possess any extensive quantity, and yet there does belong to it a quantity (and that by means of its apprehension, in which empirical consciousness can within a certain time rise from nothing=o up to its given amount), consequently an *intensive quantity*. And thus we must ascribe intensive quantity, that is, a degree of influence on sense to all objects of perception, in so far as this perception contains sensation.

All knowledge, by means of which I am enabled to know and determine *a priori* what belongs to empirical knowledge, may be called an anticipation; and without doubt this is the sense in which Epicurus employed his expression πρόληψις. But as there is in appearances something which is never known *a priori*, which on this account constitutes the proper difference between pure and empirical knowledge, that is to say, sensation (as the matter of perception), it follows that sensation is just that element in knowledge which cannot be at all anticipated. On the other hand, we might very well term the pure determinations in space and time, as well in regard to figure as to Quantity, anticipations of appearances because they represent *a priori* that which may always be give a *posteriori* in experience. But suppose that in every sensation, as sensation in general, without any particular sensation being thought of, there existed something which could be known *a priori*, this would deserve to be called anticipation in a special sense – special, because it may seem surprising to anticipate experience, in that which concerns the matter of experience, and which we can only derive from itself. Yet such really is the case here.

Apprehension, by means of sensation alone, fills only one moment, that is, if I do not take into consideration a succession of many sensations. As that in the appearance, the apprehension of which is not a successive synthesis advancing from parts to an entire representation, sensation has therefore no extensive quantity; the want of sensation in a moment of time would represent it as empty, consequently=o. That which in the empirical intuition corresponds to sensation is reality (*realitas phaenomenon*); that which corresponds to the absence of it, negation=o. Now every sensation is capable of a diminution, so that it can decrease, and thus gradually disappear. Therefore, between reality in appearance and negation, there exists a continuous connection of many possible intermediate sensations, the difference of which from each other is always smaller than that between the given sensation and zero, or complete negation. That is to say, the real in appearance has always a quantity, which however is not discoverable in apprehension, inasmuch as apprehension takes place by means of mere sensation in one instant, and not by the successive synthesis of many sensations, and therefore does not progress from parts to the whole. Consequently, it has a quantity, but not an extensive quantity.

Now that quantity which is apprehended only as unity, and in which plurality can be represented only by approximation to negation=o, I term *intensive quantity*. Consequently, reality in appearance has intensive quantity, that is, a degree. If we consider this reality as cause (be it of sensation or of another reality in the appearance, for example, a change), we call the degree of reality in its character of cause a momentum, for example, the momentum of weight; and for this reason, that the degree only indicates that quantity the apprehension of which is not successive, but instantaneous. This, however, I touch upon only in passing, for with causality I have at present nothing to do.

Accordingly, every sensation, consequently every reality in appearances, however small it may be, has a degree, that is, an intensive quantity, which may always be lessened, and between reality and negation there exists a continuous connection of possible realities, and possible smaller perceptions. Every colour – for example, red – has a degree, which, be it ever so small, is never the smallest, and so is it always with heat, the momentum of weight, etc.

This property of quantities, according to which no part of them is the smallest possible (no part simple), is called their continuity. Space and time are *quanta continua*, because no part of them can be given, without enclosing it within boundaries (points and moments), consequently, this given part is itself a space or a time. Space, therefore, consists only of spaces, and time of times. Points and moments are only boundaries, that is, the mere places or positions of their limitation. But places always presuppose intuitions which are to limit or determine them; and we cannot conceive either space or time composed of constituent parts which are given before space or time. Such quantities may also be called *flowing*, because the synthesis (of the productive imagination) in the production of these quantities is a progression in time, the continuity of which we are accustomed to indicate by the expression *flowing*.

All appearances, then, are continuous quantities, in respect both to intuition and mere perception (sensation, and with it reality). In the former case they are extensive quantities; in the latter, intensive. When the synthesis of the manifold of appearance is interrupted, there results merely an aggregate of several appearances, and not properly appearance as a quantity, which is not produced by the mere continuation of the productive synthesis of a certain kind, but by the repetition of a synthesis always ceasing. For example, if I call thirteen thalers a sum or quantity of money, I employ the term quite correctly, inasmuch as I understand by thirteen thalers the value of a mark in standard silver, which is, to be sure, a continuous quantity, in which no part is the smallest, but every part might constitute a piece of money, which would contain material for still smaller pieces. If, however, by the words thirteen thalers I understand so many coins (be their value in silver what it may), it would be quite erroneous to use the expression a quantity of thalers; on the contrary, I must call them aggregate, that is, a number of coins. And as in every number we must have unity as the foundation, so appearance taken as unity is a quantity, and as such always a continuum.

Now, seeing that all appearances, whether considered as extensive or intensive, are continous quantities, the proposition: 'all change (transition of a thing from one state into another) is continuous', might be proved here easily, and with mathematical evidence, were it not that the causality of a change lies entirely beyond the bounds of a transcendental philosophy, and presupposes empirical principles. For of the possibility of a cause which changes the condition of things, that is, which determines them to the contrary of a certain given state, the understanding gives us *a priori* no knowledge; not merely because it has no insight into the possibility of it (for such insight is absent in several instances of *a priori* knowledge), but because the notion of change concerns only certain determinations of appearances, which experience alone can acquaint us with, while their cause lies in the unchangeable. But seeing that we have nothing which we could here employ but the pure fundamental concepts of all possible experience, among which of course nothing empirical can be admitted, we cannot, without injuring the unity of our system, anticipate general natural science, which is built upon certain fundamental experiences.

Nevertheless, we are in no want of proofs of the great influence which the principle above developed exercises in the anticipation of perceptions, and even in supplying the want of them, so far as to shield us against the false conclusions which otherwise we might rashly draw.

If all reality in perception has a degree, between which and negation there is an endless sequence of ever smaller degrees, and if nevertheless every sense must have a determinate degree of receptivity for sensations; then no perception, and consequently no experience is possible, which can prove, either immediately or mediately, an entire absence of all reality in appearance; in other words, it is impossible ever to draw from experience a proof of the existence of empty space or of empty time. For in the first place, an entire absence of reality in a sensible intuition cannot of course be an object of perception; secondly, such absence cannot be inferred from the contemplation of any single appearance, and the difference of the degrees in its reality, nor ought it ever to be admitted in explanation of any appearance. For if even the complete intuition of a determinate space or time is thoroughly real, that is, if no part thereof is empty, yet because every reality has its degree, which, with the extensive quantity of the appearance unchanged, can diminish through endless gradations down to nothing (the void), there must be infinitely graduated degrees, with which space or time is filled, and the intensive quantity in different appearances may be smaller or greater, although the extensive quantity of the intuition remains equal and unaltered.

We shall give an example of this. Almost all natural philosophers, remarking a great difference in the quantity of the matter of different kinds in bodies with the same volume (partly on account of the momentum of gravity or weight, partly on account of the momentum of resistance to other bodies in motion), conclude unanimously, that this volume (extensive quantity of the appearance) must be void in all bodies, although in different proportion. But who would suspect that these for the most part mathematical and mechanical inquirers into nature should ground this conclusion solely on a metaphysical hypothesis – a sort of hypothesis which they profess to avoid? Yet this they do, in assuming that the real in space (I must not here call it impenetrability or weight, because these are empirical concepts) is always identical, and can only be distinguished according to its extensive quantity, that is, multiplicity. Now to this presupposition, for which they can have no ground in experience, and which consequently is merely metaphysical, I oppose a transcendental demonstration, which it is true will not explain the difference in the filling up of spaces, but which nevertheless completely does away with the supposed necessity of the above-mentioned presupposition that we cannot explain the said difference otherwise than by the hypothesis of empty spaces. This demonstration, moreover, has the merit of setting the understanding at liberty to conceive this distinction in a different manner, if the explanation of the fact requires any such hypothesis. For we perceive that although two equal spaces may be completely filled by matters altogether different, so that in neither of them is there left a single point wherein matter is not present, nevertheless every reality has its degree (of resistance or of weight), which, without diminution of the extensive quantity, can become less and less *ad infinitum*, before it passes into nothingness and disappears. Thus an expansion which fills a space – for example, heat, or any other reality in appearance – can decrease in its degrees to infinity, yet without leaving the smallest part of the space empty; on the contrary, filling it with those lesser degrees, as completely as another appearance could with greater. My intention here is by no means to maintain that this is really the case with the difference of matters, in regard to their specific gravity; I wish only to prove, from a principle of the pure understanding, that the nature of our perceptions makes such a mode of explanation possible, and that it is erroneous to regard the real in appearance as equal in its degree, and different only in its aggregation and extensive quantity, and this, too, on the pretended authority of an *a priori* principle of the understanding.

Nevertheless, this principle of the anticipation of perception must somewhat startle and make wonder an inquirer whom initiation into transcendental philosophy has rendered cautious. We may naturally entertain some doubt whether or not the understanding can enounce any such synthetical proposition as that respecting the degree of all reality in appearances, and consequently the possibility of the internal difference of sensation itself – abstraction being made of its empirical quality. Thus it is a question not unworthy of solution: how the understanding can pronounce synthetically and *a priori* respecting appearances, and thus anticipate these, even in that which is peculiarly and merely empirical, that, namely, which concerns sensation itself.

The quality of sensation is in all cases merely empirical, and cannot be represented *a priori* (for example, colours, taste, etc.). But the real – that which corresponds to sensation – in opposition to negation=0, only represents something the concept of which in itself contains a being, and signifies nothing but the synthesis in an empirical consciousness. That is to say, the empirical consciousness in the internal sense can be raised from 0 to every higher degree, so that the very same extensive quantity of intuition, an illuminated surface, for example, excites as great a sensation as an aggregate of many other surfaces less illuminated. We can therefore make complete abstraction of the extensive quantity of appearance, and represent to ourselves in the mere sensation in a certain momentum, a synthesis of homogeneous increase from 0 up to the given empirical consciousness. All sensations therefore as such are given only *a posteriori*, but this property thereof, namely, that they have a degree, can be known *a priori*. It is worthy of remark, that in respect to quantities in general, we can know *a priori* only a single quality, namely, continuity; but in respect to all quality (the real in appearances) we cannot know *a priori* anything more than the intensive quantity thereof, namely, that they have a degree. All else is left to experience.

3

ANALOGIES OF EXPERIENCE

The principle of these is: *Experience is possible only through the Representation of a Necessary Connection of Perceptions.*

PROOF

Experience is empirical knowledge; that is to say, knowledge which determines an object by means of perceptions. It is therefore contained in perception, but which contains the synthetical unity of the manifold of perception in a consciousness; and this unity constitutes what is essential in our knowledge of *objects* of the senses, that is, of experience (not merely of intuition or sensation). Now in experience our perceptions come together contingently, so that no character of necessity in their connection appears, or can appear from the perceptions themselves, because apprehension is only a placing together of the manifold of empirical intuition, and no representation of a necessity in the connected existence of the appearances which apprehension brings together, is to be discovered in space and time. But as experience is a knowledge of objects by means of perceptions, it follows that the relation of the existence of the manifold must be represented in experience not as it is put together in time, but as it is objectively in time. And as time itself cannot be perceived, the determination of the existence of objects in time can only take place by means of their connection in time in general, consequently only by means of *a priori* connecting concepts. Now as these concepts always possess the character of necessity, experience is possible only by means of a representation of the necessary connection of perception.

The three *modi* of time are *permanence, succession*, and *coexistence*. Accordingly, there are three rules of all relations of time in appearances, according to which the existence of every appearance is determined in respect of the unity of all time, and these antecede all experience, and render it possible.

The general principle of all three analogies rests on the necessary *unity* of apperception in relation to all possible empirical consciousness (perception) *at every time*, consequently, as this unity is the *a priori* basis, the principle rests on the synthetical unity of all appearances according to their relation in time. For the original apperception relates to our internal sense (the totality of all representations), and indeed relates *a priori* to its form, that is to say, the relation of the manifold empirical consciousness in time. Now this manifold must be united in original apperception according to relations of time – a necessity imposed by the *a priori* transcendental unity of apperception, to which is subjected all that can belong to my (i.e. my own) knowledge, and therefore all that can become an object for me. This synthetical and *a priori* determined unity in relation of perceptions in time is therefore the rule : 'All empirical determinations of time must be subject to rules of the general determination of time;' and the analogies of experience, of which we are now about to treat, must be rules of this nature.

These principles have this peculiarity, that they do not concern appearances, and the synthesis of the empirical intuition thereof, but merely the *existence* of appearances and their *relation* to each other in regard to this existence. Now the mode in which we apprehend a thing in appearance can be determined *a priori* in such a manner, that the rule of its synthesis can give, that is to say, can produce this *a priori* intuition in every empirical example. But the existence of appearances cannot be known *a priori*, and although we could arrive by this path at a conclusion of the fact of some existence, we could not know that existence determinately, that is to say, we should be incapable of anticipating in what respect the empirical intuition of it would be distinguishable from that of others.

The two principles above mentioned, which I called mathematical, in consideration of the fact of their justifying the application of mathematic to appearances, relate to these appearances only in regard to their possibility, and instruct us how appearances, as far as regards their intuition or the real in their perception, can be generated according to the rules of a mathematical synthesis. Consequently, numerical quantities, and with them the determination of appearance as a quantity, can be employed in the one case as well as in the other. Thus, for example, out of 200,000 illuminations by the moon, I might compose, and give *a priori*, that is construct, the degree of our sensations of the sunlight. We may therefore entitle these two principles constitutive.

The case is very different with those principles that are meant to subject the existence of appearances to rules *a priori*. For as existence does not admit of being constructed, it is clear that they must only concern the relations of existence, and be merely *regulative* principles. In this case, therefore, neither axioms nor anticipations are to be thought of. Thus, if a perception is given us, in a certain relation of time to other (although undetermined) perceptions, we cannot then say *a priori*, *what* and *how great* (in quantity) the other perception necessarily connected with the former is, but only *how* it is connected, as regards its existence, in this given mode of time. Analogies in philosophy mean something very different from that which they represent in mathematics. In the latter they are formulae, which enounce the equality of two relations of quantity, and are always *constitutive*, so that if two terms of the proportion are given, the third is also given, that is, can be constructed thereby. But in philosophy, analogy is not the equality of two *quantitive* but of two *qualitative* relations. In this case, from three given terms, I can give *a priori* and know the *relation* to a fourth member, but not this fourth term itself, although I certainly possess a rule to guide me in the search for this fourth term in experience, and a mark to assist me in discovering it. An analogy of experience is therefore only a rule according to which unity of experience must arise out of perceptions in respect to objects (appearances) not as a *constitutive*, but merely as a *regulative* principle. The same holds good also of the postulates of empirical thought in general, which relate to the synthesis of mere intuition (which concerns the form of appearances), and the synthesis of experience (which concerns the relation of these perceptions). For they are only regulative principles, and clearly distinguishable from the mathematical, which are constitutive, not indeed in regard to the certainty which both possess *a priori*, but in the mode of evidence thereof which in the latter case is intuitive, consequently also in the manner of demonstration.

But what has been observed of all synthetical principles, and must be particularly remarked in this place, is this, that these analogies possess significance and validity, not as principles of the transcendental, but only as principles of the empirical use of the understanding, and their truth can therefore be proved only as such, and that consequently the appearances must not be subsumed directly under the categories, but only under their schemata. For if the objects to which those principles must be applied were things in themselves, it would be quite impossible to know anything concerning them synthetically *a priori*. But they are nothing but appearances; a complete knowledge of which – a knowledge to which all principles *a priori* must at last relate – is merely possible experience. It follows that those principles can have nothing else for their aim, than the conditions of the unity of empirical knowledge in the synthesis of appearances. But this synthesis is thought only in the schema of the pure concept of the understanding, of whose unity, as that of a synthesis in general, the category contains the function unrestricted by any sensible condition. Those principles will therefore justify us to connect appearances according to an analogy, with the logical and universal unity of concepts, and consequently to employ the categories in the principles themselves; but in the application of them to experience, we shall use only their schemata, as the key to their proper application, instead of the categories, or rather the latter as restricting conditions, under the title of formulae of the former.

A: FIRST ANALOGY

PRINCIPLE OF THE PERMANENCE OF SUBSTANCE

In all Changes of Appearances, Substance is permanent, and the quantum thereof in Nature is neither increased nor diminished.

PROOF

All appearances exist in time, wherein alone as substratum, that is, as the permanent form of the internal intuition, co-existence and succession can be represented. Consequently time, in which all changes of appearances must be thought, remains and changes not, because it is that in which succession and co-existence can be represented only as determinations thereof. Now, time in itself cannot be perceived. It follows that in objects of perception, that is, in appearances, there must be found a substratum which represents time in general, and in which all change or co-existence can be perceived by means of the relation of appearances to it. But the substratum of all reality, that is, of all that pertains to the existence of things, is substance; all that pertains to existence can be thought only as a determination of substance. Consequently, the permanent, in relation to which alone all relations of time in appearances can be determined, is substance in appearances, that is, the real in appearances, that which, as the substratum of all change, remains ever the same. Accordingly, as this cannot change in existence, its quantity in nature can neither be increased nor diminished.

Our *apprehension* of the manifold in appearance is always successive, is consequently always changing. By it alone we could, therefore, never determine whether this manifold, as an object of experience, is co-existent or successive, unless it had for a foundation something that exists *always*, that is, something *fixed* and *permanent*, of the existence of which all succession and co-existence are nothing but so many modes (*modi* of time). Only in the permanent, then, are relations of time possible (for simultaneity and succession are the only relations in time); that is to say, the permanent is the *substratum* of our empirical representation of time itself, in which alone all determination of time is possible. Permanence is, in fact, just another expression for time, as the abiding correlate of all existence of appearances, and of all change, and of all co-existence. For change does not affect time itself, but only the appearances in time (just as co-existence cannot be regarded as a *modus* of time itself, seeing that in time no parts are co-existent, but all successive). If we were to attribute succession to time itself, we should be obliged to think another time, in which this succession would be possible. It is only by means of the permanent that existence in different parts of the successive series of time receives a magnitude, which we entitle *duration*. For in mere succession, existence is perpetually vanishing and recommencing, and therefore never has even the least quantity. Without the permanent, then, no relation in time is possible. Now, time in itself is not an object of perception; consequently the permanent in appearances must be regarded as the substratum of all determination of time, and consequently also as the condition of the possibility of all synthetical unity of perceptions, that is, of experience; and all existence and all change in time can only be regarded as a mode in the existence of that which abides and persists. Therefore, in all appearances, the permanent is the object *in itself*, that is, the substance (phenomenon); but all that changes or can change belongs only to the mode of the existence of this substance or substances, consequently to its determinations.

I find that in all ages not only the philosopher, but even the common understanding, has presupposed this permanence as a substratum of all change in appearances; indeed, I am compelled to believe that they will always accept this as an indubitable fact. Only the philosopher expresses himself in a more definite manner, when he says: 'In all changes in the world, the *substance* remains, and the *accidents* alone are changeable.' But of this decidedly synthetical proposition, I nowhere meet with even an attempt at proof; nay, it very rarely has the good fortune to stand, as it deserves to do, at the head of the pure and entirely *a priori* laws of nature. In truth, the statement that substance is permanent, is tautological. For this very permanence is the ground on which we apply the category of substance to appearances; and we should have been obliged to prove that in all appearances there is something permanent, of the existence of which the changeable is nothing but a determination. But because a proof of this nature cannot be dogmatical, that is, cannot be drawn from concepts, inasmuch as it concerns a synthetical proposition *a priori*, and as philosophers never reflected that such propositions are valid only in relation to possible experience, and therefore cannot be proved except by means of a deduction of the possibility of experience, it is no wonder that while it has served as the foundation of all experience (for we feel the need of it in empirical knowledge), it has never been supported by proof.

A philosopher was asked: 'What is the weight of smoke?' He answered: 'Subtract from the weight of the burnt wood the weight of the remaining ashes, and you will have the weight of the smoke.' Thus he presumed it to be incontrovertible that even in fire the matter (substance) does not perish, but that only the form of it undergoes a change. In like manner was the saying: 'From nothing comes nothing', only another inference from the principle of permanence, or rather of the ever-abiding existence of the true subject in appearances. For if that in appearance which we call substance is to be the proper substratum of all determination of time, it follows that all existence in past as well as in future time, must be determinable by means of it alone. Hence we are entitled to apply the term substance to appearance, only because we suppose its existence in all time, a notion which the word permanence does not fully express, as it seems rather to be referable to future time. However, the internal necessity perpetually to be, is inseparably connected with the necessity always to have been, and so the expression may stand as it is. '*Gigni de nihilo nihil*' – '*in nihilum nil posse reverti*', are two propositions which the ancients never parted, and which people nowadays sometimes mistakenly disjoin, because they imagine that the propositions apply to objects as things in themselves, and that the former might be inimical to the dependence (even in respect of its substance also) of the world upon a supreme cause. But this apprehension is entirely needless, for the question in this case is only of appearances in the sphere of experience, the unity of which never could be possible, if we admitted the possibility that new things (in respect of their substance) should arise. For in that case, we should lose altogether that which alone can represent the unity of time, to wit, the identity of the substratum, as that through which alone all change possesses pervasive unity. This permanence is, however, nothing but the manner in which we represent to ourselves the existence of things in appearance.

The determinations of a substance, which are only particular modes of its existence, are called *accidents*. They are always real, because they concern the existence of substance (negations are only determinations, which express the non-existence of something in the substance). Now, if to this real in the substance we ascribe a particular existence (for example, to motion as an accident of matter), this existence is called inherence, in contradistinction to the existence of substance, which we call subsistence. But hence arise many misconceptions, and it would be a more accurate and just mode of expression to designate the accident only as the mode in which the existence of a substance is positively determined. Meanwhile, by reason of the conditions of the logical exercise of our understanding, it is impossible to avoid separating, as it were, that which in the existence of a substance is subject to change, whilst the substance remains, and regarding it in relation to that category of substance stands under the title of relation, rather because it is the condition thereof, than because it contains in itself any relation.

Now, upon this notion of permanence rests the correct understanding of the concept *change*. Coming to be and ceasing to be are not changes of that which comes to be or ceases to be. Change is but a mode of existence, which follows on another mode of existence of the same object; hence all that changes is permanent, and only the condition thereof is altered. Now since this alteration affects only determinations, which can have a beginning or an end, we may say, employing an expression which seems somewhat paradoxical: 'Only the *permanent* (substance) is subject to change; the mutable suffers no change, but rather *alteration*, that is, when certain determinations cease, others begin.'

Change, then, cannot be perceived by us except in substances, and coming to be and ceasing to be in an absolute sense, that does not concern merely a determination of the permanent, cannot be a possible perception, for it is this very notion of the permanent which renders possible the representation of a transition from one state into another, and from non-being to being, which, consequently can be empirically known only as altering determinations of that which is permanent. Grant that a thing absolutely begins to be; we must then have a point of time in which it was not. But how and by what can we fix and determine this point of time, unless by that which already exists? For a void time – preceding – is not an object of perception; but if we connect this beginning with objects which existed previously, and which continue to exist till the object in question begins to be, then the latter can only be a determination of the former as the permanent. The same holds good of the notion of ceasing to be, for this presupposes the empirical representation of a time, in which appearance no longer exists.

Substances (in appearance) are the substratum of all determinations of time. The beginning of some, and the ceasing to be of other substances, would utterly do away with the only condition of the empirical unity of time; and in that case appearances would relate to two different times, in which, side by side, existence would pass; which is absurd. For there is only *one* time in which all different times must be placed, not as co-existent, but as successive.

Accordingly, permanence is a necessary condition under which alone appearances, as things or objects, are determinable in a possible experience. But as regards the empirical criterion of this necessary permanence, and with it of the substantiality of appearances, we shall find sufficient opportunity to speak in the sequel.

B: SECOND ANALOGY

PRINCIPLE OF THE SUCCESSION IN TIME ACCORDING TO THE LAW OF CAUSALITY

All Changes take place according to the law of the Connection of Cause and Effect.

PROOF

(That all appearances in the succession of time are only changes, that is, a successive being and non-being of the determinations of substance, which is permanent; consequently that a being of substance itself which follows on the non-being thereof, or a non-being of substance which follows on the being thereof, in other words, that the coming to be and ceasing to be of substance itself, is impossible – all this has been fully established in treating of the foregoing principle. This principle might have been expressed as follows: '*All alteration (succession) of appearances is merely change*'; for coming to be and passing away are not changes of substances, because the concept of change presupposes the same subject as existing with two opposite determinations, and consequently as permanent. After this preliminary reminder, we shall proceed to the proof.)

I perceive that appearances succeed one another, that is to say, a state of things exists at one time, the opposite of which existed in a former state. In this case, then, I really connect together two perceptions in time. Now connection is not an operation of mere sense and intuition, but is the product of a synthetical faculty of imagination, which determines the internal sense in respect of a relation of time. But imagination can connect these two states in two ways, so that either the one or the other may antecede in time; for time in itself cannot be perceived, and what in an object precedes and what follows cannot be empirically determined in relation to it. I am only conscious, then, that my imagination places one state before, and the other after; not that the one state antecedes the other in the object. In other words, the objective relation of the successive appearances remains quite undetermined by means of mere perception. Now in order that this relation may be known as determined, the relation between the two states must be so thought that it is thereby determined as necessary, which of them must be placed before and which after, and not conversely. But the concept which carries with it a necessity of synthetical unity, can be none other than a pure concept of the understanding which does not lie in mere perception; and in this case it is the concept of the *relation of cause and effect*, the former of which determines the latter in time, as its necessary consequence, and not as something which might possibly antecede (or which might in some cases not be perceived to follow). It follows that it is only because we subject the sequence of appearances, and consequently all change, to the law of causality, that experience itself, that is, empirical knowledge of appearances, becomes possible; and consequently, that appearances themselves, as objects of experience, are possible only by virtue of this law.

Our apprehension of the manifold of appearances is always successive. The representations of parts succeed one another. Whether they succeed one another in the object also, is a second point for reflection, which was not contained in the former. Now we may certainly give the name of the object to everything, even to every representation, so far as we are conscious thereof; but what this word may mean in the case of appearances, not merely in so far as they (as representations) are objects, but only in so far as they indicate an object, is a question requiring deeper consideration. In so far as they, regarded merely as representations, are at the same time objects of consciousness, they are not to be distinguished from apprehension, that is, reception into the synthesis of imagination, and we must therefore say: 'The manifold of appearances is always produced successively in the mind.' If appearances were things in themselves, no man would be able to conjecture from the succession of our representations how this manifold is connected in the object; for we have to do only with our representations. How things may be in themselves, without regard to the representations through which they affect us, is utterly beyond the sphere of our knowledge. Now although appearances are not things in themselves, and are nevertheless the only thing given to us to be known, it is my duty to show what sort of connection in time belongs to the manifold in appearances themselves, while the representation of this manifold in apprehension is always successive. For example, the apprehension of the manifold in the appearance of a house which stands before me, is successive. Now comes the question, whether the manifold of this house is in itself also successive – which clearly no one will be willing to grant. But, so soon as I raise my concept of an object to the transcendental signification thereof, I find that the house is not a thing in itself, but only appearance, that is, a representation, the transcendental object of which remains utterly unkown. What then am I to understand by the question: How can the manifold be connected in the appearance itself – which is nothing in itself? Here that which lies in my successive apprehension is regarded as representation, whilst the appearance which is given me, notwithstanding that it is nothing more than a totality of these representations, is regarded as the object thereof, with which my concept, drawn from the representations of apprehension, must agree. It is very soon seen that, as accordance of knowledge with its object constitutes truth, the question now before us can only relate to the formal conditions of empirical truth, and that appearance, in contrast to the representations of apprehension, can only be distinguished therefrom as the object of them, if it is subject to a rule which distinguishes it from every other apprehension, and which renders necessary a mode of connection of the manifold. That in appearance which contains the condition of this necessary rule of apprehension, is the object.

Let us now proceed to our task. That something happens, that is to say, that something or some state exists which before was not, cannot be empirically perceived, unless an appearance precedes, which does not contain in itself this state. For a reality which should follow upon an empty time, in other words, a beginning, which no state of things precedes, can just as little be apprehended as the empty time itself. Every apprehension of an event is therefore a perception which follows upon another perception. But as this is the case with all synthesis of apprehension, as I have shown above in the example of a house, my apprehension of an event is not yet sufficiently distinguished from other apprehensions. But I remark also, that if in appearance which contains an occurrence, I call the antecedent state of my perception, A, and the following state, B, the perception B can only follow A in apprehension, and the perception A cannot follow B, but only precede it. For example, I see a ship float down the stream of a river. My perception of its place lower down follows upon my perception of its place higher up the course of the river, and it is impossible that in the apprehension of this appearance, the vessel should be perceived first below and afterwards higher up the stream. Here, therefore, the order in the sequence of perceptions in apprehension is determined; and by this order apprehension is regulated. In the former example, my perceptions in the apprehension of a house might begin at the roof and end at the foundation, or vice versa; or I might apprehend the manifold in this empircal intuition, by going from left to right, and from right to left. Accordingly, in the series of these perceptions, there was no determined order, which necessitated my beginning at a certain point, in order empirically to connect the manifold. But this rule is always to be met with in the perception of that which happens, and it makes the order of the successive perceptions in the apprehension of such appearance *necessary*.

I must, therefore, in the present case, derive the *subjective sequence* of apprehension from the *objective sequence* of appearances, for otherwise the former is quite undetermined, and one appearance is not distinguishable from another. The former alone proves nothing as to the connection of the manifold in an object, for it is quite arbitrary. The latter must consist in the order of the manifold in appearance, according to which order the apprehension of one thing (that which happens) follows that of another thing (that which precedes), in conformity with a rule. In this way alone can I be justified to say of the appearance itself, and not merely of my own apprehension, that a certain order or sequence is to be found therein. That is, in other words, I cannot arrange my apprehension otherwise than in this order.

In conformity with this rule, then, it is necessary that in that which antecedes an event there be found the condition of a rule, according to which this event follows always and necessarily; but I cannot reverse this and go back from the event, and determine (by apprehension) that which antecedes it. For no appearance goes back from the succeeding point of time to the preceding point, although it does certainly relate to a preceding point of time; from a given time, on the other hand, there is always a necessary progression to the determined succeeding time. Therefore, because there certainly is something that follows, I must of necessity connect it with something else, which antecedes, and upon which it follows, in conformity with a rule, that is necessarily, so that the event, as conditioned, affords certain indication of a condition, and this condition determines the event.

Let us suppose that nothing precedes an event, upon which this event must follow in conformity with a rule. All sequence of perception would then exist only in apprehension, that is to say, would be merely subjective, and it could not thereby be objectively determined what thing ought to precede, and what ought to follow in perception. In such a case, we should have nothing but a play of representations, which would possess no application to any object. That is to say, it would not be possible through perception to distinguish one appearance from another, as regards relations of time; because the succession in the act of apprehension would always be of the same sort, and therefore there would be nothing in the appearance to determine the succession, and to render a certain sequence objectively necessary. And, in this case, I cannot say that two states in appearance follow one upon the other, but only that one apprehension follows upon another. But this is merely subjective, and does not determine an object, and consequently cannot be held to be knowledge of an object – not even in appearance.

Accordingly, when we know in experience that something happens, we always presuppose that something precedes, whereupon it follows in conformity with a rule. For otherwise I could not say of the object, that it follows; because the mere succession in my apprehension, if it be not determined by a rule in relation to something preceding, does not justify succession in the object. Only, therefore, in reference to a rule, according to which appearances are determined in their sequence, that is, as they happen, by the preceding state, can I make my subjective synthesis (of apprehension) objective, and it is only under this presupposition that even the experience of an event is possible.

No doubt it appears as if this were in thorough contradiction to all the notions which people have hitherto entertained in regard to the procedure of the human understanding. According to these opinions, it is by means of the perception and comparison of similar consequences following upon certain antecedent appearances, that the understanding is led to the discovery of a rule, according to which certain events always follow certain appearances, and it is only by this process that we attain to the concept of cause. Upon such a basis, it is clear that this concept must be merely empirical, and the rule which it furnishes us with – 'Everything that happens has a cause' – would be just as contingent as experience itself. The universality and necessity of the rule would be perfectly spurious attributes of it and would have no genuine universal validity. Indeed, it could not possess universal validity, inasmuch as it would not in this case be *a priori*, but founded on induction. But the same is the case with this rule as with other pure *a priori* representations (e.g. space and time), which we can draw in perfect clearness from experience, only because we had already placed them therein, and by that means, and by that alone, had rendered experience possible. Indeed, the logical clearness of this representation of a rule, determining the series of events, i.e. of a cause, is possible only when we have made use thereof in experience. Nevertheless, the recognition of this rule, as a condition of the synthetical unity of appearances in time, was the ground of experience itself, and consequently preceded it *a priori*.

It is then, our duty to show in the case under consideration, that we never, even in experience, attribute succession to an object (of an event – that is, the happening of something that did not exist before), and distinguish it from the subjective succession of apprehension, unless when a rule lies at the foundation, which compels us to observe this order of perception in preference to any other, and that, indeed, it is this necessity which first renders possible the representation of a succession in the object.

We have representations within us, of which also we can be conscious. But, however widely extended, however accurate and thorough-going this consciousness may be, these representations are still nothing more than representations, that is, internal determinations of the mind in this or that relation of time. Now how does it happen, that to these representations we should posit an object, or that, in addition to their subjective reality, as modifications, we should still further attribute to them a certain unknown objective reality? It is clear that objective significancy cannot consist in a relation to another representation (of that which we desire to term object), for in that case the question again arises: 'How does this other representation go beyond itself, and obtain objective significancy over and above the subjective, which is proper to it, as a determination of a state of mind?' If we try to discover what sort of new property the relation to an object gives to our subjective representations, and what new importance they thereby receive, we shall find that this relation has no other effect than that of rendering necessary the connection of our representations in a certain manner, and of subjecting them to a rule; and that conversely, it is only because a certain order is necessary in the relations of time of our representations, that objective significancy is ascribed to them.

In the synthesis of appearances, the manifold of our representations is always successive. Now hereby is not represented an object, for by means of this succession, which is common to all apprehension, no one thing is distinguished from another. But as soon as I perceive or assume, that in this succession there is a relation to an antecedent state, from which the representation follows in accordance with a rule, than I represent something as an event, or as something that happens; in other words, I know an object to which I must assign a certain determinate position in time, which cannot be altered, because of the preceding state in the object. When, therefore, I perceive that something happens, there is contained in this representation, in the first place, the fact, that something antecedes; because it is only in relation to this, that the appearance obtains its proper relation of time, in other words, exists after an antecedent time, in which it did not exist. But it can receive its determined place in time, only by the presupposition that something existed in the foregoing state, upon which it follows inevitably and always, that is, in conformity with a rule. From all this it is evident that, in the first place, I cannot reverse the order of succession, and make that which happens precede that upon which it follows; and that, in the second place, if the antecedent state be posited, a certain determinate event inevitably and necessarily follows. Hence it follows that there exists a certain order in our representations, whereby the present gives a sure indication of some previously existing state, as a correlate, though still undetermined, of the existing event which is given – a correlate which itself relates to the event as its consequence, conditions it, and connects it necessarily with itself in the series of time.

If then it be admitted as a necessary law of sensibility, and consequently a formal condition of all perception, that the preceding time necessarily determines the succeeding time (inasmuch as I cannot arrive at the succeeding time except through the preceding), it must likewise be an indispensable law of empirical representation of the series of time, that the appearances of the past determine all appearances in the succeeding time, and that the latter, as events, cannot take place, except in so far as the former determine their existence in time, that is to say, establish it according to a rule. For it is of course only in appearances that we can empirically know this continuity in the connection of times.

For all experience and for the possibility of experience, understanding is indispensable, and the first step which it takes in this sphere is not to render the representation of objects clear, but to render the representation of an object in general, possible. It does this by applying the order of time to appearances, and their existence. In other words, it assigns to each appearance, as a consequence, a place in relation to preceding appearances, determined *a priori* in time, without which it could not harmonize with time itself, which determines a place *a priori* to all its parts. This determination of place cannot be derived from the relation of appearances to absolute time (for it is not an object of perception); but, on the contrary, appearances must reciprocally determine the places in time of one another, and render these necessary in the order of time. In other words, whatever follows or happens, must follow in conformity with a universal rule upon that which was contained in the foregoing stage. Hence arises a series of appearances, which, by means of the understanding, produces and renders necessary exactly the same order and continuous connection in the series of our possible perceptions, as is found *a priori* in the form of internal intuition (time), in which all our perceptions must have place.

That something happens, then, is a perception which belongs to a possible experience, which becomes real only because I look upon the appearance as determined in regard to its place in time, consequently as an object, which can always be found by means of a rule in the connected series of my perceptions. But this rule of the determination of a thing according to succession in time is as follows: 'In what precedes may be found the condition, under which an event always (that is, necessarily) follows.' From all this it is obvious that the principle of cause and effect is the principle of possible experience, that is, of objective knowledge of appearances, in regard to their relations in the succession of time.

The proof of this proposition rests entirely on the following considerations. To all empirical knowledge belongs the synthesis of the manifold by the imagination, a synthesis which is always successive, that is, in which the representations therein always follow one another. But the order of succession in imagination is not determined, and the series of successive representations may be taken retrogressively as well as progressively. But if this synthesis is a synthesis of apprehension (of the manifold of a given appearance), then the order is determined in the object, or, to speak more accurately, there is therein an order of successive synthesis which determines an object, and according to which something necessarily precedes, and when this is posited, something else necessarily follows. If, then, my perception is to contain the knowledge of an event, that is, of something which really happens, it must be an empirical judgment, wherein we think that the succession is determined; that is, it presupposes another appearance, upon which this event follows necessarily, or in conformity with a rule. If, on the contrary, when I posited the antecedent, the event did not necessarily follow, I should be obliged to consider it merely as a subjective play of my imagination, and if in this I represented to myself anything as objective, I must look upon it as a mere dream. Thus, the relation of appearances (as possible perceptions), according to which that which happens is, as to its existence, necessarily determined in time by something which antecedes, in conformity with a rule – in other words, the relation of cause and effect – is the condition of the objective validity of our empirical judgments in regard to the sequence of perceptions, consequently of their empirical truth, and therefore of experience. The principle of the relation of causality in the succession of appearances is therefore valid for all objects of experience, subject to the conditions of succession, because it is itself the ground of the possibility of experience.

Here, however, a difficulty arises, which must be resolved. The principle of the connection of causality among appearances is limited in our formula to the succession thereof, although in practice we find that the principle applies also when the appearance exist together in the same time, and that cause and effect may be simultaneous. For example, there is heat in a room, which does not exist in the open air. I look about for the cause, and find it to be the fire. Now the fire as the cause, is simultaneous with its effect, the heat of the room. In this case, then, there is no succession as regards time, between cause and effect, but they are simultaneous; and still the law holds good. The greater part of operating causes in nature are simultaneous with their effects, and the succession in time of the latter is produced only because the cause cannot achieve the total of its effect in one moment. But at the moment when the effect *first* arises, it is always simultaneous with the causality of its cause, because if the cause had but a moment before ceased to be, the effect could not have arisen. Here it must be specially remembered, that we must consider the *order* of time, and not the *lapse* thereof. The relation remains, even though no time has elapsed. The time between the causality of the cause and its immediate effect may entirely vanish, and the cause and effect be thus simultaneous, but the relation of the one to the other remains always determinable according to time. If, for example, I consider a leaden ball, which lies upon a cushion and makes a hollow in it, as a cause, then it is simultaneous with the effect. But I distinguish the two through the relation of time of the dynamical connection of both. For if I lay the ball upon the cushion, then the hollow follows upon the before smooth surface; but supposing the cushion has, from some cause or another, a hollow, there does not thereupon follow a leaden ball.

Thus, the law of succession of time is in all instances the only empirical criterion of effect in relation to the causality of the antecedent cause. The glass is the cause of the rising of the water above its horizontal surface, although the two appearances are contemporaneous. For, as soon as I draw some water with the glass from a larger vessel, an effect follows thereupon, namely, the change of the horizontal state which the water had in the large vessel into a concave, which it assumes in the glass.

Causality leads us to the concept of action; that of action, to the concept of force; and through it, to the concept of substance. As I do not wish this critical essay, the sole purpose of which is to treat of the sources of our synthetical knowledge *a priori*, to be crowded with analyses which merely explain, but do not enlarge the sphere of our concepts, I reserve the detailed explanation of the above concepts for a future system of pure reason. Such an analysis, indeed, executed with great particularity, may already be found in well-known works on this subject. But I cannot at present refrain from making a few remarks on the empirical criterion of a substance, in so far as it seems to be more evident and more easily recognized through the concept of action, than through that of the permanence of appearance.

Where action (consequently activity and force) exists, substance also must exist, and in it alone must be sought the seat of that fruitful source of appearances. Very well. But if we are called upon to explain what we mean by substance, and wish to avoid the vice of reasoning in a circle, the answer is by no means so easy. How shall we conclude immediately from the action to the *permanence* of that which acts, this being nevertheless an essential and peculiar criterion of substance (phenomenon)? But after what has been said above, the solution of this question becomes easy enough, although by the common mode of procedure – merely analysing our concepts – it would be quite impossible. The concept of action indicates the relation of the subject of causality to the effect. Now because all effect consists in that which happens, therefore in the changeable, the last subject thereof is the *permanent*, as the substratum of all that changes, that is, substance. For according to the principle of causality, actions are always the first ground of all change in appearances, and consequently cannot be a property of a subject which itself changes, because if this were the case, other actions and another subject would be necessary to determine this change. From all this it results that action alone, as an empirical criterion, is a sufficient proof of the presence of substantiality, without any necessity on my part of endeavouring to discover the permanence of substance by comparison. Besides, by this mode of induction we could not attain to the completeness which the magnitude and strict universality of the concept requires. For that the primary subject of the causality of all coming to be and ceasing to be, all origin and extinction, cannot itself (in the sphere of appearances) come to be and cease to be, is a sound and safe conclusion, a conclusion which leads us to the concept of empirical necessity and permanence in existence, and consequently to the concept of a substance as appearance.

When something happens, the mere fact of the coming to be without regard to that which comes to be, is an object requiring investigation. The transition from the non-being of a state into that state, supposing that this state contains no quality which previously existed in the appearance, is a fact of itself demanding inquiry. Such coming to be, as has been shown in Analogy A, does not concern substance (for substance does not thus come to be), but its condition or state. It is therefore only change, and not origin from nothing. If this origin be regarded as the effect of a foreign cause, it is termed creation, which cannot be admitted as an event among appearances, because the very possibility of it would annihilate the unity of experience. If, however, I regard all things not as appearances, but as things in themselves, and objects of understanding alone, they, although substances, may be considered as dependent, in respect of their existence, on a foreign cause. But this would require a very different meaning in the words, a meaning which could not apply to appearances as objects of possible experience.

How a thing can be changed, how it is possible that upon one state existing in one point of time, an opposite state should follow in another point of time – of this we have not the smallest concept *a priori*. There is requisite for this the knowledge of real powers, which can only be given empirically; for example, knowledge of moving forces, or, in other words, of certain successive appearances (as movements) which indicate the presence of such forces. But the form of every change, the condition under which alone it can take place as the coming into existence of another state (be the content of the change, that is, the state which is changed, what it may), and consequently the succession of the states themselves, can very well be considered *a priori*, in relation to the law of causality and the conditions of time.[1]

When a substance passes from one state, A, into another state, B, the point of time in which the latter exists is different from, and subsequent to that in which the former existed. In like manner, the second state, as reality (in appearance), differs from the first, in which the reality of the second did not exist, as B from zero. That is to say, if the state B differs from the state A only in respect to quantity, the change is a coming into existence of B – A, which in the former state did not exist, and in relation to which that state is $= 0$.

Now the question arises, how a thing passes from one state $= A$, into another state $= B$. Between two moments there is always a certain time, and between two states existing in these moments there is always a difference having a certain quantity (for all parts of appearances are in their turn quantities). Consequently, every transition from one state into another is always effected in a time contained between two moments, of which the first determines the state which the thing leaves, and the second determines the state into which the thing passes. Both moments, then, are limitations of the time of a change, consequently of the intermediate state between

---

[1] It must be remarked, that I do not speak of the change of certain relations, but of the change of the state. Thus, when a body moves in a uniform manner, it does not change its state (of motion); but only when its motion increases or decreases.

both, and as such they belong to the total of the change. Now every change has a cause, which exhibits its causality in the whole time during which the change takes place. The cause, therefore, does not produce the change all at once or in one moment, but in a time, so that, as the time gradually increases from the commencing instant, A, to its completion at B, in like manner also, the quantity of the reality (B − A) is generated through the lesser degrees which are contained between the first and last. All change is therefore possible only through a continous action of the causality, which, in so far as it is uniform, we call a momentum. The change does not consist of these momenta, but is produced by them as their effect.

Such is the law of the continuity of all change, the ground of which is, that neither time itself nor any appearance in time consists of parts which are the smallest possible, but that, notwithstanding, the state of a thing passes in the process of a change through all these parts, as elements, to its second state. There is no smallest degree of reality in appearance, just as there is no smallest degree in the quantity of time; and so the new state of the reality grows up out of the former state, through all the infinite degrees thereof, the differences of which one from another, taken all together, are less than the difference between o and A.

It is not our business to inquire here into the utility of this principle in the investigation of nature. But how such a proposition, which appears so greatly to extend our knowledge of nature, is possible completely *a priori*, is indeed a question which deserves investigation, although the first view seems to demonstrate the truth and reality of the principle, and the question, how it is possible, may be considered superfluous. For there are so many groundless pretensions to the enlargement of our knowledge by pure reason, that we must take it as a general rule to be mistrustful of all such, and without a thorough deduction, to believe nothing of the sort even on the clearest dogmatical proof.

Every addition to our empirical knowledge, and every advance made in the exercise of our perception, is nothing more than an extension of the determination of the internal sense, that is to say, a progression in time, be objects themselves what they may, appearances, or pure intuitions. This progression in time determines everything, and is itself determined by nothing else. That is to say, the parts of the progression exist only in time, and by means of the synthesis thereof, and are not given antecedently to it. For this reason, every transition in perception to anything which follows upon another in time, is a determination of time by means of the production of this perception. And as this determination of time is, always and in all its parts, a quantity, the perception produced is to be considered as a quantity which proceeds through all its degrees – no one of which is the smallest possible – from zero up to its determined degree. From this we perceive the possibility of knowing *a priori* a law of changes – a law, however, which concerns their form merely. We merely anticipate our own apprehension, the formal condition of which, inasmuch as it is itself to be found in the mind antecedently to all given appearances, must certainly be capable of being known *a priori*.

Thus, as time contains the sensible condition *a priori* of the possibility of a continuous progression of that which exists to that which follows it, the understanding, by virtue of the unity of apperception, contains the condition *a priori* of the possibility of a continuous determination of the position in time of all appearances, and this by means of the series of causes and effects, the former of which necessitate the sequence of the latter, and thereby render universally and for all time, and by consequence, objectively valid the empirical knowledge of the relations of time.

C: THIRD ANALOGY

PRINCIPLE OF CO-EXISTENCE, ACCORDING TO THE LAW OF RECIPROCITY OR COMMUNITY

All Substances, in so far as they can be perceived to co-exist in Space, exist in a state of complete Reciprocity of Action.

PROOF

Things are co-existent, when in empirical intuition the perception of the one can follow upon the perception of the other, and vice versa – which cannot occur in the succession of appearances, as we have shown in the explanation of the second principle. Thus I can perceive the moon and then the earth, or conversely, first the earth and then the moon; and for the reason that my perception of these objects can reciprocally follow each other, I say, they exist contemporaneously. Now co-existence is the existence of the manifold in the same time. But time itself cannot be perceived; and therefore we cannot conclude from the fact that things are placed in the same time, the other fact, that the perceptions of these things can follow each other reciprocally. The synthesis of the imagination in apprehension would only present to us each of these perceptions as present in the subject when the other is not present, and contrariwise; but would not show that the objects are co-existent, that is to say, that, if the one exists, the other also exists at the same time, and that this is necessarily so, in order that the perceptions may be capable of following each other reciprocally. It follows that a concept of the understanding of the reciprocal sequence of the determinations of appearances (existing, as they do, apart from each other, and yet contemporaneously), is requisite to justify us in saying that the reciprocal succession of perceptions has its foundation in the object, and to enable us to represent co-existence as objective. But that relation of substances in which the one contains determinations the ground of which is in the other substance, is the relation of influence. And, when this influence is reciprocal, it is the relation of community or reciprocity. Consequently the co-existence of substances in space cannot be known in experience otherwise than under the precondition of their reciprocal action. This is therefore the condition of the possibility of things themselves as objects of experience.

Things are co-existent, in so far as they exist at one and the same time. But how can we know that they exist at one and the same time? Only by observing that the order in the synthesis of apprehension of the manifold is arbitrary and a matter of indifference, that is to say, that it can proceed from A, through B, C, D, to E, or contrariwise from E to A. For if they were successive in time (and in order, let us suppose, which begins with A), it is quite impossible for the apprehension in perception to begin with E and go backwards to A, inasmuch as A belongs to past time, and therefore cannot be an object of apprehension.

Let us assume that in a number of substances considered as appearances each is completely isolated, that is, that no one acts upon another. Then I say that the *co-existence* of these cannot be an object of possible perception, and that the existence of one cannot, by any mode of empirical synthesis, lead us to the existence of another. For we imagine them in this case to be separated by a completely void space, and thus perception, which proceeds from the one to the other in time, would indeed determine their existence by means of a following perception, but would be quite unable to distinguish whether the one phenomenon follows objectively upon the first, or is co-existent with it.

Besides the mere fact of existence, then, there must be something by means of which A determines the position of B in time, and conversely, B the position of A; because only under this condition can substances be empirically represented as existing contemporaneously. Now that alone determines the position of another thing in time which is the cause of it or of its determinations. Consequently every substance (inasmuch as it can be an effect only in respect of its determinations) must contain the causality of certain determinations in another substance, and at the same time the effects of the causality of the other in itself. That is to say, substances must stand (mediately or immediately) in dynamical community with each other, if co-existence is to be known in any possible experience. But, in regard to objects of experience, that is absolutely necessary without which the experience of these objects would itself be impossible. Consequently it is absolutely necessary that all substances in appearance, in so far as they are co-existent, stand in a relation of complete community of reciprocal action to each other.

The word community has in our language two meanings, *communio* and *commercium*. We employ it in this place in the latter sense – that of a dynamical community, without which even the community of place (*communio spatii*) could not be empirically known. In our experiences it is easy to observe, that it is only the continuous influences in all parts of space that can conduct our senses from one object to another; that the light which plays between our eyes and the heavenly bodies produces a mediating community between them and us, and thereby reveals their co-existence with us; that we cannot empirically change our position (perceive this change), unless the existence of matter throughout the whole of space rendered possible the perception of the positions we occupy; and that this perception can prove the contemporaneous existence of these places only through their reciprocal influence, and thereby also the co-existence of even the most remote objects – although in this case the proof is only mediate. Without community, every perception (of a phenomenon in space) is separated from every other and isolated, and the chain of empirical representations, that is, of experience, must, with the appearance of a new object, begin entirely anew, without the least connection with preceding representations, and without standing towards these even in the relation of time. My intention here is by no means to refute the notion of empty space; for it may exist where our perceptions cannot exist, inasmuch as they cannot reach thereto, and where, therefore, no empirical perception of co-existence takes place. But in this case it is not an object of possible experience.

The following remarks may be useful in the way of explanation. In the mind, all appearances, as contents of a possible experience, must exist in community (*communio*) of apperception, and in so far as it is requisite that objects be represented as co-existent and connected, to that extent they must reciprocally determine the position in time of each other, and thereby constitute a whole. If this subjective community is to rest upon an objective basis, or to be applied to substances as appearances, the perception of one substance must render possible the perception of another, and conversely. For otherwise succession, which is always found in perceptions as apprehensions, would be predicated of external objects, and their representation of their co-existence be thus impossible. But this is a reciprocal influence, that is to say, a real community (*commercium*) of substances, without which therefore the empirical relation of co-existence could not exist in experience. By virtue of this *commercium*, appearances, in so far as they are apart from, and nevertheless in connection with each other, constitute a composite (*compositum reale*). Such *composita* are possible in many different ways. The three dynamical relations then, from which all others spring, are those of inherence, consequence, and composition.

*

These, then, are the three analogies of experience. They are nothing more than principles of the determination of the existence of appearances in time, according to the three *modi* of this determination; to wit, the relation to time itself as a quantity (the quantity of existence, that is, duration), the relation in time as a series of succession, finally, the relation in time as the totality of all existence (simultaneity). This unity of determination in regard to time is thoroughly dynamical; that is to say, time is not considered as that in which experience determines immediately to every existence its position; for this is impossible, inasmuch as absolute time is not an object of perception, by means of which appearances can be connected with each other. On the contrary, the rule of the understanding, through which alone the existence of appearances can receive synthetical unity as regards relations of time, determines for every appearance its position in time, and consequently *a priori*, and with validity for all and every time.

By nature, in the empirical sense of the word, we understand the interconnection of appearances, in respect of their existence, according to necessary rules, that is, laws. There are therefore certain laws (which are moreover *a priori*) which make nature possible; and all empirical laws can exist only by means of experience, and by virtue of those primitive laws through which experience itself becomes possible. The purpose of the analogies is therefore to represent to us the unity of nature in the connection of all appearances under certain exponents, the only business of which is to express the relation of time (in so far as it contains all existence in itself) to the unity of apperception, which can exist in synthesis only according to rules. The combined expression of all is this: All appearances exist in one nature, and must so exist, inasmuch as without this *a priori* unity no unity of experience, and consequently no determination of objects in experience, is possible.

As regards the mode of proof which we have employed in treating of these transcendental laws of nature, and the peculiar character of it, we must make one remark, which will at the same time be important as a guide in every other attempt to demonstrate the truth of intellectual and likewise synthetical propositions *a priori*. Had we endeavoured to prove these analogies dogmatically, that is, from concepts; that is to say, had we employed this method in attempting to show that everything which exists, exists only in that which is permanent – that every event presupposes the existence of something in a preceding state, upon which it follows in conformity with a rule – lastly, that in the manifold, which is co-existent, the states co-exist in connection with each other according to a rule and are thus in a state of communion – all our labour would have been utterly in vain. For mere concepts of things, analyse them as we may, cannot enable us to conclude from the existence of one object to the existence of another or to its mode of existence. What other course was left for us to pursue? This only, to demonstrate the possibility of experience as knowledge in which ultimately all objects must be capable of being presented to us, if the representation of them is to possess any objective reality. Now in this third, this mediating term, the essential form of which consists in the synthetical unity of the apperception of all appearances, we found *a priori* conditions of the universal and necessary determination as to time of all existences in appearance, without which the empirical determination thereof as to time would itself be impossible, and we also discovered rules of synthetical unity *a priori*, by means of which we could anticipate experience. For want of this method, and from the fancy that it was possible to discover a dogmatical proof of the synthetical propositions which are requisite in the empirical employment of the understanding, has it happened, that a proof of the principle of sufficient reason has been so often attempted, and always in vain. The other two analogies nobody has ever though of, although they have always been silently employed[1] because the guiding thread furnished by the categories was wanting, the guide which alone can enable us to discover and to draw attention to every gap of the understanding both in concepts and in principles.

4
THE POSTULATES OF EMPIRICAL THOUGHT

1. That which agrees with the formal conditions (intuition and concept) of experience, is *possible*.
2. That which is connected with the material conditions of experience (sensation) is *real*.
3. That whose connection with the real is determined according to universal conditions of experience is necessary (exists necessarily).

EXPLANATION

The categories of modality possess this peculiarity, that they do not in the least determine the object, or enlarge the concept to which they are annexed as predicates, but only express its relation to the faculty of knowledge. Though my concept of a thing is in itself complete, I am still entitled to ask whether the object of it is merely possible, or whether it is also real, or, if the latter, whether it is also necessary. But hereby the object itself is not more definitely determined in thought, but the question is only in what relation it, including all its determinations, stands to the understanding and its employment in experience, to the empirical faculty of judgment, and to reason in its application to experience.

For this very reason, too, the categories of modality are nothing more than explanations of the concepts of possibility, reality, and necessity, as employed in experience, and at the same time, restrictions of all the categories to empirical use alone, not entitling the transcendental employment of them. For if they are to have

---

[1] The unity of the universe, in which all appearances must be connected, is evidently a mere consequence of the tacitly admitted principle of the community of all substances which are co-existent. For were substances isolated, they could not as parts constitute a whole, and were their connection (reciprocal action of the manifold) not necessary from the very fact of co-existence, we could not conclude from the fact of the latter as a merely ideal relation to the former as a real one. We have, however, shown in its place, that community is the proper ground of the possibility of an empirical knowledge of co-existence, and that we may therefore properly reason from the latter to the former as its condition.

something more than a merely logical significance, and to be something more than a mere analytical expression of the form of *thought*, and to have a relation to *things* and their possibility, reality or necessity, they must concern possible experience and its synthetical unity, in which alone objects of knowledge can be given.

The postulate of the possibility of things requires, that the concept of the things agree with the formal conditions of our experience in general. But this, that is to say, the objective form of experience, contains all the kinds of synthesis which are requisite for the knowledge of objects. A concept which contains a synthesis must be regarded as empty and without reference to an object, if its synthesis does not belong to experience – either as borrowed from it, and in this case it is called an *empirical concept*, or such as is the ground and *a priori* condition of experience (its form), and in this case it is a *pure concept*, a concept which nevertheless belongs to experience, inasmuch as its object can be found in this alone. For where shall we find the mark of the possibility of an object which is thought by means of an *a priori* synthetical concept, if not in the synthesis which constitutes the form of empirical knowledge of objects ? That in such a concept no contradiction exists is indeed a necessary logical condition, but very far from being sufficient to establish the objective reality of the concept, that is, the possibility of such an object as is thought in the concept. Thus, in the concept of a figure which is contained within two straight lines, there is no contradiction, for the concepts of two straight lines and of their junction contain no negation of a figure. The impossibility in such a case does not rest upon the concept in itself, but upon the construction of it in space, that is to say, upon the conditions of space and its determinations. But these have themselves objective reality, that is, they apply to possible things, because they contain *a priori* the form of experience in general.

And now we shall proceed to point out the extensive utility and influence of this postulate of possibility. When I represent to myself a thing that is permanent, so that everything in it which changes belongs merely to its state, from such a concept alone I never can know that such a thing is possible. Or, if I represent to myself something which is so constituted that, when it is posited, something else follows always and infallibly, my thought contains no self-contradiction; but whether such a property as causality is to be found in any possible thing, my thought alone affords no means of judging. Finally, I can represent to myself different things (substances) which are so constituted that the state of one carries with it a consequence in the state of the other, and reciprocally; but whether such a relation is a property of things cannot be perceived from these concepts, which contain a merely arbitrary synthesis. Only from the fact, therefore, that these concepts express *a priori* the relations of perceptions in every experience, do we know that they possess objective reality, that is, transcendental truth; and that independent of experience, though not independent of all relation to the form of an experience in general and its synthetical unity, in which alone objects can be empirically known.

But when we fashion to ourselves new concepts of substances, forces, action, and reaction, from the material presented to us by perception, without following the example of experience in their connection, we create mere chimeras, of the possibility of which we cannot discover any criterion, because we have not taken experience to instruct us, though we have borrowed the concepts from it. Such fictitious concepts derive their character of possibility not, like the categories, *a priori*, as concepts on which all experience depends, but only, *a posteriori*, as concepts given by means of experience itself, and their possibility must either be known *a posteriori* and empirically, or it cannot be known at all. A substance which is permanently present in space, yet without filling it (like that *tertium quid* between matter and the thinking subject which some have tried to introduce), or a peculiar fundamental power of the mind of intuiting the future by anticipation (instead of merely inferring it), or, finally, a power of the mind to place itself in community of thought with other men, however distant they may be – these are concepts the possibility of which has no ground to rest upon. For they are not based upon experience and its known laws; and without experience, they are a merely arbitrary conjuction of thoughts, which, though containing no internal contradiction, has no claim to objective reality, neither, consequently, to the possibility of such an object as is thought in these concepts. As far as concerns reality, it is self-evident that we cannot think such a possibility *in concreto* without the aid of experience; because reality is concerned only with sensation, as the matter of experience, and not with the form of thought, with which we can no doubt indulge in shaping fancies.

But I pass by everything which derives its possibility from reality in experience, and I consider here merely of the possibility of things by means of *a priori* concepts. I maintain, then, that the possibility of things is not derived from such concepts *per se*, but only when considered as formal and objective conditions of experience in general.

It seems, indeed, as if the possibility of a triangle could be known from the concept of it alone (which is certainly independent of experience); for we can certainly give to the concept a corresponding object completely *a priori*, that is to say, we can construct it. But as a triangle is only the form of an object, it must remain a mere product of the imagination, and the possibility of the existence of an object corresponding to it must remain doubtful, unless we can discover some other ground, unless we know that the figure can be thought under the conditions upon which all objects of experience rest. Now, the facts that space is a formal condition *a priori* of external experience, that the formative synthesis, by which we construct a triangle in imagination, is the very same as that we employ in the apprehension of an appearance for the purpose of making an empirical concept of it, are what alone connect the notion of the possibility of such a thing with the concept of it. In the same manner, the possibility of continuous quantities, indeed of quantities in general, for the concepts of them are without exception synthetical, is never evident from the concepts in themselves, but only when they are considered as the formal conditions of the determination of objects in experience. And where, indeed, should we look for objects to correspond to our concepts, if not in experience, by which alone objects are presented to us? It is, however, true that without antecedent experience we can know and characterize the possibility of things, relatively to the formal conditions, under which something is determined in experience as an object, consequently, completely *a priori*. But still this is possible only in relation to experience and within its limits.

The postulate concerning the knowledge of the *reality* of things requires *perception*, consequently conscious sensation, not indeed immediately, that is, of the object itself, whose existence is to be known, but still that the object have some connection with a real perception, in accordance with the analogies of experience, which exhibit all kinds of real connection in experience.

The *mere concept* of a thing does not contain any mark of its existence. For, let the concept be ever so complete, and containing a statement of all the determinations of the thing, the existence of it has nothing to do with all this, but only with the question – whether such a thing is given, so that the perception of it can in every case precede the concept. For the fact that the concept of it precedes the perception, merely indicates the possibility of its existence; it is perception which presents the material to the concept, that is the sole mark of reality. Prior to the perception of the thing, however, and therefore comparatively *a priori*, we are able to know its existence, provided it stands in connection with some perceptions according to the principles of the empirical conjunction of these, that is, in conformity with the analogies of perception. For, in this case, the existence of the supposed thing is connected with our perceptions in a possible experience, and we are able, with the guidance of these analogies, to reason in the series of possible perceptions from a thing which we do really perceive to the thing we do not perceive. Thus, we know the existence of a magnetic matter penetrating all bodies from the perception of the attraction of the steel-filings by the magnet, although the constitution of our organs renders an immediate perception of this matter impossible for us. For, according to the laws of sensibility and the connected context of our perceptions, we should in an experience come also on an immediate empirical intuition of this matter, if our senses were more acute – but this obtuseness does not affect the *form* of possible experience in general. Our knowledge of the existence of things reaches as far as our perceptions, and what may be inferred from them according to empirical laws, extend. If we do not set out from experience, or do not proceed according to the laws of the empirical connection of appearances, our pretensions to discover the existence of a thing which we do not immediately perceive are vain. *Idealism*, however, brings forward powerful objections to these rules for proving existence mediately. This is, therefore, the proper place for its refutation.

REFUTATION OF IDEALISM

Idealism – I mean *material* idealism – is the theory which declares the existence of objects in space outside us to be either doubtful and indemonstrable, or false and impossible. The first is the *problematical* idealism of Descartes, who admits the undoubted certainty of only one empirical assertion (*assertio*), to wit, *I am*. The second is the *dogmatical* idealism of Berkeley, who maintains that space, together with all the objects of which it is the inseparable condition, is a thing which is in itself impossible, and that consequently the objects in space are mere products of the imagination. The dogmatical theory of idealism is unavoidable, if we regard space as a property of things in themselves; for in that case it is, with all to which it serves as a condition, a nonentity. But the foundation for this kind of idealism we have already undermined in the Transcendental Aesthetic. Problematical idealism, which makes no such assertion, but only alleges our incapacity to prove the existence of anything besides ourselves by means of immediate experience, is rational and appropriate to a thorough and philosophical mode of thinking, for it observes the rule, not to form a decisive judgment before sufficient proof be shown. The desired proof must therefore demonstrate that we have *experience* and not mere fancy of external things. For this purpose, we must prove, that our internal and, to Descartes, indubitable experience is itself possible only under the previous assumption of external experience.

THESIS

The mere but empirically determined consciousness of my own existence proves the existence of external objects in space.

PROOF

I am conscious of my own existence as determined in time. All determination in regard to time presupposes the existence of *something permanent* in perception. But this permanent something cannot be something in me, for the very reason that my existence in time can itself only be determined by this permanent something. It follows that the perception of this permanent existence is possible only through a *thing* outside me, and not through the mere *representation* of a thing outside me. Consequently, the determination of my existence in time is possible only through the existence of real things that I perceive outside me. Now, consciousness in time is necessarily connected with the consciousness of the possibility of this determination in time. Hence it follows, that consciousness in time is necessarily connected also with the existence of things outside me, inasmuch as the existence of these things is the condition of determination in time. That is to say, the consciousness of my own existence is at the same time an immediate consciousness of the existence of other things outside me.

Remark I. The reader will observe, that in the foregoing proof the game which idealism plays is turned upon itself, and with more justice. It assumed, that the only immediate experience is internal, and that from this we can only *infer* the existence of external things. This inference from given effects to determinate causes is always unreliable, for it is quite possible that the cause of our representations may lie in ourselves, and that we ascribe it falsely to external things. But our proof shows that external experience is properly immediate,[1] that only by virtue of it – not, indeed, the consciousness of our own existence, but certainly the determination of our existence in time, that is, internal experience – is possible. It is true, that the representation *I am*, which is the expression of the consciousness which can accompany all my thoughts, is that which immediately includes the existence of a subject. But in this representation we cannot find any knowledge of the subject, and therefore also no empirical knowledge, that is, experience. For experience contains, in addition to the thought of something existing, intuition, and in this case it must be internal intuition, that is, time, in relation to which the subject must be determined. But the existence of external things is absolutely requisite for this purpose, so that it follows that internal experience is itself possible only mediately and through external experience.

Remark II. With this thesis all empirical use of our faculty of knowledge in the determination of time is in perfect accordance. Its truth is supported by the fact, that it is possible to perceive a determination of time only by means of a change in external relations (motion) to the permanent in space (for example, the sun's motion relative to the objects of this earth). But this is not all. We find that we possess nothing permanent on which to base the concept of a substance as intuition, except *matter*. This idea of permanence is not itself derived from external experience, but is an *a priori* necessary condition of all determination of time, consequently also of the internal sense in reference to our own existence, and that through the existence of external things. In the representation *I*, the consciousness of myself is not an intuition, but a merely intellectual representation produced by the spontaneous activity of a thinking subject. It follows, that this *I* does not have any predicate of intuition, which, being permanent, could serve as correlate to the

---

[1] The *immediate* consciousness of the existence of external things is, in the preceding thesis, not presupposed, but proved, be the possibility of this consciousness understood by us or not. The question as to the possibility of it would stand thus: Have we an internal sense, but no external sense, and is our belief in external perception a mere delusion? But it is evident that, in order merely to fancy to ourselves anything *as* external, that is, to present it to the sense in intuition, we must already possess an external sense, and must thereby distinguish immediately the mere receptivity of an external intuition from the spontaneity which characterizes every act of imagination. For merely to imagine also an external sense, would annihilate the faculty of intuition itself which is to be determined by the imagination.

determination of time in the internal sense – in the same way as impenetrability is the correlate of matter as an empirical intuition.

Remark III. From the fact that the existence of external things is a necessary condition of the possibility of a particular consciousness of ourselves, it does not follow that every intuitive representation of external things involves the existence of these things, for their representations may very well be the mere products of the imagination (in dreams as well as in madness); though, indeed, these are themselves created by the reproduction of previous external perceptions, which, as has been shown, are possible only through the reality of external objects. The sole aim of our remarks has, however, been to prove that internal experience in general is possible only through external experience in general. Whether this or that supposed experience be purely imaginary, must be discovered from its particular determinations, and by comparing these with the criteria of all real experience.

*

Finally, as regards the third postulate, it applies to material necessity in existence, and not to merely formal and logical necessity in the connection of concepts. Now as we cannot know completely *a priori* the existence of any object of the senses, though we can do so comparatively *a priori*, that is, relatively to some other previously given existence – a knowledge, however, which can only be of such an existence as must be contained in the connection of experience, of which the previously given perception is a part – the necessity of existence can never be known from concepts, but always from its connection with that which is an object of perception. But the only existence known under the condition of other given appearances, as necessary, is the existence of effects from given causes in conformity with the laws of causality. It is consequently not the necessity of the existence of things (as substances), but the necessity of the state of things that we know, and that not immediately, but by means of the existence of other states given in perception, according to empirical laws of causality. Hence it follows, that the criterion of necessity is to be found only in the law of a possible experience – that everything which happens is determined *a priori* in the appearance by its cause. Thus we know only the necessity of *effects* in nature, the causes of which are given us. Moreover, the criterion of necessity in existence possesses no application beyond the field of possible experience, and even in this it is not valid of the existence of things as substances, because these can never be considered as empirical effects, or as something that happens and has a beginning. Necessity, therefore, regards only the relations of appearances according to the dynamical law of causality, and the possibility grounded thereon, of reasoning from some given existence (of a cause) *a priori* to another existence (of an effect). *Everything that happens is hypothetically necessary*, is a principle which subjects the changes that take place in the world to a law, that is, to a rule of necessary existence, without which nature herself could not possibly exist. Hence the proposition, *Nothing happens by blind chance (in mundo non datur casus)*, is an *a priori* law of nature. The case is the same with the proposition, *Necessity in nature is not blind*, that is, it is conditioned, consequently intelligible necessity (*non datur fatum*). Both laws subject the play of change to *a nature of things* (as appearances), or, which is the same thing, to the unity of the understanding, and through the understanding alone can changes belong to an experience, as the synthetical unity of appearances. Both belong to the class of dynamical principles. The former is properly a consequence of the principle of causality – one of the analogies of experience. The latter belongs to the principles of modality, which to the determination of causality adds the concept of necessity, which is itself, however, subject to a rule of the understanding. The principle of continuity forbids any *leap* in the series of appearances regarded as changes (*in mundo non datur saltus*); and likewise, in the totality of all empirical intuitions in space, any break or gap between two appearances (*non datur hiatus*) – for we can so express the principle, that experience can admit nothing which proves the existence of a vacuum, or which even admits it as a part of an empirical synthesis. For, as regards a void, which we may think as outside and beyond the field of possible experience (the world), such a question cannot come before the tribunal of mere understanding, which decides only upon questions that concern the employment of given appearances for the construction of empirical knowledge. It is rather a problem for ideal reason, which passes beyond the sphere of a possible experience, and aims at forming a judgment of that which surrounds and circumscribes it, and the proper place for the consideration of it is the transcendental dialectic. These four propositions, *In mundo non datur hiatus, non datur saltus, non datur casus, non datur fatum*, as well as all principles of transcendental origin, we could very easily exhibit in their proper order, that is in conformity with the order of the categories, and assign to each its proper place. But the already practised reader will do this for himself, or discover the clue to such an arrangement. But the combined result of all is simply this, to admit into the empirical synthesis nothing whch might cause a break in or be foreign to the understanding and the continuous connection of all appearances, that is, the unity of the concepts of the understanding. For in the understanding alone is the unity of experience, in which all perceptions must have their assigned place, possible.

Whether the field of possibility be greater than that of reality, and whether the field of the latter be itself greater than that of necessity, are interesting enough questions, and quite capable of synthetical solution, questions, however, which come under the jurisdiction of reason alone. For they are tantamount to asking, whether all things as appearances do without exception belong to the totality and connected whole of a single experience, of which every given perception is a part which therefore cannot be conjoined with any other appearance – or, whether my perceptions can belong to more than one possible experience. The understanding gives to experience, according to the subjective and formal conditions, of sensibility as well as of apperception, the rules which alone make this experience possible. Other forms of intuition besides those of space and time, other forms of understanding besides the discursive forms of thought, or of knowledge by means of concepts, we can neither imagine nor make intelligible to ourselves; and even if we could, they would still not belong to experience, which is the only mode of knowledge by which objects are presented to us. Whether other perceptions besides those which belong to the total of our possible experience, and consequently whether some other sphere of matter exists, the understanding has no power to decide, its proper occupation being with the synthesis of that which is given. Moreover, the poverty of the usual arguments which go to prove the existence of a vast sphere of possibility, of which all that is real (every object of experience) is but a small part, is very remarkable. 'All real is possible'; from this follows naturally, according to the logical laws of conversion, the particular proposition: 'Some possible is real.' Now this seems to be equivalent to: 'Much is possible that is not real.' No doubt it does seem as if we ought to consider the sum of the possible to be greater than that of the real, from the fact that something must be added to the former to constitute the latter. But this notion of adding to the possible is absurd. For that which is not in the sum of the possible, and consequently requires to be added to it, is manifestly impossible. In addition to accordance with the formal conditions of experience, the understanding requires a connection with some perception; but that which is connected with this perception is real, even though it is not immediately perceived. But that another series of appearances, in complete coherence with that which is given in perception, consequently more than one all-embracing experience is possible, is an inference which cannot be concluded from what is given to us in experience, and still less without anything being given to us, for nothing can be thought without material. That which is possible only under conditions which are themselves merely possible, is not possible *in any respect*. And yet we can find no more certain ground on which to base the discussion of the question whether the sphere of possibility is wider than that of experience.

I have merely mentioned these questions, that in treating of the concepts of the understanding, there might be no omission of anything that, in the common opinion, belongs to them. In reality, however, the notion of absolute possibility (possibility which is valid in every respect) is not a mere concept of the understanding, and cannot in any way be employed empirically, but belongs to reason alone, which passes the bounds of all empirical use of the understanding. We have, therefore, contented ourselves with a merely critical remark, leaving the subject to be explained in the sequel.

Before concluding this fourth section, and at the same time the system of all principles of the pure understanding, it seems proper to mention the reasons which induced me to call the principles of modality postulates. This expression I do not use here in the sense which some more recent philosophers, contrary to its meaning with mathematicians, to whom the word properly belongs, attach to it – that of a proposition, namely, immediately certain, requiring neither justification nor proof. For if, in the case of synthetical propositions, however evident they may be, we accord to them without deduction, and merely on the strength of their own pretensions, unqualified assent, all critique of the understanding is entirely lost; and, as there is no want of bold pretensions, which the common belief (though this is no credential) does not reject, the understanding lies exposed to every delusion and conceit, without the power of refusing its assent to those assertions, which, though illegitimate, demand acceptance as genuine axioms. When, therefore, to the concept of a thing an *a priori* determination is synthetically added, such a proposition must obtain, if not a proof, at least a deduction of the legitimacy of its assertion.

The principles of modality are, however, not objectively synthetical, for the predicates of possibility, reality, and necessity do not in the least augment the concept of that of which they are affirmed, inasmuch as they contribute nothing to the representation of the object. But as they are, nevertheless, always synthetical, they are so merely subjectively. That is to say, they have a reflective power, and add to the concept of a thing (something real), of which, in other respects, they affirm nothing, the faculty of knowledge in which the concept originates and has its seat. So that if the concept merely agrees with the formal conditions of experience, its object is called possible; if it is in connection with perception (sensation, as the material of the senses), and determined thereby, the object is real; if it is determined according to concepts by means of the connection of perceptions, the object is called necessary. The principles of modality therefore predicate of a concept nothing more than the procedure of the faculty of knowledge which generated it. Now a postulate in mathematics is a practical proposition which contains nothing by the synthesis by which we present an object to ourselves, and produce the concept of it, for example – 'With a given line, to describe a circle upon a plane, from a given point'; and such a proposition does not admit of proof, because the procedure, which it requires, is exactly that by which alone it is possible to generate the concept of such a figure. With the same right, accordingly, can we postulate the principles of modality, because they do not augment[1] the concept of a thing, but merely indicate the manner in which it is connected with the faculty of knowledge.

GENERAL REMARK ON THE SYSTEM OF PRINCIPLES

It is very remarkable that we cannot perceive the possibility of a thing from the category alone, but must always have an intuition, by which to make evident the objective reality of the pure concept of the understanding. Take, for example, the categories of relation. How (1) a thing can exist only as a *subject*, and not as a mere determination of other things, that is, can be *substance*; or how

---

[1] When I think the *reality* of a thing, I do really think more than the possibility, but not *in the thing*; for that can never contain more in reality than was contained in its complete possibility. But while the notion of possibility is merely the notion of a position of a thing in relation to the understanding (its empirical use), reality is the conjunction of the thing with perception.

(2), because something exists, some other thing must exist, consequently how a thing can be a cause; or how (3), when several things exist, from the fact that one of these things exists, some consequence to the others follows, and reciprocally, and in this way a community of substances can be possible – are questions whose solution cannot be obtained from mere concepts. The very same is the case with the other categories; for example, how a thing can be equal to a number of things taken together, that is, can be a quantity, and so on. So long as we do not have intuition we cannot know, whether we do really think an object by the categories, and where an object can anywhere be found suited to them, and thus it is confirmed that the categories are not in themselves knowledge, but mere *forms of thought* for the construction of knowledge from given intuitions. For the same reason it is true that from categories alone no synthetical proposition can be made. For example: 'In every existence there is substance', that is, something that can exist only as a subject and not as mere predicate; or, 'Everything is a quantity' – to construct propositions such as these, we require something to enable us to go out beyond the given concept and connect another with it. For the same reason the attempt to prove a synthetical proposition by means of mere concepts, for example: 'Everything that exists contingently has a cause', has never succeeded. We could never get further than proving that, without this relation to concepts, we could *not conceive* the existence of the contingent, that is, could not *a priori* through the understanding know the existence of such a thing; but it does not hence follow that this is also the condition of the possibility of the thing itself that is said to be contingent. If, accordingly, we look back to our proof of the principle of causality, we shall find that we were able to prove it as valid only of objects of possible experience, and, indeed, only as itself the principle of the possibility of experience, consequently of the *knowledge* of an object given in *empirical intuition*, and not from mere concepts. That, however, the proposition: 'Everything that is contingent must have a cause', is evident to everyone merely from concepts, is not to be denied. But in this case the concept of the contingent is thought as involving not the category of modality (as that the non-existence of which can be *conceived*), but that of relation (as that which can exist only as the consequence of something else), and so it is really an identical proposition: 'That which can exist only as a consequence, has a cause.' In fact, when we have to give examples of contingent existence, we always refer to *changes*, and not merely to the possibility of *conceiving the oppoosite*.[1] But change is an event, which, as such, is possible only through a cause, and considered *per se* its non-existence is therefore possible, and we become cognizant of its contingency from the fact that it can exist only as the effect of a cause. Hence, if a thing is assumed to be contingent, it is an analytical proposition to say, it has a cause.

But it is still more remarkable that, to understand the possibility of things according to the categories, and thus to demonstrate the *objective reality* of the latter, we require not merely intuitions, but *external intuitions*. If, for example, we take the pure concepts of relation, we find that (1) for the purpose of presenting to the concept of *substance* something *permanent* in intuition corresponding thereto, and thus of demonstrating the objective reality of this concept, we require an intuition (of matter) in *space*, because space alone is permanent and determines things as such, while time, and with it all that is in the internal sense, is in a state of continual flow; (2) in order to represent *change* as the intuition corresponding to the concept of causality, we require motion as change in space; in fact, it is through it alone that changes, the possibility of which no pure understanding can conceive, are capable of being intuited. Change is the connection of determinations contradictorily opposed to each other in the existence of one and the same thing. Now, how it is possible that out of a given state one quite opposite to it in the same thing should follow, reason without an example can not only not conceive, but cannot even make intelligible without intuition; and this intuition is the motion of a point in space; the existence of which in different spaces (as a consequence of opposite determinations) alone makes the intuition of change possible. For, in order to make even internal change capable of being thought, we require to represent time, as the form of the internal sense, figuratively by a line, and the internal change by the drawing of that line (motion),

---

[1] We can easily conceive the non-existence of matter; but the ancients did not, therefore, infer its contingency. But even the alteration of the existence and non-existence of a given state in a thing, in which all change consists, by no means proves the contingency of that state – the ground of proof being the reality of its opposite. For example, a body is in a state of rest after motion, but we cannot infer the contingency of the motion from the fact that the former is the opposite of the latter. For this opposite is merely a logical and not a real opposite to the other. If we wish to demonstrate the contingency of the motion, what we ought to prove is, that, *instead* of the motion which took place in the preceding point of time, it was possible for the body to have been *then* in rest, not, that it is *afterwards* in rest; for, in this case, both opposites are perfectly consistent with each other.

and consequently are obliged to employ external intuition to be able to represent the successive existence of ourselves in different states. The proper ground of this fact is, that all change to be perceived as change presupposes something permanent in intuition, while in the internal sense no permanent intuition is to be found. Lastly, the objective possibility of the category of *community* cannot be conceived by mere reason, and consequentely its objective reality cannot be demonstrated without an intuition, and in particular external intuition in space. For how can we conceive the possibility of community, that is, when several substances exist, that some effect on the existence of the one follows from the existence of the other, and reciprocally, and therefore that, because something exists in the latter, something else must exist in the former, which could not be understood from its own existence alone? For this is the very essence of community – which is inconceivable as a property of things which are perfectly isolated. Hence, Leibniz, in attributing to the substances of the world – as thought by the understanding alone – a community, required the mediating aid of a deity; for, from their existence, such a property seemed to him with justice inconceivable. But we can very easily conceive the possibility of community (of substances as appearances) if we represent them to ourselves as in space, consequently in external intuition. For external intuition contains in itself *a priori* formal external relations, as the conditions of the possibility of the real relations of action and reaction, and therefore of the possibility of community. With the same ease can it be demonstrated, that the possibility of things as *quantities*, and consequently the objective reality of the category of *quantity*, can be grounded only in external intuition, and that by its means alone is the notion of quantity appropriated by the internal sense. But I must avoid prolixity, and leave the task of illustrating this by examples to the reader's own reflection.

The above remarks are of the greatest importance, not only for the confirmation of our previous refutation of idealism, but still more when the subject of *self-knowledge* by mere internal consciousness and the determination of our own nature without the aid of external empirical intuitions is under discussion, in order to indicate the limits of such knowledge.

The result of the whole of this part of this whole section is, therefore – All principles of the pure understanding are nothing more than *a priori* principles of the possibility of experience, and to experience alone do all *a priori* synthetical propositions relate — indeed, their possibility itself rests entirely on this relation.

TRANSCENDENTAL DOCTRINE OF JUDGMENT

(*Analytic of Principles*)

CHAPTER III: THE GROUND OF THE DISTINCTION OF ALL OBJECTS IN GENERAL INTO PHENOMENA AND NOUMENA

We have now not only traversed the region of the pure understanding, and carefully surveyed every part of it, but we have also measured it, and assigned to everything therein its proper place. But this land is an island, and enclosed by nature herself within unchangeable limits. It is the land of truth (an attractive word!), surrounded by a wide and stormy ocean, the region of illusion, where many a fog-bank, many an iceberg, seems to the mariner on his voyage of discovery, a new country, and while constantly deluding him with vain hopes, engages him in dangerous adventures, from which he never can desist, and which yet he never can bring to a termination. But before venturing upon this sea, in order to explore it in its whole extent, and to arrive at a certainty whether anything is to be discovered there, it will not be without advantage if we cast our eyes upon the chart of the land that we are about to leave, and to ask ourselves, firstly, whether we cannot rest perfectly contented with what it contains, or whether we must not of necessity be contented with it, if we can find nowhere else a solid foundation to build upon; and, secondly, by what title we possess this land itself, and how we hold it secure against all hostile claims. Although, in the course of the Analytic, we have already given sufficient answers to these questions, yet a summary recapitulation of these solutions may be useful in strengthening our conviction, by uniting in one point the momenta of the arguments.

We have seen that everything which the understanding draws from itself, without borrowing from experience, it nevertheless possesses only for the use in experience. The principles of the pure understanding, whether constitutive *a priori* (as the mathematical principles), or merely regulative (as the dynamical), contain nothing but the pure schema, as it were, of possible experience. For experience possesses its unity from the synthetical unity which the understanding, originally and from itself, imparts to the synthesis of the imagination in relation to apperception, and in *a priori* relation to and agreement with which appearances as data for possible knowledge, must stand. But although these rules of the understanding are not only *a priori* true, but the very source of all truth, that is, of the accordance of our knowledge with objects, and on this ground, that they contain the basis of the possibility of experience, as the totality of all knowledge, it seems to us not enough to propound what is true – we desire also to be told what we want to know. If, then, we learn nothing more by this critical examination, than what we should have practised in the merely empirical use of the understanding, without any such subtle inquiry, the presumption is, that the advantage we reap from it is not worth the labour bestowed upon it. It may certainly be answered, that no rash curiosity is more prejudicial to the enlargement of our knowledge than that which must know beforehand the utility of this or that piece of information which we seek, before we have entered on the needful investigations, and before one could form the least conception of its utility, even though it were placed before our eyes. But there is one advantage in such transcendental inquiries which can be made comprehensible to the dullest and most reluctant learner – this, namely, that the understanding which is occupied merely with empirical exercise, and does not reflect on the sources of its own knowledge, may exercise its functions very well and very successfully, but is quite unable to do one thing, and that of very great importance, to determine, namely, the bounds that limit its employment, and to know what lies within or without its own sphere. This purpose can be obtained only by such profound investigations as we have instituted. But if it cannot distinguish whether certain questions lie within its horizon or not, it can never be sure either as to its claims or possessions, but must lay its account with many humiliating corrections, when it transgresses, as it unavoidably will, the limits of its own territory, and loses itself in fanciful opinions and blinding illusions.

That the understanding, therefore, cannot make of its *a priori* principles, or even of its concepts, other than an empirical use, is a proposition which leads to the most important results. A transcendental use is made of a concept in a principle, when it is referred to things *in general* and considered as things *in themselves*; an empirical use, when it is referred merely to appearances, that is, to objects of a possible *experience*. That the latter use of a concept is the only admissible one, is evident from the following reasons. For every concept are requisite, firstly, the logical form of a concept (of thought) in general; and, secondly, the possibility of presenting to this an object to which it may apply. Failing this latter, it has no sense, and is utterly void of content, although it may contain the logical function for constructing a concept from certain data. Now an object cannot be given to a concept otherwise than by intuition, and, even if a pure intuition antecedent to the object is *a priori* possible, this pure intuition can itself obtain objective validity only from empirical intuition, of which it is itself but the form. All concepts, therefore, and with them all principles, however they may be *a priori* possible, relate to empirical intuitions, that is, to data towards a possible experience. Without this they possess no objective validity, but are mere play of imagination or of understanding with their respective representations. Let us take, for example, the concepts of mathematics, and first in its pure intuitions. 'Space has three dimensions' – 'Between two points there can only be one straight line', etc. Although all these principles, and the representation of the object with which this science occupies itself, are generated in the mind entirely *a priori*, they would nevertheless have no significance if we were not always able to exhibit their significance in and by means of appearances (empirical objects). Hence it is requisite that an abstract concept be *made sensible*, that is, that an object corresponding to it in intuition be forthcoming, otherwise the concept remains, as we say, without *sense*, that is, without meaning. Mathematics fulfils this requirement by the construction of the figure, which is an appearance evident to the senses. The same science finds support and significance in number; this in its turn finds it in the fingers, or in beads of the abacus, or in lines and points. The concept itself is always produced *a priori*, together with the synthetical principles or formulas from such concepts; but the proper employment of them, and their application to objects, can exist nowhere but in experience, the possibility of which, as regards its form, they contain *a priori*.

That this is also the case with all of the categories and the principles based upon them, is evident from the fact, that we cannot provide a real definition of any of them, hence we cannot render intelligible the possibility of an object corresponding to them without having recourse to the conditions of sensibility, consequently, to the form of appearances, to which, as their only proper objects, their use must therefore be confined, inasmuch as, if this condition is removed, all significance, that is, all relation to an object, disappears, and no example can be found to make it comprehensible what sort of things we ought to think under such concepts.

The concept of quantity cannot be explained except by saying that it is the determination of a thing whereby it can be thought how many times a unit is placed in it. But this 'how many times' is based upon successive repetition, consequently upon time and the synthesis of the homogeneous therein. Reality, in contradistinction to negation, can be explained only by thinking a time which is either filled therewith or is void. If I leave out the notion of permanence (which is existence in all time), there remains in the concept of substance nothing but the logical notion of subject, a notion of which I endeavour to realize by representing to myself something that can exist only as a subject. But not only am I perfectly ignorant of any conditions under which this logical prerogative can belong to a thing, I can make nothing out of the notion, and draw no inference from it, because no object to which to apply the concept is determined, and we consequently do not know whether it has any meaning at all. In like manner, if I leave out the notion of time, in which something follows upon some other thing in conformity with a rule, I can find nothing in the pure category, except that there is a something of such a sort that from it a conclusion may be drawn as to the existence of some other thing. But in this case it would not only be impossible to distinguish between a cause and an effect, but, as this power to make inferences requires conditions of which I am quite ignorant, the concept is not determined as to the mode in which it ought to apply to an object. The so-called principle: Everything that is contingent has a cause, comes with a gravity and self-assumed authority that seems to require no support from without. But, I ask, what is meant by contingent? The answer is, that the non-existence of which is possible. But I should like very well to know by what means this possibility of non-existence is to be known, if we do not represent to ourselves a succession in the series of appearances, and in this succession an existence which follows a non-existence, or conversely, consequently, change. For to say, that the non-existence of a thing is not self-contradictory, is a lame appeal to a logical condition, which is no doubt a necessary condition of the existence of the concept, but is far from being sufficient for the real objective possibility of non-existence. I can annihilate in thought every existing substance without self-contradiction, but I cannot infer from this their objective contingency in existence, that is to say, the possibility of their non-existence in itself. As regards the category of community, it may easily be inferred that, as the pure categories of substance and causality are incapable of a definition and explanation sufficient to determine their object without the aid of intuition, the category of reciprocal causality in the relation of substances to each other (*commercium*) is just as little susceptible thereof. Possibility, existence, and necessity nobody has ever yet been able to explain without being guilty of manifest tautology, when the definition has been drawn entirely from the pure understanding. For the substitution of the logical possibility of the *concept* – the condition of which is that it be not self-contradictory, for the transcendental possibility of *things* – the condition of which is, that there be an object corresponding to the concept, is a trick which can only deceive the inexperienced.[1]

It follows incontestably, that the pure concepts of the understanding are incapable of *transcendental*, and must always be of *empirical* use alone, and that the principles of the pure understanding relate only to the general conditions of a possible experience, to objects of the senses, and never to things in general, apart from the mode in which we intuit them.

The Transcendental Analytic has accordingly this important result, to wit, that the understanding is competent to effect nothing *a priori*, except the anticipation of the form of a possible experience in general, and, that, as that which is not appearance cannot be an object of experience, it can never overstep the limits of sensibility, within which alone objects are presented to us. Its principles are merely principles of the exposition of appearances and the proud name of an ontology, which professes to present synthetical knowledge *a priori* of things in general in a systematic doctrine (e.g. the principle of causality), must give place to the modest title of analytic of the pure understanding.

Thought is the act of referring a given intuition to an object. If the mode of this intuition is unknown to us, the object is merely

---

[1] In one word, to none of these concepts belongs a corresponding object, and consequently their real possibility cannot be demonstrated, if we take away sensible intuition – the only intuition which we possess, and there then remains nothing but the *logical* possibility, that is, the fact that the concept or thought is possible – which, however, is not the question ; what we want to know being, whether it relates to an object and thus possesses any meaning.

transcendental, and the concept of the understanding is employed only transcendentally, that is, to produce unity in the thought of a manifold in general. Now a pure category, in which all conditions of sensible intuition – as the only intuition we possess – are abstracted, does not determine an object, but merely expresses the thought of an object in general, according to different modes. Now, to employ a concept, the function of judgment is required, by which an object is subsumed under the concept, consequently the at least formal condition, under which something can be given in intuition. Failing this condition of judgment (schema), subsumption is impossible; for there is in such a case nothing given, which may be subsumed under the concept. The merely transcendental use of the categories is therefore, in fact, no use at all, and has no determined, or even, as regards its form, determinable object. Hence it follows, that the pure category is unable to establish a synthetical *a priori* principle, and that the principles of the pure understanding are only of empirical and never of transcendental use, and that beyond the sphere of possible experience no synthetical *a priori* principles are possible.

It may be advisable, therefore, to express ourselves thus. The pure categories, apart from the formal conditions of sensibility, have a merely transcendental *meaning*, but are nevertheless not of transcendental *use*, because this is in itself impossible, inasmuch as all the conditions of any employment of them (in judgments) are absent, to wit, the formal conditions of the subsumption of an object under these concepts. As, therefore, in the character of pure categories, they must be employed empirically, and cannot be employed transcendentally, they are of no use at all, when separated from sensibility, that is, they cannot be applied to an object. They are merely the pure form of the employment of the understanding in respect of objects in general and of thought, without its being at the same time possible to think or to determine any object by their means.

But there lurks at the foundation of this subject an illusion which it is difficult to avoid. The categories are not based, as regards their origin, upon sensibility, like the *forms of intuition*, space, and time; they seem, therefore, to be capable of an application beyond the sphere of sensible objects. They are nothing but mere *forms of thought*, which contain only the logical faculty of uniting *a priori* in consciousness the manifold given in intuition. Apart, then, from the only intuition possible for us, they have still less meaning than the pure sensible forms, space and time, for through them an object is at least given, while a mode of connection of the manifold, when the intuition which alone gives the manifold is wanting, has no meaning at all. At the same time, when we designate certain objects as appearances or sensible existences (phenomena), thus distinguishing our mode of intuiting them from their own nature as things in themselves, it is evident that by this very distinction we as it were place the latter, considered in this their own nature, although we do not so intuit them, in opposition to the former, or, on the other hand, we do so place other possible things, which are not objects of our senses, but are thought by the understanding alone, and call them intelligible existences (noumena). Now the question arises, whether the pure concepts of our understanding do possess significance in respect of these latter, and may possibly be a mode of knowing them.

But we are met at the very beginning with an ambiguity, which may easily occasion great misapprehension. The understanding, when it terms an object in a certain relation phenomenon, at the same time forms out of this relation a representation or notion of an *object in itself*, and hence believes that it can form also *concepts* of such objects. Now as the understanding possesses no other concepts besides the categories, it takes for granted that an object considered as a thing in itself must be capable of being thought by means of these pure concepts of the understanding, and is thereby led to hold the perfectly undetermined concept of an intelligible existence, a something outside our sensibility, for a *determinate* concept of an existence which we can know in some way or other by means of the understanding.

If, by the term noumenon, we understand a thing so far as it is *not an object of our sensible intuition*, thus making abstraction of our mode of intuiting it, this is a noumenon in the *negative* sense of the word. But if we understand by it an *object of a non-sensible intuition*, we in this case assume a peculiar mode of intuition, an intellectual intuition, to wit, which does not, however, belong to use, of the very possibility of which we have no notion – and this is a noumenon in the *positive* sense.

The doctrine of sensibility is also the doctrine of noumena in the negative sense, that is, of things which the understanding is obliged to think apart from any relation to our mode of intuition, consequently not as mere appearances, but as things in themselves. But the understanding at the same time comprehends that it cannot employ its categories for the consideration of things in themselves, because these possess significance only in relation to the unity of intuitions in space and time, and that they are competent to determine this unity by means of general *a priori* connecting concepts only on account of the pure ideality of space and time. Where this unity of time is not to be met with, as is the case with noumena, the whole use, indeed the whole meaning of the categories is entirely lost, for even the possibility of things to correspond to the categories is in this case incomprehensible. On this point, I need only refer the reader to what I have said at the commencement of the General Remark appended to the foregoing chapter. Now, the possibility of a thing can never be proved from the fact that the concept of it is not self-contradictory, but only by means of an intuition corresponding to the concept. If, therefore, we wish to apply the categories to objects which cannot be regarded as appearances, we must have an intuition different from the sensible, and in this case the objects would be noumena *in the positive sense* of the word. Now, as such an intuition, that is, an intellectual intuition, lies absolutely beyond what we could know, it is absolutely impossible for the categories to possess any application beyond the limits of experience. It may be true that there are intelligible existences to which our faculty of sensible intuition has no relation, but our concepts of the understanding, as mere forms of thought for our sensible intuition, do not extend to these. What, therefore, we call noumenon, must be understood by us as such in a *negative* sense.

If I take away from an empirical intuition all thought (by means of the categories), there remains no knowledge of any object; for by means of mere intuition nothing is thought, and from the existence of such or such an affection of sensibility in me, it does not follow that this representation has any relation to an object. But if I take away all intuition, there still remains the form of thought, that is, the mode of determining an object for the manifold of a possible intuition. Thus the categories do in some measure really extend further than sensible intuition, inasmuch as they think objects in general, without regard to the mode (of sensibility) in which these objects are given. But they do not for this reason apply to and determine a wider sphere of objects, because we cannot assume that such can be given, without presupposing the possibility of another than the sensible mode of intuition, a supposition we are not justified in making.

I call a concept problematical which contains in itself no contradiction, and which is connected with other knowledge as a limitation of given concepts, but whose objective reality cannot be known in any manner. The concept of a *noumenon*, that is, of a thing which must be thought not as an object of sense, but as a thing in itself (solely through the pure understanding), is not self-contradictory, for we are not entitled to maintain that sensibility is the only possible mode of intuition. Nay, further, this concept is necessary to prevent us from extending sensible intuition to things in themselves, and thus to limit the objective validity of sensible knowledge; for things in themselves, which lie beyond its province, are called noumena for the very purpose of indicating that knowledge does not extend its application to all that the understanding thinks. But, after all, the possibility of such noumena is quite incomprehensible, and beyond the sphere of appearances, all is for us a mere void; that is to say, we possess an understanding whose province does *problematically* extend beyond this sphere, but we do not possess an intuition, indeed, not even the concept of a possible intuition, by means of which objects beyond the region of sensibility could be given us, and in reference to which the understanding might be employed *assertorically*. The concept of a noumenon is therefore merely a *limitative concept*, and therefore only of negative use. But it is not an arbitrary or fictitious notion, but is connected with the limitation of sensibility, without, however, being capable of presenting us with any positive datum beyond this sphere.

The division of objects into phenomena and noumena, and of the world into a world of the senses and a world of the understanding is therefore quite inadmissible in a *positive sense*, although concepts do certainly admit of a division into sensible and intellectual; for the latter concepts (even in the Newtonian account of the structure of the universe) have no determinate object corresponding to them, and cannot therefore possess objective validity. If we abandon the senses, how can it be made conceivable that the categories (which are the only concepts that could serve as concepts for noumena) have any meaning at all, inasmuch as something more than the mere unity of thought, namely, a possible intuition, is requisite for their application to an object? The concept of a noumenon, considered as merely problematical, is, however, not only admissible, but, as a limitative concept of sensibility, absolutely necessary. But, in this case, a noumenon is not a particular *intelligible object* for our understanding; on the contrary, the kind of understanding to which it could belong is itself a problem, for we cannot form the most distant concept of the possibility of an understanding which should know an object, not discursively by means of categories, but intuitively in a non-sensible intuition. Our understanding attains in this way a sort of negative extension. That is to say, it is not limited by, but rather limits, sensibility, by giving the name of noumena to things, not considered as appearances, but as things in themselves. But it at the same time prescribes limits to itself, for it confesses itself unable to know these by means of categories, and hence is compelled to think them merely as an unknown something.

I find, however, in the writings of modern authors, an entirely different use of the expressions, *mundus sensibilis* and *intelligibilis*, which quite departs from the meaning of the ancients – a meaning in which, indeed, there is to be found no difficulty, but which at the same time depends on mere verbal quibbling. According to this meaning, some have chosen to call the totality of appearances, in so far as it is intuited, *mundus sensibilis*, but in so far as the connection thereof is thought according to general laws of thought, *mundus intelligibilis*. Astronomy, in so far as we mean by the word the mere observation of the starry heaven, may represent the former; a system of astronomy, such as the Copernican or Newtonian, the latter. But such twisting of words is a mere sophistical subterfuge, to avoid a difficult question, by modifying its meaning to suit our own convenience. To be sure, understanding and reason are employed in the knowledge of appearances; but the question is, whether these can be applied when the object is not a phenomenon (noumenon) – and in this sense we regard it if it is thought as given to the understanding alone, and not to the senses. The question therefore is, whether over and above the empirical use of the understanding, a transcendental use is possible, which applies to the noumenon as an object. This question we have answered in the negative.

When therefore we say, the senses represent objects *as they appear*, the understanding *as they are*, the latter statement must not be understood in a transcendental, but only in an empirical significa-cation, that is, as they must be represented in the complete connection of appearances, and not according to what they may be, apart from their relation to possible experience, hence to senses in general, consequently not as objects of the pure understanding. For this must ever remain unknown to us. Nay, it is also quite unknown to us, whether any such transcendental or extraordinary knowledge is possible under any circumstances, at least, whether it is possible by means of our categories. *Understanding* and *sensibility*, with us, can determine objects only *in conjunction*. If we separate them, we have intuitions without concepts, or concepts without intuitions; in both cases, representations, which we cannot apply to any determinate object.

If, after all our inquiries and explanations, any one still hesitates to abandon the mere transcendental use of the categories, let him attempt to construct with them a synthetical proposition. It would, of course, be unnecessary for this purpose to construct an analytical proposition, for that does not extend the understanding, but, being concerned only about what is thought in the concept itself, it leaves it quite undecided whether the concept has any relation to objects, or merely indicates the unity of thought – complete abstraction being made of the ways in which an object may be given: in such a proposition, it is sufficient for the understanding to know what lies in the concept – to what it applies, is to it indifferent. The attempt must therefore be made with a synthetical and so-called transcendental principle, for example: Everything that exists, exists as substance or as a determination of substance, or, Everything that is contingent exists as an effect of some other thing, viz. of its cause. Now I ask, whence can the understanding draw these synthetical propositions, when the concepts contained therein do not relate to possible experience but to things in themselves (noumena)? Where is to be found the *third something*, which is always requisite in a synthetical proposition, which may connect in the same proposition concepts which have no logical (analytical) connection with each other? The proposition never will be demonstrated, nay, more, the possibility of any such pure assertion never can be shown, without making reference to the empirical use of the understanding, and thus, *ipso facto*, completely renouncing pure and non-sensible judgment. Thus the concept of pure and merely intelligible objects is completely empty of all principles of its application, because we cannot imagine any mode in which they might be given, and the problematical thought which leaves a place open for them serves only, like an empty space, to limit the use of empirical principles, without containing at the same time any other object of knowledge beyond their sphere.

APPENDIX: THE AMPHIBOLY OF THE CONCEPTS OF
REFLECTION ARISING FROM THE CONFUSION OF THE
TRANSCENDENTAL WITH THE EMPIRICAL USE OF THE
UNDERSTANDING

Reflection (*reflexio*) is not occupied with objects themselves, for the
purpose of directly obtaining concepts of them, but is that state of
the mind in which we set ourselves to discover the subjective
conditions under which we obtain concepts. It is the consciousness
of the relation of given representations to the different sources or
faculties of knowledge, by which alone their relation to each other
can be rightly determined. The first question which occurs in
considering our representations is, to what faculty of knowledge do
they belong? To the understanding or to the senses? Many judgments are admitted to be true from mere habit; but, because
reflection neither precedes nor follows, it is held to be a judgment
that has its origin in the understanding. Not all judgments require
examination, that is, investigation into the grounds of their truth.
For, when they are immediately certain (for example: Between two
points there can be only one straight line), no better or less mediate
test of their truth can be found than that which they themselves
contain and express. But all judgment, nay, all comparisons require
reflection, that is, a distinction of the faculty of knowledge to which
the given concepts belong. The act whereby I compare my representations with the faculty of knowledge which originates them, and
whereby I distinguish whether they are compared with each other
as belonging to the pure understanding or to sensible intuition, I
term *transcendental reflection*. Now, the relations in which concepts
can stand to each other are those of *identity* and *difference*,
agreement and *opposition*, of the *internal* and *external*, finally, of
the *determinable* and the *determining* (matter and form). The
proper determination of these relations rests on the question, to
what faculty of knowledge they *subjectively* belong, whether to
sensibility or understanding. For, on the manner in which we solve
this question depends the manner in which we must think these
relations.

Before constructing any objective judgment, we compare the
concepts and observe whether there exists *identity* (of many representations in one concept), if a *general* judgment is to be constructed, or *difference*, if a *particular*; whether there is *agreement*
when *affirmative*, and *opposition* when *negative* judgments are to

be constructed, and so on. For this reason we ought to call these concepts, concepts of comparison (*conceptus comparationis*). But as, when the question is not as to the logical form, but as to the content of concepts, that is to say, whether the things themselves are identical or different, in agreement or opposition, and so on, the things can have a twofold relation to our faculty of knowledge, to wit, a relation either to sensibility or to the understanding, and as on this relation depends their relation to each other, transcendental reflection, that is, the relation of given representations to one or the other faculty of knowledge, can alone determine this latter relation. Thus we shall not be able to discover whether the things are identical or different, in agreement or opposition, etc., from the mere concept of the things by means of comparison (*comparatio*), but only by distinguishing the mode of knowledge to which they belong, in other words, by means of transcendental reflection. We may, therefore, with justice say, that *logical reflection* is mere comparison, for in it no account is taken of the faculty of knowledge to which the given concepts belong, and they are consequently, as far as regards their origin, to be treated as homogeneous; while *transcendental reflection* (which applies to the objects themselves) contains the ground of the possibility of objective comparison of representations with each other, and is therefore very different from the former, because the faculties of knowledge to which they belong are not even the same. Transcendental reflection is a duty which no one can neglect who wishes to establish an *a priori* judgment upon things. We shall now proceed to fulfil this duty, and thereby throw not a little light on the question as to the determination of the proper business of the understanding.

1. *Identity and Difference.* When an object is presented to us several times, but always with the same internal determinations (*qualitas et quantitas*), it, if an object of pure understanding, is always the same, not several things, but only one thing (*numerica identitas*); but if it is an appearance, it is not a matter of comparing concepts, and although everything may be the same as far as concepts are concerned, the difference of place of appearances at the same time is a sufficient ground for asserting the *numerical difference* of the object (of sense). Thus, in the case of two drops of water, we may make complete abstraction of all internal difference (quality and quantity), and, the fact that they are intuited at the same time in different places, is sufficient to justify us in holding them to be numerically different. Leibniz regarded appearances as

things in themselves, consequently as *intelligibilia*, that is, objects of pure understanding (although, on account of the confused nature of their representations, he gave them the name of phenomena), and in this case his principle of indiscernibles (*principium identatis indiscernibilium*) is not to be impugned. But, as appearances are objects of sensibility, and, as the understanding, in respect of them, must be employed empirically and not purely or transcendentally, plurality and numerical difference are given by space itself as the condition of external appearances. For one part of space, although it may be perfectly similar and equal to another part, is still outside it, and for this reason alone is different from the latter, which is added to it in order to make up a greater space. It follows that this must hold good of all things that are in the different parts of space at the same time, however similar and equal one may be to another.

2. *Agreement and Opposition.* When reality is represented by the pure understanding (*realitas noumenon*), opposition between realities is inconceivable – such a relation, that is, that when these realities are connected in one subject, they annihilate the effects of each other, and may be represented in the formula $3-3=0$. On the other hand, the real in an appearance (*realitas phaenomenon*) may very well be in mutual opposition, and, when united in the same subject, the one may completely or in part annihilate the *consequence of the other*; as in the case of two moving forces in the same straight line drawing or impelling a point in opposite directions, or in the case of a pleasure counterbalancing a certain amount of pain.

3. *The Internal and External.* In an object of the pure understanding, only that is internal which has no relation (as regards its existence) to anything different from itself. On the other hand, the internal determinations of a *substantia phaenomenon* in space are nothing but relations, and it is itself nothing more than a totality of mere relations. Substance in space we are cognisant of only through forces operative in it, either drawing others towards itself (attraction), or preventing others from penetrating into it (repulsion and impenetrability). We know no other properties that make up the concept of substance in space, and which we term matter. On the other hand, as an object of the pure understanding, every substance must have internal determination and forces. But what other internal attributes of such an object can I think than those which my internal sense presents to me? That, to wit, which is either itself *thought*, or something analogous to it. Hence Leibniz, who looked

upon things as noumena, after denying them everything like external relation, and therefore also *composition*, declared that all substances, even the component parts of matter, were simple substances with powers of representation, in one word, *monads*.

4. *Matter and Form*. These two concepts lie at the foundation of all other reflection, so inseparably are they connected with every mode of exercising the understanding. The former denotes the determinable in general, the second its determination, both in a transcendental sense, abstraction being made of every difference in that which is given, and of the mode in which it is determined. Logicians formerly termed the universal, matter, the specific difference, form. In a judgment one may call the given concepts logical matter (for the judgment), the relation of these to each other (by means of the copula), the form of the judgment. In an object, the composite parts thereof (*essentialia*) are the matter; the mode in which they are connected in the object, the form. In respect to things in general, unlimited reality was regarded as the matter of all possibility, the limitation thereof (negation) as the form, by which one thing is distinguished from another according to transcendental concepts. The understanding demands that something be given (at least in the concept), in order to be able to determine it in a certain manner. Hence, in a concept of the pure understanding, the matter precedes the form, and for this reason Leibniz first assumed the existence of things (monads) and of an internal power of representation in them, in order to found upon this their external relation and the community of their state (that is, of their representations). Hence, with him, space and time were possible – the former through the relation of substances, the latter through the connection of their determinations with each other, as grounds and consequences. And so would it really be, if the pure understanding were capable of an immediate application to objects, and if space and time were determinations of things in themselves. But being merely sensible intuitions, in which we determine all objects solely as appearances, the form of intuition (as a subjective property of sensibility) must antecede all matter (sensations), consequently space and time must antecede all appearances and all data of experience, and rather make experience itself possible. But the intellectual philosopher could not endure that the form should precede the things themselves, and determine their possibility; an objection perfectly correct, if we assume that we intuit things as they are, although with confused representation. But as sensible intuition is a peculiar

subjective condition, which is *a priori* at the foundation of all perception, and the form of which is primitive, the form must be given *per se*, and so far from matter (or the things themselves which appear) lying at the foundation of experience (as we must conclude, if we judge by mere concepts), the very possibility of itself presupposes, on the contrary, a given formal intuition (space and time) as given in advance.

Remark on the Amphiboly of the Concepts of Reflection

Let me be allowed to term the position which we assign to a concept either in the sensibility or in the pure understanding, the *transcendental place*. In this manner, the appointment of the position which must be taken by each concept according to the difference in its use, and the directions for determining this place to all concepts according to rules, would be a *transcendental topic*, a doctrine which would thoroughly shield us from the surreptitious devices of the pure understanding and the delusions which thence arise, as it would always distinguish to what faculty of knowledge each concept properly belonged. Every concept, every title, under which many pieces of knowledge rank together, may be called a *logical place*. Upon this is based the *logical topic* of Aristotle, of which teachers and rhetoricians could avail themselves, in order, under certain titles of thought, to observe what would best suit the matter they had to treat, and thus enable themselves to quibble and talk with fluency and an appearance of profundity.

Transcendental topic, on the contrary, contains nothing more than the above-mentioned four titles of all comparison and distinction, which differ from categories in this respect, that they do not represent the object according to that which constitutes its concept (quantity, reality), but set forth merely the comparison of representations, which precedes our concepts of things. But this comparison requires a previous reflection, that is, a determination of the place to which the representations of the things which are compared belong, whether, to wit, they are thought by the pure understanding, or given by sensibility in appearance.

Concepts may be logically compared without the trouble of inquiring to what faculty their objects belong, whether as noumena, to the understanding, or as phenomena, to sensibility. If, however, we wish to employ these concepts in respect of objects, previous transcendental reflection is necessary. Without this reflection I should make a very unsafe use of these concepts, and construct pretended synthetical propositions which critical reason cannot acknowledge, and which are based solely upon a transcendental amphiboly, that is, upon confusing an object of pure understanding for an appearance.

For want of this doctrine of transcendental topic, and consequently deceived by the amphiboly of the concepts of reflection, the celebrated Leibniz constructed an *intellectual system of the world*, or rather, believed himself competent to know of the internal nature of things, by comparing all objects merely with the understanding and the abstract formal concepts of thought. Our table of the concepts of reflection gives us the unexpected advantage of being able to exhibit the distinctive peculiarities of his system in all its parts, and at the same time of exposing the fundamental principle of this peculiar mode of thought, which rested upon nothing but a misconception. He compared all things with each other merely by means of concepts, and naturally found no other differences than those by which the understanding distinguishes its pure concepts one from another. The conditions of sensible intuition, which contain in themselves their own means of distinction, he did not look upon as primitive, because sensibility was to him but a confused mode of representation, and not any particular source of representations. An appearance was for him the representation of the thing in itself, although distinguished from knowledge by the understanding only in respect of the logical form – the former with its usual want of analysis containing, according to him, a certain mixture of accompanying representations in its concept of a thing, which it is the duty of the understanding to separate and distinguish. In one word, Leibniz *intellectualized* appearances, just as Locke, in his system of *noogony* (if I may be allowed to make use of such expressions), *sensualized* the concepts of the understanding, that is to say, declared them to be nothing more than empirical or abstracted concepts of reflection. Instead of seeking in the understanding and sensibility two different sources of representations, which, however, can present us with objectively valid judgments of things only in *conjunction*, each of these great men recognized but one of these faculties, which, in their opinion, applied immediately to things in themselves, the other having no duty but that of confusing or arranging the representations of the former.

Accordingly, the objects of sense were compared by Leibniz as things in general merely in the understanding.

First, he compared them in regard to their identity or difference – as judged by the understanding. As, therefore, he considered merely the concepts of objects, and not their position in intuition, in which alone objects can be given, and left quite out of sight the transcendental *place* of these concepts – whether, that is, their object ought to be classed among appearances, or among things in themselves, it was to be expected that he should extend the application of the principle of indiscernibles, which is valid solely of concepts of things in general, to objects of sense (*mundus phaenomenon*), and that he should believe that he had thereby contributed in no small degree to extend our knowledge of nature. In truth, if I know in all its inner determinations a drop of water as a thing in itself, I cannot look upon one drop of water as different from another, if the concept of the one is completely identical with that of the other. But if it is an appearance in space, it has a place not merely in the understanding (among concepts), but also in sensible external intuition (in space), and in this case, the physical *place* is a matter of indifference in regard to the internal determinations of things, and one place, B, may contain a thing which is perfectly similar and equal to another in a place, A, just as well as if the two things were in every respect different from each other. Difference of place without any other conditions, makes the plurality and distinctness of objects as appearance, not only possible in itself, but even necessary. Consequently, the above so-called law is not a law of nature. It is merely an analytical rule for the comparison of things by means of mere concepts.

Secondly, the principle: 'Realities (as simply affirmations) never logically contradict each other', is a proposition perfectly true respecting the relation of concepts, but, as regards nature, or things in themselves (of which we have not the slightest concept), is without any the least meaning. For real opposition, in which A – B is $=0$, exists everywhere, an opposition, that is, in which one reality united with another in the same subject annihilates the effects of the other – a fact which is constantly brought before our eyes by the different antagonistic actions and operations in nature, which, nevertheless, as depending on forces, must be called *realitates phaenomena*. General mechanics can even present us with the empirical condition of this opposition in an *a priori* rule, as it directs its attention to the opposition in the direction of forces – a condition of which the transcendental concept of reality can tell us nothing. Although Herr von Leibniz did not announce this proposition with precisely the pomp of a new principle, he yet employed it for the establishment of new propositions, and his followers introduced it into their Leibniz-Wolffian system of philosophy. According to this principle, for example, all evils are but consequences of the limited nature of created beings, that is, negations, because these are the only opposite of reality. (In the mere concept of a thing in general this is really the case, but not in things as appearances.) In like manner, the upholders of this system deem it not only possible, but natural also, to connect and unite all reality in one being, because they acknowledge no other sort of opposition than that of contradiction (by which the concept itself of a thing is annihilated), and find themselves unable to conceive an opposition of reciprocal destruction, so to speak, in which one real cause destroys the effect of another, and the conditions of whose representation we meet with only in sensibility.

Thirdly, the Leibnizian Monadology has really no better foundation than on this philosopher's mode of falsely representing the difference of the internal and external solely in relation to the understanding. Substances, in general, must have something *inward*, which is therefore free from external relations, consequently from that of composition also. The *simple* is therefore the foundation of that which is internal in things in themselves. The internal state of substances cannot therefore consist in place, shape, contact, or motion, determinations which are all external relations, and we can ascribe to them no other than that whereby we internally determine our faculty of sense itself, that is to say, the state of representation. Thus, then, were constructed the monads, which were to form the elements of the universe, the active force of which consists in representation, the effects of this force being thus entirely confined to themselves.

For the same reason, his view of the possible community of substances could not represent it but as a *pre-established harmony*, and by no means as a physical influence. For inasmuch as everything is occupied only internally, that is, with its own representations, the state of the representations of one substance could not stand in active and living connection with that of another, but some third cause operating on all without exception was necessary to make the different states correspond with one another. And this did not happen by means of assistance applied in each particular case (*systema assistentiae*), but through the unity of the idea of a cause valid for all substances, in which they necessarily had to receive their existence and permanence, consequently also reciprocal correspondence, according to universal laws.

Fourthly, this philosopher's celebrated *doctrine of space and time*, in which he intellectualized these forms of sensibility, originated in the same illusion of transcendental reflection. If I attempt to represent by the mere understanding, the external relations of things, I can do so only by employing the concept of their reciprocal action, and if I wish to connect one state of the same thing with another state, I must avail myself of the notion of the order of ground and consequence. And thus Leibniz regarded space as a certain order in the community of substances, and time as the dynamical sequence of their states. That which space and time possess proper to themselves and independent of things, he ascribed to a necessary *confusion* in their concepts, whereby that which is a mere form of dynamical relations is held to be a self-existent intuition, antecedent even to things themselves. Thus space and time were the intelligible form of the connection of things (substances and their states) in themselves. But things were intelligible substances (*substantiae noumena*). At the same time, he made these concepts valid of appearances, because he did not allow to sensibility a peculiar mode of intuition, but sought all, even the empirical representation of objects, in the understanding, and left to sense nothing but the despicable task of confusing and distorting the representations of the former.

But even if we could frame any synthetical proposition concerning things in themselves by means of the pure understanding (which is impossible), it could not apply to appearances, which do not represent things in themselves. In dealing with appearances we are therefore obliged in transcendental reflection to compare our concepts only under the conditions of sensibility, and so space and time are not determinations of things in themselves, but of appearances. What things may be in themselves, I know not, and need not know, because a thing is never presented to me otherwise than in appearance.

I must adopt the same mode of procedure with the other concepts of reflection. Matter is *substantia phaenomenon*. That in it which is eternal I seek to discover in all parts of space which it occupies, and in all the effects it performs, and which are indeed never anything but appearances of the external sense. I cannot therefore find anything that is absolutely, but only what is comparatively internal, and which itself consists of external relations. The absolutely internal in matter, and as it should be according to the pure understanding, is a mere chimera, for matter is not an object for the pure understanding. But the transcendental object, which is the foundation of the appearance which we call matter, is a mere *something*, the nature of which we could not understand, even though someone were found able to tell us. For we can understand nothing that does not bring with it something in intuition corresponding to the expressions employed. If by the complaint of being *unable to perceive the internal nature of things*, it meant that we do not comprehend by the pure understanding what the things which appear to us may be in themselves, it is a silly and unreasonable complaint; for those who talk thus, really desire that we should be able to know, consequently to intuit things without senses, and therefore wish that we possessed a faculty of knowledge perfectly different from the human faculty, not merely in degree, but even as regards intuition and in kind, so that thus we should not be human beings, but belong to a class of beings, the possibility of whose existence, much less their nature and constitution, we have no means of knowing. By observation and analysis of appearances we penetrate into the interior of nature, and no one can say what progress this knowledge may make in time. But those transcendental questions which pass beyond the limits of nature, we could never answer, even although all nature were laid open to us, and we do not even have the power of observing our own mind with any other intuition than that of our internal sense. For herein lies the mystery of the origin and source of our faculty of sensibility. Its application to an object, and the transcendental ground of this unity of subjective and objective, lie too deeply concealed for us, who know ourselves only through the internal sense, consequently as appearances, to be able to discover in our existence anything but appearances, the non-sensible cause of which we at the same time earnestly desire to penetrate to.

The great utility of this critique of conclusions arrived at by the processes of mere reflection, consists in its clear demonstration of the nullity of all conclusions respecting objects which are compared with each other in the understanding alone, while it at the same time confirms what we particularly insisted on, namely, that, although appearances are not included as things in themselves among the objects of the pure understanding, they are nevertheless the only things by which our knowledge can possess objective reality, that is to say, which give us intuitions to correspond with our concepts.

When we reflect in a purely logical manner, we do nothing more than compare concepts in our understanding, to discover whether both have the same content, whether they are self-contradictory or not, whether anything is contained in the concept or is an addition from outside the conception, which of the two is given, and which is merely a mode of thinking that given. But if I apply these concepts to an object in general (in the transcendental sense), without first determining whether it is an object of sensible or intellectual intuition, certain limitations present themselves, which forbid us to pass beyond the concepts, and render all empirical use of them impossible. And thus these limitations prove, that the representation of an object as a thing in general is not only *insufficient*, but, without sensible determination and independently of empirical conditions, *incoherent*; that we must therefore make abstraction of all objects, as in logic, or, admitting them, must think them under conditions of sensible intuition; that, consequently, the intelligible requires an altogether peculiar intuition, which we do not possess, and in the absence of which it is for us nothing; while, on the other hand, appearances cannot be objects in themselves. For, when I merely think things in general, the difference in their external relations cannot constitute a difference in the things themselves; on the contrary, the former presupposes the latter, and if the concept of one of two things is not internally different from that of the other, I am merely thinking the same thing in different relations. Further, by the addition of one affirmation (reality) to the other, the positive therein is really augmented, and nothing is taken from it; hence the real in things cannot be in conflict with itself – and so on.

*

As a result of a certain misconception, the concepts of reflection have, as we have shown, had such an influence on the use of the understanding that they have been able to mislead even the most acute of all philosophers to offer a supposed system of intellectual knowledge capable of determining its objects without the assistance of the senses. For this reason, the exposition of the deceptive cause of the amphiboly of these concepts, as the origin of these false principles, is of great utility in determining with certainty the proper limits of the understanding.

It is right to say that what universally belongs to or contradicts a concept does also belong to or contradict everything particular contained uner the concept (*dictum de omni et nullo*); but it would be absurd so to alter this logical proposition, as to say, whatever is not contained in a general concept, is likewise not contained in the particular concepts which rank under it; for the latter are particular concepts, for the very reason that their content is greater than that which is thought in the general concept. And yet the whole intellectual system of Leibniz is based upon this false principle, and with it must necessarily collapse, together with all the ambiguity in the employment of the understanding which have thence originated.

The principle of the identity of indiscernibles is really based on the presupposition, that, if in the concept of a thing a certain distinction is not to be found, it is also not to be met with in things themselves; that, consequently, all things are completely identical (*numero eadem*) which are not distinguishable from each other (as to quality or quantity) in our concepts of them. But, as in the mere concept of anything abstraction has been made of many necessary conditions of intuition, that of which abstraction has been made is rashly held to be non-existent, and nothing is attributed to the thing but what is contained in its concept.

The concept of a cubic foot of space, however I may think it, is in itself completely identical. But two cubic feet in space are nevertheless distinct from each other from the sole fact of their being in different places (they are *numero diversa*); and these places are conditions of intuition, wherein the object of this concept is given, and which do not belong to the concept, but to the faculty of sensibility. In like manner, there is in the concept of a thing no contradiction when a negation is not connected with an affirmation; and merely affirmative concepts cannot, in conjunction, produce any cancellation. But in sensible intuition, wherein reality (take for example, motion) is given, we find conditions (opposite directions) – of which abstraction has been made in the concept of motion in general – which render possible a conflict (not indeed of a logical kind) – and which from pure positives produce zero=0. We are therefore not justified in saying, that because no contradiction is discoverable among its concepts all reality is in perfect agreement and harmony with itself.[1] According to mere concepts, that which is internal is the substratum of all relations or external

---

[1] If any one wishes here to have recourse to the usual subterfuge, and to say, that at least *realitates noumena* cannot be in opposition to each other, it will be requisite for him to adduce an example of this pure and non-sensible reality, that it may be understood whether the notion represents something or nothing. But an example cannot be found except in experience, which never presents to us anything more than *phenomena*; and thus the proposition means nothing more than that the concept which contains only affirmatives, does not contain anything negative – a proposition nobody ever doubted.

determinations. When, therefore, I abstract all conditions of intuition, and confine myself solely to the concept of a thing in general, I can make abstraction of all external relations, and there must nevertheless remain a concept of that which indicates no relation, but merely internal determinations. Now it seems to follow, that in everything (substance) there is something which is absolutely internal, and which antecedes all external determinations, inasmuch as it renders them possible; and that therefore this substratum is something which does not contain any external relations, and is consequently simple (for corporeal things are never anything but relations, at least of their parts external to each other); and inasmuch as we know of no other absolutely internal determinations than those of the internal sense, this substratum is not only simple, but also, analogously with our internal sense, determined through *representations*, that is to say, all things are properly *monads*, or simple beings endowed with the power of representation. Now all this would be perfectly correct, if the concept of a thing were the only necessary condition of the presentation of objects of external intuition. It is, on the contrary, manifest that a permanent appearance in space (impenetrable extension) can contain mere relations, and nothing that is absolutely internal, and yet be the primary substratum of all external perception. By mere concepts I cannot think anything external, without, at the same time, thinking something internal, for the reason that concepts of relations presuppose given things, and without these are impossible. But, as in intuition there is something (that is, space, which, with all it contains, consists of purely formal, or, indeed, real relations) which is not found in the mere concept of a thing in general, and this presents to us the substratum which could not be known through concepts alone, I cannot say: Because a thing cannot be represented *by mere concepts* without something absolutely internal, there is also, in the things themselves which are contained under these concepts, and in *their intuition* nothing external to which something absolutely internal does not serve as the foundation. For, when we have made abstraction of all the conditions of intuition, there certainly remains in the mere concept nothing but the internal in general, through which alone the external is possible. But this necessity, which is grounded upon abstraction alone, does not obtain in the case of things themselves, in so far as they are given in intuition with such determinations as express mere relations, without having anything internal as their foundation; for they are not things in themselves, but only appearances. What we know in matter is nothing but relations. (What we call its internal determinations are but comparatively internal.) But there are some self-subsistent and permanent, through which a determined object is given. That I, when abstraction if made of these relations, have nothing more to think, does not destroy the concept of a thing as appearance, nor the concept of an object *in abstracto*, but it does away with the possibility of an object that is determinable according to mere concepts, that is, of a noumenon. It is certainly startling to hear that a thing consists solely of relations; but this thing is simply an appearance, and cannot be thought by means of the mere categories: it does itself consist in the mere relation of something in general to the senses. In the same way, we cannot think relations of things *in abstracto*, if we commence with concepts alone, in any other manner than that one is the cause of determinations in the other; for that is itself the concept of the understanding of relation. But, as in this case we make abstraction of all intuition, we lose altogether the mode in which the manifold determines to each of its parts its place, that is, the form of sensibility (space); and yet this mode antecedes all empirical causality.

If by intelligible objects we understand things which can be thought by means of the pure categories, without the need of the schemata of sensibility, such objects are impossible. For the condition of the objective use of all our concepts of understanding is the mode of our sensible intuition, whereby objects are given; and, if we make abstraction of the latter, the former can have no relation to an object. And even if we should suppose a different kind of intuition from our own sensible intuition, still our functions of thought would have no use or signification in respect thereof. But if we understand by the term, objects of a non-sensible intuition, in respect of which our categories are not valid, and of which we can accordingly have no knowledge (neither intuition nor concept), in this merely negative sense noumena must be admitted. For this is no more than saying that our mode of intuition is not applicable to all things, but only to objects of our senses, that consequently its objective validity is limited, and that room is therefore left for another kind of intuition, and thus also for things that may be objects of it. But in this sense the concept of a noumenon is problematical, that is to say, it is the notion of a thing of which we can neither say that it is possible, nor that it is impossible, inasmuch as we do not know of any mode of intuition besides the sensible, or of any other sort of concepts than the categories – a mode of intuition and a kind of concept neither of which is applicable to a non-sensible object. We cannot, therefore, extend the sphere of our objects of thought beyond the conditions of our sensibility, and to assume the existence of objects of pure thought, that is, of noumena, inasmuch as these have no true positive signification. For it must be confessed of the categories, that they are not of themselves sufficient for the knowledge of things in themselves, and without the data of sensibility are mere subjective forms of the unity of the understanding. Thought is certainly not a product of the senses, and in so far is not limited by them, but it does not therefore follow that it may be employed purely and without the intervention of sensibility, for it would then be without reference to an object. And we cannot call a noumenon an object of pure thought; for the representation thereof is but the problematical concept of an object for a perfectly different intuition and a perfectly different understanding from ours, both of which are consequently themselves problematical. The concept of a noumenon is therefore not the concept of an object, but merely a problematical concept inseparably connected with the limitation of our sensibility. That is to say, this concept contains the answer to the question – Are there objects quite unconnected with, and independent of, our intuition? – a question to which only an indeterminate answer can be given. That answer is: Inasmuch as sensible intuition does not apply to all things without distinction, there remains room for other and different objects. The existence of these problematical objects is therefore not absolutely denied, in the absence of a determinate concept of them, but, as no category is valid in respect of them, neither must they be admitted as objects for our understanding.

Understanding accordingly limits sensibility, without at the same time enlarging its own field. While, moreover, it forbids sensibility to apply its forms and modes to things in themselves and restricts it to the sphere of appearances, it thinks an object in itself, only, however, as a transcendental object, which is the cause of appearances (consequently not itself an appearance), and which cannot be thought either as a quantity or as reality, or as substance (because these concepts always require sensible forms in which to determine an object) – an object, therefore, of which we are quite unable to say whether it can be met with in ourselves or outside us, whether it would be annihilated with the annihilation of sensibility, or, if this were taken away, would continue to exist. If we wish to call this object a noumenon, because the representation of it is non-sensible, we are at liberty to do so. But as we can apply to it none of our concepts of the understanding, the representation is for us quite empty, and is available only for the indication of the limits of our sensible intuition, thereby leaving at the same time an empty space, which we are competent to fill by the aid neither of possible experience, nor of the pure understanding.

The critique of the pure understanding, accordingly, does not permit us to create for ourselves a new field of objects beyond those which are presented to us as appearances, and to stray into intelligible worlds; nay, it does not even allow us to endeavour to form so much as a concept of them. The error which leads to this – and which is excusable but not justifiable – lies in the fact that the employment of the understanding, contrary to its proper purpose and destination, is made transcendental, and objects, that is, possible intuitions, are made to regulate themselves according to concepts, instead of the concepts regulating themselves according to the intuitions, on which alone their own objective validity rests. Now the reason of this again is, that apperception, and with it, thought, antecedes all possible determinate arrangement of representations. Accordingly we think something in general, and determine it on the one hand sensibly, but, on the other, distinguish the general and *in abstracto* represented object from this particular mode of intuiting it. In this case there remains a mode of determining the object by mere thought, which is really but a logical form without content, which, however, seems to us to be a mode of the existence of the object in itself (noumenon), without regard to intuition which is limited to our senses.

*

Before ending this Transcendental Analytic, we must make an addition, which, although in itself of no particular importance, seems to be necessary to the completeness of the system. The highest concept, with which a transcendental philosophy commonly begins, is the division into possible and impossible. But as all division presupposes a divided concept, a higher one must exist, and this is the conception of an object in general – problematically understood, and without its being decided whether it is something or nothing. As the categories are the only concepts, which apply to objects in general, the distinguishing of an object, whether it is something or nothing, must proceed according to the order and direction of the categories.

1. To the concepts of all, many, and one, the concept which annihilates all, that is, the concept of *none*, is opposed. And thus the object of a concept, to which no intuition can be found to correspond, is =nothing. That is, it is a concept without an object (*ens rationis*), like noumena, which cannot be considered possible in the sphere of reality, though they must not therefore be held to be impossible – or like certain new fundamental forces, the existence of which is capable of being thought without contradiction, though, as examples from experience are not forthcoming, they must not be regarded as possible.

2. Reality is *something*; negation is *nothing*, that is, a concept of the absence of an object, as cold, a shadow (*nihil privativum*).

3. The mere form of intuition, without substance, is in itself no object, but the merely formal condition of an object (as appearance), as pure space and pure time. These are certainly something, as forms of intuition, but are not themselves objects which are intuited (*ens imaginarium*).

4.The object of a concept which is self-contradictory, is nothing, because the concept is nothing – is impossible, as a figure composed of two straight lines (*nihil negativum*).

The table of this division of the concept of *nothing* (the corresponding division of the concept of *something* follows directly from it) must therefore be arranged as follows:

NOTHING

AS

1

Empty concept without object,
ens rationis

2	3
Empty object of a concept	Empty intuition without object,
nihil privativum	*ens imaginarium*

4

Empty object without concept
nihil negativum

We see that the *ens rationis* is distinguished from the *nihil negativum* by the consideration, that the former must not be reckoned among possibilities, because it is a mere fiction – though not self-contradictory, while the latter is completely opposed to all possibility, inasmuch as the concept annihilates itself. Both, however, are empty concepts. On the other hand, the *nihil privativum* and *ens imaginarium* are empty *data* for concepts. If light be not given to the senses we cannot represent to ourselves darkness, and if extended objects are not perceived, we cannot represent space. Neither the negation, nor the mere form of intuition can, without something real, be an object.

TRANSCENDENTAL LOGIC: SECOND DIVISION

TRANSCENDENTAL DIALECTIC: INTRODUCTION
I: TRANSCENDENTAL ILLUSION

We termed dialectic in general a logic of illusion. This does not signify a doctrine of *probability*; for probability is truth, only known upon insufficient grounds, and though the information it gives us is imperfect, it is not therefore deceitful. Hence it must not be separated from the analytical part of logic. Still less must appearance and illusion be held to be identical. For truth or illusory appearance does not reside in the object, in so far as it is intuited, but in the judgment upon the object in so far as it is thought. It is therefore quite correct to say that the senses do not err, not because they always judge correctly, but because *they do not* judge at all. Hence truth and error, consequently also, illusion as the cause of error, are only to be found in a judgment, that is, in the relation of an object to our understanding. In that knowledge, which completely harmonizes with the laws of the understanding, no error can exist. In a representation of the senses – since it does not contain any judgment – there is also no error. But no power of nature can of itself deviate from its own laws. Hence neither the understanding *per se* (without the influence of another cause), nor the senses *per se*, would fall into error; the former could not, because, if it acts only according to its own laws, the effect (the judgment) must necessarily accord with these laws. But in accordance with the laws of the understanding consists the formal element in all truth. In the senses there is no judgment – neither a true nor a false one. But, as we have no source of knowledge besides these two, it follows that error is caused solely by the unnoticed influence of the sensibility upon the understanding. And thus it happens that the subjective grounds of a judgment blend and are confounded with the objective, and cause them to deviate from their proper determination,[1] just as a body in motion would always of itself proceed in a straight line, but if another impetus gives to it a different direction, it will then start off into a curvilinear line of motion. To distinguish the peculiar action of the understanding from the power which mingles with it, it is necessary to consider an erroneous judgment as the diagonal between two forces, that determine the judgment in two different directions, which, as it were, form an angle, and to resolve this composite operation into the simple ones of the understanding and the sensibility. In pure *a priori* judgments this must be done by means of transcendental reflection, whereby, as has been already shown, each representation has its place appointed in the corresponding faculty of knowledge, and consequently the influence of the one faculty upon the other is distinguished.

It is not at present our business to treat of empirical illusion (for example, optical illusion), which occurs in the empirical application of otherwise correct rules of the understanding, and in which the judgment is misled by the influence of imagination. Our purpose is to speak of *transcendental illusion*, which influences principles – that are not even applied to experience, for in this case we should possess a sure test of their correctness – but which leads us, in disregard of all the warnings of criticism, completely beyond the empirical employment of the categories, and deludes us with the chimera of an extension of the sphere of the *pure understanding*. We shall term those principles, the application of which is confined entirely within the limits of possible experience, *immanent*; those, on the other hand, which transgress these limits, we shall call *transcendent* principles. But by these latter I do not understand principles of the *transcendental* use or misuse of the categories, which is in reality a mere fault of the judgment when not under due restraint from criticism, and therefore not paying sufficient attention to the limits of the sphere in which the pure understanding is allowed to exercise its functions; but real principles which exhort us to break down all those barriers, and to lay claim to a perfectly new field of knowlede, which recognizes no line of demarcation.

---

[1] Sensibility, subjected to the understanding, as the object upon which the understanding employs its functions, is the source of real knowledge. But, in so far as it exercises an influence upon the action of the understanding, and determines it to judgment, sensibility is itself the cause of error.

Thus *transcendental* and *transcendent* are not identical terms. The principles of the pure understanding, which we have already propounded, ought to be of empirical and not of transcendental use, that is, they are not applicable to any object beyond the sphere of experience. A principle which removes these limits, nay, which commands us to overstep them, is called *transcendent*. If our criticism can succeed in exposing the illusion in these pretended principles, those which are limited in their employment to the sphere of experience, may be called, in opposition to the others, *immanent* principles of the pure understanding.

Logical illusion, which consists merely in the imitation of the form of reason (the illusion of invalid reasoning), arises entirely from a want of due attention to logical rules. So soon as the attention is awakened to the case before us, this illusion totally disappears. Transcendental illusion, on the contrary, does not cease to exist, even after it has been exposed, and its nothingness clearly perceived by means of transcendental criticism. Take, for example, the illusion in the proposition : 'The world must have a beginning in time.' The cause of this is as follows. In our reason, subjectively considered as a faculty of human knowledge, there exist fundamental rules and maxims of its exercise, which have completely the appearance of objective principles. Now from this cause it happens, that the subjective necessity of a certain connection of our concepts, is regarded as an objective necessity of the determination of things in themselves. This illusion it is impossible to avoid, just as we cannot avoid perceiving that the sea appears to be higher at a distance than it is near the shore, because we see the former by means of higher rays than the latter, or, which is a still stronger case, as even the astronomer cannot prevent himself from seeing the moon larger at its rising than some time afterwards, although he is not deceived by this illusion.

Transcendental dialectic will therefore content itself with exposing the illusion in transcendental judgments, and guarding us against it ; but to make it, as in the case of logical illusion, entirely disappear and cease to be illusion, is utterly beyond its power. For we have here to do with a *natural* and unavoidable illusion, which rests upon subjective principles, and imposes these upon us as objective, while logical dialectic, in the detection of sophisms, has to do merely with an error in the logical consequence of the propositions, or with an artificially constructed illusion, in imitation of the natural error. There is, therefore, a natural and unavoidable dialectic of pure reason – not that in which the bungler, from want of the requisite knowledge, involves himself, nor that which the sophist devises for the purpose of misleading, but that which is inseparable from human reason, and which, even after its illusions have been exposed, does not cease to play tricks on reason, and continually to lead reason into momentary aberrations, which it becomes necessary continually to remove.

II : PURE REASON AS THE SEAT OF TRANSCENDENTAL ILLUSION

A : Reason in General

All our knowledge begins with sense, proceeds thence to understanding, and ends with reason, beyond which nothing higher can be discovered in us for elaborating the matter of intuition and subjecting it to the highest unity of thought. At this stage of our inquiry it is my duty to give an explanation of this, the highest faculty of knowledge, and I confess I find myself here in some difficulty. Of reason, as of the understanding, there is a merely formal, that is, logical use, in which it makes abstraction of all content of knowledge; but there is also a real use, inasmuch as it contains in itself the source of certain concepts and principles, which it does not borrow either from the senses or the understanding. The former faculty has been long defined by logicians as the faculty of mediate conclusion in contradistinction to immediate conclusions (*consequentiae immediatae*); but the nature of the latter, which itself generates concepts, is not to be understood from this definition. Now as a division of reason into a logical and a transcendental faculty presents itself here, it becomes necessary to seek for a higher concept of this source of knowledge which shall comprehend both concepts. In this we may expect, according to the analogy of the concepts of the understanding, that the logical concept will give us the key to the transcendental, and that the table of the functions of the former will present us with the clue to the concepts of reason.

In the former part of our transcendental logic, we defined the understanding to be the faculty of rules; reason may be distinguished from understanding as the *faculty of principles*.

The term *principle* is ambiguous, and commonly signifies merely that knowledge that may be employed as a principle, although it is not in itself, and as regards its proper origin, a principle. Every general proposition, even if derived from experience by the process of induction, may serve as the major in a syllogism; but it is not for that reason a principle. Mathematical axioms (for example, there can be only one straight line between two points) are general *a priori* knowledge, and are therefore rightly denominated principles, relatively to the cases which can be subsumed under them. But I cannot for this reason say that I know this property of a straight line from principles – I know it only in pure intuition.

Knowledge from principles, then, is that knowledge in which I know the particular in the general by means of concepts. Thus every inference is a form of the deduction of knowledge from a principle. For the major always gives a concept, through which everything that is subsumed under the condition thereof, is known according to a principle. Now as every general knowledge may serve as the major in an inference, and the understanding presents us with such general *a priori* propositions, they may be termed principles, in respect of their possible use.

But if we consider these principles of the pure understanding in relation to their origin, we shall find them to be anything rather than knowledge from concepts. For they would not even be possible *a priori*, if we could not rely on the assistance of pure intuition (in mathematics), or on that of the conditions of a possible experience. That everything that happens has a cause, cannot be concluded from the general concept of that which happens; on the contrary the principle of causality instructs us as to the mode of obtaining a determinate empirical concept of that which happens.

Synthetical knowledge from concepts the understanding cannot supply, and such knowledge alone is entitled to be called principles. At the same time, all general propositions may be termed comparative principles.

It has been a long-cherished wish – that (who knows how late) may one day be happily accomplished – that the principles of the endless variety of civil laws should be investigated and exposed; for in this way alone can we find the secret of simplifying legislation. But in this case, laws are nothing more than limitations of our freedom upon conditions under which it subsists in perfect harmony with itself; they consequently have for their object that which is completely our own work, and of which we ourselves may be the cause by means of these concepts. But how objects as things in themselves – how the nature of things is subordinated to principles and is to be determined according to concepts, is a demand which, if not impossible, is at least contrary to good sense. Be this, however, as it may – for on this point our investigation is yet to be made – it is at least manifest from what we have said, that knowledge from principles is something very different from knowledge by means of the understanding, which may indeed precede other knowledge in the form of a principle, but in itself – in so far as it is synthetical – is neither based upon mere thought, nor contains a universal drawn from concepts alone.

The understanding may be a faculty for the production of unity of appearances by virtue of rules; reason is a faculty for the production of unity of the rules of the understanding under principles. Reason, therefore, never applies directly to experience, or to any sensible object; rather it applies to the understanding, in order to provide the multiple knowledge of the understanding with *a priori* unity by means of concepts – a unity which may be called rational unity, and which is of a nature very different from that of the unity produced by the understanding.

The above is the general concept of the faculty of reason, in so far as it has been possible to make it comprehensible in the absence of examples. These will be given in the sequel.

B: *The Logical Use of Reason*

A distinction is commonly made between that which is immediately known and that which is inferred. That in a figure which is bounded by three straight lines there are three angles, is immediate knowledge; but that these angles are together equal to two right angles, is an inference. Now, as we are in constant need of making inferences, and have thus become quite accustomed to it, we no longer remark the above distinction, and, as in the case of the so-called sense-deceptions, consider as immediately perceived, what has really been inferred. In every reasoning, there is a fundamental proposition, then a second inferred from it, and finally the inference itself, which inseparably connects the truth in the first with the truth in the second. If the judgment inferred is so contained in the first proposition, that it can be deduced from it without the mediation of a third representation, the inference is called immediate (*consequentia immediata*); I prefer the term inference of the understanding. But if, in addition to the fundamental inference, a second judgment is necessary for the production of the conclusion, it is called an inference of reason. In the proposition: *All men are mortal*, are contained the propositions: *Some men are mortal, some mortal beings are men, Nothing that is not mortal is a man,* and these are therefore immediate inferences from the first. On the other hand, the proposition: *All the learned are mortal,* is not contained in the main proposition (for the concept of a learned man does not occur in it), and it can be deduced from the main proposition only by means of a mediating judgment.

In every syllogism I first think a *rule (the major)* by means of the *understanding.* In the next place I *subsume* some knowledge under the condition of the rule (and this is the *minor*) by means of *judgment.* And finally I *determine* my knowledge by means of the predicate of the rule (*conclusio*), consequently, I determine it *a priori* by means of *reason.* The relations, therefore, which the major proposition, as the rule, represents between some knowledge and its condition, constitute the different kinds of syllogisms. These are just threefold – analogously with all judgments, in so far as they differ in the mode of expressing the relation of knowledge in the understanding – namely, *categorical, hypothetical, and disjunctive.*

When, as often happens, the conclusion is a judgment which may follow from other given judgments, through which a perfectly different object is thought, I endeavour to discover in the understanding whether the assertion in this conclusion does not stand under certain conditions according to a general rule. If I find such a condition, and if the object mentioned in the conclusion can be subsumed under the given condition, then this conclusion follows from a rule which is also valid for other objects of knowledge. From this we see that reason endeavours to subject the great variety of the knowledge of the understanding to the smallest possible number of principles (general conditions), and thus to produce in it the highest unity.

C: The Pure Use of Reason

Can we isolate reason, and, if so, is it in this case a peculiar source of concepts and jugments which spring from it alone, and through which it can be applied to objects; or is it merely a subordinate faculty, whose duty it is to give a certain form to given knowledge – a form which is called logical, and through which the knowledge of the understanding are subordinated to each other, and lower rules to higher (those, to wit, whose condition comprises in its sphere the condition of the others), in so far as this can be done by comparison? This is the question which we have at present to answer. Multiplicity of rules and unity of principles is a requirement of reason, for the purpose of bringing the understanding into complete accordance with itself, just as understanding subjects the manifold of intuition to concepts, and thereby introduces connection into it. But this principle prescribes no law to objects, and does not contain any ground of the possibility of knowing, or of determining them as such, but is merely a subjective law for the proper arrangement of the content of the understanding. The purpose of this law is, by a comparison of the concepts of the understanding, to reduce their general to the smallest possible number, although, at the same time, it does not justify us in demanding from objects themselves such a uniformity as might contribute to the convenience and the enlargement of the sphere of the understanding, or in entitling us to ascribe objective validity to the maxim. In one word, the question is, does reason in itself, that is, does pure reason contain *a priori* synthetical principles and rules, and what are those principles?

The formal and logical procedure of reason in syllogisms gives us sufficient information in regard to the ground on which the transcendental principle of reason in its pure synthetical knowledge will rest.

First, rational inferences are not applicable to intuitions, for the purpose of subjecting them to rules – for this is the province of the understanding with its categories – but to concepts and judgments. If pure reason does apply to objects and the intuition of them, it does so not immediately, but mediately – through the understanding and its judgments, which have a direct relation to the senses and their intuition, for the purpose of determining their objects. The unity of reason is therefore not the unity of a possible experience, but is essentially different from this unity, which is that of the understanding. That everything which happens has a cause, is not a principle known and prescribed by reason. This principle makes the unity of experience possible and borrows nothing from reason, which, without a reference to possible experience, could never have produced by means of mere concepts any such synthetical unity.

Secondly, reason in its logical use, endeavours to discover the general condition of its judgment (the conclusion), and a syllogism is itself nothing but a judgment by means of the subsumption of its condition under a general rule (the major). Now as this rule may itself be subjected to the same process of reason, and thus the condition of the condition be sought (by means of a prosyllogism) as long as the process can be continued, it is very manifest that the peculiar principle of reason in its logical use is – to find for the conditioned knowledge of the understanding the unconditioned whereby the unity of the former is completed.

But this logical maxim cannot be a principle of *pure reason*, unless we admit that, if the conditioned is given, the whole series of conditions subordinated to one another – a series which is consequently itself unconditioned – is also given, that is, contained in the object and its connection.

But this principle of pure reason is evidently *synthetical*; for analytically, the conditioned certainly relates to some condition, but not to the unconditioned. From this principle also there must originate different synthetical propositions, of which the pure understanding is perfectly ignorant, for it has to do only with objects of a possible experience, the knowledge and synthesis of which are always conditioned. The unconditioned, if it does really exist, must be especially considered in regard to the determinations which distinguish it from whatever is conditioned, and will thus afford us material for many *a priori* synthetical propositions.

The principles resulting from this highest principle of pure reason will, however, be *transcendent* in relation to all appearances, that is to say, it will be impossible to make any adequate empirical use of this principle. It is therefore completely different from all principles of the understanding, the use made of which is entirely *immanent*, their object and purpose being merely the possibility of experience. Now our duty in the transcendental dialectic is as follows. To discover whether the principle, that the series of conditions (in the synthesis of appearances, or of thought in general) extends to the unconditioned, is objectively correct, or not; what consequences result therefrom affecting the empirical use of the understanding, or rather whether there exists any such objectively valid proposition of reason, and whether it is not, on the contrary, a merely logical precept which directs us to ascend perpetually to still higher conditions, to approach completeness in the series of them, and thus to introduce into our knowledge the highest possible unity of reason. We must ascertain, I say, whether this requirement of reason has not been regarded, by a misunderstanding, as a transcendental principle of pure reason, which postulates a thorough completeness in the series of conditions in objects themselves. We must show, moreover, the misconceptions and illusions that intrude into syllogisms, the major proposition of which pure reason has supplied – a proposition which has perhaps more of the character of *an assumption* than of a *postulate* – and that proceed from experience upwards to its conditions. The solution of these problems is our task in transcendental dialectic, which we are about to expose even at its source, that lies deep in human reason. We shall divide it into two parts, the first of which will treat of the *transcendent concepts* of pure reason, the second of transcendent and *dialectical inferences*.

TRANSCENDENTAL DIALECTIC: BOOK I

THE CONCEPTS OF PURE REASON

The concepts of pure reason – we do not here speak of the possibility of them – are not obtained by reflection, but by inference. The concepts of understanding are also thought *a priori* antecedently to experience, and render it possible; but they contain nothing but the unity of reflection upon appearances, in so far as these must necessarily belong to a possible empirical consciousness. Through them alone are knowledge and the determination of an object possible. It is from them, accordingly, that we receive material for reasoning, and antecedently to them we possess no *a priori* concepts of objects from which they might be deduced. On the other hand, the sole basis of their objective consists in the fact that, since they constitute the intellectual form of all experience, their application must always be capable of being exhibited in experience.

But the term, *concept of reason*, itself indicates that it does not confine itself within the limits of experience, because its object-matter is a knowledge, of which every empirical knowledge is but a part – nay, the whole of possible experience may be itself but a part of it – a knowledge to which no actual experience ever fully attains, although it does always belong to it. Concepts of reason enable us to conceive, concepts of the understanding to understand (perceptions). If they contain the unconditioned, they relate to that to which all experience is subordinate, but which is never itself an object of experience – that towards which reason tends in all its conclusions from experience, and by the standard of which it estimates the degree of their empirical use, but which is never itself an element in an empirical synthesis. If, notwithstanding, such concepts possess objective validity, they may be called *conceptus ratiocinati* (concepts legitimately inferred); in cases where they do not, they have been admitted on account of having the appearance of being correctly inferred, and may be called *conceptus ratiocinantes* (sophistical concepts). But as this can only be sufficiently demonstrated in that part of our treatise which relates to the dialectical inferences of reason, we shall omit any consideration of it in this place. As we called the pure concepts of the understanding categories, we shall also distinguish those of pure reason by a new name, and call them transcendental ideas. These terms, however, we must in the first place explain and justify.

Section I : Ideas in general

Despite the great wealth of our languages, the thinker finds himself often at a loss for an expression exactly suited to his concept, for want of which he is unable to make himself intelligible either to others or to himself. To coin new words is a pretension to legislation in language which is seldom successful; and, before recourse is taken to so desperate an expedient, it is advisable to examine the dead and learned languages, with the hope that we may there meet with some adequate expression of our concept. In this case, even if the original meaning of the word has become somewhat uncertain, from carelessness on the part of the authors of it, it is always better to adhere to and confirm its proper meaning – even although it may be doubtful whether it was formerly used in exactly this sense – than to make our labour vain by want of sufficient care to render ourselves intelligible.

For this reason, when it happens that there exists only a single word to express a certain concept, and this word, in its usual acceptation, is thoroughly adequate to the concept, the accurate distinction of which from related concepts is of great importance, we ought not to employ the expression in a profligate way, or, for the sake of variety and elegance of style, use it as a synonym for other cognate words. It is our duty, on the contrary, carefully to preserve its peculiar signification, as otherwise it easily happens that when the attention of the reader is no longer particularly attracted to the expression, and it is lost amid the multitude of other words of very different import, the thought which it alone conveyed, is lost with it.

Plato employed the expression *idea* in a way that plainly showed he meant by it something which is never derived from the senses, but which far transcends even the concepts of the understanding (with which Aristotle occupied himself), inasmuch as in experience nothing perfectly corresponding to them could be found. Ideas are, according to Plato, archetypes of things themselves, and not merely keys to possible experiences, like the categories. In his view they flow from the highest reason, by which they have been imparted to human reason, which, however, exists no longer in its original state, but is obliged with great labour to recollect – which is called philosophy – the old but now sadly obscured ideas. I will not here enter upon any literary investigation of the sense which this sublime philosopher attached to this expression. I shall content myself with remarking that it is nothing unusual, in common conversation as well as in written works, by comparing the thoughts which an author has delivered upon a subject, to understand him better than he understood himself – inasmuch as he may not have sufficiently determined his concept, and thus have sometimes spoken, nay even thought, in opposition to his own intention.

Plato perceived very clearly that our faculty of knowledge feels a much higher need than that of merely spelling out appearances according to synthetical unity, for the purpose of being able to read them as experience, and that our reason naturally raises itself to knowledge far too elevated to admit of the possibility of an object given by experience corresponding to them – knowledge which is nevertheless real, and not mere phantoms of the brain.

Plato found his ideas especially in all that is practical,[1] that is, which rests upon freedom, which in its turn ranks under knowledge that is the peculiar product of reason. He who would derive from experience the concept of virtue, who would make (as many have really done) that, which at best can but serve as an imperfectly illustrative example, a pattern from which to derive knowledge, would in fact transform virtue into a nonentity changeable according to time and circumstance, and utterly incapable of being employed as a rule. On the contrary, every one is conscious that, when any one is held up to him as a model of virtue, he compares this so-called model with the true original which he possesses in his own mind, and values him according to this model. But this model is the idea of virtue, in relation to which all possible objects of experience are indeed serviceable as examples – proofs of the practicability in a certain degree of that which the concept of virtue demands – but certainly not as archetypes. That the actions of man will never be in perfect accordance with the pure idea of virtue, does not prove the thought to be chimerical. For only through this idea are all judgments as to moral merit or demerit possible; it

---

[1] He certainly extended the application of his concept to speculative knowledge also, provided they were given pure and completely *a priori*, nay, even to mathematics, although this science cannot possess an object otherwise than in *possible* experience. I cannot follow him in this, and as little can I follow him in his mystical deduction of these ideas, or in his hypostatization of them: although, in truth, the elevated and exaggerated language which he employed in describing them is quite capable of an interpretation more subdued and more in accordance with the nature of things.

consequently lies at the foundation of every approach to moral perfection, however far removed from it the obstacles in human nature – indeterminable as to degree – may keep us.

The Republic of Plato has become proverbial as an example – and a striking one – of imaginary perfection, such as can exist only in the brain of the idle thinker; and Brucker ridicules the philosopher for maintaining that a prince can never govern well, unless he is participant in *the ideas*. But we should do better to follow up this thought, and, where this admirable thinker leaves us without assistance, employ new efforts to place it in clearer light, rather than carelessly fling it aside as useless, under the very miserable and pernicious pretext of impracticability. A constitution of *greatest possible human freedom* according to laws, by which *the freedom of every individual is consistent with the freedom of every other* (not of the greatest possible happiness, for this follows necessarily from the former), is, to say the least, a necessary idea, which must be placed at the foundation not only of the first plan of the constitution of a state, but of all its laws. And in this, it is not necessary at the outset to take account of the obstacles which lie in our way – obstacles which perhaps do not necessarily arise from the character of human nature, but rather from the previous neglect of true ideas in legislation. For there is nothing more pernicious and more unworthy of a philosopher, than the vulgar appeal to a so-called adverse experience, which indeed would not have existed, if those institutions had been established at the proper time and in accordance with ideas; while instead of this, concepts, crude for the very reason that they have been drawn from experience, have marred and frustrated all our better views and intentions. The more legislation and government are in harmony with this idea, the more rare do punishments become, and thus it is quite reasonable to maintain, as Plato did, that in a perfect state no punishments at all would be necessary. Now although a perfect state may never exist, the idea is not on that account the less right, which holds up this *maximum* as the archetype of a constitution, in order to bring legislative government always nearer and nearer to the greatest possible perfection. For at what precise degree human nature must stop in its progress, and how wide must be the chasm which must necessarily exist between the idea and its realization, are problems which no one can or ought to determine – and for this reason, that it is the destination of freedom to overstep all assigned limits.

But not only in that wherein human reason is a real causal agent and where ideas are operative causes (of actions and their objects), that is to say, in the region of ethics, but also in regard to nature herself, Plato saw clear proofs of an origin from ideas. A plant, an animal, the regular order of nature – probably also the disposition of the whole universe – give manifest evidence that they are possible only by means of and according to ideas; that, indeed, no one creature, under the individual conditions of its existence, perfectly harmonizes with the idea of the most perfect of its kind – just as little as man with the idea of humanity, which nevertheless he bears in his soul as the archetypal standard of his actions; that, notwithstanding, these ideas are in the highest sense individuals, unchangeable, and completely determined, and are the original cause of things; and that the totality of connected objects in the universe is alone fully adequate to that idea. Setting aside the exaggerations of expression in the writings of this philosopher, the mental power exhibited in this ascent from the ectypal mode of regarding the physical world to the architectonic connection thereof according to ends, that is, ideas, is an effort which deserves imitation and claims respect. But as regards the principles of ethics, of legislation, and of religion, spheres in which ideas alone render experience possible, although they never attain to full expression therein, Plato's position is position of peculiar merit, which is not appreciated only because it is judged by the very empirical rules, the validity of which as principles is destroyed by ideas. For as regards nature, experience presents us with rules and is the source of truth, but in relation to ethical laws experience is the parent of illusion, and it is in the highest degree reprehensible to limit or to deduce the laws which dictate what I *ought to do*, from what *is done*.

We must, however, omit the consideration of these important subjects, the development of which is in reality the peculiar duty and dignity of philosophy, and confine ourselves for the present to the more humble but not less useful task of preparing a firm foundation for those majestic edifices of moral science. For this foundation has been hitherto insecure from the many subterranean passages which reason in its confident but vain search for treasures has made in all directions. Our present duty is to make ourselves perfectly acquainted with the transcendental use made of pure reason, its principles and ideas, that we may be able properly to determine and value its influence and real worth. But before bringing these introductory remarks to a close, I beg those who really have philosophy at heart – and their number is but small – if they shall find themselves convinced by the considerations following as well as by those above, to exert themselves to preserve to the expression *idea* its original signification, and to take care that it be not lost among those other expressions by which all sorts of representations are loosely designated – that the interests of science may not thereby suffer. We are in no want of words to denominate adequately every mode of representation, without the necessity of encroaching upon terms which are proper to others. The following is a serial arrangement of them. The genus is *representation* in general *(representatio)*. Under it stands representation with consciousness *(perceptio)*. A *perception* which relates solely to the subject as a modification of its state, is a *sensation (sensatio)*, an objective perception is *knowledge (cognitio)*. A cognition is either an *intuition* or a *concept (intuitus vel conceptus)*. The former has an immediate relation to the object and is singular; the latter has but a mediate relation, by means of a characteristic mark which may be common to several things. A concept is either *empirical* or *pure*. A pure concept, in so far as it has its origin in the understanding alone, and is not the concept of a pure sensible image, is called *notio*. A concept formed from notions, which transcends the possibility of experience, is an *idea*, or a concept of reason. To one who has accustomed himself to these distinctions, it must be quite intolerable to hear the representation of the colour red called an idea. It ought not even to be called a notion or concept of understanding.

TRANSCENDENTAL DIALECTIC : BOOK I

Section II : Transcendental Ideas

The Transcendental Analytic showed us how the mere logical form of our knowledge can contain the origin of pure concepts *a priori*, concepts which represent objects antecedently to all experience, or rather, indicate the synthetical unity which alone renders possible an empirical knowledge of objects. The form of judgments – converted into a concept of the synthesis of intuitions – produced the categories, which direct the employment of the understanding in experience. This consideration warrants us to expect that the form of syllogisms, when applied to synthetical unity of intuitions, following the rule of the categories, will contain the origin of particular *a priori* concepts, which we may call pure concepts of reason or transcendental ideas, and which will determine the use of the understanding in the totality of experience according to principles.

The function of reason in arguments consists in the universality of knowledge according to concepts, and the syllogism itself is a judgment which is determined *a priori* in the whole extent of its condition. The proposition: 'Caius is mortal', may be obtained from experience by the aid of the understanding alone; but my wish is to find a concept which contains the condition under which the predicate of this judgment is given – in this case, the concept of *man* – and after subsuming under this condition, taken in its whole extent (all men are mortal), I determine according to it the knowledge of the object thought, and say: 'Caius is mortal.'

Hence, in the conclusion of a syllogism we restrict a predicate to a certain object, afer having thought it in the major in its whole extent under a certain condition. This complete quantity of the extent in relation to such a condition is called *universality (universalitas)*. To this corresponds *totality (universitas)* of conditions in the synthesis of intuitions. The transcendental concept of reason is therefore nothing else than the concept of the *totality of the conditions* of a given conditioned. Now as the *unconditioned* alone renders possible a totality of conditions, and, conversely, the totality of conditions is itself always unconditioned; a pure rational concept in general can be defined and explained by means of the concept of the unconditioned, in so far as it contains a basis for the synthesis of the conditioned.

To the number of modes of relation which the understanding thinks by means of the categories, the number of pure rational concepts will correspond. We must therefore seek for, first, an *unconditioned* of the *categorical* synthesis in a *subject*; secondly, of the *hypothetical* synthesis of the members of a *series*; thirdly, of the *disjunctive* synthesis of parts in a *system*.

There are exactly the same number of modes of syllogisms, each of which proceeds through prosyllogisms to the unconditioned – one to the subject which cannot be employed as predicate, another to the presupposition which supposes nothing higher than itself, and the third to an aggregate of the members of the complete division of a concept. Hence the pure rational concepts of totality in the synthesis of conditions have a necessary foundation in the nature of human reason – at least as modes of elevating the unity of the understanding to the unconditioned. They may have no valid application, corresponding to their transcendental employment, *in concreto*, and be thus of no greater utility than to direct the understanding, while extending them as widely as possible, to maintain its exercise and application in perfect consistence and harmony.

But, while speaking here of the totality of conditions and of the unconditioned as the common title of all concepts of reason, we again light upon an expression which we find it impossible to dispense with, and which nevertheless, owing to the ambiguity attaching to it from long abuse, we cannot employ with safety. The word *absolute* is one of the few words which, in its original signification, was perfectly adequate to the concept it was intended to convey – a concept which no other word in the same language exactly suits, and the loss – or, which is the same thing, the incautious and loose employment – of which must be followed by the loss of the concept itself. And, as it is a concept which occupies much of the attention of reason, its loss would be greatly to the detriment of all transcendental philosophy. The word *absolute* is at present frequently used to denote that something is true of a thing considered *in itself* and intrinsically. In this sense *absolutely possible* would signify that which is possible in itself *(interne)* – which is, in fact, the *least* that one can say of an object. On the other hand, it is sometimes employed to indicate that something is valid in all respects (without limitation) – for example, absolute sovereignty. *Absolutely possible* would in this sense signify that which is *possible in all relations* and in every respect; and this is the most that can be said of the possibility of a thing. Now these significations do in truth frequently coincide. Thus, for example, that which is intrinsically impossible, is also impossible in all relations, that is, absolutely impossible. But in most cases they entirely differ from each other *toto caelo*, and I can by no means conclude that, because a thing is in itself possible, it is also possible in all relations, and therefore absolutely. Nay, more, I shall in the sequel show, that absolute necessity does not by any means depend on internal necessity, and that therefore it must not be considered as synonymous with it. If the opposite of something is intrinsically impossible, we may affirm that it is in all respects impossible, and that consequently the thing itself, of which this is the opposite, is absolutely necessary; but I cannot reason conversely and say, the opposite of that which is absolutely necessary is intrinsically impossible, that is, that the *absolute* necessity of things is an *internal* necessity. For this internal necessity is in certain cases a mere empty word with which the least concept cannot be connected, while the concept of the necessity of a thing in all relations possesses very peculiar determinations. Now as the loss of a concept of great utility in speculative science cannot be a matter of indifference to the philosopher, I trust that the proper determination and careful preservation of the expression on which the concept depends will likewise be not indifferent to him.

In this enlarged signification then shall I employ the word *absolute*, in opposition to that which is valid only comparatively or in some particular respect; for the latter is restricted by conditions, the former is valid without any restriction whatever.

Now the transcendental concept of reason has for its object nothing else than absolute totality in the synthesis of conditions, and does not rest satisfied till it has attained to the absolutely, that is, in all respects, unconditioned. For pure reason leaves to the understanding everything that immediately relates to the object of intuition or rather to their synthesis in imagination. The former restricts itself to the absolute totality in the employment of the concepts of the understanding, and aims at carrying out the synthetical unity which is thought in the category, even to the absolutely unconditioned. This unity may hence be called the *rational unity* of appearances, as the other, which the category expresses, may be termed the *unity of the understanding*. Reason, therefore, has an immediate relation to the use of the understanding, not indeed so far as the latter contains the ground of possible experience (for the concept of the absolute totality of conditions is not a concept that can be employed in experience, because no experience is unconditioned), but solely for the purpose of directing the understanding to a certain unity, of which the understanding has no conception, and the aim of which is to collect into an *absolute whole* all acts of the understanding with regard to every object. Hence the objective employment of the pure concepts of reason is always *transcendent*, while that of the pure concepts of the understanding must, according to their nature, be always *immanent*, inasmuch as they are limited to possible experience.

I understand by idea a necessary concept of reason, to which no corresponding object can be discovered in sense-experience. Accordingly, the pure concepts of reason at present under consideration are *transcendental ideas*. They are concepts of pure reason, for they regard all empirical knowledge as determined by means of an absolute totality of conditions. They are not mere fictions, but natural products of reason, and have hence a necessary relation to the whole exercise of the understanding. And finally, they are transcendent, and overstep the limits of all experience, in which, consequently, no object can ever be presented that would be perfectly adequate to a transcendental idea. When we use the word *idea*, we say, as regards its object (an object of the pure understanding), a great deal, but as regards its subject (that is, in respect of its reality under empirical conditions of experience), exceedingly little, because the idea, as the concept of a maximum, can never be completely and adequately presented *in concreto*. Now, as in the merely speculative employment of reason the latter is properly the sole aim, and as in this case the approximation to a concept, which is never attained in practice, is the same thing as if the concept were non-existent – it is commonly said of the concept of this kind, *it is only an idea*. So we might very well say, the absolute whole of all appearances is only an idea, for as we never can present an adequate image of it, it remains for us a *problem* incapable of solution. On the other hand, as in the practical use of the understanding we have only to do with practice according to rules, an idea of pure reason can always be given really *in concreto*, although only partially, nay, it is the indispensable condition of all practical employment of reason. The practice of the idea is always limited and defective, but nevertheless within indeterminable boundaries, consequently always under the influence of the concept of an absolute completeness. And thus the practical idea is always in the highest degree fruitful, and in relation to real actions indispensably necessary. In the idea, pure reason possesses even causality and the power of producing that which its concept contains. Hence we cannot say of wisdom, in a disparaging way, *it is only an idea*. For, for the very reason that it is the idea of the necessary unity of all possible aims, it must be for all practical exertions and endeavours the primitive condition and rule – a rule which is at least limitative.

Now, although we must say of the transcendental concepts of reason, *they are only ideas*, we must not, on this account, look upon them as superfluous and empty. For, although no object can be determined by them, they can be of great utility, unobserved and at the basis of the edifice of the understanding, as the canon for its extended and self-consistent exercise – a canon which, indeed, does not enable it to know more in an object than it would know by the help of its own concepts, but which guides it more securely in its knowledge. Not to mention that they perhaps render possible a transition from our concepts of nature to the practical concepts, and thus produce support for even ethical ideas, and bringing them into connection with the speculative knowledge of reason. The explication of all this must be looked for in the sequel.

But setting aside, in conformity with our original purpose, the consideration of the practical ideas, we proceed to contemplate reason in its speculative use alone, nay, in a still more restricted sphere, to wit, in the transcendental use; and here must strike into the same path which we followed in our deduction of the categories. That is to say, we shall consider the logical form of the knowledge of reason, that we may see whether reason may not be thereby a source of concepts which enables us to regard objects in themselves as determined synthetically *a priori*, in relation to one or other of the functions of reason.

Reason, considered as the faculty of a certain logical form of knowledge, is the faculty of inference, that is, of mediate judgment – by means of the subsumption of the condition of a possible judgment under the condition of a given judgment. The given judgment is the general rule (major). The subsumption of the condition of another possible judgment under the condition of the rule is the minor. The actual judgment, which enounces the assertion of the rule in the subsumed case, is the conclusion (*conclusio*). The rule predicates something generally under a certain condition. The condition of the rule is satisfied in some particular case. It follows, that what was valid in general under that condition must also be considered as valid in the particular case which satisfies this condition. It is very plain that reason attains to knowledge, by means of acts of the understanding which constitute a series of conditions. When I arrive at the proposition, 'All bodies are changeable', by beginning with the more remote knowledge (in which the concept of body does not appear, but which nevertheless contains the condition of that concept), 'Everything composite is changeable', by proceeding from this to a less remote knowledge, which stands under the condition of the former, 'Bodies are composite', and hence to a third, which at length connects for me the remote knowledge (changeable) with the one before me, 'Consequently, bodies are changeable' – I have arrived at a knowledge (conclusion) through a series of conditions (premisses). Now every series, whose exponent (of the categorical or hypothetical judgment) is given, can be continued; consequently the same procedure of reason conducts us to the *ratiocinatio poly-syllogistica*, which is a series of syllogisms, that can be continued either on the side of the conditions (*per prosyllogismos*) or of the conditioned (*per episyllogismos*) indefinitely.

But we very soon perceive that the chain or series of pro-syllogisms, that is, of inferred knowledge on the side of the grounds or conditions of a given knowledge, in other words, the *ascending series* of syllogisms must have a very different relation to the faculty of reason from that of the *descending series*, that is, the progressive procedure of reason on the side of the conditioned by means of episyllogisms. For, as in the former case the knowledge (*conclusio*) is given only as conditioned, reason can attain to this knowledge only under the presupposition that all the members of the series on the side of the conditions are given (totality in the series of premisses), because only under this supposition is the judgment under consideration possible *a priori*; while on the side of the conditioned or the inferences, only an incomplete and *becoming*, and not a presupposed or given series, consequently only a potential progression, is thought. Hence, when knowledge is contemplated as conditioned, reason is compelled to consider the series of conditions in an ascending line as completed and given in their totality. But if the very same knowledge is considered at the same time as the condition of other knowledge, which together constitute a series of inferences in a descending line, reason may preserve a perfect indifference, as to how far this progression may extend *a parte posteriori*, and whether the totality of this series is possible, because it stands in no need of such a series for the purpose of arriving at the conclusion before it, inasmuch as this conclusion is sufficiently guaranteed and determined on grounds *a parte priori*. It may be the case, that upon the side of the conditions the series of premisses has a *first* or highest condition, or it may not possess this, and so be *a parte priori* unlimited; but it must nevertheless contain totality of conditions, even admitting that we never could succeed in completely apprehending it; and the whole series must be unconditionally true, if the conditioned, which is considered as an inference resulting from it, is to be held as true. This is a requirement of reason, which announces its knowledge as determined *a priori* and as necessary, either in itself – and in this case it needs no grounds to rest upon – or, if it is derivative, as a member of a series of grounds, which is itself unconditionally true.

TRANSCENDENTAL DIALECTIC : BOOK I

Section III : System of Transcendental Ideas

We are not at present engaged with a logical dialectic which makes complete abstraction of the content of knowledge, and aims only at uncovering the illusion in the form of rational inferences. Our subject is transcendental dialectic, which must contain, completely *a priori*, the origin of certain knowledge drawn from pure reason, and the origin of certain inferred concepts, the object of which cannot be given empirically, and which therefore lie beyond the sphere of the faculty of understanding. We have observed, from the natural relation which the transcendental use of our knowledge, in inferences as well as in judgments, must have to the logical, that there are three kinds of dialectical inferences, corresponding to the three modes of inference, by which reason attains to knowledge on principles; and that in all it is the business of reason to ascend from the conditioned synthesis, beyond which the understanding never proceeds, to the unconditioned which the understanding never can reach.

Now the most general relations which can exist in our representations are: 1st, the relation to the subject; 2nd, the relation to objects, either as appearances, or as objects of thought in general. If we connect this subdivision with the main division, all the relations of our representations, of which we can form either a concept or an idea, are threefold: 1. The relation to the subject; 2. The relation to the manifold of the object in appearance; 3. The relation to all things in general.

Now all pure concepts have to do in general with the synthetical unity of representations; concepts of pure reason (transcendental ideas), on the other hand, with the unconditional synthetical unity of all conditions. It follows that all transcendental ideas arrange themselves in three classes, the *first* of which contains the absolute (unconditioned) *unity of the thinking subject*, the *second* the absolute *unity of the series of the conditions* of an appearance, the *third* the absolute *unity of the condition of all objects of thought* in general.

The thinking subject is the concern of *psychology*; the sum total of all appearances (the world) is the concern of *cosmology*; and the thing which contains the highest condition of the possibility of all that is capable of being thought (the being of all beings) is the concern of all *theology*. Thus pure reason presents us with the idea of a transcendental doctrine of the soul (*psychologia rationalis*), of a transcendental science of the world (*cosmologia rationalis*), and finally of a transcendental doctrine of God (*theologia transcendentalis*). Understanding cannot originate even the outline of any of these sciences, even when connected with the highest logical use of reason, that is, all conceivable inferences – for the purpose of proceeding from one object (appearance) to all others, even to the utmost limits of the empirical synthesis. They are, on the contrary, pure and genuine products, or problems, of pure reason.

What modi of the pure concepts of reason these transcendental ideas are, will be fully exposed in the following chapter. They follow the guiding thread of the categories. For pure reason never relates immediately to objects, but to the concepts of these contained in the understanding. In like manner, it will be made manifest in the detailed explanation of these ideas – how reason, merely through the synthetical use of the same function which it employs in a categorical inference, necessarily attains to the concept of the absolute unity of the *thinking subject* – how the logical procedure in hypothetical ideas necessarily produces the idea of the absolutely unconditioned *in a series* of given conditions, and finally – how the mere form of the disjunctive inference involves the highest concept of a *being of all beings* : a thought which at first sight seems in the highest degree paradoxical.

An *objective deduction*, such as we were able to present in the case of the categories, is impossible as regards these transcendental ideas. For they have, in truth, no relation to any object, in experience, for the very reason that they are only ideas. But a subjective deduction of them from the nature of our reason is possible, and has been given in the present chapter.

It is easy to perceive that the sole aim of pure reason is the absolute totality of the synthesis *on the side of the conditions*, and that it does not concern itself with the absolute completeness *on the part of the conditioned*. For of the former alone does reason stand in need, in order to presuppose the whole series of conditions, and thus present them to the understanding *a priori*. But if we once have a completely (and unconditionally) given condition, there is no further necessity, in proceeding with the series, for a concept of reason ; for the understanding takes of itself every step downward, from the condition to the conditioned. Thus the transcendental ideas are available only for *ascending* in the series of conditions, till we reach the unconditioned, that is, principles. As regards *descend-*

ing to the conditioned, on the other hand, we find that there is a widely extensive logical use which reason makes of the laws of the understanding, but that a transcendental use thereof is impossible; and, that when we form an idea of the absolute totality of such a synthesis (of the regressus), for example, of the whole series of all *future* changes in the world, this idea is a mere entity of the mind (*ens rationis*), an arbitrary fiction of thought, and not a necessary presupposition of reason. For the possibility of the conditioned presupposes the totality of its conditions, but not of its consequences. Consequently, this concept is not a transcendental idea — and it is with these alone that we are at present occupied.

Finally, it is obvious, that there exists among the transcendental ideas a certain connection and unity, and that pure reason, by means of them, collects all its knowledge into one system. From the knowledge of oneself (the soul) to the knowledge of the world, and through these to the supreme being, the progression is so natural, that it seems to resemble the logical advance of reason from the premisses to the conclusion.[1] Now whether there lies unobserved at the foundation of these ideas an analogy of the same kind as exists between the logical and transcendental procedure of reason, is another of those questions, the answer to which we must not expect till we arrive at a more advanced stage in our inquiries. In this cursory and preliminary view, we have, meanwhile, reached our aim. For we have dispelled the ambiguity which attached to the transcendental concepts of reason, from their being commonly mixed up with other concepts in the systems of philosophers, and not properly distinguished from the concepts of the understanding; we have exposed their origin, and thereby at the same time their determinate number, and presented them in a systematic

---

[1] Metaphysics has for the proper object of its inquiries only three ideas: GOD, FREEDOM, and IMMORTALITY, and it aims at showing, that the second concept, conjoined with the first, must lead to the third, as a necessary conclusion. All the other subjects with which it occupies itself, are merely means for the attainment and realization of these ideas. It does not require these ideas for the construction of a science of nature, but, on the contrary, for the purpose of passing beyond the sphere of nature. A complete insight into and comprehension of them would render *Theology, Morals*, and, through the conjunction of both, *Religion*, solely dependent on the speculative faculty of reason. In a systematic representation of these ideas the above-mentioned arrangement — the *synthetical* one — would be the most suitable; but in the investigation which must necessarily precede it, the *analytical*, which reverses this arrangement, would be better adapted to our purpose, as in it we should proceed from that which experience immediately presents to us — psychology, — to cosmology, and thence to theology.

connection, and have thus marked out and enclosed a definite sphere for pure reason.

TRANSCENDENTAL DIALECTIC: BOOK II

THE DIALECTICAL INFERENCES OF PURE REASON

It may be said that the object of a merely transcendental idea is something of which we have no concept, although the idea may be a necessary product of reason according to its original laws. For, in fact, a concept of an object that is adequate to the idea given by reason, is impossible. For such an object must be capable of being presented and intuited in a possible experience. But we should express our meaning better, and with less risk of being misunderstood, if we said that we can have no knowledge of an object, which perfectly corresponds to an idea, although we may possess a problematical concept thereof.

Now the transcendental (subjective) reality at least of the pure concepts of reason rests upon the fact that we are led to such ideas by a necessary inference of reason. There must therefore be inferences which contain no empirical premisses, and by means of which we infer from something that we do know, to something of which we do not even possess a concept, to which we, nevertheless, by an unavoidable illusion, ascribe objective reality. Such inferences are, as regards their result, rather to be termed sophisms than inferences, although indeed, as regards their origin, they are very well entitled to the latter name, inasmuch as they are not fictions or accidental products of reason, but are necessitated by its very nature. They are sophistications, not of men, but of pure reason itself, from which the wisest cannot free himself. After long labour he may be able to guard against the error, but he can never be thoroughly rid of the illusion which continually mocks and misleads him.

Of these dialectical inferences there are three kinds, corresponding to the number of the ideas which their conclusions present. In the inference of the *first class*, I infer from the transcendental concept of the subject which contains no manifold, the absolute unity of the subject itself, of which I cannot in this manner attain to a concept. This dialectical inference I shall call the transcendental *paralogism*. The *second class* of sophistical inferences is occupied with the transcendental concept of the absolute totality of the series of conditions for a given appearance, and I infer, from the fact that I have always a self-contradictory concept of the unconditioned synthetical unity of the series upon one side, the truth of the opposite unity, of which I have nevertheless no concept. The state of reason in these dialectical inferences, I shall term the *antinomy* of pure reason. Finally, according to the *third* kind of sophistical inference, I infer, from the totality of the conditions for thinking objects in general, in so far as they can be given to me, the absolute synthetical unity of all conditions of the possibility of things in general; that is, from things which I do not know in their mere transcendental concept, I infer a being of all beings which I know still less by means of a transcendental concept, and of whose unconditioned necessity I can form no concept whatever. This dialectical inference I shall call the *ideal* of pure reason.

CHAPTER I – THE PARALOGISMS OF PURE REASON

The logical paralogism consists in the falsity of an inference of reason in respect of its form, be the content what it may. But a transcendental paralogism has a transcendental ground: to make a formally fallacious inference. In this manner the fallacy is grounded in the nature of human reason, and is the parent of an unavoidable, though not insoluble, illusion.

We now come to a concept which was not inserted in the general list of transcendental concepts, and yet must be reckoned with them, but at the same time without in the least altering, or indicating a deficiency in that table. This is the concept, or, if the term is preferred, the judgment, *I think*. But it is readily perceived that this is the vehicle of all concepts in general, and consequently of transcendental concepts also, and that it is therefore regarded as a transcendental concept. But it does not come under any one particular heading, inasmuch as its only use is to indicate that all thought belongs to consciousness. At the same time, pure as this concept is from all empirical content (impressions of the senses), it enables us to distinguish two different kinds of objects through the nature of our faculty of representations. *I*, as thinking, am an object of the internal sense, and am called soul. That which is an object of the external senses is called body. Thus the expression, I, as a thinking being, designates the concern of psychology, which may be called the rational doctrine of the soul, inasmuch as in this science I desire to know nothing of the soul but what, independently of all experience (which determines me *in concreto*), may be inferred from this concept *I*, in so far as it appears in all thought.

Now, the *rational* doctrine of the soul is really an undertaking of this kind. For if the smallest empirical element of thought, if any particular perception of my internal state, were to be introduced among the grounds of knowledge of this science, it would not be a rational, but an *empirical* doctrine of the soul. We have thus before us a supposed science, raised upon the single proposition, the *I think*, whose foundation or want of foundation we may very properly, and agreeably with the nature of a transcendental philosophy, here examine. It ought not to be objected that in this proposition, which expresses the perception of oneself, an internal experience is asserted, and that consequently the rational doctrine of the soul which is founded upon it, is not pure, but partly founded upon an empirical principle. For this internal perception is nothing more than the mere apperception, *I think*, which in fact renders all transcendental concepts possible, in which we say, I think substance, cause, etc. For internal experience in general and its possibility, or perception in general, and its relation to other perceptions, unless some particular distinction or determination thereof is empirically given, cannot be regarded as empirical knowledge, but as knowledge of the empirical in general, and belongs to the investigation of the possibility of every experience, which is certainly transcendental. The smallest object of perception (for example, only pleasure or pain), that should be included in the general representation of self-consciousness, would immediately change rational psychology into an empirical psychology.

The *I think* is therefore the only text of rational psychology, from which it must develop its whole wisdom. It is manifest that this thought, when applied to an object (myself), can contain nothing but transcendental predicates thereof; because the least empirical predicate would destroy the purity of the science and its independence of all experience.

But we shall have to follow here the guidance of the categories — only, as in the present case a thing, I, as thinking being, is at first given, we shall — not indeed change the order of the categories as it stands in the table — but begin at the category of substance, by which a thing in itself is represented, and proceed backwards through the series. The topic of the rational doctrine of the soul, from which everything else it may contain must be derived, is accordingly as follows:

1
The soul is SUBSTANCE

2
As regards its quality,
it is SIMPLE

3
As regards the different times
in which it exists, it is
numerically identical, that is
UNITY, not Plurality

4
It is in relation to *possible*
objects in space[1]

From these elements originate all the concepts of pure psychology, by combination alone, without the aid of any other principle. This substance, merely as an object of the internal sense, gives the concept of *immateriality*; as simple substance, that of *incorruptibility*; its identity, as intellectual substance, gives the concept of *personality*; all these three together, *spirituality*. Its relation to objects in space gives us the concept of connection (*commercium*) with bodies. Thus it represents thinking substance as the principle of life in matter, that is, as a soul (*anima*), and as the ground of *animality*; and thus, limited by the concept of spirituality, gives us that of *immortality*.

Now to these concepts relate four paralogisms of a transcendental psychology, which is falsely held to be a science of pure reason, concerning the nature of our thinking being. We can, however, lay at the foundation of this science nothing but the simple and in itself perfectly contentless representation *I*, which cannot even be called a concept, but merely a consciousness which accompanies all concepts. By this I, or he or it, who or which thinks, nothing more is represented than a transcendental subject of thought=*x*, which is known only by means of the thoughts that are its predicates, and of

---

[1] The reader, who may not so easily perceive the psychological sense of these expressions – taken here in their transcendental abstraction, and cannot guess why the latter attribute of the soul belongs to category of *existence*, will find the expressions sufficiently explained and justified in the sequel. I have, moreover, to apologize for the Latin terms which have been employed, instead of their German synonyms, contrary to good taste. But I judged it better to sacrifice elegance to perspicuity.

which, apart from these, we cannot form the least concept. Hence we are obliged to move in a perpetual circle, inasmuch as we must always employ it, in order to frame any judgment respecting it. And this inconvenience we find it impossible to rid ourselves of, because consciousness in itself is not so much a representation distinguishing a particular object, as a form of representation in general, in so far as it may be termed knowledge; for in and by knowledge alone do I think anything.

It must, however, appear extraordinary at first sight that the condition under which I think, and which is consequently a property of my subject, should be held to be likewise valid for every existence which thinks, and that we can presume to base upon seemingly empirical proposition a judgment which is apodeictic and universal, to wit, that everything which thinks is constituted as the voice of my consciousness declares it to be, that is, as a self-conscious being. The cause of this belief is to be found in the fact, that we necessarily attribute to things *a priori* all the properties which constitute conditions under which alone we can think them. Now I cannot obtain the least representation of a thinking being by means of external experience, but solely through self-consciousness. Such objects are consequently nothing more than the transference of this consciousness of mine to other things which can only thus be represented as thinking beings. The proposition, *I think*, is, in the present case, understood in a problematical sense, not in so far as it contains a perception of an existence (like the Cartesian *Cogito, ergo sum*), but in regard to its mere possibility – for the purpose of discovering what properties may be inferred from so simple a proposition and predicated of the subject of it.

If at the foundation of our pure rational knowledge of thinking beings there lay more than the mere *Cogito* – if we could likewise call in aid observations on the play of our thoughts, and the thence derived natural laws of the thinking self, there would arise an empirical psychology which would be a kind of physiology of the internal sense, and might possibly be capable of explaining the appearances of that sense. But it could never be available for discovering those properties which do not belong to possible experience (such as simplicity), nor could it make any apodeictic statement on the nature of thinking beings: it would therefore not be a rational psychology.

Now, as the proposition *I think* (in the problematical sense) contains the form of every judgment of the understanding in general, and is the constant accompaniment of all the categories as their vehicle; it is manifest, that inferences are drawn from it only by a transcendental employment of the understanding. This use of the understanding excludes all empirical elements; and we cannot, as has been shown above, have any favourable concept beforehand of its procedure. We shall therefore follow with a critical eye this proposition through all the predicaments of pure psychology; but we shall, for brevity's sake, allow this examination to proceed in an uninterrupted connection.

Before entering on this task, however, the following general remark may help to sharpen our attention to this mode of inference. It is not merely through my thinking that I know an object, but only through my determining a given intuition in relation to the untiy of consciousness in which all thinking consists. It follows that I know myself, not through my being conscious of myself as thinking, but only when I am conscious of the intuition of myself as determined in relation to the function of thought. All the modi of self-consciousness in thought are hence not concepts of objects (of the understanding – categories); they are mere logical functions, which do not present to thought an object to be known, and cannot therefore present myself as an object. Not the consciousness of the *determining*, but only that of the *determinable* self, that is, of my internal intuition (in so far as the manifold contained in it can be connected conformably with the general condition of the unity of apperception in thought), is the object.

1. In all judgments I am the *determining* subject of that relation which constitutes a judgment. But that the I which thinks, must be considered as in thought always a *subject*, and as a thing which cannot be a predicate to thought, is an apodeictic and *identical* proposition. But this proposition does not signify that I, as an object, am, for myself, a *self-subsistent being* or *substance*. This latter statement – an ambitious one – requires to be supported by data which are not to be discovered in thought; and are perhaps (in so far as I consider the thinking self merely *as such*) not to be discovered in thought at all.

2. That the I of apperception, and consequently in all thought, is *singular*, and cannot be resolved into a plurality of subjects, and therefore indicates a logically simple subject – this already lies in the concept of thinking, and is consequently an analytical prop-osition. But this is not tantamount to declaring that the thinking I is a simple *substance* – for this would be a synthetical proposition.

The concept of substance always relates to intuitions, which with me cannot be other than sensible, and which consequently lie completely outside the sphere of the understanding and its thought: but to this sphere belongs the affirmation that the I is simple in thought. It would indeed be surprising, if the concept of substance, which in other cases requires so much labour to distinguish from the other elements presented by intuition – so much trouble, too, to discover whether it can be simple (as in the case of the parts of matter) – should be presented immediately to me, as if by revelation, in the poorest representation of all.

3. The proposition of the identity of myself amidst all the manifold representations of which I am conscious, is likewise a proposition lying in the concepts themselves, and is consequently analytical. But this identity of the subject, of which I am conscious in all its representations, does not relate to the intuition of the subject, by which it is given as an object. This proposition cannot therefore enounce the identity of the person, by which is understood the consciousness of the identity of its own substance as a thinking being in all change and variation of circumstances. To prove this, we should require not a mere analysis of the proposition, but synthetical judgments based upon a given intuition.

4. I distinguish my own existence, as that of a thinking being, from that of other things external to me – among which my body also is reckoned. This is also an analytical proposition, for *other* things are exactly those which I think as different or *distinguished* from myself. But whether this consciousness of myself is possible *without* things external to me; and whether therefore I can exist merely as a thinking being (without being human) – cannot be known from this proposition.

Thus we have gained nothing as regards the knowledge of myself as object, by the analysis of the consciousness of myself in thought. The logical exposition of thought in general is mistaken for a metaphysical determination of the object.

Our *Critique* would meet a real stumbling-block, if there existed a possibility of proving *a priori*, that all thinking beings are in themselves simple substances, as such, therefore (for this follows from the same mode of proof), possess the inseparable attribute of personality, and are conscious of their existence distinct from matter. For we should thus have taken a step beyond the world of sense, and have penetrated into the sphere of *noumena*; and in this case the right could not be denied us of extending our knowledge in this sphere, of establishing ourselves, and, under a favouring star, appropriating to ourselves possessions in it. For the proposition: 'Every thinking being, as such, is simple substance', is an *a priori* synthetical proposition; because in the first place it goes beyond the concept which is the subject of it, and adds to the mere notion of a thinking being the *mode of its existence*, and in the second place annexes a predicate (that of simplicity) to the latter concept – a predicate which it could not have discovered in the sphere of experience. It would follow that *a priori* synthetical propositions are possible and legitimate, not only, as we have maintained, in relation to objects of possible experience, and as principles of the possibility of this experience itself, but are applicable to things as things in themselves – an inference which makes an end of the whole of this *Critique*, and obliges us to fall back on the old mode of metaphysical procedure. But indeed the danger is not so great, if we look a little closer into the question.

There lies in the procedure of rational psychology a paralogism, which is represented in the following inference:

That which cannot be thought otherwise than as subject, does not exist otherwise than as subject, and is therefore substance.

A thinking being, considered merely as such, cannot be thought otherwise than as subject.

Therefore it exists also as such, that is, as substance.

In the major we speak of a being that can be thought generally and in every relation, consequently as it may be given in intuition. But in the minor we speak of the same being only in so far as it regards itself as subject, relatively to thought and the unity of consciousness, but not in relation to intuition, by which it is presented as an object to thought. Thus the conclusion is here arrived at by a *sophisma figurae dictionis*.[1]

That this famous argument is a mere paralogism, will be plain to anyone who will consider the general remark which precedes our

---

[1] *Thought* is taken in the two premisses in two totally different senses. In the major it is considered as relating and applying to objects in general, consequently to objects of intuition also. In the minor, we understand it as relating merely to self-consciousness. In this sense, we do not think an object, but merely the relation to the self-consciousness of the subject, as the form of thought. In the former premiss we speak of things which cannot be thought otherwise than as subjects. In the second, we do not spek of *things*, but of *thought* (all objects being abstracted), in which the *I* is always the subject of consciousness. Hence the conclusion cannot be, 'I cannot exist otherwise than as subject;' but only 'I can, in thinking my existence, employ myself only as the subject of the judgment.' But this is an identical proposition, and throws no light on the mode of my existence.

systematic presentation of the principles and the section on noumena. For it was there proved that the concept of a thing, which can exist *per se* – only as a subject and never as a predicate, possesses no objective reality ; that is to say, we can never know whether there exists any object to correspond to the concept, since we do not have means of deciding whether such a mode of existence is possible, so that the concept does not afford any knowledge at all. If this concept is to indicate by the term *substance*, an object that can be given, if it is to become knowledge, we must have at the foundation of the knowledge a permanent intuition, as the indispensable condition of its objective reality. For through intuition alone can an object be given. But in internal intuition there is nothing permanent, for the *I* is but the consciousness of my thought. If, then, we appeal merely to thought, we cannot discover the necessary condition of the application of the concept of substance – that is, of a subject existing *per se* – to the subject as a thinking being. And thus the concept of the simple nature of substance, which is connected with the objective reality of this concept, is shown to be also invalid, and to be, in fact, nothing more than the logical qualitative unity of self-consciousness in thought in general ; whilst we remain perfectly ignorant whether the subject is composite or not.

Refutation of the Proof of Mendelssohn for the Permanence of the Soul

This acute philosopher easily perceived the insufficiency of the common argument which attempts to prove that the soul – if one grants that it is a simple being – cannot perish by *dissolution* ; he saw it is not impossible for it to cease to be by *disappearance*. He endeavoured to prove in his *Phaedo*, that the soul cannot be annihilated, by showing that a simple being cannot cease to exist. Inasmuch as, he said, a simple existence cannot diminish, nor gradually lose portions of its being, and thus be by degrees reduced to nothing (for it possesses no parts, and therefore no multiplicity), between the moment in which it is, and the moment in which it is not, no time can be discovered – which is impossible. But this philosopher did not consider, that, granting the soul to possess this simple nature, which contains no parts external to each other, and consequently no extensive quantity, we cannot refuse to it any less than to any other being, intensive quantity, that is, a degree of reality in regard to all its faculties, nay, to all that constitutes its existence. But this degree of reality can become less and less through an infinite series of smaller degrees. It follows, therefore, that this supposed substance – this thing, the permanence of which is not assured in any other way, may, if not by decomposition, then by gradual loss *(remissio)* of its powers (consequently by elanguescence, if I may employ this expression), be changed into nothing. For consciousness itself has always a degree, which may be lessened.[1] Consequently the faculty of being conscious may be diminished; and so with all other faculties. The permanence of the soul, therefore, as an object of the internal sense, remains undemonstrated, nay, even indemonstrable. Its permanence in life is evident *per se,* inasmuch as the thinking being (as man) is to itself, at the same time, an object of the external senses. But this does not suffice for the rational psychologist to affirm, from mere concepts, its absolute permanence.[2]

[1] Clearness is not, as logicians maintain, the consciousness of a representation. For a certain degree of consciousness, which may not, however, be sufficient for recollection, is to be met with in many dim representations. For without any consciousness at all, we should not be able to recognize any difference in the obscure representations we connect; as we really can do with many concepts, such as those of right and equity, and those of the musician, who strikes at once several notes in improvising a piece of music. But a representation is clear, in which our consciousness is sufficient for the *consciousness of the difference* of this representation from others. If we are only conscious that there is a difference, but are not conscious of the difference – that is, what the difference is – the representation must still be termed obscure. There is, consequently, an infinite series of degrees of consciousness down to its entire disappearance.

[2] There are some who think they have done enough to establish a new possibility in the mode of the existence of souls, when they have shown that there is no contradiction in their hypotheses on this subject. Such are those who affirm the possibility of thought – of which they have no other knowledge than what they derive from its use in connecting empirical intuitions presented in this our human life – after this life has ceased. But it is very easy to embarrass them by the introduction of counter-possibilities, which rest upon quite as good a foundation. Such, for example, is the possibility of the division of a *simple substance* into several substances; and conversely, of the coalition of several into one simple substance. For, although divisibility presupposes composition, it does not necessarily require a composition of substances, but only of the degrees (of the several faculties) of one and the same substance. Now we can think all the power and faculties of the soul – even that of consciousness – as diminished by one half, the substance still remaining. In the same way we can represent to ourselves without contradiction, this obliterated half as preserved, not in the soul, but outside it; and we can believe that, as in this case everything that is real in the soul, and has a degree – consequently its entire existence – has been halved, a particular substance would arise out of the soul. For the multiplicity, which has been divided, formerly existed, but not as a multiplicity of substances, but of every reality as the quantum of existence in it; and the unity of substance was merely a mode of existence, which by this division alone has been transformed into a plurality of subsistence. In the same manner several simple substances

If, now, we take the above propositions – as they must be accepted as valid for all thinking beings in the system of rational psychology – in synthetical connection, and proceed, from the category of relation, with the proposition : 'All thinking beings are, as such, substances', backwards through the series, till the circle is completed ; we come at last to the existence of these things. Now in this system of rational psychology the thinking beings are not only conscious of their own existence independently of external things, they can even determine that existence by themselves with regard to the permanence that is a necessary characteristic of substance. It follows that *idealism* – at least problematical idealism – is perfectly unavoidable in this rationalistic system. And, if the existence of outward things is not held to be requisite to the determination of one's own existence in time, the existence of these outward things at all, is a gratuitous assumption which remains without the possibility of a proof.

But if we proceed *analytically* – the 'I think' as a proposition containing in itself an existence as given, consequently modality being the principle – and analyse this proposition, in order to ascertain its content, and discover whether and how this *I* determines its existence in time and space solely through that content, the propositions of rationalistic psychology would not begin with the concept of a thinking being, but with a reality, and the properties of a thinking being in general would be derived from the mode in which this reality is thought, after everything empirical had been abstracted ; as is shown in the following table :

might coalesce into one, without anything being lost except the plurality of subsistence, inasmuch as the one substance would contain the degree of reality of all the former substances. Perhaps, indeed, the simple substances, which appear under the form of matter, might (not indeed by a mechanical or chemical influence upon each other, but by an unknown influence, of which the former would be but the appearance), by means of such a *dynamical* division of the parent-souls, as *intensive quantities,* produce other souls, while the former repaired the loss thus sustained with new matter of the same sort. I am far from allowing any value to such chimeras ; and the principles of our analytic have clearly proved that no other than an empirical use of the categories – that of substance, for example – is possible. But if the rationalist is bold enough to construct, on the mere authority of the faculty of thought – without any intuition, whereby an object is given – a self-subsistent being, merely because the unity of apperception in thought cannot allow him to believe it a composite being, instead of declaring, as he ought to do, that he is unable to explain the possibility of a thinking nature ; what ought to hinder the *materialist*, with as complete an independence of experience, to employ the principle of the rationalist in a directly opposite manner – still preserving the formal unity required by his opponent ?

1
I think

2
as Subject

3
as simple subject,

4
as identical subject,
in every state
of my thought.

Now, inasmuch as it is not determined in this second proposition, whether I can exist and be thought only as subject, and not also as a predicate of another being, the concept of a subject is here taken in a merely logical sense; and its remains undetermined, whether substance is to be thought under the concept or not. But in the third proposition, the absolute unity of apperception – the simple *I* in the representation to which all connection and separation, which constitute thought, relate, is of itself important; even though it presents us with no information about the constitution or subsistence of the subject. Apperception is something real, and the simplicity of its nature is given in the very fact of its possibility. Now in space there is nothing real that is at the same time simple; for points, which are the only simple things in space, are merely limits, but not constituent parts of space. From this follows the impossibility of a definition on the basis of materialism of the constitution of myself as a merely thinking subject. But, because my existence is considered in the first proposition as given, for it does not mean, 'Every thinking being exists' (for this would be predicating of them absolute necessity), but only, '*I exist* thinking'; the proposition is quite empirical, and contains the determinability of my existence merely in relation to my representations in time. But as I require for this purpose something that is permanent, such as is not given in internal intuition; the mode of my existence, whether as substance or as accident, cannot be determined by means of this simple self-consciousness. Thus, if materialism is inadequate to explain the mode in which I exist, spiritualism is likewise as insufficient; and the conclusion is, that we are utterly unable to attain to any knowledge of the constitution of the soul, in so far as the possibility of its separate existence is concerned.

And, indeed, how should it be possible, merely by the aid of the unity of consciousness – which we know only for the reason that it is indispensable to the possibility of experience – to pass the bounds of experience (our existence in this life); and to extend our knowledge to the nature of all thinking beings by means of the empirical – but in relation to every sort of intuition, perfectly undetermined – proposition, 'I think'?

There does not then exist any rational psychology as a *doctrine* furnishing any addition to our knowledge of ourselves. It is nothing more than a *discipline*, which sets impassable limits to speculative reason in this region of thought, to prevent it, on the one hand, from throwing itself into the arms of a soulless materialism, and, on the other, from losing itself while alive, in a baseless spiritualism. It teaches us to consider this refusal of our reason to give any satisfactory answer to questions which reach beyond the limits of this our present life, as a hint to abandon fruitless and extravagant speculation; and to direct, to a fruitful use, our knowledge of ourselves – which, although applicable only to objects of experience, receives its principles from a higher source, and regulates our conduct as if our destiny reached far beyond the boundaries of experience and hence of the present life.

From all this it is evident that rational psychology has its origin in a mere misunderstanding. The unity of consciousness, which lies at the basis of the categories, is considered to be an intuition of the subject as an object; and the category of substance is applied to the intuition. But this unity is nothing more than the unity in *thought*, by which no object is given; to which therefore the category of substance – which always presupposes a given intuition – cannot be applied. Consequently, the subject cannot be known. The subject of the categories cannot, therefore, for the very reason that it thought these, frame any conception of itself as an object of the categories; for, to think these, it must lay at the foundation its own pure self-consciousness – the very thing that it wishes to explain and describe. In like manner, the subject, in which the representation of time has its basis, cannot determine, for this very reason, its own existence in time. Now, if the latter is impossible, the former, as an attempt to determine itself by means of the categories as a thinking being in general, is no less so.[1]

*

[1] The 'I think' is, as has already been stated, an empirical proposition, and contains the proposition 'I exist'. But I cannot say, 'Everything, which thinks, exists'; for in this case the property of thought would turn all beings possessing it into necessary beings. Hence my existence cannot be considered as an inference from the proposition, 'I think', as Descartes maintained – because in this case the major premiss, 'Everything, which thinks, exists',

Thus disappointed expectation is the result of the attempt to extend knowledge beyond the limits of possible experience and yet in the highest interest of mankind, at least if such knowledge is to be the gift of speculative philosophy. But, in this interest of thought, the severity of criticism has rendered to reason a not unimportant service, by the demonstration of the impossibility of making any dogmatical affirmation concerning an object of experience beyond the boundaries of experience. Criticism has thus fortified reason against all affirmations of the contrary. Now, this can be accomplished in only two ways. Either our proposition must be proved apodeictically; or, if this is unsuccessful, the sources of this inability must be sought for, and if these are discovered to exist in the natural and necessary limitation of our reason, our opponents must submit to the same law of renunciation, and refrain from advancing claims to dogmatic assertion.

But the right, and even the necessity to admit a future life, upon principles of the practical conjoined with the speculative use of reason, has lost nothing by this renunciation; for the merely speculative proof has never had any influence upon the common reason of men. It stands upon the point of a hair, so that even the schools have been able to preserve it from falling only by incessantly discussing it and spinning it like a top; and even in their eyes it has never been able to present any safe foundation for the erection of anything. The proofs which have been current among men, preserve their value undiminished; nay, rather gain in clearness and unsophisticated power, by the rejection of the dogmatical assumptions. For reason is thus confined within its own peculiar province – the

---

must precede – but the two propositions are identical. The proposition, 'I think,' expresses an undetermined empirical intuition, that is, perception (proving consequently that sensation, which must belong to sensibility, lies at the foundation of this proposition); but it precedes experience, whose province it is to determine an object of perception by means of the categories in relation to time; and existence in this proposition is not a category, as it does not apply to an undetermined given object, but only to one of which we have a concept, and about which we wish to know whether it does or does not exist outside this concept. An undetermined perception signifies here merely something real that has been given, only, however, to thought in general – but not as an appearance, nor as a thing in itself (noumenon), but only as something that actually exists, and is designated as such in the proposition, 'I think'. For it must be remarked that, when I call the proposition 'I think', an empirical proposition, I do not thereby mean that the *I* in the proposition is an empirical representation; on the contrary, it is purely intellectual, because it belongs to thought in general. But without some empirical representation, which presents to the mind material for thought, the act, 'I think', would not take place; and the empirical is only the condition of the application or employment of the pure intellectual faculty.

arrangement of ends or aims, which is at the same time the arrangement of nature; and, as a practical faculty, without limiting itself to the latter, it is justified in extending the former, and with it our own existence, beyond the boundaries of experience and life. If we turn our attention to the *analogy of the nature* of living beings in this world, in the consideration of which reason is obliged to accept as a principle, that no organ, no faculty, no appetite, nothing whatsoever is useless, and that nothing is superfluous, nothing disproportionate to its use, nothing unsuited to its end; but that, on the contrary, everything is perfectly conformed to its destination in life – we shall find that man, who alone is the final end of this order, is still the only animal that seems to be excepted from it. For his natural gifts, not merely as regards the talents and motives that may incite him to employ them – but especially the moral law in him, stretch so far beyond all utility and advantage that he could derive from it in this life, that he feels himself bound to prize the mere consciousnes of probity, apart from all advantageous consequences – even the shadowy gift of posthumous fame – above everything; and he is conscious of an inward call to make himself fit, by his conduct in this world – and through renunciation of much advantage – to be the citizen of a better world, which he knows as an idea. This mighty, irresistible proof – accompanied by an ever-increasing knowledge of the conformability to a purpose in everything we see around us, by the contemplation of the boundless immensity of creation, by the consciousness of a certain illimitableness in the possible extension of our knowledge, and by a desire commensurate therewith – still remains, even after the theoretical knowledge of ourselves has failed to establish the necessity of an existence after death.

Conclusion of the Solution of the Psychological Paralogism

The dialectical illusion in rational psychology arises from our confusing an idea of reason (of a pure intelligence) with the concept – in every respect undetermined – of a thinking being in general. I think myself on behalf of a possible experience; at the same time making abstraction of all actual experience: and infer therefrom that I can be conscious of myself apart from experience and its empirical conditions. I consequently confound the possible *abstraction* of my empirically determined existence with the supposed consciousness of a possible *separate* existence of my thinking self;

and I believe that I know what is substantial in myself as a transcendental subject, when I have nothing more in thought than the unity of consciousness, which lies at the basis of all determination of knowledge.

The task of explaining the community of the soul with the body does not properly belong to the psychology of which we are here speaking; because this psychology proposes to prove the personality of the soul even apart from this communion (after death), and is therefore *transcendent* in the proper sense of the word; although occupying itself with an object of experience it does so only in so far, however, as it ceases to be an object of experience. But a sufficient answer may be found to the question in our teaching. The difficulty which lies in the execution of this task consists, as is well known, in the presupposed heterogeneity of the object of the internal sense (the soul) and the objects of the external senses; inasmuch as the formal condition of the intuition of the one is time, and of that of the other space also. But if we consider that both kinds of objects do not differ internally, but only in so far as the one *appears* externally to the other – consequently, that which lies at the basis of appearances, as a thing in itself, may not be heterogeneous; this difficulty disappears. There then remains no other difficulty than is to be found in the question – how a community of substances is possible; a question which lies outside the region of psychology, and which the reader, after what in our Analytic has been said of primitive forces and faculties, will easily judge to be also beyond the region of human knowledge.

General Remark on the Transition from Rational Psychology to Cosmology

The proposition, 'I think', or, 'I exist thinking', is an empirical proposition. But such a proposition must be based on empirical intuition, hence also the object thought as an appearance; and thus our theory appears to maintain that the soul, even in thought, is turned into an appearance; and in this way our consciousness itself being an illusion, must amount to nothing.

Thought, *per se*, is merely the purely spontaneous logical function which operates to connect the manifold of a possible intuition; and it does not represent the subject of consciousness as an appearance – for this reason alone, that it pays no attention to the question whether the mode of intuiting it is sensible or intellectual. I therefore do not represent myself in thought either as I am, or as I appear to myself; I merely think myself as an object in general, of the mode of intuiting which I make abstraction. When I represent myself as the *subject* of thought, or as the *ground* of thought, these modes of representation are not related to the categories of substance or of cause; for these are functions of thought applicable only to our sensible intuition. The application of these categories to the *I* would, however, be necessary, if I wished to make myself an object of knowledge. But I wish to be conscious of myself only as thinking; in what mode my own self is given in intuition, I do not consider, and it may be that I, who think, am an appearance – although not in so far as I am a thinking being; but in the consciousness of myself in mere thought I am a being, though this consciousness does not present to me any property of this being as material for thought.

But the proposition, 'I think', in so far as it declares, '*I exist* thinking', is not a mere logical function. It determines the subject (which is in this case an object also) in relation to existence; and it cannot be given without the aid of the internal sense, whose intuition presents to us an object, not as a thing in itself, but always as an appearance. In this proposition there is therefore something more to be found than the mere spontaneity of thought; there is also the receptivity of intuition, that is, my thought of myself applied to the empirical intuition of myself. Now in this intuition the thinking self must seek the conditions of the employment of its logical functions as categories of substance, cause, and so forth; not merely for the purpose of distinguishing itself as an object in itself by means of the representation *I*, but also for the purpose of determining the mode of its existence, that is, to know itself as noumenon. But this is impossible, for the internal empirical intuition is sensible, and presents us with nothing but phenomenal data, which do not assist the object of pure consciousness in its attempt to know itself as a separate existence, but are only for the sake of experience.

But, let it be granted that we could discover, not in experience, but in certain (not merely logical) firmly-established *a priori* laws of the use of pure reason – laws relating to our existence, ground to consider ourselves as legislating *a priori* in relation to our own existence and as determining this existence; we should, on this supposition, find ourselves possessed of a spontaneity, by which our actual existence would be determinable, without the aid of the conditions of empirical intuition. We should also become aware, that in the consciousness of our existence there was *a priori* something present which would serve to determine our own existence – an existence only sensibly determinable – relatively, however, to a certain internal faculty in relation to an intelligible world, though of course a world that is merely thought.

But this would not give the least help to the attempts of rational psychology. For this wonderful faculty, which the consciousness of the moral law in me reveals, would present me with a principle of the determination of my own existence which is purely intellectual – but by what predicates? By none other than those which are given in sensible intuition. Thus I should find myself in the same position in rational psychology which I formerly occupied, that is to say, I should find myself still in need of sensible intuitions, in order to give significance to my concepts of the understanding of substance, cause, etc., by means of which alone I can possess a knowledge of myself: but these intuitions can never raise me above the sphere of experience. I should be justified, however, in applying these concepts, in regard to their practical use, which is always directed to objects of experience – in conformity with their analogical significance when employed theoretically – to freedom and its subject. At the same time, I should understand by them merely the logical functions of subject and predicate, of ground and consequence, in conformity with which all actions are so determined, that they are capable of being explained along with the laws of nature, conformably to the categories of substance and cause, although they orginate from a very different principle. We have made these observations for the purpose of guarding against misunderstanding, to which the doctrine of our intuition of ourself as an appearance is exposed. We shall have occasion to perceive their utility in the sequel.

FIRST PARALOGISM : SUBSTANTIALITY

Substance is that whose representation is the absolute subject of our judgments, hence it cannot be used as a determination of any other thing.

I am, as a thinking being, the absolute subject of all my possible judgments and this representation of myself cannot be used as a predicate of any other thing.

I am, therefore, as a thinking being (soul), a substance.

CRITICISM OF THE FIRST PARALOGISM OF PURE PSYCHOLOGY

In the Analytic of the Transcendental Logic we have shown that pure categories (including the category of substance) do not have any objective meaning by themselves, unless they are supplied with an intuition on whose manifold they can be applied as functions of synthetic unity. Otherwise they are solely functions of judgment, without any content. I may say of anything whatever that it is substance in so far as I distinguish if from mere predicates and determinations of things. Now the *I* is the subject in all our thinking, thoughts merely inhering in it as determinations, and this *I* cannot be used as a determination of any other thing. Hence everybody must necessarily consider themselves as a substance and must consider thinking as only so many accidents of his existence and determinations of his state.

But what use am I to make of this concept of a substance? I cannot in any way infer from it that I will go on existing or that it is in the nature of things that I neither come into existence nor pass out of existence. But surely that was the whole point of the concept of the substantiality of my thinking subject. Without it I might as well dispense with the concept.

The mere pure category of substance is far from providing a basis for inferring these properties, rather the persistence of a given object must be based on experience if we want to apply the empirically applicable concept of a substance to the object. Now in the case of the claim we are considering, we did not base it on experience, rather we drew our inference merely from the concept of the relation in which all thinking stands to the *I* as the common subject in which it inheres. Nor would there be any reliable observation on which we could establish such a permanence, if we should want to turn to experience instead. For, although the *I* is present in all thoughts, this representation is not tied to any intuition at all, an intuition which could serve to distinguish it from other objects in intuition. So, although we may note that this representation is invariably present in all thinking, we cannot observe that there is a permanent and abiding intuition in which thoughts (being changeable) come and go.

It follows from the above that the first rational inference of transcendental psychology gives us only the pretence of new insight. It does so by mistaking the abiding logical subject of thought for knowledge of a real inner subject. Of this real subject we do not have, nor could have, any knowledge whatsoever. For consciousness is the only thing that turns representations into thoughts, hence all our perceptions must, by virtue of belonging to the transcendental subject, exist in consciousness; but we do not, except for this *I* in its logical meaning, have any knowledge of the subject in itself, as a substratum underlying this *I* as well as all thoughts. This is not to say that one need give up the proposition that the soul is a substance, provided that one adopts a moderate stance and admits that this concept does not lead a single step further and could not demonstrate any of the inferences commonly drawn in the pseudo-science of [rational] psychlogy, such as the everlastingness of the soul in the face of all change and even in the face of the person's death. This concept designates a substance only as an idea, not in reality.

SECOND PARALOGISM : SIMPLICITY

A thing is simple if its action cannot ever be considered as the concurrence of several things acting.

Now the soul, or the thinking *I*, is like that.

It follows that, etc.

CRITICISM OF THE SECOND PARALOGISM OF
TRANSCENDENTAL PSYCHOLOGY

This is the Achilles of all dialectical inferences of pure psychology. It is not a mere sophistical game contrived by some dogmatic thinker in order to endow his claims with a fleeting appeal; rather it is an inference which appears to withstand subjection to the sharpest examination and to the most considered inquiry. Here it is.

Every composite substance is an aggregate of several substances, and the action of a composite substance, or of what inheres in it in so far as it is composite, is an aggregate of several actions or accidents distributed among the set of substances. Now it is possible that an effect should arise from the concurrence of several acting substances, provided that the effect is merely external. (For example, the movement of a body is the united movement of all its parts.) But the same is not true with regard to thoughts, which are accidents belonging inherently to a thinking being. For suppose that something composite could think. In that case each part of it would contain a part of the thought while the whole thought would be contained only in all of them together. But this is incoherent. For since representations distributed among different beings can never constitute a whole thought (say a line in a poem), thoughts cannot inhere in something composite as composite. It follows that thoughts are possible only within a unitary substance which is not an aggregate of several substances, hence which is absolutely simple.[1]

The so-called *nervus probandi* of this argument is the thesis that several representations can constitute a thought only if they are contained in the absolute unity of the thinking subject. But nobody can prove this thesis on the basis of concepts [alone]. For how could he go about the task? The proposition 'A thought can be the effect only of the absolute unity of the thinking being' cannot be treated as being analytic. For the unity of a thought, since thoughts consist of several representations, is a collective unity which, as far as mere concepts make out, can rely just as much on the collective unity of the substances involved (just as the movement of a body is the

[1] It is straightforward to give this proof a properly scholarly appearance. But for my purpose it suffices if we have only the basis of the proof in front of us, even if merely popularly presented.

composite movement of all its parts) as on the absolute unity of the subject. Thus the law of identity cannot establish the necessity of presupposing a simple substance for every composite thought. On the other hand, nobody who appreciates the bases we have offered for the possibility of synthetic *a priori* propositions will take on the burden of asserting that the proposition in question can be known on the basis of concepts alone to be synthetic yet fully *a priori*.

Now it is equally impossible to derive this necessary unity of the subject, as the condition for the possibility of all thoughts, from experience. For through experience we do not apprehend any necessity, not to mention the fact that the concept of an absolute unity goes far beyond the domain of experience. From where, then, are we to derive this proposition, on whose basis the entire psychological rational inference relies?

It is clear that if one wants to imagine a thinking being, one has to place oneself in its position. Thus one has to lend one's own subject to the object that one wants to consider. (This is not true in any other kind of inquiry.) This is the only reason why we recognize absolute unity of the subject for every thought, since otherwise one could not say 'I am thinking (the manifold in a representation)'. For although the whole thought could be divided and distributed among several subjects, the subjective *I* cannot be divided and distinguished, and it is precisely this *I* that we presuppose in all thinking.

Here, then, just as in the case of the previous paralogism, the formal expression of apperception – the 'I think' – remains the sole basis on which rational psychology ventures to extend its knowledge. This presupposition is not an experience, it is the form of all apperception attaching to and preceding all experience, while at the same time it must always be considered in relation to possible experience in general, since it is merely its subjective condition. We go wrong if we turn this condition into a condition for the possibility of knowing an object, that is to say if we turn it into a concept of a thinking being, something we are inclined to do because we cannot imagine a thinking being without placing ourselves, including the formula of our consiousness, in the position of every other intelligent being.

Moreover, the simplicity of myself (as soul) is not something to be inferred from the proposition 'I think', rather it is present in every thought itself. The proposition 'I am simple' must be regarded as a direct expression of apperception, just as the supposed

Cartesian inference 'cognito, ergo sum' is in fact a tautology since the cogito (sum cogitans) directly asserts existence. But 'I am simple' means only that this representation, the 'I', does not include any multiplicity whatsoever and that it is absolute unity, albeit only logical unity.

Thus the famous psychological proof is based merely on the indivisible unity of a representation, a representation serving only to relate the verb [i.e. thinking] to a person. But it is clear that the subject of inherence is only transcendentally characterized by means of the *I* attaching to thoughts and that we do not thereby observe any of its properties whatsoever or in general have any acquaintance or knowledge of it. The *I* designates a something in general (the transcendental subject), whose representation must certainly be simple, but only because we are not thereby determining anything about the subject, just as nothing more simple can be represented than by means of the concept of a mere something. The simplicity of the representation of a subject is not the same as knowledge of the simplicity of the subject itself. In referring to a subject merely through the expression *I*, which is utterly devoid of content (and which can be applied to every thinking subject), we are entirely abstracting from the properties of the subject.

This much is certain, that the *I* always serves me to think of an absolute but logical unity of the subject (simplicity); it does not serve me to know that my subject is actually simple. Just as the proposition 'I am a substance' refers only to the pure category, which I cannot make use of *in concreto*, so I am equally entitled to say 'I am a simple substance', that is to say a substance the representation of which never contains any synthesis of the manifold. But this concept, or this proposition, does not tell us anything at all with regard to myself as an object of experience since the concept of a substance itself is being used only as a function of synthesis here, without intuition being supplied, hence without an object, and it applies only to the condition of our knowledge and not to any object that one might care to mention. Let us consider the supposed usefulness of this proposition through the following experiment.

Everybody will admit that the postulate of the simple nature of the soul is of any value only to the extent that we are thereby able to distinguish this subject from all matter and hence to exempt if from perishing, to which matter is always subject. This is indeed how the above proposition was intended, which is why it is also commonly expressed as 'The soul is not corporeal'. Now suppose that I am able to show that even if one grants full objective validity to this cardinal thesis of rational psychology in its pure meaning as a mere rational judgment (from pure categories) and one says that everything that thinks is a simple substance, still this thesis cannot be put to any use whatever as regards the dissimilarity or else affinity between the thinking substance and matter. In that case I should have banished this supposed psychological insight to the realm of mere ideas, lacking in the reality provided by objective use.

In the Transcendental Aesthetic we undeniably demonstrated that bodies are mere appearances of our external sense and not things in themselves. We are, therefore, justified in saying that our thinking subject is not corporeal, that is to say since we represent it as an object of inner sense, it cannot, in so far as it thinks, be an object of outer sense, i.e. an appearance in space. This means that we can never encounter thinking beings, as such, among external appearances, or that we cannot intuit their thoughts, their consciousness, their desires, etc., by means of external intuition, such things belonging to internal sense. This does indeed appear to be the natural and popular argument, whch appears always to have struck even the most common sense and which from very early on made it regard souls as beings that are entirely different from bodies.

Now, it is true that extension, impenetrability, cohesion [compositeness] and motion, in short everything that external senses can deliver us, are not thoughts, feelings, inclinations or decisions, nor do they contain these since these are never objects of external intuition. But it might still be the case that this something, which underlies the external appearances and which affects our sense in such a way that it receives the representations of space, matter, shape, etc., considered as noumenon (or better, as transcendental object), is at the same time the subject of thoughts, although it affects our external sense in such a way that we do not receive any intuition of representation, volition, etc., but merely of space and its determinations. But this something is not extended, not impenetrable, not composite, because all these predicates are the province only of sensibility and its intuition by virtue of being affected by such objects (otherwise unknown to us). At the same time, these expressions do not at all reveal what kind of object this is, but only that these predicates of external appearances cannot be attributed to it in so far as it is considered in itself as such and not in relation to external senses. However, the predicates of inner sense – representation and thoughts – do not contradict it. Hence the human soul is not, even if one grants the simplicity of its nature, sufficiently distinguished from the substratum of matter, assuming, that is, that one considers matter merely as appearance, as indeed one should.

If matter were a thing in itself, it would, being something composite, be entirely distinct from the soul, which is something simple. But in fact matter is merely external appearance whose substratum cannot be known through any available predicate. It follows that I may well assume that the substratum is in itself simple but that it affects our senses in such a way that the intuition of something extended and hence composite is produced. Hence the substance which in relation to our external sense is extended, is in itself the locus of thoughts which, through their own inner sense, can be represented with consciousness. According to this line of thought, the very same thing which is called corporeal with regard to one relation would with regard to a different relation be a thinking being, the signs of whose thoughts, though not the thoughts themselves, we can intuit in appearance. But then it would be wrong to say that only souls (as peculiar kinds of substance) think. Rather, we should adopt to the common expression that it is human beings who think, that is to say, the very same thing which as external intuition is extended is internally (in itself) a subject which is not composite but rather simple and thinking.

However, we need not allow for such hypotheses in order to observe in a general way that if by a soul one means the thinking being itself, it is misplaced to ask whether or not the soul is the same kind of thing as matter (matter not being a thing in itself but only a kind of representation in us). For it is plain that a thing in itself is of a different nature than the determinations that merely serve to make up its state.

If, on the other hand, we compare the thinking I not with the matter but with that which is intelligible and which underlies the external intuition that we call matter, we equally cannot say that the soul is somehow internally distinct from this, for we know nothing about it.

Thus the fact that consciousness is simple does not mean that we are acquainted with the simple nature of our subject, if that means that we are meant to distinguish this subject from matter, which is something composite.

But although this concept proves of no use in precisely the one case where it would be useful, namely in order to compare myself with objects of external experience so as to establish what is peculiar and distinctive about my nature, one might still pretend to know that the thinking I, the soul (which is what the transcendental object of inner sense is called) is simple. But this expression does not thereby become applicable to real objects, hence it cannot extend our knowledge in the least.

Thus collapses the main pillar supporting rational psychology and with it collapses entire rational psychology. Here too, as in every other area, we have no hope of extending our insight through concepts alone (let alone through the mere subjective form of all our concepts, that is to say consciousness), without relating them to possible experience. So much more since the fundamental concept of a simple nature is such that we cannot encounter it in any experience, hence there is no way of turning it into an objectively valid concept.

THIRD PARALOGISM : PERSONALITY

That which is conscious of its numerical identity at different times is to that extent a person.

Now the soul is conscious, etc.

Therefore, the soul is a person.

CRITICISM OF THE THIRD PARALOGISM OF TRANSCENDENTAL PSYCHOLOGY

If I want to know the numerical identity of an external object through experience, I need to attend to the persistence of the appearance which serves as the subject to which everything else relates as determination, and I need to note the identity of this subject over time and in the midst of changing determinations. But I am myself an object of inner sense and all time is only the form of inner sense. Consequently, I relate each and every one of my successive determinations to the numerically identical self in all time, i.e. in the form of the inner intuition of myself. But in that case the personality of the soul is not even something that needs to be inferred, rather it ought to be considered as a fully identical proposition about self-consciousness in time, which is also why it is valid *a priori*. For all it says is that during the whole time in which

I am conscious of myself, I am conscious of that time as belonging to the unity of myself. It amounts to the same whether I say that this whole time is in me, as an individual unity, or that I am, including my numerical identity, present in all that time.

Personal identity is thus invariably present in my own consciousness. When, however, I consider myself from the perspective of someone else (as an object of his external intuition), then, and only then, this external observer considers me *in* time, for in apperception time is really represented only *in me*. It follows that, whether he realizes it, he will not infer my objective persistence from the *I* which at every time accompanies all representations in my consciousness and does so with full identity. For since the time in which the observer places me is not the time in my own sensibility but the time in his sensibility, it follows that the identity which is necessarily connected with my consciousness is not for that reason connected with his consciousness, i.e. with the external intuition of my subject.

The identity of the consciousness of myself at different times is only a formal condition of my thoughts and their connection, and it in no way proves the numerical identity of my subject. Notwithstanding the logical identity of the *I*, my subject might undergo such change as would prevent it from retaining its identity, and this despite the fact that the univocal *I* is still to be assigned to it, an *I* which would, in every new state and even in the transformation of the subject, be able to retain the thoughts of the previous subject and thus pass them on to the next.[1]

Although the thesis of some ancient schools – everything in the world is in flux and nothing in it persists or abides – cannot be upheld as soon as one assumes the existence of substances, yet the unity of self-consciousness cannot be used to refute it. For we cannot use our own consciousness to assess whether or not we persist in so far as we are souls. For it is only what we are conscious

---

[1] An elastic ball hitting a similar ball in a direct line will communicate to it all its motion, hence all its state (if we attend only to positions in space). Now let us assume, on the analogy of such bodies, the existence of substances each communicating representations, as well as the consciousness of them, to the next. We may then imagine a whole series of such substances, the first communicating its state, as well as the consciousness of it, to the second, the second communicating its state, along with the state of the previous substance, to the third, and likewise the third communicating both its state and the state of all the previous ones. In this way the final substance would be conscious of all the states of the previously changed substances as its own states since these states, together with the consciousness of them, would have been passed on to it. Nonetheless, it would not have been the same person in all these states.

of that we count as belonging to our identical self, hence we must necessarily judge that we remain the same during the whole time of which we are conscious. From the standpoint of an outsider, however, we cannot declare the same to be true. For since we cannot discover any persistent appearance of the soul but only the representation *I* which accompanies and connects all the appearances, we can never make out whether this *I* (a mere thought) is not just as much in a state of flux as all the other thoughts which it serves to tie together.

It is noteworthy that the personality of the soul, hence the persistence which personality presupposes, as well as its substantiality, still require proof at this late stage. For if these [properties] could be presupposed, the possibility of a lasting consciousness in an abiding subject would follow, though not the [actual] lastingness of consciousness, and this suffices for a personality since a personality does not at once cease to exist if its influence happens to be interrupted for a time. However, we are in no position whatever to draw on this persistence prior to the numerical identity of our self, an identity we infer from the identical apperception. Rather the persistence would have to be inferred from the identity of the *I* in the first place (and the concept of a substance would, for the argument to be properly conducted, have to be inferred from the numerical identity of the *I*). But in fact the identity of a person does not in any way follow from the identity of the *I* in the consciousness of all the time in which I recognize myself. Hence the substantiality of the soul could equally not have been made out previously, as resting on the identity of the *I*.

We may, however, retain the concept of personality, just as we may retain the concept of substance and of something simple, provided it is merely transcendental, i.e. it signifies unity of the subject, a subject that is otherwise unknown to us, though its determinations are pervasively connected through apperception. To that extent the concept is both required and sufficient for practical employment. But it can no longer serve us to extend the knowledge of ourself by means of pure reason, reason which through the mere concept of the identical self deludes us into believing in an unbroken lastingness of the subject. For this concept keeps revolving around itself and does not bring us a single step further with regard to any question directed at synthetic knowledge. It is certainly utterly unknown to us what kind of thing matter is in itself (transcendental object), and yet the persistence of matter as appearance is something we can observe since it is represented as something external. But if I want to observe the pure *I* in the midst of all the changing representations, I have no other correlate for my comparisons than precisely myself, including the general conditions for my consciousness. Hence all I have to offer in reply to any question is tautological answers, and this I do by [tacitly] supplying my concept and its unity with properties that belong to myself as object and by presupposing that we wanted to know in the first place.

FOURTH PARALOGISM: IDEALITY (WITH REGARD TO EXTERNAL RELATION)

That whose existence can only be inferred as a cause of given perceptions has a merely doubtful existence.

Now all external appearances are such that their existence cannot be directly perceived, rather they can only be inferred as the cause of given perceptions.

It follows that the existence of all objects of external senses is doubtful. This uncertainty I call the ideality of external appearances and the doctrine of this ideality is called idealism, compared to which the claim of a possible certainty of objects of external senses is called dualism.

CRITICISM OF THE FOURTH PARALOGISM OF TRANSCENDENTAL PSYCHOLOGY

Let us begin by examining the premises. We may rightly claim that only that which is in ourselves can be directly perceived and that only my own experience can be the object of a mere perception. Thus the existence of a real object outside me (taking the word in its intellectual sense) is never directly given in perception, rather it has to be added in thought, hence it has to be inferred as the external cause of the perception, the perception being only a modification of inner sense. Hence too Descartes was right in confining all perception, in the narrowest sense [of 'perception'] to the proposition 'I am (as a thinking being)'. For it is clear that since what is external is not in me, I cannot encounter it in my apperception nor, therefore, in any perception, perception being really only the way apperception is determined.

Thus properly speaking I cannot perceive external things, I can only infer their existence from my inner perception in so far as I regard the perception as the effect of which something external is the immediate cause. But an inference from a given effect to a particular cause is always uncertain since the effect can arise from more than one cause. Thus it always remains doubtful, with regard to the relation between the perception and its cause, whether the cause is internal or external, hence whether all so-called external perceptions are a mere play of our internal sense or whether they relate to real external objects as their cause. At least the existence of external objects is merely inferred and runs the danger of all inferences, while, by contrast, the object of inner sense (myself including all my representations) is directly perceived and its existence does not admit of any doubt.

Thus an idealist ought not to be understood as somebody who denies the existence of external objects of the senses, but rather as somebody who does not admit that this existence can be known through direct perception and who then goes on to infer from this that we can never, through any possible experience, be fully certain of their existence.

Before proceeding to lay bare the deceptive appeal of our paralogism, I need to begin by observing that it is necessary to distinguish two kinds of idealism, transcendental idealism and empirical idealism. By the transcendental idealism of all appearances I mean the doctrine that regards all appearances as mere representations and not as things in themselves and according to which time and space are ony sensible forms of our intuition and not determinations given in themselves or conditions of objects as things in themselves. This idealism is opposed to transcendental realism which regards time and space as things in themselves (independently of our sensibility). Thus the transcendental realist conceives external appearances (if their existence is admitted) as things in themselves which exist independently of us and our sensibility, hence which would be outside us even according to the pure concepts of the understanding. It is in fact this transcendental realist who later assumes the guise of empirical idealist and who, having first falsely assumed that objects of the senses, if they are to be external, must be capable of existing in themselves, even without senses, goes on from this perspective to find all sense-representations insufficient for certifying the reality of external objects.

The transcendental idealist may, by contrast, be an empirical realist, hence what is called a dualist, i.e. he may concede the existence of matter without going beyond mere self-consciousness and without assuming anything more than the certainty of the representations in me, hence anything more than the *cogito ergo sum*. For since he allows for matter and even for its inherent possibility only as appearance, which is nothing in separation from our sensibility, matter is for him only a kind of representation (intuition), called external; not as if the representations related to external objects in themselves, but rather because they relate perceptions to space, in which all things exist outside one another, while space itself is in us.

We have from the beginning declared ourselves in favour of this transcendental idealism. Thus, according to our doctrine, we ought not to have any scruples in assuming and declaring that the existence of matter is proven on the testimony of our mere self-consciousness, just as we in the same way assume and declare proven the existence of myself as a thinking being. For I am certainly conscious of my representations, hence they exist just as much as I exist myself who have them. But external objects (bodies) are merely appearance, hence they are nothing other than a kind of my representations and their objects are something only by virtue of these representations and are nothing in separation from them. Thus external objects exist just as much as I exist myself and both exist on the direct testimony of my self-consciousness. But there is this difference, that the representation of myself as a thinking subject relates merely to inner sense whereas the representations designating extended being relate to outer sense. I need just as little rely on inference with regard to the reality of external objects as I need to rely on inference with regard to the reality of the object of my inner sense (my thoughts). For they are both nothing but representations, the direct perception (consciousness) of which is at once sufficient proof of their reality.

Thus the transcendental idealist is an empirical realist and concedes the reality of matter as appearance, a reality that ought not to be inferred but is rather directly perceived. Transcendental realism, by contrast, is forced into an embarrassing situation and sees itself compelled to give way to empirical idealism because it regards the objects of the external senses as distinct from the senses themselves and regards appearances as independent entities existing outside us. No wonder then that, even considering our best consciousness of our representations of these things, it us far from certain that if the representation exists, its corresponding object will also exist. In our system, by contrast, these external objects, that is to say matter, in all shapes and variations, are nothing but mere appearances, i.e. representations in us, of whose reality we become directly conscious.

Now since, if I am not mistaken, all psychologists who subscribe to empirical idealism are transcendental realists, they at least have been consequential in attributing great significance to empirical idealism as being one of the problems from which human reason is hard put to extricate itself. For it is quite true that if one regards external appearances as representations produced by their objects, these objects being conceived as existing in themselves outside us, then it is hard to see how one could know their existence except by inferring cause from effect, an inference that must always leave it doubtful whether the cause is in us or outside us. Now we may grant that there may be something outside us, in the transcendental meaning [of 'outside us'] which is the cause of our external intuitions, but this is not what we mean by the object associated with the representations of matter and corporeal things. For they are merely appearances, i.e. mere ways of representing, and they always exist in us, their reality resting on direct awareness, just as does the reality of my own thoughts. The transcendental object is equally unknown, whether in relation to inner or to outer intuition. But then neither is this what we are concerned with, rather we are concerned with empirical objects, and they are called external if represented in space and internal if represented merely in the relation of time. But space and time are both in us.

The expression 'outside us' is unavoidably ambiguous, sometimes meaning something distinct from us as a thing itself, sometimes meaning what belongs merely to external appearance. Let us therefore, by way of unequivocally giving the latter meaning to the concept (this being in fact the meaning the psychological question concerning the reality of our external intuition) distinguish empirically external objects from objects one might call external in the transcendental sense by straightforwardly calling the former objects things to be encountered in space.

It is true that space and time are *a priori* representations at home in us as forms of our sensible intuition prior to any real objects having determined our sense through sensation and thereby having been represented under these sensible relationships. However, this material or real something, this something to be intuited in space, necessarily presupposes perception and cannot be invented and produced by the imagination, independently of perception, perception serving to indicate the reality of something in space. Thus it is sensation which designates something real in space or time by relating in either way to sensible intuition. Once sensation is present (which is called perception if it is applied to an object in general and without determining the object), the manifold present in it allows us to invent various objects according to our fancy, for which there is no room in space or time, or outside our fancy. Whether one considers the sensations pleasure and pain or else external sensations such as colour, warmth, etc., this much is certain, that we need to be given perception to begin with in order to possess the material for thinking of objects of sensible intuition. Thus perception represents something real in space (confirming ourselves to external intuitions here). For, first, perception is the representation of something real, just as space is the representation of the mere possibility of co-existence. Secondly, this real something is represented as being in front of the external sense, i.e. as being in space. Thirdly, space itself is nothing but mere representation, hence something counts as being real in it only if it is represented as being in it;[1] and, conversely, something that is given in it, i.e. something is represented in it through perception, is at the same time real in it. For if it were not real in it, i.e. if it were not given directly through empirical intuition, it could equally not be invented since what is real in intuitions cannot be invented *a priori*.

Thus all external perception directly proves something real in space, or rather it proves reality itself, which implies that empirical realism is beyond doubt, i.e. there corresponds something real in space to our external intuitions. To be sure, space itself, including all its appearances, are nothing but representation in me, and yet it is in this space that what is real, what serves as the material for all objects of external intuition, is really given, independently of all invention. Nor is it possible that something outside us (in the transcendental sense [of 'outside us']) should be given in this space

---

[1] This paradoxical but correct proposition needs to be emphasized: nothing exists in space except what is represented as being in it. For space itself is nothing other than representation, hence what is contained in it must be contained in representation, hence there is nothing in space except what is actually represented as being in it. It does indeed sound strange to say that something can exist only in the representation of it, but it ceases to offend if we recall that the things that concern us are not things in themselves but only appearances, i.e. representations.

since space itself is nothing outside our sensibility. Thus not even the most exacting idealist can demand of us that we should prove that the object outside us (in the strict meaning [of 'outside us']) corresponds to our representation. For, if there were such things, they could not be represented or intuited as being outside us since this presupposes space itself while what is real in space, space being a mere representation, is nothing other than perception itself. What is real about external appearances is thus real only with regard to perception and this is the only way it can be real.

Perceptions serve to produce knowledge of objects, either through a mere play of fancy or else through experience. Here it is certainly true that deceptive representations may arise, to which objects do not correspond, and the illusion may be due either to an illusion of fancy (as in dreams) or to a misuse of judgment (as in so-called sense-deception). In order to avoid such false appearances we proceed according to the rule that something is real if it is connected to a perception according to empirical laws. But such illusion, as well as the precaution against it, affects idealism and dualism equally, since it is only a matter of the form of experience. In order to refute empirical idealism, which is a false reservation concerning the objective reality of our external perceptions, it suffices to show that external perception provides direct proof of something real in space while space, although in itself it is mere form of representations, possesses objective reality with regard to all external appearances (which are also nothing but mere representations); and to show that not even invention or dreaming is possible without perception, hence that our external senses, according to the data that can produce experience, have real objects corresponding to them in space.

A dogmatic idealist would be somebody who denies the existence of matter while a sceptical idealist doubts its existence because he thinks it cannot be established. The only reason the former could have for being a dogmatic idealist is that he believes himself to have found some contradiction in the possibility of matter in general, and this does not concern us here. The following section on dialectical inferences, which presents reason in its internal conflict with regard to the concepts concerning the possibility of what belongs to the interconnection of experience, will provide the remedy for this difficulty too. The sceptical idealist, on the other hand, who merely challenges the basis of our claim and who declares inadequate our conviction in the existence of matter, which we believe ourselves to have grounded in immediate perception, [this sceptical idealist] is a benefactor of human reason in so far as he forces us properly to open our eyes even in making the smallest step in our common experience and not immediately to take possession and to think that we have properly acquired something when in fact we may have obtained it by illegitimate means. The benefit provided by these idealist objections should be clear by now. They compel us to the view that if we want to avoid becoming caught up in the most groundless assertions, we need to regard all perceptions, whether internal or external, as a mere consciousness of what belongs to our sensibility and to regard the external objects of our sensibility not as things in themselves but only as representations. Just as with every other representation, we can become directly conscious of these representations, and they are called external because they belong to the sense which we call external sense, space being its intuition, but which is itself nothing other than an inner way of representing in which certain perceptions are connected with others.

If we allow external objects to count as things in themselves, then there is absolutely no way of understanding how we can come to know their reality outside us by relying merely on representation, which is in us. For surely one cannot sense outside oneself but only in oneself, hence the entire self-consciousness does not supply us with anything except merely our own determinations. This sceptical idealism forces us to take up the only recourse left to us, namely the ideality of all appearances, something we established in the Transcendental Aesthetic independently of these consequences which we could not then have foreseen. Now if one asks whether this implies that dualism alone is allowed to count in psychology, the answer is Precisely so! – but only in the empirical sense [of 'dualism']. That is to say, in connection with experience matter is really given to external sense as substance in appearance, just as the *I* is given to inner sense also as substance in appearance. Appearances, whether inner or outer, must be connected to each other according to the rules that the category of substance introduces by way of connecting our external as well as our internal perception into a single [unitary] experience. If, on the other hand, we should desire, as commonly happens, to extend the concept of dualism and use it in the transcendental sense, then there would not be any basis at all either for dualism or indeed for the position it stands opposed to: spiritualism on the one hand and materialism on the other. For in that case one would fail in the definition of one's concepts and would mistake a difference in the way we represent objects – objects which, according to what they are in themselves, remain unknown to us – for a difference in the things themselves. It is true that I, in so far as I am represented through inner sense as being in time, and objects in space, [in so far as they are represented as being] outside me, are entirely different appearances in kind, but they are not for that reason conceived as different things. The transcendental object, which underlies both external appearances and internal intuition, is in itself neither matter nor a thinking being, rather it is a, to us, unknown basis for appearances, appearances that supply the concepts of both matter and thinking beings.

If, then, as the present criticism manifestly compels us to do, we remain faithful to the rule that we laid down above and do not extend our questions beyond the point where possible experience can provide them with an object, we shall not even dream of inquiring beyond the objects of our senses and to ask what they may be in themselves, i.e. independently of all relation to the senses. On the other hand, when psychologists regard appearances as things in themselves, it is quite irrelevant whether what they adopt as their doctrine about things in themselves is materialism, allowing only for matter, or spiritualism, allowing merely for thinking being (of course according to the form of inner sense), or else dualism, allowing for both. They are in every case wedded to a misconception which makes them engage in pseudo-reasoning about the way in which something might exist in itself while in fact that thing is not a thing in itself but only the appearance of a thing in general.

CONSIDERATION OF PURE PSYCHOLOGY AS A WHOLE,
IN VIEW OF THESE PARALOGISMS

If we compare psychology ['the science of the soul'] with the science of bodies as a physiology of the objects of outer sense, we find, in addition to the fact that there is much to be known empirically in both cases, a remarkable difference, for while the latter science affords much synthetic *a priori* knowledge from the mere concept of an extended and impenetrable being, the former science does not afford any synthetic *a priori* knowledge from the concept of a thinking being. The reason is as follows. Although they are both appearances, there is something permanent or abiding to the appearance in front of outer sense which provides a substratum as the basis for the changeable determinations, hence there is a synthetic concept, namely the concept of space and of an appearance. On the other hand, there is nothing abiding to time, which is the sole form of inner intuition, hence time presents us only with changing determinations and not with a determinable object. For all that is present in what we call the soul is in a state of constant flux and there is nothing abiding there – except perhaps (if one insists) for the simple *I*, which is so simple [only] because this representation is devoid of content, hence devoid of a manifold, which is also why it seems to represent a simple object, or rather to designate such an object. In order for it to have been possible to arrive at pure rational knowledge of the nature of a thinking being in general, this *I* would have to be an intuition which, since it is presupposed (prior to all experience) in all thinking, would, being an *a priori* intuition, supply synthetic *a priori* propositions. But this *I* is not [in fact] intuition, just as little as it is a concept of an object, rather it is the mere form of our consciousness which accompanies both kinds of representations [i.e. intuitions and concepts] and is in this way capable of turning them into knowledge; for now something further is present in intuition which serves to supply the material for a representation of an object. In this way rational psychology collapses in its entirety, being a science that surpasses all the power of human reason, and there is nothing left for us but to study our soul at the guidance of experience and to limit ourselves to questions that do not go beyond the point where possible inner experience can supply them with content.

But although rational psychology is useless for extending our knowledge and as such consists solely of paralogisms, still one cannot deny that it is of important negative use, provided that it does not pretend to be more than a critical treatment of our dialectical inferences, which indeed belong to common and natural reason.

Why do we need a psychology based merely on pure rational principles? Undoubtedly primarily in order to safeguard our thinking subject against the danger of materialism. But this is achieved by the rational concept that we have offered of our thinking self. For far from our concept leaving us with the apprehension that if one took away matter, all thinking and even the existence of thinking beings would become null, we have rather shown manifestly that if one took away the thinking subject, the entire material world would have to fall away likewise since it is nothing but appearances in the sensibilility of our subject and a kind of representation by our subject.

To be sure, this is not a way of improving our knowledge of this thinking self with regard to its properties, nor am I capable of apprehending its persistence or even the independence of its existence from the supposed transcendental substratum underlying external appearances; for both these things are unknown to me. However, it is still possible that there should be a source other than mere speculative reason for trusting in an independent and persistent existence of my thinking nature amidst all possible changes of my state. It is threfore a great advantge if, while freely conceding my own ignorance, I can still fend off the dogmatic advances of a speculative opponent and show him that he is never in a better position to know something about the nature of my subject in order to undermine the possibility of my expectations, than I am in order to remain true to them.

Nevertheless, this transcendental illusion of our psychological concepts is the basis for three dialectical questions which make up the real aim of rational psychology and which cannot be settled in any other way than through the above investigation. First, the question concerning the possibility of the soul standing in communion with an organic body, i.e. concerning the animality of the soul and the state of the soul in the life of a human being. Secondly, concerning the beginning of this communion, i.e. concerning the soul at the moment of and prior to the birth of the human being. Thirdly, concerning the end of the communion, i.e. concerning the soul at the moment of and subsequent to the death of the human being (the question of immortality).

I am claiming, then, that all the difficulties that one believes oneself to encounter in these questions and which serve one well as dogmatic objections to the attempt to assume a guise of deeper insight into the nature of things than common sense can afford, rest on mere illusion. When under this illusion one hypostatizes what exists merely in our thoughts and assumes it to be a real object outside the thinking subject. Thus one regards extension, which is nothing but appearance, as a property, subsisting even independently of our sensibility, of external things and one regards motion as its effect which again really occurs in itself apart from our senses. For matter, whose communion with the soul causes such scruples, is nothing but a mere form, a certain way of representing an unknown object through the intuition called external sense. There may then well be something outside us to which the appearance that we call matter corresponds, but as appearance it is not outside us but merely a thought in us, although this thought, through the mentioned sense, represents it as being outside us. Thus matter is not to be understood as a substance entirely different and heterogeneous in kind from the object of our inner sense (soul), rather it is to be understood as the way in which the appearances of objects (in themselves unknown to us), whose representations we call external, differ in kind compared to the appearances that we count as belonging to inner sense, although both belong just as much to the thinking subject as does every thought. It is merely that these representations [i.e. of external sense] have something misleading about them in that, since they represent objects in space, they as it were make themselves independent of the soul and appear to hover outside it, whereas in fact space itself, in which the objects are intuited, is nothing but a representation whose corresponding image it is equally impossible to encounter apart from the soul. The question no longer concerns the communion of the soul with other substances that we know but that differ in kind from it, rather it concerns merely the connection of the representations of inner sense with the modifications of our external sensibility, i.e. how they may become connected with each other according to unchanging laws so as to become interconnected into one unitary experience.

As long as we connect internal and external appearances as mere representations in experience, we do not come up gainst anything strange or anything that would turn the communion between the two kinds of senses into something strange. But as soon as we hypostatize external appearances and no longer regard them as representations but as things in themselves outside us in the same manner as they are also in us, whilst at the same time we relate to our thinking subject the actions which they perform as appearances in relation to each other, then we become stuck with a kind of efficient cause outside us that will not fit in with its effect in us. For then the cause relates merely to external senses while the effect relates to inner sense, and these, though they are united in one subject, are yet highly different in kind. Thus in the one case [i.e. outside us] there are external effects other than changes of place and no other forces but efforts terminating in spatial relations as their effect. In ourselves, by contrast, the effects are thoughts, which do not include among themselves any place, movement, shape, or in general any spatial determinations, so that we shall entirely have lost trace of the causes in the effects, effects which were supposed to reveal themselves in inner sense proceeding from the causes.

However, we ought to recall that bodies are not in themselves objects that we encounter, rather they are mere appearance, whose object is unknown; [further we ought to recall] that motion is not the effect of this unknown cause but merely the appearance of its influence on our senses; and that both [bodies and motion] are not anything outside us but merely representations in us; hence that the motion of matter does not produce representations in us, rather motion itself (hence the matter that it serves to reveal) is mere representation. Thus, to sum up, the entire invented difficulty issues in the question of how and by what cause the representations of our sensibility are connected with one another in such a way that those of them which we call external intuitions can be represented as objects outside us according to empirical laws. But this question in no way contains the supposed difficulty of explaining the origin of representations of strange efficient causes that lie outside us, [a difficulty that arises] because we regard the appearances of an unknown cause as the cause [itself] outside us, which only serves to create confusion. When one is faced with views containing a misconception that has become well-entrenched through long-standing habit, it is impossible immediately to render the remedy as easily graspable, as one may demand in other cases, cases where concepts have not become confused through such unavoidable illusion. Hence the way we are proposing to liberate reason from sophistical theories will hardly at once possess the clarity that is requisite for its proper satisfaction.

I think clarity can be served in the following way.

All objections can be divided into dogmatic, critical and sceptical objections. An objection is dogmatic if it is directed against a thesis and it is critical if it is directed against the proof of a thesis. The dogmatic objection requires insight into the constitution of the nature of the subject-matter in order that one may assert the opposite about the subject-matter than is asserted by the thesis, hence it is itself dogmatic and pretends to have better knowledge of the constitution under consideration than does the opposing view. The critical objection, since it does not interfere with the value, or lack of it, of the thesis but challenges only its proof, does not require better knowledge of the subject-matter or the pretence to such knowledge. It only shows that the assertion is groundless, not that it is wrong. The sceptical objection places thesis and antithesis in mutual opposition as two equally weighty mutual objections, each serving alternately as dogma and the other as its objection. Hence the sceptical objection appears to be dogmatic on both sides, all for the sake of utterly destroying all judgment about the subject matter. Thus both the dogmatic and the sceptical objection must pretend as much insight into the subject-matter as is needed in order to assert or deny something about it. Only the critical objection is such that it undermines a theory by undermining its presumed foundation, i.e. by showing that one's assertion rests on a useless and merely imaginary assumption, without, however, wanting to make out anything else about the constitution of the subject-matter.

Now, the common view of reason with regard to the communion between our thinking subject and things outside us is dogmatic and it regards these things as genuine objects subsisting independently of us. [This view arises] as a result of a certain transcendental dualism which does not count these external appearances as representations belonging to the subject but rather places them, just as they are supplied to us in intuition, outside us as objects and thus fully separates them from the thinking subject. It is precisely this subreption that serves as the foundation of all theories about the communion between soul and body. It is never asked whether indeed this objective reality of appearances is correct, but rather this reality is assumed to be something already agreed upon and instead one engages in pseudo-reasoning about how it is to be explained and understood. Three systems are commonly invented in response, and they are indeed the only possible ones: physical interaction; pre-established harmony; and super-natural assistance.

The two latter ways of explaining the communion of soul and matter rely on objections against the first explanation, which is the view of common sense. The objection is that what appears as matter cannot through its direct influence be the cause of representations, these being a wholly heterogeneous kind of effect. In that case, however, these latter explanations cannot associate what they mean by 'an object of the external sense' with the conception of matter as nothing but appearance, hence as already in itself mere representation produced by some exernal object. For to do so they would have to say that the representations of external objects (appearances) cannot be the external causes of representations in our mind; but that would be a wholly senseless objection since nobody would dream of regarding as an external cause something that he has already recognized to be a mere representation. Thus, according to our principles, these explanations must have their theory say that it is the genuine (transcendental) object of our external senses that cannot be the cause of the representations (appearances) that we call matter. But now, since nobody can justifiably pretend to know anything about the transcendental cause of our representations of the external senses, their assertion is wholly groundless. But suppose, on the other hand, that these supposed improvers of the doctrine of physical interaction, following the way that transcendental dualism commonly views the issue, wanted to regard matter as such as a thing in itself (and not as mere appearance of an unknown thing) and then wanted to show through their objection that an external object whose causal influence is restricted to movement could never be the efficient cause of representations and that consequently we need to posit an intermediary third being so as to establish, if not mutual interaction, at least agreement and harmony. In that case they would, as part of their dualism, base their refutation on the asumption, the *proton pseudos*, of physical interaction, and so they would through their own objection refute not so much a natural interaction as their own dualist presupposition. For all the dificulties that mark the connection of a thinking nature with matter arise without exception solely from the illegitimate dualist view that matter as such is not appearance, i.e. mere representation of the mind to which there corresponds an unknown object, but is an object in itself existing outside us independently of all sensibility.

There is thus no room for making a dogmatic objection against the commonly accepted view of physical interaction. For, if the opponent assumes that matter and its movement are mere appearances, hence are themselves only representations, then the only place where he can claim to find a difficulty is in the idea that the unknown object of our sensibility can be the cause of representations. But then nothing whatsoever can justify this idea to him since nobody can discover of an unknown object what it is or is not capable of doing. But, according to our proofs above, he has no option but to concede this transcendental idealism, unless he is openly prepared to hypostatize representations and to locate them outside himself as genuine things.

It is nevertheless possible to raise a justifed critical objection to the commonly held doctrine of physical interaction. [The doctrine of] such a supposed communion between two kinds of substances, thinking substances and extended substances, is based on a crude dualism which turns extended substances, which are nothing but mere representations by the thinking subject, into things existing in themselves. Hence the mistaken [doctrine of] physical interaction can be fully undermined by one's revealing its proof to be null and void.

Thus the notorious issue about the communion between what thinks and what is extended would, once cleared of all illusion, merely result in the inquiry: How is it at all possible that external intuition, namely the intuition of space (including its content, shape and motion) should occur in a thinking subject? But it is impossible for any human being to give an answer to this question and this gap in our knowledge can never be filled, rather one can only draw attention to it by ascribing external appearances to a transcendental object serving as the cause of this kind of representation, but one which we do not know at all nor will we ever possess a single concept of it. With regard to all the questions that arise within the empirical realm we treat appearances as things in themselves without concerning ourselves with the ultimate basis for their possibility (as appearances), but as soon as we go beyond the limits of experience the concept of a transcendental object becomes necessary.

These reminders concerning the communion between thinking and extended beings immediately imply the resolution of all disputes or objections about the state of a thinking nature prior to this communion (life) or subsequent to the termination of the commun- ion (death). The opinion that the thinking subject is capable of thought prior to all communion with bodies would now express itself as follows. Before the beginning of this kind of sensibility, by means of which things in space appear to us, the very same transcendental objects that in our present state appear as bodies were capable of being intuited in a wholly different manner. On the other hand, the opinion that the soul, after all communion with the material world has come to an end, can still continue to think, would express itself as follows. Even if the kind of sensibility by means of which transcendental objects appear as a material world and which are at present wholly unknown to us has come to an end, this does not imply that all intuition of these transcendental objects must equally come to an end and it is quite possible that the very same unknown objects should continue to be known to the thinking subject, albeit of course no longer as bodies.

Now it is certainy true that nobody can have the least reason, based on speculative principles, for such a claim, indeed it is not even possible to demonstrate its possibility [in this way] but only to presuppose its possibility. On the other hand, neither can anybody raise any valid objections against the claim. For, whoever he may be, he knows just as little about the absolute and inner cause of external and corporeal appearance as I do or anybody else does. He cannot justifiably pretend to know what the reality of external appearances is based on in our present state (in life); hence he equally cannot justifiably pretend to know that the condition of all external intuition, or the thinking subject itself, would cease after life has ceased (in death).

Thus all dispute about the nature of our thinking being and its connection with the material world is merely the result of filling the unavoidable gap in one's knowledge with paralogisms of reason by way of hypostatizing one's thoughts and turning them into things. This gives rise to imaginary science involving either positive or negative assertions. Here everybody either pretends to know something about objects about which nobody in fact has any concept, or he turns his own representations into objects, in this way being caught up in an eternal circle of ambiguities and contradictions. Only the sobriety of a rigorous but just criticism can liberate us from this dogmatic illusion, which is keeping so many people tied to theories and systems with a view to an imaginary salvation, and can limit all our speculative demands to the realm of possible experience. This is not a matter of adding hollow mockery to so much fruitless endeavour, nor of raising pious sighs at the bounds of our reason; it is a matter of determining the limits of reason according to certain principles. The determiniation of the limits of reason serve to fasten as reliably as possible its *nihil ulterius* onto the Herculean pillar, a pillar that nature itself has erected in order to prevent the voyage of our reason from taking us beyond the continuous shores of experience, lest we venture out into a boundless sea which, while presenting us with delusive views, eventually forces us to give up as hopeless all the difficult and arduous endeavour.

*

We still need to provide a clear and general discussion of the transcendental but natural illusion present in the paralogisms of pure reason as well as to justify ordering the paralogisms systematically in a way parallel to the table of the categories. This would have been impossible at the beginning of the section without running the risk of obscurity and without improper anticipation. Let us then try to meet this obligation.

An illusion consists in mistaking the subjective condition of thinking for the knowledge of an object. Moreover, we showed in the introduction to the Transcendental Dialectic that pure reason is concerned merely with the totality in the synthesis of the conditions for something conditioned which has been given. Since the dialectical illusion of pure reason cannot be an empirical illusion which occurs with regard to certain empirical knowledge, it will concern the conditions of thinking in general and there will be just three cases where pure reason is used dialectically:

1. The synthesis of the conditions for thinking in general;
2. The synthesis of the conditions for empirical thinking;
3. The synthesis of the conditions for pure thinking.

In all three cases pure reason is concerned merely with the absolute totality of this synthesis, i.e. with the condition that is itself unconditioned. This division also serves as the basis for the three-fold transcendental illusion, which gives rise to three sections of dialectic and an equal number of illusory sciences of pure reason: transcendental psychology; transcendental cosmology; and transcendental theology. Only the first concerns us here.

In considering thinking in general we abstract from all relation of thoughts to an object (whether of the senses or of pure intellect). Hence the synthesis of the conditions for a thought in general (no. 1) is not objective at all, it is merely a synthesis of thought with the subject, which is wrongly thought to be a synthetic representation of an object.

It follows that the dialectical inference directed at the condition for all thinking in general, a condition itself unconditioned, is mistaken not in its content (for it abstracts from all content of objects) but only in its form, hence it deserves to be called a 'paralogism'.

Further, since the *I*, the only condition that accompanies all thinking, is at issue in the universal proposition 'I think', reason is also concerned with this condition in so far as it is unconditioned. But this is a formal condition, namely the logical unity of every thought in abstraction from all objects. Still, it is wrongly regarded as an object about which I am thinking, namely myself, and its unconditioned unity.

If somebody should present me with the question, 'How is a

thinking thing constituted?', I would not in the least know *a priori* what to reply since the answer is meant to be synthetic. (An analytic answer may perhaps explain what thinking is, but it does not extend our knowledge about what the basis for thinking is which serves to make thinking possible.) Now every synthetic answer requires intuition, which is wholly absent from the question stated as generally as that. It is equally impossible to answer the general question, 'What must a thing be like in order to be movable?' For in that case no impenetrable extension (matter) has been made available. But, despite the fact that in general one has nothing to say in response to that question, it still seems to one that in one's own case one can provide an answer, namely through the proposition expressing self-consciousness: 'I think'. For this is the ultimate subject, i.e. it is substance, it is simple, etc. Now these would have to be empirical propositions. On the other hand, empirical propositions could not contain these kinds of predicates (which are not empirical) without a general rule stating *a priori* the conditions for the possibility of thinking in the first place. In this way one becomes suspicious of the initially so plausible insight into the nature of a thinking being on the basis of concepts alone, even if I have not as yet discovered where the mistake lies.

We may, however, discover the mistake by inquiring further into the origin of these attributes that I ascribe to myself as a thinking being in general. They are nothing but pure categories, which never serve to think any particular object, but only to think the unity of representations [necessary] in order to determine an object for them. A category alone, without an underlying intuition, can never provide a concept of an object; for an object is given only through intuition, though the object is consequently thought in conformity with the category. In declaring a thing to be a substance in appearance, I need first to be given predicates for its intuition which allow me to distinguish what persists from what changes, to distinguish the substratum (the very thing) from the accidents. In calling a thing simple in appearance, I mean that its intuition, though it is a part of the appearance, cannot be divided, etc. If, on the other hand, something is recognized as simple not in appearance but in its concept, this really does not afford any knowledge of the object, but only of my concept, a concept which is of something general and does not admit of any intuition proper. All one is saying in that case is that one is simply thinking something, for all one can say about it is that it is something.

Now mere apperception (*I*) is substance in its concept, it is simple in its concept, etc., hence all the psychological theses are undeniably right. But still this is not a way of knowing what we actually wanted to know about the soul, for all these predicates are not applicable to intuition at all, hence they cannot have any consequences that would be applied to objects in experience. They are, therefore, entirely empty. The concept of a substance does not tell me that the soul persists by itself, that it is a part of external appearances that cannot itself be further divided, hence can neither come into existence nor pass out of existence as a result of any change in nature – properties that would all reveal the soul in its relationship to experience and with regard to its origin and future state. But in using the mere category to say that the soul is a simple substance, it is clear that since the naked concept of the understanding, the concept of a substance, says merely that a thing is to be represented as a subject and without in turn being the predicate of anything else, nothing follows about persistence, the attribute of simplicity certainly not being capable of adding such persistence, hence we have not in the least been told what might happen to the soul as a result of changes in the world. If we could be told that the soul is a simple part of matter, we would be able to derive persistence from what experience informs us about the soul and we would in conjunction with its simple nature, be able to derive its indestructibility. But the concept of the *I* in the psychological axiom (I think) tells us nothing of the sort.

It is for the following reason that the being that thinks in us is under the impression that it can know itself through pure categories and in particular through the categories that express absolute unity under every title of category. Apperception is itself the basis for the possibility of the categories, while the categories for their part represent nothing but the synthesis of the manifold of intuition in so far as the manifold possesses unity in apperception. For this reason self-consciousness in general is the representation of the condition of all unity while being iself unconditioned. We may, therefore, say the following of the thinking *I* (the soul), the *I* that thinks itself as substance, as simple, as numerically identical at all time, and as the correlate of all existence from which all other existence must be inferred: the *I* does not so much know itself through categories, rather it knows the categories in the absolute unity of apperception, and through them all objects, hence it knows [these things] through itself. Now it is manifest that I cannot know something as an object if I have to presuppose that thing in order to know any object in the first place, hence the determining self (thinking) is distinguished from the determinable self (the thinking subject) as knowledge is distinguished from its object. Still there is nothing more natural and tempting than the illusion of mistaking the unity in the synthesis of thought for a perceived unity in the subject of these thoughts. We might call this the subreption of the hypostatized consciousness (*apperceptionis substantiatae*).

Should we desire to bring under a logical heading the paralogism present in the dialectical inferences of reason in rational psychology, since these inferences still contain correct premisses, we may call it a *sophisma figurae dictionis*. Here the major premiss makes a purely transcendental use of a category with a view to [the soul as] condition whereas the minor premiss and the conclusion make empirical use of the very same category with a view to the soul as subsumed under this condition. Thus, for example, the concept of a substance in the paralogism of simplicity is a pure intellectual concept which, unless it is provided with conditions in sensible intuition, is of mere transcendental use, i.e. of no use at all. In the minor premiss, on the other hand, the very same concept is applied to the object of all inner experience, but it is so applied without having first been provided with the condition for its application *in concreto*, namely with the persistence of its object. Hence the concept has been used empirically here, but illegitimately.

Let us finally point out the following, by way of showing the systematic interconnectedness of all these dialectical claims into a pseudo-science of rational psychology and into a unitary order of pure reason, hence by way of showing their completeness. Apperception has been carried through with regard to all sets of categories, but only with regard to those particular pure concepts of the understanding which serve in each set to provide the others with the basis for unity in a possible perception. They are: subsistence, reality, unity (not plurality) and existence – bearing in mind that reason considers these as conditions for the possibility of a thinking being here, conditions themselves unconditioned. Thus the soul knows itself as

1. The unconditioned unity of relation, i.e. not as inhering but as subsisting;

2. The unconditioned unity of quality, i.e. not as a real whole but as simple;[1]

3. The unconditioned unity in the plurality in time, i.e. not as numerically different at different times but as one and the same subject;

4. The unconditioned unity of existence in space, i.e. not as the consciousness of many things outside it but as consciousness only of its own existence and of other things merely as its representations.

Reason is the capacity for principles. The claims of rational psychology do not contain empirical predicates of the soul, but only predicates that, if there are any such predicates, are supposed to determine an object in itself and independently of experience, hence to determine it by mere reason. The claims ought therefore to be based on principles and general concepts about thinking natures in general. Instead, however, we find that they are governed by the single representation 'I think' which, since it expresses the pure formula of all my experience (indeterminate), presents itself as a general proposition applicable to all thinking beings. On the other hand, since it is still in all respects singular, it carries with it the illusion of an absolute unity in the conditions of thinking in general, in this way extending itself further than any possible experience could reach.

---

[1] I cannot yet show how what is simple can still correspond to the category of reality. This will be shown in the next chapter, in connection with a different rational use of this same concept.

THE TRANSCENDENTAL DIALECTIC:
BOOK II

CHAPTER II – THE ANTINOMY OF PURE REASON

We showed in the introduction to this part of our work, that all transcendental illusion of pure reason arose from dialectical inferences, the schema of which logic gives us in its three formal species of inferences – just as the categories find their logical schema in the four functions of all judgments. The first kind of these sophistical arguments related to the unconditioned unity of the *subjective* conditions of all representations in general (of the subject or soul), in correspondence with the *categorical* inferences, the major of which, as the principle, enounces the relation of a predicate to a subject. The second kind of dialectical argument will therefore be concerned, following the analogy with *hypothetical* inferences, with the unconditioned unity of the objective conditions in the appearance; and, in this way, the theme of the third kind to be treated of in the following chapter, will be the unconditioned unity of the objective conditions of the possibility of objects in general.

But it is worthy of remark, that the transcendental paralogism produced in the mind only a one-sided illusion, in regard to the idea of the subject of our thought; and the concepts of reason gave no ground to maintain the contrary assertion. The advantage is completely on the side of pneumatism; although this theory iself passes into naught, in the crucible of pure reason.

Very different is the case when we apply reason to the *objective synthesis* of appearances. Here, certainly, reason establishes, with much plausibility, its principle of unconditioned unity; but it very soon falls into such contradictions, that it is compelled, in relation to cosmology, to renounce its pretensions.

For here a new phenomenon of human reason meets us – a perfectly natural antithetic, which does not require to be sought for by subtle sophistry, but into which reason of itself unavoidably falls. It is thereby preserved, to be sure, from the slumber of a fancied conviction – which a merely one-sided illusion produces; but it is at the same time compelled, either, on the one hand, to abandon itself to a despairing scepticism, or, on the other, to assume a dogmatical confidence and obstinate persistence in certain assertions, without granting a fair hearing to the other side of the question. Either is the death of a sound philosophy, although the former might perhaps deserve the title of the euthanasia of pure reason.

Before entering this region of discord and confusion, which the conflict of the laws of pure reason (antinomy) produces, we shall present the reader with some considerations, in explanation and justification of the method we intend to follow in our treatment of this subject. I term all transcendental ideas, in so far as they relate to the absolute totality in the synthesis of appearances, *cosmical concepts*; partly on account of this unconditioned totality, on which the concept of the world-whole is based – a concept which is itself an idea – partly because they relate solely to the synthesis of appearances – the empirical synthesis; while, on the other hand, the absolute totality in the synthesis of the conditions of all possible things gives rise to an ideal of pure reason, which is quite distinct from the cosmical concept, although it stands in relation with it. Hence, as the paralogism of pure reason laid the foundation for a dialectical psychology, the antinomy of pure reason will present us with the transcendental principles of a pretended pure (rational) cosmology – not, howwever, to declare it valid and to appropriate it but – as the very term of a conflict of reason sufficiently indicates, to present it as an idea which cannot be reconciled with appearances and experience.

THE ANTINOMY OF PURE REASON

Section I : System of Cosmological Ideas

That we may be able to numerate with sytematic precision these ideas according to a principle, we must remark, *in the first place,* that it is from the understanding alone that pure and transcendental concepts take their origin; that the reason does not provide any concept, but only frees the appearance of the understanding from the unavoidable limitation of a possible experience, and thus endeavours to raise it above the empirical, though it must still be in connection with it. This happens from the fact, that for a given conditioned, reason demands absolute totality on the side of the conditions (to which, as conditions of systematic unity, the understanding submits all appearances), and thus makes of the category a transcendental idea. This it does that it may be able to give absolute completeness to the empirical synthesis, by continuing it to the unconditioned (which is not to be found in experience, but only in the idea). Reason requires this according to the principle: *If the conditioned is given, the whole of the conditions, and consequently the absolutely unconditioned, is also given*, whereby alone the former was possible. *First*, then, the transcendental ideas are properly nothing but categories elevated to the unconditioned; and they may be arranged in a table according to the title of the latter. But, *secondly*, all the categories are not available for this purpose, but only those in which the synthesis constitutes a series – of conditions subordinated to, not co-ordinated with, each other. Absolute totality is required of reason only in so far as concerns the ascending series of the conditions of a conditioned; not, consequently, when the question relates to the descending series of consequences, or to the aggregate of the co-ordinated conditions of these consequences. For, in relation to a given conditioned, conditions are presupposed and considered to be given along with it. On the other hand, as the consequences do not render possible their conditions, but rather presuppose them – in the consideration of the procession of consequences (or in the descent from the given condition to the conditioned), we may be quite unconcerned whether the series ceases or not; and their totality is not a necessary demand of reason.

Thus we necessarily think – a given time completely elapsed up to a given moment, although that time is not determinable by us. But as regards time future, which is not the condition of arriving at the present, in order to conceive it; it is quite indifferent whether we consider future time as ceasing at some point, or as prolonging itself to infinity. Take, for example, the series *m, n, o,* in which *n* is given as conditioned in relation to *m,* but at the same time as the condition of *o,* and let the series proceed upwards from the conditioned *n* to *m (l, k, i,* etc), and also downwards from the condition *n* to the conditioned *o (p, q, r,* etc) – I must presuppose the former series, to be able to consider *n* as given, and *n* is according to reason (the totality of conditions) possible only by means of that series. But its possibility does not rest on the following series *o, p, q, r,* which for this reason cannot be regarded as given, but only as capable of being given (*dabilis*).

I shall term the synthesis of the series on the side of the conditions – from that nearest to the given appearance up to the more remote – *regressive*; that which proceeds on the side of the conditioned, from the immediate consequence to the more remote, I shall call the *progressive* synthesis. The former proceeds *in antecedentia*, the latter *in consequentia*. The cosmological ideas are therefore occupied with the totality of the regressive synthesis, and proceed *in antecedentia*, not *in consequentia*. When the latter takes place, it is an arbitrary and not a necessary problem of pure reason; for we require, for the complete understanding of what is given in an appearance, not the consequences which succeed, but the grounds which precede.

In order to construct the table of ideas in correspondence with the table of categories, we take first the two primitive *quanta* of all our intuitions, time and space. Time is in itself a series (and the formal condition of all series), and hence, in relation to a given present, we must distinguish *a priori* in it the *antecedentia* as conditions (time past) from the *consequentia* (time future). Consequently, the transcendental idea of the absolute totality of the series of the conditions of a given conditioned, relates merely to all past time. According to the idea of reason, the whole past time, as the condition of the given moment, is necessarily thought as given. But as regards space, there exists in it no distinction between *progressus* and *regressus*; for it is an *aggregate* and not a series – its parts existing together at the same time. I can consider a given point of time in relation to past time only as conditioned, because this given moment comes into existence only through the past time – or rather through the passing of the preceding time. But as the parts of space are not subordinated, but co-ordinated to each other, one part cannot be the condition of the possibility of the other; and space is not in itself, like time, a series. But the synthesis of the manifold parts of space – (the syntheses whereby we apprehend space) – is nevertheless successive; and it takes place, therefore, in time, and contains a series. And as in this series of aggregated spaces (for example, the feet in a rood), beginning with a given portion of space, those which continue to be annexed form the *condition of the limits* of the former – the measurement of a space must also be regarded as a synthesis of the series of the conditions of a given conditioned. It differs, however, in this respect from that of time, that the side of the conditioned is not in itself distinguishable from the side of the condition; and, consequently, *regressus* and *progressus* in space sesm to be identical. But, inasmuch as one part of space is not given, but only limited, by and through another, we must also consider every limited space as conditioned, in so far as it presupposes some other space as the condition of its limitation, and so on. As regards limitation, therefore, our procedure in space is also a *regressus*, and the transcendental idea of the absolute totality of the synthesis in a series of conditions applies to space also; reason is entitled to demand the absolute totality of the synthesis of appearances in space as well as in lapsed time. Whether my demand can be satisfied, is a question to be answered in the sequel.

Secondly, the real in space – that is, matter, is conditioned. Its internal conditions are its parts, and the parts of parts its remote conditions; so that in this case we find a regressive synthesis, the absolute totality of which is a demand of reason. But this cannot be obtained otherwise than by a complete division of parts, whereby the real in matter becomes either nothing or that which is not matter, that is to say, the simple. Consequently we find here also a series of conditions and a progress to the unconditioned.

Thirdly, as regards the categories of a real relation between appearances, the category *of substance* and its accidents is not suitable for the formation of a transcendental idea; that is to say, reason has no ground, in regard to it, to proceed regressively with conditions. For accidents (in so far as they inhere in a substance) are co-ordinated with each other, and do not constitute a series. And, in relation to substance, they are not properly subordinated to it, but are the mode of existence of the substance itself. The concept of the *substantial* might nevertheless seem to be an idea of the transcendental reason. But, as this signifies nothing more than the concept of an object in general, which subsists in so far as we think in it merely a transcendental subject without any predicates; and as the question here is of an unconditioned in the series of appearances – it is clear that the substantial can form no member thereof. The same holds good of substances in community, which are mere aggregates, and do not form a series. For they are not subordinated to each other as conditions of the possibility of each other; which, however, may be affirmed of spaces, the limits of which are never determined in themselves, but always by some other space. It is, therefore, only in the category of *causality* that we can find a series of causes to a given effect, and in which we ascend from the latter, as the conditioned, to the former as the conditions, and thus answer the question of reason.

Fourthly, the concept of the *possible*, the *actual*, and the *necessary* do not conduct us to any series – excepting only in so far as the contingent in existence must always be regarded as conditioned, and as indicating, according to a law of the understanding, a condition, under which it is necessary to rise to a higher, till in the totality of the series, reason arrives at unconditional *necessity*.

There are, accordingly, only four cosmological ideas, corresponding with the four titles of the categories. For we can select only such as necessarily furnish us with a series in the synthesis of the manifold.

I

Absolute Completeness
of the
COMPOSITION
of the given whole
of all appearances

<table>
<tr><td>

2

Absolute Completeness
in the
DIVISION
of a given whole
in an appearance

</td><td>

3

Absolute Completeness
in the
ORIGINATION
of an appearance

</td></tr>
</table>

4

Absolute Completeness
as regards DEPENDENCE *of the* EXISTENCE
of what is changeable in appearance

We must here remark, in the first place, that the idea of absolute totality relates to nothing but the exposition of *appearances*, and therefore not to the pure concept of the understanding of a whole of things. Appearances are here, therefore, regarded as given, and reason requires the absolute completeness of the conditions of their possibility, in so far as these conditions constitute a series – consequently an absolutely (that is, in every respect) complete synthesis, whereby an appearance can be exhibited according to the laws of understanding.

Secondly, it is properly the unconditioned alone, that reason seeks in this serially and regressively conducted synthesis of conditions. It wishes, to speak in another way, to attain to completeness in the series of premises, so as to render it unnecessary to presuppose others. This *unconditioned* is always contained in the *absolute totality of the series*, when we endeavour to form a representation of it in thought. But this absolutely complete synthesis is itself but an idea; for it is impossible, at least beforehand, to know whether any such synthesis is possible in the case of appearances. When we represent all existence in thought by means of pure concepts of the understanding, without any conditions of sensible intuition, we may say with justice that for a given conditioned the whole series of conditions subordinated to each other is also given; for the former is only given through the latter. But we find in the case of appearances a particular limitation of the mode in which conditions are given, that is, through the sucessive synthesis of the manifold of intuition, which must be complete in the regress. Now whether this completeness is sensibly possible, is a problem. But the idea of it lies in the reason – be it possible or impossible to connect with the idea adequate empirical concepts. Therefore, as in the absolute totality of the regressive synthesis of the manifold in an appearance (following the guidance of the categories, which represent it as a series of conditions to a given conditioned) the unconditioned is necessarily contained – it being still left unascertained whether and how this totality exists; reason sets out from the idea of totality, although its proper and final aim is the *unconditioned* – of the whole series, or of a part thereof.

This unconditioned may be thought – either as existing only in the entire series, all the members of which therefore would be without exception conditioned and only the totality absolutely unconditioned – and in this case the *regressus* is called infinite, or the absolutely unconditioned is only a part of the series, to which the other members are subordinated, but which is not itself subject to any other condition.[1] In the former case the series is *a parte priori* unlimited (without beginning), that is, infinite,and nevertheless completely given. But the regress in it is never completed, and can only be called *potentially* infinite. In the second case there exists a first member in the series. This first is called, in relation to past time, the *beginning of the world*; in relation to space the *limit of the world*; in relation to the parts of a given limited whole, the *simple*; in relation to causes, absolute *spontaneity*; and in relation to the existence of changeable things, absolute *necessity*.

---

[1] The absolute totality of the series of conditions to a given conditioned is always unconditioned: because beyond it there exist no other conditions, on which it might depend. But the absolute totality of such a series is only an idea, or rather a problematical concept, the possibility of which must be investigated – particularly in relation to the mode in which the unconditioned, as the transcendental idea which is the real subject of inquiry, may be contained therein.

We possess two expressions, *world* and *nature*, which are generally interchanged. The first denotes the mathematical total of all appearances and the totality of their synthesis in the great and in the small – in its progress by means of composition, as well as by division. And the world is termed nature,[1] when it is regarded as a dynamical whole – when our attention is not directed to the aggregation in space and time, for the purpose of thinking it as a quantity, but to the unity in the *existence* of appearances. In this case the condition of that which happens is called a cause; the unconditioned causality of the cause in an appearance is termed freedom; the conditioned cause is called in a more limited sense a natural cause. The conditioned in existence is termed contingent, and the unconditioned necessary. The unconditioned necessity of appearances may be called *natural necessity*.

The ideas which we are at present engaged in discussing I have called cosmological ideas; partly because by the term *world* is understood the totality of all appearances, and our ideas are directed solely to the unconditioned among appearances; partly also, because *world*, in the transcendental sense, signifies the absolute totality of the sum of existing things, and we are directing our attention only to the completeness of the synthesis – although, properly, only in regression. In regards to the fact that these ideas are all transcendent, and, although they do not transcend appearances as regards their mode, but are concerned solely with the world of sense (and not with noumena), nevertheless carry their synthesis to a degree beyond all possible experience – it still seems to me that we can, with perfect propriety, designate them *cosmical concepts*. As regards the distinction between the mathematically and the dynamically unconditioned which is the aim of the regression of the synthesis, I should call the two former, in a more limited signification, cosmical concepts, the remaining two *transcendent natural concepts*. This distinction does not at present seem to be of particular importance, but we shall afterwards find it to be of some value.

---

[1] Nature, understood adjectivally (*formaliter*), signifies the connection of the determinations of a thing, connected according to an internal principle of causality. On the other hand, we understand by nature, *substantively (materialiter)*, the sum total of appearances, in so far as they, by virtue of an internal principle of causality, are connected with each other throughout. In the former sense we speak of the nature of liquid matter, of fire, etc., and employ the word only *adjectivally*; while, if speaking of the objects of nature, we have in our minds the idea of a subsisting whole.

THE ANTINOMY OF PURE REASON

Section II : Antithetic of Pure Reason

Thetic is the term applied to any body of dogmatical doctrine. By antithetic I do not understand dogmatical assertions of the opposite, but the conflict of seemingly dogmatical knowledge (*thesis cum antithesi*), in none of which we can discover any decided superiority. Antithetic is not therefore occupied with one-sided statements, but is engaged in considering the conflicts of the general knowledge of reason, and its causes. Transcendental antithetic is an investigation into the antinomy of pure reason, its causes and result. If we employ our reason not merely in the application of the principles of the understanding to objects of experience, but venture with it beyond these boundaries, there arise certain sophistical doctrines. These assertions have the following peculiarities : They can find neither confirmation not refutation in experience ; and each is in itself not only self-consistent, but possesses conditions of its necessity in the very nature of reason – only that, unluckily, there exist just as valid and necessary grounds for maintaining the contrary proposition.

The questions which naturally arise in the consideration of this dialectic of pure reason, are therefore : 1st. In what propositions is pure reason unavoidably subject to an antinomy ? 2nd. What are the causes of this antinomy ? 3rd. Whether and in what way can reason free itself from this conflict and find a way to certainty ?

A dialectical doctrine of pure reason must, according to what has been said, be distinguished from all sophistical propositions, by the fact that it is not an answer to an arbitary question, which may be raised at the mere pleasure of any person, but to one which human reason must necessarily encounter in its progress. In the second place, a dialectical proposition, with its opposite, does not carry the appearance of a merely artificial illusion, which disappears as soon as it is investigated, but a natural and unavoidable illusion, which, even when we are no longer deceived by it, continues to mock us, and, although rendered harmless, can be completely removed.

This dialectical doctrine will not relate to the unity of understanding in empirical concept, but to the unity of reason in pure ideas. The conditions of this doctrine are – inasmuch as it must, as a synthesis according to rules, be conformable to the understanding, and at the same time as the absolute unity of the synthesis, to reason – that, if it is adequate to the unity of reason, it is too great for the understanding, if according with the understanding, it is too small for reason. Hence arises a mutual opposition, which cannot be avoided, do what we will.

These sophistical assertions of dialetic open, as it were, a battle-field, where that side obtains the victory which has been permitted to make the attack, and he is compelled to yield who has been unfortunately obliged to stand on the defensive. And hence, champions of ability, whether on the right or on the wrong side, are certain to carry away the crown of victory, if they only take care to have the right to make the last attack, and are not obliged to sustain another onset from their opponent. We can easily believe that this arena has been often trampled by the feet of combatants, that many victories have been obtained on both sides, but that the last victory, decisive of the affair between the contending parties, was won by him who fought for the right, only if his adversary was forbidden to continue the tourney. As impartial umpires, we must lay aside entirely the consideration whether the combatants are fighting for the right or for the wrong side, and allow the combat to be first decided. Perhaps, after they have wearied more than injured each other, they will discover the nothingness of their cause of quarrel, and part good friends.

This method of watching, or rather of provoking, a conflict of assertions, not for the purpose of finally deciding in favour of either side, but to discover whether the object of the struggle is not a mere illusion, which each strives in vain to reach, but which would be no gain even when reached – this procedure, I say, may be termed the *sceptical method*. It is thoroughly distinct from *scepticism* – the principle of a technical and scientific ignorance, which undermines the foundations of all knowledge, in order, if possible, to destroy our belief and confidence therein. For the sceptical method aims at certainty, by endeavouring to discover in a conflict of this kind, conducted honestly and intelligently on both sides, the point of misunderstanding; just as wise legislators derive, from the embarrassment of judges in lawsuits, information in regard to the defective and ill-defined parts of their statutes. The antinomy which reveals itself in the application of laws, is for our limited wisdom the best criterion of legislation. For the attention of reason, which in abstract speculation does not easily become conscious of its errors, is thus roused to the momenta in the dermination of its principles.

But this sceptical method is essentially peculiar to transcendental philosophy, and can perhaps be dispensed with in every other field of investigation. In mathematics its use would be inappropriate; because in it no false assertions can long remain hidden, inasmuch as its demonstrations must always proceed under the guidance of pure intuition, and by means of an always evident synthesis. In experimental philosophy doubt and delay may be very useful; but no misunderstanding is possible, which cannot be easily removed; and in experience means of solving the difficulty and putting an end to the dissension must at last be found, whether sooner or later. Moral philosophy can always exhibit its principles, with their practical consequences, *in concreto* – at least in possible experiences, and thus escape the mistake of abstraction. But transcendental propositions, which lay claim to extending our insight beyond the region of possible experience, cannot, on the one hand, exhibit their abstract synthesis in any *a priori* intuition, nor, on the other, expose a lurking error by the help of experience. Transcendental reason, therefore, presents us with no other criterion, than that of an attempt to reconcile assertions among themselves, and for this purpose to permit a free and unrestrained conflict between them. And this we now proceed to arrange.[1]

THE ANTINOMY OF PURE REASON

FIRST CONFLICT OF THE TRANSCENDENTAL IDEAS

Thesis	*Antithesis*
The world has a beginning in time, and is also limited in regard to space.	The world has no beginning, and no limits in space, but is, in relation both to time and space, infinite.
PROOF	
Let us assume, that the world has no beginning in time; up to every given moment of time, an eternity must have elapsed, and therewith passed away an infinite series of successive states of things in the world.	**PROOF**
	For let us assume, that it has a beginning. A beginning is an existence which is preceded by a time in which the thing does not exist. On the above supposition, it follows that

[1] The antinomies stand in the order of the four transcendental ideas above detailed.

Thesis	*Antithesis*

Now the infinity of a series consists in the fact, that it never can be completed by means of a successive synthesis. It follows that an infinite series already elapsed is impossible, and that consequently a beginning of the world is a necessary condition of its existence. And this was the first thing to be proved.

As regards the second, let us assume the opposite. In this case, the world must be an infinite given whole of coexistent things. Now we cannot think the magnitude of a quantity, which is not given within certain limits of an intuition,[1] in any other way than by means of the synthesis of its parts, and the whole of such a quantity only by means of a completed synthesis, or the repeated addition of unity to itself. Accordingly, to think the world, which fills all spaces, as a whole, the successive synthesis of the parts of an infinite world must be looked upon as completed, that is to say, an infinite time must be regarded as having elapsed in

[1] We may consider an undetermined quantity as a whole, when it is enclosed within limits, although we cannot construct its totality by measurement, that is, by the successive synthesis of its parts. For its limits of themselves determine its completeness as a whole by cutting off anything further.

there must have been a time in which the world did not exist, that is, an empty time. But in an empty time the origination of a thing is impossible; because no part of any such time contains a distinctive condition of being, in preference to that of non-being (whether the supposed thing originate of itself, or by means of some other cause). Consequently, many series of things may have a beginning in the world, but the world itself cannot have a beginning, and is, therefore, in relation to past time, infinite.

As regards the second statement, let us first assume the opposite – that the world is finite and limited in space; it follows that it must exist in an empty space, which is not limited. We should therefore meet not only with a relation of things *in space*, but also a relation of things *to space*. Now, as the world is an absolute whole, beyond which no object of intuition, and consequently no correlate to which can be discovered, this relation of the world to an empty space is a relation to *no object*. But such a relation, and consequently the limitation of the world by empty space, is nothing. Consequently, the world, as regards space, is not

Thesis

the enumeration of all co-existing things; which is impossible. For this reason an infinite aggregate of actual things cannot be considered as a given whole, consequently, not as co-existing. The world is consequently, as regards extension in space, *not infinite*, but enclosed in limits. And this was the second thing to be proved.

Antithesis

limited, that is, it is infinite in regard to extension.[1]

[1] Space is merely the form of external intuition (formal intuition), and not a real object which can be externally intuited. Space, prior to all things which determine it (fill or limit it), or, rather, which present an *empirical intuition* conformable to it, is, under the title of absolute space, nothing but the mere possibility of external appearances, in so far as they either exist in themselves, or can annex themselves to given intuitions. Empirical intuition is therefore not a composition of appearances and space (of perception and empty intuition). The one is not the correlate of the other in a synthesis, but they are connected in the same empirical intuition, as matter and form. If we wish to set one of these two apart from the other – space from appearances – there arise all sorts of empty determinations of external intuition, which are very far from being possible perceptions. For example, motion or rest of the world in an infinite empty space, or a determination of the mutual relation of both, cannot possibly be perceived, and is therefore merely the predicate of a notional entity.

OBSERVATIONS ON THE FIRST ANTINOMY

On the Thesis

In bringing forward these conflicting arguments, I have not been on the search for sophisms, for the purpose of availing myself of special pleading, which takes advantage of the carelessness of the opposite party, appeals to a misunderstood law, and erects its unrighteous claims upon the

On the Antithesis

The proof in favour of the infinity of the given world-series and the world-whole is based upon the consideration, that, in the opposite case, an empty time and an empty space must constitute the limits of the world. Now I am not unaware, that there is any way of escaping this conclusion. It

Thesis

refutation of that law. Both proofs originate from the nature of the case, and the advantage presented by the mistakes of the dogmatists of both parties had been completely set aside.

The thesis might also have been unfairly demonstrated, by the introduction of an erroneous concept of the infinity of a given quantity, as the dogmatists usually do. A quantity is infinite, if a greater than itself cannot possibly exist. The quantity is measured by the number of given units contained in it. Now no number can be the greatest, because one or more units can always be added. It follows that an infinite given quantity, consequently an infinite world (both as regards time and extension) is impossible. It is, therefore, limited in both respects. In this manner I might have conducted my proof; but the concept given in it does not agree with the true concept of an infinite whole. In this there is no representation of how large it is; consequently its concept is not the concept of a *maximum*. We think in it merely its relation to an arbitrarily assumed unit, in relation to which it is greater than any number. Now, just as the unit which is taken is greater or

Antithesis

may, for example, be alleged, that a limit to the world, as regards both space and time, is quite possible, without at the same time holding the existence of an absolute time before the beginning of the world, or an absolute space extending beyond the actual world – which is impossible. I am quite well satisfied with the latter part of this opinion of the philosophers of the Leibnizian school. Space is merely the form of external intuition, but not a real object which can itself be externally intuited; it is not a correlate of appearances, it is the form of appearances itself. Space, therefore, cannot be regarded as absolutely and in itself something determinative of the existence of things, because it is not itself an object, but only the form of possible objects. Consquently, things, as appearances, determine space; that is to say, they render it possible that, of all the possible predicates of space (size and relation), certain may belong to reality. But we cannot affirm the converse, that space, as something self-subsistent, can determine real things in regard to size or shape, for it is in itself not a real thing. Space (filled or empty)[1] may therefore be

[1] It is evident that what is meant here is, that empty space, in so far as it is limited

Thesis

smaller, the infinite will be greater or smaller; but the infinity, which consists merely in the relation to this given unit, must remain always the same, although the absolute quantity of the whole is not thereby known.

The true (transcendental) concept of infinity is: that the successive synthesis of unity in the measurement of a given quantum can never be completed.[1] Hence it follows, without possibility of mistake, that an eternity of actual successive states up to a given (the present) moment cannot have elapsed, and that the world must therefore have a beginning.

In regard to the second part of the thesis, the difficulty as to an infinite and yet elapsed series disappears; for the manifold of a world infinite in extension is contemporaneously given. But, in order to think the totality of this set, as we cannot have the aid of limits constituting by themselves this totality in intuition, we are obliged to give some account of our concept, which in this case cannot proceed from the whole to the determined set of the parts, but

Antithesis

limited by appearances, but appearances cannot be limited by an empty space outside them. This is true of time also. All this being granted, it is nevertheless indisputable, that we must assume these two nonentities, empty space outside the world and empty time before the world, if we assume the existence of a world-limit, relatively to space or time.

For, as regards the subterfuge adopted by those who endeavour to evade the consequence – that, if the world is limited as to space and time, the infinite void must determine the existence of actual things in regard to their magnitude – it arises solely from the fact that, instead of a *sensible world*, an *intelligible world* – of which nothing is known – is thought; further, that instead of a real beginning (an existence, which is preceded by a period in which nothing exists), an existence is thought which presupposes *no other condition*; and, instead of limits of extension, boundaries of the universe are thought. But

[1] The quantum in this sense contains a set of given units, which is greater than any number – and this is the mathematical concept of the infinite.

by appearances – space, that is, *within* the world – does not at least contradict transcendental principles, and may therefore, as regards them, be admitted, although its possibility cannot on that account be affirmed.

Thesis	*Antithesis*
must demonstrate the possibility of a whole by means of a successive synthesis of the parts. But as this synthesis must constitute a series that cannot be completed, it is impossible for us to think prior to it, and consequently not by means of it, a totality. For the concept of totality itself is in the present case the representation of a completed synthesis of the parts; and this completion, and consequently its concept, is impossible.	we are concerned with the *mundus phaenomenon*, and its magnitude; and in this case we cannot make abstraction of the conditions of sensibility, without doing away with the essential reality of this world. The world of sense, if it is limited, must necessarily lie in the infinite void. If this, and with it space as the *a priori* condition of the possibility of appearances, is left out of view, the whole world of sense disappears. In our problem is this alone considered as given. The *mundus intelligibilis* is nothing but the general concept of a world, in which abstraction has been made of all conditions of intuition, and in relation to which no synthetical proposition – either affirmative or negative – is possible.

SECOND CONFLICT OF THE TRANSCENDENTAL IDEAS

Thesis	*Antithesis*
Every composite substance in the world consists of simple parts; and there exists nothing that is not either itself simple, or composed of simple parts.	No composite thing in the world consists of simple parts; and there does not exist in the world anything simple.
PROOF	PROOF
For, suppose that composite substances do not consist of simple parts; in this case, if all composition were annihilated in thought, no composite part,	Let it be supposed that a composite thing (as substance) consists of simple parts. Inasmuch as all external relation, consequently all composition of substances, is

Thesis

and (as, by the supposition, there do not exist simple parts) no simple part would exist. Consequently, no susbstance; consequently, nothing, would exist. Either, then, it is impossible to annihilate composition in thought; or, after such annihilation, there must remain something that subsists without composition, that is, something that is simple. But in the former case the composite could not itself consist of substances, because with substances composition is merely a contingent relation, apart from which they must still exist as self-subsistent permanent beings. Now, as this case contradicts the supposition, the second must obtain that the substantial composite in the world consists of simple parts.

It follows immediately, that the things in the world are all, without exception, simple beings – that composition is merely an external condition pertaining to them – and that, although we never can separate and isolate the elementary substances from the state of composition, reason must think these as the primary subjects of all composition, and consequently, as prior thereto – and as simple substances.

Antithesis

possible only in space; the space, occupied by that which is composite, must consist of the same number of parts as is contained in the composite. But space does not consist of simple parts, but of spaces. Therefore, every part of the composite must occupy a space. But the absolutely primary parts of what is composite are simple. It follows that what is simple occupies a space. Now, as everything real that occupies a space, contains a manifold, the parts of which are external to each other, and is consequently composite – and a real composite, not of accidents (for these cannot exist external to each other apart from substance), but of substances – it follows that the simple must be a substantial composite, which is self-contradictory.

The second proposition of the antithesis – that there exists in the world nothing that is simple – is here equivalent to the following: The existence of the absolutely simple cannot be demonstrated from any experience or perception either external or internal; hence the absolutely simple is a mere idea, the objective reality of which cannot be demonstrated in any possible experience; it is consequently, in the exposition of appearances, without

Thesis	*Antithesis*
	application and object. For, let us take for granted that an object may be found in experience for this transcendental idea; the empirical intuition of such an object must then be recognized to contain absolutely no manifold with its parts external to each other, and connected into unity. Now, as we cannot reason from our lack of consciousness of such a manifold to the impossibility of its existence in the intuition of an object, and as the proof of this impossibility is necessary for the establishment and proof of absolute simplicity; it follows, that this simplicity cannot be inferred from any perception whatever. As, therefore, an absolutely simple object cannot be given in any experience, and the sensible world must be considered as the sum total of all possible experiences: nothing simple exists in the world.

This second proposition in the antithesis goes far beyond the first. The first merely banishes the simple from the intuition of the composite; while the second drives it entirely out of nature. Hence we were unable to demonstrate it from the concept of a given object of external intuition (of the composite), but we were

Thesis	*Antithesis*
	obliged to prove it from the relation of a given object to a possible experience in general.

OBSERVATIONS ON THE SECOND ANTINOMY

On the Thesis	*On the Antithesis*

On the Thesis

When I speak of a *whole*, which necessarily consists of simple parts, I understand thereby only a substantial whole, as the true composite; that is to say, I understand that contingent unity of the manifold which is given as perfectly isolated (at least in thought), placed in reciprocal connection, and thus constitutes a unity. Space ought not to be called a *compositum* but a *totum*, for its parts are possible in the whole, and not the whole by means of the parts. It might perhaps be called a *compositum ideale*, but not a *compositum reale*. But this is of no importance. As space is not a composite of substances (and not even of real accidents), if I abstract all composition therein – nothing, not even a point, remains; for a point is possible only as the limit of a space – consequently of a composite. Space and time, therefore, do not consist of simple parts. That which belongs only to the state of a substance, even although it possesses a

On the Antithesis

Against the proposition of the infinite divisibility of matter, whose ground of proof is purely mathematical, objections have been alleged by the Monadists. These objections lay themselves open, at first sight, to suspicion, from the fact that they do not recognize the clearest mathematical proofs as propositions relating to the constitution of space, in so far as it is really the formal condition of the possibility of all matter, but regard them merely as inferences from abstract but arbitrary concept, which cannot have any application to real things. Just as if it were possible to imagine another mode of intuition than that given in the primitive intuition of space; and just as if its *a priori* determinations did not apply to everything, the existence of which is possible, from the fact alone of its filling space. If we listen to them, we shall find ourselves required to think, in addition to the mathematical point, which is

Thesis

magnitude (motion or change, for example), likewise does not consist of simple parts. That is to say, a certain degree of change does not originate from the addition of many simple changes. Our inference of the simple from the composite is valid only of self-subsisting things. But the accidents of a state are not self-subsistent. The proof, then, for the necessity of the simple, as the component part of all that is substantial and composite, may prove a failure, and the whole case of this thesis be lost, if we carry the proposition too far, and wish to make it valid of everything that is composite without distinction – as indeed has really now and then happened.

Besides, I am here speaking only of the simple, in so far as it is necessarily given in the composite – the latter being capable of solution into the former as its component parts. The proper signification of the word *monas* (as employed by Leibniz) ought to relate to the simple, given *immediately* as simple substance (for example, in self-consciousness), and not as an element of the composite. As an element, the term *atomus* would be more appropriate. And as I wish to prove the existence of simple substances,

Antithesis

simple – not, however, a part, but a mere limit of space – physical points, which are indeed likewise simple, but possess the peculiar property, as parts of space, of filling it merely by their aggregation. I shall not repeat here the common and clear refutations of this absurdity, which are to be found everywhere in numbers : every one knows that it is impossible to undermine the evidence of mathematics by mere discursive concept ; I shall only remark, that, if in this case philosophy meddles with mathematics, it is because it forgets that the discussion relates solely to appearances and their conditions. It is not sufficient to find the concept of the simple for the pure concept of the composite, but we must discover for the *intuition* of the composite (matter), the intuition of the simple. Now this, according to the laws of sensibility, and consequently in the case of objects of sense, is utterly impossible. In the case of a whole composed of substances, which is thought solely by the pure understanding, it may be necessary to be in possession of the simple before composition is possible. But this does not hold good of the *totum substantiale phaenomenon*,

Thesis

only in relation to, and as the elements of, the composite, I might term the antithesis of the Second Antinomy, transcendental *atomistic*. But as this word has long been employed to designate a particular theory of corporeal appearances (*moleculae*), and thus presupposes empirical concepts, I prefer calling it the dialectical principle of *Monadology*.

Antithesis

which, as an empirical intuition in space, possesses the necessary property of containing no simple part, for the very reason, that no part of space is simple. Meanwhile, the Monadists have been subtle enough to escape from this difficulty, by presupposing bodies and the dynamical relation of substances as the condition of the possibility of space, instead of regarding space as the condition of the possibility of the objects of external intuition, that is, of bodies. Now we have a concept of bodies only as appearances, and, as such, they necessarily presuppose space as the condition of all external appearances. The evasion is therefore in vain; as, indeed, we have sufficiently shown in our Aesthetic. If bodies were *things in themselves*, the proof of the Monadists would be unexceptionable.

The second dialectical assertion possesses the peculiarity of having opposed to it a dogmatical proposition, which, among all such sophistical statements, is the only one that undertakes to prove in the case of an object of experience, that which is properly a transcendental idea – the absolute simplicity of substance. The proposition is, that the object of the internal

Thesis   *Antithesis*

sense, the thinking I, is an absolute simple substance. Without at present entering upon this subject – as it has been considered at length above – I shall merely remark, that, if something is merely thought as an object, without the addition of any synthetical determination of its intuition – as happens in the case of the bare representation, *I* – it is of course obvious that no manifold and no composition can be perceived in such a representation. As, moreover, the predicates whereby I think this object are merely intuitions of the internal sense, there cannot be discovered in them anything to prove the existence of a manifold whose parts are external to each other, and consequently, nothing to prove the existence of real composition. Consciousness, therefore, is so constituted, that, inasmuch as the thinking subject is at the same time its own object, it cannot divide itself – although it can divide its inhering determinations. For every object in relation to itself is absolute unity. Nevertheless, if the subject is regarded *externally*, as an object of intuition, it must, in its character of appearance, possess the property of composition in appearance.

Thesis

Antithesis

And it must always be regarded in this manner, if we wish to know whether there is or is not contained in it a manifold whose parts are external to each other.

THIRD CONFLICT OF THE TRANSCENDENTAL IDEAS

Thesis

Causality according to the laws of nature, is not the only causality operating to originate the appearances of the world. A causality of freedom is also necessary to account for these appearances.

PROOF

Let it be supposed, that there is no other kind of causality than that according to the laws of nature. Consequently, everything that happens presupposes a previous condition, which it follows invariably, in conformity with a rule. But this previous condition must itself be something that has happened (that has arisen in time, as it did not exist before), for, if it has always been in existence, its consequence or effect would not thus originate for the first time, but would likewise have always existed. The causality, therefore, of a cause, whereby something happens, is itself a thing that

Antithesis

There is no such thing as freedom, but everything in the world happens solely according to the laws of nature.

PROOF

Suppose that there does exist *freedom* in the transcendental sense, as a peculiar kind of causality, operating to produce events in the world – a faculty, that is to say, of absolutely originating a state, and consequently a series of consequences from that state. In this case, not only the series originated by this spontaneity, but the determination of this spontaneity itself to the production of the series, that is to say, the causality itself must have an absolute beginning, such, that nothing can precede to determine this action according to unvarying laws. But every beginning of action presupposes in the acting cause a state of inaction; and a dynamically primal beginning

Thesis	*Antithesis*
has *happened.* Now this again presupposes, in conformity with the law of nature, a previous condition and its causality, and this another anterior to the former, and so on. If, then, everything happens solely in accordance with the laws of nature, there cannot be any real first beginning of things, but only a subaltern or comparative beginning. There cannot, therefore, be a completeness of series on the side of the causes which originate the one from the other. But the law of nature is, that nothing can happen without a sufficient *a priori* determined cause. The proposition, therefore – if all causality is possible only in accordance with the laws of nature – is, when taken in its unlimited universality, self-contradictory. It follows that this cannot be the only kind of causality.	of action presupposes a state, which has no connection – as regards causality – with the preceding state of the cause – which does not, that is, in any wise result from it. Transcendental freedom is therefore opposed to the natural law of cause and effect, and such a connection of succesive states in effective causes is destructive of the possibility of unity in experience, and for that reason not to be found in experience – is consequently a mere fiction of thought.
From what has been said, it follows that a causality must be admitted, by means of which something happens, without its cause being determined according to necessary laws by some other cause preceding. That is to say, there must exist an *absolute spontaneity* of cause, which of itself originates a series of appearances which proceeds according to natural laws – consequently	We have, therefore, nothing but nature to which we must look for connection and order in world-events. Freedom – independence of the laws of nature – is certainly a deliverance from restraint, but it is also a relinquishing of the guidance of all rules. For it cannot be alleged, that, instead of the laws of nature, laws of freedom may be introduced into the causality of the course of nature. For, if freedom were determined according to laws, it would be no longer freedom, but merely nature. Nature, therefore, and transcendental freedom are distinguishable as conformity to law and lawlessness. The former imposes upon understanding the difficulty of seeking the origin

Thesis	*Antithesis*
transcendental freedom, without which even in the course of nature the succession of appearances on the side of causes is never complete.	of events ever higher in the series of causes, inasmuch as causality is always conditioned thereby ; while it compensates this labour by the guarantee of a unity complete and in conformity with law. The illusion of freedom, on the contrary, holds out to the searching understanding the promise of a point of rest in the chain of causes, by conducting it to an unconditioned causality, which professes to have the power of spontaneous origination, but which, in its blindness, deprives it of the guidance of rules, by which alone a completely connected experience is possible.

OBSERVATIONS ON THE THIRD ANTINOMY

On the Thesis	*On the Antithesis*
The transcendental idea of freedom is far from constituting the entire content of the psychological concept so termed, which is for the most part empirical. It merely presents us with the concept of spontaneity of action, as the proper ground for its imputability. It is, however, the true stumbling-stone to philosophy, which meets with unconquerable difficulties in the way of its admitting this kind of unconditioned causality. That	The defender of the all-sufficiency of nature in regard to causality (transcendental *physiocracy*), in opposition to the doctrine of freedom, would defend his view as follows. He would say, in answer to the sophistical inferences of the opposite party : *If you do not accept a mathematical first, in relation to time, you have no need to seek a dynamical first, in regard to causality.* Who compelled you to imagine an absolutely primal condition of

Thesis

element in the question of the freedom of the will, which has for so long a time placed speculative reason in such perplexity, is properly only transcendental, and concerns the question, whether there must be held to exist a faculty of *spontaneous* origination of a series of successive things or states by themselves. How such a faculty is possible, is not a necessary inquiry; for in the case of natural causality itself, we are obliged to content ourselves with the *a priori* knowledge that such a causality must be presupposed, although we are quite incapable of comprehending how the being of one thing is possible through the being of another, but must for this information look entirely to experience. Now we have demonstrated this necessity of a free first beginning of a series of appearances, only in so far as it is required for the comprehension of an origin of the world, all following states being regarded as a succession according to laws of nature alone. But, as there has thus been proved the existence of a faculty which can of itself originate a series in time – although we are unable to explain how – we feel ourselves authorized to admit, even in the

Antithesis

the world, and therewith an absolute beginning of the gradually progressing series of appearances – and, as some resting-point for this fancy of yours, to set bounds to unbounded nature? Inasmuch as the substances in the world have always existed – at least the unity of experience renders such a supposition quite necessary – there is no difficulty in believing also, that the changes in the states of these substances have always existed; and, consequently, that a first beginning, mathematical or dynamical, is by no means required. The possibility of such an infinite derivation, without any initial member from which all the others result, is incomprehensible. But if you deny this enigma of nature for this reason, you will find yourselves obliged to deny also the existence of many synthetic fundamental properties of natural objects (fundamental forces), which you can just as little comprehend; and even the possibility of change in general must present to you insuperable difficulties. For if experience did not teach you that it was real, you never could conceive *a priori* the possibility of this ceaseless sequence of being and non-being.

But if the existence of a

Thesis

midst of the natural course of events, a beginning, as regards causality, of different series of appearances, and at the same time to attribute to their substances a faculty of free action. But we ought in this case not to allow ourselves to fall into a common misunderstanding, and to suppose that, because a successive series in the world can only have a comparatively first beginning – another state or condition of things always preceding – an absolutely first beginning of a series in the course of the world is impossible. For we are not speaking here of an absolutely first beginning in relation to time, but as regards causality alone. When, for example, I, completely of my own free will, and independently of the necessarily determinative influence of natural causes, rise from my chair, there commences with this event, including its natural consequences *in infinitum*, an absolutely new series; although, in relation to time, this event is merely the continuation of a preceding series. For this resolution and act of mine do not form part of the succession of effects in nature, and are not mere continuations of it; on the

Antithesis

transcendental faculty of freedom is granted – a faculty of originating changes in the world – this faculty must at least exist outside the world; although it is certainly a bold presumption, that, over and above the sum total of all possible intuitions, there still exists an object which cannot be presented in any possible perception. But, to attribute to substances in the world itself such a faculty, is quite inadmissible; for, in this case, the connection of appearances reciprocally determining and determined according to general laws, which is termed nature, and along with it the criteria of empirical truth, which enable us to distinguish experience from dreaming, would almost entirely disappear. Next to such a lawless faculty of freedom, a system of nature is hardly conceivable; for the laws of the later would be continually subject to the intrusive influences of the former, and the course of appearances, which would, according to nature, proceed regularly and uniformly, would become thereby confused and disconnected.

Thesis

contrary, the determining causes of nature cease to operate in reference to this event, which certainly *succeeds* the acts of nature, but does not *proceed* from them. For these reasons, the action of a free agent must be termed, in regard to causality, if not in relation to time, an absolutely primal beginning of a series of appearances.

The confirmation of this need of reason to rely upon a free act as the first beginning of the series of natural causes, is evident from the fact, that all philosophers of antiquity (with the exception of the Epicurean school) felt themselves obliged, when constructing a theory of the motions of the universe, to accept a *prime mover*, that is, a freely acting cause, which spontaneously and prior to all other causes began this series of states. They always felt the need of going beyond mere nature, for the purpose of making a first beginning comprehensible.

FOURTH CONFLICT OF THE TRANSCENDENTAL IDEAS

Thesis	*Antithesis*
There belongs to the world something, either as a part of it, or as the cause of it – is an absolutely necessary being.	An absolutely necessary being does not exist, either in the world, or outside as its cause.

Thesis	*Antithesis*
PROOF	PROOF

The world of sense, as the sum total of all appearances, contains a series of changes. For, without such a series, the representation of the series of time itself, as a condition of the possibility of the sensible world, could not be presented to us.[1] But every change stands under its condition, which precedes it in time and renders it necessary. Now the existence of a given condition presupposes a complete series of conditions up to the absolutely unconditioned, which alone is absolutely necessary. It follows that something that is absolutely necessary must exist, if change exists as its consequence. But this necessary thing itself belongs to the sensible world. For suppose it to exist outside it, the series of world-changes would receive from it a beginning, and yet this necessary cause would not itself belong to the world of sense. But this is impossible. For, as the beginning of a series in time is determined only by that which precedes it in time, the supreme condition of the

Suppose that either the world itself is necessary, or that there is contained in it a necessary existence. Two cases are then possible. *First*, there must either be in the series of world-changes a beginning, which is unconditionally necessary, and therefore uncaused – which is at variance with the dynamical law of the determination of all appearances in time; or *secondly*, the series itself is without beginning, and, although contingent and conditioned in all its parts, is nevertheless absolutely necessary and unconditioned as a whole – which is self-contradictory. For the existence of an aggregate cannot be necessary, if no single part of it possesses necessary existence.

Grant, on the other hand, that an absolutely necessary cause of the world exists outside the world. This cause, as the highest member in the series of the causes of world-changes, must begin[1] the existence of the latter and their series. In this case it must also

---

[1] *Objectively*, time, as the formal condition of the possibility of change, precedes all changes; but *subjectively*, and in consciousness, the representation of time, like every other, is given solely by *occasion* of perception.

[1] The word *begin* is taken in two senses. The first is active – the cause beginning a series of conditions as its effect (*infit*). The second is passive – the causality in the cause itself beginning to operate (*fit*). I reason here from the first to the second.

Thesis

beginning of a series of changes must exist in the time in which this series itself did not exist; for a beginning presupposes a time preceding, in which the thing that begins to be was not in existence. The causality of the necessary cause of changes, and consequently the cause itself, must for these reasons belong to time – and to appearances, time being possible only as the form of appearances. Consequently, it cannot be thought as separated from the world of sense – the sum total of all appearances. There is, therefore, contained in the world, something that is absolutely necessary – whether it be the whole world-series itself, or only a part of it.

Antithesis

begin to act, and its causality would therefore belong to time, and consequently to the sum total of appearances, that is, to the world. It follows that the cause cannot be outside the world; which is contradictory to the hypothesis. Therefore, neither in the world, nor outside it (but in causal connection with it), does there exist any absolutely necessary being.

OBSERVATIONS ON THE FOURTH ANTINOMY

On the Thesis

To demonstrate the existence of a necessary being, I cannot be permitted in this place to employ any other than the *cosmological* argument, which ascends from the conditioned in appearances to the unconditioned in concept – the unconditioned being considered the necessary condition of the absolute totality of the series. The proof, from the mere idea of a supreme being, belongs to another principle of reason, and

On the Antithesis

The difficulties which meet us, in our attempt to rise through the series of appearances to the existence of an absolutely necessary supreme cause, must not originate from our mere concepts of the necessary existence of a thing. That is to say, our objections must not be ontological, but must be directed against the causal connection with a series of appearances of a condition which is itself unconditioned. In

Thesis

requires separate discussion.

The pure cosmological proof demonstrates the existence of a necessary being, but at the same time leaves it quite unsettled, whether this being is the world itself, or quite distinct from it. To establish the truth of the latter view, principles are requisite, which are not cosmological, and do not proceed in the series of appearances. We should require to introduce into our proof concepts of contingent beings in general – regarded merely as objects of the understanding, and also a principle which enables us to connect these, by means of mere concepts, with a necessary being. But the proper place for all such arguments is a *transcendent* philosophy, which is not here at issue.

But, if we begin our proof cosmologically, by laying at the foundation of it the series of appearances, and the regress in it according to empirical laws of causality, we are not at liberty to break off from this mode of demonstration and to pass over to something which is not itself a member of the series. The condition must be taken in exactly the same signification as the relation of the conditioned to its condition in the series has been taken, for the series must conduct us in an

Antithesis

one word, they must be cosmological, and relate to empirical laws. We must show that the regress in the series of causes (in the world of sense) cannot conclude with an empirically unconditioned condition, and that the cosmological argument from the contingency of the world-states – a contingency alleged to arise from change – does not justify us in accepting a first cause, that is, an absolute prime originator of the series.

The reader will observe in this antinomy a remarkable contrast. The very same grounds of proof which established in the thesis the existence of a supreme being, demonstrated in the antithesis – and with equal rigour – the non-existence of such a being. We found, first, that *a necessary being exists*, because the whole time past contains the series of all conditions, and with it, therefore, the unconditioned (the necessary); secondly, that *there does not exist any necessary being*, for the same reason, that the whole time past contains the series of all conditions – which are themselves therefore, collectively, conditioned. The cause is as follows. We attend, in the first argument, solely to the *absolute totality* of the series

Thesis

unbroken regress to this supreme condition. But if this relation is sensible, and belongs to the possible empirical employment of the understanding, the supreme condition or cause must close the regressive series according to the laws of sensibility, and consequently must belong to the series of time. It follows that this necessary existence must be regarded as the highest member of the world-series.

Certain philosophers have, nevertheless, allowed themselves the liberty of making such a jump (μετάβασις εἰς ἄλλο γένος). From the changes in the world they have concluded their empirical contingency, that is, their dependence on empirically-determined causes, and they thus admitted an ascending series of empirical conditions: and in this they are quite right. But as they could not find in this series any primal beginning or any highest member, they passed suddenly from the empirical concept of contingency to the pure category, which presents us with merely intellectual a series whose completeness does certainly rest upon the existence of an absolutely necessary cause. Nay, more, this intellectual series is not tied to

Antithesis

of conditions, the one of which determines the other in time, and thus arrive at something necessary and unconditioned. In the second argument, we consider, on the contrary, the *contingency* of everything that is determined in the *series of time* – for every event is preceded by a time, in which the condition itself must be determined as conditioned – and thus everything that is unconditioned or absolutely necessary disappears. In both, the mode of proof is quite in accordance with the common procedure of human reason, which often falls into discord with itself, from considering an object from two different points of view. Herr von Mairan regarded the controversy between two celebrated astronomers, which arose from a similar difficulty as to the choice of a proper standpoint, as a phenomenon of sufficient importance to warrant a separate treatise on the subject. The one concluded: *the moon revolves on its own axis*, because it constantly presents the same side to the earth; the other declared that *the moon does not revolve on its own axis*, for the same reason. Both conclusions were perfectly correct, according to the point of view from which the motions of the moon were considered.

Thesis   *Antithesis*

any sensible conditions; and is therefore free from the condition of time, which requires that its causality should itself have a beginning. But such a procedure is perfectly inadmissible, as will be made plain from what follows.

In the pure sense of the categories, that is contingent the contradictory opposite of which is possible. Now we cannot reason from empirical contingency to intellectual. The opposite of that which is changed – the opposite of its state – is actual at another time, and is therefore possible. Consequently, it is not the contradictory opposite of the former state. To be *that*, it is necessary that in the same time in which the preceding state existed, its opposite could have existed in its place; but this is not something we could know through the mere appearance of change. A body that was in motion=A, comes into a state of rest=*non-A*. Now it cannot be concluded from the fact that a state opposite to the state A follows it, that the contradictory opposite of A is possible; and that A is therefore contingent. To prove this, we should require to know that the state of rest could have existed in the very same time in

Thesis   *Antithesis*

which the motion took place.
Now we know nothing more
than that the state of rest was
actual in the time that followed
the state of motion ;
consequently, that it was also
possible. But motion at one
time, and rest at another time,
are not contradictorily opposed
to each other. It follows from
what has been said, that the
succession of opposite
determinations, that is, change,
does not demonstrate the fact
of contingency as represented in
the concepts of the pure
understanding ; and that it
cannot, therefore, conduct us to
the fact of the existence of a
necessary being according to
pure concepts of the
understanding. Change proves
merely empirical contingency,
that is to say, that the new state
could not have existed without
a cause, which belongs to the
preceding time, which is what
the law of causality requires.
This cause – even although it is
regarded as absolutely
necessary – must be present in
this way in time, and must
belong to the series of
appearances.

THE ANTINOMY OF PURE REASON

Section III: The Interest of Reason in these Conflicts

We have thus completely before us the dialectical play of the cosmological ideas. No possible experience can present us with an object adequate to them. Nay, more, reason itself cannot think them as according with the general laws of experience. And yet they are not arbitrary fictions of thought. On the contrary, reason, in its uninterrupted progress in the empirical synthesis, is necessarily conducted to them, when it endeavours to free from all conditions and to comprehend in its unconditioned totality, that which can only be determined conditionally in accordance with rules of experience. These dialectical propositions are so many attempts to solve four natural and unavoidable problems of reason. There are neither more, nor can there be less, than this number, because there are no other series of synthetical presuppositions, limiting *a priori* the empirical synthesis.

The brilliant claims of reason striving to extend its dominion beyond the limits of experience, have been represented above only in dry formulae, which contain merely the grounds of its pretensions. They have, besides, in conformity with the character of a transcendental philosophy, been freed from every empirical element; although the full splendours of the promises they hold out, and of the anticipations they excite, manifest themselves only when in connection with empirical knowledge. In the application of them, however, and in the advancing enlargement of the employment of reason, while struggling to rise from the region of experience and to soar to those sublime ideas, philosophy discovers a value and a dignity, which, if it could but make good its assertions, would raise it far above all other departments of human knowledge – professing, as it does, to present a sure foundation for our highest hopes and the ultimate aims of all the exertions of reason. The questions: whether the world has a beginning and a limit to its extension in space; whether there exists anywhere, or perhaps, in my own thinking self, an indivisible and indestructible unity – or whether nothing but what is divisible and transitory exists; whether I am a free agent, or, like other beings, am bound in the chains of nature and fate; whether, finally, there is a supreme cause of the world, or all our thought and speculation must end with nature and its orderliness – are questions for the solution of which the mathematician would willingly exchange his whole science; for in it there is no satisfaction for the highest aspirations and more ardent desires of humanity. Nay, it may even be said that the true value of mathematics – that pride of human reason – consists in this: that it guides reason to the knowledge of nature – in its greater, as well as in its lesser manifestations – in its beautiful order and regularity – guides it, moreover, to an insight into the wonderful unity of the moving forces in the operations of nature, far beyond the expectations of a philosophy building only on experience; and that it thus encourages philosophy to extend the province of reason beyond all experience, and at the same time provides it with the most excellent materials for supporting its investigations, in so far as their nature admits, by adequate intuitions.

Unfortunately for speculation – but perhaps fortunately for the practical interests of humanity – reason, in the midst of its highest anticipations, find itself jostled by claims and counterclaims, from which neither its honour nor its safety will permit it to draw back. Nor can it regard these conflicting trains of reasoning with indifference as mere passages at arms, still less can it command peace; for in the subject of the conflict it has a deep interest. There is no other course left open to it, than to reflect with itself upon the origin of this disunion in reason – whether it may not arise from a mere misunderstanding. After such an inquiry, arrogant claims would perhaps have to be given up on both sides, and instead a lasting and peaceful reign of reason over the understanding and the senses would be inaugurated.

We shall at present defer this radical inquiry, and in the meantime consider for a little – what side in the controversy we should most willingly take, if we were obliged to become partisans at all. As, in this case, we leave out of sight altogether the logical criterion of truth, and merely consult our own interest in reference to the question, these considerations, although inadequate to settle the question of right in either party, will enable us to comprehend how those who have taken part in the struggle, adopt the one view rather than the other – no special insight into the subject, however, having influenced their choice. They will, at the same time, explain to us many other things by the way – for example, the fiery zeal on the one side and the sober claims on the other; why the one party has met with the warmest approbations, and the other has always been repulsed by irreconcilable prejudices.

There is one thing, however, that determines the proper point of view, from which alone this preliminary inquiry can be instituted and carried on with the proper thoroughness – and that is the comparison of the principles from which both sides, thesis and antithesis, proceed. My readers would remark in the propositions of the antithesis a complete uniformity in the mode of thought and a perfect unity of principle. Its principle was that of pure empiricism, not only in the explication of the appearances in the world, but also in the solution of the transcendental ideas, even of that of the universe itself. The affirmations of the thesis, on the contrary, was based, in addition to the empirical mode of explanation employed in the series of appearances, on intellectual bases and its maxim was in so far not simple. I shall term the thesis, in view of its essential characteristic, the *dogmatism* of pure reason.

On the side of *dogmatism* or of the thesis, therefore, in the determination of the cosmological ideas, we find:

1. A *practical interest*, which must be very dear to every right-thinking man. That the world has a beginning – that the nature of my thinking self is simple, and therefore indestructible – that I am a free agent, and raised above the compulsion of nature – and, finally, that the entire order of things, which form the world, is dependent upon a Supremem Being, from which everything receives unity and teleological connection – these are so many foundation-stones of morality and religion. The antithesis deprives us of all these supports – or, at least, seems so to deprive us.

2. A *speculative interest* of reason manifests itself on this side. For, if we take the transcendental ideas and employ them in the manner which the thesis directs, we can grasp completely *a priori* the entire chain of conditions, and understand the derivation of the conditioned – beginning from the unconditioned. This the antithesis does not achieve; and for this reason does not meet with so welcome a reception. For it can give no answer to our question respecting the conditions of its synthesis – except such as must be supplemented by another question, and so on to infinity. According to it, we must rise from a given beginning to one still higher; every part conducts us to a still smaller one; every event is preceded by another event which is its cause; and the conditions of existence rest always upon other and still higher conditions, and find neither end nor basis in some self-subsistent thing as the primal being.

3. This side has also the advantage of *popularity*; and this constitutes no small part of its claim to favour. The common understanding does not find the least difficulty in the idea of the

unconditioned beginning of all synthesis – accustomed, as it is, rather to descend progressively along the consequences than to ascend regressively in search for grounds. In the concept of an absolute first, moreover – the possibility of which it does not inquire into – it is gratified to find a fixed point of departure to guide its steps; while in the restless and continuous ascent from the conditioned to the condition, always with one foot in the air, it can find no satisfaction.

On the side of the antithesis, or *empiricism*, in the determination of the cosmological ideas:

1. We cannot discover any such practical interest arising from pure principles of reason, as morality and religion present. On the contrary, pure empiricism seems to empty them of all their power and influence. If there does not exist a Supreme Being distinct from the world – if the world is without beginning, consequently without a Creator – if our wills are not free, and the soul is divisible and subject to corruption just like matter – the ideas and principles of morality lose all validity, and fall with the transcendental ideas which constituted their theoretical support.

2. But empiricism, in compensation, holds out to reason, in its speculative interests, certain important advantages, far exceeding any that the dogmatist can promise us. For, when employed by the empiricist, understanding is always upon its proper ground of investigation – the field of possible experience, the laws of which it can explore, and thus extend its knowledge securely and with clear intelligence without being stopped by limits in any direction. Here can it and ought it to present to intuition its proper object – not only in itself, but in all its relations; or, if it employ concepts, upon this ground it can always present the corresponding images in clear and unmistakable intuitions. It is quite unnecessary for it to leave behind the chain of natural order, to attach itself to ideas, the objects of which it cannot know; because, as mere intellectual entities, they cannot be presented in any intuition. On the contrary, it is not even permitted to abandon its proper occupation, under the pretence that it has been brought to a conclusion, and to pass into the region of idealizing reason and transcendent concepts, where it is not required to observe and explore the laws of nature, but merely to *think* and to invent – secure from being contradicted by facts, because they have not been called as witnesses, but passed by, or perhaps subordinated to the so-called higher interests and considerations of pure reason.

Hence the empiricist will never allow himself to accept any epoch of nature for the absolutely primal state; he will not believe that there can be limits to his outlook into its wide domains, nor pass from the objects of nature, which he can satisfactorily explain by means of observation and mathematical thought – which he can determine synthetically in intuition (extension), to those which neither sense nor imagination can ever present *in concreto* (simplicity); he will not concede the existence of a faculty in nature, operating independently of the laws of nature (freedom) – a concession which would tresspass into the procedure of the understanding, which is to investigate the origin of appearances under the guidance of necessary rules; nor, finally, will he permit himself to seek a cause beyond nature (primal being), inasmuch as we know nothing but it, and from it alone receive an objective basis for all our concepts and instruction in the unvarying laws of things.

In truth, if the empirical philosopher had no other purpose in the establishment of his antithesis, than to check the presumption of a reason which mistakes its true destination, which boasts of its insight and its knowledge, just where all insight and knowledge cease to exist, and regards that which is valid only in relation to a practical interest, as an advancement of the speculative interests (in order, when it is convenient for itself, to break the thread of our physical investigations, and, under pretence of extending our knowledge, connect them with transcendental ideas, by means of which we really know only that we know nothing) – if, I say, the empiricist rested satisfied with this benefit, the principle advanced by him would be a maxim recommending moderation in the pretensions of reason and modesty in its affirmations, and at the same time would direct us to the right mode of extending the province of the understanding, by the help of the only true teacher, experience. In obedience to this advice, intellectual *hypotheses* and *faith* would not be called in aid of our practical interests; nor should we introduce them under the pompous titles of science and reason. For speculative knowledge can find an objective basis only in experience; and, when we overstep its limits, our synthesis, which requires ever new knowledge independent of experience, has no substratum of intuition upon which to apply itself.

But if – as often happens – empiricism, in relation to ideas, becomes itself dogmatic, and boldly denies that which is above the sphere of its intuitive knowledge, it falls itself into the error of intemperance – an error which is here all the more reprehensible, as thereby the practical interest of reason receives an irreparable injury.

And this constitutes the opposition between Epicureanism[1] and Platonism.

Both Epicurus and Plato assert more than they know. The former encourages and advances science – although to the prejudice of the practical; the latter presents us with excellent principles for the investigation of the practical, but, in relation to everything regarding which we can attain to speculative knowledge, permits reason to append idealistic explanations of natural phenomena, to the neglect of physical investigation.

3. In regard to the third motive for the preliminary choice of a party in this conflict of assertions, it seems very extraordinary that empiricism should be utterly unpopular. We should be inclined to believe, that the common understanding would receive it with pleasure – promising as it does to satisfy it without passing the bounds of experience and its connected order; while transcendental dogmatism obliges it to rise to concepts which far surpass the intelligence and rational ability of the most practised thinkers. But in this, in truth, is to be found its real motive. For the common understanding thus finds itself in a situation where not even the most learned can have the advantage of it. If it understands little or nothing about these transcendental concepts, no one can boast of understanding any more; and although it may not express itself in so scholastically correct a manner as others, it can busy itself with reasoning and arguments without end, wandering among mere ideas, about which one can always be very eloquent, because we know nothing about them; while, in the observation and investigation of nature, it would be forced to remain dumb and to confess its utter ignorance. Thus indolence and vanity form of themselves

---

[1] It is, however, still a matter of doubt whether Epicurus ever propounded these principles as objective claims. If, instead, they were nothing more than maxims for the speculative exercise of reason, he gives evidence therein of a more genuine philosophic spirit than any of the philosophers of antiquity. That, in the explanation of appearances, we must proceed as if the field of inquiry had neither limits in space nor commencement in time; that we must be satisfied with the teaching of experience in reference to the material of which the world is composed; that we must not look for any other mode of the origination of events than that which is determined by the unalterable laws of nature; and finally, that we must not employ the hypothesis of a cause distinct from the world are principles for the extension of speculative philosophy, just as the principles of morals can be discovered without the aid of alien sources. At the same time, any one desirous of *ignoring*, in mere speculation, these dogmatical propositions, need not for that reason be accused of *denying* them.

strong recommendations of these principles. Besides, although it is a hard thing for a philosopher to assume a principle, of which he can give to himself no reasonable account, and still more to employ concepts, the objective reality of which cannot be established, nothing is more usual with the common understanding. It wants something which will allow it to go to work with confidence. The difficulty of even comprehending a supposition does not disquiet it, because – not knowing what comprehending means – it never even thinks of the supposition it may be adopting as a principle; and regards as known, that with which it has become familiar from constant use. And, at last, all speculative interests disappear before the practical interests which it holds dear; and it fancies that it understands and knows what its necessities and hopes incite it to assume or to believe. Thus the empiricism which transcendentally idealizes reason is robbed of all popularity; and, however prejudicial it may be to the highest practical principles, there is no fear that it will ever pass the limits of the schools, or acquire any favour or influence in society or with the multitude.

Human reason is by nature architectonic. That is to say, it regards all knowledge as parts of a possible system, and hence accepts only such principles as at least do not incapacitate a knowledge to which we may have attained from being placed along with others in a general system. But the propositions of the antithesis are of a character which renders the completion of an edifice of knowledge impossible. According to these, beyond one state of the world there is always to be found one more ancient; in every part always other parts themselves divisible; preceding every event another, the origin of which must itself be sought still higher; and everything in existence is conditioned, and still not dependent on an unconditioned and primal existence. As, therefore, the antithesis will not concede the existence of a first beginning which might be available as a foundation, a complete edifice of knowledge, in the presence of such hypotheses, is utterly impossible. Thus the architectonic interest of reason, which requires a unity – not empirical, but *a priori* and rational, forms a natural recommendation for the assertions of the thesis.

But if any one could free himself entirely from all considerations of interest, and weigh without partiality the assertions of reason, attending only to their content, irrespective of the consequences which follow from them; such a person, on the supposition that he knew no other way out of the confusion than to settle the truth of one or other of the conflicting doctrines, would live in a state of continual hesitation. Today, he would feel convinced that the human will is free; tomorrow, considering the indissoluble chain of nature, he would look on freedom as a mere illusion and declare *nature* to be everything there is. But, if he were called to action, the play of the merely speculative reason would disappear like the shapes of a dream, and practical interest would dictate his choice of principles. But, as it well befits a reflective and inquiring being to devote certain periods of time to the examination of its own reason – to divest itself of all partiality, and frankly to communicate its observations for the judgment and opinion of others; so no one can be blamed for, much less prevented from placing both parties on their trial, with permission to defend themselves, free from intimidation, before a sworn jury of equal condition with themselves – the condition of weak and fallible men.

THE ANTINOMY OF PURE REASON

Section IV: The Absolute Necessity of being able to Resolve the Transcendental Problems of Pure Reason

To avow an ability to solve all problems and to answer all questions, would be a profession certain to convict any philosopher of extravagant boasting and self-conceit, and at once to destroy the confidence that might otherwise have been reposed in him. There are, however, sciences so constituted, that every question arising within their sphere must necessarily be capable of receiving an answer from the knowledge already possessed, for the answer must be received from the same sources whence the question arose. In such sciences it is not allowable to excuse ourselves on the plea of unavoidable ignorance; a solution is absolutely requisite. The rule of *right* and *wrong* must help us to the knowledge of what is right or wrong in all possible cases; otherwise, the idea of obligation would be utterly null, for we cannot have any obligation to that *which we cannot know*. On the other hand, in our investigations of the appearances of nature, much must remain uncertain, and many questions continue insoluble; because what we know of nature is far from being sufficient to explain everything. Now the question is: Whether there is in transcendental philosophy any question, relating to an object presented to pure reason, which is unanswerable by this reason; and whether we must regard the subject of the question as quite uncertain – so far as our knowledge extends, and must give it a place among those subjects, of which we have just so much conception as is sufficient to enable us to raise a question – faculty or materials failing us, however, when we attempt an answer.

Now I maintain, that among all speculative knowledge, the peculiarity of transcendental philosophy is, that there is no question, relating to an object presented to pure reason, which is insoluble by this reason; and that the profession of unavoidable ignorance – the problem being alleged to be beyond our reach – cannot free us from the obligation to present a complete and satisfactory answer. For the very concept, which enables us to raise the question, must give us the power of answering it; inasmuch as the object, as in the case of right and wrong, is not to be discovered outside the concept.

But, in transcendental philosophy, it is only the cosmological questions to which we can demand a satisfactory answer in relation to the constitution of their object; and the philosopher is not permitted to avail himself of the pretext of impenetrable obscurity. These questions relate solely to the cosmological ideas. For the object must be given in experience, and the question relates to the adequateness of the object to an idea. If the object is transcendental, and therefore itself unknown; if the question, for example, is whether the object – the something, the appearance of which (internal – in ourselves) is thought – that is to say, the soul, is in itself a simple being; or whether there is a cause of all things, which is absolutely necessary – in such cases we are seeking for our idea an object, of which we may confess that it is unknown to us, though we must not on that account assert that it is impossible.[1] The cosmological ideas alone possess the peculiarity, that we can presuppose the object of them and the empirical synthesis requisite for the concept of that object to be given; and the question, which

[1] The question, What is the constitution of a transcendental object? is unanswerable – we are unable to say *what it is*; but we can perceive that the *question* itself *is nothing*; because it does not relate to any object that can be presented to us. For this reason, we must consider all the questions raised in transcendental psychology as answerable, and as really answered; for they relate to the transcendental subject of all internal appearances, which is not itself appearance, and consequently not given as an object, in which, moreover, none of the categories – and it is to them that the question is properly directed – find any conditions of its application. Here, therefore, is a case where no answer is the only proper answer. For a question regarding the constitution of a something which cannot be thought by any determined predicate – being completely beyond the sphere of objects and experience, is perfectly null and void.

arises from these ideas, relates merely to the progress of this synthesis, in so far as it must contain absolute totality – which, however, is not empirical, as it cannot be given in any experience. Now, as the question here is solely in regard to a thing as the object of a possible experience, and not as a thing in itself, the answer to the transcendental cosmological question need not be sought outside the idea, for the question does not regard an object in itself. The question in relation to a possible experience, is not, what can given in an experience *in concreto* – but what is contained in the idea, to which the empirical synthesis must approximate. The question must therefore be capable of solution from the idea alone. For the idea is a creation of reason itself, which therefore cannot disclaim the obligation to answer or refer us to the unknown object.

It is not so extraordinary as it at first sight appears, that a science should demand and expect assured answers to all the questions that may arise within its own sphere (*questiones domesticae*), although, up to a certain time, these answers may not have been discovered. There are, in addition to transcendental philosophy, only two pure sciences of reason; the one with a speculative, the other with a practical content – *pure mathematics* and *pure ethics*. Has any one ever heard it alleged that, from our complete and necessary ignorance of the conditions, it is *uncertain* what exact relation the diameter of a circle bears to the circle in rational or irrational numbers? The relation cannot be stated in rational numbers, and it had not yet been discovered in terms of irrational numbers, so it was supposed that the impossibility of such a solution could be known with certainty, which is what Lambert went on to show. In the general principles of morals there can be nothing uncertain, for the propositions are either utterly without meaning, or must originate solely in our rational concepts. On the other hand, there must be in physical science an infinite number of conjectures, which can never become certainties; because the appearances of nature are not given as objects dependent on our concepts. The key to the solution of such questions cannot therefore be found in our concepts or in pure thought, but must lie outside us, and for that reason is in many cases not to be discovered; and consequently a satisfactory solution cannot be expected. The questions of the Transcendental Analytic, which relate to the deduction of our pure knowledge, are not to be regarded as of the same kind as those mentioned above; for we are not at present treating of the certainty of judgments in relation to the origin of our concepts, but only of that certainty in relation to objects.

We cannot, therefore, escape the responsibility of at least a critical solution of the questions of reason, by complaints of the limited nature of our faculties, and the seemingly humble confession that it is beyond the power of our reason to decide, whether the world has existed from all eternity or had a beginning – whether it is infinitely extended, or enclosed within certain limits – whether anything in the world is simple, or whether everything must be capable of infinite divisibility – whether freedom can originate appearances, or whether everything is absolutely dependent on the laws and order of nature – and, finally, whether there exists a being that is completely unconditioned and necessary, or whether the existence of everything is conditioned and consequently dependent on something external to itself, and therefore in its own nature contingent. For all these questions relate to an object, which can be given nowhere else than in thought. This object is the absolutely unconditioned totality of the synthesis of appearances. If our own concepts in our minds do not assist us to some certain result in regard to these problems, we must not defend ourselves on the plea that the object itself remains hidden from and unknown to us. For no such thing or object can be given – it is not to be found outside of our idea itself. We must seek the cause of our failure in our idea itself, which is an insoluble problem, and in regard to which we obstinately assume that there exists a real object corresponding and adequate to it. A clear explanation of the dialectic which lies in our concept, would very soon enable us to come to full certainty in regard to such a question.

The pretext, that we are unable to arrive at certainty in regard to these problems, may be met with this question, which requires at least a plain answer: From what source do the ideas originate, the solution of which involves you in such difficulties? Are you seeking for an explanation of certain appearances; and do you expect these ideas to give you the principles or the rules of this explanation? Let it be granted, that all nature was laid open before you; that nothing of what is presented in our intuition was hid from your senses and your consciousness. Still, you could not know *in concreto* the object of your ideas in any experience. For what is demanded, is, not only this full and complete intuition, but also a complete synthesis and the consciousness of its absolute totality; and this is not possible by means of any empirical knowledge. It follows that your question –

your idea – is by no means necessary for the explanation of any appearance; and the idea cannot have been in any sense given by the object itself. For such an object can never be presented to us, because it cannot be given by any possible experience. Whatever perceptions you may attain to, you are still confined to *conditions* – in space, or in time – and you cannot discover anything unconditioned; nor can you decide whether this unconditioned is to be placed in an absolute beginning of the synthesis, or in an absolute totality of the series without beginning. A whole, in the empirical signification of the term, is always merely comparative. Concerning the absolute whole of quantity (the universe), of division, of derivation, of the condition of existence, with the question of whether it is to be produced by finite or infinite synthesis, no possible experience can instruct us. You will not, for example, be able to explain the appearances of a body in the least degree better, whether you believe it to consist of simple, or of composite parts; for a simple appearance – and just as little an infinite composition – can never be presented to you. Appearances require and admit of explanation, only in so far as the conditions of that explanation are given in perception; but the sum total of that which is given in appearances, considered as an absolute whole, is itself not a perception – and we cannot therefore seek for explanations of this whole beyond itself, in other perceptions. The explanation of this whole is the proper object of the transcendental problems of pure reason.

Although, therefore, the solution of these problems is unattainable through experience, we must not permit ourselves to say, that it is uncertain how the object of our inquiries is constituted. For the object is in our own mind, and cannot be discovered in experience; and we have only to take care that our thoughts are consistent with each other, and to avoid falling into the amphiboly of regarding our idea as a representation of an object empirically given, and therefore to be known according to the laws of experience. A dogmatical solution is therefore not only unsatisfactory, but impossible. The critical solution, which is a perfectly certain one, does not consider the question objectively, but proceeds by inquiring into the basis of the knowledge upon which the question rests.

THE ANTINOMY OF PURE REASON

Section V: Sceptical Exposition of the Cosmological Questions presented in the four Transcendental Ideas

We should be quite willing to desist from the demand of a dogmatical answer to our questions, if we understood beforehand that, be the answer what it may, it would only serve to increase our ignorance, to throw us from one incomprehensibility into another, from one obscurity into another still greater, and perhaps lead us into irreconcilable contradictions. If a dogmatical affirmative or negative answer is demanded, is it at all prudent to set aside the probable grounds of a solution which lie before us, and to take into consideration what advantage we shall gain, if the answer is to favour the one side or the other? If it happens that in both cases the answer is mere nonsense, we have in this an irresistible summons to institute a critical investigation of the question, for the purpose of discovering whether it is based on a groundless presupposition, and relates to an idea, the falsity of which would be more easily exposed in its application and consequences, than in its separate representation. This is the great utility of the sceptical mode of treating the questions addressed by pure reason to itself. By this method we easily rid ourselves of the confusions of dogmatism, and establish in its place a temperate criticism, which, as a genuine cathartic, will successfully remove the presumption and its consequence, polymathy.

If, then, I could understand the nature of a cosmological idea, and perceive, that, whatever side of the question regarding the unconditioned of the regressive synthesis of appearances it favoured, it must either be *too great* or *too small* for every *concept of the understanding* – I would be able to comprehend how the idea, which relates to an object of experience – an experience which must be adequate to a possible concept of the understanding – must be completely void and without significance, inasmuch as its object is inadequate, consider it as we may. And this is acutally the case with all cosmological concept, which, for the reason above mentioned, involve reason, so long as it remains attached to them, in an unavoidable antinomy. For suppose:

First, that *the world has no beginning* – in this case it is too large for our concept; for this concept, which consists in a successive regress, cannot fathom the whole eternity that has elapsed. Grant that *it has a beginning*, it is then too small for the concept of the understanding. For, as a beginning presupposes a time preceding, it cannot be unconditioned; and the law of the empirical employment of the understanding imposes the necessity of looking for a higher condition of time; and the world is, therefore, evidently too small for this law.

The same is the case with the double answer to the question regarding the magnitude, in space, of the world. For, if it is *infinite* and unlimited, it must be *too large* for every possible empirical concept. If it is *finite* and limited, we have a right to ask – what determines these limits? Empty space is not a self-subsistent correlate of things, and cannot be a final condition – and still less an empirical condition, forming a part of a possible experience. For how can we have any experience or perception of an absolute void? But the absolute totality of the empirical synthesis requires that the unconditioned be an empirical concept. Consequently, a finite world is *too small* for our concept.

Second, if every appearance (matter) in space consists of an *infinite number of parts*, the regress of the division is always too great for our concept; and if the *division* of space must *cease* with some member of the division (the simple), it is too small for the idea of the unconditioned. For the member at which we have discontinued our division still admits a regress to many more parts contained in the object.

Third, suppose that every event in the world happens in accordance with the laws of nature; the causality of a cause must itself be an event, and necessitates a regress to a still higher cause, and consequently the unceasing prolongation of the series of conditions *a parte priori*. Operative nature is therefore too large for every concept we can form in the synthesis of world-events.

If we admit the existence of *spontaneously* produced events, that is of *free* agency, we are driven, in our search for sufficient reasons, on an unavoidable law of nature, and are conpelled to appeal to the empirical law of causality, and we find that any such totality of connection in our synthesis is too small for our necessary empirical concept.

Fourthly, if we assume the existence of an *absolutely necessary being* – whether it be the world or something in the world, or the cause of the world; we must place it in a time at an infinite distance from any given moment; for, otherwise, it must be dependent on some other and higher existence. Such an existence is, in this case, too large for our empirical concept, and unattainable by the continued regress of any synthesis.

But if we believe that everything in the world – be it condition or conditioned – is *contingent*; every given existence is too small for our concept. For in this case we are compelled to seek for some other existence upon which the former depends.

We have said that in all these cases the cosmological idea is either too great or too small for the empirical regress in a synthesis, and consequently for every possible concept of the understanding. Why did we not express ourselves in a manner exactly the reverse of this, and, instead of accusing the cosmological idea of overstepping or of falling short of its true aim – possible experience, say that, in the first case, the empirical concept is always too small for the idea, and in the second too great, and thus attach the blame of these conflicts to the empirical regress? The reason is this. Possible experience can alone give reality to our concepts; without it a concept is merely an idea, without truth or relation to an object. Hence a possible empirical concept must be the standard by which we are to judge whether an idea is anything more than an idea and fiction of thought, or whether it relates to an object in the world. If we say of a thing that in relation to some other thing it is too large or too small, the former is considered as existing for the sake of the latter, and requiring to be adapted to it. Among the trivial subjects of discussion in the old schools of dialectics was this question: If a ball cannot pass through a hole, shall we say that the ball is too large or the hole too small? In this case it is indifferent what expression we employ; for we do not know which exists for the sake of the other. On the other hand, we cannot say: The man is too long for his coat – but: The coat is too short for the man.

We are thus led to the well-founded suspicion, that the cosmological ideas, and all the conflicting sophistical assertions connected with them, are based upon an empty and fictitious concept of the mode in which the object of these ideas is presented to us; and this suspicion will probably direct us how to expose the illusion that has so long led us astray.

THE ANTINOMY OF PURE REASON

Section VI: Transcendental Idealism as the Key to the Solution of Cosmological Dialectic

In the transcendental aesthetic we proved, that everything intuited in space and time – all objects of a possible experience – are nothing but appearances, that is, mere representations; and that these, as presented to us – as extended bodies, or as series of changes – have no self-subsistent existence apart from our thought. This doctrine I call *transcendental idealism*.[1] The realist in the transcendental sense regards these modifications of our sensibility – these mere representations – as things subsisting in themselves.

It would be unjust to accuse us of holding the long-decried theory of empirical idealism, which, while admitting the reality of space, denies, or at least doubts, the existence of bodies extended in it, and thus leaves us without a sufficient criterion of reality and illusion. The supporters of this theory find no difficulty in admitting the reality of the appearance of the internal sense in time; nay, they go to the length of maintaining that this internal experience is of itself a sufficient proof of the real existence of its object as a thing in itself with all this time-determination.

Transcendental idealism allows that the objects of external intuition – as intuited in space, and all changes in time – as represented by the internal sense, are real. For, as space is the form of that intuition which we call external, and without objects in space, no empirical representation could be given us; we can and ought to regard extended bodies in it as real. The case is the same with representations in time. But time and space, with all appearances therein, are not in themselves *things*. They are nothing but representations, and cannot exist outside of and apart from the mind. Nay, the sensible internal intuition of the mind (as the object of consciousness), the determination of which is represented by the succession of different states in time, is not the real, proper self, as it exists in itself – not the transcendental subject, but only an appearance, which is presented to the sensibility of this, to us, unknown being. This internal appearance cannot be admitted to be a self-subsisting thing; for its condition is time, and time cannot be the condition of a thing in itself. But the empirical truth of appearances in space and time is guaranteed beyond the possibility of doubt, and sufficiently distinguished from the illusion of dreams – although both have a proper and thorough connection in an experience according to empirical laws.

The objects of experience then are not things in themselves, but

---

[1] I have elsewhere termed this theory *formal* idealism, to distinguish it from *material* idealism, which doubts or denies the existence of external things. To avoid ambiguity, it seems advisable in many cases to employ this term instead of that mentioned in the text.

are given only in experience, and have no existence apart from and independently of experience. That there may be inhabitants in the moon, although no one has ever observed them, must certainly be admitted; but this assertion means only, that we may in the possible progress of experience discover them at some future time. For that, which stands in connection with a perception according to the laws of the progress of experience, is real. They are therefore really existent, if they stand in empirical connection with my actual or real consciousness, although they are not in themselves real, that is, apart from the progress of experience.

There is nothing actually given to us, except a perception and the empirical progression from it to other possible perceptions. For appearances, as mere representations, are real only in perception; and perception is, in fact, nothing but the reality of an empirical representation, that is, an appearance. To call appearance a real thing prior to perception, means either that we must meet with this appearance in the progress of experience, or it means nothing at all. For I can say only of a thing in itself that it exists without relation to the senses and experience. But we are speaking here merely of appearances in space and time, both of which are determinations of sensibility, and not of things in themselves. It follows that appearances are not things in themselves, but are mere representations, which, if not given in us – in perception, are non-existent.

The faculty of sensible intuition is properly a receptivity – a capacity of being affected in a certain manner by representations, the relation of which to each other is a pure intuition of space and time – the pure forms of sensibility. These representations, in so far as they are connected and determinable in this relation (in space and time) according to laws of the unity of experience, are called *objects*. The non-sensible cause of these representations is completely unknown to us, and hence cannot be intuited as an object. For such an object could not be represented either in space or in time (as mere conditions of sensible representation); and without these conditions intuition is impossible. We may, at the same time, term the non-sensible (intelligible) cause of appearances the transcendental object – but merely as a mental correlate to sensibility, considered as a receptivity. To this transcendental object we may attribute the whole connection and extent of our possible perceptions, and say that it is given and exists in itself prior to all experience. But the appearances, corresponding to it, are not given as things in themselves, but in experience alone. For they are mere representations, receiving from perceptions alone significance and relation to a real object, under the condition that this or that perception – indicating an object – is in complete connection with all others in accordance with the rules of the unity of experience. Thus we can say: the things that really existed in past time, are given in the transcendental object of experience. But these are to me real objects, only in so far as I can represent to myself, that a regressive series of possible perceptions – following the indications of history, or the footsteps of cause and effect – in accordance with empirical laws – that, in one word, the course of the world conducts us to an elapsed series of time as the condition of the present time. This series in past time is represented as real, not in itself, but only in connection with a possible experience. Thus, when I say that certain events occurred in past time, I merely assert the possibility of prolonging the chain of experience, from the present perception, upwards to the conditions that determine it according to time.

If I represent to myself all objects existing in all space and time, I do not thereby place these in space and time prior to all experience; on the contrary, such a representation is nothing more than the notion of a possible experience, in its absolute completeness. In experience alone are those objects, which are nothing but representations, given. But, when I say, they existed prior to my experience: this means only that I must begin with the perception present to me, and follow the track indicated, until I discover them in some part or region of experience. The cause of the empirical condition of this progression – and consequently at what member therein I must stop, and at which point in the regress I am to find this member – is transcendental, and hence necessarily incapable of being known. But this is not our concern; our concern is only with the law of progression in experience, in which objects, that is, appearances, are given. It is a matter of indifference, whether I say: I may in the progress of experience discover stars, at a hundred times greater distance that the most distant of those now visible – or Stars at this distance may be met in space, although no one has, or ever will discover them. For, if they were given as things in themselves, without any relation to possible experience, they would be for me nothing, consequently, are not objects, for they are not contained in the regressive series of experience. But, if these appearances are employed in relation the cosmological idea of an absolute whole – and, when we are discussing a question that oversteps the limits of possible experience, the proper distinction of the different theories of the reality of sensible objects is of great importance, in order to avoid the illusion which must necessarily arise from the misinterpretation of our empirical concepts.

THE ANTINOMY OF PURE REASON

Section VII: Critical Solution of the Cosmological Conflict of Reason with itself

The antinomy of pure reason is based upon the following dialectical argument: If that which is conditioned is given, the whole series of its conditions is also given; but sensible objects are given as conditioned; consequently ... This syllogism, the major of which seems so natural and evident, introduces as many cosmological ideas as there are different kinds of conditions in the synthesis of appearances, in so far as these conditions constitute a series. These ideas postulate absolute totality in the series, and thus place reason in unavoidable conflict with itself. Before proceeding to expose the fallacy in this dialectical argument, it will be necessary to have a correct understanding of certain concepts that appear in it.

In the first place, the following proposition is evident, and indubitably certain: If the conditioned is given, a regress in the series of all its conditions is thereby set as a task. For the very concept of a conditioned is a concept of something related to a condition, and, if this condition is itself conditioned, to another condition — and so on through all the members of the series. This proposition is, therefore, analytical, and has nothing to fear from transcendental criticism. It is a logical postulate of reason: to pursue, as far as possible, the connection of a concept with its conditions which results from the concept itself.

If, in the second place, both the conditioned and the condition are things in themselves, and if the former is given, not only is the regress to the latter requisite, but the latter is really *given with* the former. Now, as this is true of all the members of the series, the entire series of conditions, and with them the unconditioned, is at the same time given in the very fact of the conditioned, the existence of which is possible only in and through that series, being given. In this case, the synthesis of the conditioned with its condition, is a synthesis of the understanding merely, which represents things *as they are*, without regarding whether and how we can know them. But if I have to do with appearances, which, in their character of mere representations, are not given, if I do not attain to a knowledge of them (in other words, to themselves, for they are nothing more than empirical knowledge), I am not entitled to say: If the conditioned is given, all its conditions (as appearances) are also given. I cannot, therefore, from the fact of a conditioned being given, infer the absolute totality of the series of its conditions. For appearances are nothing but an empirical synthesis in apprehension (in space and time), and are therefore given only in it. Now, in speaking of appearances, it does not follow, that, if the conditioned is given, the synthesis which constitutes its empirical condition is also thereby given and presupposed; such a synthesis can be established only by an actual regress in the series of conditions. But we are entitled to say in this case: that a *regress* to the conditions of a conditioned, in other words, that a continuous empirical synthesis is enjoined; that, if the conditions are not *given*, they are at least enjoined and set for us as a task; and that this regress cannot fail to supply conditions.

We can now see that the major in the above cosmological inference, takes the conditioned in the transcendental signification which it has in the pure category, while the minor speaks of it in the empirical signification which it has in the category as applied to appearances. There is, therefore, a dialectical fallacy in the syllogism – a *sophisma figurae dictionis*. But this fallacy is not a consciously devised one, but a perfectly natural illusion of the common reason. For, when a thing is given as conditioned, we presuppose in the major its conditions and their series, unperceived, as it were, and unseen; because this is nothing more than the logical requirement of complete and satisfactory premisses for a given conclusion. In this case, time is altogether left out in the connection of the conditioned with the condition; they are supposed to be given in themselves, and *contemporaneously*. It is, moreover, just as natural to regard appearances (in the minor) as things in themselves and as objects presented to the pure understanding, as in the major, in which complete abstraction was made of all conditions of intuition. But it is under these conditions alone that objects are given. Now we overlook a remarkable distinction between the concepts. The synthesis of the conditioned with its condition, and the complete series of the latter (in the major) are not limited by time, and do not contain the concept of succession. On the contrary, the empirical synthesis, and the series of conditions in appearance – subsumed in the minor – are necessarily successive, and given in time alone. It follows that I cannot presuppose in the minor, as I did in the major, the absolute *totality* of the synthesis and of the series therein represented; for in the major all the members of the series are given as things in themselves — without any limitations or conditions in time, while in the minor they are possible only in and through a successive regress, which cannot exist, except if it is actually carried out.

After this proof of the viciousness of the argument commonly employed in maintaining cosmological assertions, both parties may now be justly dismissed, as advancing claims without grounds or title. But the process had not been ended, by convincing them that one or both were in the wrong, and had maintained an assertion which was without valid grounds of proof. Nothing seems to be clearer than that, if one maintains: the world has a beginning, and another: the world has no beginning, one of the two must be right. But it is likewise clear, that, if the evidence on both sides is equal, it is impossible to discover on what side the truth lies; and the controversy continues, although the parties have been recommended to peace before the tribunal of reason. There remains, then, no other means of settling the question than to convince the parties, who refute each other with such conclusiveness and ability, that they are disputing about nothing, and that a transcendental illusion has been mocking them with visions of reality where there is none. This mode of adjusting a dispute which cannot be decided upon its own merits, we shall now proceed to lay before our readers.

*

Zeno of Elea, a subtle dialectician, was severely reprimanded by Plato as a sophist, who, merely in order to exhibit his skill in discussion, maintained and subverted the same proposition by arguments as powerful and convincing on the one side as on the other. He maintained, for example, that God (who was probably nothing more, in his view, than the world) is neither finite nor infinite, neither in motion nor in rest, neither similar nor dissimilar to any other thing. It seemed to those philosophers who criticized his mode of discussion, that his purpose was to deny completely both of two mutually conflicting propositions — which is absurd. But I cannot believe that there is any justice in this accusation. The first of these propositions I shall presently consider in a more detailed manner. With regard to the others if by the word *God* he understood merely the *universe*, his meaning must have been, that it cannot be permanently present in one place — that is, at rest, nor be capable of changing its place — that is, of moving, because all places are in the universe, and the universe itself is, therefore, in no place. Again, if the universe contains in itself everything that exists, it cannot be similar or dissimilar to any *other* thing, because there is, in fact, no *other* thing with which it can be compared. If two opposite judgments presuppose an inadmissible condition, both – in spite of their conflict (which is, however, not properly a contradiction) – fall away; because the condition, which ensured the validity of both, has itself disappeared.

If we say: every body has either a good or a bad smell, we have omitted a third possible judgment – it has no smell at all; and thus both conflicting statements may be false. If we say: it is either good-smelling or not good-smelling (*vel suaveolens vel non-suaveolens*), both judgments are contradictorily opposed; and the contradictory opposite of the former judgment – some bodies are not good-smelling – embraces also those bodies which have no smell at all. In the preceding pair of opposed judgments (*per disparata*), the contingent condition of the concept of body (smell) attached to both conflicting statements, instead of having been omitted in the latter, which is consequently not the contradictory opposite of the former.

If, accordingly, we say: The world is either infinite in extension, or it is not infinite (*non est infinitus*); and if the former proposition is false, its contradictory opposite – The world is not infinite – must be true. And thus I should deny the existence of an infinite, without however, affirming the existence of a finite world. But if we construct our proposition thus: The world is either infinite or finite (non-infinite) – both statements may be false. For, in this case, we consider the world as *per se* determined in regard to magnitude, and while, in the one judgement, we deny its infinite and consequently, perhaps, its independent existence; in the other, we append to the world, regarded as a thing in itself, a certain determination – that of finitude; and the latter may be false as well as the former, if the world is not given as a *thing in itself*, and thus neither as finite nor as infinite in magnitude. This kind of opposition I may be allowed to term *dialectical*; that of contradictories may be called *analytical opposition*. Thus then, of two dialectically opposed judgments both may be false, from the fact, that the one is not a mere contradictory of the other, but actually says more than is requisite for a contradiction.

When we regard the two propositions – The world is infinite in magnitude, and, The world is finite in magnitude – as contradictory opposites, we are assuming that the world – the complete series of appearances – is a thing in itself. For it remains as a permanent magnitude, whether I deny the infinite or the finite regress in the series of its appearances. But if we dismiss this assumption – this transcendental illusion, and deny that it is a thing in itself, the contradictory opposition is changed into a merely dialectial one; and the world, as not existing in itself – independently of the regressive series of my representations, exists in like manner neither as a whole which is infinite nor as a whole which is finite in itself. The universe exists for me only in the empirical regress of the series of appearances, and not *per se*. If, then, it is always conditioned, it is never given completely or as a whole; and it is, therefore, not an unconditioned whole, and does not exist as such, either with an infinite, or with a finite magnitude.

What we have here said of the first cosmological idea – that of the absolute totality of magnitude in appearances, applies also to the others. The series of conditions is discoverable only in the regressive synthesis itself, and not in the appearance considered as a thing in itself – given prior to all regress. Hence I am compelled to say: The aggregate of parts in a given appearance is in itself neither finite nor infinite; and these parts are given only in the regressive synthesis of decomposition – a synthesis which is never given in absolute *completeness*, either as finite, or as infinite. The same is the case with the series of subordinated causes, or of the conditioned up to the unconditioned and necessary existence, which can never be regarded as in itself, and in its totality, either as finite or as infinite; because, as a series of subordinate representations, it subsists only in the dynamical regress, and cannot be regarded as existing previously to this regress, or as a self-subsistent series of things.

Thus the antinomy of pure reason in its cosmological ideas disappears. For the above demonstration has established the fact that it is merely the product of a dialectical and illusory opposition, which arises from the application of the idea of absolute totality – admissible only as a condition of things in themselves, to appearances, which exist only in our representations, and – when constituting a series – in a successive regress. This antinomy of reason may, however, be really profitable to our speculative interests, not in the way of contributing any dogmatical addition, but as presenting to us another material support in our critical investigations. For it furnishes us with an indirect proof of the transcendental ideality of appearances, if we were not completely satisfied with the direct proof set forth in the Transcendental Aesthetic. The proof would proceed in the following dilemma. If the world is a whole existing in itself, it must be either finite or infinite. But it is neither finite nor infinite – as has been shown, on the one side, by the thesis, on the other, by the antithesis. Therefore the world – the totality of all appearances – is not a whole existing in itself. It follows that appearances are nothing, apart from our representations. And this is what we mean by transcendental ideality.

This remark is of some importance. It enables us to see that the proofs of the fourfold antinomy are not mere sophistries but well grounded on the nature of reason, under the supposition that appearances are things in themselves. The opposition of the judgments which follow makes it evident that a fallacy lay in the initial supposition, and thus helps us to discover the true constitution of objects of sense. This transcendental dialectic does not favour scepticism, but it does favour sceptical method, the great utility of which is apparent in the antinomy, where the arguments of reason were allowed to confront each other with unrestricted freedom. And although the result of these conflicts of reason is not what we expected, we have still reaped a great advantage in the correction of our judgments.

THE ANTINOMY OF PURE REASON

Section VIII: Regulative Principle of Pure Reason in Relation to the Cosmological Ideas

The cosmological principle of totality does not give us any *maximum* in the series of conditions in the world of sense; considered as a thing in itself, it merely sets us the task towards this maximum through the regress in the series of conditions. This principle of pure reason, therefore, may still be considered as valid – not as an *axiom* enabling us to think totality in the object as actual, but as a *problem* for the understanding, which requires it to institute and to continue, in conformity with the idea of totality in the mind, the regress in the series of the conditions of a given conditioned. For in sensibility, that is, in space and time, every condition which we discover in our investigation of appearance is itself conditioned; because sensible objects are not things in themselves (in which case an absolutely unconditioned might be reached), but are merely empirical representations, the conditions of which must always be found in intuition. The principle of reason is therefore properly a mere rule – prescribing a regress in the series of conditions for given appearances, and prohibiting any pause or rest on an absolutely unconditioned. It is, therefore, not a principle of the possibility of experience or of the empirical knowledge of sensible objects – consequently not a principle of the understanding; for every experience is confined within its limits in accord with the given intuition. Still less is it a *constitutive principle* of reason authorizing us to extend our concepts of the sensible world beyond all possible experience. It is merely a principle for the enlargement and extension of experience as far as is possible. It forbids us to consider any empirical limits as absolute. It is, hence, a principle of reason, which, as a *rule*, dictates how we ought to proceed in our empirical regress, but is unable to *anticipate* prior to the regress what is given in the object itself. I have termed it for this reason a *regulative* principle of reason; while the principle of the absolute totality of the series of conditions, as existing in itself and given in the object, is a constitutive cosmological principle. This distinction will at once demonstrate the falsehood of the constitutive principle, and prevent us from attributing (by a transcendental subreption) objective reality to an idea, which is valid only as a rule.

In order to understand the proper meaning of this rule of pure reason, we must notice first, that it cannot tell us *what the object is*, but only *how the empirical regress is to be proceeded with* in order to attain to the complete concept of the object. If it gave us any information in respect to the former statement, it would be a constitutive principle – a principle impossible from the nature of pure reason. It will not therefore enable us to establish any such conclusions as – the series of conditions for a given conditioned is in itself infinite, or, it is infinite. For, in this case, we should be thinking in the mere idea of absolute totality, an object which is not and cannot be given in experience; inasmuch as we should be attributing a reality objective and independent of the empirical synthesis, to a series of appearances. This idea of reason cannot then be regarded as valid – except as a rule for the regressive synthesis in the series of conditions, according to which we must proceed from the conditioned, through all subordinate conditions, up to the unconditioned; although this goal will never be attained. For the absolutely unconditioned cannot be discovered in the sphere of experience.

We now proceed to determine clearly our notion of a synthesis which can never be complete. There are two terms commonly employed for this purpose. These terms are regarded as expressions of different and distinguishable notions, although the ground of the distinction has never been clearly exposed. The term employed by the mathematicians is *progressus in infinitum*. The philosophers who explore concepts prefer the expression *progressus in indefinitum*. Without detaining the reader with an examination of the reasons for such a distinction, or with remarks on the right or wrong use of the terms, I shall endeavour clearly to determine these concepts, so far as it is necessary for our purpose.

We may, with propriety, say of a straight line, that it may be extended to infinity. In this case the distinction between a *progressus in infinitum* and a *progressus in indefinitum* is a mere piece of subtlety. For, although when we say, Extend a straight line – it is more correct to say *in indefinitum* than *in infinitum* because the former means, Extend it as far as far as you *please*, the second, You *must* not cease to extend it; the expression *in infinitum* is, when we are speaking of the *power* to do it, perfectly correct, for we can always make it longer if we please – on to infinity. And this remark holds good in all cases, when we speak of a *progressus*, that is, an advancement from the condition to the conditioned; this possible advancement always proceeds to infinity. We may proceed from a given pair in the descending line of generation from father to son, and think a never-ending line of descendants from it. For in such a case reason does not demand absolute totality in the series, because it does not presuppose it as a condition and as given (*datum*), but merely as conditioned, and as capable of being given (*dabile*) and is without end.

Very different is the case with the problem of how far the regress, which ascends from the given conditioned to the conditions, must extend; whether I can say, It is a *regress in infinitum*, or only *in indefinitum*; and whether, for example, setting out from the human beings at present alive in the world, I may ascend in the series of their ancestors, *in infinitum* – or whether all that can be said is, that so far as I have proceeded, I have discovered no empirical ground for considering the series limited, so that I am justified, and indeed, obliged to search for ancestors still further back, although I am not obliged by the idea of reason to presuppose them.

My answer to this question is: If the series is given in empirical intuition as a whole, the regress in the series of its internal conditions proceeds *in infinitum*; but, if only one member of the series is given, from which the regress is to proceed to absolute totality, the regress is possible only *in indefinitum*. For example, the division of a portion of matter given within certain limits – of a body, that is – proceeds *in infinitum*. For, as the condition of this whole is its part, and the condition of the part a part of the part, and so on, and as in this regress of decomposition an unconditioned indivisible member of the series of conditions is not to be found; there are no grounds in experience for stopping in the division, but, on the contrary, the more remote members of the division are actually and empirically given prior to this division. That is to say, the division proceeds to infinity. On the other hand, the series of ancestors of any given human being is not given, in its absolute totality, in any experience, and yet the regress proceeds from every genealogical member of this series to one still higher, and does not meet with any empirical limit presenting an absolutely unconditioned member of the series. But as the members of such a series are not continued in the empirical intuition of the whole, prior to the regress, this regress does not proceed to infinity, but only *in indefinitum*, that is, we are called upon to discover other and higher members, which are themselves always conditioned.

In neither case – the *regressus in infinitum*, nor the *regressus in indefinitum*, is the series of conditions to be considered as actually infinite in the object itself. This might be true of things in themselves, but it cannot be asserted of appearances, which, as conditions of each other, are only given in the empirical regress itself. Hence, the question no longer is, How large is this series of conditions in itself – is it finite or infinite? for it is nothing in itself; but, How is the empirical regress to be commenced, and how far ought we to proceed with it? And here a signal distinction in the application of this rule becomes apparent. If the whole is given empirically, it is possible to recede in the series of its internal conditions *to infinity*. But if the whole is not given, and can only be given through the empirical regress, I can only say – it is *possible to infinity*, to proceed to still higher conditions in the series. In the first case, I am justified in asserting that more members are empirically given in the object than I attain to in the regress (of decomposition). In the second case, I am justified only in saying, that I can always proceed further in the regress, because no member of the series is given as absolutely conditioned, and thus a higher member is possible, and an inquiry with regard to it is necessary. In the one case it is necessary to *find* other members of the series, in the other it is necessary to *inquire* for others, inasmuch as experience presents no absolute limitation of the regress. For, either you do not possess a perception which absolutely limits your empirical regress, and in this case the regress cannot be regarded as complete; or, you do possess such a limitative perception, in which case it is not a part of your series (for that which *limits* must be distinct from that which is *limited* by it), and it is incumbent on you to continue your regress up to this condition, and so on.

These remarks will be placed in their proper light by their application in the following section.

THE ANTINOMY OF PURE REASON

Section IX: The Empirical Use of the Regulative Principle of Reason with regard to all the Cosmological Ideas

We have shown that no transcendental use can be made either of the pure concepts of reason or of understanding. We have shown, likewise, that the demand of absolute totality in the series of conditions in the world of sense arises from a transcendental employment of reason, resting on the opinion that appearances are to be regarded as things in themselves. It follows that we are not required to answer the question respecting the absolute magnitude of a series – whether it is *in itself* limited or unlimited. We are only called upon to determine how far we must proceed in the empirical regress from condition to condition, in order to discover, in conformity with the rule of reason, a full and correct answer to the questions proposed by reason itself.

This principle of reason is hence valid only as a rule for the *extension* and magnitude of a possible experience – its invalidity as a principle constitute of appearances in themselves having been sufficiently demonstrated. And thus, too, the antinomial conflict of reason with itself is completely put an end to; inasmuch as we have not only presented a critical solution of the illusion behind the conflict of reason, but have shown the true meaning of the ideas which gave rise to these statements. The *dialectical* principle of reason has, therefore, been changed into a *doctrinal* principle. But in fact, if this principle, in the subjective signification which we have shown to be its only true sense, may be guaranteed as a principle of the unceasing extension of the employment of our understanding in experience with a view to determine its objects appropriately, its influence and value are just as great as if it were an axiom or the *a priori* determination of objects (which cannot be determined by pure reason). For such an axiom could not exert a stronger influence on the extension and rectification of our knowledge, otherwise than by procuring for the principles of the understanding the most widely expanded employment in the field of experience.

I : Solution of the Cosmological Idea of the Totality of the Composition of Appearances in the Universe

Here, as well as in the case of the other cosmological problems, the ground of the regulative principle of reason is the proposition, that in our empirical regress *no experience of an absolute limit*, and consequently no experience of a condition, which is itself *absolutely unconditioned*, is discoverable. And the truth of this proposition itself rests upon the consideration, that such an experience would have to represent to us appearances as limited by nothing or the mere void, which our continued regress by means of perception would have to be able to encounter – which is impossible.

Now this proposition, which declared that every condition attained in the empirical regress must itself be considered empirically conditioned, contains the rule *in terminis*, which requires me, to whatever extent I may have proceeded in the ascending series, always to look for some higher member in the series – whether this member is to become known to me through experience, or not.

Nothing further is necessary, then, for the solution of the first cosmological problem, than to decide, whether, in the regress to the unconditioned magnitude of the universe (as regards space and time), this never-limited ascent ought to be called a *regressus in infinitum* or *in indefinitum*.

The general representation of the series of all past states or conditions of the world, or of all the things which at present exist in it, is itself nothing more than a *possible* empirical regress, which is thought – although in an undetermined manner – in us, and which gives rise to the concept of a series of conditions for a given object.[1] Now I have a concept of the universe, but not an intuition

---

[1] The world-series can neither be greater nor smaller than the possible empirical regress, upon which its concept is based. And as this regress cannot be a determinate infinite regress, still less a determinate finite (absolutely limited), it is evident, that we cannot regard the world as either finite or infinite, because the regress, which gives us the representation of the world, is neither finite nor infinite.

– that is, not an intuition of it as a whole. Thus I cannot infer the magnitude of the regress from the magnitude of the world, and determine the former by means of the latter; on the contrary, I must first of all form a concept of the magnitude of the world from the magnitude of the empirical regress. But of this regress I know nothing more, than that I ought to proceed from every given member of the series of conditions to one still higher. But the magnitude of the universe is not thereby determined, and we cannot affirm that this regress proceeds *in infinitum*. Such an affirmation would *anticipate* the members of the series which has not yet been reached, and represent the number of them as beyond the grasp of any empirical synthesis; it would consequently *determine* the magnitude of the world prior to the regress (although only in a negative manner) – which is impossible. For the world is not given in its totality in any intuition: consequently its magnitude cannot be given prior to the regress. It follows that we are unable to make any declaration respecting the magnitude of the world in itself – not even that the regress in it is a regress *in infinitum*; we must only endeavour to attain to a concept of the quantity of the universe, in conformity with the rule which determines the empirical regress in it. But this rule merely requires us never to admit an absolute limit to our series – how far soever we may have proceeded in it – but always, on the contrary, to subordinate every appearance to some other as its condition, and consequently to proceed to this higher appearance. Such a regress is, therefore, the *regressus in indefinitum*, which, as not determining a magnitude in the object, is clearly distinguishable from the *regressus in infinitum*.

It follows from what we have said that we are not justified in declaring the world to be infinite in space, or as regards past time. For this concept of an infinite given magnitude is empirical; but we cannot apply the concept of an infinite magnitude to the world as an object of the senses. I cannot say, the regress from a given perception to everything limited either in space or time, proceeds *in infinitum* – for this presupposes an infinite magnitude of the world; neither can I say, it is *finite* – for an absolute limit is likewise impossible in experience. It follows that I am not entitled to make any assertion at all respecting the whole object of experience – the world of sense – I must limit my declarations to the rule, according to which experience or empirical knowledge is to be attained.

To the question, therefore, respecting the magnitude of the world, the first and negative answer is: The world has no beginning in time, and no absolute limit in space.

For, in the contrary case, it would be limited by an empty time on the one hand, and by an empty space on the other. Now, since the world, as an appearance, cannot be thus limited in itself – for an appearance is not a thing in itself – it would have to be possible for us to have a perception of this limitation by an empty time and an empty space. But such a perception – such an experience – is impossible; because it has no content. Consequently, an absolute world limit is empirically, and therefore absolutely, impossible.[1]

The above rule does not prescribe an unceasing regress in one kind of appearances. It does not, for example, forbid us, in our ascent from an individual human being through the line of his ancestors, to expect that we shall discover at some point of the regress a primeval pair, or to admit, in the series of heavenly bodies, a sun at the farthest possible distance from some centre. All that it demands is a perpetual progress from appearances to appearances, even although an actual perception is not presented by them (as in the case of our perceptions being too weak in degree for our consciousness), since they, nevertheless, belong to possible experience.

Every beginning is in time, and all limits to extension are in space. But space and time are in the world of sense. Consequently appearances *in the world* are conditionally limited, but *the world* itself is not limited, either conditionally or unconditionally.

For this reason, and because neither the world nor the series of conditions to a given conditioned can be *completely given*, our concept of the world magnitude is given only in and through the regress and not prior to it – in a collective intuition. But the regress itself is really nothing more than the *determining* of the world magnitude, and cannot therefore give us any *determined* concept of it – still less a concept of a magnitude which is, in relation to a certain standard, infinite. The regress does not, therefore, proceed to infinity (an infinity given), but only to an indefinite extent, for

---

[1] The reader will remark that the proof presented above is very different from the dogmatical demonstration given in the antithesis of the first antinomy. In that demonstration, it was taken for granted that the world is a thing in itself – given in its totality prior to all regress – and a determined position in space and time was denied to it – if it was not considered as occupying all time and all space. Hence our conclusion differed from that given above; for we inferred in the antithesis the actual infinity of the world.

the purpose of presenting to us a magnitude (of experience) – realized only in and through the regress itself.

II: Solution of the Cosmological Idea of the Totality of the Division of a Whole given in Intuition

When I divide a whole which is given in intuition, I proceed from a conditioned to its conditions. The division of the parts of the whole (*subdivisio* or *decompositio*) is a regress in the series of these conditions. The absolute totality of this series would be actually given, only if the regress could arrive at *simple* parts. But if all the parts in a continuous decomposition are themselves divisible, the division, that is to say, the regress, proceeds from the conditioned to its conditions *in infinitum*; because the conditions (the parts) are themselves contained in the conditioned, and, as the latter is given in a limited intuition, the former are all given along with it. This regress cannot, therefore, be called a *regressus in indefinitum*, as happened in the case of the preceding cosmological idea, the regress in which proceeded from the conditioned to the conditions not given contemporaneously and along with it, but discoverable only through the empirical regress. We are not, however, entitled to affirm of a whole of this kind, which is divisible *in infinitum*, that *it consists of an infinite number of parts*. For, although all the parts are contained in the intuition of the whole, the *whole division* is not contained therein. The division is contained only in the progressing decomposition – in the regress itself, which is what makes the series real in the first place. Now, as this regress is infinite, all the members (parts) to which it attains must be contained in the given whole as an *aggregate*. But the complete *series of division* is not contained therein. For this series, being infinite in succession and always incomplete, cannot represent an infinite number of members, and still less a composition of these members into a whole.

To apply this remark to space, every limited part of space presented to intuition is a whole, the parts of which are always spaces – to whatever extend subdivided. Every limited space is hence divisible to infinity.

Let us again apply the remark to an external appearance enclosed in limits, that is, a body. The divisibility of a body rests upon the divisibility of space, which is the condition of the possibility of the body as an extended whole. A body is consequently divisible to infinity, though it does not, for that reason, consist of infinitely many parts.

It certainly seems that, as a body must be thought as substance in space, the law of divisibility would not be applicable to it as substance. For we may and ought to grant, in the case of space, that division or decomposition, to any extent, never can utterly annihilate composition (that is to say, the smallest part of space must still consist of spaces); otherwise space would entirely cease to exist — which is impossible. But, the assertion on the other hand, that when all composition in matter is annihilated in thought, nothing remains, does not seem to harmonize with the concept of substance, which must be properly the subject of all composition and must remain, even after the conjunction of its attributes in space — which constituted a body — is annihilated in thought. But this is not the case with substance in appearance, which is not a thing in itself thought by the pure concept of the understanding. Phenomenal substance is not an absolute subject: it is merely a permanent sensible image, and nothing more than an intuition, in which the unconditioned is not to be found.

But, although this rule of progress to infinity is applicable to the subdivision of an appearance, as a mere filling of space, it is not applicable to a whole consisting of a number of distinct parts and constituting a *quantum discretum* — that is to say, an organized body. It cannot be admitted that every part in an organized whole is itself organized, and that, in analysing it to infinity, we must always meet with organized parts; although we may allow that the parts of the matter which we decompose *in infinitum, may* be organized. For the infinity of the division of an appearance in space rests altogether on the fact that the divisibility of an appearance is given only in and through this infinity, that is, an undetermined number of parts is given, while the parts themselves are given and determined only in and through the subdivision; in a word, the infinity of the division necessarily presupposes that the whole is not already divided *in se*. Hence our division determines a number of parts in the whole — a number which extends just as far as the actual regress in the division; while, on the other hand, the very notion of a body organized to infinity represents the whole as already and in itself divided. We expect, therefore, to find in it a determinate, but, at the same time, infinite, number of parts — which is self-contradictory. For we should thus have a hole containing a series of members which could not be completed in any regress

– which is infinite, and at the same time complete in an organized composite. Infinite divisibility is applicable only to a *quantum continuum*, and is based entirely on the infinite divisibility of space. But in a *quantum discretum* the multitude of parts or units is always determined, and hence always equal to some number. To what extent a body may be organized, experience alone can inform us; and although, so far as our experience of this or that body has extended, we may not have discovered any inorganic part, such parts must exist in possible experience. But how far the transcendental division of an appearance must extend, we cannot know from experience – it is a question which experience cannot answer; it is answered only by the principle of reason which forbids us to consider the empirical regress, in the analysis of extended body, as ever absolutely complete.

Concluding Remark on the Solution of the Transcendental Mathematical Ideas – and Preliminary Observation to the Solution of the Transcendental Dynamical Ideas

We presented the antinomy of pure reason in a tabular form, and we endeavoured to show the ground of this conflict on the part of reason, and the only means of bringing it to a conclusion – namely, by declaring both conflicting statements to be false. We represented in these antinomies the conditions of appearances as belonging to the conditioned according to relations of space and time – which is the usual supposition of the common understanding. In this respect, all dialectical representations of totality, in the series of conditions to a given conditioned, were perfectly *homogeneous*. The condition was always a member of the series along with the conditioned, and thus the homogeneity of the whole series was assured. In this case the regress could never be thought as complete; or, if this was the case, a member really conditioned was falsely regarded as a primal member, consequently as unconditioned. In such an antinomy, therefore, we did not consider the object, that is, the conditioned, but the series of conditions belonging to the object, and the magnitude of that series. And thus arose the difficulty – a difficulty not to be settled by any decision regarding the claims of the two parties, but simply by cutting the knot – by declaring the series proposed by reason to be either *too long* or *too short* for the understanding, which could in neither be equal to the prescribed ideas.

But we have overlooked, up to this point, an essential difference existing between the concepts of the understanding which reason endeavours to raise to the rank of ideas – two of these indicating a *mathematical*, and two a *dynamical* synthesis of appearances. Hitherto, it was not necessary to signalize this distinction; for, just as in our general representation of all transcendental ideas, we considered them under conditions in appearance, so, in the two mathematical ideas, our discussion is concerned solely with an object in appearance. But as we are now about to proceed to the consideration of the *dynamical* concepts of the understanding, and their adequateness with ideas, we must not lose sight of this distinction. We shall find that it opens up to us an entirely new view of the conflict in which reason is involved. For, while in the first two antinomies, both parties were *dismissed*, on the ground of having advanced statements based upon false hypotheses; in the present case the hope appears of discovering a hypothesis which may be consistent with the demands of reason, and, the judge completing the statement of the grounds of claim, which both parties had left in an unsatisfactory state, the question may be settled on its own merits, not by dismissing the claimants, but by a *comparison* of the arguments on both sides, which was impossible in the conflict of the mathematical antinomies.

If we consider merely their *extension*, and whether they are adequate with ideas, the series of conditions may be regarded as all homogeneous. But the concept of the understanding which lies at the basis of these ideas, contains either a *synthesis of the homogeneous* (presupposed in every magnitude – in its composition as well as in its division) or of the *heterogeneous*, which is the case in the dynamical synthesis of cause and effect, as well as of the necessary with the contingent.

Thus it happens, that in the mathematical series of appearances no other than a sensible condition is admissible – a condition which is itself a member of the series; while the dynamical series of sensible conditions admits a heterogenous condition, which is not a member of the series, but, as purely *intelligible*, lies outside it. And thus reason is satisfied, and an unconditioned placed at the head of the series of appearances, without introducing confusion into or discontinuing it, contrary to the principles of the understanding.

Now, from the fact that the dynamical ideas admit a condition of appearances which does not form a part of the series of appearances, arises a result which we should not have expected from an antinomy. In former cases, the result was that both conflicting dialectical statements had to be false. In the present case, we find the conditioned in the dynamical series connected with an empirically unconditioned, but *non-sensible* condition; and thus satisfaction is done to the *understanding* on the one hand and to the *reason* on the other.[1] While, moreover, the dialectical arguments for unconditioned totality in mere appearances fall to the ground, *both* propositions of reason may be shown to be true in their proper signification. This could not happen in the case of the cosmological ideas which demanded a mathematically unconditioned unity; for no condition could be placed at the head of the series of appearances, except one which was itself an appearance, and consequently a member of the series.

III: Solution of the Cosmological Idea of the Totality of the Derivation of World Events from their Causes

There are only two modes of causality – the causality of *nature*, or of *freedom*. The first is the conjunction of a particular state with another preceding it in the world of sense, the former following the latter by virtue of a law. Now, as the causality of appearance is subject to conditions of time, and the preceding state, if it had always existed, could not have produced an effect which would make its first appearance at a particular time, the causality of a cause must itself be an effect – must itself have *begun to be*, and therefore, according to the principle of the understanding itself requires a cause.

We must understand, on the contrary, by the term freedom, in the cosmological sense, a faculty of the *spontaneous* origination of a state; the causality of which, therefore, is not subordinated to another cause determining it in time. Freedom is in this sense a pure transcendental idea, which, in the first place, contains no empirical element; the object of which, in the second place, cannot be given or determined in any experience, because it is a universal law of the very possibility of experience, that everything which happens must have a cause, that consequently the causality of a cause, being itself

---

[1] For the understanding cannot admit *among phenomena* a condition which is itself empirically unconditioned. But if it is possible to think an *intelligible* condition – one which is not a member of the series of appearances – for a conditioned appearance, without breaking the series of empirical conditions, such a condition may be admissible as *empirically unconditioned*, and the empirical regress continue without break.

something that has *happened*, must also have a cause. In this view of the case, the whole field of experience, how far soever it may extend, contains nothing that is not subject to the laws of nature. But, as we cannot by this means attain to an absolute totality of conditions in reference to the series of causes and effects, reason creates the idea of spontaneity, which can begin to act of itself, and without any external cause determining it to action, according to the law of causality.

It is especially remarkable that the practical concept of freedom is based upon the *transcendental idea*, and that the question of the possibility of the former is difficult only as it involves the consideration of the truth of the latter. Freedom, in the *practical sense*, is the independence of the will of *coercion* by sensible impulses. A will is sensible, in so far as it is *pathologically affected* (by sensible impulses); it is termed *animal* (*arbitrium brutum*), when it is *pathologically necessitated*. The human will is certainly an *arbitrium sensitivum*, not *brutum*, but *liberum*; because sensibility does not necessitate its action, a faculty existing in man of self-determination, independently of all sensible coercion.

It is plain, that, if all causality in the world of sense were natural – and natural only – every event would be determined by another according to necessary laws, and that consequently, appearances, in so far as they determine the will, must necessitate every action as a natural effect from themselves; and thus all practical freedom would fall to the ground with the transcendental idea. For the latter presupposes that, although a certain thing has not happened, it *ought* to have happened, and that, consequently, its phenomenal cause was not so powerful and determinative as to exclude the causality of our will – a causality capable of producing effects independently of and even in opposition to the power of natural causes, and capable, consequently, of *spontaneously* originating a series of events.

Here, too, we find it to be the case, as we generally found in the conflicts of a reason which strives to pass the bounds of possible experience, that the problem is properly not *physiological*, but *transcendental*. The question of the possibility of freedom does not indeed concern psychology; but, as it rests upon dialectical arguments of pure reason, its solution must engage the attention of transcendental philosophy. Before attempting this solution, a task which transcendental philosophy cannot decline, it will be advisable to make a remark with regard to its procedure in the settlement of the question.

If appearances were things in themselves, and time and space forms of the existence of things, condition and conditioned would always be members of the same series; and thus would arise in the present case the antinomy common to all transcendental ideas – that their series is either too great or too small for the understanding. The dynamical ideas, which we are about to discuss in this and the following section, possess the peculiarity of relating to an object, not considered as a magnitude, but as an *existence*; and thus, in the discussion of the present question, we may make abstraction of the magnitude of the series of conditions, and consider merely the dynamical relation of the condition to the conditioned. The question, then, suggests itself, whether freedom is possible; and, if it is, whether it can consist with the universality of the natural law of causality; and, consequently, whether we enounce a proper disjunctive proposition when we say, Every effect must have its origin either in nature or in freedom – or whether *both* cannot exist together in the same event in different relations. The principle of an unbroken connection between all events in the phenomenal world, in accordance with the unchangeable laws of nature, is a well-established principle of the Transcendental Analytic which admits of no exception. The question, therefore, is: Whether an effect, determined according to the laws of nature, can at the same time be produced by a free agent, or whether freedom and nature mutually exclude each other? And here, the common, but fallacious hypothesis of the *absolute reality* of appearances manifests its injurious influence in embarrassing the procedure of reason. For if appearances are things in themselves, freedom is impossible. In this case, nature is the complete and all-sufficient cause of every event; and condition and conditioned, cause and effect, are contained in the same series, and necessitated by the same law. If, on the contrary, appearances are held to be, as they are in fact, nothing more than mere representations, connected with each other in accordance with empirical laws, they must have a ground which is *not* phenomenal. But the causality of such an intelligible cause is not determined by appearances; although its effects, as appearances, can be determined by other appearances. This cause and its causality exist therefore outside the series of appearances; while its effects do exist and are discoverable in the series of empirical conditions. Such an effect may therefore be considered to be free in relation to its intelligible cause, and necessary in relation to the appearances from which it is a necessary consequence – a distinction which, stated in this perfectly general and abstract manner, must appear in the highest degree subtle and obscure. The sequel will explain. It is sufficient, at present, to remark that, as the complete and unbroken connection of appearances is an unalterable law of nature, freedom would be impossible – on the supposition that appearances are real existences. Hence those who adhere to the common opinion on this subject can never succeed in reconciling nature with freedom.

Possibility of Causality through Freedom in Harmony with the Universal Law of Natural Necessity

That element in a sensible object which is not itself sensible, I term *intelligible*. If, accordingly, an object which must be regarded as a sensible appearance possesses a faculty which is not an object of sensible intuition, but by means of which it is capable of being the cause of appearances, the *causality* of a being of this kind may be regarded from two different points of view. It may be considered to be *intelligible*, as regards its *action* – the action of a thing which is a thing in itself, and it may be considered sensible as regards its *effects* – the effects of an appearance belonging to the sensible world. We should, accordingly, have to form both an empirical and an intellectual concept of its causality – both, however, having reference to the same effect. This twofold manner of thinking a power residing in a sensible object does not run counter to any of the concepts which we ought to form of the world of appearances or of a possible experience. Appearances – not being things in themselves – must have a transcendental object as a foundation, which determines them as mere representations ; and there seems to be no reason why we should not ascribe to this transcendental object, in addition to the property of appearing, a *causality* whose effects are to be met with in the world of appearances, although it is not itself an appearance. But every effective cause must possess a *character*, that is to say, a law of its causality, without which it would cease to be a cause. In the above case, then, every sensible object would possess an *empirical* character, which guaranteed that its actions, as appearances, stand in complete and harmonious connection, conformably to unvarying natural laws, with all other appearances, and can be derived from these, as conditions, and that they do thus, in connection with these, constitute a series in the order of nature. This sensible object must, in the second place, possess an *intelligible character*, which guarantees it to be the cause of those actions, as appearances, although it is not itself an appearance nor subordinate to the conditions of the world of sense. The former may be termed the character of the thing as an appearance, the latter the character of the thing as a thing in itself.

Now this active subject would, in its character of intelligible subject, be subordinate to no conditions of time, for time is only a condition of appearances, and not of things in themselves. No *action* would *begin* or *cease* to be in this subject; it would consequently be free from the law of all determination of time – the law of change, namely, that everything *which happens* must have a cause in the appearances of a preceding state. In one word, the causality of the subject, in so far as it is intelligible, would not form part of the series of empirical conditions which necessitate an event in the world of sense. Again, this intelligible character of a thing cannot be immediately known, because we can perceive nothing but appearances, but it must be capable of being thought in harmony with the empirical character; for we always find ourselves compelled to place, in thought, a transcendental object at the basis of appearances, although we can never know what this object is in itself.

In virtue of its empirical character, this subject would at the same time be subordinate to all the empirical laws of causality, and, as an appearance and member of the sensible world, its effects would have to be accounted for by preceding appearances. External appearances must be capable of influencing it; and its actions, in accordance with natural laws, must explain to us how its empirical character, that is, the law of its causality, is to be known in and by means of experience. In a word, all requisites for a complete and necessary determination of these actions must be presented to us by experience.

In virtue of its intelligible character, on the other hand (although we possess only a general concept of this character), the subject must be regarded as free from all sensible influences, and from all determination in appearance. Moreover, as nothing *happens* in this subject – for it is a *noumenon*, and there does not consequently exist in it any change, demanding the dynamical determination of time, and for the same reason no connection with appearances as causes – this active existence must in its actions be free from and independent of natural necessity, for this necessity exists only in the world of appearances. It would be quite correct to say, that it originates or begins its effects in the world of sense *from itself*, although the action productive of these effects does not begin *in it*. We should not be in this case affirming that these sensible effects began to exist of themselves, because they are always determined by prior empirical conditions – by virtue of the empirical character, which is the appearance of the intelligible character – and are possible only as constituting a continuation of the series of natural causes. And thus nature and freedom, each in the complete and absolute signification of these terms, can exist, without conflict, in the same action depending on whether the actions are referred to their intelligible or to their sensible cause.

Exposition of the Cosmological Idea of Freedom in its Connection with Universal Natural Necessity

I have thought it advisable to lay before the reader at first merely a sketch of the solution of this transcendental problem, in order to enable him to form with greater ease a clear conception of the course which reason must adopt in the solution. I shall now proceed to exhibit the several momenta of this solution, and to consider them in their order.

The natural law, that everything which happens must have a cause, that the causality of this cause, that is, the action of the cause (which cannot always have existed, but must itself have happened, for it precedes in time some effect which it has originated), must have itself a phenomenal cause, by which it is determined, and, consequently, that all events are empirically determined in an order of nature – this law, I say, which lies at the foundation of the possibility of experience, and of a connected system of appearances or *nature*, is a law of the understanding, from which no departure, and to which no exception, can be admitted. For to except even a single appearance from its operation, is to exclude it from the sphere of possible experience, and thus to admit it to be a mere fiction of thought or phantom of the brain.

Thus we are obliged to acknowledge the existence of a chain of causes, in which, however, *absolute totality* cannot be found. But we need not detain ourselves with this question, for it has already been sufficiently answered in our discussion of the antinomies into which reason falls, when it attempts to reach the unconditioned in the series of appearances. If we permit ourselves to be deceived by the illusion of transcendental realism, we shall find that neither nature nor freedom exists. Now the question is: Whether, admitting the existence of natural necessity in the world of appearances, it is possible to consider an effect as at the same time an effect of nature and an effect of freedom – or, whether these two modes of causality are contradictory and incompatible.

No cause in appearance can absolutely and of itself begin a series. Every action, in so far as it is productive of an event, is itself an event or occurrence, and presupposes another preceding state, in which its cause existed. Thus everything that happens is but a continuation of a series, and an absolute beginning is impossible in the sensible world. The actions of natural causes are, accordingly, themselves effects, and presuppose causes preceding them in time. A *primal* action – an action which forms an absolute beginning – is beyond the causal power of appearances.

Now, is it absolutely necessary that, granting that all effects are appearances, the causality of the cause of these effects must also be an appearance, and be merely empirical? Is it not rather possible that, although every effect in the phenomenal world must be connected with an empirical cause, according to the universal law of nature, this empirical causality may be itself the effect of a non-empirical and intelligible causality – its connection with natural causes remaining nevertheless intact? Such a causality would be considered, in reference to appearances, as the primal action of a cause, which is so far, therefore, not phenomenal, but, by reason of this power, intelligible; although it must, at the same time, as a link in the chain of nature, be regarded as belonging to the sensible world.

The principle of the causal connection of appearances is required, if we are required to look for and to present the natural conditions of natural events, that is to say, their causes. This being admitted as unexceptionably valid, the requirements of the understanding, which recognizes nothing but nature in the region of appearances, are satisfied, and our physical explanations of physical phenomena may proceed in their regular course, without hindrance and conflict. But it is no stumbling-block in the way, even assuming the idea to be a pure fiction, to admit that there are some natural causes in the possession of a faculty which is not empirical, but intelligible, inasmuch as it is not determined to action by empirical conditions, but purely and solely upon grounds brought forward by the understanding – this action being still, when the cause is in the field of appearance, in perfect accordance with the laws of empirical causality. Thus the acting subject, as a *causal* appearance, would continue to preserve a complete connection with nature and natural conditions; and the *phenomenon* only of the subject (with all its causality in appearance) would contain certain conditions, which, if we ascend from the empirical to the transcendental object, must necessarily be regarded as intelligible. For, if we attend, in our inquiries with regard to causes in the world of appearances, to the directions of nature alone, we need not trouble ourselves about the relation in which the transcendental subject, which is completely unknown to us, stands to these appearances and their connection in nature. The intelligible ground of appearances in this subject does not concern empirical questions. It has to do only with pure thought; and, although the effects of this thought and action of the pure understanding are discoverable in appearances, these appearances must nevertheless be capable of a full and complete explanation, upon purely physical grounds, and in accordance with natural laws. And in this case we attend solely to their empirical, and omit all consideration of their intelligible character (which is the transcendental cause of the former), as completely unknown, except in so far as it is exhibited by the latter as its sensible sign. Now let us apply this to experience. Man is an appearance in the sensible world, and at the same time, therefore, a natural cause, the causality of which must be regulated by empirical laws. As such, he must possess an empirical character, like all other natural appearances. We remark this empirical character in his actions, which reveal the presence of certain powers and faculties. If we consider inanimate, or merely animal nature, we can discover no reason for ascribing to ourselves any other than a faculty which is determined in a purely sensible manner. But man, to whom nature reveals herself only through sense, knows himself not only by his senses, but also through pure apperception; and this in actions and internal determinations, which he cannot regard as sensible impressions. He is thus to himself, on the one hand, an appearance, but on the other hand, in respect of certain faculties, a purely intelligible object – intelligible, because its action cannot be ascribed to the receptivity of sensibility. These faculties are understanding and reason. The latter, especially, is in a peculiar manner distinct from all empirically-conditioned faculties, for it employs ideas alone in the consideration of its objects, and by means of these determines the understanding, which then proceeds to make an empirical use of its own concepts, which, like the ideas of reason, are pure concepts.

That reason possesses the faculty of causality, or that at least we are compelled so to represent it, is evident from the *imperatives*, which in the sphere of the practical we impose as rules on our active powers. The words *I ought* express a species of necessity, and imply a connection with grounds which nature does not contain. Understanding knows nothing in nature but that *which is* or has been, or will be. It would be absurd to say that anything in nature *ought* to be other than it is in the relations of time in which it stands; indeed, the *ought*, when we consider merely the course of nature, has neither application nor meaning. The question, What ought to happen in the sphere of nature? is just as absurd as the question, What ought to be the properties of a circle? All that we are entitled to ask is, What takes place in nature? or, in the latter case, What *are* the properties of a circle?

This *ought* indicates a possible action, the ground of which is a pure concept; while the ground of a merely natural action is, on the contrary, always an appearance. This action must certainly be possible under physical conditions, if it is prescribed by the moral imperative *ought*; but these physical or natural conditions do not concern the determination of the will itself, they relate to its effect alone, and the consequences of the effect in the world of appearances. Whatever number of motives nature may present to my will, whatever sensible impulses – the moral *ought* it is beyond their power to produce. They may produce a volition, which, so far from being necessary, is always conditioned – a volition to which the *ought* enunciated by reason, sets an aim and a standard, gives permission or prohibition. Be the object what it may, purely sensible – as pleasure, or presented by pure reason – as good, reason will not yield to grounds which have an empirical origin. Reason will not follow the order of things presented by experience, but, with perfect spontaneity, arranges them according to ideas, with which it compels empirical conditions to agree. It declares, in the name of these ideas, certain actions to be necessary which nevertheless *have not taken place*, and which perhaps never will take place; and yet presupposes that it possesses the faculty of causality in relation to these actions. For, in the absence of this supposition, it could not expect its ideas to produce effects in the world of experience.

Now, let us stop here, and admit it to be at least possible, that reason does not stand in a really causal relation to appearances. In this case it must – though it is pure reason – exhibit an empirical character. For every cause presupposes a rule, according to which certain appearances follow as effects from the cause, and every rule requires uniformity in these effects; and this is the proper ground of the concept of a cause – as a power. Now this concept (of a cause) may be termed the empirical character of reason; and this character is a permanent one, while the effects produced appear, in conformity with the various conditions which accompany and partly limit them, in various forms.

Thus the will of every man has an empirical character, which is nothing more than the causality of his reason, in so far as its effects in the phenomenal world manifest the presence of a rule, according to which we are enabled to examine, in their several kinds and degrees, the actions of this causality and the grounds for these actions, and in this way to decide upon the subjective principles of his will. Now we learn what this empirical character is only from phenomenal effects, and from the rule of these which is presented by experience; and for this reason all the actions of man in the world of appearances are determined by his empirical character, and the co-operative causes of nature. If, then, we could investigate all the appearances of the human will to their very ground, there would be no action which we could not anticipate with certainty, and recognize to be absolutely necessary from its preceding conditions. So far as relates to this empirical character, therefore, there can be no freedom; and it is only in the light of this character that we can consider the human will, when we confine ourselves to simple *observation*, and, as is the case in anthropology, institute a physiological investigation of the motive causes of human actions.

But when we consider the same actions in relation to reason – not for the purpose of *explaining* their origin, that is, in relation to speculative reason – but to practical reason, as the producing cause of these actions, we shall discover a rule and an order very different from those of nature. For here it may be that what *has* taken place and could not but take place in the course of nature, *ought not* to have taken place. Sometimes, too, we discover, or believe that we discover, that the ideas of reason did actually stand in a causal relation to certain actions of man; and that these actions have taken place because they were determined, not by empirical causes, but by the act of the will upon grounds of reason.

Now, granting that reason stands in a causal relation to appearances; can an action of reason be called free, when we know that sensibly – in its empirical character, it is completely determined and absolutely necessary? But this empirical character is itself determined by the intelligible character. The latter we cannot know; we can only indicate it by means of appearances, which enable us to have an immediate knowledge only of the empirical character.[1] An action, then, in so far as it is to be ascribed to an intelligible cause, does not result from it in accordance with empirical laws. That is to say, not the conditions of pure reason, but only their effects in the internal sense, precede the act. Pure reason, as a purely intelligible faculty, is not subject to the conditions of time. The causality of reason in its intelligible character *does not begin to be*; it does not make its appearance at a certain time, for the purpose of producing an effect. If this were not the case, the causality of reason would be subservient to the natural law of appearances, which determines them according to time, and as a series of causes and effects in time; it would consequently cease to be freedom, and become a part of nature. We are therefore justified in saying: If reason stands in a causal relation to appearances, it is a faculty which originates the sensible condition of an empirical series of effects. For the condition, which resides in reason, is non-sensible, and therefore cannot be originated, or begin to be. And thus we find – what we could not discover in any empirical series – a *condition* of a successive series of events itself empirically unconditioned. For, in the present case, the condition stands outside the series of appearances – it is intelligible, and it consequently cannot be subjected to any sensible condition, or to any time-determination by a preceding cause.

But, in another respect, the same cause belongs also to the series of appearances. Man is himself an appearance. His will has an empirical character, which is the empirical cause of all his actions. There is no condition – determining man in conformity with this character – which does not itself form part of the series of effects in nature, and is subject to their law – the law according to which an empirically undetermined cause of an event in time cannot exist. For this reason no given action can have an absolute and spontaneous origination, all actions being appearances, and belonging

---

[1] The real morality of actions – their merit or demerit, and even that of our own conduct, is completely unknown to us. Our estimates can relate only to their empirical character. How much is the result of the action of freedom, how much is to be ascribed to nature and to blameless error, or to a happy constitution of temperament (*merito fortunae*), no one can discover, nor, for this reason, determine with perfect justice.

to the world of experience. But it cannot be said of reason, that the state in which it determines the will is always preceded by some other state determining it. For reason is not an appearance, and therefore not subject to sensible conditions; and, consequently, even in relation to its causality, the sequence or conditions of time do not influence reason, nor can the dynamical law of nature, which determines the sequence of time according to certain rules, be applied to it.

Reason is consequently the permanent condition of all actions of the will under which man appears. Each action is determined in the empirical character of the man, even before it has taken place. The intelligible character, of which the former is but the sensible schema, knows no *before* or *after*; and every action, irrespective of the time-relation in which its stands with other appearances, is the immediate effect of the intelligible character of pure reason, which, consequently, enjoys freedom of action, and is not dynamically determined either by internal or external preceding conditions. This freedom must not be described, in a merely negative manner, as independence of empirical conditions, for in this case the faculty of reason would cease to be a cause of appearances; but it must be regarded, positively, as a faculty which can spontaneously originate a series of events. At the same time, it must not be supposed that any beginning can take place in reason; on the contrary, reason, as the unconditioned condition of all action of the will, admits of no time-conditions, although its effect does really begin in a series of appearances – a beginning which is not, however, absolutely primal.

I shall illustrate this regulative principle of reason by an example from its employment in the world of experience; proved it cannot be by any amount of experience, or by any number of facts, for such arguments cannot establish the truth of transcendental propositions. Let us take a voluntary action – for example, a malicious lie – by means of which a man has introduced a certain degree of confusion into society and which is first examined according to its motive while then we go on to assess how the action and its consequences can be imputed to the offender. We at first proceed to examine the empirical character of the offence, and for this purpose we endeavour to penetrate to the sources of that character, such as a defective education, bad company, a shameless and wicked disposition, frivolity, and want of reflection – not forgetting also the occasioning causes which prevailed at the moment of the transgression. In this the procedure is exactly the same as that pursued in the investigation of the series of causes which determine a given physical effect. Now, although we believe the action to have been determined by all these circumstances, we do not the less blame the offender. We do not blame him for his unhappy disposition, nor for the circumstances which influenced him, nay, not even for his former course of life; for we presuppose that all these considerations may be set aside, that the series of preceding conditions may be regarded as having never existed, and that the action may be considered as completely unconditioned in relation to any state preceding, just as if the agent commenced with it an entirely new series of effects. Our blame of the offender is grounded upon a law of reason, which requires us to regard this faculty as a cause, which could have and ought to have otherwise determined the behaviour of the offender, independently of all empirical conditions. This causality of reason we do not regard as a co-operating agency, but as complete in itself. It matters not whether the sensible impulses favoured or opposed the action of this causality, the offence is estimated according to its intelligible character – the offender is decidedly worthy of blame, the moment he utters a lie. It follows that we regard reason, irrespective of the empirical conditions of the act, as completely free, and therefore, as in the present case, culpable.

Such imputation shows that we consider reason not to be affected by sensible conditions. In it no change takes place – although its appearances, in other words, the mode in which it appears in its effects, are subject to change – that in it no preceding state determines the following, and, consequently, that it does not form a member of the series of such imputations shows that we consider conditions which necessitate appearances according to natural laws. Reason is present and the same in all human actions, and at all times; but it does not itself exist in time, and therefore does not enter upon any state in which it did not formerly exist. It is, relatively to new states or conditions, *determining*, but not *determinable*. Hence we cannot ask: Why did not reason determine itself in a different manner? The question ought to be thus stated: Why did not reason employ its power of causality to determine certain appearances in a different manner? But this is a question which admits of no answer. For a different intelligible character would have exhibited a different empirical character; and, when we say that, in spite of the course which his whole former life has taken, the offender could have refrained from uttering the lie, this means merely that the act was subject to the power and authority of reason. Now, reason is not subject in its causality to any conditions of appearances or of time; and a difference in time may produce a difference in the relation of appearances to each other – for these are not things, and therefore not causes in themselves – but it cannot produce any difference in the relation in which the action stands to the faculty of reason.

Thus, then, in our investigation into free actions and the causal power which produced them, we arrive at an intelligible cause, beyond which, however, we cannot go; although we can recognize that it is free, that is, independent of all sensible conditions, and that, in this way, it may be the sensibly unconditioned condition of appearances. But for what reason the intelligible character generates such and such appearances, and exhibits such and such an empirical character under certain circumstances, it is beyond the power of our reason to decide. The question is as much above the power and the sphere of reason as the following would be: Why does the transcendental object of our external sensible intuition allow of no other form than that of intuition *in space*? But the problem, which we were called upon to solve, does not require us to entertain any such questions. The problem was merely this – whether freedom and natural necessity can exist without conflict in the same action. To this question we have given a sufficient answer; for we have shown that, as the former stands in a relation to a different kind of conditions from those of the latter, the law of the one does not affect the law of the other, and that, consequently, both can exist together in independence of and without interference with each other.

*

The reader must be careful to remark that my intention in the above remarks has not been to prove the *actual existence* of freedom, as a faculty in which resides the cause of certain sensible appearances. For, not to mention that such an argument would not have a transcendental character, nor have been limited to the discussion of pure concepts – all attempts at inferring from experience what cannot be thought in accordance with its laws, must ever be unsuccessful. Nay, more, I have not even aimed at demonstrating the *possibility* of freedom; for this too would have been a vain endeavour, inasmuch as it is beyond the power of the mind to know the possibility of any real ground or its causality by the aid of mere *a priori* concepts. Freedom has been considered in the foregoing remarks only as a transcendental idea, by means of which reason aims at originating a series of conditions in the world of appearances with the help of that which is sensibly unconditioned, involving itself, however, in an antinomy with the laws which it itself prescribes for the empirical conduct of the understanding. That this antinomy is based upon a mere illusion, and that nature and freedom are at least *not opposed* – this was the only thing in our power to prove, and the question which it was our task to solve.

IV: Solution of the Cosmological Idea of the Totality of the Dependence of Appearances as regards their Existence in general

In the preceding remarks, we considered the changes in the world of sense as constituting a dynamical series, in which each member is subordinated to another – as its cause. Our present purpose is to avail ourselves of this series of states or conditions as a guide to an existence which may be the highest condition of everything change-able, that is, to a *necessary being*. Our endeavour is to reach, not the unconditioned causality, but the unconditioned existence, of substance. The series before us is therefore a series of concepts, and not of intuitions (in which the one intuition is the condition of the other).

But it is evident that, as all appearances are subject to change, and conditioned in their existence, the series of dependent existences cannot embrace an unconditioned member, the existence of which would be absolutely necessary. It follows that, if appearances were things in themselves, and – as an immediate consequence from this supposition – condition and conditioned belonged to the same series of appearances, the existence of a necessary being, as the condition of the existence of sensible appearances, would be per-fectly impossible.

An important distinction, however, exists between the dynamical and the mathematical regress. The latter is engaged solely with the combination of parts into a whole, or with the division of a whole into its parts; and therefore are the conditions of its series parts of the series, and to be consequently regarded as homogeneous, and for this reason, as consisting, without exception, of appearances. In the former regress, on the contrary, the aim of which is not to establish the possibility of an unconditioned whole consisting of given parts, or of an unconditioned part of a given whole, but to demonstrate the possibility of the derivation of a certain state from its cause, or of the contingent existence of substance from that which exists necessarily, it is not requisite that the condition should form part of an empirical series along with the conditioned.

In the case of the apparent antinomy with which we are at present dealing, there exists a way of escape from the difficulty; for it is not impossible that both of the conflicting statements may be true in different relations. All sensible appearances may be contingent, and consequently possess only an empirically conditioned existence, and yet there may also exist a non-empirical condition of the whole series, or, in other words, a necessary being. For this necessary being, as an intelligible condition, would not form a member – not even the highest member – of the series; the whole world of sense would be left in its empirically determined existence uninterfered with and uninfluenced. This would also form a ground of distinction between the modes of solution employed for the third and fourth antinomies. For, while in the consideration of freedom in the former antinomy, the thing itself – the cause (*substantia phaenomenon*) – was regarded as belonging to the series of conditions, and only its *causality* to the intelligible world, we are obliged in the present case to think this necessary being as purely intelligible and as existing entirely apart from the world of sense (as an *ens extramundanum*); for otherwise it would be subject to the phenomenal law of contingency and dependence of all appearances.

In relation to the present problem, therefore, the *regulative principle* of reason is that everything in the sensible world possesses an empirically conditioned existence – that no property of the sensible world possess unconditioned necessity – that we are bound to expect, and, so far as is possible, to seek for the empirical condition of every member in the series of conditions – and that there is no sufficient reason to justify us in deriving any existence from a condition which lies outside of and beyond the empirical series, or in regarding any existence as independent and self-subsistent; although this should not prevent us from recognizing the possibility of the whole series being based upon a being which is intelligible, and for this reason free from all empirical conditions, and rather contains the basis for the possibility of all appearances.

But it has been far from my intention, in these remarks, to prove the existence of this unconditioned and necessary being, or even to evidence the possibility of a purely intelligible condition of the existence of all sensible appearances. As bounds were set to reason, to prevent it from leaving the guiding thread of empirical conditions, and losing itself in *transcendent* theories which are incapable of *concrete* presentation; so it was my purpose, on the other hand, to set bounds to the law of the purely empirical understanding, and to protest against any attempts on its part at deciding on the possibility of things, or declaring the existence of the intelligible to be *impossible*, merely on the ground that it is not available for the explanation of appearances. It has been shown, at the same time, that the contingency of all the appearances of nature and their empirical conditions is quite consistent with the arbitrary hypothesis of a necessary, although purely intelligible condition, that no real contradiction exists between them, and that, consequently, *both may be true*. The existence of such an absolutely necessary being may be impossible; and this can never be demonstrated from the universal contingency and dependence of sensible appearances, nor from the principle which forbids us to discontinue the series at some member of it, or to seek for its cause in some sphere of existence beyond the world of nature. Reason goes its way in the empirical world, and follows, too, its peculiar path in the sphere of the transcendental.

The sensible world contains nothing but appearances, which are mere representations, and always sensibly conditioned; things in themselves are not, and cannot be, objects to us. It is not to be wondered at, therefore, that we are not justified in leaping from some member of an empirical series beyond the world of sense, as if empirical representations were things in themselves, existing apart from their transcendental ground and the cause of whose existence may be sought outside of the empirical series. This would certainly be the case with contingent *things*; but it cannot be with mere *representations* of things, the contingency of which is itself merely a phenomenon, and can relate to no other regress than that which determines phenomena, that is, the empirical. But to think an intelligible ground of appearances, as free, moreover, from the contingency of the latter, conflicts neither with the unlimited nature of the empirical regress, nor with the complete contingency of appearances. And the demonstration of this was the only thing necessary for the solution of this apparent antinomy. For if the condition of every conditioned – as regards its existence – is sensible, and for this reason a part of the same series, it must be itself conditioned, as was shown in the Antithesis of the fourth Antinomy. The embarrassments into which a reason, which postulates the unconditioned, necessarily falls, must, therefore, continue to exist; or the unconditioned must be placed in the sphere of the intelligible. In this way, its necessity does not require, nor does it even permit, the presence of an empirical condition: and it is, consequently, unconditionally necessary as far as appearances are concerned.

The empirical employent of reason, with regard to the conditions of existence in the sensible world, is not affected by the assumption of a purely intelligible being; it continues its operations on the principle of the contingency of all appearances, proceeding from empirical conditions to still higher and higher conditions, themselves empirical. Just as little does this regulative principle exclude the assumption of an intelligible cause, when the question regards merely the pure employment of reason – in relation to ends or aims. For, in this case, an intelligible cause signifies merely the transcendental and to us unknown ground of the possibility of sensible appearances, and its existence necessary and independent of all sensible conditions, does not conflict with the contingency of appearances, or with the unlimited possibility of regress which exists in the series of empirical conditions.

Concluding Remarks on the whole Antinomy of Pure Reason

So long as the object of our rational concept is the totality of conditions in the world of appearances, and the satisfaction from this source, of the requirements of reason, to that extent our ideas are at once transcendental and *cosmological*. But when we set the unconditioned – which is the aim of all our inquiries – in a sphere which lies outside the world of sense and possible experience, our ideas become *transcendent*. They are then not merely serviceable towards the completion of the exercise of reason (which remains an idea, never executed, but always to be pursued); they detach themselves completely from experience, and construct for themselves objects, the material of which has not been presented by experience, and the objective reality of which is not based upon the completion of the empirical series, but upon pure *a priori* concepts. The intelligible object of these transcendent ideas may be conceded, as a transcendental object. But we cannot think it as a thing determinable by certain distinct predicates relating to its internal nature, for it has no connection with empirical concepts; nor are we justified in affirming the existence of any such object. It is, consequently, a mere product of thought alone. Of all the cosmological ideas, however, it is that occasioning the fourth antinomy which compels us to venture upon this step. For the existence of appearances, always conditioned and never self-subsistent, requires us to look for an object different from appearances – an intelligible object, with which all contingency must cease. But, as we have allowed ourselves to assume the existence of a self-subsistent reality outside the field of experience, and are therefore obliged to regard appearances as merely a contingent mode of representing intelligible objects employed by beings which are themselves intelligences – no other course remains for us than to follow analogy, and employ the same mode in forming some concept of intelligible things, of which we have not the least knowledge. Experience made us acquainted with the contingent. But we are at present engaged in the discussion of things which are not objects of experience; and must, therefore, derive our knowledge of them from that which is necessary absolutely and in itself, that is, from pure concepts. Hence the first step which we take outside the world of sense obliges us to begin our system of new knowledge with the investigation of a necessary being, and to derive from our concepts of it, all our concepts of intelligible things. This we propose to attempt in the following chapter.

TRANSCENDENTAL DIALECTIC: BOOK II

Chapter III – The Ideal of Pure Reason

Section I: The Ideal in general

We have seen that pure concepts of the understanding do not represent objects, except under sensible conditions; because the conditions of objective reality do not exist in these concepts, which contain, in fact, nothing but the mere form of thought. They may, however, when applied to appearances, be presented *in concreto*; for it is appearances that present to them the materials for the formation of empirical concepts, which are nothing more than concrete forms of the concepts of the understanding. But *ideas* are still further removed from objective reality than *categories*; for no appearance can ever present them to the human mind *in concreto*. They contain a certain perfection, attainable by no possible empirical knowledge; and they give to reason a systematic unity, to which the unity of experience attempts to approximate, but can never completely attain.

But still further removed from objective reality than the idea is the *ideal*, by which term I understand the idea, not *in concreto*, but *in individuo* – as an individual thing, determinable or even determined by the idea alone. The idea of humanity in its complete perfection supposes not only the advancement of all the powers and faculties, which constitute our concept of human nature, to a complete attainment of their final aims, but also everything which is requisite for the complete determination of the idea; for of all contradictory predicates, only one can conform with the idea of the perfect man. What I have termed an idea, was in Plato's philosophy an *idea of the divine mind* – an individual object present to its pure intuition, the most perfect of every kind of possible beings, and the archetype of all the copies in appearance.

Without rising to these speculative heights, we are bound to confess that human reason contains not only ideas, but ideals, which possess, not, like those of Plato, creative, but certainly *practical* power – as regulative principles, and form the basis of the perfectibility of certain *actions*. Moral concepts are not perfectly pure concentrations of reason, because an empirical element – of pleasure or pain – lies at the foundation of them. In relation, however, to the principle, whereby reason sets bounds to a freedom which is in itself without law, and consequently when we attend merely to their form, they may be considered as pure concepts of reason. Virtue and wisdom in their perfect purity, are ideas. But the wise man of the Stoics is an ideal, that is to say, a human being existing only in thought, and in complete conformity with the idea of wisdom. As the idea provides a rule, so the ideal serves as an *archetype* for the perfect and complete determination of the copy. Thus the conduct of this wise and divine man serves us as a standard of action, with which we may compare and judge ourselves, which may help us to reform ourselves, although the perfection it demands can never be attained by us. Although we cannot concede objective reality to these ideals, they are not to be considered as chimeras; on the contrary, they provide reason with a standard, which enables it to estimate, by comparison, the degree of incompleteness in the objects presented to it. But to aim at realizing the ideal in an example in the world of experience – to describe, for instance, the character of the perfectly wise man in a novel, is impracticable. Nay more, there is something absurd in the attempt; and the result must be little edifying, as the natural limitations which are continually breaking in upon the perfection and completeness of the idea, destroy the illusion in the story, and throw an air of suspicion even on what is good in the idea, which hence appears fictitious and unreal.

Such in the constitution of the ideal of reason, which is always based upon determinate concepts, and serves as a rule and a model for imitation or for criticism. Very different is the nature of the ideals of the imagination. Of these it is impossible to present an intelligible concept; they are a kind of *monogram*, drawn according to no determinate rule, and forming rather a vague picture – the production of many diverse experiences – than a determinate image. Such are the ideals which painters and physiognomists profess to have in their minds, and which can serve neither as a model for production nor as a standard for appreciation. They may be termed, though improperly, sensible ideals, as they are declared to be models of certain possible empirical intuitions. They cannot, however, furnish rules or standards for explanation or examination.

In its ideals, reason aims at complete and perfect determination according to *a priori* rules; and hence it thinks an object, which must be completely determinable in conformity with principles, although all empirical conditions are absent, and the concept of the object is on this account transcendent.

CHAPTER III

Section II: The Transcendental Ideal

(*Prototypon Transcendentale*)

Every concept is, in relation to that which is not contained in it, undetermined and subject to the principle of *determinability*. This principle is, that of *every two* contradictorily opposed predicates, only one can belong to a concept. It is a purely logical principle, itself based upon the principle of contradiction; inasmuch as it makes complete abstraction of the content, and attends merely to the logical form of knowledge.

But again, everything, as regards its possibility, is also subject to the principle of complete determination, according to which for every possible pair of contradictory predicates, one in each pair must belong to it. This principle is not based merely upon that of contradiction; for, in addition to the relation between two contradictory predicates, it regards everything as standing in a relation to the *sum of possibilities*, as the sum total of all predicates of things, and, while presupposing this sum as an *a priori* condition, presents to the mind everything as receiving the possibility of its individual existence from the relation it bears to, and the share it possesses in the aforesaid sum of possibilities.[1] The principle of complete determination relates therefore to the content and not to the logical form. It is the principle of the synthesis of all the predicates which are required to constitute the complete concept of a thing, and not a mere principle of analytical representation, which enounces that one of two contradictory predicates must belong to a concept. It contains, moreover, a transcendental presupposition – that, namely, of the material for *all possibility*, which must contain *a priori* the data for this or that *particular possibility*.

The proposition, *Everything which exists is completely determined*, means not only that one of every pair of *given* contradictory predicates, but that one of all *possible*, always belongs of the thing; in it the predicates are not merely compared logically with each other, but the thing itself is transcendentally compared with the sum total of all possible predicates. The proposition is equivalent to saying: To attain to a complete knowledge of a thing, it is necessary to possess a knowledge of everything that is possible, and to determine the thing thereby in a positive or negative manner. The concept of complete determination is consequently a concept which cannot be presented in its totality *in concreto*, and is therefore based upon an idea, which has its seat in reason – the faculty which prescribes to the understanding the laws of its harmonious and perfect exercise.

Now, although the idea of the *sum total of all possibility*, in so far as it forms the condition of the complete determination of everything, is itself undetermined in relation to the predicates which may constitute this sum total, and we think in it merely the sum total of all possible predicates – we nevertheless find, upon closer examination, that this idea, as a primitive concept of the mind, excludes a large number of predicates – those derived and those incompatible with others, and that it is evolved as a concept

---

[1] Thus this principle declares everything to possess a relation to a common correlate – the sum total of possibility, which (i.e. the material for all possible predicates), if discovered to exist in the idea of one individual thing, would establish the affinity of all possible things, from the identity of the ground of their complete determination. The *determinability* of every concept is subordinate to the *universality (universalitas)* of the principle of excluded middle; the *determination* of a *thing* to the *totality (universitas)* of all possible predicates.

completely determined *a priori*. Thus it becomes the concept of an individual object, which is completely determined by and through the mere idea, and must consequently be termed an ideal of pure reason.

When we consider all possible predicates, not merely logically, but transcendentally, that is to say, with reference to the content which may be thought as existing in them *a priori*, we shall find that some indicate a being, others merely a non-being. The logical negation expressed in the word *not*, does not properly belong to a concept but only to the relation of one concept to another in a judgment, and is consequently quite insufficient to present to the mind the content of a concept. The expression *not mortal* does not indicate that a non-being is thought in the object; it does not concern the content at all. A transcendental negation, on the contrary, indicates non-being in itself, and is opposed to transcendental affirmation, the concept of which of itself expresses a being. Hence this affirmation indicates a reality, because in and through it objects are considered to be something – to be things; while the opposite negation, on the other hand, indicates a mere privation and, where such negations alone are attached to a representation, the non-existence of anything corresponding to the representation.

Now a negation cannot be thought as determined, without thinking at the same time the opposite affirmation. The man born blind has not the least notion of darkness, because he has none of light; the savage knows nothing of poverty, because he has never known wealth,[1] the ignorant man has no concept of his ignorance, because he has no concepts of knowledge. All concepts of negatives are accordingly derived; and realities contain the *data*, and, so to speak, the material or transcendental content of the possibility and complete determination of all things.

If, therefore, a transcendental substratum lies at the foundation of the complete determination of things – a substratum which is to form the fund from which all possible predicates of things are to be supplied, this substratum cannot be anything else than the idea of a sum total of reality (*omnitudo realitatis*). In this view, negations are

---

[1] The investigations and calculations of astronomers have taught us much that is wonderful; but the most important lesson we have received from them is the discovery of the abyss of our *ignorance* in relation to the universe – an ignorance, the magnitude of which reason, without the information thus derived, could never have conceived. This discovery of our deficiencies must produce a great change in the determination of the aims of human reason.

nothing but *limitations* – a term which could not, with propriety, be applied to them, if the unlimited (the all) did not form the true basis of our concept.

This concept of a sum total of reality is the concept of a *thing in itself*, regarded as completely determined; and the concept of an *ens realissimum* is the concept of an individual being, inasmuch as it is determined by that predicate of all possible contradictory predicates, which indicates and belongs to *being*. It is therefore a transcendental *ideal* which forms the basis of the complete determination of everything that exists, and is the highest material condition of its possibility – a condition on which must rest the thinking of all objects with respect to their content. Nay, more, this ideal is the only proper ideal of which reason is capable; because in this case alone a general concept of a thing is completely determined by and through itself, and known as the representation of an individuum.

The logical determination of a concept is based upon a disjunctive inference, the major of which contains the logical division of the extent of a general concept, the minor limits this extent to a certain part, while the conclusion determines the concept by this part. The general concept of a reality cannot be divided *a priori*, because, without the aid of experience, we cannot know any determinate kinds of reality, standing under the former as the genus. The transcendental principle of the complete determination of all things is therefore merely the representation of the sum total of all reality; it is not a concept which is the genus of all predicates *under itself*, but one which comprehends them all *within itself*. The complete determination of a thing is consequently based upon the limitation of this *total* of reality, so much being predicated of the thing, while all that remains over is excluded – a procedure which is in exact agreement with that of the disjunctive inference and the determination of the object in the conclusion by one of the members of the division. It follows that reason, in laying the transcendental ideal at the foundation of its determination of all possible things, takes a course in exact analogy with that which it pursues in disjunctive syllogisms – a proposition which formed the basis of the systematic division of all transcendental ideas, according to which they are produced in complete parallelism with the three modes of syllogistic reasoning.

It is self-evident that reason, in thinking the necessary complete determination of things, does not presuppose the existence of a being corresponding to its ideal, but merely the idea of such a thing – for the purpose of deducing from the unconditioned totality of complete determination, the conditioned, that is, the totality of limited things. The ideal is therefore the prototype of all things, which, as defective copies (*ectypa*), receive from it the material of their possibility, and approximate to it more or less, though it is impossible that they can ever attain to its perfection.

The possibility of things must therefore be regarded as derived (that is, of the synthesis of the manifold in respect of its content) – except that of the thing which contains in itself all reality, which must be considered to be primitive. For all negations – and they are the only predicates by means of which all other things can be distinguished from the *ens realissimum* – are mere limitations of a greater and a higher – nay, the highest reality; and they consequently presuppose this reality, and are, as regards their content, derived from it. The manifold nature of things is only an infinitely various mode of limiting the concept of the highest reality, which is their common substratum; just as all figures are possible only as different modes of limiting infinite space. The object of the ideal of reason – an object existing only in reason itself – is also termed the *primal being* (*ens originarium*); as having no existence superior to him, the *supreme being* (*ens summum*); and as being the condition of all other beings, which rank under it, the *being of all beings* (*ens entium*). But none of these terms indicate the objective relation of an actually existing object to other things, but merely that of an *idea to concepts*; and all our investigations into this subject still leave us in perfect uncertainty with regard to the existence of this being.

A primal being cannot be said to consist of many other beings with an existence which is derivative, for the latter presuppose the former, and therefore cannot be constitutive parts of it. It follows that the ideal of the primal being must be thought as simple.

The derivation of the possibility of all other things from this primal being cannot, strictly speaking, be considered as a *limitation*, or as a kind of *division* of its reality; for this would be regarding the primal being as a mere aggregate – which has been shown to be impossible, although it was so represented in our first rough sketch. The highest reality must be regarded rather as the *ground* than as the *sum total* of the possibility of all things, and the manifold nature of things be based, not upon the limitation of the primal being itself, but upon the complete series of effects which flow from it.

And thus all our sensibility, as well as all phenomenal reality, may be with propriety regarded as belonging to this series of effects, while they could not have formed parts of the idea, considered as an aggregate.

Pursuing this track, and hypostatizing this idea, we shall determine our notion of the Supreme Being by means of the mere concept of a highest reality, as one, simple, all-efficient, eternal, and so on – in one word, to determine it in its unconditioned completeness by the aid of every possible predicate. The concept of such a being is the concept of *God* in its transcendental sense, and thus the ideal of pure reason is the object-matter of a transcendental *theology*.

But, by such an employment of the transcendental idea, we should be overstepping the limits of its validity and purpose. For reason placed it, as the concept of all reality, at the basis of the complete determination of things, without requiring that this concept be regarded as the concept of an objective existence. Such an existence would be purely fictitous, and the hypostatizing of the content of the idea into an ideal, as an individual being, is a step perfectly illegitimate. Nay, more, we are not even called upon to assume the possibility of such an hypothesis, as none of the deductions drawn from such an ideal would affect the complete determination of things in general – for the sake of which alone is the idea necessary.

It is not sufficient to circumscribe the procedure and the dialectic of reason; we must also endeavour to discover the sources of this dialectic, that we may have it in our power to give a rational explanation of this illusion, as a phenomenon of the understanding. For the ideal, of which we are at present speaking, is based, not upon an arbitrary, but upon a natural, idea. The question hence arises: How happens it that reason regards the possibility of all things as derived from a single possibility, that, to wit, of the highest reality, and presupposes this as existing in an individual and primal being?

The answer is ready; its is at once presented by the procedure of transcendental analytic. The possibility of sensible objects is a relation of these objects to thought, in which something (the empirical form) may be thought *a priori*; while that which constitutes the matter – the reality of the appearance (that element which corresponds to sensation) – must be given from outside, as otherwise it could not even be thought by, nor could its possibility be represented. Now, a sensible object is completely determined, when it has been compared with all phenomenal predicates, and represented by means of these either positively or negatively. But, as that which constitutes the thing itself – the real in an appearance – must be given, and that, in which the real of *all appearances* is given, is experience, one, sole, and all-embracing – the material of the possibility of all sensible objects must be presupposed as given in a whole, and it is upon the limitation of this whole that the possibility of all empirical objects, their distinction from each other and their complete determination, are based. Now, no other objects are presented to us besides sensible objects, and these can be given only in connection with a possible experience; it follows that a thing is not an object *to us*, unless it presupposes the whole or sum total of empirical reality as the condition of its possibility. Now, a natural illusion leads us to consider this principle, which is valid only of sensible objects, as valid with regard to things in general. And thus we are induced to hold the empirical principle of our concepts of the possibility of things, as appearances, by leaving out this limitative condition, to be a transcendental principle of the possibility of things in general.

We proceed afterwards to hypostatize the idea of the sum-total of all reality, by changing the *distributive* unity of the empirical exercise of the understanding into the *collective* unity of an empirical whole – a dialectical illusion, and by thinking this whole of experience as an individual thing, containing in itself all empirical reality. This individual being is then, by means of the above-mentioned transcendental subreption, substituted for our notion of a thing which stands at the head of the possibility of all things, the real conditions of whose complete determination it presents.[1]

CHAPTER III

Section III : The Arguments of Speculative Reason in Proof of the Existence of a Supreme Being

Notwithstanding the pressing necessity which reason feels, to form some presupposition that shall serve the understanding as a proper

---

[1] This ideal of the *ens realissimum* – although merely a representation – is first realized, that is, has an objective existence attributed to it, then *hypostatized*, and finally, by the natural progess of reason to the completion of unity, *personified*, as we shall show presently. For the regulative unity of experience is not based upon appearances themselves in sensibility, but upon the connection of the manifold of appearances by the *understanding* in a *consciousness*, and thus the unity of the supreme reality and the complete determinability of all things, seems to reside ina supreme understanding, and consequently, in an intelligence.

basis for the complete determination of its concepts, the idealistic and factitious nature of such a presupposition is too evident to allow reason for a moment to persuade itself into belief of the objective existence of a mere creation of its own thought. But there are other considerations which compel reason to seek out some resting-place in the regress from the conditioned to the unconditioned, which is not given as an actual existence from the mere concept of it, although it alone can give completeness to the series of conditions. And this is the natural course of every human reason, even of the most uneducated, although the path at first entered it does not always continue to follow. It does not begin from concepts, but from common experience, and requires a basis in actual existence. But this basis is insecure, unless it rests upon the immovable rock of the absolutely necessary. And this foundation itself unworthy of trust, if it leave under and above it empty space, if it do not fill all, and leave no room for a *why*, if it be not, in one word, infinite in its reality.

If we admit the existence of some one thing, whatever it may be, we must also admit that there is something which exists *necessarily*. For what is contingent exists only under the condition of some other thing, which is its cause; and from this we must go on to conclude the existence of a cause which is not contingent, and which consequently exists necessarily and unconditionally. Such is the argument by which reason justifies its advances towards a primal being.

Now reason looks round for the concept of a being that may be admitted to be worthy of the attribute of absolute necessity, not for the purpose of inferring *a priori*, from the concept of such a being, its objective existence (for if reason allowed itself to take this course, it would not require a basis in given and actual existence, but merely the support of pure concepts, but for the purpose of discovering, among all our concepts of possible things, that concept which possesses no element conflicting with the idea of absolute necessity. For that there must be some absolutely necessary existence, it regards as a truth already established. Now, if it can remove every existence incapable of supporting the attribute of absolute necessity, excepting one – this must be the absolutely necessary being, whether its necessity is comprehensible by us, that is, derivable from the concept of it alone, or not.

Now that, the concept of which contains a *therefore* to every why, which is not defective in any respect whatever, which is all-sufficient as a condition, seems to be the being of which we can justly predicate absolute necessity – for this reason, that, possessing the conditions of all that is possible, it does not and cannot itself require any condition. And thus it satisfies, in one respect at least, the requirements of the concept of absolute necessity. In this view, it is superior to all other concepts, which, as deficient and incomplete, do not possess the characteristic of independence of all higher conditions. It is true that we cannot argue that what does not contain in itself the supreme and complete condition – the condition of all other things, must possess only a conditioned existence; but as little can we assert the contrary, for this supposed being does not possess the only characteristic which can enable reason to know by means of an *a priori* concept the unconditioned and necessary nature of its existence.

The concept of an *ens realissimum* is that which best agrees with the concept of an unconditioned and necessary being. The former concept does not satisfy all the requirements of the latter; but we have no choice, we are obliged to adhere to it, for we find that we cannot do without the existence of a necessary being; and even although we admit, we find it beyond our power to discover in the whole sphere of possibility any being that can advance well-grounded claims to such a distinction.

The following is, therefore, the natural course of human reason. It begins by persuading itself of the existence of some necessary being. In this being it recognizes the characteristics of unconditioned existence. It then seeks the concept of that which is independent of all conditions, and finds it in that which is itself the sufficient condition of all other things – in other words, in that which contains all reality. But the unlimited all is an absolute unity, and is conceived as a being one and supreme; and thus reason concludes that the Supreme Being, as the primal basis of all things, possesses an existence which is absolutely necessary.

This concept must be regarded as in some degree satisfactory, if we admit the existence of a necessary being, and consider that there exists a necessity for a definite and final answer to these questions. In such a case, we cannot make a better choice, or rather we have no choice at all, but feel ourselves obliged to declare in favour of the absolute unity of complete reality, as the highest source of the possibility of things. But if there exists no motive for coming to a definite conclusion, and we may leave the question unanswered till we have fully weighed both sides – in other words, when we are merely called upon to decide how much we happen to know about the question, and how much we merely flatter ourselves that we know – the above conclusion does not appear to so great advantage, but, on the contrary, seems defective in the grounds upon which it is supported.

For, admitting the truth of all that has been said, that, namely, the inference from a given existence (my own, for example) to the existence of an unconditioned and necessary being is valid and unassailable; that, in the second place, we must consider a being which contains all reality, and consequently all the conditions of other things, to be absolutely unconditioned; and admitting too, that we have thus discovered the concept of a thing to which may be attributed, without inconsistency, absolute necessity – it does not follow from all this that the concept of a limited being, in which the supreme reality does not reside, is therefore incompatible with the idea of absolute necessity. For, although I do not discover the element of the unconditioned in the concept of such a being – an element which is manifestly existent in the sum total of all conditions, I am not entitled to conclude that its existence is therefore conditioned; just as I am not entitled to affirm, in a hypothetical inference, that where a certain condition does not exist (in the present, completeness, as far as pure concepts are concerned), the conditioned does not exist either. On the contrary, we are free to consider all limited beings as likewise unconditionally necessary, although we are unable to infer this form the general concept which we have of them. Thus conducted, this argument is incapable of giving us the least notion of the properties of a necessary being, and must be in every respect without result.

This argument continues, however, to possess a weight and an authority, which, in spite of its objective insufficiency, it has never been divested of. For, granting that certain obligations lie upon us, which, as based on the ideas of reason, deserve to be respected and submitted to, although they are incapable of a real or practical application to our nature, or, in other words, would be obligations without motives, except upon the supposition of a Supreme Being to give effect and influence to the practical laws: in such a case we should be bound to obey our concepts, which, although objectively insufficient, do, according to the standard of reason, preponderate over and are superior to any claims that may be advanced from any other quarter. The equilibrium of doubt would in this case be destroyed by a practical addition; indeed, reason would be compelled to condemn itself, if it refused to comply with the demands of the judgment, no superior to which we know – however defective its understanding of the grounds of these demands might be.

This argument, although in fact transcendental, inasmuch as it rests upon the intrinsic insufficiency of the contingent, is so simple and natural, that the commonest understanding can appreciate its value. We see things around us change, arise, and pass away; they, or their condition, must therefore have a cause. The same demand must again be made of the cause itself – as a datum of experience. Now it is natural that we should place the *highest* causality just where we place *supreme* causality, in that being, which contains the conditions of all possible effects, and the concept of which is so simple as that of an all-embracing reality. This highest cause, then, we regard as absolutely necessary, because we find it absolutely necessary to rise to it, and do not discover any reason for proceeding beyond it. Thus, among all nations, through the darkest polytheism glimmer some faint sparks of monotheism, to which one is led, not from reflection and profound thought, but by the study and natural progress of the common understanding.

> There are only three modes of proving the existence of God,
> on the grounds of speculative reason.

All the paths conducting to this end, begin either from determinate experience and the peculiar constitution of the world of sense, and rise, according to the laws of causality, from it to the highest cause existing apart from the world – or from a purely indeterminate experience, that is, some empirical existence – or abstraction is made of all experience, and the existence of a supreme cause is concluded from *a priori* concepts alone. The first is the *physico-theological* argument, the second the *cosmological*, and the third the *ontological*. More there are not, and more there cannot be.

I shall show it is as unsuccessful on the one path – the empirical, as on the other – the transcendendal, and that it stretches its wings in vain, to soar beyond the world of sense by the mere might of speculative thought. As regards the order in which we must discuss those arguments, it will be exactly the reverse of that in which reason, in the progress of its development, attains to them – the order in which they are placed above. For it will be made manifest to the reader, that, although experience presents the occasion and the starting-point, it is the *transcendental idea* of reason which guides it in its pilgrimage, and is the goal of all its struggles. I shall therefore begin with an examination of the transcendental argument, and afterwards inquire, what additional strength has accrued to this mode of proof from the addition of the empirical element.

CHAPTER III

Section IV: The Impossibility of an Ontological Proof of the Existence of God

It is evident from what has been said, that the concept of an absolutely necessary being is a mere concept of reason, i.e. a mere idea, the objective reality of which is far from being established by the mere fact that it is a need of reason. On the contrary, this idea serves merely to indicate a certain unattainable perfection, and rather limits the operations than, by the presentation of new objects, extends the sphere of the understanding. But a strange anomaly meets us at the very threshold; for the inference from a given existence in general to an absolutely necessary existence, seems to be correct and unavoidable, while the conditions of the *understanding* refuse to aid us in forming any concept of such a being.

Philosophers have always talked of an *absolutely necessary* being, and have nevertheless declined to take the trouble of conceiving, whether – and how – a being of this nature is even capable of being thought, not to mention that its existence is actually demonstrable. A verbal definition of the concept is certainly easy enough: it is something, the non-existence of which is impossible. But does this definition throw any light upon the conditions which render it impossible to think the non-existence of a thing – conditions which we wish to ascertain, that we may discover whether we think anything in the concept of such a being or not? For the mere fact that I throw away, by means of the word *unconditioned*, all the conditions which the understanding habitually requires in order to regard anything as necessary, is very far from making clear whether by means of the concept of the unconditionally necessary I think of something, or really of nothing at all.

Nay, more, this chance-concept, now become so current, many have endeavoured to explain by examples which seemed to render any inquiries regarding its intelligibility quite needless. Every geometrical proposition – a triangle has three angles – it was said, is absolutely necessary; and thus people talked of an object which lay out of the sphere of our understanding as if it were perfectly plain what the concept of such a being meant.

All the examples adduced have been drawn, without exception, from *judgments*, and not from *things*. But the unconditioned necessity of a judgment is not the absolute necessity of a thing. On the contrary, the absolute necessity of a judgment is only a conditioned necessity of a thing, or of the predicate in a judgment. The proposition above-mentioned does not enounce that three angles necessarily exist, but, upon condition that a triangle exists, three angles must necessarily exist – in it. And thus this logical necessity has been the source of the greatest delusions. Having formed an *a priori* concept of a thing, the content of which was made to embrace existence, we believed ourselves safe in concluding that, because existence belongs necessarily to the object of the concept (that is, under the condition of my positing this thing as given), the existence of the thing is also posited necessarily (according to the law of identity), and that it is therefore absolutely necessary – merely because its existence has been thought in the concept which is assumed arbitrarily and on account of what we posit the object.

If, in an identical judgment, I annihilate the predicate in thought, and retain the subject, a contradiction is the result : and hence I say, The former belongs necessarily to the latter. But if I suppress both subject and predicate in thought, no contradiction arises ; for there *is nothing* at all, and therefore no means of forming a contradiction. To suppose the existence of a triangle and not that of its three angles, is self-contradictory ; but to suppose the non-existence of both triangle and angles is perfectly admissible. And so is it with the concept of an absolutely necessary being. Annihilate its existence in thought, and you annihilate the thing itself with all its predicates ; how then can there be any room for contradiction ? Externally, there is nothing to give rise to a contradiction, for a thing cannot be necessary externally ; nor internally, for, by the annihilation or suppression of the thing itself, its internal properties are also annihilated. God is omnipotent – that is a necessary judgment. His omnipotence cannot be denied, if the existence of God is posited – the existence, that is, of an infinite being, the two concepts being identical. But when you say, *God does not exist*, neither omnipotence nor any other predicate is affirmed ; they must all disappear with the subject, and in this judgment there cannot exist the least self-contradiction.

You have thus seen, that when the predicate of a judgment is annihilated in thought along with the subject, no internal contradiction can arise, be the predicate what it may. There is no possibility of evading the conclusion – you find yourselves compelled to declare: There are certain subjects which cannot be annihilated in thought. But this is nothing more than saying: There exist subjects which are absolutely necessary – the very hypothesis which you are called upon to establish and which I am drawing into question. For I find myself unable to form the slightest concept of a thing which, when annihilated in thought with all its predicates, leaves behind a contradiction; and contradiction is the only criterion of impossibility, in the sphere of pure *a priori* concepts.

Against these general considerations, the justice of which no one can dispute, one argument is adduced, which is regarded as furnishing a satisfactory demonstration from the fact. It is affirmed, that there is one and only one concept, in which the non-being or annihilation of the object is self-contradictory, and this is the concept of an *ens realissimum*. It possesses, you say, all reality, and you feel yourselves justified in admitting the possibility of such a being. (This I am willing to grant for the present, although the existence of a concept which is not self-contradictory is far from being sufficient to prove the possibility of an object.[1]) Now the notion of all reality embraces in it that of existence; the notion of existence lies, therefore, in the concept of this possible thing. If this thing is annihilated in thought, the internal possibility of the thing is also annihilated, which is self-contradictory.

I answer: It is absurd to introduce – under whatever term disguised – into the concept of a thing, which is to be thought solely in reference to its possibility, the concept of its existence. If this is admitted, you will have apparently gained the day, but in reality have enounced nothing but a mere tautology. I ask, is the proposition, *this or that thing* (which I am admitting to be possible) *exists*, an analytical or a synthetical propostion? If the former, there is no addition made to the subject of your thought by the affirmation of its existence; but either then the concept in your minds is identical with the thing itself, or you have supposed the existence of a thing to be possible, and then inferred its existence from its

---

[1] A concept is always possible, if it is not self-contradictory. This is the logical criterion of possibility, distinguishing the object of such a concept from the *nihil negativum*. But it may be, notwithstanding, an empty concept, unless the objective reality of this synthesis, by which it is generated, is demonstrated; and a proof of this kind must be based upon principles of possible experience, and not upon the principle of analysis or contradiction. This remark may be serviceable as a warning against concluding, from the possibility of a concept – which is logical possibility, the possibility of a thing – which is real possibility.

internal possibility – which is but a miserable tautology. The word *reality* in the concept of the thing, and the word *existence* in the concept of the predicate, will not help you out of the difficulty. For, supposing you were to term all positing of a thing, reality, you have thereby posited the thing with all its predicates in the concept of the subject and asumed its actual existence, and this you merely repeat in the predicate. But if you confess, as every reasonable person must, that every existential proposition is synthetical, how can it be maintained that the predicate of existence cannot be denied without contradiction ? – a property which is the characteristic of analytical propositions, alone.

I should have a reasonable hope of putting an end for ever to this sophistical mode of argumentation, by a strict definition of the concept of existence, did not my own experience teach me that the illusion arising from our confounding a logical with a real predicate (a predicate which determines a thing) resists almost all instruction. A *logical predicate* may be what you please, even the subject may be predicated of itself ; for logic pays no regard to the content of a judgment. But the determination of a concept is a predicate, which adds to and enlarges the concept. It must not, therefore, be contained in the concept.

Being is evidently not a real predicate, that is, a concept of something which is added to the concept of a thing. It is merely the positing of a thing, or of certain determinations in it. Logically, it is merely the copula of a judgment. The proposition, *God is omnipotent*, contains two concepts, which have a certain object, God and omnipotence ; the word *is*, is no additional predicate – it merely indicates the relation of the predicate to the subject. Now, if I take the subject (God) with all its predicates (omnipotence being one), and say : *God is*, or, *There is a God*, I add no new predicate to the concept of God, I merely posit or affirm the existence of the subject with all its predicates – I posit the *object* in relation to my concept. The content of both is the same ; and there is no addition made to the concept which expresses merely the possibility of the object, by my thinking the object – in the expression, it *is* – as absolutely given or existing. Thus the real contains no more than the possible. A hundred thalers contain no more than a hundred possible dollars. For, as the latter indicate the concept, and the former the object, on the supposition that the content of the former was greater than that of the latter, my concept would not be an expression of the whole object, and would consequently be an inadequate concept of it. But in reckoning my wealth there may be said to be more in a hundred real thalers than in a hundred possible thalers – that is, in the mere concept of them. For the real object – the thalers – is not analytically contained in my concept, but forms a synthetical addition to my concept (which is merely a determination of my mental state), although this objective reality – this existence – apart from my concepts, does not in the least degree increase the aforesaid hundred thalers themselves.

By whatever and by whatever number of predicates – even to the complete determination of it – I may think a thing, I do not in the least augment the object of my concept by the addition of the statement, this thing exists. Otherwise, not exactly the same, but something more than what was thought in my concept, would exist, and I could not affirm that the exact object of my concept had real existence. If I think a thing as containing all modes of reality except one, the mode of reality which is absent is not added to the concept of the thing by the affirmation that the thing exists; on the contrary, the thing exists – if it exist at all – with the same defect as that thought in its concept; otherwise not that which was thought, but something different would exist. Now, if I think a being as the highest reality, without defect or imperfection, the question still remains – whether this being exists or not. For although no element is wanting in the possible real content of my concept, there is a defect in its relation to my mental state, that is, I am ignorant whether the knowledge of the object indicated by the concept is possible a *posteriori*. And here the cause of the present difficulty becomes apparent. If the question regarded an object of sense merely, it would be impossible for me to confound the concept with the existence of a thing. For the concept merely enables me to think an object as according with the general conditions of experience; while the existence of the object permits me to think it as contained in the sphere of actual experience. At the same time, this connection with the world of experience does not in the least augment the concept, although a possible perception has been added to our thought. But if we think existence by the pure category alone, it is not to be wondered at, that we should find ourselves unable to present any criterion sufficient to distinguish it from mere possibility.

Whatever be the content of our concept of an object, it is necessary to go beyond it, if we wish to ascribe existence of the object. In the case of sensible objects, this is attained by their connection according to empirical laws with some one of my perceptions; but there is no means of knowing the existence of objects of pure thought, because it must be known completely *a priori*. But all our knowledge of existence (be it immediately by perception, or by inferences connecting some object with a perception) belongs entirely to the sphere of experience – which is in perfect unity with itself; and although an existence outside this sphere cannot be absolutely declared to be impossible, it is a hypothesis the truth of which we have no means of justifying.

The notion of a Supreme Being is in many respects a highly useful idea; but for the very reason that it is an idea, it is incapable of enlarging our knowledge with regard to the existence of things. It is not even sufficient to instruct us as to the possibility of an additional being. The analytical criterion of possibility, which consists in the absence of contradiction in propositions, cannot be denied it. But the connection of all real properties in a thing is a synthesis of the possibility of which an *a priori* judgment cannot be formed, because these realities are not presented to us specifically; and even if this were to happen, a judgment would still be impossible, because the criterion of the possibility of synthetical knowledge must be sought for only in experience, to which the object of an idea cannot belong. And thus the celebrated Leibniz has utterly failed in his attempt to establish upon *a priori* grounds the possibility of this sublime ideal being.

The celebrated ontological or Cartesian argument for the existence of a Supreme Being is therefore insufficient; and we may as well hope to increase our stock of knowlege by the aid of mere ideas, as the merchant to augment his wealth by the addition of noughts to his cash-account.

CHAPTER III

Section V: The Impossibility of a Cosmological Proof of the Existence of God

It was by no means a natural course of proceeding, but, on the contrary, an invention entirely due to the subtlety of the schools, to attempt to draw from a mere idea a proof of the existence of an object corresponding to it. Such a course would never have been pursued, were it not for that need of reason which requires it to suppose the existence of a necessary being as a terminus for the regress, and that, as this necessity must be unconditioned and *a priori*, reason is bound to discover a concept which shall satisfy, if possible, this requirement, and enable us to attain to the *a priori* knowledge of such a being. This concept was though to be found in the idea of an *ens realissimum*, and thus this idea was employed for the attainment of a better defined knowledge of a necessary being, of the existence of which we were convinced, or persuaded, on other grounds. Thus reason was seduced from her natural course; and, instead of concluding with the concept of an *ens realissimum*, an attempt was made to begin with it, for the purpose of inferring from it that idea of a necessary existence which it was in fact called in to complete. Thus arose that unfortunate ontological argument, which neither satisfies the healthy common sense of humanity, nor a rigorous academic examination.

The *cosmological proof*, which we are about to examine, retains the connection between absolute necessity and the highest reality; but, instead of reasoning from this highest reality to a necessary existence, like the preceding argument, it concludes from the given unconditioned necessity of some being its unlimited reality. The track it pursues, whether rational or sophistical, is at least natural, and not only goes far to persuade the common understanding, but shows itself deserving of respect from the speculative intellect; while it contains, at the same time, the outlines of all the arguments employed in natural theology – arguments which always have been, and still will be, in use and authority. These, however adorned, and hid under whatever embellishments of rhetoric and sentiment, are at bottom identical with the arguments we are at present to discuss. This proof, termed by Leibniz the *argumentum a contingentia mundi*, I shall now lay before the reader, and subject to a strict examination.

It is framed in the following manner: If something exists, an absolutely necessary being must likewise exist. Now I, at least, exist. Consequently, there exists an absolutely necessary being. The minor contains an experience, the major reasons from a general experience to the existence of a necessary being.[1] Thus this argument really begins at experience, and is not completely *a priori*, or

---

[1] This inference is too well known to require more detailed discussion. It is based upon the supposed transcendental law of causality, that everything which is *contingent* has a cause, which, if itself contingent, must also have a cause; and so on, till the series of subordinated causes must end with an absolutely necessary cause, without which it would not possess completeness.

ontological. The object of all possible experience being the world, it is called the *cosmological* proof. It contains no reference to any peculiar property of sensible objects, by which this world of sense might be distinguished from other possible worlds; and in this respect it differs from the physico-theological proof, which is based upon the consideration of the peculiar constitution of our sensible world.

The proof proceeds thus: A necessary being can be determined only in one way, that is, it can be determined by only one of all possible opposed predicates; consequently, it must be *completely* determined in and by its concept. But there is only a single concept of a thing possible, which completely determines the thing *a priori*: that is, the concept of the *ens realissimum*. It follows that the concept of the *ens realissimum* is the only concept by which we can think a necessary being. Consequently, a Supreme Being necessarily exists.

In this cosmological argument are assembled so many sophistical propositions, that speculative reason seems to have exerted in it all her dialectical skill to produce a transcendental illusion of the most extreme character. We shall postpone an investigation of this argument for the present, and confine ourselves to exposing the stratagem by which it imposes upon us an old argument in a new dress, and appeals to the agreement of two witnesses, the one with the credentials of pure reason, and the other with those of empiricism; while, in fact, it is only the former who has changed his dress and voice, for the purpose of passing himself off for an additional witness. That it may possess a secure foundation, it bases its conclusions upon experience, and thus appears to be completely distinct from the ontological argument, which places its confidence entirely in pure *a priori* concepts. But this experience merely aids reason in making one step – to the existence of a necessary being. What the properties of this being are, cannot be learned from experience; and therefore reason abandons it altogether, and pursues its inquiries in the sphere of pure concepts, for the purpose of discovering what the properties of an absolutely necessary being ought to be, that is, what among all possible things contain the conditions (*requisita*) of absolute necessity. Reason believes that it has discovered these requisites in the concept of an *ens realissimum* – and in it alone, and hence concludes: The *ens realissimum* is an absolutely necessary being. But it is evident that reason has here presupposed that the concept of an *ens realissimum* is perfectly adequate to the concept of a being of absolute necessity, that is, that we may infer the existence of the latter from that of the former – a proposition which formed the basis of the ontological argument, and which is now employed in the support of the cosmological argument, contrary to the profession of its inventors. For the existence of an absolutely necessary being is given in concepts alone. But if I say : The concept of the *ens realissimum* is a concept of this kind, and in fact the only concept which is adequate to our idea of a necessary being – I am obliged to admit, that the latter may be inferred from the former. Thus it is properly the ontological argument which figures in the cosmological, and constitutes the whole strength of the latter ; while the supposed basis of experience has been of no further use than to conduct us to the concept of absolute necessity, being utterly insufficient to demonstrate the presence of this attribute in any determinate existence or thing. For when we propose to ourselves an aim of this character, we must abandon the sphere of experience, and rise to that of pure concepts, which we examine with the purpose of discovering whether any one contains the conditions of the possibility of an absolutely necessary being. But if the possibility of such a being is thus demonstrated, its existence is also proved ; for we may then assert that, of all possible beings there is one which possesses the attribute of absolute necessity – in other words, this being possesses an absolutely necessary existence.

All illusions in an argument are more easily detected when they are presented in a properly formal manner which we now proceed to do.

If the proposition : Every absolutely necessary being is likewise an *ens realissimum*, is correct (and it is this which constitutes the *nervus probandi* of the cosmological argument), it must, like all affirmative judgments, be capable of conversion – the *conversio per accidens*, at least. It follows, then, that some *entia realissima* are absolutely necessary beings. But no *ens realissimum* is in any respect different from another, and what is valid of some, is valid of all. In this present case, therefore, I may employ simple conversion, and say : Every *ens realissimum* is a necessary being. But as this proposition is determined *a priori* by the concept contained in it, the mere concept of an *ens realissimum* must possess the additional attribute of absolute necessity. But this is exactly what was maintained in the ontological argument, and not recognized by the cosmological, although it formed the real ground of its disguised reasoning.

Thus the second mode employed by speculative reason of demonstrating the existence of a Supreme Being, is not only like the first, illusory and inadequate, but possesses the additional blemish of an *ignoratio elenchi* – professing to conduct us by a new road to the desired goal, but bringing us back, after a short circuit, to the old path which we had deserted at its call.

I mentioned above, that this cosmological argument contains a perfect nest of dialectical assumptions, which transcendental criticism does not find it difficult to expose and to dissipate. I shall merely enumerate these, leaving it to the reader, who must by this time be well practised in such matters, to investigate the fallacies residing therein.

The following fallacies, for example, are discoverable in this mode of proof: 1. The transcendental principle: Everything that is contingent must have a cause – a principle without significance, except in the sensible world. For the purely intellectual concept of the contingent cannot produce any synthetical proposition, like that of causality, which is itself without significance or distinguishing characteristic except in the sensible world. But in the present case it is employed to help us beyond the limits of its sphere. 2. From the impossibility of an infinite ascending series of causes in the world of sense a first cause is inferred; a conclusion which the principles of the employment of reason do not justify even in the sphere of experience, and still less when an attempt is made to pass the limits of this sphere. 3. Reason allows itself to be satisfied upon insufficient grounds, with regard to the completion of this series. It removes all conditions (without which, however, no concept of necessity can take place); and, as after this it is beyond our power to form any other concept, it accepts this as a completion of the concept it wishes to form of the series. 4. The logical possibility of a concept of the total of reality (without inner contradiction) is confounded with the transcendental, which requires a principle of the practicability of such a synthesis – a principle which again refers us to the world of experience. And so on.

The aim of the cosmological argument is to avoid the necessity of proving the existence of a necessary being *a priori* from mere concepts – a proof which must be ontological, and of which we feel ourselves quite incapable. With this purpose, we reason from an actual existence – an experience in general, to an absolutely necessary condition of that existence. It is in this case unnecessary to demonstrate its possibility. For after having proved that it exists, the question regarding its possibility is superfluous. Now when we wish to define more strictly the nature of this necessary being, we do not look out for some being the concept of which would enable us to comprehend the necessity of its being – for if we could do this, an empirical presupposition would be unnecessary; no, we try to discover merely the negative condition (*conditio sine qua non*), without which a being would not be absolutely necessary. Now this would be perfectly admissible in every sort of reasoning, from a consequence to its ground; but in the present case it unfortunately happens that the condition of absolute necessity can be discovered in but a single being, the concept of which must consequently contain all that is requisite for demonstrating the presence of absolute necessity, and thus entitle me to infer this absolute necessity *a priori*. That is, it must be possible to reason conversely, and say – the thing, to which the concept of the highest reality belongs, is absolutely necessary. But if I cannot reason thus – and I cannot, unless I believe in the sufficiency of the ontological argument – I find insurmountable obstacles in my new path, and am really no farther than the point from which I set out. The concept of a Supreme Being satisfies all questions *a priori* regarding the internal determinations of a thing, and is for this reason an ideal without equal or parallel, the general concept of it indicating it as at the same time an *ens individuum* among all possible things. But the concept does not satisfy the question regarding its existence – which was the purpose of all our inquiries; and, although the existence of a necessary being were admitted, we should find it impossible to answer the question: What of all things in the world must be regarded as such?

It is certainly allowable to *admit* the existence of an all-sufficient being – a cause of all possible effects, for the purpose of enabling reason to introduce unity into its mode and grounds of explanation. But to assert that such a being *necessarily exists*, is no longer the modest enunciation of an admissible hypothesis, but the boldest declaration of an apodeictic certainty; for the knowledge of that which is absolutely necessary, must itself possess that character.

The aim of the transcendental ideal formed by the mind is, either to find a concept when the absolute necessity is given, or to find the absolute necessity of something when the concept of that thing is given. If the one is possible, so is the other; for reason recognizes that alone as absolutely necessary, which is necessary from its concept. But both attempts are equally beyond our power – we find it impossible to *satisfy* the understanding upon this point, and as impossible to induce it to remain at rest in relation to this incapacity.

Unconditioned necessity, which, as the ultimate support of all existing things, is an indispensable requirement, is an abyss on the verge of which human reason trembles in dismay. Even the idea of eternity, terrible and sublime as it is, as depicted by Haller, does not produce upon the mind such a feeling of giddiness; for, although it *measures* the duration of things, it does not *support* them. We cannot bear, nor can we rid ourselves of the thought, that a being, which we regard as the greatest of all possible existences, should *say to himself*: I am from eternity to eternity; beside me there is nothing, except that which exists by my will; *but whence then am I*? Here all sinks away from under us; and the greatest, as the smallest, perfection, hovers without stay or footing in presence of the speculative reason, which finds it as easy to part with the one as with the other.

Many natural powers, which evidence their existence by their effects, are perfectly inscrutable in their nature; they elude all our powers of observation. The transcendental object which forms the basis of appearances, and, in connection with it, the reason why our sensibility possesses this rather than that particular kind of conditions, are and must ever remain hidden from us; the fact is there, the reason of the fact we cannot se. But an ideal of pure reason cannot be termed *inscrutable*, because the only credential of its reality is the need of it felt by reason, for the purpose of giving completeness to the world of synthetical unity. An ideal is not even given as an *object* capable of being thought, and therefore cannot be inscrutable; on the contrary, it must, as a mere idea, be based on the constitution of reason itself, and on this account must be capable of explanation and solution. For the very essence of reason consists in its ability to give an account of all our concepts, opinions, and assertions – upon objective, or, when they happen to be illusory, upon subjective grounds.

Detection and Explanation of the Dialectical Illusion in all Transcendental Proofs of the Existence of a Necessary Being

Both of the above arguments are transcendental; in other words, they are independent of empirical principles. For, although the cosmological argument professed to lay a basis of experience for its edifice of reasoning, it did not ground its procedure upon the peculiar constitution of experience, but upon pure principles of reason – in relation to an existence given by empirical consciousness; utterly abandoning the guidance of experience, however, for the purpose of supporting its assertions entirely upon pure concepts. Now what is the cause, in these transcendental arguments, of the dialectical, but natural, illusion, which connects the concepts of necessity and supreme reality, and hypostatizes that which cannot be anything but an idea? What is the cause of this unavoidable step on the part of reason, of admitting that some one among all existing things must be necessary, while it falls back from the assertion of the existence of such a being as from an abyss? And how does reason proceed to explain this anomaly to itself, and from the wavering condition of a timid and reluctant approbation – always again withdrawn, arrive at a calm and settled insight into its cause?

It is something very remarkable that, on the supposition that something exists, I cannot avoid the inference, that something exists necessarily. Upon this perfectly natural – but not on that account reliable – inference does the cosmological argument rest. But, let me form any concept whatever of a thing, I find that I cannot think the existence of the thing as absolutely necessary, and that nothing prevents me – be the thing or being what it may – from thinking its non-existence. I may thus be obliged to admit that all existing things have a necessary basis, while I cannot think any single or individual thing as necessary. In other words, I can never *complete* the regress through the conditions of existence, without admitting the existence of a necessary being; but, on the other hand, I cannot begin from this being.

If I must think something as existing necessarily as the basis of existing things, and yet am not permitted to think any individual thing as in itself necessary, the inevitable inference is, that necessity and contingency are not properties of things themselves – otherwise a contradiction would result; that consequently neither of these principles is objective, but that they are merely subjective principles of reason – the one requiring us to seek for a necessary ground for everything that exists, that is, to be satisfied with no other explanation than that which is complete *a priori*, the other forbidding us ever to hope for the attainment of this completeness, that is, to regard no member of the empirical world as unconditioned. In this mode of viewing them, both principles, in their purely heuristic and regulative character, and as concerning merely the formal interest of reason, are quite consistent with each other. The one says, You must philosophize upon nature, as if there existed a necessary primal basis of all existing things, solely for the purpose of introducing systematic unity into your knowledge, by pursuing an idea of this character – a foundation which is arbitrarily admitted to be ultimate; while the other warns you to consider no individual determination, concerning the existence of things, as such an ultimate foundation, that is, as absolutely necessary, but to keep the way always open for further progress in the derivation, and to treat every determination as determined by some other. But if all that we perceive must be regarded as conditionally necessary, it is impossible that anything which is empirically given should be absolutely necessary.

It follows from this, that you must accept the absolutely necessary as outside the world, inasmuch as it is useful only as a principle of the highest possible unity in experience, and you cannot discover any such necessary existence in the *world*, the second rule requiring you to regard all empirical causes of unity as themselves derived.

The philosophers of antiquity regarded all form[s] of nature as contingent; while matter was considered by them, in accordance with the judgment of common reason, as primal and necessary. But if they had regarded matter, not relatively – as the substratum of appearances, but absolutely and *in itself* as an independent existence, this idea of absolute necessity would have immediately disappeared. For there is nothing absolutely connecting reason with such an existence; on the contrary, it can annihilate it in thought, always and without self-contradiction. But in thought alone lay the idea of absolute necessity. A regulative principle must, therefore, have been at the foundation of this opinion. In fact, extension and impenetrability – which together constitute our concept of matter – form the supreme empirical principle of the unity of appearances, and this principle, in so far as it is empirically unconditioned, possesses the property of a regulative principle. But, as every determination of matter which constitutes what is real in it – and consequently impenetrability – is an effect, which must have a cause, and is for this reason always derived, the notion of matter cannot harmonize with the idea of a necessary being, in its character of the principle of all derived unity. For every one of its real properties, being derived, must be only conditionally necessary, and can therefore be annihilated in thought; and thus the whole existence of matter can be so annihilated. If this were not the case, we should have found in the world of appearances the highest ground or condition of unity – which is impossible, according to the second regulative principle. It follows, that matter, and, in general, all that forms part of the world of sense, cannot be a necessary primal being, nor even a principle of empirical unity, but that this being or principle must have its place assigned outside the world. And, in this way, we can proceed in perfect confidence to derive the appearances of the world and their existence from other appearances, just as if there existed no necessary being; and we can at the same time, strive without ceasing towards the attainment of completeness for our derivation, just as if such a being – the supreme condition of all existences – were presupposed by the mind.

These remarks will have made it evident to the reader that the ideal of the Supreme Being, far from being an enouncement of the existence of a being in itself necessary, is nothing more than a *regulative principle* of reason, requiring us to regard all connection existing between appearances as if it had its origin from an all-sufficient necessary cause, and basing upon this the rule of a systematic and necessary unity in the explanation of appearances. We cannot, at the same time, avoid regarding, by a transcendental subreption, this formal principle as constitutive or avoid hypostatizing this unity. Precisely similar is the case with our notion of space. Space is the primal condition of all shapes, which are properly just so many different limitations of it; and thus, although it is merely a principle of sensibility, we cannot help regarding it as an absolutely necessary and self-subsistent thing – as an object given *a priori* in itself. In the same way, it is quite natural that, as the systematic unity of nature cannot be established as a principle for the empirical employment of reason, unless it is based upon the idea of an *ens realissimum*, as the supreme cause, we should regard this idea as a real object, and this object, in its character of supreme condition, as absolutely necessary, and that in this way a *regulative* should be transformed into a *constitutive* principle. This interchange becomes evident when I regard this supreme being, which, relatively to the world, was absolutely (unconditionally) necessary, as a thing *per se*. In this case, I find it impossible to represent this necessity by any concept, and it exists merely in my own mind, as the formal condition of thought, but not as a material and hypostatic condition of existence.

CHAPTER III

Section VI: The Impossibility of a Physico-Theological Proof of the Existence of God

If, then, neither the concept of things in general nor the experience of an existing being can provide a sufficient basis for the proof of the existence of God, we can make the attempt by the only other mode – that of grounding our argument upon a *determinate experience* of the things of the present world, their constitution and disposition, and discover whether we can thus attain to a sound conviction of the existence of a Supreme Being. This argument we shall term the *physico-theological* argument. If it is shown to fail, speculative reason cannot present us with any satisfactory proof of the existence of a being corresponding to our transcendental idea.

It is evident from the remarks that have been made in the preceding sections, that an answer to this question will be easy and convincing. For how can any experience be adequate with an idea? The very essence of an idea consists in the fact that no experience can ever be discovered congruent or adequate with it. The transcendental idea of a necessary and all-sufficient being is so immeasurably great, so high above all that is empirical, which is always conditioned, that we hope in vain to find materials in the sphere of experience sufficiently ample for our concept, and in vain seek the unconditioned among things that are conditioned, while examples, nay, even guidance is denied us by the laws of empirical synthesis.

If the Supreme Being forms a link in the chain of empirical conditions, it must be a member of the empirical series, and, like the lower members which it precedes, have its origin in some higher member of the series. If, on the other hand, we disengage it from the chain, and think it as an intelligible being, apart from the series of natural causes – how shall reason bridge the gap that separates the latter from the former? All laws respecting the regress from effects to causes, all synthetical additions to our knowledge relate solely to possible experience and the objects of the sensible world, and, apart from them, are without significance.

The world around us opens before our view so magnificent a spectacle of order, variety, beauty, and conformity to ends, that whether we pursue our observations into the infinity of space in the one direction, or into its illimitable divisions in the other, whether we regard the world in its greatest or its least manifestations – even after we have attained to the highest summit of knowledge which our weak minds can reach, we find that language in the presence of wonders so inconceivable has lost its force, and number its power to reckon, nay, even thought fails to conceive adequately, and our concept of the whole dissolves into an astonishment without the power of expression – all the more eloquent that it is dumb. Everywhere around us we observe a chain of causes and effects, of means and ends, of death and birth; and, as nothing has entered of itself into the condition in which we find it, we are constantly referred to some other thing, which itself suggests the same inquiry regarding its cause, and thus the universe must sink into the abyss of nothingness, unless we admit that, besides this infinite chain of contingencies, there exists something that is primal and self-subsistent – something which, as the cause of this phenomenal world, secures its continuance and preservation.

This highest cause – what magnitude shall we attribute to it? Of the content of the world we are ignorant; still less can we estimate its magnitude by comparison with the sphere of the possible. But this supreme cause being a necessity of the human mind, what is there to prevent us from attributing to it such a degree of perfection as to place it above the sphere of *all else that is possible*? This we can easily do, although only by the aid of the faint outline of an abstract concept, by representing this being to ourselves as containing in itself, as an individual substance, all possible perfection – a concept which satisfies that requirement of reason which demands parsimony in principles, which is free from self-contradiction, which even contributes to the extension of the employment of reason in experience, by means of the guidance afforded by this idea to order and system, and which in no respect conflicts with any law of experience.

This argument always deserves to be mentioned with respect. It is the oldest, the clearest, and that most in conformity with the common reason of humanity. It animates the study of nature, as it itself derives its existence and draws ever new strength from that source. It introduces aims and ends into a sphere in which our observation could not of itself have discovered them, and extends our knowledge of nature, by directing our attention to a unity, the principle of which lies beyond nature. This knowledge of nature again reacts upon this idea – its cause; and thus our belief in a divine author of the universe rises to the power of an irresistible conviction.

For these reasons it would be utterly hopeless to attempt to rob this argument of the authority it has always enjoyed. Reason, unceasingly elevated by these considerations, which, although empirical, are so remarkably powerful, and continually adding to their force, will not suffer itself to be depressed by the doubts suggested by subtle speculation; it tears itself out of this state of uncertainty, the moment it casts a look upon the wondrous forms of nature and the majesty of the universe, and rises from height to height, from condition to condition, till it has elevated itself to the supreme and unconditioned author of all.

But although we have nothing to object to the reasonableness and utility of this procedure, but have rather to commend and encourage it, we cannot approve of the claims which this argument advances to demonstrative certainty and to a reception upon its own merits, apart from favour or support by other arguments. Nor can it injure the good cause to endeavour to lower the tone of the arrogant sophist, and to teach him that modesty and moderation which are the properties of a belief that brings calm and content, without prescribing to it an unworthy subjection. I maintain, then, that the physico-theological argument is insufficient of itself to prove the existence of a Supreme Being, that it must entrust this to the ontological argument – to which it serves merely as an introduction, and that, consequently, the ontological argument contains the *only possible ground of proof* (possessed by speculative reason) for the existence of this being, with which reason can never dispense.

The chief momenta in the physico-theological argument are as follow: 1. We observe in the world manifest signs of an arrangement full of purpose, executed with great wisdom, and existing in a whole of a content indescribably various, and of an extent without limits. 2. This arrangement of means and ends is entirely foreign to the things existing in the world – it belongs to them merely as a contingent attribute; in other words, the nature of different things could not of itself, whatever means were employed, harmoniously tend towards certain purposes, were they not chosen and directed for these purposes by a rational and disposing principle, in accordance with certain fundamental ideas. 3. There exists therefore, a sublime and wise cause (or several), which is not merely a blind, all-powerful nature, producing the beings and events which fill the world in unconscious *fecundity*, but a *free* and intelligent cause of the world. 4. The unity of this cause may be inferred from the unity of the reciprocal relation existing between the parts of the world, as portions of an artistic edifice – an inference which all our observation favours, and all principles of analogy support.

In the above argument, it is inferred from the analogy of certain products of nature with those of human art, when it compels nature to bend herself to its purposes, as in the case of a house, a ship, or a watch, that the same kind of causality – namely, understanding and will – resides in nature. It is also declared that the internal possibility of this freely-acting nature (which is the source of all art, and perhaps also of human reason) is derivable from another and superhuman art – a conclusion which would perhaps be found incapable of standing the test of subtle transcendental criticism. But to neither of these opinions shall we at present object. We shall only remark that it must be confessed that, if we are to discuss the subject of cause at all, we cannot proceed more securely than with the guidance of the analogy subsisting between nature and such products of design – these being the only products whose causes and modes of origination are completely known to us. Reason would be unable to satisfy its own requirements, if it passed from a causality which it does know, to obscure and indemonstrable principles of explanation which it does not know.

According to the physico-theological argument, the conformity to ends existing in the world evidence the contingency of the form merely, but not of the matter, that is, of the substance of the world. To establish the truth of the latter opinion, it would be necessary to prove that all things would be in themselves incapable of this harmony and order, unless they were, even as regards their *substance*, the product of a supreme wisdom. But this would require very different grounds of proof from those presented by the analogy with human art. This proof can at most, therefore, demonstrate the existence of an *architect of the world*, whose efforts are limited by the capabilities of the material with which he works, but not of a *creator of the world*, to whom all things are subject. Thus this argument is utterly insufficient for the task before us – a demonstration of the existence of an all-sufficient being. If we wish to prove the contingency of matter, we must have recourse to a transcendental argument, which the physico-theological was constructed expressly to avoid.

We infer, from the order and conformity to ends visible in the universe, as a disposition of a thoroughly contingent character, the existence of a cause *proportionate thereto*. The concept of this cause must contain certain *determinate* qualities, and it must therefore be regarded as the concept of a being which possesses all power, wisdom, and so on, in one word, all perfection – the concept, that is, of an all-sufficient being. For the predicates of *very great*, astonishing, or immeasurable power and excellence, give us no determinate concept of the thing, nor do they inform us what the thing may be in itself. They merely indicate the relation existing between the magnitude of the object and the observer, who compares it with himself and with his own power of comprehension, and are mere expressions of praise and reverence, by which the object is either magnified, or the observing subject depreciated in relation to the object. Where we have to do with the magnitude (of the perfection) of a thing, we can discover no determinate concept, except that which comprehends all possible perfection or completeness, and it is only the total (*omnitudo*) of reality which is completely determined in and through its concept alone.

Now it cannot be expected that any one will be bold enough to declare that he has a perfect insight into the relation which the magnitude of the world he contemplates, bears (in its extent as well as in its content) to omnipotence, into that of the order and conformity to ends in the world to the highest wisdom, and that of the unity of the world to the absolute unity of a Supreme Being. Physico-theology is therefore incapable of presenting a determinate concept of a supreme cause of the world, and is therefore insufficient as a principle of theology – a theology which is itself to be the basis of religion.

The attainment of absolute totality is completely impossible on the path of empiricism. And yet this is the path pursued in the physico-theological argument. What means shall we employ to bridge the gap?

After elevating ourselves to admiration of the magnitude of the power, wisdom, and other attributes of the author of the world, and finding we can advance no further, we leave the argument on empirical grounds, and proceed to infer the contingency of the world from the order and conformity to ends that are observable in it. From this contingency we infer, by the help of transcendental concepts alone, the existence of something absolutely necessary; and, still advancing, proceed from the concept of the absolute necessity of the first cause to the completely determined or determining concept thereof – the concept of an all-embracing reality. Thus the physico-theological, failing in its undertaking, recurs in its embarrassment to the cosmological argument; and, as this is merely the ontological argument in disguise, it executes its design solely by the aid of pure reason, although it at first professed to have no connection with this faculty, and to base its entire procedure upon experience alone.

The physico-theologians have therefore no reason to regard with such contempt the transcendental mode of argument, and to look down upon it, with the conceit of clear-sighted observers of nature, as the cobweb of obscure speculatists. For if they reflect upon and examine their own arguments, they will find that, after following for some time the path of nature and experience, and discovering themselves no nearer their object, they suddenly leave this path and pass into the region of pure possibility, where they hope to reach upon the wings of ideas what had eluded all their empirical investigations. Gaining, as they think, a firm footing after this immense leap, they extend their determinate concept – into the possession of which they have come, they know not how – over the whole sphere of creation, and explain their ideal, which is entirely a product of pure reason, by illustrations drawn from experience – though in a degree entirely unworthy of the grandeur of the object, while they refuse to acknowledge that they have arrived at this knowledge or hypothesis by a very different road from that of experience.

Thus the physico-theological is based upon the cosmological, and this upon the ontological proof of the existence of a Supreme Being; and as besides these three there is no other path open to speculative reason, the ontological proof, on the ground of pure concepts of reason, is the only possible one, if any proof of a proposition so far transcending the empirical exercise of the understanding is possible at all.

CHAPTER III

Section VII : Critique of all Theology based upon
Speculative Principles of Reason

If by the term *theology* I understand the knowledge of a primal being, that knowledge is based either upon reason alone (*theologia rationalis*) or upon revelation (*theologia revelata*). The former thinks its object either by means of pure transcendental concepts, as an *ens originarium, realissimum, ens entium,* and is termed transcendental theology; or, by means of a concept derived from the nature of our own mind, as a supreme intelligence, and must then be entitled *natural* theology. The person who believes in a transcendental theology alone, is termed a *deist*; he who acknowledges the possibility of a *natural* theology also, a *theist*. The former admits that we can know by pure reason alone the existence of a Supreme Being, but at the same time maintains that our concept of this being is purely transcendental, and that all we can say of it is, that it possesses all reality, without being able to define it more closely. The second asserts that reason is capable of presenting us, from the analogy with nature, with a more definite concept of this being, and that its operations, as the cause of all things, are the results of intelligence and free will. The former regards the Supreme Being as the *cause of the world* – whether by the necessity of his nature, or as a free agent, is left undetermined; the latter considers this being as the *author of the world*.

Transcendental theology aims either at inferring the existence of a Supreme Being from a general experience – without any closer reference to the world to which this experience belongs, and in this case it is called *cosmotheology*; or it endeavours to know the existence of such a being, through mere concepts, without the aid of experience, and is then termed *ontotheology*.

Natural theology infers the attributes and the existence of an author of the world, from the constitution of, the order and unity observable in, the world, in which two modes of causality must be admitted to exist – those of nature and freedom. Thus it rises from this world to a supreme intelligence, either as the principle of all natural, or of all moral order and perfection. In the former case it is termed physico-theology, in the latter, ethical or moral-theology.[1]

As we are wont to understand by the term *God* not merely an eternal nature, the operations of which are insensate and blind, but a Supreme Being, who is the free and intelligent author of all things, and as it is this latter view alone that can be of interest to humanity,

---

[1] Not theological ethics; for this science contains laws, which *presuppose* the existence of a Supreme Governor of the world; while moral-theology, on the contrary, is the expression of a conviction of the existence of a Supreme Being, founded upon moral laws.

we might, in strict rigour, deny to the *deist* any belief in God at all, and regard him merely as a maintainer of the existence of a primal being or thing – the supreme cause of all other things. But, as no one ought to be blamed, merely because he does not feel himself justified in maintaining a certain opinion, as if he altogether denied its truth and asserted the opposite, it is more correct – as it is less harsh – to say, the deist believes in a God, the theist in a *living God* (*summa intelligentia*). We shall now proceed to investigate the sources of all these attempts of reason to establish the existence of a Supreme Being.

It may be sufficient in this place to define theoretical knowledge as knowledge of that which *is*, and practical knowledge as knowledge of that which *ought to be*. In this view, the theoretical employment of reason is that by which I know *a priori* (as necessary) that something is, while the practical is that by which I know *a priori* what ought to happen. Now, if it is an indubitably certain, though at the same time an entirely conditioned truth, that something is, or ought to happen, either a certain determinate condition of this truth is absolutely necessary, or such a condition may be arbitrarily presupposed. In the former case the condition is postulated (*per thesin*), in the latter supposed (*per hypothesin*). There are certain practical laws – those of morality – which are absolutely necessary. Now, if these laws necessarily presuppose the existence of some being, as the condition of the possibility of their *obligatory* power, this being must be *postulated*, because the conditioned, from which we reason to this determinate condition, is itself known *a priori* as absolutely necessary. We shall at some future time show that the moral laws not merely presuppose the existence of a Supreme Being, but also, as themselves absolutely necessary in a different relation, demand or postulate it – although only from a practical point of view. The discussion of this argument we postpone for the present.

When the question relates merely to that which is, not to that which ought to be, the conditioned which is presented in experience is always thought as contingent. For this reason its condition cannot be regarded as absolutely necessary, but merely as relatively necessary, or rather as *needful*; the condition is in itself and *a priori* a mere arbitrary presupposition in aid of the knowledge, by reason, of the conditioned. If, then, we are to possess a theoretical knowledge of the absolute necessity of a thing, we cannot attain to this knowledge otherwise than *a priori* by means of concepts; while it is impossible in this way to know the existence of a cause which bears any relation to an existence given in experience.

Theoretical knowledge is *speculative* when it relates to an object or certain concepts of an object which is not given and cannot be discovered by means of experience. It is opposed to the *thinking of nature*, which concerns only those objects or predicates which can be presented in a possible experience.

The principle that everything which happens (the *empirically* contingent) must have a cause, is a principle of the knowledge of nature, but not of speculative knowledge. For, if we change it into an abstract principle, and deprive it of its reference to experience and the empirical, we shall find that it cannot with justice be regarded any longer as a synthetical proposition, and that it is impossible to discover any mode of transition from that which exists to something entirely different – termed cause. Nay, more, the concept of a cause – as likewise that of the contingent – loses, in this speculative mode of employing it, all significance, for its objective reality and meaning are comprehensible from experience alone.

When from the existence of things in the world the existence of a cause of the world is inferred, reason is proceeding not in the *natural*, but in the *speculative* method. For the principle of the former enounces, not that things themselves or substances, but only that which *happens* or their *states* – as empirically contingent – have a cause: the assertion that the existence of substance itself is contingent is not justified by experience, it is the assertion of a reason employing its principles in a speculative manner. If, again, I infer from the form of the world, from the way in which all things are connected and act and react upon each other, the existence of a cause entirely distinct from the world – this would again be a judgment of purely speculative reason; because the object in this case – the cause – can never be an object of possible experience. In both these cases the principle of causality, which is valid only in the field of experience – useless and even meaningless beyond this region, would be diverted from its proper destination.

Now I maintain that all attempts of reason to establish a theology by the aid of speculation alone are fruitless, that the principles of reason as applied to nature do not conduct us to any theological truths, and, consequently, that a rational theology can have no existence, unless it is founded upon the laws of morality. For all synthetical principles of the understanding are valid only as *imma-*

nent; while the knowledge of a Supreme Being necessitates their being employed transcendentally, and of this the understanding is quite incapable. If the empirical law of causality is to conduct us to a Supreme Being this Being must belong to the chain of empirical objects – in which case it would be, like all appearances, itself conditioned. If the possibility of passing the limits of experience be admitted, by means of the dynamical law of the relation of an effect to its cause, what kind of concept shall we obtain by this procedure ? Certainly not the concept of a Supreme Being, because experience never presents us with the greatest of all possible effects, and it is only an effect of this character that could witness to the existence of a corresponding cause. If, for the purpose of fully satisfying the requirements of Reason, we recognize its right to assert the existence of a perfect and absolutely necessary being, this can be admitted only from favour, and cannot be regarded as the result or irresistible demonstration. The physico-theological proof may add weight to others – if other proofs there are – by connecting speculation with experience; but in itself it rather prepares the mind for theological knowledge, and gives it a right and natural direction, than establishes a sure foundation for theology.

It is now perfectly evident that transcendental questions admit only of transcendental answers – those presented *a priori* by pure concepts without the least empirical admixture. But the question in the present case is evidently synthetical – it aims at the extension of our knowledge beyond the bounds of experience – it requires an assurance respecting the existence of a being corresponding with the idea in our minds, to which no experience can ever be adequate. Now it has been abundantly proved that all *a priori* synthetical knowledge is possible only as the expression of the formal conditions of a possible experience; and that the validity of all principles depends upon their immanence in the field of experience, that is, their relation to objects of empirical knowledge, that is appearances. Thus all transcendental procedure in reference to speculative theology is in vain.

If any one prefers doubting the conclusiveness of the proofs of our Analytic to losing the persuasion of the validity of these old and time-honoured arguments, he at least cannot decline answering the question – how he can pass the limits of all possible experience by the help of mere ideas. If he talks of new arguments, or of improvements upon old arguments – I request him to spare me. There is certainly no great choice in this sphere of discussion, as all speculative arguments must at last look for support to the ontological, and I have, therefore, very little to fear from the argumentative fecundity of the dogmatical defenders of a non-sensible reason. Without looking upon myself as a remarkably combative person, I shall not decline the challenge to detect the fallacy and destroy the pretensions of every attempt of speculative theology. And yet the hope of better fortune never deserts those who are accustomed to the dogmatical mode of procedure. I shall, therefore, restrict myself to the simple and equitable demand that such reasoners will demonstrate, from the nature of the human understanding as well as from that of the other sources of knowledge, how we are to proceed to extend our knowledge completely *a priori*, and to carry it to that point where experience abandons us, and no means exist of guaranteeing the objective reality of our concepts. In whatever way the understanding may have attained to a concept, the existence of the object of the concept cannot be discovered in it by analysis, because the knowledge of the *existence* of the object depends upon the object's being posited and given in itself *apart from the concept*. But it is utterly impossible to go beyond our concept, without the aid of experience – which presents to the mind nothing but appearances, or to attain by the help of mere concepts to a conviction of the existence of new kinds of objects or supernatural beings.

But although pure speculative reason is far from sufficient to demonstrate the existence of a Supreme Being, it is of the highest utility in *correcting* our concept of this being – on the supposition that we can attain to the knowledge of it by some other means – in making it consistent with itself and with all other concepts of intelligible objects, clearing it from all that is incompatible with the concept of a primal being, and eliminating from it all limitations or admixture of empirical elements.

Transcendental theology is still therefore, notwithstanding its objective insufficiency, of importance in a negative respect; it is useful as a test of the procedure of reason when engaged with pure ideas, no other than a transcendental standard being in this case admissible. For if, from a practical point of view, the hypothesis of a Supreme and all-sufficient Being is to maintain its validity without objection, it must be of the highest importance to define this concept in a correct and rigorous manner – as the transcendental concept of a necessary being, to eliminate all phenomenal elements (anthropomorphism in its most extended signification), and at the same time to clear away all contradictory assertions – be they *atheistic, deistic,* or *anthropomorphic.* This is of course very easy; as the same arguments which demonstrated the inability of human reason to *affirm* the existence of a Supreme Being must be alike sufficient to prove the invalidity of its denial. For it is impossible to gain from the pure speculation of reason demonstration that there exists no Supreme Being, as the ground of all that exists, or that this being possesses none of those properties which we regard as analogical with the dynamical qualities of a thinking being, or that, as the anthropomorphists would have us believe, it is subject to all the limitations which sensibility imposes upon those intelligences which exist in the world of experience.

A Supreme Being is, therefore, for the speculative reason, a mere ideal, though a *faultless* one – a concept which perfects and crowns the system of human knowledge, but the objective reality of which can neither be proved nor disproved by pure reason. If this defect is ever supplied by a moral theology, the problematic transcendental theology which has preceded, will have been at least serviceable as demonstrating the necessity existing for the concept, by the complete determination of it which it has furnished, and the ceaseless testing of the conclusions of a reason often disappointed by sensibility, and not always in harmony with its own ideas. The attributes of necessity, infinitude, unity, existence apart from the world (and not as a world-soul), eternity – free from conditions of time, omnipresence – free from conditions of space, omnipotence, and others, are pure transcendental predicates; and thus the accurate concept of a Supreme Being, which every theology requires, is furnished by transcendental theology alone.

APPENDIX TO TRANSCENDENTAL DIALECTIC

The Regulative Employment of the Ideas of Pure Reason

The result of all the dialectical attempts of pure reason not only confirms the truth of what we have already proved in our Transcendental Analytic, namely, that all inferences which would lead us beyond the limits of experience are fallacious and groundless, but it at the same time teaches us this important lesson, that human reason has a natural inclination to overstep these limits, and that transcendental ideas are as much the natural property of the reason as categories are of the understanding. There exists this difference, however, that while the categories never mislead us, outward objects being always in perfect harmony therewith, ideas are the parents of irresistible illusions, the severest and most subtle criticism being required to save us from the fallacies which they induce.

Whatever is grounded in the nature of our powers, will be found to be in harmony with the final purpose and proper employment of these powers, when once we have discovered their true direction and aim. We are entitled to suppose, therefore, that there exists a mode of employing transcendental ideas which is proper and *immanent*; although, when we mistake their meaning, and regard them as concepts of actual things, their mode of application is *transcendent* and delusive. For it is not the idea itself, but only the employment of the idea in relation to possible experience, that is transcendent or immanent. An idea is employed transcendently, when it is applied to an object falsely believed to be adequate with and to correspond to it; immanently, when it is applied solely to the employment of the *understanding* in the sphere of experience. Thus all errors of *subreption* – of misapplication, are to be ascribed to defects of judgment, and not to understanding or reason.

Reason never has an immediate relation to an object; it relates immediately to the understanding alone. It is only through the understanding that it can be employed in the field of experience. It does not *form* concepts of objects, it merely *arranges* them and gives to them that unity which they are capable of possessing when the sphere of their application has been extended as widely as possible. Reason avails itself of the concepts of the understanding for the sole purpose of producing totality in the different series. This totality the understanding does not concern itself with; its only occupation is the connection of experiences, by which *series* of conditions in accordance with concepts are established. The object of reason is therefore the understanding and its proper destination. As the latter brings unity into the diversity of objects by means of its concepts, so the former brings unity into the diversity of concepts by means of ideas; as it sets the final aim of a collective unity to the operations of the understanding, which without this occupies itself with a distributive unity alone.

I accordingly maintain, that transcendental ideas can never be employed constitutively, that they cannot be concepts of objects, and that, when thus considered, they assumed a fallacious and dialectical character. But, on the other hand, they are capable of an admirable and indispensably necessary application to objects – as regulative ideas, directing the understanding to a certain aim, the guiding lines towards which all its laws follow, and in which they all meet in one point. This point – though a mere idea (*focus imaginarius*), that is, not a point from which the concepts of the understanding do really proceed, for it lies beyond the sphere of possible experience – serves notwithstanding to give the greatest possible extension. Hence arises the natural illusion which induces us to believe that these lines proceed from an object which lies outside the sphere of empirical knowledge, just as objects reflected in a mirror appear to be behind it. But this illusion – which we may hinder from imposing upon us – is necessary and unavoidable, if we desire to see, not only those objects which lie before us, but those which are at a great distance behind us; that is to say, when, in the present case, we direct the aims of the understanding, beyond every given experience, towards an extension as great as can possibly be attained.

If we review our knowledge in its entire extent, we shall find that the peculiar business of reason is to arrange it into a *system*, that is to say, to give it connection according to a principle. This unity presupposes an idea – the idea of the form of a whole (of knowledge), prior to the determinate knowledge of the parts, and containing the conditions which determine *a priori* to every part its place and relation to the other parts of the whole system. This idea accordingly demands complete unity in the knowledge of the understanding – not the unity of a contingent aggregate, but that of a system connected according to necessary laws. It cannot be affirmed with propriety that this idea is a concept of an object; it is merely a concept of the complete unity of the concepts of objects, in so far as this unity is available to the understanding as a rule. Such concepts of reason are not derived from nature; on the contrary, we employ them for the interrogation and investigation of nature, and regard our knowledge as defective so long as it is not adequate to them. We admit that such a thing as *pure earth, pure water*, or *pure air*, is not to be discovered. And yet we require these concepts (which have their origin in the reason, so far as regards their absolute purity and completeness) for the purpose of determining the share which each of these natural causes has in every appearance. Thus the different kinds of matter are all referred to earths, as mere weight; to salts and inflammable bodies, as pure force; and finally, to water and air – as the vehicle of the former, or the machines employed by them in their operations – for the purpose of explaining the chemical action and reaction of bodies in accordance with the idea of a mechanism. For, although not actually so expressed, the influence of such ideas of reason is very observable in the procedure of natural scientists.

If reason is the faculty of deriving the particular from the general, and if the general be certain in itself and given, it is only necessary that the *judgment* should subsume the particular under the general, the particular being thus necessarily determined. I shall term this the apodeictic employment of reason. If, however, the general is admitted as *problematical* only, and is a mere idea, the particular case is certain, but the universality of the rule which applies to this particular case remains a problem. Several particular cases, the certainty of which is beyond doubt, are then taken and examined, for the purpose of discovering whether the rule is applicable to them; and if it appears that all the particular cases which can be collected follow from the rule, its universality is inferred, and at the same time, all the causes which have not, or cannot be presented to our observation, are concluded to be of the same character with those which we have observed. This I shall term the hypothetical employment of the reason.

The hypothetical exercise of reason by the aid of ideas employed as problematical concepts is properly not *constitutive*. That is to say, if we consider the subject strictly, the truth of the rule, which has been employed as an hypothesis, does not follow from the use that is made of it by reason. For how can we know all the possible cases that may arise? – some of which may, however, prove exceptions to the universality of the rule. This employment of reason is merely regulative, and its sole aim is the introduction of unity into the aggregate of our particular knowledge, and thereby the *approximating* of the rule to universality.

The aim of the hypothetical employment of reason is therefore the systematic unity of the understanding; and this unity is the *criterion* of the *truth* of a rule. On the other hand, this systematic unity – as a mere idea – is in fact merely a unity *projected*, not to be regarded as given, but only in the light of a problem – a problem which serves, however, as a principle for the various and particular exercise of the understanding in experience, directs it with regard to those cases which are not presented to our observation, and introduces connection into all its operation.

All that we can be certain of from the above considerations is, that this systematic unity is a logical principle, whose aim is to assist the understanding, where it cannot of itself attain to rules, by means of ideas, to bring all these various rules under one principle, and thus to ensure the most complete connection that can be attained. But the assertion that objects and the understanding by which they are known are so constituted as to be determined to systematic unity, that this may be postulated *a priori*, without any reference to the interest of reason, and that we are justified in declaring all possible knowledge – empirical and other – to possess systematic unity, and to be subject to general principles from which, notwithstanding its various character, it is all derivable – such an assertion can be founded only upon a *transcendental* principle of reason, which would render this systematic unity not subjectively and logically – in its character of a method, but objectively necessary.

We shall illustrate this by an example. The concepts of the understanding make us acquainted, among many other kinds of unity, with that of the causality of a substance, which is termed *power*. The different appearances of the same substance appear at first view to be so very dissimilar, that we are inclined to assume the existence of just as many different powers as there are different effects – as, in the case of the human mind, we have feeling, consciousness, imagination, memory, wit, analysis, pleasure, desire, and so on. Now we are required by a logical maxim to reduce these differences to as small a number as possible, by comparing them and discovering the hidden identity which exists. We must inquire, for example, whether or not imagination (connected with consciousness), memory, wit, and analysis are not merely different forms of understanding and reason. The idea of a *fundamental power*, the existence of which no effort of logic can assure us of, is the problem to be solved, for the systematic representation of the existing variety of powers. The logical principle of reason requires us to produce as great a unity as is possible in the system of our knowledge; and the more the appearances of this and the other power are found to be identical, the more probable does it become, that they are nothing but different manifestations of one and the same power, which may be called, relatively speaking, a *fundamental power*. And so with other cases.

These relatively fundamental powers must again be compared with each other, to discover, if possible, the one radical and *absolutely* fundamental power of which they are but the manifestations. But this unity is purely hypothetical. It is not maintained, that this unity does really exist, but that we must, in the interest of reason, that is, for the establishment of principles for the various rules presented by experience, try to discover and introduce it, so far as is practicable, into the sphere of our knowledge

But the transcendental employment of the understanding would lead us to believe that this idea of a fundamental power is not problematical, but that it possesses objective reality, and thus the systematic unity of the various powers or forces in a substance is demanded by the understanding and erected into an apodeictic principle. For, without having attempted to discover the unity of the various powers existing in nature, nay, even after all our attempts have failed, we notwithstanding presuppose that it does exist, and may be, sooner or later, discovered. And this reason does, not only, as in the case above adduced, with regard to the unity of substance, but where many substances, although all to a certain extent homogeneous, are discoverable, as in the case of matter in general. Here also does reason presuppose the existence of the systematic unity of various powers – inasmuch as particular laws of nature are subordinate to general laws; and parsimony in principles is not merely an economical principle of reason, but an essential law of nature.

We cannot understand, in fact, how a logical principle of unity can of right exist, unless we presuppose a transcendental principle, by which such a systematic unity – as a property of objects themselves – is regarded as necessary *a priori*. For with what right can reason, in its logical exercise, require us to regard the variety of forces which nature displays, as in effect a disguised unity, and to derive them from one fundamental power, when it is free to admit that it is just as possible that all forces should be different in kind, and that a systematic unity is not conformable to the design of nature? In this view of the case, reason would be proceeding in direct opposition to its own destination, by setting as an aim an idea which entirely conflicts with the procedure and arrangement of nature. Neither can we assert that reason has previously inferred this unity from the contingent nature of appearances. For the law of reason which requires us to seek for this unity is a necessary law, inasmuch as without it we should not possess a faculty of reason, nor without reason a unified and connected mode of employing the understanding, nor, in the absence of this, any proper and sufficient criterion of empirical truth. In relation to this criterion, therefore, we must suppose the idea of the systematic unity of nature to possess objective validity and necessity.

We find this transcendental presupposition lurking in different forms in the principles of philosophers, although they have neither recognized it nor confessed to themselves its presence. That the diversities of individual things do not exclude identity of species, that the various species must be considered as merely different determinations of a few *genera*, and these again as divisions of still higher *races*, and so on – that, accordingly, a certain systematic unity of all possible empirical concepts, in so far as they can be derived from higher and more general concepts, must be sought for – is a scholastic maxim or logical principle, without which reason could not be employed by us. For we can infer the particular from the general, only in so far as general properties of things constitute the foundation upon which the particular rest.

That the same unity exists in nature is presupposed by philosophers in the well-known scholastic maxim, which forbids us unnecessarily to augment the number of principles (*entia praeter necessitatem non esse multiplicanda*). This maxim asserts that nature herself assists in the establishment of this unity of reason, and that the seemingly infinite diversity of appearances should not deter us from the expectation of discovering beneath this diversity a unity of fundamental properties, of which the aforesaid variety is but a more or less determined form. This unity, although a mere idea, has been always pursued with so much zeal, that thinkers have found it necessary rather to moderate the desire than to encourage it. It is considered a great step when chemists were able to reduce all salts to two main genera – acids and alkalis; and they regard this difference as itself a mere variety, or different manifestation of one and the same fundamental material. The different kinds of earths (stones and even metals) chemists have endeavoured to reduce to three, and afterwards to two; but still, not content with this advance, they cannot but think that behind these diversities there lurks but one genus – nay, that even salts and earths have a common principle. It might be conjectured that this is merely an economical plan of reason, for the purpose of sparing itself trouble, and an attempt of a purely hypothetical character, which, when successful, gives an appearance of probability to the principle of explanation employed by reason. But a selfish purpose of this kind is easily to be distinguished from the idea, according to which every one presupposes that this unity is in accordance with the laws of nature, and that reason does not in this case *request*, but *requires*, although we are quite unable to determine the proper limits of this unity.

If the diversity existing in appearance – a diversity not of form (for in this they may be similar) but of content – were so great that the subtlest human reason could never by comparison discover in them the least similarity (which is not impossible), in this case the logical law of genera would be without foundation, the concept of a genus, nay, all general concepts would be impossible, and the faculty of the understanding, the exercise of which is restricted to the world of concepts, could not exist. The logical principle of genera, accordingly, if it is to be applied to nature (by which I mean objects presented to us), presupposes a transcendental principle. In accordance with this principle, homogeneity is necessarily presupposed in the variety of appearances (although we are unable to determine *a priori* the degree of this homogeneity), because without it no empirical concepts and consequently no experience, would be possible.

The logical principle of genera, which demands identity in appearances, is balanced by another principle – that of *species*, which requires multiplicity and diversity in things, notwithstanding their accordance in the same genus, and directs the understanding to attend to the one no less than to the other. This principle (of the faculty of distinction) acts as a check upon the levity of the former (the faculty of wit) ; and reason exhibits in this respect a double and conflicting interest – on the one hand the interest in the *extent* (the interest of generality) in relation to genera, on the other that of the *content* (the interest of determinatenesss) in relation to the variety of species. In the former case, the understanding thinks more *under* its concepts, in the latter it thinks more *in* them. This distinction manifests itself likewise in the habits of thought peculiar to natural scientists, some of whom – the remarkably speculative heads – may be said to be hostile to heterogeneity in appearances, and have their eyes always fixed on the unity of genera, while others – with a strong empirical tendency – aim unceasingly at the analysis of appearances, and almost destroy in us the hope of ever being able to estimate the character of these according to general principles.

The latter mode of thought is evidently based upon a logical principle, the aim of which is the systematic completeness of all knowledge. This principle authorizes me, beginning at the genus, to descend to the multiple and diverse contained under it ; and in this way extension, as in the former case unity, is assured to the system. For if we merely examine the sphere of the concept which indicates a genus, we cannot discover how far it is possible to proceed in the division of that sphere; just as it is impossible, from the consideration of the space occupied by matter, to determine how far we can proceed in the division of it. Hence every *genus* must contain different *species*, and these again different *sub-species*; and as each of the latter must itself contain a sphere (must be of a certain extent, as a *conceptus communis*), reason demands that no species or subspecies is to be considered as the lowest possible. For a species or sub-species, being always a concept, which contains only what is common to a number of different things, does not completely determine any individual thing, or relate immediately to it, and must consequently contain other concepts, that is, other sub-species under it. This law of specification may be thus expressed: *Entium varietates non temere sunt minuendas*.

But it is easy to see that this logical law would likewise be without sense or application, were it not based upon a transcendental *law of specification*, which certainly does not require that the differences existing in appearances should be *infinite* in number, for the logical principle, which merely maintains the *indeterminateness* of the logical sphere of a concept, in relation to its possible division, does not demand as much; while it does impose upon the understanding the duty of searching for sub-species to every species, and minor differences in every difference. For, were there no lower concepts, neither could there be any higher. Now the understanding knows only by means of concepts consequently, how far soever it may proceed in division, never by mere intuition, but always by lower and lower concepts. The knowledge of appearances in their complete determination (which is possible only by means of the understanding) requires an unceasingly continued specification of concepts, and a progression to ever smaller differences, of which abstraction had been made in the concept of the species, and still more in that of the genus.

This law of specification cannot be derived from experience; it can never present us with a principle of so universal an application. Empirical specification very soon stops in its distinction of diversities, and requires the guidance of the transcendental law, as a principle of the reason – a law which imposes on us the necessity of never ceasing in our search for differences, even although these may not present themselves to the senses. That absorbent earths are of different kinds, could only be discovered by obeying the anticipatory law of reason, which imposes upon the understanding the task of discovering the differences existing between these earths, and supposes that nature is richer in substances than our senses would indicate. The faculty of the understanding belongs to us just as much under the presupposition of differences in the objects of nature, as under the condition that these objects are homogeneous, because we could not possess concepts, nor make any use of our understanding, were not the appearances included under these concepts in some respects dissimilar, as well as similar, in their character.

Reason thus prepares the sphere of the understanding for the operations of this faculty: 1. By the principle of the *homogeneity* of the diverse in higher genera; 2. By the principle of the *variety* of the homogeneous in lower species; and, to complete the systematic unity, it adds, 3. A law of the *affinity* of all concepts which prescribes a continuous transition from one species to every other by the gradual increase of diversity. We may term these the principles of the *homogeneity*, the *specification*, and the *continuity* of forms. The latter results from the union of the two former, inasmuch as we regard the systematic connection as complete in thought, in the ascent to higher genera, as well as in the descent to lower species. For all diversities must be related to each other, as they all spring from one highest genus, descending through the different gradations of a more and more extended determination.

We may illustrate the systematic unity produced by the three logical principles in the following manner. Every concept may be regarded as a point, which, as the standpoint of a spectator, has a certain horizon, which may be said to enclose a number of things, that may be viewed, so to speak, from that centre. Within this horizon there must be an infinite number of other points, each of which has its own horizon, smaller and more circumscribed; in other words, every species contains sub-species, according to the principle of specification, and the logical horizon consists of smaller horizons (sub-species), but not of points (individuals), which possess no extent. But different horizons or genera, which include under them so many concepts, may have one common horizon, from which, as from a mid-point, they may be surveyed; and we may proceed thus, till we arrive at the highest genus, or universal and true horizon, which is determined by the highest concept, and which contains under itself all differences and varieties, as genera, species, and sub-species.

To this highest standpoint I am conducted by the law of homogeneity, while to all lower and more variously-determined standpoints, I am conducted by the law of specification. Now as in this way there exists no void in the whole extent of all possible concepts and as outside the sphere of these we can discover nothing, there arises from the presupposition of the universal horizon above mentioned, and its complete division, the principle: *Non datur vacuum formarum*. This principle asserts that there are not different primitive and highest genera, which stand isolated, so to speak, from each other, but all the various genera are mere divisions and limitations of one highest and universal genus; and hence follows immediately the principle: *Datur continuum formarum*. This principle indicates that all differences of species limit each other, and do not admit of transition from one to another by a jump, but only through smaller degrees of the difference between the one species and the other. In one word, there are no species or sub-species which (in the view of reason) are the nearest possible to each other; intermediate species or sub-species being always possible, the difference of which from each of the former is always smaller than the difference existing between these.

The first law, therefore, directs us to avoid the notion that there exist different primal genera, and enounces the fact of perfect homogeneity; the second imposes a check upon this tendency to unity and prescribes the distinction of sub-species, before proceeding to apply our general concepts to individuals. The third unites both the former, by enouncing the fact of homogeneity as existing even in the most various diversity, by means of the gradual transition from one species to another. Thus it indicates a relationship between the different branches or species, in so far as they all spring from the same stem.

But this logical law of the *continuum specierum (formarum logicarum)* presupposes a transcendental principle (*lex continui in natura*), without which the understanding might be led into error, by following the guidance of the former and thus perhaps pursuing a path contrary to that prescribed by nature. This law must consequently be based upon pure transcendental, and not upon empirical considerations. For, in the latter case, it would come later than the system; whereas it is really itself the parent of all that is systematic in our knowledge of nature. These priciples are not mere hypotheses employed for the purpose of experimenting upon nature; although when any such connection is discovered, it forms a solid ground for regarding the hypothetical unity as valid in the sphere of nature – and thus they are in this respect not without their use. But we go farther, and maintain that it is manifest that these principles of parsimony in fundamental causes, variety in effects, and affinity in appearances, are in accordance both with reason and nature, and that they are not mere methodological devices but carry their recommendations directly in themselves.

But it is plain that this continuity of forms is a mere idea, to which no adequate object can be discovered in experience. And this for two reasons. First, because the species in nature are really divided, and hence form *quanta discreta*, and, if the gradual progression through their affinity were continuous, the intermediate members lying between two given species must be infinite in number, which is impossible. Second, because we cannot make any determinate empirical use of this law, inasmuch as it does not present us with any criterion of affinity which could aid us in determining how far we ought to pursue the graduation of differences: it merely contains a general indication that it is our duty to seek for and, if possible, to discover them.

When we arrange these priciples of systematic unity in the order conformable to their employment in experience, they will stand thus: *variety, affinity, unity*, each of them, as ideas, being taken in the highest degree of their completeness. Reason presupposes the existence of knowledge of the understanding, which has a direct relation to experience, and it aims at the ideal unity of this – a unity which far transcends all experience or empirical notion. The affinity of the diverse, notwithstanding the differences existing between its parts, has a relation to things, but a still closer one to the mere properties and powers of things. For example, imperfect experience may represent the orbits of the planets as circular. But we discover variations from this course, and we proceed to suppose that the planets revolve in a path which, if not a circle, is of a character very similar to it. That is to say, the movements of those planets which do not form a circle will approximate more or less to the properties of a circle, and probably form an ellipse. The paths of comets exhibit still greater variations, for, so far as our observation extends, they do not return upon their own course in a circle or ellipse. But we proceed to the conjecture that comets describe a parabola, a figure which is closely allied to the ellipse. In fact, a parabola is merely an ellipse, with its longer axis produced to an indefinite extent. Thus these principles conduct us to a unity in the genera of the forms of these orbits, and, proceeding farther, to a unity as regards the cause of the motions of the heavenly bodies – that is, gravitation. But we go on extending our conquests over nature, and endeavour to explain all seeming deviations from these rules, and even make additions to our system which no experience can ever substantiate – for example, the theory, in affinity with that of ellipses, of hyperbolic paths of comets, pursuing which, these bodies leave our solar system, and, passing from sun to sun, unite the most distant parts of the infinite universe, which is held together by the same moving power.

The most remarkable circumstance connected with these principles is, that they seem to be transcendental, and, although only containing ideas for the guidance of the empirical exercise of reason, and although this empirical employment stands to these ideas in an asymptotic relation alone, that is; continually approximate, without ever being able to attain to them, they possess, notwithstanding, as *a priori* synthetical propositions, objective though undetermined validity, and are available as rules for possible experience. In the elaboration of our experience, they may also be employed with great advantage, as heuristic principles. A transcendental deduction of them cannot be made; such a deduction being always impossible in the case of ideas, as has been already shown.

We distinguished, in the Transcendental Analytic, the *dynamical* principles of the understanding, which are regulative principles of *intuition*, from the mathematical, which are constitutive principles of intuition. These dynamical laws are, however, constitutive in relation to *experience*, inasmuch as they render the concepts without which experience could not exist, possible *a priori*. But the principles of pure reason cannot be constitutive even in regard to empirical *concepts*, because no sensible schema corresponding to them can be discovered, and they cannot therefore have an object *in concreto*. Now, if I grant that they cannot be employed in the sphere of experience, as constitutive principles, how shall I secure for them employment and objective validity as regulative principles, and in what way can they be so employed?

The understanding is the object of reason, as sensibility is the object of the understanding. The production of systematic unity in all the empirical operation of the understanding is the proper occupation of reason; just as it is the business of the understanding to connect the manifold of appearances by means of concepts, and subject them to empirical laws. But the operations of the understanding are, without the schemata of sensibility, *undetermined*; and, in the same manner, the unity of reason is perfectly *undetermined* as regards the conditions under which, and the extent to which, the understanding ought to carry the systematic connection of its concepts. But, although it is impossible to discover in *intuition* a schema for the complete systematic unity of all the concepts of the understanding, there must be some *analogon* of this schema. This analogon is the idea of the *maximum* of the division and the connection of our knowledge in one principle. For we may have a determinate notion of a *maximum* and an absolutely perfect, all the restrictive conditions which are connected with an indeterminate and multiple content having been abstracted. Thus the idea of reason is analogous with a sensible schema, with this difference, that the application of the categories to the schema of reason does not present a knowledge of any object (as is the case with the application of the categories to sensible schemata), but merely provides us with a rule or principle for the systematic unity of the exercise of the understanding. Now, as every principle which imposes upon the exercise of the understanding *a priori* compliance with the rule of systematic unity, also relates, although only in an indirect manner, to an object of experience, the principles of pure reason will also possess objective reality in relation to experience. But they will not aim at *determining* our knowledge in regard to any empirical object; they will merely indicate the procedure, following which, the empirical and determinate exercise of the understanding may be in complete harmony and connection with itself – a result which is produced by its being brought into harmony with the principle of systematic unity, so far as that is possible, and derived from it.

I term all subjective principles, which are not derived from observation of the constitution of an object, but from the interest which reason has in producing a certain completeness in its knowledge of that object, *maxims* of reason. Thus there are maxims of speculative reason, which are based solely upon its speculative interest, although they appear to be objective principles.

When principles which are really regulative are regarded as constitutive, and employed as objective priciples, they may conflict; but if they are considered as mere maxims, there is no room for contradictions of any kind, as they then merely indicate the different interests of reason, which occasion differences in the mode of thought. In effect, reason has only one single interest, and the seeming conflict existing between its maxims merely indicates a difference in, and a reciprocal limitation of, the methods by which this interest is satisfied.

This reasoner has at its heart the interest of *diversity* – in accordance with the principle of specification; another, the interest of *unity* – in accordance with the principle of aggregation. Each believes that his judgment rests upon a thorough insight into the subject he is examining, and yet it has been influenced solely by a greater or less degree of adherence to some one of the two principles, neither of which is objective, but originates solely from the interest of reason, and on this account to be termed maxims rather than principles. When I observe intelligent men disputing about the distinctive characteristics, of men, animals, or plants, and even of minerals, those on the one side assuming the existence of certain national characteristics, certain well-defined and hereditary distinctions of family, race, and so on, while the other side maintain that nature had endowed all races of men with the same faculties and dispositions, and that all difference are but the result of external and accidental circumstances – I have only to consider for a moment the real nature of the subject of discussion, to arrive at the conclusion that it is a subject far too deep for us to judge of, and that there is little probability of either party being able to speak from a perfect insight into and understanding of the nature of the subject itself. Both have, in reality, been struggling for the twofold interest of reason; the one maintaining the one interest, the other the other. But this difference between the maxims of diversity and unity may easily be reconciled and adjusted; although, so long as they are regarded as objective principles, they must occasion not only conflict, but place hindrances in the way of the advancement of truth, until some means is discovered of reconciling these conflicting interests, and thus satisfy the interests of reason.

The same is the case with the so-called law propounded by Leibniz, and supported with remarkable ability by Bonnet – the law of the *continuous gradation* of created beings, which is nothing more than an inference from the principle of affiniy; for observation and insight into the order of nature could never present it as an objective truth. The steps of this ladder, as they appear in experience, are too far apart from each other, and the so-called petty differences between different kinds of animals are in nature commonly so wide separations that no confidence can be placed in such views (particularly when we reflect on the great variety of things, and the ease with which we can discover resemblances), and no faith in the laws which are said to express the aims and purposes of nature. On the other hand, the method of investigating the order of nature in the light of this principle, and the maxim which requires us to regard this order – it being still undetermined how far it extends – as really existing in nature, is beyond doubt a legitimate and excellent principle of reason – a principle which extends farther than any experience or observation of ours, and which, without giving us any positive knowledge of anything in the region of experience, guides us to the goal of systematic unity.

The Ultimate Purpose of the Natural Dialectic of Human Reason

The ideas of pure reason cannot be, of themselves and in their own nature, dialectical; it is from their misemployment alone that fallacies and illusions arise. For they originate in the nature of reason itself, and it is impossible that this supreme tribunal for all the rights and claims of speculation should be itself undeserving of confidence and promotive of error. It is to be expected, therefore, that these ideas have a genuine and legitimate aim. It is true, the mob of sophists raise against reason the cry of inconsistency and contradiction, and affect to despise the government of that faculty, because they cannot understand its constitution, while it is to its beneficial influences alone that they owe the position and the inteligence which enable them to criticize and to blame its procedure.

We cannot employ an *a priori* concept with certainty, until we have made a transcendental deduction thereof. The ideas of pure reason do not admit of the same kind of deduction as the categories. But if they are to possess the least objective validity, and to represent anything but mere creations of thought (*entia rationis ratiocinantis*), a deduction of them must be possible. This deduction will complete the critical task imposed upon pure reason; and it is to this part of our labours that we now proceed.

There is a great difference between a thing's being presented to reason as an *object in an absolute sense*, or merely as an *object in the idea*. In the former case I employ my concepts to determine the object; in the latter case nothing is present but a mere schema, which does not relate directly to an object, not even in a hypothetical sense, but which is useful only for the purpose of representing other objects, in a mediate and indirect manner, by means of their relation to the idea. Thus I say, the concept of a supreme intelligence is a mere idea; that is to say, its objective reality does not consist in the fact that it has an immediate relation to an object (for in this sense we have no means of establishing its objective validity), it is merely a schema constructed according to the necessary conditions of the unity of reason – the schema of a thing in general, which is useful towards the production of the highest degree of systematic unity in the empirical exercise of reason, in which we derive this or that object of experience from the imaginary object of this idea, as the ground or cause of the said object of experience. In this way, the idea is properly a heuristic, and not an ostensive concept; it does not give any information respecting the constitution of an object, it merely indicates how, under the guidance of the idea, we ought to *investigate* the constitution and the relations of objects in the world of experience. Now, if it can be shown that the three kinds of transcendental ideas (psychological, cosmological, and theological), although not relating directly to any object nor determining it, do nevertheless, on the supposition of the existence of an *object in the idea*, produce systematic unity in the laws of the empirical employment of the reason, and extend our empirical knowledge, without ever being in conflict with it – it must be a necessary *maxim* of reason to regulate its procedure according to these ideas. And this forms the transcendental deduction of all speculative ideas, not as *constitutive* principles of the extension of our knowledge beyond the limits of our experience, but as *regulative* principles of the systematic unity of empirical knowledge, which is by the aid of these ideas arranged and emended within its own proper limits, to an extent unattainable by the operation of the principles of the understanding alone.

I shall make this plainer. Guided by the principles involved in these ideas, we must, in the *first* place, so connect all the appearances, actions, and feelings of the mind, as if it were a simple substance, which, endowed with personal identity, possesses a permanent existence (in this life at least), while its states, among which those of the body are to be included as external conditions, are in continual change. *Secondly*, in cosmology, we must investigate the conditions of all natural appearances, internal as well as external, as if they belonged to a chain infinite and without any prime or supreme member, while we do not, on this account, deny the existence of intelligible grounds of these appearances, although we never employ them to explain appearances, for the simple reason that they are not objects of our knowledge. *Thirdly*, in the sphere of theology, we must regard the whole system of possible experience as forming an absolute, but dependent and sensibly-conditioned unity, and at the same time as based upon a sole, supreme, and all-sufficient ground existing apart from the world itself – a ground which is a self-subsistent, primal and creative reason, in relation to which we so employ our reason in the field of experience, as if all objects drew their origin from that archetype of all reason. In other words, we ought not to derive the internal appearances of the soul from a simple thinking substance, but derive them from each other under the guidance of the regulative idea of a simple being; we ought not to derive the appearances, order, and unity of the universe from a supreme intelligence, but merely draw from this idea of a supremely wise cause the rules which must guide reason in its connection of causes and effects.

Now there is nothing to hinder us from assuming these ideas to possess an objective and hypostatic existence, except the cosmological ideas, which lead reason into an antinomy; while the psychological and theological ideas are not antinomial. They contain no contradiction; how then can anyone dispute their objective reality, since he who denies it knows as little about their possibility as we who affirm? And yet, when we wish to admit the existence of a thing, it is not sufficient to convince ourselves that there is no positive obstacle in the way; for it cannot be allowed to regard mere creations of thought, which transcend, though they do not contradict, all our concepts, as real and determinate objects, solely upon the authority of a speculative reason striving to compass its own aims. They cannot, therefore, be admitted to be real in themselves; they can only serve as analogues of real things – that of a schema of the regulative principle of the systematic unity of all knowledge. We abstract from the object of the idea all the conditions which limit the exercise of our understanding, but which, on the other hand, are the sole conditions of our possessing a determinate concept of anything. And thus we think a something, of the real nature of which we have not the least concept, but which we represent to ourselves as standing in a relation to the whole system of appearances, analogous to that in which appearances stand to each other.

By admitting these ideal beings, we do not really extend our knowledge beyond the objects of possible experience; we extend merely the empirical unity of our experience, by the aid of systematic unity, the schema of which is furnished by the idea, which is therefore valid – not as a constitutive, but as a regulative principle. For although we posit a thing corresponding to the idea – a something, an actual existence – we do not on that account aim at the extension of our knowledge by means of transcendent concepts. This existence is purely ideal, and not objective; it is the mere expression of the systematic unity which is to be the guide of reason in the field of experience. There are no attempts made at deciding what the ground of this unity may be, or what the real nature of this imaginary being.

Thus the transcendental and only determinate concept of God, which is presented to us by speculative reason, is in the strictest sense *deistic*. In other words, reason does not assure us of the objective validity of the concept; it merely gives us the idea of something, on which the supreme and necessary unity of all experience is based. This something we cannot, following the analogy of a real substance, think otherwise than as the cause of all things operating in accordance with rational laws, if we regard it as an individual object; although we should rest contented with the idea alone as a regulative principle of reason, and make no attempt at completing the sum of the conditions imposed by thought. This attempt is, indeed, inconsistent with the aim of complete systematic unity in the sphere of knowledge – a unity to which no bounds are set by reason.

Hence it happens that, admitting a divine being, I can have no concept of the internal possibility of its perfection, or of the necessity of its existence. The only advantage of this admission is, that it enables me to answer all other questions relating to the contingent, and to give reason the most complete satisfaction as regards the unity which it aims at attaining in the world of experience. But I cannot satisfy reason with regard to this hypothesis itself; and this proves that it is not its intelligence and insight into the subject, but its speculative interest alone which induces it to proceed from a point lying far beyond the sphere of our knowledge, for the purpose of being able to consider all objects as parts of a systematic whole.

Here a distinction presents itself, in regard to the way in which we may think a presupposition – a distinction which is somewhat subtle, but of great importance in transcendental philosophy. I may have sufficient grounds to admit something, or the existence of something, in a relative point of view (*suppositio relativa*) without being justified in admitting it in an absolute sense (*suppositio absoluta*). This distinction is undoubtedly requisite, in the case of a regulative principle, the necessity of which we recognize though we are ignorant of the source of that necessity and which we assume to be based upon some ultimate ground, for the purpose of being able to think the universality of the principle in a more determinate way. For example, I think the existence of a being corresponding to a pure transcendental idea. But I cannot admit that this being exists absolutely and in itself, because all of the concepts, by which I can think an object in a determinate manner, fall short of assuring me of its existence; nay, the conditions of the objective validity of my concepts are excluded by the idea – by the very fact of its being an idea. The concept of reality, substance, causality, nay, even that of necessity in existence, have no significance outide the sphere of empirical knowledge, and cannot, beyond that sphere, determine any object. They may, accordingly, be employed to explain the possibility of things in the world of sense, but they are utterly inadequate to explain the possibility of the *world itself* considered as a whole; because in this case the ground of explanation must lie outside the world, and cannot, therefore, be an object of possible experience. Now, I may admit the existence of an incomprehensible being of this nature – the object of a mere idea, relatively to the world of sense; although I have no ground to admit its existence absolutely and in itself. For if an idea (that of a systematic and complete unity, of which I shall presently speak more particularly) lies at the foundation of the most extended empirical employment of reason, and if this idea cannot be adequately represented *in concreto*, although it is indispensably necessary for the approximation of empirical unity to the highest possible degree – I am not only authorized, but compelled to realize this idea, that is, to posit a real object corresponding thereto. But I cannot profess to know this object; it is to me merely a something, to which, as the ground of systematic unity in knowledge, I attribute such properties as are analogous to the concepts employed by the understanding in the sphere of experience. Following the analogy of the notions of reality, substance, causality, and necessity, I think a being, which possesses all these attributes in the highest degree; and, as this idea is the offspring of my reason alone, I think this being as *self-subsistent reason*, and as the cause of the universe operating by means of ideas of the greatest possible harmony and unity. Thus I abstract all conditions that would limit my idea, solely for the purpose of rendering systematic unity possible in the world of empirical diversity, and thus securing the widest possible extension for the exercise of reason in that sphere. This I am enabled to do, by regarding all connections and relations in the world of sense, *as if* they were the dispositions of a supreme reason, to which our reason is but a faint image. I then proceed to think this Supreme Being by concepts which have, properly, no meaning or application, except in the world of sense. But as I am authorized to employ the transcendental hypothesis of such a being in a relative respect alone, that is, as the substratum of the greatest possible unity in experience – I may attribute to a being which I regard as distinct from the world, such properties as belong solely to the sphere of sense and experience. For I do not desire, and am not justified in desiring, to know this object of my idea, as it exists in itself; for I possess no concepts sufficient for this task, those of reality, substance, causality, nay, even that of necessity in existence, losing all significance, and becoming merely the title of concepts, without content, when I attempt to carry them beyond the limits of the world of sense. I think merely the relation of a perfectly unknown being to the greatest possible systematic unity of experience, solely for the purpose of employing it as the schema of the regulative principle which directs reason in its empirical exercise.

It is evident, at the first view, that we cannot presuppose the reality of this transcendental object, by means of the concepts of reality, substance, causality, and so on; because these concepts cannot be applied to anything that is distinct from the world of sense. Thus the supposition of a Supreme Being or cause is purely relative; it is thought only in behalf of the systematic unity of experience; such a being is but a something, of whose existence in itself we have not the least concept. Thus, too, it becomes sufficiently manifest, why we required the idea of a necessary being in relation to ojects given by sense, although we can never have the least concept of this being, or of its absolute necessity.

And now we can clearly perceive the result of our transcendental dialectic, and the proper aim of the ideas of pure reason – which become dialectical solely from misunderstanding and inconsiderateness. Pure reason is, in fact, occupied with itself, and not with any object. Objects are not presented to it to be embraced in the unity of an empirical concept; it is only the concepts of the understanding that are presented to it, for the purpose of receiving the unity of a rational concept, that is, of being connected according to a principle. The unity of reason is the unity of system; and this systematic unity is not an objective principle, extending its dominion over objects, but a subjective maxim, extending its authority over the empirical knowledge of objects. The systematic connection which reason gives to the empirical employment of the understanding, not only advances the extension of that employment, but ensures its correctness, and thus the principle of a systematic unity of this nature is also objective, although only in an indefinite respect (*principium vagum*). It is not, however, a constitutive principle, determining an object to which it directly relates; it is merely a regulative principle or maxim, advancing and strengthening the empirical exercise of reason, by the opening up of new paths of which the understanding is ignorant, while it never conflicts with the laws of its exercise in the sphere of experience.

But reason cannot think this systematic unity, without at the same time thinking an object of the idea – an object that cannot be presented in any experience, which contains no concrete example of a complete systematic unity. This being (*ens rationis ratiocinatae*) is therefore a mere idea, and is not assumed to be a thing which is real absolutely and in itself. On the contrary, it forms merely the problematical foundation of the connection which the mind introduces among the appearances of the sensible world. We look upon this connection, in the light of the above-mentioned idea, as if it drew its origin from the supposed being which corresponds to the idea. And yet all we aim at is the possession of this idea as a secure foundation for the systematic unity of experience – a unity indispensable to reason, advantageous to the understanding, and promotive of the interests of empirical knowledge.

We mistake the true meaning of this idea, when we regard it as an enouncement, or even as a hypothetical declaration of the existence of a real thing, which we are to regard as the origin or ground of a systematic constitution of the universe. On the contrary, it is left completely undetermined what the nature or properties of this so-called ground may be. The idea is merely to be adopted as a point of view, from which this unity, so essential to reason and so beneficial to the understanding, my be regarded as radiating. In one word, this transcendental thing is merely the schema of a regulative principle, by means of which reason, so far as it is capable, extends the dominion of systematic unity over the whole sphere of experience.

The first object of an idea of this kind is myself, considered merely as a thinking nature or soul. If I wish to investigate the properties of a thinking being, I must interrogate experience. But I find that I can apply none of the categories to this object, the schema of these categories, which is the condition of their application, being given only in sensible intuition. But I cannot thus attain to the knowledge of a systematic unity of all the appearances of the internal sense. Instead, therefore, of an empirical concept of what the soul really is, reason takes the concept of the empirical unity of all thought, and, by thinking this unity as unconditioned and primitive, constructs the rational concept or idea of a simple substance which is in itself unchangeable, possessing personal identity, and in connection with other real things external to it; in one word, it constructs the idea of a simple self-subsistent intelligence. But the real aim of reason in this procedure is the attainment of principles of systematic unity for the explanation of the appearances of the soul. That is, reason desires to be able to represent all the determinations of the internal sense, as existing in one subject, all powers as derived from one fundamental power, all changes as mere varieties in the condition of a being which is permanent and always the same, and all appearances in space as entirely different in their nature from the procedure of thought. Simplicity is regarded as the mere schema of this regulative principle; it is not assumed that it is the actual ground of the properties of the soul. For these properties may rest upon quite different grounds, of which we are completely ignorant; just as the above predicates could not give us any knowledge of the soul as it is in itself, even if we regarded them as valid in respect of it, inasmuch as they constitute a mere idea, which cannot be represented *in concreto*. Nothing but good can result from a psychological idea of this kind, if we only take proper care not to consider it as more than an idea; that is, if we regard it as valid merely in relation to the employment of reason, in the sphere of the appearances of the soul. Under the guidance of this idea, or principle, no empirical laws of corporeal appearances are called in to explain that which is a appearance of the *internal sense* alone; no windy hypothesis of the generation, annihilation, and palingenesis of souls are admitted. Thus the consideration of this object of the internal sense is kept pure, and unmixed with heterogeneous elements; while the investigation of reason aims at reducing all the grounds of explanation employed in this sphere of knowledge to a single principle. All this is best effected, nay, cannot be effected otherwise than by means of such a schema, which requires us to regard this ideal thing as an actual existence. The psychological idea is therefore meaningless and inapplicable, except as the schema of a regulative concept. For, if I ask whether the soul is not in itself of a spiritual nature – it is a question which has no meaning. From such a concept has been abstracted, not merely all corporeal nature, but all nature, that is, all the predicates of a possible experience; and consequently, all the conditions which enable us to think an object to this concept have disappeared. But, if these conditions are absent, it is evident that the concept is meaningless.

The second regulative idea of speculative reason is the concept of the universe. For nature is properly the only object presented to us, in regard to which reason requires regulative principles. Nature is twofold – thinking and corporeal nature. To think the latter in regard to its internal possibility, that is, to determine the application of the categories to it, no idea is required – no representation which transcends experience. In this sphere, therefore, an idea is impossible, sensible intuition being our only guide; while, in the sphere of psychology, we require the fundamental idea (*I*), which contains *a priori* a certain for of thought, namely, the unity of the *I*. Pure reason has therefore nothing left but nature in general, and the completeness of conditions in nature in accordance with some principle. The absolute totality of the series of these conditions is an idea, which can never be fully realized in the empirical exercise of reason, while it is serviceable as a rule for the procedure of reason in relation to that totality. It requires us, in the explanation of given appearances (in the regress or ascent in the series), to proceed as if the series were infinite in itself, that is, were prolonged *in indefinitum*; while, on the other hand, where reason is regarded as itself the determining cause (in the region of freedom), we are required to proceed as if we had not before us an object of sense, but of the pure understanding. In this latter case, the conditions do not exist in the series of appearances, but may be placed quite outside of and beyond it, and the series of conditions may be regarded as if it had an absolute beginning from an intelligible cause. All this proves that the cosmological ideas are nothing but regulative principles, and not constitutive; and that their aim is not to realize an actual totality in such series. The full discussion of this subject will be found in its proper place in the chapter on the antinomy of pure reason.

The third idea of pure reason, containing the hypothesis of a being which is valid merely as a relative hypothesis, is that of the one and all-sufficient cause of all cosmological series, in other words, the idea of God. We have not the slightest ground absolutely to admit the existence of an object corresponding to this idea; for what can empower or authorize us to affirm the existence of a being of the highest perfection – a being whose existence is absolutely necessary, merely because we possess the concept of such a being? The answer is – it is the existence of the world which renders this hypothesis necessary. But this answer makes it perfectly evident, that the idea of this being, like all other speculative ideas, is essentially nothing more than a demand upon reason that it shall regulate the connection which it and its subordinate faculties introduce into the appearances of the world by principles of systematic unity, and consequently, that it shall regard all appearances as originating from one all-embracing being, as the supreme and all-sufficient cause. From that it is plain that the only aim of reason in this procedure is the establishment of its own formal rule for the extension of its dominion in the world of experience; that it does not aim at an extension of its knowledge *beyond the limits of experience*; and that, consequently, this idea does not contain any constitutive principle.

The highest formal unity, which is based upon ideas alone, is the unity of all things – a unity in accordance with their conformity to ends; and the speculative interest of reason renders it necessary to regard all order in the world as if it originated from the intention and design of a supreme reason. This principle unfolds to the view of reason in the sphere of experience new and enlarged prospects, and invites it to connect the appearances of the world according to teleological laws, and in this way to attain to the highest possible degree of systematic unity. The hypothesis of a supreme intelligence, as the sole cause of the universe – an intelligence which has for us no more than an ideal existence, is accordingly always of the greatest service to reason. Thus, if we presuppose, in relation to the figure of the earth (which is round, but somewhat flattened at the poles),[1] or that of mountains or seas, wise designs on the part of an

---

[1] The advantages which a circular form, in the case of the earth, has over every other, are well known. But few are aware that the slight flattening at the poles, which gives it the

author of the universe, we cannot fail to make, by the light of this supposition, a great number of interesting discoveries. If we keep to this hypothesis, as a principle which is purely regulative, even error cannot be very detrimental. For, in this case, error can have no more serious consequences than that, were we expected to discover a teleological connection (*nexus finalis*), only a mechanical or physical connection appears (*nexus effectivus*). In such a case, we merely fail to find the additional form of unity we expected, but we do not lose the rational unity which reason requires in its procedure in experience. But even a miscarriage of this sort cannot affect the law in its general and teleological relations. For although we may convict an anatomist of an error, when he connects the limb of some animal with a certain purpose; it is quite impossible to *prove* in a single case, that any arrangement of nature, be it what it may, is entirely without aim or end. And thus medical physiology, by the aid of a principle presented to it by pure reason, extends its very limited empirical knowledge of the purposes of the different parts of an organized body so far, that it may be asserted with the utmost confidence, and with the approbation of all reflecting men, that every organ or bodily part of an animal has its use and answers a certain aim. Now, this is a supposition, which, if regarded as of a constitutive character, goes much farther than any experience or observation of ours can justify. Hence it is evident that it is nothing more than a regulative principle of reason, which aims at the highest degree of systematic unity, by the aid of the idea of a causality according to design in a supreme cause – a cause which it regards as the highest intelligence.

If, however, we neglect this restriction of the idea to a purely regulative influence, reason is betrayed into numerous errors. For it has then left the ground of experience, in which alone are to be found the criteria of truth, and has ventured into the region of the incomprehensible and unsearchable, on the heights of which it loses all sobriety, because it has completely severed its connection with experience.

---

figure of a spheroid, is the only cause which prevents the elevations of continents or even of mountains, perhaps thrown up by some internal convulsion, from continually altering the position of the axis of the earth – and that to some considerable degree in a short time. The great protuberance of the earth under the Equator serves to overbalance the impetus of all other masses of earth, and thus to preserve the axis of the earth, so far as we can observe, in its present position. And yet this wise arrangement has been unthinkingly explained from the equilibrium of the formerly fluid mass.

The first error which arises from our employing the idea of a Supreme Being as a constitutive (in repugnance to the very nature of an idea), and not as a regulative principle, is the error of idle reason (*ignava ratio*[1]). We may so term every principle which requires us to regard our investigations of nature as absolutely complete, and allows reason to cease its inquiries, as if it had fully executed its task. Thus the psychological idea of the *I*, when employed as a constitutive principle for the explanation of the appearances of the soul, and for the extension of our knowledge regarding this subject beyond the limits of experience – even to the condition of the soul after death, is convenient enough for the purposes of pure reason, but detrimental and even ruinous to its interests in the sphere of nature and experience. The dogmatizing spiritualist explains the unchanging unity of our personality through all changes of condition from the unity of a thinking substance, the interest which we take in things and events that can happen only after our death, from a consciousness of the immaterial nature of our thinking subject, and so on. Thus he dispenses with all empirical investigations into the cause of these internal appearances, and with all possible explanations of them upon purely natural grounds; while, at the dictation of a transcendent reason, he passes by the immanent sources of knowledge in experience, greatly to his own ease and convenience, but to the sacrifice of all genuine insight and intelligence. These prejudicial consequences become still more evident, in the case of the dogmatical treatment of our idea of a Supreme Intelligence, and the theological system of nature (physico-theology) which is falsely based upon it. For, in this case, the aims which we observe in nature, and often those which we merely fancy to exist, make the investigation of causes a very easy task, by directing us to refer such and such appearances immediately to the unsearchable will and counsel of the Supreme Wisdom, while we ought to investigate their causes in the general laws of the mechanism of matter. We are thus recommended to consider the labour of reason as ended, when we have merely dispensed with its employment, which is guided surely and safely, only by the order of nature and the series of changes in the world – which are arranged

---

[1] This was the term applied by the old dialecticians to a sophistical argument, which ran thus: If it is your fate to die of this disease, you will die, whether you employ a physician or not. Cicero says that this mode of reasoning has received this appellation, because, if followed, it puts an end to the employment of reason in the affairs of life. For a similar reason I have applied this designation to the sophistical argument of pure reason.

according to immanent and general laws. This error may be avoided, if we do not merely consider from the view-point of final aims certain parts of nature, such as the division and structure of a continent, the constitution and direction of certain mountain-chains, or even the organization existing in the vegetable and animal kingdoms, but look upon this systematic unity of nature in a perfectly *general* way, in relation to the idea of a Supreme Intelligence. If we pursue this advice, we lay as a foundation for all investigation the conformity to aims of all appearances of nature in accordance with univeral laws, from which no particular arrangement of nature is exempt, but only known by us with more or less difficulty; and we possess a regulative principle of the systematic unity of a teleological connection, which we do not attempt to anticipate or predetermine. All that we do, and ought to do, is to follow out the physio-mechanical connection in nature according to general laws, with the hope of discovering, sooner or later, the teleological connection also. Thus, and thus only, can the principle of final unity aid in the extension of the employment of reason in the sphere of experience, without being in any case detrimental to it interests.

The second error whch arises from the misconception of the principle of systematic unity is that of perverted reason (*perversa ratio*, ὕστερον πρότερον *rationis*). The idea of systematic unity is available as a regulative principle in the connection of appearances according to general natural laws; and, how far soever we have to travel upon the path of experience to discover some fact or event, this idea requires us to believe that we have approached all the more nearly to the completion of its use in the sphere of nature, although that completion can never be attained. But this error reverses the procedure of reason. We begin by hypostatizing the principle of teleological unity, and by giving an anthropomorphic determination to the concept of a Supreme Intelligence, and then proceed forcibly to impose aims upon nature. Thus not only does teleology, which ought to aid in the completion of unity in accordance with general laws, operate to the destruction of its influence, but it hinders reason from attaining its proper aim, that is, the proof, upon natural grounds, of the existence of a supreme intelligent cause. For, if we cannot presuppose supreme teleology in nature *a priori*, that is, as essentially belonging to nature, how can we be directed to endeavour to discover this unity, and, rising gradually through its different degrees, to approach the supreme perfection of an author of all – a perfection which is absolutely necessary, and therefore capable of *a priori*? The regulative principle directs us to presuppose systematic unity absolutely, and, consequently, as following from the essential nature of things – but only as a *unity of nature*, not merely known empirically, but presupposed *a priori*, although not only in an indeterminate manner. But if I insist on basing nature upon the foundation of a supreme ordaining Being, the unity of nature is in effect lost. For, in this case, it is quite foreign and unessential to the nature of things, and cannot be known from the general laws of nature. And thus arises a vicious circular argument, what ought to have been proved having been presupposed.

To take the regulative principle of systematic unity in nature for a constitutive principle, and to hypostatize and make a cause out of that which is properly the ideal ground of the consistent and harmonious exercise of reason, involves reason in inextricable embarrassments. The investigation of nature pursues its own path under the guidance of the chain of natural causes, in accordance with the general laws of nature, and ever follows the light of the idea of an author of the universe – not for the purpose of deriving the finality, which it constantly pursues, from this Supreme Being, but to attain to the knowledge of his existence from the finality which it seeks in the existence of the appearances of nature, and, if possible, in that of all things – to know this being, consequently, as absolutely necessary. Whether this latter purpose succeed or not, the idea is and must always be correct in iself, and in its employment, provided it is merely regulative.

Complete unity, in conformity with aims, constitutes absolute perfection. But if we do not find this unity in the nature of the things which go to constitute the world of experience, that is, of objective knowledge, consequently in the universal and necessary laws of nature, how can we infer from this unity the idea of the supreme and absolutely necessary perfection of a primal being, which is the origin of all causality? The greatest systematic unity, and consequently teleological unity, constitutes the very foundation of the possibility of the most extended employment of human reason. The idea of unity is therefore essentially and indissolubly connected with the nature of our reason. This idea is a legislative one; and hence it is very natural that we should assume the existence of a legislative reason corresponding to it, from which the systematic unity of nature – the object of the operations of reason – must be derived.

In the course of our discussion of the antinomies, we stated that it is always possible to answer all the questions which pure reason may raise; and that the plea of the limited nature of our knowledge, which is unavoidable and proper in many questions regarding natural inquiries, cannot in this case be admitted, because the questions raised do not relate to the nature of things, but are necessarily originated by the nature of reason itself, and relate to its own internal constitution. We can now establish this assertion, which at first sight appeared so rash, in relation to the two questions in which reason takes the greatest interest, and thus complete our discussion of the dialectic of pure reason.

If, then, the question is asked, in relation to transcendental theology,[1] *first*, whether there is anything distinct from the world, which contains the ground of world-order and connection according to general laws, the answer is: *Certainly*. For the world is a sum of appearances; there must therefore be some transcendental basis of these appearances, that is, a basis capable of being thought by the pure understanding alone. If, *second*, the question is asked, whether this being is substance, whether it is of the greatest reality, whether it is necessary, and so forth, I answer that *this question is utterly without meaning*. For all the categories which aid me in forming a concept of an object, cannot be employed except in the world of sense, and are without meaning when not applied to objects of actual or possible experience. Outside this sphere, they are not properly concepts, but the mere titles or indices of concepts, which we may admit, although they cannot, without the help of experience, help us to understand any subject or thing. If, *third*, the question is, whether we may not think this being, which is distinct from the world, in analogy with the objects of experience, the answer is *undoubtedly*, but only as an ideal, and not as a real object. That is, we must think it only as an unknown substratum of the systematic unity, order, and finality of the world – a unity which reason must employ as the regulative principle of its investigation of nature. Nay, more, we may admit into the idea certain anthro-

---

[1] After what has been said of the psychological idea and its proper employment as a regulative principle of the operation of reason, I need not enter into detail regarding the transcendental illusion by which the systematic unity of all the manifold of the internal sense is hypostatized. The procedure is in this case very similar to that which has been discussed in our remarks on the theological ideal.

pomorphic elements, which are promotive of the interests of this regulative principle. For it is no more than an idea, which does not relate directly to a being distinct from the world, but to the regulative principle of the systematic unity of the world, by means, however, of a schema of this unity – the schema of a Supreme Intelligence, who is the wisely-designing author of the universe. What this basis of world-unity may be in itself, we know not – we cannot discover from the idea; we merely know how we ought to employ the idea of this unity, in relation to the systematic operation of reason in the sphere of experience.

But, it will be asked again, *can* we on these grounds, admit the existence of a wise and omnipotent author of the world? *Without doubt*; and not only so, but we *must* assume the existence of such a being. But do we thus extend the limits of our knowledge beyond the field of possible experience? *By no means*. For we have merely presupposed a something, of which we have no concept, which we do not know as it is in itself; but, in relation to the systematic disposition of the universe, which we must presuppose in all our observation of nature, we have thought this unknown being *in analogy* with an intelligent existence (an empirical concept), that is to say, we have endowed it with those attributes, which, judging from the nature of our own reason, may contain the ground of such a systematic unity. This idea is therefore valid only relatively to the employment in experience of our reason. But if we attribute to it absolute and objective validity, we overlook the fact that it is merely an ideal being that we think; and, by setting out from a basis which is not determinable by consideration drawn from experience, we place ourselves in a position which incapacitates us from applying this principle to the empirical employment of reason.

But, it will be asked further, can I make any use of this concept and hypothesis in my investigations into the world and nature? *Yes*, for this very purpose was the idea established by reason as a fundamental basis. But may I regard certain arrangements, which seemed to have been made in conformity wih some fixed aim, as the arrangements of design, and look upon them as proceeding from the divine will, with the intervention, however, of certain other particular arrangemnts disposed to that end? Yes, you may do so; but at the same time you must regard it as indifferent, whether it is asserted that divine wisdom has disposed all things in conformity with his highest aims, or that the idea of supreme wisdom is a regulative principle in the investigation of nature, and at the same time a principle of the systematic unity of nature according to general laws, even in those cases where we are unable to discover that unity. In other words, it must be perfectly indifferent to you, whether you say, when you have discovered this unity – God has wisely willed it so, or, nature has wisely arranged this. For it was nothing but the systematic unity, which reason requires as a basis for the investigation of nature, that justified you in accepting the idea of a supreme intelligence as a schema for a regulative principle; and, the further you advance in the discovery of design and finality, the more certain the legitimacy of your idea. But, as the whole aim of this regulative principle was the discovery of a necessary and systematic unity in nature, we have, in so far as we attain this, to attribute our success to the idea of a Supreme Being; while, at the same time, we cannot, without involving ourselves in contradictions, overlook the general laws of nature, as it was in reference to them alone that this idea was employed. We cannot, I say, overlook the general laws of nature, and regard this conformity to aims observable in nature as contingent or hyperphysical in its origin; inasmuch as there is no ground which can justify us in the admission of a being with such properties distinct from and above nature. All that we are authorized to assert is, that this idea may be employed as a principle, and that the properties of the being which is assumed to correspond to it may be regarded as systematically connected in analogy with the causal determination of appearances.

For the same reasons we are justified in introducing into the idea of the supreme cause not only a subtle anthropomorphism (for without this we could not predicate anything of it); we may think this cause as a being with understanding, the feelings of pleasure and displeasure, and facultes of desire and will corresponding to these. At the same time, we may attribute to this being infinite perfection – a perfection which necessarily transcends that which our knowledge of the order and design in the world would authorize us to predicate of it. For the regulative law of systematic unity requires us to study nature on the supposition that systematic and final unity *in infinitum* is everywhere discoverable, even in the highest diversity. For, although we may discover little of this cosmical perfection, it belongs to the legislative prerogative of reason, to require us always to seek for and to expect it; while it must always be beneficial to institute all inquiries into nature in accordance with this principle. But it is evident that, by this idea of a supreme author of all, which I place as the foundation of all inquiries into nature, I do not mean to assert the existence of such a being, or that I have any knowledge of its existence; and, consequently, I do not really derive anyhing from the existence of this being, but merely from its idea, that is to say, from the nature of things in this world, in accordance with this idea. A certain dim consciousness of the true use of this idea seems to have dictated to the philosophers of all times the moderate language used by them regarding the cause of the world. We find them employing the expressions, wisdom and care of nature, and divine wisdom, as synonymous – nay, in purely speculative discussions, preferring the former, because it does not carry the appearance of greater pretensions than such as we are entitled to make, and at the same time directs reason to its proper field of action – nature and its appearances.

Thus, pure reason, which at first seemed to promise us nothing less than the extension of our knowledge beyond the limits of experience, is found, when thoroughly examined, to contain nothing but regulative principles, the virtue and function of which is to introduce into our knowledge a higher degree of unity than the understanding could of itself. These principles, by placing the goal of all our struggles at so great a distance, realize for us the most thorough connection between the different parts of our knowlege, and the highest degree of systematic unity. But, on the other hand, if misunderstood and employed as constitutive principles of transcendent knowledge, they become the parents of illusions and contradictions, while pretending to introduce us to new regions of knowledge.

Thus all human knowledge begins with intuitions, proceeds from these to concepts, and ends with ideas. Although it possesses in relation to all three elements, sources of knowledge *a priori*, which seem at first to transcend the limits of all experience, a thoroughgoing criticism demonstrates, that speculative reason can never, by the aid of these elements, pass the bounds of possible experience, and that the proper destination of this highest faculty of knowledge is to emply all methods, and all the principles of these methods, for the purpose of penetrating into the innermost secrets of nature, by the aid of the principles of unity (among all kinds of which teleological unity is the highest), while it ought not to attempt to soar above the sphere of experience, beyond which there lies nothing for us but emptiness. The critical examination, in our Transcendental Analytic, of all the propositions which professed to

CRITIQUE OF PURE REASON

extend knowledge beyond the sphere of experience, completely demonstrated that they can only conduct us to a possible experience. If we were not distrustful even of the clearest abstract doctrines, if we were not allured by specious and inviting prospects to escape from the constraining power of their evidence, we might spare ourselves the laborious examination of all the dilectical arguments which a transcendent reason adduces in support of its pretensions; for we should know with the most complete certainty that, however honest such professions might be, they are null and valueless, because they relate to a kind of knowledge to which nobody can by any possibility attain. But, as there is no end to discussion, if we cannot discover the true cause of the illusions by which even the wisest are deceived, and as the analysis of all our transcendent knowledge into its elements is of itself of no slight value as a psychological study, while it is a duty incumbent on every philosopher – it was found necessary to investigate the dialectical procedure of reason in its primary sources. And as the inferences of which this dialectic is the parent, are not only deceitful, but naturally possess a profound interest for humanity, it was advisable at the same time, to give a full account of the momenta of this dialectical procedure, and to deposit it in the archives of human reason, in order to prevent future errors of the same kind.

II : TRANSCENDENTAL DOCTRINE OF METHOD

If we regard the sum of the knowledge of pure speculative reason as an edifice, the idea of which, at least, exists in the human mind, it may be said that we have in the Transcendental Doctrine of Elements examined the materials and determined to what edifice these belong, and what its height and stability. We have found, indeed, that, although we had purposed to build for ourselves a tower which should reach to heaven, the supply of materials sufficed merely for a habitation, which was spacious enough for all terrestrial purposes, and high enough to enable us to survey the level plain of experience, but that the bold undertaking designed necessarily failed for want of materials – not to mention the confusion of tongue, which gave rise to endless disputes among the labourers on the plan of the edifice, and at last scattered them over all the world, each to erect a separate building for himself, according to his own plans and his own inclinations. Our present task relates not to the materials, but to the plan of an edifice; and, as we have had sufficient warning not to venture blindly upon a design which may be found to transcend our natual powers, while, at the same time, we cannot give up the intention of erecting a secure abode, we must proportion our design to the material which is presented to us, and which is, at the same time, sufficient for all our wants.

I understand, then, by the transcendental doctrine of method, the determination of the formal conditions of a complete system of pure reason. We shall accordingly have to treat of the *discipline*, the *canon*, the *architectonic*, and, finally, the *history* of pure reason. This part of our *Critique* will accomplish, from the transcendental point of view, what has been usually attempted, but miserably executed, under the name of *practical logic*. It has been badly executed, I say, because general logic, not being limited to any particular kind of knowledge (not even to the pure knowledge of the understanding) nor to any particular objects, it cannot, without borrowing from other sciences, do more than present merely the titles of *possible methods* and the technical expressions, which are employed in the systematic parts of all sciences; and thus the pupil is made acquainted with names, the meaning and application of which he is to learn only at some future time.

CHAPTER I: THE DISCIPLINE OF PURE REASON

Negative judgments – those which are so not merely as regards their logical form, but in respect of their content – are not commonly held in especial respect. They are, on the contrary, regarded as jealous enemies of our insatiable desire for knowledge; and it almost requires an apology to induce us to tolerate, much less to prize and to respect them.

All propositions, indeed, may be *logically* expressed in a negative form; but, in relation to the content of our knowledge, the peculiar province of negative judgments is solely to *prevent error*. For this reason, too, negative propositions, which are framed for the purpose of correcting false cognitions, where error is absolutely impossible, are, undoubtedly true, but senseless; that is, they are in reality purposeless, and for this reason often very ridiculous. Such is the proposition of the schoolman, that Alexander could not have subdued any countries without an army.

But where the limits of our possible knowledge are very narrow, the attraction to new fields of knowledge great, the illusions to which the mind is subject of the most deceptive character, and the harmful consequences of error of no inconsiderable magnitude – the *negative* element in knowledge, which is useful only to guard us against error, is of far more importance than much of that positive instruction which makes additions to the sum of our knowledge. The *restraint* which is employed to repress, and finally to extirpate the constant inclination to depart from certain rules, is termed *discipline*. It is distinguished from *culture*, which aims at the formation of a certain degree of skill, without attempting to destroy any already existing. In the cultivation of a talent, which has given evidence of an impulse towards self-development, discipline takes a negative,[1] culture and doctrine a positive, part.

That natural dispositions and talents (such as imagination and wit), which ask a free and unlimited development, require in many respects the corrective influence of discipline, every one will readily

---

[1] I am well aware that, in the language of the schools, the term *discipline* is usually employed as synonymous with *instruction*. But there are so many cases in which it is necessary to distinguish the notion of the former, as a course of corrective training, from that of the latter, as the communication of knowledge, and the nature of things itself demands the appropriation of the most suitable expressions for this distinction, that it is my desire that the former term should never be employed in any other than a negative signification.

grant. But it may well appear strange, that reason, whose proper duty it is to prescribe rules of discipline to all endeavours, should itself require this corrective. It has, in fact, hitherto escaped this humiliation, only because, in presence of its magnificent pretensions and high position, no one could readily suspect it to be capable of substituting fancies for concepts, and words for things.

Reason, when employed in the field of experience, does not stand in need of criticism, because its principles are subjected to the continual test of empirical observation. Nor is criticism requisite in the sphere of mathematics, where the concepts of reason must always be presented *in concreto* in pure intuition, and baseless or arbitrary assertions are discovered without difficulty. But where reason is not held in a plain track by the influence of empirical or of pure intuition, that is, when it is employed in the transcendental sphere of pure concept, it stands in great need of discipline, to restrain its propensity to overstep the limits of possible experience, and to keep it from wandering into error. In fact, the utility of the philosophy of pure reason is entirely of this negative character. Particular errors may be corrected by particular animadversions, and the causes of these errors may be eradicated by criticism. But where we find, as in the case of pure reason, a complete system of illusions and fallacies, closely connected with each other and depending upon general principles, there seems to be required a peculiar and negative code of mental legislation, which, under the denomination of a *discipline*, and founded upon the nature of reason and the objects of its exercise, shall constitute a system of thorough examinations and testing, which no fallacy will be able to withstand or escape from, under whatever disguise it may lurk.

But the reader must remark that, in this the second division of our Transcendental Critique, the discipline of pure reason is not directed to the content, but to the method of the knowledge of pure reason. The former task has been completed in the Doctrine of Elements. But there is so much similarity in the mode of employing the faculty of reason, whatever be the object to which it is applied, while, at the same time, its employment in the transcendental sphere is so essentially different in kind from every other, that, without the warning negative influence of a discipline specially directed to that end, the errors are unavoidable which spring from the improper employment of the methods which are originated by reason but which are out of place in this sphere.

Section I: The Discipline of Pure Reason in its Dogmatic Use

Mathematics presents the most splendid example of the extension of the sphere of pure reason without the aid of experience. Examples are always contagious; and they exert an especial influence on the same faculty, which naturally flatters itself that it will have the same good fortune in other case as fell to its lot in one fortunate instance. Hence pure reason hopes to be able to extend its empire in the transcendental sphere with equal success and security, especially when it applies the same method which was attended with such results in the science of mathematics. It is, therefore, of the highest importance for us to know, whether the method of arriving at demonstrative certainty, which is termed *mathematical*, be identical with that by which we endeavour to attain the same degree of certainty in philosophy, and which is termed in that science *dogmatical*.

Philosophical knowledge is the *knowledge* of *reason* by means of concepts; mathematical knowledge is knowledge by means of the *construction* of concepts. The *construction* of a concept is the presentation *a priori* of the intuition which corresponds to the concept. For this purpose a *non-empirical* intuition is requisite, which, as an intuition, is an *individual* object; while, as the construction of a concept (a general representation), it must be seen to be universally valid for all the possible intuitions which rank under that concept. Thus I construct a triangle, by the presentation of the object which corresponds to this concept, either by mere imagination, in pure intuition; or upon paper, in empirical intuition – in both cases completely *a priori*, without borrowing the type of that figure from any experience. The individual figure drawn upon paper is empirical; but it serves, notwithstanding, to indicate the concept, even in its universality, because in this empirical intuition we keep our eye merely on the act of the construction of the concept, and pay no attention to the various modes of determining it, for example, its size, the length of its sides, the size of its angles, these not in the least affecting the essential character of the concept.

Philosophical knowledge, accordingly, regards the particular only in the general; mathematical the general in the particular, nay, in the individual. This is done, however, entirely *a priori* and by means of pure reason, so that, as this individual figure is determined under certain universal conditions of construction, the object of the concept, to which this individual figure corresponds as its schema, must be thought as universally determined.

The essential difference of these two modes of knowledge consists, therefore, in this formal quality; it does not regard the difference of the matter or objects of both. Those thinkers who aim at distinguishing philosophy from mathematics by asserting that the former has to do with *quality* merely, and the latter with *quantity*, have mistaken the effect for the cause. The reason why mathematical knowledge can relate only to quantity, is to be found in its form alone. For it is the concept of quantities only that is capable of being constructed, that is, presented *a priori* in intuition; while qualities cannot be given in any other than an empirical intuition. Hence the knowledge of qualities by reason is possible only through concepts. No one can find an intuition which shall correspond to the concept of reality, except in experience; it cannot be presented to the mind *a priori* and antecedently to the empirical consciousness of a reality. We can form an intuition, by means of the mere concept of it, of a cone, without the aid of experience; but the colour of the cone we cannot know except from experience. I cannot present an intuition of a cause, except in an example, which experience offers to me. Besides, philosophy, as well as mathematics, treats of quantities; as, for example, of totality, infinity, and so on. Mathematics, too, treats of the difference of lines and surfaces – as spaces of different quality, of the continuity of extension – as a quality thereof. But, although in such cases they have a common object, the mode in which reason considers that object is very different in philosophy from what it is in mathematics. The former confines itself to the general concepts; the latter can do nothing with a mere concept, it hastens to intuition. In this intuition it regards the concept *in concreto*, not empirically, but in an *a priori* intuition, which it has constructed; and in which, all the results which follow from the general conditions of the construction of the concept, are in all cases valid for the object of the constructed concept.

Suppose that the concept of a triangle is given to a philosopher, and that he is required to discover, by the philosophical method, what relation the sum of its angles bears to a right angle. He has nothing before him but the concept of a figure enclosed within three straight lines, and, consequently, with the same number of angles. He may analyse the concept of a straight line, of an angle or of the number three as long as he pleases, but he will not discover any properties not contained in these concepts. But, if this question is proposed to a geometrician, he at once begins by constructing a triangle. He knows that two right angles are equal to the sum of all the contiguous angles which proceed from one point in a straight line; and he goes on to produce one side of his triangle, thus forming two adjacent angles which are together equal to two right angles. He then divides the exterior of these angles, by drawing a line parallel with the opposite idea of the triangle, and immediately perceives that he had thus got an exterior adjacent angle which is equal to the interior. Proceeding in this way, through a chain of inferences, and always on the ground of intuition, he arrives at a clear and universally valid solution of the question.

But mathematics does not confine itself to the construction of quantities (*quanta*), as in the case of geometry; it occupies itself with pure quantity also (*quantitas*), as in the case of algebra, where complete abstraction is made of the properties of the object indicated by the concept of quantity. In algebra, a certain method of notation by signs is adopted, and these indicate the different possible constructions of quantities, the extraction of roots, and so on. After having this denoted the general concept of quantities, according to their different relations, the different operations by which quantity or number is increased or diminished are presented in intuition in accordance with general rules. Thus, when one quantity is to be divided by another, the signs which denote both are placed in the form peculiar to the operation of division; and thus algebra, by means of a symbolical construction of quantity, just as geometry, with its ostensive or geometrical construction (a construction of the objects themselves), arrives at results which discursive knowledge cannot hope to reach by the aid of mere concepts.

Now, what is the cause of this difference in the fortune of the philosopher and the mathematician, the former of whom follows the path of concepts, while the latter pursues that of intuitions, which he represents, *a priori*, in correspondence with his concepts? The cause is evident from what has been already presented in our fundamental transcendental doctrines. We do not, in the present case, want to discover analytical propositions, which may be produced merely by analysing our concepts – for in this the philosopher would have the advantage over his rival; we aim at the discovery of synthetical propositions – such synthetical propositions, moreover, as can be known *a priori*. I must not confine myself to that which I actually think in my concept of a triangle, for this is nothing more than the mere definition; I must try to go beyond that, and to arrive at properties which are not contained in, although they belong to, the concept. Now, this is impossible, unless I determine the object present according to the conditions, either of empirical, or of pure intuition. In the former case, I should have an empirical proposition (arrived at by actual measurement of the angles of the triangle), which would possess neither universality nor necessity; but that would be of no value. In the latter, I proceed by geometrical construction, by means of which I collect, in a pure intuition, just as I would in an empirical intuition, all the various properties which belong to the schema of a triangle in general, and consequently to its concept, and thus construct synthetical propositions which possess the attribute of universality.

It would be vain to philosophize upon the triangle, that is, to reflect on it discursively; I should get no further than the definition with which I had been obliged to set out. There are certainly transcendental synthetical propositions which are framed by means of pure concepts, and which form the peculiar distinction of philosophy; but these do not relate to any particular thing, but to a thing in general, and enounce the conditions under which the perception of it may become a part of possible experience. But the science of mathematics has nothing to do with such questions, nor with the question of existence in any fashion; it is concerned merely with the properties of objects in themselves, only in so far as these are connected with the concepts of the objects.

In the above example, we have merely attempted to show the great difference which exists between the discursive employment of reason in the sphere of concepts, and its intuitive exercise by means of the construction of concepts. The question naturally arises — What is the cause which necessitates this twofold exercise of reason, and how are we to discover whether it is the philosophical or the mathematical method which reason is pursuing in an argument?

All our knowledge relates, finally, to possible intuitions, for it is these alone that present objects. An *a priori* or non-empirical concept contains either a pure intuition — and in this case it can be constructed; or it contains nothing but the synthesis of possible intuitions, which are not given *a priori*. In this latter case, it may help us to form synthetical *a priori* judgments, but only in the discursive method, by concepts, not in the intuitive, by means of the construction of concepts.

The only *a priori* intuition is that of the pure form of appearance

– space and time. A concept of space and time as *quanta* may be presented *a priori* in intuition, that is, constructed, either alone with their quality (figure), or as pure quantity (the mere synthesis of the homogeneous), by means of number. But the matter of appearance, by which *things* are given in space and time, can be presented only in perception, *a posteriori*. The only concept which represents *a priori* this empirical content of appearances, is the concept of a *thing* in general; and the *a priori* synthetical knowledge of this concept can give us nothing more than the rule for the synthesis of that which may be contained in the corresponding *a posteriori* perception; it is utterly inadequate to present an *a priori* intuition of the real object, which must necessarily be empirical.

Synthetical propositions, which relate to *things* in general, an *a priori* intuition of which is impossible, are transcendental. For this reason transcendental propositions cannot be framed by means of the construction of concepts, they are *a priori*, and based entirely on concepts themselves. They contain merely the rule, by which we are to seek in the world of perception or experience the synthetical unity of that which cannot be intuited *a priori*. But they are incompetent to present any of the concepts which appear in them in an *a priori* intuition; these can be given only *a posteriori*, in experience, which, however, is itself possible only through these synthetical principles.

If we are to form a synthetical judgment regarding a concept, we must go beyond it, to the intuition in which it is given. If we keep to what is contained in the concept, the judgment is merely analytical – it is merely an explanation of what we have thought in the concept. But I can pass from the concept to the pure or empirical intuition which corresponds to it. I can proceed to examine my concept *in concreto*, and to know, either *a priori* or *a posteriori*, what I find in the object of the concept. The former – *a priori* knowledge – is rational and mathematical knowledge by means of the construction of the concept; the latter – *a posteriori* knowledge – is purely empirical knowledge, which can never supply necessary and apodeictic propositions. Thus I may analyse the concept I have of gold; but I gain no new information from this analysis. I merely enumerate the different properties which I had connected with the notion indicated by the word. My knowledge has gained in logical clearness and arrangement, but no addition has been made to it. But if I take the matter which is indicated by this name, and submit it to the examintion of my senses, I am enabled to form several synthetical – although still empirical – propositions. The mathematical concept of a triangle I should construct, that is, present *a priori* in intuition, and in this way attain to rational but synthetical knowledge. But when the transcendental concept of reality, or substance, or power is presented, I find that it does not indicate either an empirical or pure intuition, but that it indicates merely the synthesis of empirical intuitions, which cannot of course be given *a priori*. The synthesis in such a concept cannot proceed *a priori* – without the aid of experience – to the intuition which corresponds to the concept; and, for this reason, none of these concepts can produce a determinative synthetical proposition, they can never present more than a principle of the synthesis[1] of possible empirical intuitions. A transcendental proposition is, therefore, a synthetical knowledge of reason by means of pure concepts, and the discursive method, and it renders possible all synthetical unity in empirical knowledge, though it cannot present us with any intuition *a priori*.

There is thus a twofold exercise of reason. Both modes have the properties of universality and an *a priori* origin in common, but are, in their procedure, of widely different character. The reason of this is, that in the world of appearances, in which alone objects are presented, there are two main elements: the form of intuition (space and time), which can be known and determined completely *a priori*; and the matter or content – that which is presented in space and time, and which, consequently, contains a something – an existence corresponding to our powers of sensation. As regards the latter, which can never be given in a determinate mode except by experience, there are no *a priori* notions which relate to it, except the undetermined concepts of the synthesis of possible sensations, in so far as these belong (in a possible experience) to the unity of consciousness. As regards the former, we can determine our concepts *a priori* in intuition, inasmuch as we are ourselves the creators of the objects of the concepts in space and time – these objects being regarded simply as *quanta*. In the one case, reason

---

[1] In the case of the concept of cause, I do really go beyond the empirical concept of an event – but not to the intuition which presents this concept *in concreto*, but only to the time-conditions, which may be found in experience to correspond to the concept. My procedure is, therefore, strictly according to concepts; I cannot in a case of this kind employ the construction of concepts, because the concept is merely a rule for the synthesis of perceptions, which are not pure intuitions, and which, therefore, cannot be given *a priori*.

proceeds according to concepts, and can do nothing more than subject appearances to these – which can only be determined empirically, that is, *a posteriori* – in conformity, however, with those concepts as the rules of all empirical synthesis. In the other case, reason proceeds by the construction of concepts; and, as these concepts relation to an *a priori* intuition, they may be given and determined in pure intuition *a priori*, and without the aid of empirical data. The examination and consideration of everything that exists in space or time – whether it is a quantum or not, in how far the particular something (which fills space or time) is a primary substratum, or a mere determination of some other exist-ence, whether it relates to anything else – either as cause or effect, whether its existence is isolated or in reciprocal connection with and dependence upon others, the possibility of this existence, its reality and necessity or their opposites – all these form part of the *knowledge of reason* on the ground of concepts, and this knowledge is termed *philosophical*. But to determine *a priori* an intuition in space (its figure), to divide time into periods, or merely to know the quantity of an intuition in space and time, and to determine it by number – all this is an *operation of reason* by means of the construction of concepts, and is called *mathematical*.

The success which attends the efforts of reason in the sphere of mathematics, naturally fosters the expectation that the same good fortune will be its lot, if it applies the mathematical method in other regions of mental endeavour besides that of quantities. Its success is thus great, because it can support all its concepts by *a priori* intuitions, and in this way, make itself a master, as it were, over nature; while pure philosophy, with its *a priori* discursive concepts, bungles about in the world of nature, and cannot accredit or show any *a priori* evidence of the reality of these concepts. Masters in the science of mathematics are confident of the success of this method; indeed, it is a common persuasion, that it is capable of being applied to any subject of human thought. They have hardly ever reflected on their favourite science – a task of great difficulty – and the specific difference between the two modes of employing the faculty of reason has never entered their thoughts. Rules current in the field of common experience, and which common sense stamps every-where with its approval, are regarded by them as axiomatic. From what source the concepts of space and time, with which (as the only primitive quanta) they have to deal, enter their minds, is a question which they do not trouble themselves to answer; and they think it just as unnecessary to examine into the origin of the pure concepts of the understanding and the extent of their validity. All they have to do with them is to employ them. In all this they are perfectly right, if they do not overstep the limits of the sphere of *nature*. But they pass, unconsciously, from the world of sense, to the insecure ground of pure transcendental concepts (*instabilis tellus, innabilis unda*), where they can neither stand nor swim, and where the tracks of their footsteps are obliterated by time; while the march of mathematics is pursued on a broad and magnificent highway, which the latest posterity shall frequent without fear of danger or impediment.

As we have taken upon us the task of determining, clearly and certainly, the limits of pure reason in the sphere of transcendentalism, and as the efforts of reason in this direction are persisted in, even after the plainest and most expressive warnings, hope still beckoning us past the limits of experience into the splendours of the intellectual world – it becomes necessary to cut away the last anchor of this fallacious and fantastic hope. We shall accordingly show that the mathematical method is unattended in the sphere of philosophy by the least advantage – except, perhaps, that it more plainly exhibits its own inadequacy – that geometry and philosophy are two quite different things, although they go hand in hand in the field of natural science, and, consequently, that the procedure of the one can never be imitated by the other.

The evidence of mathematics rests upon definitions, axioms, and demonstrations. I shall be satisfied with showing that none of these forms can be employed or imitated in philosophy in the sense in which they are understood by mathematicians; and that the geometrician, if he employs his method in philosophy, will succeed only in building card-castles, while the employment of the philosophical method in mathematics can result in nothing but mere verbiage. The essential business of philosophy, indeed, is to mark out the limits of the science; and even the mathematician, unless his talent is naturally circumscribed and limited to this particular department of knowledge, cannot turn a deaf ear to the warnings of philosophy, or set himself above its direction.

I. *Definitions.* A *definition* is, as the term itself indicates, the representation, upon primary grounds, of the complete concept of a thing within its own limits.[1] Accordingly, an *empirical* concept

---

[1] The definition must describe the concept *completely*, that is, omit none of the marks of which it is composed; *within its own limits*, that is, it must be precise, and enumerate no

cannot be defined, it can only be *explicated*. For, as there are in such a concept only a certain number of marks or signs, which denote a certain class of sensible objects, we can ever be sure that we do not think under the word which indicates the same object, at one time a greater, at another a smaller number of signs. Thus, one person may think in his concept of gold, in addition to its properties of weight, colour, malleability, that of resisting rust, while another person may be ignorant of this quality. We employ certain signs only so long as we require them for the sake of distinction; new observations abstract some and add new ones, so that an empirical concept never remains within permanent limits. It is, in fact, useless to define a concept of this kind. If, for example, we are speaking of water and its properties, we do not stop at what we actually think by the word *water*, but proceed to observation and experiment; and the word, with the few signs attached to it, is more properly a *designation* than a concept of the thing. A definition in this case would evidently be nothing more than a determination of the word. In the second place, no *a priori* concept, such as those of substance, cause, right, fairness, and so on, can be defined. For I can never be sure, that the clear representation of a given concept (which is given in a confused state) has been fully developed, until I know that the representation is adequate with its object. But, inasmuch as the concept, as it is given, may contain a number of obscure representations, which we do not observe in our analysis, although we employ them in our application of the concept, I can never be sure that my analysis is complete, while examples may make this probable, although they can never demonstrate the fact. Instead of the word *definition*, I should rather employ the term *exposition* – a more modest expression, which the critic may accept without surrendering his doubts as to the completeness of the analysis of any such concepts. As, therefore, neither empirical nor *a priori* concepts are capable of definition, we have to see whether the only other kind of concepts – arbitrary concepts – can be subjected to this mental operation. Such an arbitrarily thought concept can always be defined; for I must know thoroughly what I wished to think in it, as it was I who created it, and it was not given to me either by the nature of my understanding or by experience.

more signs than belong to the concept; and *on primary grounds*, that is to say, the limitation of the bounds of the concept must not be derived from other concepts, as in this case a proof would be necessary, and the so-called definition would be incapable of taking its place at the head of all the judgments we have to form regarding an object.

At the same time, I cannot say that, by such a definition, I have defined a real object. If the concept is based upon empirical conditions, if, for example, I have a concept of a clock for a ship, this arbitrary concept does not assure me of the existence or even of the possibility of the object. My definition of such a concept would with more propriety be termed a declaration of a project than a definition of an object. There are no further concepts which can bear definition, except those which contain an arbitrary synthesis, which can be constructed *a priori*. Consequently, the science of mathematics alone posseses definitions. For the object here thought is presented *a priori* in intuition ; and thus it can never contain more or less than the concept, because the concept of the object has been given by the definition – and primarily, that is, without deriving the definition from any other source. Philosophical definitions are, therefore, merely expositions of given concepts, while mathematical definitions are constructions of concepts originally formed ; the former are produced by analysis, the completeness of which is never demonstratively certain, the latter by a synthesis. In a mathematical definition the concept is *formed*, in a philosophical definition it is only *explained*. From this it follows :

(*a*) That we must not imitate, in philosophy, the mathemtical usage of commencing with definitions – except by way of hypothesis or experiment. For, as all so-called philosophical definitions are merely analyses of given concepts, these concepts, although only in a confused form, must precede the analysis ; and the incomplete exposition must precede the complete, so that we may be able to draw certain inferences from the characteristics which an incomplete analysis has enabled us to discover, before we attain to the complete exposition or definition of the concept. In one word, a full and clear definition ought, in philosophy, rather to form the conclusion than the commencement of our labours.[1] In mathematics, on the contrary, we cannot have a concept prior to the definition ; it is the definition which gives us the concept, and it

---

[1] Philosophy abounds in faulty definitions, especially such as contain some of the elements requisite to form a complete definition. If a concept could not be employed in reasoning before it had been defined, it would fare ill with all philosophical thought. But, as incompletely defined concepts may always be employed without detriment to truth, so far as our analysis of the elements contained in them proceeds, imperfect definitions, that is, propositions which are properly not definitions, but merely approximations thereto, may be used with great advantage. In mathematics, definition belongs *ad esse*, in philosophy *ad melius esse*. It is a difficult task to construct a proper definition. Jurists are still without a complete definition of the concept of right.

must for this reason form the commencement of every chain of mathematical reasoning.

(b) Mathematical definitions cannot be erroneous. For the concept is given only in and through the definition, and thus it contains only what has been thought in the definition. But although a definition cannot be incorrect, as regards its content, an error may sometimes, although seldom, creep into the form. This error consists in a want of precision. Thus the common definition of a circle – that is a curved line, every point in which is equally distant from another point called the centre – is faulty, from the fact that the determination indicated by the word *curved* is superfluous. For there ought to be a particular theorem, which may be easily proved from the definition, to the effect that every line, which has all its points at equal distances from another point, must be a curved line – that is, that not even the smallest part of it can be straight. Analytical definitions, on the other hand, may be erroneous in many respects, either by the introduction of signs which do not actually exist in the concept, or by wanting in that completeness which forms the essential of a definition. The latter case arises because we can never be fully certain of the completeness of our analysis. For these reasons, the method of definition employed in mathematics cannot be imitated in philosophy.

2. *Axioms*. These, in so far as they are immediately certain, are *a priori* synthetical principles. Now, one concept cannot be connected synthetically and yet immediately with another; because if we wish to proceed beyond a concept, a third mediating knowledge is necessary. And, as philosophy is a knowledge of reason by the aid of concepts alone, there is to be found in it no principle which deserves to be called an axiom. Mathematics, on the other hand, may possess axioms, because it can always connect the predicates of an object *a priori*, and without any mediating term, by means of the construction of concepts in intuition. Such is the case with the proposition: Three points can always lie in a plane. On the other hand, no synthetical principle which is based upon concepts, can ever be immediately certain (for example, the proposition: Everything that happens has a cause), because I require a mediating term to connect the two concepts of event and cause – namely, the condition of time-determination in an experience – and I cannot know any such principle immediately and from concept alone. Discursive principles are, accordingly, very different from intuitive principles or axioms. The former always require deduction, which

in the case of the latter may be altogether dispensed with. Axioms are, for this reason, always self-evident, while philosophical principles, whatever may be the degree of certainty they possess, cannot lay any claim to such a distinction. No synthetical proposition of pure transcendental reason can be so evident, as is often rashly enough declared, as the statement, *twice two are four*. It is true that in the Analytic I introduced into the list of principles of the pure understanding, certain axioms of intuition; but the principle there discussed was not itself an axiom, but served merely to present the principle of the possibility of axioms in general, while it was really nothing more than a principle based upon concepts. For it is one part of the duty of transcendental philosophy to establish the possibility of mathematics itself. Philosophy possesses, then, no axioms, and has no right to impose its *a priori* principles upon thought, until it has established their authority by a thorough-going deduction.

3. *Demonstrations*. Only an apodeictic proof, based upon intuition, can be termed a demonstration. Experience teaches us what is, but it cannot convince us that it might have been otherwise. Hence a proof upon empirical grounds cannot be apodeictic. *A priori* concepts, in discursive knowledge, can never produce intuitive certainty, i.e. self-evidence, however certain the judgment they present may be. Mathematics alone, therefore, contains demonstrations, because it does not derive its knowledge from concepts, but from the construction of concepts, that is, from intuition, which can be given *a priori* in accordance with concepts. The method of algebra, in equations, from which the correct answer is derived by reduction, is a kind of construction – not geometrical, but by symbols – in which all concepts, especially those of the relations of quantities, are represented in intuition by signs; and thus the conclusions in that science are secured from errors by the fact that every proof is submitted to ocular evidence. Philosophical knowledge does not possess this advantage, it being required to consider the general always *in abstracto* (by means of concepts), while mathematics can always consider it *in concreto* (in an individual intuition), and at the same time by means of *a priori* representation, whereby all errors are rendered manifest to the senses. The former – discursive proofs – ought to be termed *acroamatic proofs*, rather than *demonstrations*, as only words are employed in them, while demonstrations proper, as the term itself indicates, always require a reference to the intuition of the object.

It follows from all these considerations, that it is not consonant with the nature of philosophy, especially in the sphere of pure reason, to employ the dogmatical method, and to adorn itself with the titles and insignia of mathematical science. It does not belong to that order, and can only hope for a fraternal union with that science. Its attempts at mathematical evidence are vain pretensions, which can only keep it back from its true aim, which is to detect the illusory procedure of reason when transgressing is proper limits, and by sufficiently elucidating our concepts, to conduct us from the dim regions of speculation, to the clear region of modest self-knowledge. Reason must not, therefore, in its transcendental endeavours, look forward with such confidence, as if the path it is pursuing led straight to its aim, nor reckon with such security upon its premisses, as to consider it unnecessary to take a step back, or to keep a strict watch for errors, which, overlooked in the principles, may be detected in the arguments themselves – in which case it may be requisite either to determine these principles with greater strictness, or to change them entirely.

I divide all apodeictic propositions, whether demonstrable or immediately certain, into – dogmata and *mathemata*. A direct synthetical proposition, based on concepts, is a *dogma*; a proposition of the same kind, based on the construction of concepts, is a *mathema*. Analytical judgments do not teach us any more about an object than what was contained in the concept we had of it; because they do not extend our knowledge beyond our concept of an object, they merely elucidate the concept. They cannot therefore be with propriety termed dogmas. Of the two kinds of *a priori* synthetical propositions above mentioned, only those which are employed in philosophy can, according to the general mode of speech, bear this name; those of arithmetic or geometry would not be rightly so denominated. Thus the customary mode of speaking confirms the explanation given above, and the conclusion arrived at, that only those judgments which are based upon concepts, not on the construction of concepts, can be termed dogmatical.

Thus, pure reason, in the sphere of speculation, does not contain a single direct synthetical judgment based upon concepts. By means of ideas, it is, as we have shown, incapable of producing synthetical judgments, which are objectively valid; by means of the concepts of the understanding, it establishes certain indubitable principles, not, however, directly on the basis of concepts, but only indirectly by means of the relation of these concepts to something of a purely contingent nature, namely, possible experience. When experience is presupposed, these principles are apodeictically certain, but in themselves, and directly, they cannot even be known *a priori*. Thus the given concepts of *cause* and *event* will not be sufficient for the demonstration of the proposition: Every event has a cause. For this reason, it is not a dogma; although from another point of view, that of experience, it is capable of being proved to demonstration. The proper term for such a proposition is *principle*, and not *theorem* (although it does require to be proved), because it possesses the remarkable peculiarity of being the condition of the possibility of its own ground of proof, that is, experience, and of forming a necessary presupposition in all empirical observation.

If then, in the speculative sphere of pure reason, no dogmata are to be found; all *dogmatical* methods, whether borrowed from mathematics, or invented by philosophical thinkers, are alike improper. They only serve to conceal errors and fallacies, and to deceive philosophy, whose duty it is to see that reason pursues a safe and straight path. A philosophical method may, however, be *systematical*. For our reason is, subjectively considered, itself a system, and, in the sphere of mere concepts, a system of investigation according to principles of unity, the material being supplied by experience alone. But this is not the proper place for discussing the peculiar method of transcendental philosophy, as our present task is simply to examine whether our faculties are capable of erecting an edifice on the basis of pure reason, and how far they may proceed with the materials at their command.

Section II: The Dicipline of Pure Reason in its Polemical Use

Reason must subject itself, in all its undertakings, to criticism, and cannot limit the freedom of such criticism by prohibitions, without harming itself and incurring a damaging suspicion. There is nothing, however useful, however sacred it may be, that can claim exemption from the searching examination of this supreme tribunal, which has no respect of persons. The very existence of reason depends upon this freedom; for the voice of reason is not that of a dictatorial and despotic power, it is rather like the vote of the citizens of a free state, every member of which must have the privilege of giving free expression to his doubts, and possess even the right of *veto*.

But while reason can never decline to submit itself to the tribunal of criticism, it does not always have cause to fear it. Pure reason, however, in its dogmatic use, is not so thoroughly conscious of a strict observance of its highest laws, as to appear before a higher judicial reason with perfect confidence ready to renounce its dogmatical pretensions.

Very different is the case, when it has to defend itself, not before a judge, but against an equal. If dogmatical assertions are advanced on the negative side, in opposition to those made by reason on the positive side, its justification κατ' ἄνθρωπον is complete, although the proof of its propositions is κατ' ἀλήθειαν unsatisfactory.

By the polemic of pure reason I mean the defence of its propositions made by reason, in opposition to the dogmatical counter-claims. The question here is not whether its own statements may not also be false; it merely regards the fact that reason proves that the opposite cannot be established with demonstrative certainty, nor even asserted with a higher degree of plausability. Reason does not hold its possessions upon sufferance; for, although it cannot show a perfectly satisfactory title to them, no one can prove that it is *not* the rightful possessor.

It is a grievous and depressing reflection, that reason, in its highest exercise, falls into an antithetic; and that the supreme tribunal for the settlement of differences should not be at union with itself. It is true that we had to discuss the question of an apparent antithetic, but we found that it was based upon a misconception. In conformity with the common prejudice, appearances were regarded as things in themselves, and thus an absolute completeness in their synthesis was required in the one mode or in the other (it was shown to be impossible in both); a demand entirely out of place in regard to appearances. There was, then, no real contradiction of reason in the propositions – The series of appearances *given in themselves* has an absolutely first beginning, and, This series is absolutely and *in itself* without beginning. The two propositions are perfectly consistent with each other, because appearances as appearances are *in themselves* nothing, and consequently the hypothesis that they are things in themselves, must lead to self-contradictory inferences.

But there are cases in which a similar misunderstanding cannot be provided against, and the dispute must remain unsettled. Take, for example, the theistic proposition: There is a Supreme Being; and on the other hand, the atheistic counter-statement: There exists no Supreme Being; or, in psychology: Everything that thinks, possesses the attribute of absolute and permanent unity, which is utterly different from the transitory unity of material appearance; and the counter-proposition: The soul is not an immaterial unity, and its nature is transitory, like that of appearances. The objects of these questions contain no foreign elements contradicting the object in question, for they relate to *things in themselves*, and not to appearances. There would arise, indeed, a real conflict, if reason came forward with a statement on the negative side of these questions alone. As regards the criticism to which the grounds of proof on the affirmative side must be subjected, it may be freely admitted, without necessitating the surrender of the affirmative propositions, which have, at least, the interest of reason in their favour – an advantage which the opposite party cannot lay claim to.

I cannot agree with the opinion of several admirable thinkers – Sulzer, for example – that in spite of the weakness of the arguments hitherto in use, we may hope, one day, to see sufficient demonstrations of the two cardinal propositions of pure reason – the existence of a Supreme Being, and the immortality of the soul. I am certain, on the contrary, that this will never be the case. For on what ground can reason base such synthetical propositions, which do not relate to the objects of experience and their internal possibility, let alone assert dogmatically? – But it is also demonstratively certain that no one will ever be able to maintain the contrary with the least show of plausibility. For, as he can attempt such a proof solely upon the basis of pure reason, he is bound to prove that a Supreme Being, and a thinking subject in the character of a pure inteligence, are *impossible*. But where will he find the knowledge which can enable him to enounce synthetical judgments in regard to things which transcend the region of experience? We may, therefore, rest assured that the opposite never will be demonstrated. We need not, then, have recourse to scholastic arguments; we may always admit the truth of those propositions which are consistent with the speculative interests of reason in the sphere of experience, and form, moreover, the only means of uniting the speculative with the practical interest. Our opponent, who must not be considered here as a critic solely, we can be ready to meet with a *non liquet* which cannot fail to disconcert him; while we cannot deny his right to a similar retort, as we have on our side the advantage of the support of the subjective maxim of reason, and can therefore look upon all his sophistical arguments with calm indifference.

From this point of view, there is properly no antithetic of pure reason. For the only arena for such a struggle would be upon the field of pure theology and psychology; but on this ground there can appear no combatant whom we need to fear. Ridicule and boasting can be his only weapons; and these may be laughed at as mere child's play. This consideration restores to reason its courage; for what source of confidence could be found, if it, whose vocation it is to destroy error, were at variance with itself and without any reasonable hope of ever reaching a state of permanent repose?

Everything in nature is good for some purpose. Even poisons are serviceable; they destroy the evil effects of other poisons generated in our system, and must always find a place in every complete pharmacopoeia. The objections raised against the fallacies and sophistries of speculative reason, are objections given by the nature of this reason itself, and must therefore have a destination and purpose which can only be for the good of humanity. For what purpose has providence raised many objects, in which we have the deepest interest, so far above us, that we vainly try to know them with certainty, and our powers are rather excited than satisfied by the glimpses we may chance to seize? It is very doubtful whether it is for our benefit to advance bold affirmations regarding subjects involved in such obscurity; perhaps it would even be detrimental to our best interests. But it is undoubtedly always beneficial to leave the investigating, as well as the critical reason, in perfect freedom, and permit it to take charge of its own interests, which are advanced as much by its limitation, as by its extension of its views, and which always suffer by the interference of foreign powers forcing it, against its natural tendencies, to bend to certain preconceived designs.

Allow your opponent to say what he thinks reasonable, and combat him only with the weapons of reason. Have no anxiety for the practical interests of humanity – these are never imperilled in a purely speculative dispute. Such a dispute serves merely to disclose the antinomy of reason, which, as it had its source in the nature of reason, ought to be thoroughly investigated. Reason is benefited by the examination of a subject on both sides, and its judgments are corrected by being limited. It is not the *latter* that may give occasion to dispute, but the *manner*. For it is perfectly permissible to employ, in the presence of reason, the language of a firmly-rooted *faith*, even after we have been obliged to renounce all pretensions to *knowledge*.

[A743/B771]

If we were to ask the dispassionate *David Hume* – a philosopher endowed, in a degree that few are, with a well-balanced judgment: What motive induced you to spend so much labour and thought in undermining the consoling and beneficial persuasion that reason is capable of assuring us of the existence, and presenting us with a determinate concept of a Supreme Being? – his answer would be: Nothing but the desire of teaching reason to know its own powers better, and, at the same time, a dislike of the procedure by which that faculty was compelled to support foregone conclusions, and prevented from confessing the internal weaknesses which it cannot but feel when it enters upon a rigid self-examination. If, on the other hand, we were to ask *Priestley* – a philosopher who had no taste for transcendental speculation, but was entirely devoted to the principles of *empiricism* – what his motives were for overturning those two main pillars of religion – the doctrines of the freedom of the will and the immortality of the soul (in his view the hope of a future life is but the expectation of the miracle of resurrection) – this philosopher, himself a zealous and pious teacher of religion, could give no other answer than this: I acted in the interest of reason, which always suffers, when certain objects are explained and judged by a reference to other supposed laws than those of material nature – the only laws which we know in a determinate manner. It would be unfair to decry the latter philosopher, who endeavoured to harmonize his paradoxical opinions with the interests of religion, and to undervalue an honest and reflecting man, because he finds himself at a loss the moment he has left the field of natural science. The same grace must be accorded to Hume, a man not less well-disposed, and quite as blameless in his moral character, and who pushed his abstract speculations to an extreme length, because, as he rightly believed, the object of them lies entirely beyond the bounds of natural science, and within the sphere of pure ideas.

What is to be done to provide against the danger which seems in the present case to menace the best interest of humanity? The course to be pursued in reference to this subject is a perfectly plain and natural one. Let each thinker pursue his own path; if he shows talent, if he gives evidence of profound thought, in one word, if he shows that he possesses the power of reasoning – reason is always the gainer. If you have recourse to other means, if you attempt to coerce reason, if you raise the cry of treason to humanity if you excite the feelings of the crowd, which can neither understand nor sympathize with such subtle speculations – you will only make yourself ridiculous. For the question does not concern the advantage or disadvantage which we are now expected to reap from such inquiries; the question is merely, how far reason can advance in the field of speculation, apart from all kinds of interest, and whether we may depend upon the exertions of speculative reason, or must renounce all reliance on it. Instead of joining the combatants, it is your part to be a tranquil spectator of the struggle – a laborious struggle for the parties engaged, but attended, in its progress as well as in its result, with the most advantageous consequences for the interests of thought and knowledge. It is absurd to expect to be enlightened by reason, and at the same time to prescribe to it what side of the question it must adopt. Moreover, reason is sufficiently held in check by its own power, the limits imposed on it by it own nature are sufficient; it is unnecessary for you to place over it additional guards, as if its power were dangerous to the constitution of the intellectual state. In the dialectic of reason there is no victory gained, which need in the least disturb your tranquillity.

The strife of dialectic is a necessity of reason, and we cannot but wish that it had been conducted long before this with that perfect freedom which ought to be its essential condition. In this case, we should have had at an earlier period a matured and profound criticism, which must have put an end to all dialectical disputes, by exposing the illusions and prejudices in which they originated.

There is in human nature an unworthy propensity – a propensity which, like everything that springs from nature, must in its final purpose be conducive to the good of humanity – to conceal our real sentiments, and to give expression only to certain received opinions, which are regarded as at once safe and promotive of the common good. It is true, this tendency, not only to conceal our real sentiments, but to profess those which may gain us favour in the eyes of society, has not only *civilized*, but, in a certain measure, *moralized* us; as no one can break through the outward covering of respectability, honour, and modesty, and thus the seemingly-good examples which we see around us, form an excellent school for moral improvement, so long as our belief in their genuineness remains unshaken. But this disposition to represent ourselves as better than we are, and to utter opinions which are not our own, can be nothing more than a kind of *provisionary* arrangement of nature to lead us from the rudeness of an uncivilized state, and to teach us how to assume at least the appearance and *manner*, of the good we see. But when true principles have been developed, and have obtained a sure foundation in our habit of thought, this conventionalism must be attacked with earnest vigour, otherwise it corrupts the heart, and checks the growth of good dispositions with the mischevious weed of fair appearances.

I am sorry to remark the same tendency to misrepresentation and hypocrisy in the sphere of speculative discussion, where there is less temptation to restrain the free expression of thought. For what can be more prejudicial to the interests of intelligence, than to falsify our real sentiments, to conceal the doubts which we feel in regard to our statements, or to maintain the validity of grounds of proof which we well know to be insufficient? So long as mere personal vanity is the source of these unworthy artifices – and this is generally the case in speculative discussions, which are mostly destitute of practical interest, and are incapable of complete demonstration – the vanity of the opposite party exaggerates as much on the other side; and thus the result is the same, although it is not brought about so soon as if the dispute had been conducted in a sincere and upright spirit. But where the mass entertains the notion that the aim of certain subtle speculators is nothing less than to shake the very foundations of public welfare and morality – it seems not only prudent, but even praiseworthy, to maintain the good cause by illusory arguments, rather than to give to our supposed opponents the advantage of lowering our declarations to the moderate tone of a merely practical coviction, and of compelling us to confess our inability to attain to apodeictic certainty in speculative subjects. But we ought to reflect that there is nothing in the world more fatal to the maintenance of a good cause than deceit, misrepresentation, and falsehood. That the strictest laws of honesty should be observed in the discussion of a purely speculative subject, is the least requirement that can be made. If we could reckon with security even upon so little, the conflict of speculative reason regarding the imporant questions of God, immortality, and freedom, would have been either decided long go, or would very soon be brought to a conclusion. But, in general, the uprightness of the defence stands in an inverse ratio to the goodness of the cause; and perhaps more honesty and fairness are shown by those who deny, then by those who uphold these doctrines.

I shall persuade myself, then, that I have readers who do not wish to see a righteous cause defended by unfair arguments. Such will not recognize the fact that, according to the principles of this

Critique, if we consider not what is, but what ought to be the case, there can be really no polemic of pure reason. For how can two persons dispute about a thing, the reality of which neither can present in actual or even in possible experience? Each adopts the plan of meditating on his idea for the purpose of drawing from the idea, if he can, what is *more than the idea*, that is, the reality of the object which it indicates. How shall they settle the dispute, since neither is able to make his assertions directly comprehensible and certain, but must restrict himself to attacking and confuting those of his opponent? All statements enounced by pure reason transcend the conditions of possible experience, beyond the sphere of which we can discover no criterion of truth, while they are at the same time framed in accordance with the laws of the understanding, which are applicable only to experience; and thus it is the fate of all such speculative discussions, that while the one party attacks the weaker idea of his opponent, he infallibly lays open his own weaknesses.

The critique of pure reason may be regarded as the highest tribunal for all speculative disputes; for it is not involved in these disputes, which have an immediate relation to certain objects, but is instituted for the purpose of determining the rights and limits of reason.

Without the control of criticism reason is, as it were, in a state of nature, and can only establish its claims and assertions by *war*. Criticism, on the contrary, deciding all questions according to the fundamental laws of its own institution, secures to us the peace of law and order, and enables us to discuss all differences in the more tranquil manner of a legal *process*. In the former case, disputes are ended by *victory*, which both sides may claim, and which is followed by a hollow armistice; in the latter, by a *verdict*, which, as it strikes at the root of all speculative differences, ensures to all concerned a lasting peace. The endless disputes of a dogmatizing reason compel us to look for some mode of arriving at a settled decision by a critical investigation of reason itself; just as Hobbes maintains that the state of nature is a state of injustice and violence, and that we must leave it and submit ourselves to the constraint of law, which indeed limits individual freedom, but only that it may co-exist with the freedom of others and with the common good of all.

This freedom will, among other things, permit of our openly stating the difficulties and doubts which we are ourselves unable to solve, without being decried on that account as turbulent and dangerous citizens. This privilege forms part of the native rights of human reason, which recognizes no other judge than the universal reason of humanity; and as this reason is the source of all progress and improvement, such a privilege is to be held sacred and inviolable. It is unwise, moreover, to denounce as dangerous, any bold assertions against, or rash attacks upon, an opinion which is held by the largest and most moral class of the community; for that would be giving them an importance which they do not deserve. When I hear that the freedom of the will, the hope of a future life, and the existence of God have been overthrown by the arguments of some able writer, I feel a strong desire to read his book; for I expect that he will add to my knowledge, and impart greater clearness and distinctness to my views by the argumentative power shown in his writings. But I am perfectly certain, even before I have opened the book, that he has not succeeded in a single point, not because I believe I am in possession of irrefutable demonstrations of these important propositions, but because this transcendental critique, which has disclosed to me the power and the limits of pure reason, has fully convinced me that, as it is insufficient to establish the affirmative, it is as powerless, and even more so, to assure us of the truth of the negative answer to these questions. From what source does this free-thinker derive his knowledge that there is, for example, no Supreme Being? This proposition lies outside the field of possible experience, and, therefore, beyond the limits of human knowledge. But I would not read at all the answers which the dogmatical maintainer of the good cause makes to his opponent, because I know well beforehand, that he will merely attack the fallacious grounds of his adversary, without being able to establish his own assertions. Besides, a new illusory argument, in the construction of which talent and acuteness are shown, is suggestive of new ideas and new trains of reasoning, and in this respect the old and everyday sophistries are quite useless. Again, the dogmatical opponent of religion gives employment to criticism, and enables us to test and correct its principles, while there is no occasion for anxiety in regard to the influence and results of his reasoning.

But, it will be said, must we not warn the youth entrusted to academical care against such writings, must we not preserve them from the knowledge of these dangerous assertions, until their judgment is ripened, or rather until the doctrines which we wish to inculcate are so firmly rooted in them as to withstand all attempts at instilling the contrary dogmas, from whatever quarter they may come?

If we are to confine ourselves to the dogmatical procedure in the sphere of pure reason, and find ourselves unable to settle such disputes otherwise than by becoming a party in them, and setting counter-assertions against the statements advanced by our opponents, there is certainly no plan more advisable *for the moment*, but, at the same time, none more absurd and inefficient *for the future*, than this retaining of the youthful mind under guardianship for a time, and thus preserving it – for so long at least – from seduction into error. But when, at a later period, either curiosity, or the prevalent fashion of thought, places such writings in their hands, will the so-called convictions of their youth stand firm? The young thinker, who has in his armoury none but dogmatical weapons with which to resist the attacks of his opponent, and who cannot detect the latent dialectic which lies in his own opinions as well as in those of the opposite party, sees the advance of illusory arguments and grounds of proof which have the advantage of novelty, against as illusory grounds of proof destitute of this advantage, and which, perhaps, excite the suspicion that the natural credulity of his youth has been abused by his instructors. He thinks he can find no better means of showing that he has outgrown the discipline of his minority, than by despising those well-meant warnings, and, knowing no system of thought but that of dogmatism, he drinks deep draughts of the poison that is to sap the principles in which his early years were trained.

Exactly the opposite of the system here recommended ought to be pursued in academical instruction. This can only be effected, however, by a thorough training in the critical investigation of pure reason. For, in order to bring the principles of this critique into exercise as soon as possible, and to demonstrate their perfect sufficiency, even in the presence of the highest degree of dialectical illusion, the student ought to examine the assertions made on both sides of speculative questions step by step, and to test them by these priciples. It cannot be a difficult task for him to show the fallacies inherent in these propositions, and thus he begins early to feel his own power of securing himself against the influence of such sophistical arguments, which must finally lose, for him, all their illusory power. And, although the same blows which overturn the edifice of his opponent are as fatal to his own speculative structures, if such he has wished to rear; he need not feel any sorrow in regard to this seeming misfortune, as he has now before him a fair propect into the practical region, in which he may reasonably hope to find a more secure foundation for a rational system.

There is, accordingly, no proper polemic in the sphere of pure reason. Both parties beat the air and fight with their own shadows, as they pass beyond the limits of nature, and can find no tangible point of attack – no firm footing for their dogmatical conflict. Fight as vigorously as they may, the shadows which they hew down, immediately start up again, like the heroes in Walhalla, and renew the bloodless and unceasing contest.

But neither can we admit that there is any proper sceptical employment of pure reason, such as might be based upon the principle of *neutrality* in all speculative disputes. To excite reason against itself, to place weapons in the hands of the party on the one side as well as in those of the other, and to remain an undisturbed and sarcastic spectator of the fierce struggle that ensues, seems, from the dogmatical point of view, to be a part fitting only a malevolent disposition. But, when the sophist evidences an invincible obstinacy and blindness, and a pride which no criticism can moderate, there is no other practicable course than to oppose to this pride and obstinacy similar feelings and pretensions on the other side, equally well or ill founded, so that reason, staggered by the reflections thus forced upon it, finds it necessary to moderate its confidence in such pretensions, and to listen to the advices of criticism. But we cannot stop at these doubts, much less regard the conviction of our ignorance, not only as a cure for the conceit natural to dogmatism, but as the settlement of the disputes in which reason is involved with itself. On the contrary, scepticism is merely a means of awakening reason from its dogmatic dreams, and exciting it to a more careful investigation into its own powers and pretensions. But, as scepticism appears to be the shortest road to a permanent peace in the domain of philosophy, and as it is the tract pursued by the many who aim at giving a philosophical colouring to their contemptuous dislike of all inquiries of this kind, I think it necessary to present to my readers this mode of thought in its true light.

The Impossibility of a Sceptical Satisfaction of Pure Reason in its Internal Conflicts

The consciousness of ignorance – unless this ignorance is recognized to be absolutely necessary – ought, instead of forming the conclusion of my inquiries, to be the strongest motive to the pursuit of them. All ignorance is either ignorance of things, or of the limits of knowledge. If my ignorance is accidental and not necessary, it must incite me, in the first case, to a *dogmatical* inquiry regarding the objects of which I am ignorant; in the second, to a *critical* investigation into the bounds of all possible knowledge. But that my ignorance is absolutely necessary and unavoidable, and that it consequently absolves from the duty of all further investigation, is a fact which cannot be made out upon empirical grounds – from *observation* – but upon critical grounds alone, that is, by a thorough-going *investigation* into the primary sources knowledge. It follows that the determination of the bounds of reason can be made only on *a priori* grounds; while the empirical limitation of reason, which is merely an indeterminate knowledge of an ignorance that can never be completely removed, can take place only *a posteriori*. In other words, our empirical knowledge is limited by that which yet remains for us to know. The former knowledge of our ignorance, which is possible only on a rational basis, is a *science*; the latter is merely a *perception*, and we cannot say how far this surface extends. But experience teaches me that, how far soever I go, I always see before me a space in which I can proceed farther; and thus I know the limits – of my actual knowledge of the earth, although I am ignorant of the limits of the earth itself. But if I have got so far as to know that the earth is a sphere, and that its surface is spherical, I can know *a priori* and determine upon principles, from my knowledge of a small part of this surface – say to the extent of a degree – the diameter and circumference of the earth; and although I am ignorant of the objects which this surface contains, I have a perfect knowledge of its limits and extent.

The sum of all the possible objects of our knowledge seems to us to be a level surface, with an apparent horizon – that which forms the limit of its extent, and which has been termed by us the idea of unconditioned totality. To reach this limit by empirical means is impossible, and all attempts to determine it *a priori* according to a priciple, are alike in vain. But all the questions raised by pure reason relate to that which lies beyond this horizon, or, at least, in its boundary line.

The celebrated David Hume was one of those geographers of human reason who believe that they have given a sufficient answer to all such questions, by declaring them to lie beyond the horizon of our knowledge – a horizon which, however, Hume was unable to determine. His attention especially was directed to the principle of causality; and he remarked with perfect justice, that the truth of this principle, and even the objective validity of the concept of a cause, was not commonly based upon clear insight, that is, upon *a priori* knowledge. Hence he concluded that this law does not derive its authority from its universality and necessity, but merely from its general applicability in the course of experience, and a kind of subjective necessity thence arising, which he termed *habit*. From the inability of reason to establish this principle as a necessary law for the acquisition of all experience, he inferred the nullity of all the attempts of reason to pass the region of the empirical.

This procedure, of subjecting the *facta* of reason to examination, and, if necessary, to disapproval, may be termed the *censura* of reason. This *censura* must inevitably lead us to *doubts* regading *all* transcendent employment of principles. But this is only the second step in our inquiry. The first step in regard to this subject of pure reason, and which marks the infancy of that faculty, is that of *dogmatism*. The second, which we have just mentioned, is that of *scepticism*, and it gives evidence that our judgment has been improved by experience. But a third step is necessary – indicative of the maturity and manhood of the judgment, which now lays a firm foundation upon universal and necessary principles. This is the period of *criticism*, in which we do not examine the *facta* of reason, but reason itself, in the whole extent of its powers, and in regard to its capability of *a priori* knowledge; and thus we determine not merely the empirical and ever-shifting bounds of our knowledge, but its necessary and eternal limits. We demonstrate from indubitable principles, not merely our ignorance in respect to this or that subject, but in regard to all possible questions of a certain class. Thus scepticism is a resting-place for reason, in which it may reflect on its dogmatical wanderings, and gain some knowledge of the region in which it happens to be, that it may pursue its way with greater certainty; but it cannot be its permanent dwelling-place. It must take up its abode only in the region of complete certitude, whether this relates to the knowledge of objects themselves, or to the limits which bound all our knowledge.

Reason is not to be considered an an indefinitely extended plane, of the bounds of which we have only a general knowledge; it ought rather to be compared to a sphere, the radius of which may be found from the curvature of its surface – that is, the nature of *a priori* synthetical propositions – and, consequently, its circumference and extent. Beyond the sphere of experience there are no objects which it can know; nay, even questions regarding such supposititious objects relate only to the subjective principles of a complete determination of the relations which exist between the concepts of the understanding which lie within this sphere.

We are actually in possession of *a priori* synthetical knowledge, as if proved by the existence of the principles of the understanding, which anticipate experience. If any one cannot comprehend the possibility of these principles, he may have some reason to doubt whether they are really *a priori*; but he cannot on this account declare them to be impossible, and affirm the nullity of the steps which reason may have taken under their guidance. He can only say: If we perceived their origin and their authenticity, we should be able to determine the extent and limits of reason; but, till we can do this, all propositions regarding the latter are mere random assertions. In this view, the doubt respecting all dogmatical philosophy, which proceeds without the guidance of criticism, is well grounded; but we cannot therefore deny to reason the ability to construct a sound philosophy, when the way has been prepared by a thorough critical investigation. All the concepts produced, and all the questions raised, by pure reason, do not lie in the sphere of experience, but in that of reason itself, and hence they must be solved, and shown to be either valid or inadmissible, by that faculty. We have no right to decline the solution of such problems, on the ground that the solution can be discovered only from the nature of things, and under pretence of the limitation of human faculties, for reason is the sole creator of all these ideas, and is therefore bound either to establish their validity or to expose their illusory nature.

The polemic of scepticism is properly directed against the dogmatist, who erects a system of philosophy without having examined the fundamental objective principles on which it is based, for the purpose of evidencing the futility of his design, and thus bringing him to a knowlege of his own powers. But, in itself, scepticism does not give us any certain information in regard to the bounds of our knowledge. All unsuccesful dogmatical attempts of reason are *facta*, which it is always useful to submit to the censure of the sceptic. But this cannot help us to any decision regarding the expectations which reason cherishes of better success in future endeavours; the investigations of scepticism cannot, therefore, settle the dispute regarding the rights and powers of human reason.

Hume is perhaps the ablest and most ingenious of all sceptical philosophers, and his writings have, undoubtedly, exerted the most powerful influence in awakening reason to a thorough investigation into its own powers. It will, therefore, well repay our labours to consider for a little the course of reasoning which he followed, and the errors into which he strayed, although setting out on the path of truth and certitude.

Hume was probably aware, although he never clearly developed the notion, that we proceed in judgments of a certain class beyond our concept of the object. I have termed this kind of judgments synthetical. As regards the manner in which I pass beyond my concept by the aid of experience, no doubts can be entertained. Experience is itself a synthesis of perceptions; and it employs perceptions to increment the concept, which I obtain by means of another perception. But we think that we are able to proceed beyond a concept, and to extend our knowledge *a priori*. We attempt this in two ways – either, through the pure understanding, in relation to that which may become an *object of experience*, or, through pure reason, in relation to such properties of things, or of the existence of things, as can never be presented in any experience. This sceptical philosopher did not distinguish these two kinds of judgments, as he ought to have done, but regarded this augmentation of concepts, and, if we may so express ourselves, the spontaneous generation of understanding and reason, independently of the impregnation of experience, as altogether impossible. The so-called *a priori* principles of these faculties he consequently held to be invalid and imaginary, and regarded them as nothing but subjective habits of thought originating in experience, and therefore purely empirical and contingent rules, to which we attribute a spurious necessity and universality. In support of this strange assertion, he referred us to the generally acknowledged principle of the relation between cause and effect. No faculty of the mind can conduct us from the concept of a thing to the existence of something else; and hence he believed he could infer that, without experience, we possess no source from which we can augment a concept that is to extend our knowledge *a priori*. That the light of the sun, which shines upon a piece of wax, at the same time melts it, while it hardens clay, no power of the understanding could infer from the concepts which we previously possessed of these substances; much less is there any *a priori* law that could conduct us to such a conclusion, which experience alone can certify. On the other hand, we have seen in our discussion of Transcendental Logic, that, although we can never proceed *immediately* beyond the content of the concept which is given is, we can always know completely *a priori* – in relation, however, to a third term, namely, *possible* experience – the law of its connection with other things. For example, if I observe that a piece of wax melts, I can know *a priori* that there must have been something (the sun's heat) preceding, which this effect follows according to a fixed law; although, without the aid of experience, I could not know *a priori* and in a *determinate* manner, either the cause from the effect, or the effect from the cause. Hume was therefore wrong in inferring, from the contingency of the determination *according to law*, the contingency of *the law* itself; and the passing beyond the concept of a thing to possible experience (which is an *a priori* proceeding, constituting the objective reality of the concept), he confounded with our synthesis of objects in actual experience, which is always, of course, empirical. Thus, too, he regarded the principle of affinity, which has its seat in the understanding and indicates a necessary connection, as a mere rule of association, lying in the imitative faculty of imagination, which can present only contingent, and not objective connections.

The sceptical errors of this remarkably acute thinker arose principally from a defect, which was common to him with the dogmatists, namely, that he had never made a systematic review of all the different kinds of *a priori* synthesis performed by the understanding. Had he done so, he would have found, to take one example among many, that the *principle of permanence* was of this character, and that it, as well as the principle of causality, anticipates experience. In this way he might have been able to describe the determinate limits of the *a priori* operations of understanding and reason. But he merely declared the understanding to be limited, instead of showing what its limits were; he created a general mistrust in the power of our faculties, without giving us any determinate knowledge of the bounds of our necessary and unavoidable ignorance; he examined and condemned some of the principles of the understanding, without investigating all its powers with the completeness necessary to criticism. He denies, with truth, certain powers to the understanding, but he goes further, and declares it to be utterly inadequate to the *a priori* extension of knowledge, although he has not fully examined all the powers which reside in the faculty; and thus the fate which always overtakes scepticism meets him too. That is to say, his own declarations are doubted, for his objections were based upon *facta*, which are contingent, and not upon principles, which can alone demonstrate the necessary invalidity of all dogmatical assertions.

As Hume makes no distinction between the well-grounded claims of the understanding and the dialectical pretensions of reason, against which, however, his attacks are mainly directed, reason does not feel itself shut out from all attempts at the extension of *a priori* knowledge, and hence it refuses, in spite of a few checks in this or that quarter, to relinquish such efforts. For one naturally arms oneself to resist an attack, and becomes more obstinate in the resolve to establish the claims he had advanced. But a complete review of the powers of reason, and the conviction thence arising that we are in possession of a limited field of action, while we must admit the vanity of higher claims, puts an end to all doubt and dispute, and induces reason to rest satisfied with the undisturbed possession of its limited domain.

To the uncritical dogmatist, who has not surveyed the sphere of his understanding, nor determined, in accordance with principles, the limits of possible knowledge, who, consequently, is ignorant of his own powers, and believes he will discover them by the attempts he makes in the field of knowledge, these attacks of scepticism are not only dangerous, but destructive. For if there is one proposition in his chain of reasoning which he cannot prove, or the fallacy in which he cannot evolve in accordance with a principle, suspicion falls on all his statements, however plausible they may appear.

And thus scepticism, the bane of dogmatical philosophy, conducts us to a sound investigation into the understanding and the reason. When we are thus far advanced, we need fear no further attacks; for the limits of our domain are clearly marked out, and we can make no claims nor become involved in any disputes regarding the region that lies beyond these limits. Thus the sceptical procedure in philosophy does not present any *solution* of the problems of reason, but it forms an excellent *exercise* for its powers, awakening its circumspection, and indicating the means whereby it may most fully establish its claims to its legitimate possessions.

Section III : The Discipline of Pure Reason in Regard to Hypotheses

This critique of reason has now taught us that all its efforts to extend the bounds of knowledge, by means of pure speculation, are utterly fruitless. So much the wider field, it may appear, lies open to hypothesis; as, where we cannot know with certainty, we are at liberty to make guesses, and to form suppositions.

Imagination may be allowed, under the strict surveillance of reason, to invent suppositions; but, these must be based on something that it perfectly certain – and that is the *possibility* of the object. It we are well assured upon this point, it is allowable to have recourse to supposition in regard to the reality of the object; but this supposition must, unless it is utterly groundless, be connected, as its ground of explanation, with that which is really given and absolutely certain. Such a supposition is termed a *hypothesis*.

It is beyond our power to form the least concept *a priori* of the possibility of dynamical connection in appearances; and the category of the pure understanding will not enable us to excogitate any such connection, but merely helps us to understand it, when we meet with it in experience. For this reason we cannot, in accordance with the categories, imagine or invent any object or any property of an object not given, or that may not be given in experience, and employ it in a hypothesis; otherwise, we should be basing our chain of reasoning upon mere chimerical fancies, and not upon concepts of things. Thus, we have no right to assume the existence of new powers, not existing in nature – for example, an understanding with a non-sensible intuition, a force of attraction without contact, or some new kind of substances occupying space, and yet without the property of impenetrability; and, consequently, we cannot assume that there is any other kind of community among substances than that observable in experience, any kind of presence than that in space, or any kind of duration than that in time. In one word, the conditions of possible experience are for reason the only conditions of the possibility of things; reason cannot venture to form, independently of these conditions, any concepts of things, because such concepts, although not self-contradictory, are without object and without application.

The concepts of reason are, as we have already shown, mere ideas, and do not relate to any object in any kind of experience. At the same time, they do not indicate imaginary or possible objects. They are purely problematical in their nature, and, as aids to the heuristic exercise of the faculties, form the basis of the regulative principles for the systematic employment of the understanding in the field of experience. If we leave this ground of experience, they become mere fictions of thought, the possibility of which is quite indemonstrable; and they cannot consequently be employed, as hypotheses, in the explanation of real appearances. It is quite admissible to think the soul as simple, for the purpose of enabling ourselves to employ the idea of a perfect and necessary unity of all the faculties of the mind as the principle of all our inquiries into its internal appearances, although we cannot know this unit *in concreto*. But to *assume* that the soul is a simple substance (a transcendental concept) would be enouncing a proposition which is not only indemonstrable – as many physical hypotheses are – but a proposition which is purely arbitrary, and in the highest degree rash. The simple is never presented in experience; and, if by substance is here meant the permanent object of sensible intuition, the possibility of a *simple appearance* is perfectly inconceivable. Reason affords no good grounds for admitting the existence of intelligible beings, or of intelligible properties of sensible things, although – as we have no concept either of their possibility or of their impossibility – it will always be out of our power to affirm dogmatically that they do not exist. In the explanation of given appearances, no other things and no other grounds of explanation can be employed, than those which stand in connection with the given appearances according to the known laws of experience. A *transcendental hypothesis*, in which a mere idea of reason is employed to explain the appearance of nature, would not give us any better insight into an appearance, as we should be trying to explain what we do not sufficiently understand from known empirical principles, by what we do not understand at all. The principles of such a hypothesis might conduce to the satisfaction of reason, but it would not assist the understanding in its application to objects. Order and conformity to aims in the sphere of nature must be themselves explained upon natural grounds and according to natural laws; and the wildest hypotheses, if they are only physical, are here more admissible than a hyperphysical hypothesis, such as that of a divine author. For such a hypothesis would introduce the principle of idle reason (*ignava ratio*), which requires us to give up the search for causes that might be discovered in the course of experience, and to rest satisfied with a mere idea. As regards the absolute totality of the grounds of explanation in the series of these causes, this can be no hindrance to the understanding in the case of appearances; because, as they are to us nothing more than appearances, we have no right to look for anything like completeness in the synthesis of the series of their conditions.

Transcendental hypotheses are therefore inadmissible; and we cannot use the liberty of employing, in the absence of physical, hyperphysical grounds of explanation. And this for two reasons;

first, because such hypotheses do not advance reason, but rather stop it in its progress; second, because this licence would render fruitless all its exertions in its own proper sphere, which is that of experience. For, when the explanation of nature happens to be difficult, we have constantly at hand a transcendental ground of explanation, which lifts us above the necessity of investigating nature; and our inquiries are brought to a close not because we have obtained all the requisite knowledge, but because we abut upon a principle, which is incomprehensible, and which, indeed, is so far back in the track of thought, as to contain the concept of the absolutely primal being.

The next requisite for the admissibility of a hypothesis is its sufficiency. That is, it must determine *a priori* the consequences which are given in experience, and which are supposed to follow from the hypothesis itself. If we require to employ auxiliary hypotheses, the suspicion naturally arises that they are mere fictions; because the necessity for each of them requires the same justification as in the case of the original hypothesis, and thus their testimony is invalid. If we suppose the existence of an infinitely perfect cause, we possess sufficient grounds for the explanation of the conformity to aims, the order and the greatness which we observe in the universe; but we find ourselves obliged, when we observe the evil in the world and the exceptions to these laws, to employ new hypotheses in support of the original one. We employ the idea of the simple nature of the human soul as the foundation of all the theories we may form of its appearances; but when we meet with difficulties in our way, when we observe in the soul appearances similar to the changes which take place in matter, we require to call in new auxiliary hypotheses. These may, indeed, not be false, but we do not know them to be true, because the only witness to their certitude is the hypothesis which they themselves have been called in to explain.

We are not discussing the above-mentioned assertions regarding the immaterial unity of the soul and the existence of a Supreme Being, as dogmata, which certain philosophers profess to demonstrate *a priori*; but purely as hypotheses. In the former case, the dogmatist must take care that his arguments possess the apodeictic certainty of a demonstration. For the assertion that the reality of such ideas is *probable*, is as absurd as a proof of the probability of a proposition in geometry. Pure abstract reason, apart from all experience, can either know a proposition entirely *a priori*, and as necessary, or it can know nothing at all; and hence the judgments it enounces are never mere opinions, they are either apodeictic certainties, or declarations that nothing can be known on the subject. Opinions and probable judgments on the nature of things can only be employed to explain given appearances, or they may relate to the effect, in accordance with empirical laws, of an actually existing cause. In other words, we must restrict the sphere of opinion to the world of experience and nature. Beyond this region *opinion* is mere invention; unless we are groping about for the truth on a path not yet fully known, and have some hopes of stumbling upon it by chance.

But, although hypotheses are inadmissible in answers to the questions of pure speculative reason, they may be employed in the defence of these answers. That is to say, hypotheses are admissible in polemic, but not in the sphere of dogmatism. By the defence of statements of this character, I do not mean an attempt at discovering new grounds for their support, but merely the refutation of the arguments of opponents. All *a priori* synthetical propositions possess the peculiarity, that, although the philosopher who maintains the reality of the ideas contained in the proposition, is not in possession of sufficient knowledge to establish the certainty of his statements, his opponent is as little able to prove the truth of the opposite. This equality of fortune does not allow the one party to be superior to the other in the sphere of speculative knowledge; and it is this sphere accordingly that is the proper arena of these endless speculative conflicts. But we shall afterwards show that, in relation to its *practical exercise*, reason has the right of admitting what, in the field of pure speculation, it would not be justified in supposing, except upon perfectly sufficient grounds; because all such suppositions destroy the necessary completeness of speculation – a condition which the practical reason, however, does not consider to be requisite. In this sphere, therefore, reason has a title to which it does not require to prove – which, in fact, it could not do. The burden of proof accordingly rests upon the opponent. But as he has just as little knowledge regarding the subject discussed, and is as little able to prove the non-existence of the object of an idea, as the philosopher on the other side is to demonstrate its reality, it is evident that there is an advantage on the side of the philosopher who maintains his proposition as a practically necessary supposition (*melior est conditio possidentis*). For he is at liberty to employ, in self-defence, the same weapons as his opponent makes use of in attacking him; that is, he has a right to use hypothese not for the purpose of supporting the arguments in favour of his own propositions, but to show that his opponent knows no more than himself regarding the subject under discussion, and cannot boast of any speculative advantage.

Hypotheses are, therefore, admissible in the sphere of pure reason, only as weapons for self-defence, and not as supports to dogmatical assertions. But the opposing party we must always seek for in ourselves. For speculative reason is, in its transcendental use, dialectical *in its own nature*. The difficulties and objections we have to fear lie in ourselves. They are like old but never superannuated claims; and we must seek them out, and settle them once and for ever, if we are to expect a permanent peace. External tranquillity is hollow and unreal. The root of these disturbances, which lies in the nature of human reason, must be destroyed; and this can only be done by giving it, in the first instance, freedom to grow, nay, by nourishing it, that it may send out shoots, and thus betray its own existence. It is our duty, therefore, to try to discover new objections, to put weapons in the hands of our opponent, and to grant him the most favourable position in the arena that he can wish. We have nothing to fear from these concessions; on the contrary, we may rather hope that we shall thus make ourselves master of a possession which no one will ever venture to dispute.

The thinker requires, to be fully equipped, the hypotheses of pure reason, which, although but leaden weapons (for they have not been steeled in the armoury of experience), are as useful as any that can be employed by his opponents. If, accordingly, we have assumed, from a non-speculative point of view, the immaterial nature of the soul, and are met by the objection that experience seems to prove that the growth and decay of our mental faculties are mere modifications of the sensible organism – we can weaken the force of this objection, by the assumption that the body is nothing but the fundamental appearance, to which, as a necessary condition, all sensibility, and consequently all thought, relates in the present state of our existence; and that the separation of soul and body forms the conclusion of the sensible exercise of our power of knowledge, and the beginning of the intellectual. The body would, in this view of the question, be regarded, not as the cause of thought, but merely as its restrictive condition, as promotive of the sensitive and animal, but as a hindrance to the pure and spiritual life; and the dependence of the animal life on the constitution of the body, would not prove that the *whole* life of man was also dependent on the state of the organism. We might go still farther, and discover new objections, or carry out to their extreme consequences those which have already been adduced.

Generation, in the human race as well as among the irrational animals, depends on so many accidents – of occasion, of proper sustenance, of the laws enacted by the government of a country of vice even, that it is difficult to believe in the eternal existence of a being, whose life has begun under circumstances so mean and trivial, and so entirely dependent upon our own control. As regards the continuance of the existence of the whole race, we need have no difficulties, for accident in single cases is subject to general laws; but, in the case of each individual, it would seem as if we could hardly expect so wonderful an effect from causes so insignificant. But, in answer to these objections, we may adduce the transcendental hypothesis, that all life is properly intelligible, and not subject to changes in time, and that it neither began in birth, nor will end in death. We may assume that this life is nothing more than a sensible representation of pure spiritual life; that the whole world of sense is but an image, hovering before the faculty of cognition which we exercise in this sphere, and with no more objective reality than a dream; and that if we could intuit ourselves and other things as they really are, we should see ourselves in a world of spiritual natures, our connection with which did not begin at our birth, and will not cease with the destruction of the body. And so on.

We cannot be said to know what has been above asserted, nor do we seriously maintain the truth of these assertions; and the notions therein indicated are not even ideas of reason, they are purely *fictitious* concepts. But this hypothetical procedure is in perfect conformity with the laws of reason. Our opponent mistakes the absence of empirical conditions for a proof of the complete impossibility of all that we have asserted; and we have to show him that he has not exhausted the whole sphere of possibility, and that he can as little compass that sphere by the laws of experience and nature, as we can lay a secure foundation for the operations of reason beyond the region of experience. Such hypothetical defences against the pretensions of an opponent must not be regarded as declarations of opinion. The philosopher abandons them, so soon as the opposite party renounces its dogmatical conceit. To maintain a simply negative position in relation to propositions which rest on an insecure foundation, well befits the moderation of a true philosopher; but to uphold the objections urged against an opponent as proofs of the opposite statement, is a proceeding just as unwarrantable and arrogant as it is to attack the position of a philosopher who advances affirmative propositions regarding such a subject.

It is evident, therefore, that hypotheses, in the speculative sphere, are valid, not as independent propositions, but only relatively to opposite transcendent assumptions. For, to make the principles of possible experience conditions of the possibility of things in general is just as transcendent a procedure as to maintain the objective reality of ideas which can be applied to no objects except such as lie without the limits of possible experience. The judgments enounced by pure reason must be necessary, or they must not be enounced at all. Reason cannot trouble itself with opinions. But the hypotheses we have been discussing are merely problematical judgments, which can neither be refuted nor proved; while, therefore, they are not personal opinions, they are indispensable as answers to objections which are liable to be raised. But we must take care to confine them to this function, and guard against any assumption on their part of absolute validity, a proceeding which would involve reason in inextricable difficulties and contradictions.

CHAPTER I

Section IV: The Discipline of Pure Reason in Regard to its Proofs

It is a peculiarity which distinguishes the proofs of transcendental synthetical propositions from those of all other *a priori* synthetical knowledge, that reason, in the case of the former, does not apply its concepts directly to an object, but is first obliged to prove, *a priori*, the objective validity of these concepts and the possibility of their syntheses. This is not merely a prudential rule, it is essential to the very possibility of the proof of a transcendental proposition. If I am required to pass, *a priori*, beyond the concept of an object, I find that it is utterly impossible without the guidance of something which is not contained in the concept. In mathematics, it is *a priori* intuition that guides my synthesis; and, in this case, all our conclusions may be drawn immediately from pure intuition. In transcendental knowledge, so long as we are dealing only with concepts of the understanding, we are guided by possible experience. That is to say, a proof in the sphere of transcendental knowledge does not show that the given concept (that of an event, for example) leads directly to another concept (that of a cause) –

for this would be a jump which nothing can justify; but it shows that experience itself, and consequently the object of experience, is impossible without the connection indicated by these concepts. it follows that such a proof must demonstrate the possibility of arriving, synthetically and *a priori*, at a certain knowledge of things, which was not contained in our concepts of these things. Unless we pay particular attention to this requirement, our proofs, instead of pursuing the straight path indicated by reason, follow the tortuous road of mere subjective association. The illusory conviction, which rests upon subjective causes of association, and which is considered as resulting from the perception of a real and objective natural affinity, is always open to doubt and suspicion. For this reason, all the attempts which have been made to prove the principle of sufficient reason, have, according to the univeral admission of philosophers, been quite unsuccessful; and, before the appearance of transcendental criticism, it was considered better, as this principle could not be abandoned, to appeal boldly to the common sense of mankind (a proceeding which always proves that the problem, which reason ought to solve, is one in which philosophers find great difficulties), rather than attempt to discover new dogmatical proofs.

But, if the proposition to be proved is a proposition of pure reason, and if I aim at passing beyond my empirical concepts by the aid of mere ideas, it is necessary that the proof should first show that such a step in synthesis is possible (which it is not), before it proceeds to prove the truth of the proposition itself. The so-called proof of the simple nature of the soul from the unity of apperception, is a very plausible one. But it contains no answer to the objection, that, as the notion of absolute simplicity is not a concept which is directly applicable to a perception, but is an idea which must be inferred – if at all from observation, it is by no means evident, how the mere fact of consciousness, which is contained *in all thought*, although in so far a simple representation, can conduct me to the consciousness and knowledge of a thing which is purely a thinking substance. When I represent to my mind the power of my body as in motion, my body in this thought is so far absolute unity, and my representation of it is a simple one; and hence I can indicate this representation by the motion of a point, because I have made abstraction of the size or volume of the body. But I cannot hence infer that, given merely the moving power of a body, the body may be thought as simple substance, merely because the representation in my mind takes no account of its content in space, and is consequently simple. The simple, in abstraction, is very different from the objectively simple; and hence the *I*, which is simple in the first sense, may, in the second sense, as indicating the soul itself, be a very complex concept, with a very various content. Thus it is evident, that in all such arguments there lurks a paralogism. We guess (for without some such surmise our suspicion would not be excited in reference to a proof of this character) at the presence of the paralogism, by keeping ever before us a criterion of the possibility of those synthetical propositions which aim at proving more than experience can teach us. This criterion is obtained from the observation that such proofs do not lead us directly from the subject of the proposition to be proved to the required predicate, but find it necessary to presuppose the possibility of extending our knowledge *a priori* by means of ideas. We must, accordingly, always use the greatest caution; we require, before attempting any proof, to consider how it is possible to extend the sphere of knowledge by the operations of pure reason, and from what source we are to derive knowledge, which is not obtained from the analysis of concepts, nor relates, by anticipation, to possible experience. We shall thus spare ourselves much severe and fruitless labour, by not expecting from reason what is beyond its power, or rather by subjecting it to discipline, and teaching it to moderate its vehement desires for the extension of the sphere of knowledge.

The first rule for our guidance is, therefore, not to attempt a transcendental proof, before we have considered from what source we are to derive the principles upon which the proof is to be based, and what right we have to expect that our conclusions from these principles will be veracious. If they are principles of the understanding, it is vain to expect that we should attain by their means to ideas of pure reason; for these principles are valid only in regard to objects of possible experience. If they are principles of pure reason, our labour is alike in vain. For the principles of reason, if employed as objective, are without exception dialectical, and possess no validity or truth, except as regulative principles of the systematic employment of reason in experience. But when such delusive proofs are presented to us, it is our duty to meet them with the *non liquet* of a matured judgment; and, although we are unable to expose the particular sophism upon which the proof is based, we have a right to demand a deduction of the principles employed in it; and, if these principles have their origin in pure reason alone, such a deduction is absolutely impossible. And thus it is unnecessary that we should trouble ourselves with the exposure and refutation of every sophistical illusion; we may, at once, bring all dialectic, which is inexhaustible in the production of fallacies, before the bar of critical reason, which tests the principles upon which all dialectical procedure is based. The second peculiarity of transcendental proof is, that a transcendental proposition cannot rest upon more than *a single* proof. If I am drawing conclusions, not from concepts, but from intuition corresponding to a concept, be it pure intuition, as in mathematics, or empirical, as in natural science, the intuition which forms the basis of my inferences, presents me with materials for many synthetical propositions, which I can connect in various modes, while, as it is allowable to proceed from different points in the intention, I can arrive by different paths at the same proposition.

But every transcendental proposition sets out from a concept, and posits the synthetical condition of the possibility of an object according to this concept. There must, therefore, be but one ground of proof, because it is the concept alone which determines the object; and thus the proof cannot contain anything more than the determination of the object according to the concept. In our Transcendental Analytic, for example, we inferred the principle: Every event has a cause, from the only condition of the objective possibility of our concept of an event. This is, that an event cannot be determined in time, and consequently cannot form a part of experience, unless it stands under this dynamical law. This is the only possible ground of proof; for our concept of an event possesses objective validity, that is, is a true concept, only because the law of casuality determines an object to which it can refer. Other arguments in support of this principle have been attempted – such as that from the contingent nature of a phenomenon; but when this argument is considered, we can discover no criterion of contingency, except the fact of an event – of something *happening*, that is to say, the existence which is preceded by the non-existence of an object, and thus we fall back on the very thing to be proved. If the proposition: Every thinking being is simple, is to be proved, we keep to the concept of the *I*, which is simple, and to which all thought has a relation. The same is the case with the transcendental proof of the existence of God, which is based solely upon the harmony and reciprocal fitness of the concept of an *ens realissimum* and a necessary being, and cannot be attempted in any other manner.

This caution serves to simplify very much the criticism of all propositions of reason. When reason employs concept alone, only one proof of its thesis is possible, if any. When, therefore, the dogmatist advances with ten arguments in favour of a proposition, we may be sure that not one of them is conclusive. For if he possessed one which proved the proposition he brings forward to demonstration – as must always be the case with the propositions of pure reason – what need is there for any more ? His intention can only be similar to that of the advocate, who had different arguments for different judges; thus availing himself of the weakness of those who examine his arguments, who, without going into any profound investigation, adopt the view of the case which seems most probable at first sight, and decide according to it.

The third rule for the guidance of pure reason in the conduct of a proof is, that all transcendental proofs must never be *apagogic* or indirect, but always ostensive or direct. The direct or ostensive proof not only establishes the truth of the proposition to be proved, but exposes the grounds of its truth; the apagogic, on the other hand, may assure us of the truth of the proposition, but it cannot enable us to comprehend the grounds of its possibility. The latter is, accordingly, rather an auxiliary to an argument, than a strictly philosophical and rational mode of procedure. In one respect, however, they have an advantage over direct proofs, from the fact that the mode of arguing by contradiction, which they employ, renders our understanding of the question more clear, and approximates the proof to the certainty of an intuitional demonstration.

The true reason why indirect proofs are employed in different sciences is this. When the ground upon which we seek to base knowledge are too various or too profound, we try whether or not we may not discover the truth of our knowledge from its consequences. The *modus ponens* of reasoning from the truth of its inferences to the truth of a proposition, would be admissible if all the inferences that can be drawn from it are known to be true; for in this case there can only be one possible ground for these inferences, and that is the true one. But this is a quite impracticable procedure, as it surpasses all our powers to discover all the possible inferences that can be drawn from a proposition. But this mode of reasoning is employed, under favour, when we wish to prove the truth of an hypothesis; in which case we admit the truth of the conclusion – which is supported by analogy – that, if all the inferences we have drawn and examined agree with the proposition assumed, all other possible inferences will also agree with it. But, in this way, an hypothesis can never be established as a demonstrated truth. The *modus tollens* of reasoning from known inferences to the unknown proposition, is not only a rigorous, but a very easy mode of proof. For, if it can be shown that but one inference from a proposition is false, then the proposition must itself be false. Instead, then, of examining, in an ostensive argument, the whole series of the grounds on which the truth of a proposition rests, we need only take the opposite of this proposition, and if one inference from it be false, then must the opposite be itself false; and, consequently, the proposition which we wished to prove, must be true.

The apagogic method of proof is admissible only in those sciences where it is impossible to mistake a subjective representation for objective knowledge. Where this is possible, it is plain that the opposite of a given proposition may contradict merely the subjective conditions of thought, and not the objective knowledge; or it may happen that both propositions contradict each other only under a subjective condition, which is incorrectly considered to be objective, and, as the condition is itself false, both propositions may be false, and it will, consequently, be impossible to conclude the truth of the one from the falseness of the other.

In mathematics such subreptions are impossible; and it is in this science, accordingly, that the indirect mode of proof has its true place. In the science of nature, where all assertion is based upon empirical intuition, such subreptions may be guarded against by the repeated comparison of observations; but this mode of proof is of little value in this sphere of knowledge. But the transcendental efforts of pure reason are all made in the sphere of the subjective, which is the real medium of all dialectical illusion; and thus reason endeavours, in its premisses, to impose upon us subjective representations for objective knowledge. In the transcendental sphere of pure reason, then, and in the case of synthetical propositions, it is inadmissible to support a statement by disproving the counter-statement. For only two cases are possible; either, the counter-statement is nothing but the enouncement of the inconsistency of the opposite opinion with the subjective conditions of reason, which does not affect the real case (for example, we cannot comprehend the unconditioned necessity of the existence of a being, and hence every speculative proof of the existence of such a being must be opposed on *subjective* grounds, while the possibility of this being *in itself* cannot with justice be denied); or, both propositions, being dialectical in their nature, are based upon an impossible concept. In this latter case the rule applies – *non entis nulla sunt predicta*; that is to say, what we affirm and what we deny, respecting such an object, are equally untrue, and the apagogic mode of arriving at the truth is in this case impossible. If, for example, we presuppose that the world of sense is given *in itself* in its totality, it is false, *either* that it is infinite, *or* that it is finite and limited in space. Both are false, because the hypothesis is false. For the notion of appearances (as mere representations) which are given *in themselves* (as objects) is self-contradictory; and the infinitude of this imaginary whole would, indeed, be unconditioned, but would be inconsistent (as everything in appearance is conditioned) with the unconditioned determination and finitude of quantities which is presupposed in our concept.

The apagogic mode of proof is the true source of those illusions which have always had so strong an attraction for the admirers of dogmatical philosophy. It may be compared to a champion, who maintains the honour and claims of the party he had adopted, by offering battle to all who doubt the validity of these claims and the purity of that honour; while nothing can be proved in this way, except the respective strength of the combatants, and the advantage, in this respect, is always on the side of the attacking party. Spectators, observing that each party is alternately conqueror and conquered, are led to regard the subject of dispute as beyond the power of man to decide upon. But such an opinion cannot be justified; and it is sufficient to apply to these reasoners the remark:

> Non defensoribus istis
> Tempus eget.

Each must try to establish his assertions by a transcendental deduction of the grounds of proof employed in his argument, and thus enable us to see in what way the claims of reason may be supported. If an opponent bases his assertions upon subjective grounds, he may be refuted with ease; not, however to the advantage of the dogmatist, who likewise depends upon subjective sources of cognition, and is in like manner driven into a corner by his opponent. But, if parties employ the direct method of procedure, they will soon discover the difficulty, nay, the impossibility of proving their assertions, and will be forced to appeal to prescription and precedence; or they will, by the help of criticism, discover with ease the dogmatical illusions by which they had been mocked, and compel reason to renounce its exaggerated pretensions to speculative insight, and to confine itself within the limits of its proper sphere – that of practical principles.

CHAPTER II : THE CANON OF PURE REASON

It is a humiliating consideration for human reason, that it is incompetent to discover truth by means of pure speculation, but, on the contrary, stands in need of discipline to check its deviations from the straight path, and to expose the illusions which it originates. But, on the other hand, this consideration ought to elevate and to give it confidence, for this discipline is exercised by itself alone, and it is subject to the censure of no other power. The bounds, moreover, which it is forced to set to its speculative exercise, form likewise a check upon the fallacious pretensions of opponents ; and thus what remains of its possessions, after these exaggerated claims have been disallowed, is secure from attack or usurpation. The greatest, and perhaps the only, use of all philosophy of pure reason is, accordingly, of a purely negative character. It is not an organon for the extension, but a discipline for the determination of the limits of its exercise ; and without laying claim to the discovery of new truth, it has the modest merit of guarding against error.

At the same time, there must be some source of positive knowledge which belongs to the domain of pure reason, and which becomes the cause of error, only from our mistaking its true character, while it forms the goal towards which reason continually strives. How else can we account for the inextinguishable desire in the human mind to find a firm footing in some region beyond the limits of the world of experience? It hopes to attain to the possession of a knowledge in which it has the deepest interest. It enters upon the path of pure speculation; but in vain. We have some reason, however, to expect that, in the only other way that lies open to it – the path of *practical* reason – it may meet with better success.

I understand by a canon a list of the *a priori* principles of the proper employment of certain faculties of knowledge. Thus general logic, in its analytical department, is a formal canon for the faculties of understanding and reason. In the same way, Transcendental Analytic was seen to be a canon of the pure *understanding*; for it

alone is competent to enounce true *a priori* synthetical knowledge.
But, when no proper employment of a faculty of knowledge is
possible, no canon can exist. But the synthetical knowledge of pure
speculative *reason* is, as has been shown, completely impossible.
There cannot, therefore, exist any canon for the speculative exercise
of this faculty – for its speculative exercise is entirely dialectical;
and consequently, transcendental logic, in this respect, is merely a
discipline, and not a canon. If, then, there is any proper mode of
employing the faculty of pure reason – in which case there must be
a canon for this faculty – this canon will relate, not to the
speculative, but to the *practical use of reason*. This canon we now
proceed to investigate.

Section I: The Ultimate End of the Pure Use of Reason

There exists in the faculty of reason a natural desire to venture
beyond the field of experience, to attempt to reach the utmost
bounds of all knowledge by the help of ideas alone, and not to rest
satisfied, until it has fulfilled its course and raised the sum of its
knowledge into a self-subsistent systematic whole. Is the motive for
this endeavour to be found in its speculative, or in its practical
interests alone?

Setting aside, at present, the results of the labours of pure reason
in its speculative exercise, I shall merely inquire regarding the
problems, the solution of which forms its ultimate aim – whether
reached or not, and in relations to which all other aims are but
partial and intermediate. These highest aims must, from the nature
of reason, possess complete unity; otherwise the highest interest of
humanity could not be successfully promoted.

The transcendental speculation of reason relates to three things:
the freedom of the will, the immortality of the soul, and the
existence of God. The speculative interest which reason has in those
questions is very small; and, for its sake alone, we should not
undertake the labour of transcendental investigation – a labour full
of toil and ceaseless struggle. We should be loath to undertake this
labour, because the discoveries we might make would not be of the
smallest use in the sphere of concrete or physical investigation. We
may find out that the will is free, but this knowledge only relates to
the intelligible cause of our will. As regards the appearance or
expressions of this will, that is, our actions, we are bound, in
obedience to an inviolable maxim, without which reason cannot be

employed in the sphere of experience, to explain these in the same way as we explain all the other appearances of nature, that is to say, according to its unchangeable laws. We may have discovered the spirituality and immortality of the soul, but we cannot employ this knowledge to explain the appearances of this life, nor the peculiar nature of the future, because our concept of an incorporeal nature is purely negative and does not add anything to our knowledge, and the only inferences to be drawn from it are purely fictitious. If, again, we prove the existence of a supreme intelligence, we should be able from it to make the conformity to aims existing in the arrangement of the world comprehensible; but we should not be justified in inferring from it any particular arrangement or disposition, or, inferring any, where it is not perceived. For it is a necessary rule of the speculative use of reason, that we must not overlook natural causes, or refuse to listen to the teaching of experience, for the sake of inferring what we know and perceive from something that transcends all our knowledge. In one word, these three propositions are, for the speculative reason, always transcendent, and cannot be employed as immanent principles in relation to the objects of experience; they are, consequently, of no use to us in this sphere, being but the valueless results of the severe but unprofitable efforts of reason.

If, then, the actual *knowledge* of these three cardinal propositions is perfectly useless, while reason uses its utmost endeavours to induce us to admit them, it is plain that their real value and importance relate to our *practical*, and not to our speculative interest.

I term all that is possible through free will, practical. But if the conditions of the exercise of free will are empirical, reason can have only a regulative, and not a constitutive, influence upon it, and is serviceable merely for the introduction of unity into its empirical laws. In the moral philosophy of prudence, for example, the sole business of reason is to bring about a union of all the ends, which are aimed at by our inclinations, into one ultimate end – that of *happiness*, and to show the agreement which should exist among the means of attaining that end. In this sphere, accordingly, reason cannot present to us any other than *pragmatical* laws of free action, for our guidance towards the aims set up by the senses, and is incompetent to give us laws which are pure and determined completely *a priori*. On the other hand, pure practical laws, the ends of which have been given by reason entirely *a priori*, and which are not empirically conditioned, but are, on the contrary, absolutely imperative in their nature, would be products of pure reason. Such are the *moral* laws; and these alone belong to the sphere of the practical exercise of reason, and admit of a canon.

All the powers of reason, in the sphere of what may be termed pure philosophy, are, in fact, directed to the three above-mentioned problems alone. These again have a still higher end – the answer to the question, *what we ought to do*, if the will is free, if there is a God, and a future world. Now, as this problem relates to our conduct, in reference to the highest aim of humanity, it is evident that the ultimate intention of nature, in the constitution of our reason, has been directed to our *moral* interests alone.

We must take care, however, in turning our attention to an object which is foreign[1] to the sphere of transcendental philosophy, not to injure the unity of our system by digressions, nor, on the other hand, to fail in clearness, by saying too little on the new subject of discussion. I hope to avoid both extremes, by keeping as close as possible to the transcendental, and excluding all psychological, that is, empirical elements.

I have to remark, in the first place, that at present I treat of the concept of freedom in the practical sense only, and set aside the corresponding transcendental concept, which cannot be employed as a ground of explanation in appearances, but is itself a problem for pure reason. A will is purely *animal (arbitrium brutum)* when it is determined by sensible impulses or instincts only, that is, when it is determined in a *pathological* manner. A will, which can be determined independently of sensitive impulses, consequently by motives presented by reason alone, is called a *free will (arbitrium liberum)*; and everything which is connected with this free will, either as principle or consequence, is termed *practical*. The existence of practical freedom can be proved from experience alone. For the human will is not determined by that alone which immediately affects the senses; on the contrary, we have the power, by calling up the notion of what is useful or hurtful in a more distant relation, of overcoming the immediate impressions on our sensible faculty of

---

[1] All practical concept relate to objects of pleasure and pain, and consequently – in an indirect manner, at least – to objects of feeling. But as feeling is not a faculty of representation, but lies outside the sphere of our powers of concept, the elements of our judgments, in so far as they relate to pleasure or pain, that is, the elements of our practical judgments, do not belong to transcendental philosophy, which has to do with pure *a priori* knowledge alone.

desire. But these considerations of what is desirable in relation to our whole state, that is, is in the end good and useful, are based entirely upon reason. This faculty, accordingly, enounces laws, which are imperative or objective *laws of freedom*, and which tell us what *ought to take place*, thus distinguishing themselves from the *laws of nature*, which relate to that which *does take place*. The laws of freedom or of free will are hence termed practical laws.

Whether reason is not itself, in the actual delivery of these laws, determined in its turn by other influences, and whether the action which, in relation to sensible impulses, we call free, may not, in relation to higher and more remote operative causes, really form a part of *nature* – these are questions which do not here concern us. They are purely speculative questions; and all we have to do, in the practical sphere, is to inquire into the *rule* of conduct which reason has to present. Experience demonstrates to us the existence of practical freedom as one of the causes which exist in nature, that is, it shows the causal power of reason in the determination of the will. The idea of transcendental freedom, on the contrary, requires that reason – in relation to its causal power of commencing a series of appearances – should be independent of all sensible determining causes; and thus it seems to be in opposition to the law of nature and to all possible experience. It therefore remains a problem for the human mind. But this problem does not concern reason in its practical use; and we have, therefore, in a canon of pure reason, to do with only two questions, which relate to the practical interest of pure reason – Is there a God? and, Is there a future life? The question of transcendental freedom is purely speculative, and we may therefore set it entirely aside when we come to treat of practical reason. Besides, we have already fully discussed this subject in the Antinomy of Pure Reason.

Section II: The Ideal of the Highest Good as a Determining Ground of the Ultimate End of Pure Reason

Reason conducted us, in its speculative use, through the field of experience, and, as it can never find complete satisfaction in that sphere, from thence to speculative ideas – which, however, in the end brought us back again to experience, and thus fulfilled the purpose of reason, in a manner which, though useful, was not at all in accordance with our expectations. It now remains for us to consider whether pure reason can be employed in a practical sphere, and whether it will here conduct us to those ideas which attain the highest ends of pure reason, as we have just stated them. We shall thus ascertain whether, from the point of view of its practical interest, reason may not be able to supply us with that which, on the speculative side, it wholly denies us.

The whole interest of reason, speculative as well as practical, is centred in the three following questions:

1. WHAT CAN I KNOW?
2. WHAT OUGHT I TO DO?
3. WHAT MAY I HOPE?

The first question is purely speculative. We have, as I flatter myself, exhausted all the replies of which it is susceptible, and have at last found the reply with which reason must content itself, and with which it ought to be content, so long as it pays no regard to the practical. But from the two great ends to the attainment of which all these efforts of pure reason were in fact directed, we remain just as far removed as if we have consulted our ease, and declined the task at the outset. So far, then, as *knowledge* is concerned, thus much, at least, is established, that, in regard to those two problems, it lies beyond our reach.

The second question is purely practical. As such it may indeed fall within the province of pure reason, but still it is not transcendental, but moral, and consequently cannot in itself form the subject of our criticism.

The third question: If I act as I ought to do, what may I then hope? – is at once practical and theoretical. The practical forms a clue to the answer of the theoretical, and – in its highest form – speculative question. For all *hoping* has happiness for its object, and stands in precisely the same relation to the practical and the law of morality, as *knowing* to the theoretical knowledge of things and the law of nature. The former arrives finally at the conclusion that *something is* (which determines the ultimate end), because *something ought to take place*; the latter, that *something is* (which operates as the highest cause), because *something does take place*.

Happiness is the satisfaction of all our desires; *extensive*, in regard to their multiplicity; *intensive*, in regard to their degree; and *protensive*, in regard to their duration. The practical law based on the motive of *happiness*, I term a pragmatical law (or prudential rule); but that law, assuming such to exist, which has no other motive than the *worthiness of being happy*, I term a moral or ethical law. The first tells us what we have to do, if we wish to become possessed of happiness; the second dictates how we ought to act, in order to deserve happiness. The first is based upon empirical principles; for it is only by experience that I can learn either what inclinations exist which desire satisfaction, or what are the natural means of satisfying them. The second takes no account of our desires or the means of satisfying them, and regards only the freedom of a rational being, and the necessary conditions under which alone this freedom can harmonize with the distribution of happiness according to principles. This second law may therefore rest upon mere ideas of pure reason, and may be known *a priori*.

I assume that there are pure moral laws which determine, entirely *a priori* (without regard to empirical motives, that is, to happiness), the conduct of a rational being, or in other words, the use which it makes of its freedom, and that these laws are *absolutely* imperative (not merely hypothetically, on the supposition of other empirical ends), and therefore in all respects necessary. I am warranted in assuming this, not only by the arguments of the most enlightened moralists, but by the moral judgment of every man who will make the attempt to form a distinct concept of such a law.

Pure reason, then, contains, not indeed in its speculative, but in its practical, or, more strictly, its moral use, principles of the *possibility of experience*, of such actions, namely, as, in accordance with ethical precepts, *might* be met with in the *history* of man. For since reason commands that such actions should take place, it must be possible for them to take place; and hence a particular kind of systematic unity – the moral, must be possible. We have found, it is true, that the systematic unity of nature could not be established according to speculative principles of reason, because, while reason possesses a causal power in relation to freedom, it has none in relation to the whole sphere of nature; and, while moral principles of reason can produce free actions, they cannot produce natural laws. It is, then, in its practical, but especially in its moral use, that the principles of pure reason possess objective reality.

I call the world *a moral world*, in so far as it may be in accordance with all the ethical laws – which, by virtue of the *freedom* of reasonable beings, it *can* be, and according to the necessary laws of *morality* it *ought to be*. But this world must be conceived only as an intelligible world, inasmuch as abstraction is therein made of all conditions (ends), and even of all impediments to morality (the weakness or pravity of human nature). So far, then, it is a mere idea

[A806/B834]

– though still a practical idea – which may have, and ought to have, an influence on the world of sense, so as to bring it as far as possible into conformity with itself. The idea of a moral world has, therefore, objective reality, not as referring to an object of intelligible intuition – for of such an object we can form no concept whatever – but to the world of sense – conceived, however, as an object of pure reason in its practical use – and to a *corpus mysticum* of rational beings in it, in so far as the *liberum arbitrium* of the individual is placed, under and by virtue of moral laws, in complete systematic unity both with itself, and with the freedom of all others.

That is the answer to the first of the two questions of pure reason which relate to its practical interest: *Do that which will render thee worthy of happiness*. The second question is this: If I conduct myself so as not to be unworthy of happiness, may I hope thereby to obtain happiness? In order to arrive at the solution of this question, we must inquire whether the principles of pure reason, which prescribe *a priori* the law, necessarily also connect this hope with it.

I say, then, that just as the moral principles are necessary according to reason in its *practical* use, so it is equally necessary according to reason in its *theoretical* use, to assume that every one has ground to hope for happiness in the measure in which he has made himself worthy of it in his conduct, and that therefore the system of morality is inseparably (though only in the idea of pure reason) connected with that of happiness.

Now in an intelligible, that is, in the moral world, in the concept of which we make abstraction of all the impediments to morality (sensitive desires), such a system of happiness, connected with and proportioned to morality, may be conceived as necessary, because freedom of the will – partly incited, and partly restrained by moral laws – would be itself the cause of general happiness; and thus rational beings, under the guidance of such principles, would be themselves the authors both of their own enduring welfare and that of others. But such a system of self-rewarding morality is only an idea, the carrying out of which depends upon the condition that every one acts as he ought; in other words, that all actions of reasonable beings be such as they would be if they sprang from a Supreme Will, comprehending in, or under, itself all particular wills. But since the moral law is binding on each individual in the use of his freedom of the will, even if others should not act in conformity with this law, neither the nature of things, nor the causality of actions and their relation to morality, determine how the consequences of these actions will be related to happiness; and the necessary connection of the hope of happiness with the inceasing endeavour to become worthy of happiness, cannot be known by reason, if we take nature alone for our guide. This connection can be hoped for only on the assumption that the cause of nature is a supreme reason, which governs according to moral laws.

I term the idea of an intelligence in which the morally most perfect will, united with supreme blessedness, is the cause of all happiness in the world, so far as happiness stands in strict relation to morality (as the worthiness of being happy), *the ideal of the supreme good*. It is only, then, in the ideal of the supreme *original* good, that pure reason can find the ground of the practically necessary connection of both elements of the highest *derivative* good, and accordinly of an intelligible, that is, *moral* world. Now since we are necessitated by reason to conceive ourselves as belonging to such a world, while the senses present to us nothing but appearances, we must assume the former as a consequence of our conduct in the world of sense (since the world of sense gives us no hint of it), and therefore as future in relation to us. Thus God and a future life are two hypotheses which, according to the principles of pure reason, are inseparable from the obligation which this reason imposes upon us.

Morality *per se* constitutes a system. But we can form no system of happiness, except in so far as it is dispensed in strict proportion to morality. But this is only possible in the intelligible world, under a wise author and ruler. Such a ruler, together with life in such a world, which we must look upon as future, reason finds itself compelled to assume; or it must regard the moral laws as idle dreams, since the necessary consequence which this same reason connects with them, must, without this hypothesis, collapse. Hence also the moral laws are universally regarded as *commands*, which they could not be, did they not connect *a priori* adequate consequences with their dictates, and thus carry with them *promises* and *threats*. But this, again, they could not do, did they not reside in a necessary being, as the supreme good, which alone can render such a teleological unity possible.

Leibniz termed the world, when viewed in relation to the rational beings which it contains, and the moral relations in which they stand to each other, under the government of the supreme good, *the kingdom of grace*, and distinguished it from the *kingdom of nature*, in which these rational beings live, under moral laws, indeed, but expect no other consequencies from their actions than such as follows according to the course of nature in the world of sense. To view ourselves, therefore, as in the kingdom of grace, in which all happiness awaits us, except in so far as we ourselves limit our participation in it by actions which render us unworthy of happiness, is a practically necessary idea of reason.

Practical laws, in so far as they are subjective grounds of actions, that is, subjective principles, are termed *maxims*. The *judgments* of morality, in its purity and ultimate results, are framed according to *ideas*; the *observance* of its laws, according to *maxims*.

The whole course of our life must be subject to moral maxims; but this is impossible, unless with the moral law, which is a mere idea, reason connects an efficient cause which ordains to all conduct which is in conformity with the moral law an issue either in this or in another life, which is in exact conformity with our highest aims. Thus, without a God and without a world, invisible to us now, but hoped for, the glorious ideas of morality are, indeed, objects of approbation and of admiration, but cannot be the springs of purpose and action. For they do not satisfy all the aims which are natural to every rational being, and which are determined *a priori* by pure reason itself, and necessary.

Happiness alone is, in the view of reason, far from being the complete good. Reason does not approve of it (however much inclination may desire it), except as united with desert. On the other hand, morality alone, and with it, mere *desert*, is likewise far from being the complete good. To make it complete, he who conducts himself in a manner not unworthy of happiness, must be able to hope for the possession of happiness. Even reason, unbiased by private ends, or interested considerations, cannot judge otherwise, if it puts itself in the place of a being whose business it is to dispense all happiness to others. For in the practical idea both points are essentially combined, though in such a way that participation in happiness is rendered possible by the moral disposition by the prospect of happiness. For a disposition which should require the prospect of happiness as its necessary condition, would not be moral, and hence also would not be worthy of complete happiness – a happiness which, in the view of reason, recognizes no limitation but such as arises from our own immoral conduct.

Happiness, therefore, in exact proportion with the morality of rational beings (whereby they are made worthy of happiness), constitutes alone the supreme good of a world into which we absolutely must transport ourselves according to the commands of pure but practical reason. This world is, it is true, only an intelligible world; for such a systematic unity of ends as it requires, the world of sense gives us no hint. Its reality can be based on nothing else but the hypothesis of a supreme original good. In it independent reason, equipped with all the sufficiency of a supreme cause, founds, maintains, and fulfils the universal order to things, with the most perfect teleological harmony, however much this order may be hidden from us in the world of sense.

This moral theology has the peculiar advantage, in contrast with speculative theology, of leading inevitably to the conception of a *sole, perfect*, and *rational* First Cause, whereof speculative theology does not give us any *indication* on objective grounds, far less any convincing *evidence*. For we find neither in transcendental nor in natural theology, however far reason may lead us in these, any ground to warrant us in assuming the existence of *one only* Being, which stands at the head of all natural causes, and on which these are entirely dependent. On the other hand, if we take our stand on moral unity as a necessary law of the universe, and from this point of view consider what is necessary to give this law adequate efficiency and, for us, obligatory force, we must come to the conclusion that there is one only supreme will, which comprehends all these laws in itself. For how, under different wills, should we find complete unity of ends ? This will must be omnipotent, that all nature and its relation to morality in the world may be subject to it; omniscient, that it may have knowledge of the most secret feelings and their moral worth; omnipresent, that it may be at hand to supply every necessity to which the highest weal of the world may give rise; eternal, that this harmony of nature and liberty may never fail; and so on.

But this systematic unity of ends in this world of intelligences – which, as mere nature, is only a world of sense, but as a system of freedom of the will, may be termed an intelligible, that is, moral world (*regnum gratiae*) – leads inevitably also to the teleological unity of all things which constitute this great whole, according to universal natural laws – just as the unity of the former is according to universal and necessary moral laws – and units the practical with the speculative reason. The world must be represented as having originated from an idea, if it is to harmonize with that use of reason without which we cannot even consider ourselves as worthy of reason – namely, the moral use, which rests entirely on the idea of the supreme good. Hence the investigation of nature receives a teleological direction, and becomes, in its widest extension, physico-theology. But this, taking its rise in moral order as a unity founded on the essence of freedom, and not accidentally instituted by external commands, establishes the teleological view of nature on grounds which must be inseparably connected with the internal possibility of things. This gives rise to a *transcendental theology*, which takes the ideal of the highest ontological perfection as a principle of systematic unity; and this principle connects all things according to univeral and necessary natural laws, because all things have their origin in the absolute necessity of the one only Primal Being.

What *use* can we make of our understanding, even in respect of experience, if we do not propose ends to ourselves? But the highest ends are those of morality, and it is only pure reason that can give us the knowledge of these. Though supplied with these, and putting ourselves under their guidance, we can make no teleological use of the knowledge of nature, as regards *knowledge*, unless nature itself has established teleological unity. For without this unity we should not even possess reason, because we should have no school for reason, and no cultivation through objects which afford the materials for is concepts. But teleological unity is a necessary unity, and founded on the essence of the individual will itself. Hence this will, which is the condition of the application of this unity *in concreto*, must be so likewise. In this way the transcendental enlargement of our rational knowledge would be, not the cause, but merely the effect of the practical teleology, which pure reason imposes upon us.

Hence, also, we find in the history of human reason that, before the moral concepts were sufficiently purified and determined, and before men had attained to a perception of the systematic unity of ends according to these concepts and from necessary principles, the knowledge of nature, and even a considerable amount of intellectual culture in many other sciences, could produce only rude and vague concepts of God, sometimes even admitting of an astonishing indifference with regard to this question altogether. But the more enlarged treatment of moral ideas, which was rendered necessary by the extremely pure moral law of our religion, awakened the interest, and thereby quickened the perceptions of reason in relation to this object. In this way, and without the help either of an extended acquaintance with nature, or of a reliable transcendental insight (for these have been wanting in all ages), a concept of God was arrived at, which we now hold to be the correct one, not because speculative reason convinces us of its correctness, but because it accords with the moral principles of reason. Thus it is to pure reason, but only in its practical use, that we must ascribe the merit of having connected with out highest interest a knowledge, of which mere speculation was able only to form a conjecture, but the validity of which it was unable to establish – and of having thereby rendered it, not indeed a demonstrated dogma, but a hypothesis absolutely necessary to the essential ends of reason.

But if practical reason has reached this elevation, and has attained to the conception of a sole Primal Being, as the supreme good, it must not, therefore, imagine that it has transcended the empirical conditions of its application, and risen to the immediate knowledge of new objects; it must not presume to start from the concept which it has gained, and to derive from it the moral laws themselves. For it was these very laws, the *internal* practical necessity of which led us to the hypothesis of an independent cause, or of a wise rule of the universe, who should give them effect. Hence we are not entitled to regard them as accidental and derived from the mere will of the rule, especially as we have no concept of such a will, except as formed in accordance with these laws. So far, then, as practical reason as the right to conduct us, we shall not look upon actions as binding on us, because they are the commands of God, but we shall regard them as divine commands, because we are internally bound by them. We shall study freedom under the teleological unity which accords with principles of reason; we shall look upon ourselves as acting in conformity with the divine will only in so far as we hold sacred the moral law which reason teaches us from the nature of actions themselves, and we shall believe that we can obey that will only by promoting the weal of the universe in ourselves and in others. Moral theology is, therefore, only of immanent use. It teaches us to fulfil our destiny here in the world, by placing ourselves in harmony with the general system of ends, and warns us against the fanaticism, nay, the crime of depriving reason of its legislative authority in the moral conduct of life, for the purpose of directly connecting this authority with the idea of the Supreme Being. For this would be, not an immanent, but a transcendent use of moral theology, and, like the transcendent use of mere speculation, would inevitably pervert and frustrate the ultimate ends of reason.

Section III: Opinion, Knowledge, and Belief

The holding of a thing to be true, is a occurrence in our understanding which may rest on objective grounds, but requires, also subjective causes in the mind of the person judging. If a judgment is valid for every rational being, then its ground is objectively sufficient, and it is termed a *conviction*. If, on the other hand, it has its ground in the particular character of the subject, it is termed a *persuasion*.

Persuasion is a mere illusion, the ground of the judgment, which lies solely in the subject, being regarded as objective. Hence a judgment of this kind has only private validity – is only valid for the individual who judges, and the holding of a thing to be true in this way cannot be communicated. But truth depends upon agreement with the object, and consequently the judgments of all understandings, if true, must be in agreement with each other (*consentientia uni tertio consentiunt inter se*). Conviction may, therefore, be distinguished, from an external point of view, from persuasion, by the possibility of communicating it, and by showing its validity for the reason of every man; for in this case the presumption, at least, arises, that the agreement of all judgments with each other, in spite of the different characters of individuals, rests upon the common ground of the agreement of each with the object, and thus the correctness of the judgment is established.

Persuasion, accordingly, cannot be *subjectively* distinguished from conviction, that is, so long as the subject views its judgment simply as an occurence of its own mind. But if we inquire whether the grounds of our judgment, which are valid for us, produce the same effect on the reason of others as on our own, we have then the means, though only subjective means, not, indeed, of producing conviction, but of detecting the merely private validity of the judgment; in other words, of discovering that there is in it the element of mere persuasion.

If we can, in addition to this, develop the *subjective causes* of the judgment, which we have taken for its *objective grounds*, and thus explain the deceptive judgment as an occurrence in our mind, apart altogether from the objective character of the object, we can then expose the illusion and need be no longer deceived by it, although, if its subjective cause lies in our nature, we cannot hope altogether to escape its influence.

I can only *maintain*, that is, affirm as necessarily valid for every one, that which produces conviction. Persuasion I may keep for myself, if it is agreeable to me; but I cannot, and ought not, to attempt to impose it as binding upon others.

Holding for true, or the subjective validity of a judgment in relation to conviction (which is, at the same time, objectively valid), has the three following degrees: *opinion, belief*, and *knowledge*. Opinion is a consciously insufficient judgment, subjectively as well as objectively. Belief is subjectively sufficient, but is recognized as being objectively insufficient. Knowledge is both subjectively and objectively sufficient. Subjective sufficiency is termed *conviction* (for myself); objective sufficiency is termed *certainty* (for all). I need not dwell longer on the explanation of such simple concepts.

I must never venture to *be of opinion*, without *knowing* something, at least, by which my judgment, in itself merely problematical, is brought into connection with the truth – which connection, although not perfect, is still something more than an arbitrary fiction. Moreover, the law of such a connection must be certain. For if, in relation to this law, I have nothing more than opinion, my judgment is but a play of the imagination, without the least relation to truth. In the judgments of pure reason, opinion has no place. For as they do not rest on empirical grounds, and as the sphere of pure reason is that of necessary truth and *a priori* knowledge, the principle of connection in it requires universality and necessity, and consequently perfect certainty – otherwise we should have no guide to the truth at all. Hence it is absurd to have an opinion in pure mathematics; we must know, or abstain from forming a judgment altogether. The case is the same with the maxims of morality. For we must not hazard an action on the mere opinion that it is allowed, but we must know it to be so.

In the transcendental sphere of reason, on the other hand, the term opinion is too weak, while the word knowledge is too strong. From the merely speculative point of view, therefore, we cannot form a judgment at all. For the subjective grounds of a judgment, such as produce belief, cannot be admitted in speculative inquiries, inasmuch as they cannot stand without empirical support, and are incapable of being communicated to others in equal measure.

But it is only from the *practical* point of view that a *theoretically* insufficient judgment can be termed belief. Now the practical reference is either to *skill* or to *morality*; to the former, when the end proposed is arbitrary and accidental, to the latter, when it is absolutely necessary.

If we propose to ourselves any end whatever, the conditions of its attainment are hypothetically necessary. The necessity is subjectively, but still only comparatively, sufficient, if I am acquainted with no other conditions under which the end can be attained. On the other hand, it is sufficient, absolutely, and for every one, if I know for certain that no one can be acquainted with any other conditions, under which the attainment of the proposed end would be possible. In the former case my supposition – my judgment with regard to certain conditions, is a merely accidental belief; in the latter it is a necessary belief. The physician must pursue some course in the case of a patient who is in danger, but is ignorant of the nature of the disease. He observes the symptoms, and concludes, according to the best of his judgment, that it is a case of phthisis. His belief is, even in his own judgment, only contingent: another man might, perhaps, come nearer the truth. Such a belief, contingent indeed, but still forming the ground of the actual use of means for the attainment of certain ends, I term *pragmatical belief*.

The usual test, whether that which any one maintains is merely his persuasion, or his subjective conviction at least, that is, his firm belief, is a *bet*. It frequently happens that a man delivers his opinions with so much boldness and assurance, that he appears to be under no apprehension as to the possibility of his being in error. The offer of a bet startles him, and makes him pause. Sometimes it turns out that his persuasion may be valued at a ducat, but not at ten. For he does not hesitate, perhaps, to venture a ducat, but if it is proposed to stake ten, he immediately becomes aware of the possibility of his being mistaken – a possibility which has hitherto escaped his observation. If we imagine to ourselves that we have to stake the happiness of our whole life on the truth of any proposition, our judgment drops its air of triumph, we take the alarm, and discover the actual strength of our belief. Thus pragmatical belief has degrees, varying in proportion to the interest at stake.

Now, in cases where we cannot enter upon any course of action in reference to some object, and where, accordingly, our judgment is purely theoretical, we can still represent to ourselves, in thought, the possibility of a course of action, for which we suppose that we have sufficient grounds, if any means existed of ascertaining the truth of the matter. Thus we find in purely theoretical judgments an *analogon* of practical judgments, to which the word *belief* may properly be applied, and which we may term *doctrinal belief*. I should not hesitate to stake my all on the truth of the proposition – if there were any possibility of bringing it to the test of experience – that, at least, some one of the planets, which we see, is inhabited. Hence I say that I have not merely the opinion, but the strong belief, on the correctness of which I would stake even many of the advantages of life, that there are inhabitants in other worlds.

Now we must admit that the doctrine of the existence of God belongs to doctrinal belief. For, although in respect to the theoretical knowledge of the universe I do not require to form any theory which necessarily involves this idea, as the condition of my explanation of the appearances which the universe presents, but, on the contrary, am rather bound so to use my reason as if everything were mere nature, still teleological unity is so important a condition of the application of my reason to nature, that it is impossible for me to ignore it – especially since, in addition to these considerations, abundant examples of it are supplied by experience. But the sole condition, so far as my knowledge extends, under which this unity can be my guide in the investigation of nature, is the assumption that a supreme intelligence has ordered all things according to the wisest ends. Consequently the hypothesis of a wise author of the universe is necessary for my guidance in the investigation of nature – is the condition under which alone I can fulfil an end which is contingent indeed, but by no means unimportant. Moreover, since the result of my attempts so frequently confirms the utility of this assumption, and since nothing decisive can be adduced against it, it follows that it would be saying far too little to term my judgment, in this case, a mere opinion, and that, even in this theoretical connection, I may assert that I firmly believe in God. Still, if we use words strictly, this must not be called a practical, but a doctrinal belief, which the theology of nature (physico-theology) must also produce in my mind. In the wisdom of a Supreme Being, and in the shortness of life, so inadequate to the development of the glorious powers of human nature, we may find equally sufficient grounds for a doctrinal belief in the future life of the human soul.

The expression of belief is, in such cases, an expression of modesty from the *objective* point of view, but, at the same time, of firm confidence, from the *subjective*. If I should venture to term this merely theoretical judgment even so much as a hypothesis which I am entitled to assume; a more complete concept, with regard to another world and to the cause of the world, might then be justly required of me than I am, in reality, able to give. For, if I assume anything, even as a mere hypothesis, I must, at least, know so much of the properties of *such* a being as will enable me, not to form the *concept*, but to imagine the *existence* of it. But the word *belief* refers only to the guidance which an idea gives me, and to its subjective influence on the conduct of my reason, which forces me to hold it fast, though I may not be in a position to give a speculative account of it.

But mere doctrinal belief is, to some extent, wanting in stability. We often quit our hold of it, in consequence of the difficulties which occur in speculation, though in the end we inevitably return to it again.

It is quite otherwise with *moral belief*. For in this sphere action is absolutely necessary, that is, I must act in obedience to the moral law in all points. The end is here incontrovertibly established, and there is only one condition possible, according to the best of my perception, under which this end can harmonize with all other ends, and so have practical validity – namely, the existence of a God and of a future world. I know also, to a certainty, that no one can be acquainted with any other conditions which conduct to the same unity of ends under the moral law. But since the moral precept is, at the same time, my maxim (as reason requires that it should be), I am irresistibly constrained to believe in the existence of God and in a future life; and I am sure that nothing can make me waver in this belief, since I should thereby overthrow my moral maxims, the renunciation of which would render me hateful in my own eyes.

Thus, while all the ambitious attempts of reason to penetrate beyond the limits of experience end in disappointment, there is still enough left to satisfy us in a practical point of view. No one, it is true, will be able to boast that he knows that there is a God and a future life; for, if he knows this, he is just the man whom I have long wished to find. All knowledge would receive this wonderful extension, through the instrumentality of his instruction. No, my conviction is not *logical*, but *moral* certainty; and since it rests on subjective grounds (of the moral sentiment), I must not even say: *It is* morally certain that there is a God, etc., but: *I am* morally certain, that is, my belief in God and in another world is so interwoven with my moral nature, that I am under as little apprehension of having the former torn from me as of losing the latter.

The only point in this argument that may appear open to suspicion, is that this rational belief presupposes the existence of moral sentiments. If we give up this assumption, and take a man who is entirely indifferent with regard to moral laws, the question which reason proposed, becomes then merely a problem for speculation, and may, indeed, be supported by strong grounds from analogy, but not by such as will compel the most obstinate scepticism to give way.[1] But in these questions no man is free from all interest. For though the want of good sentiments may place him beyond the influence of moral interests, still even in this case enough may be left to make him *fear* the existence of God and a future life. For he cannot pretend to any *certainty* of God and a future life. For he cannot pretend to any *certainty* of the non-existence of God and of a future life, unless – since it could only be proved by mere reason, and therefore apodeictically – he is prepared to establish the *impossibility* of both, which certainly no reasonable man would undertake to do. This would be a *negative* belief, which could not, indeed, produce morality and good sentiments, but still could produce an analogon of these, by operating as a powerful restraint on the outbreak of evil dispositions.

But, it will be said, is this all that pure reason can effect, in opening up prospects beyond the limits of experience? Nothing more than two articles of belief? Common sense could have done as much as this, without taking the philosophers to counsel in the matter!

I shall not here eulogize philosphy for the benefits which the laborious efforts of its criticism have conferred on human reason – even granting that its merit should turn out in the end to be only negative – for on this point something more will be said in the next section. But I ask, do you require that that knowledge which concerns all men, should transcend the common understanding, and should only be revealed to you by philosophers? The very circumstance which has called forth your censure, is the best confirmation of the correctness of our previous assertions, since it discloses, what could not have been foreseen, that Nature is not

---

[1] The human mind (as, I believe, every rational being must of necessity do) takes a natural interest in morality, although this interest is not undivided, and may not be practically in preponderance. If you strengthen and increase it, you will find the reason become docile, more enlightened, and more capable of uniting the speculative interest with the practical. But if you do not take care at the outset, or at least midway, to make men good, you will never force them into an honest belief.

chargeable with any partial distribution of her gifts in those matters which concern all men without distinction, and that in respect to the essential ends of human nature, we cannot advance further with the help of the highest philosophy, than under the guidance which nature has vouchsafed to the meanest understanding.

CHAPTER III : THE ARCHITECTONIC OF PURE REASON

By the term *architectonic* I mean the art of constructing a system. Without systematic unity, our knowledge cannot become science; it will be an aggregate, and not a system. Thus architectonic is the doctrine of the scientific in knowledge, and therefore necessarily forms part of our method.

Reason cannot permit our knowledge to remain in an unconnected and rhapsodic state, but requires that the sum of our knowledge should constitute a system. It is thus alone that they can advance the ends of reason. By a system I mean the unity of various knowledge under one idea. This idea is the concept – given by reason – of the form of a whole, in so far as the concept determines *a priori* not only the limits of its content, but the place which each of its parts is to occupy. The scientific idea contains, therefore, the end, and the form of the whole which is in accordance with that end. The unity of the end, to which all the parts of the system relate, and through which all have a relation to each other communicates unity to the whole system, so that the absence of any part can be immediately detected from our knowledge of the rest; and it determines *a priori* the limits of the system, thus excluding all contingent or arbitrary additions. The whole is thus an organism (*articulatio*), and not an aggregate (*coacervatio*); it may grow from within (*per intussusceptionem*), but it cannot increase by external additions (*per appositionem*). It is thus like an animal body, the growth of which does not add any limb, but, without changing their proportions, makes each in its sphere stronger and more active.

We require, for the execution of the idea of a system, a *schema*, that is, a content and an arrangement of parts determined *a priori* by the principle which the aim of the system prescribes. A schema which is not projected in accordance with an idea, that is, from the standpoint of the highest aim of reason, but merely empirically, in accordance with accidental aims and purposes (the number of which cannot be predetermined), can give us nothing more than *technical* unity. But the schema which is originated from an idea (in which case reason presents us with aims *a priori*, and does not look for them to experience), forms the basis of *architectonical unity. A science, in the proper acceptation of that term, cannot be formed technically*, that is, from observation of the similarity existing between different objects, and the purely contingent use we make of our knowledge *in concreto* with reference to all kinds of arbitrary external aims; its constitution must be framed on architectonical principles, that is, its parts must be shown to possess an essential affinity, and be capable of being derived from one supreme and internal aim or end, which forms the condition of the possibility of the scientific whole. The schema of a science must give *a priori* the plan of it (*monogramma*), and the division of the whole into parts, in conformity with the idea of the science; and it must also distinguish this whole from all others, according to certain understood principles.

No one will attempt to construct a science, unless he have some idea to rest on as a proper basis. But, in the elaboration of the science, he finds that the schema, nay, even the definition which he at first gave of the science, rarely corresponds with his idea; for this idea lies, like a germ, in our reason, its parts undeveloped and hid even from microscopial observation. For this reason, we ought to explain and define sciences, not according to the description which the originator gives of them, but according to the idea which we find based in reason itself, and which is suggested by the natural unity of the parts of the science already accumulated. For it will often be found, that the originator of a science, and even his latest successors, remain attached to an erroneous idea, which they cannot render clear to themselves, and that they thus fail in determining the true content, the articulation or systematic unity, and the limits of their science.

It is unfortunate that, only after having occupied ourselves for a long time in the collection of materials, under the guidance of an idea which lies undeveloped in the mind, but not according to any definite plan of arrangement – nay, only after we have spent much time and labour in the technical disposition of our materials, does it become possible to view the idea of a science in a clear light, and to project, according to architectonial principles, a plan of the whole, in accordance with the aims of reason. Systems seem, like certain worms, to be formed by a kind of *generatio aequivoca* – by the mere confluence of concepts, and to gain completeness only with the progress of time. But the schema or germ of all lies in reason; and thus is not only every system organized according to its own idea, but all are united into one grand system of human knowledge, of which they form members. For this reason, it is possible to frame an architectonic of all human knowledge, the formation of which, at the present time, considering the immense materials collected or to be found in the ruins of old systems, would not indeed be very difficult. Our purpose at present is merely to sketch the plan of the *architectonic* of all knowledge given by *pure reason*; and we begin from the point where the main root of human knowledge divides into two, one of which is *reason*. By reason I understand here the whole higher faculty of knowledge, the *rational* being placed in contradistinction to the *empirical*.

If I make complete abstraction of the content of knowledge, objectively considered, all knowledge is, from a subjective point of view, either historical or rational. Historical knowledge is *cognitio ex datis*, rational, *cognitio ex principiis*. Whatever may be the original source of knowledge, it is, in relation to the person who possesses it, merely historical, if he knows only what has been given him from another quarter, whether that knowledge was communicated by direct experience or by instruction. This the person who has *learned* a system of philosophy – say the Wolffian – although he has a perfect knowledge of all the principles, definitions, and arguments in that philosophy, as well as of the divisions that have been made of that philosphy, as well as of the divisions that have been made of the system, he possesses really no more than an *historical* knowledge of the Wolffian system; he knows only what has been told him, his judgments are only those which he has received from his teachers. Dispute the validity of a definition, and he is completely at a loss to find another. He had formed his mind on another's; but the imitative faculty is not the productive. His knowledge has not been drawn from reason; and although, objectively considered, it is rational knowledge, subjectively, it is merely historical. He has learned this or that philosophy, and is merely a plaster-cast of a living man. Rational knowledge which is objective, that is, which has its source in reason, can be so termed from a subjective point of view, only when it has been drawn by the individual himself from the sources of reason, that is, from principles; and it is in this way alone that criticism, or even the rejection of what has been already learned, can spring up in the mind.

All rational knowledge is, again, based either on concepts, or on the construction of concepts. The former is termed philosophical, the latter mathematical. I have already shown the essential difference of these two methods of knowledge in the first chapter. Knowledge may be objectively philosophical and subjectively historical – as is the case with the majority of scholars and those who cannot look beyond the limits of their system, and who remain in a state of pupillage all their lives. But it is remarkable that mathematical knowledge, when committed to memory, is valid, from the subjective point of view, as rational knowledge also, and that the same distinction cannot be drawn here as in the case of philosophical knowledge. The reason is, that the only way of arriving at this knowledge is through the essential principles of reason, and thus it is always certain and indisputable; because reason is employed *in concreto* – but at the same time *a priori* – that is, in pure, and therefore, infallible intuition; and thus all causes of illusion and error are excluded. Of all the *a priori* sciences of reason, therefore, mathematics alone can be learned. Philosophy – unless it be in an historical manner – cannot be learned; we can at most learn to *philosophize*.

Philosophy is the system of all philosophical knowledge. We must use this term in an objective sense, if we understand by it the archetype of all attempts at philosophizing, and the standard by which all subjective philosophies are to be judged. In this sense, philosophy is merely the idea of a possible science, which does not exist *in concreto*, but to which we endeavour in various ways to approximate, until we have discovered the right path to pursue – a path overgrown by the errors and illusions of sense – and the image we have hitherto tried to shape in vain, has become a perfect copy of the great prototype. Until that time, we cannot learn philosophy – it does not exist; if it does, where is it, who possesses it, and how shall we know it? We can only learn to philosophize, in other words, we can only exercise our powers of reasoning in accordance with general principles, retaining at the same time, the right of investigating the sources of these principles, of testing, and even of rejecting them.

Until then, our concept of philosophy is only a *scholastic concept* – a concept, that is, of a system of knowledge which we are trying to elaborate into a science; all that we at present know, being the systematic unity of this knowledge, and consequently the *logical* completeness of the knowledge for the desired end. But which has always formed the true basis of this term, especially when philosophy was personified and presented to us in the ideal of a *philosopher*. In this view, philosophy is the science of the relation of all knowledge to the ultimate and essential aims of human reason (*teleologia rationis humanae*), and the philosopher is not merely an artist, who occupies himself with concepts; but a law-giver, legislating for human reason. In this sense of the word, it would be in the highest degree arrogant to assume the title of philosopher, and to pretend that we had reached the perfection of the prototype which lies in the idea alone.

The mathematician, the natural philosopher, and the logician – how far soever the first may have advanced in rational, and the two latter in philosophical knowledge – are merely artists, engaged in the arrangement and formation of concepts; they cannot be termed philosophers. Above them all, there is the ideal teacher, who employs them as instruments for the advancement of the essential aims of human reason. Him alone can we call philospher; but he nowhere exists. But the idea of his legislative power resides in the mind of every man, and it alone teaches us what kind of systematic unity philosophy demands in view of the ultimate aims of reason. This idea is, therefore, a cosmical concept.[1]

In view of the complete systematic unity of reason, there can only be one ultimate end. To this all other aims are subordinate, and nothing more than means for its attainment. This ultimate end is the destination of man, and the philosophy which relates to it is termed moral philosophy. The superior position occupied by moral philosophy, above all other spheres for the operations of reason, sufficiently indicates the reason why the ancients always included the idea – and in an especial manner – of moralist in that of philosopher. Even at the present day, we call a man who appears to have the power of self-government, even although his knowledge may be very limited, by the name of philospher.

The legislation of human reason, or philosophy, has two objects – nature and freedom, and thus contains not only the laws of nature, but also those of ethics, at first in two separate systems, which, finally, merge into one grand philosophical system of cognition. The philosophy of nature relates to that *which is*, that of ethics to that which *ought to be*.

[1] By a *cosmical concept*, I mean one in which all men necessarily take an interest; the *aim* of a science must accordingly be determined according to *scholastic* concepts, if it is regarded merely as a means to certain arbitrarily proposed ends.

But all philosophy is either knowledge on the basis of pure reason, or the knowledge of reason on the basis of empirical principles. The former is termed pure, the latter empirical philosphy.

The philosophy of pure reason is either *propaedeutic*, that is, an inquiry into the power of reason in regard to pure *a priori* knowledge, and is termed critical philosophy; or it is, secondly, the system of pure reason – a science containing the systematic presentation of the whole body of philosophical knowledge, true as well as illusory, given by pure reason – and is called metaphysics. This name may, however, be also given to the whole system of pure philosophy, critical philosophy included, and may designate the investigation into the sources or possibility of *a priori* knowledge, as well as the presentation of the *a priori* knowledge which forms a system of pure philosophy – excluding, at the same time, all empirical and mathematical elements.

Metaphysics is divided into that of the *speculative* and that of the *practical* use of pure reason, and is, accordingly, either the *metaphysic of nature*, or the *metaphysic of ethics*. The former contains all the pure rational principles – based upon concepts alone (and this excluding mathematics) – of all *theoretical* concepts; the latter, the principles which determine and necessitate *a prior* all *action*. Now moral philosophy alone contains a code of laws – for the regulation of our actions – which are derived from principles entirely *a priori*. Hence the metaphysics of ethics is the only pure moral philosophy, as it is not based upon anthropological or other empirical considerations. The metaphysic of speculative reason is what is commonly called metaphysics in the more limited sense. But as pure moral philosophy properly forms a part of this system of cognition, we must allow it to retain the name of metaphysics, although it is not requisite that we should insist on so terming it in our present discussion.

It is of the highest importance to separate that knowledge which differs from others both in kind and in origin, and to take great care that it is not confounded with those with which they are generally found connected. What the chemist does in the analysis of substances, what the mathematician in pure mathematics, is, in a still higher degree, the duty of the philospher, that the value of each different kind of knowledge, and the part it takes in the operations of the mind, may be clearly defined. Human reason has never wanted a metaphysics of some kind, since it attained the power of thought, or rather of reflection; but is has never been able to keep this sphere of thought and knowledge pure from all admixture of foreign elements. The idea of a science of this kind is as old as speculation itself; and what mind does not speculate – either in the scholastic or in the popular fashion? At the same time, it must be admitted that even thinkers by profession have been unable clearly to explain the distinction between the two elements of our knowledge – the one completely *a priori*, the other *a posteriori*; and hence the proper definition of a peculiar kind of knowledge, and with it the just idea of a science which has so long and so deeply engaged the attention of the human mind, has never been established. When it was said – Metaphysics is the science of the first principles of human knowledge, this definition did not signalize a peculiarity in kind, but only a difference in degree; these first principles were thus declared to be more general than others, but no criterion of distinction from empirical principles was given. Of these some are more general, and therefore higher, than others; and – as we cannot distinguish what is completely *a priori* from that which is known to be *a posteriori* – where shall we draw the line which is to separate the higher and so-called first principles, from the lower and subordinate principles of knowledge? What would be said if we were asked to be satisfied with a division of the epochs of the world into the earlier centuries and those following them? Does the fifth, or the tenth century belong to the earlier centuries? it would be asked. In the same way I ask: Does the concept of extension belong to metaphysics? You answer, Yes. Well, that of body too? Yes. And that of a fluid body? You stop, you are unprepared to admit this; for if you do, everything will belong to metaphysics. From this it is evident that the mere degree of subordination – of the particular to the general – cannot determine the limits of a science; and that, in the present case, we must expect to find a difference in the concepts of metaphysics both in kind and in origin. The fundamental idea of metaphysics was obscured on another side, by the fact that this kind of *a priori* knowledge showed a certain similarity in character with the science of mathematics. Both have the property in common of possessing an *a priori* origin; but, in the one, our knowledge is based upon concepts, in the other, on the construction of concepts. Thus a decided dissimilarity between philosophical and mathematical knowledge comes out – a dissimilarity which was always felt, but which could not be made distinct for want of an insight into the criteria of the difference. And thus it happened that, as philosophers themselves failed in the proper development of the idea of their science, the elaboration of the science could not proceed with a definite aim, or under trustworthy guidance. Thus, too, philosophers, ignorant of the path they ought to pursue, and always disputing with each other regarding the discoveries which each asserted he had made, brought their science into disrepute with the rest of the world, and finally, even among themselves.

All pure *a priori* knowledge forms, therefore, in view of the peculiar faculty which originates it, a peculiar and distinct unity; and metaphysics is the term applied to the philosophy which attempts to represent that knowledge in this systematic unity. The speculative part of metaphysics, which has especially appropriated this appellation – that which we have called the *metaphysics of nature* – and which considers everything, as it is (not as it ought to be), by means of *a priori* concepts, is divided in the following manner.

Metaphysics, in the more limited acceptation of the term, consists of two parts – *transcendental philosophy* and the *physiology* of *pure reason*. The former presents the system of all the concepts and principles belonging to the understanding and the reason, and which relate to objects in general, but not to any particular given objects (*ontologia*); the latter has *nature* for its subject-matter, that is, the sum of given objects – whether given to the senses, or, if we will, to some other kind of intuition – and is accordingly *physiology*, although only *rationalis*. But the use of the faculty of reason in this rational mode of regarding nature is either physical or hyperphysical, or, more properly speaking, *immanent* or *transcendent*. The former relates to nature, in so far as our knowledge regarding it may be applied in experience (*in concreto*); the latter to the connection of the objects of experience, which transcends all experience. *Transcendent physiology* has, again, an *internal* and an *external* connection with its object, both, however, transcending possible experience; the former is the physiology of nature as a whole, or *transcendental knowledge of the world*, the latter of the connection of the whole of nature with a being above nature, or transcendental *knowledge of God*.

Immanent physiology, on the contrary, consider nature as the sum of all sensible objects, consequently, as it is presented to us – but still according to *a priori* conditions, for it is under these alone that nature can be presented to our minds at all. The objects of immanent physiology are of two kinds: 1. Those of the external senses, or *corporeal nature*; 2. The object of the internal sense, the soul, or, in accordance with our fundamental concepts of it, *thinking nature*. The metaphysics of corporeal nature if called *physics*, but, as it must contain only the principles of an *a priori* knowledge of nature, we must term it *rational physics*. The metaphysics of thinking nature is called *psychology*, and for the same reason it is to be regarded as merely the *rational knowledge* of the soul.

Thus the whole system of metaphysics consists of four principal parts: 1. *Ontology*: 2. *Rational Physiology*; 3. *Rational Cosmology*; and 4. *Rational Theology*. The second part – that of the rational doctrine of nature – may be subdivided into two, *physica rationalis*[1] and *psychologia rationalis*.

The fundamental idea of a philosophy of pure reason of necessity dictates this division; it is, therefore, *architectonical* – in accordance with the highest aims of reason, and not merely *technical*, or according to certain accidentally-observed similarities existing between the different parts of the whole science. For this reason, also, is the division immutable and of legislative authority. But the reader may observe in it a few points to which he ought to demur, and which may weaken his conviction of its truth and legitimacy.

In the first place, how can I desire an *a priori* knowledge or metaphysics of objects, in so far as they are given *a posteriori*? and how is it possible to know the nature of things according to *a priori* principles, and to attain to a *rational* physiology? The answer is this. We take from experience nothing more than is requisite to present us with an object (in general) of the external, or of the internal sense; in the former case, by the mere concept of matter (impenetrable and inanimate extension), in the latter, by the concept of a thinking being – given in the internal empirical representation, *I think*. As to the rest, we must not employ in our metaphysics of these objects any empirical principles (which add to the content of

---

[1] It must not be supposed that I mean by this appellation what is generally called *physica generalis*, and which is rather mathematics, than a philosophy of nature. For the metaphysics of nature is completely different from mathematics, nor is it so rich in results, although it is of great importance as a critical test of the application of pure concepts of the understanding to nature. For want of its guidance, even mathematicians, adopting certain common notions – which are, in fact, metaphysical – have unconsciously crowded their theories of nature with hypotheses, the fallacy of which becomes evident upon the application of the principles of this metaphysics, without detriment, however, to the employment of mathematics in this sphere of knowledge.

our concepts by means of experience), for the purpose of forming by their help any judgments respecting these objects.

Secondly, what place shall we assign to *empirical psychology*, which has always been considered a part of metaphysics, and from which in our time such important philosophical results have been expected, after the hope of constructing an *a priori* system of knowledge had been abandoned? I answer: It must be placed by the side of empirical physics or physics proper; that is, it must be regarded as forming a part of *applied* philosophy, which is therefore connected, although it must not be confounded, with psychology. Empirical psychology must therefore be banished from the sphere of metaphysics, and is indeed excluded by the very idea of that science. In conformity, however, with scholastic usage, we must permit it to occupy a place in metaphysics – but only as an appendix to it. We adopt this course from motives of economy; as psychology is not as yet full enough to occupy our attention as an independent study, while it is, at the same time, of too great importance to be entirely excluded or placed where it has still less affinity than it has with the subject of metaphysics. It is a stranger who has been long a guest; and we make it welcome to stay, until it can take up a more suitable abode in a complete system of anthropology – the pendant to empirical physics.

The above is the general idea of metaphysics, which, as more was expected from it than could be looked for with justice, and as these pleasant expectations were unfortunately never realized, fell into general disrepute. Our *Critique* must have fully convinced the reader, that, although metaphysics cannot form the foundation of religion, it must always be one of its most important bulwarks, and that human reason, which naturally pursues a dialectical course, cannot do without this science, which checks its tendencies towards dialectic, and, by elevating reason to a scientific and clear self-knowledge, prevents the ravages which a lawless speculative reason would infallibly commit in the sphere of morals as well as in that of religion. We may be sure, therefore, whatever contempt may be thrown upon metaphysics by those who judge a science not by its own nature, but according to the accidental effects it may have produced, that it can never be completely abandoned, that we must always return to it as to a beloved one who has been for a time estranged, because the questions with which it is engaged relate to the highest aims of humanity, and reason must always labour either to attain to settled views in regard to these, or to destroy those which others have already established.

Metaphysics, therefore – that of nature, as well as that of ethics, but in an especial manner the criticism which forms the propaedeutic to all the operation of reason – forms properly that department of knowledge which may be termed, in the truest sense of the word, philosophy. The path which it pursues is that of science, which, when it has once been discovered, is never lost, and never misleads. Mathematics, natural science, the common experience of men, have a high value as means, for the most part, to accidental ends – but at last also, to those which are necessary and essential to the existence of humanity. But to guide them to this high goal, they require the aid of rational knowledge on the basis of pure concepts, which, be it termed as it may, is properly nothing but metaphysics.

For the same reason, metaphysics forms likewise the completion of the *culture* of human reason. In this respect, it is indispensable, setting aside altogether the influence which it exerts as a science. For its subject-matter is the elements and highest maxims of reason, which form the basis of the *possibility* of some sciences and of the *use* of all. That, as a purely speculative science, it is more useful in preventing error, than in the extension of knowledge, does not detract from its value; on the contrary, the supreme office of censor which it occupies, assures to it the highest authority and importance. This office it administers for the purpose of securing order, harmony, and well-being to science, and of directing its noble and fruitful labours to the highest possible aim – the happiness of all mankind.

CHAPTER IV: THE HISTORY OF PURE REASON

This title is placed here merely for the purpose of designating a division of the system of pure reason, of which I do not intend to treat at present. I shall content myself with casting a cursory glance, from a purely transcendental point of view – that of the nature of pure reason – on the labours of philosophers up to the present time. They have aimed at erecting an edifice of philosophy; but to my eye this edifice appears to be in a very ruinous condition.

It is very remarkable, although naturally it could not have been otherwise, that, in the infancy of philosophy, the study of the nature of God, and the hope, or even the study, of the constitution of a future world, was the starting-point rather than the proper end.

However rude the religious conceptions generated by the remains of the old manners and customs of a less cultivated time, the intelligent classes were not thereby presented from devoting themselves to free inquiry into the existence and nature of God; and they easily saw that there could be no surer way of pleasing the invisible ruler of the world, and of attaining to happiness in another world at least, than a good and honest course of life in this. Thus theology and morals formed the two chief motives, or rather the points of attraction in all abstract inquiries. But it was the former that especially occupied the attention of speculative reason, and which afterwards became so celebrated under the name of metaphysics.

I shall not at present indicate the periods of time at which the greatest changes in metaphysics took place, but shall merely give a hasty sketch of the different ideas which occasioned the most important revolutions in this sphere of thought. There are three different ends, in relation to which these revolutions have taken place.

1. *In relation to the object* of the cognition of reason, philosophers may be divided into *sensualists* and *intellectualists*. *Epicurus* may be regarded as the head of the former, *Plato* of the latter. The distinction here signalized, subtle as it is, dates from the earliest times, and was long maintained. The former asserted, that reality resides in sensible objects alone, and that everything else is merely imaginary; the latter, that the senses are the parents of illusion, and that truth is to be found in the understanding alone. The former did not deny to the concepts of the understanding a certain kind of reality; but with them it was merely *logical*, with the others it was *mystical*. The former admitted *intellectual* concepts, but declared that sensuous objects alone possessed real existence. The latter maintained that all real objects were *intelligible*, and believed that the pure understanding possessed a faculty of *intuition* apart from sense, which, in their opinion, served only to confuse the pure understanding.

2. *In relation to the origin* of the pure knowledge of reason, we find one school maintaining that they are derived entirely from experience, and another, that they have their origin in reason alone. *Aristotle* may be regarded as the head of the *empiricists*, and *Plato* of the *noologists*. *Locke*, the follower of Aristotle in modern times, and *Leibniz* of Plato (although he cannot be said to have imitated him in his mysticism), have not been able to bring this question to

a settled conclusion. The procedure of Epicurus in his sensual system, in which he always restricted his conclusions to the sphere of experience, was much more consequent than that of Aristotle and Locke. The latter especially, after having derived all the concept and principle from experience, goes so far, in the employment of these concepts and principles, as to maintain that we can prove the existence of God and the immortality of the soul – both of them objects lying beyond the limits of possible experience – with the same force of demonstration as any mathematical proposition.

3. *In relation to method.* Method is procedure *according to principles.* We may divide the methods at present employed in the field of inquiry into the *naturalistic* and the *scientific.* The *naturalist* of pure reason lays it down as his principle, that common reason, without the aid of science – which he calls sound reason, or common sense – can give a more satisfactory answer to the most important questions of metaphysics than speculation is able to do. He must maintain, therefore, that we can determine the content and circumference of the moon more certainly by the naked eye, than by the aid of mathematical reasoning. But this system is mere misology reduced to principles; and, what is the most absurd thing in this doctrine, the neglect of all scientific means is paraded as a *peculiar method* of extending our knowledge. As regards those who are *naturalists* because they know no better, they are certainly not to be blamed. They follow common sense, without parading their ignorance as a method which is to teach us the wonderful secret, how we are to find the truth which lies at the bottom of the well of Democritus.

Quod sapio est mihi, non ego curo
Esse quod Arcesilas aerumnosique Solones

PERSIUS

is their motto, under which they may lead a pleasant and praise-worthy life, without troubling themselves with science or troubling science with them.

As regards those who wish to pursue a *scientific* method, they have now the choice of following either the *dogmatical* or the *sceptical*, while they are bound never to desert the *systematic* mode of procedure. When I mention, in relation to the former, the celebrated *Wolff*, and as regards the latter, *David Hume*, I may leave, in accordance with my present intention, all others unnamed. The *critical* path alone is still open. If my reader has been kind and patient enough to accompany me on this hitherto untravelled route, he can now judge whether, if he and others will contribute their exertions towards making this narrow footpath a high road of thought, that, which many centuries have failed to accomplish, may not be executed before the close of the present – namely, to bring reason to perfect contentment in regard to that which has always, but without permanent results, occupied its powers and engaged its ardent desire for knowledge.

SUGGESTIONS FOR FURTHER READING

Kant's collected works

Kant's gesammelte Schriften, edited by Königlich Preussische (subsequently: Deutsche) Akademie der Wissenschaften, in twenty-nine volumes. The standard edition of Kant's works and the edition referred to in standard pagination.

W. Weischedel, ed., *Werke in zwölf Bänden*, Frankfurt am Main, 1968.

Kant's individual works with English translations

1755 *Allgemeine Naturgeschichte und Theorie des Himmels* (*Universal Natural History and Theory of the Heavens*, trans. W. Hastie, Michigan, 1969).

1755 *Principiorum primorum cognitionis metaphysicae nova dilucidatio* (*New Exposition of the First Principles of Metaphysical Knowledge*, trans. in *Kant's Latin Writings* by L. W. Beck, M. J. Gregor, R. Meerbote and J. A. Reuscher, New York, 1986).

1763 *Der einzig mögliche Beweisgrund zu einer Demonstration des Daseins Gottes* (*The One Possible Basis for a Demonstration of the Existence of God*, trans. G. Treash, New York, 1979).

1764 *Beobachtungen über das Gefühl des Schönen und Erhabenen* (*Observation on the Feeling of the Beautiful and Sublime*, trans. J. Goldthwait, Calif., 1960).

1764 *Untersuchungen über die Deutlichkeit der Grundsätze der natürlichen Theologie und der Moral* (*An Inquiry into the Distinctness of the Principles of Natural Theology and Morals*, trans. G. B. Kerferd and D. E. Walford in *Kant's Selected Pre-Critical Writings*, Manchester, 1968).

1766 *Träume eines Geistersehers, erläutert durch die Träume der Metaphysik* (*Dreams of a Spirit-Seer, illustrated by Dreams of Metaphysics*, trans. E. F. Gorwitz, London, 1900).

1770 *De mundi sensibilis atque intelligibilis forma et pricipiis* (Inaugural dissertation: *On the Form and Principles of the Sensible and Intelligible World*, trans. G. B. Kerferd and D. E. Walford in *Kant's Selected Pre-Critical Writings*, Manchester, 1968).

1781 *Kritik der reinen Vernunft* (*Critique of Pure Reason*, trans. N. Kemp Smith, London, 1929).

1783 *Prolegomena ~u einer jeden künftigen Metaphysik* (*Prolegomena to Any Future Metaphysics*, trans. L. W. Beck, London, 1950).

1784 *Idee zu einer allgemeinen Geschichte in weltbürgerlicher Absicht* (*Idea for a Universal History from a Cosmopolitan Point of View*, trans. H. B. Nisbet in *Kant's Political Writings*, ed. H. Reiss, Cambridge, 1970).

1785 *Grundlegung zur Metaphysik der Sitten* (*The Groundwork of the Metaphysics of Morals*, trans. H. J. Paton, London, 1949; and *Foundations of the Metaphysics of Morals*, trans. L. W. Beck, Indianapolis, 1959).

1786 *Metaphysische Anfangsgründe der Naturwissenschaft* (*Metaphysical Foundations of Natural Science*, trans. J. Ellington, Indianapolis, 1970).

1787 *Kritik der reinen Vernunft*, second edition *Critique of Pure Reason*, trans. N. Kemp Smith, London, 1929).

1788 *Kritik der praktischen Vernunft* (*Critique of Practical Reason*, trans. L. W. Beck, Indianapolis, 1956).

1790 *Kritik der Urteilkraft* (*Critique of Judgment*, trans. J. C. Meredith, Oxford, 1952).

1793 *Religion innerhalb der Grenzen der blossen Vernunft* (*Religion within the Limits of Reason Alone*, trans. T. M. Greene and H. H. Hudson, New York, 1960).

1795 *Zum ewigen Frieden* (*Perpetual Peace*, trans. L. W. Beck, Indianapolis, 1957).

1797 *Metaphysik der Sitten* (*Metaphysics of Morals*; Part I translated as *The Metaphysical Elements of Justice* by J. Ladd, Indianapolis, 1965; Part II translated as *The Metaphysical Principles of Virtue* by J. Ellington, Indianapolis, 1964, and as *The Doctrine of Virtue* by M. J. Gregor, New York, 1964).

1798 *Anthropologie in pragmatischer Hinsicht* (*Anthropology from a Pragmatic Point of View*, trans. M. J. Gregor, The Hague, 1974).

1804 *Über die Fortschritte der Metaphysik seit Leibniz und Wolff* (*What Real Progress has Metaphysics Made in Germany since the Time of Leibniz and Wolff?*, trans. T. Humphrey, New York, 1983).

Currently under preparation is The Cambridge Edition of the Works of Immanuel Kant, which will provide new or revised translations of all the works.

Life and Letters

Gulyga, A., *Immanuel Kant: His Life and Thought*, Boston, 1987.

Vorländer, K., *Immanuel Kant's Leben*, Leipzig, 1924; Hamburg, 1986.

Zweig, A., *Kant's Philosophical Correspondence*, Chicago and London, 1967.

Background and Context

Beck, L. W., *Early German Philosophy: Kant and his Predecessors*, Cambr., Mass., 1969.
Beiser, F. C., *The Fate of Reason: German Philosophy from Kant to Fichte*, Cambr., Mass., 1987.
Beiser, F. C., *Enlightenment, Revolution and Romanticism*, Cambr., Mass., 1992.
Buchdahl, G., *Metaphysics and the Philosophy of Science: The Classical Origins Descartes to Kant*, Oxford, 1969.

General Introductions

Hartnack, J., *Kant's Theory of Knowledge*, London, 1967 (on the *Critique of Pure Reason* only).
Kemp, J., *The Philosophy of Kant*, Oxford, 1968.
Körner, S., *Kant*, Penguin, 1955.
Walker, R., *Kant*, London, 1978.

Commentaries on the Critique of Pure Reason

Ewing, A. C., *A Short Commentary on Kant's Critique of Pure Reason*, Chicago, 1938.
Heimsoeth, H. *Tranzendentale Dialectic: Ein Kommentar zu Kant's Kritik der reinen Vernunft*, Berlin, 1966–71.
Kemp Smith, N., *A Commentary to Kant's Critique of Pure Reason*, London, 1923.
Vaihinger, H., *Commentar zu Kant's Kritik der reinen Vernunft*, Stuttgart, 1881–92.

Collections of articles on the Critique of Pure Reason

Beck, L. W. (ed.), *Kant Studies Today*, LaSalle, Ill., 1967.
Beck, L. W. (ed.), *Kant's Theory of Knowledge*, Dordrecht, 1974.
Guyer, P. (ed.), *The Cambridge Companion to Kant*, 1992.
Penelhum, T. and J. J. MacIntosh (eds), *The First Critique*, Belmont, 1969.
Schaper, E. and W. Vossenkuhl (eds), *Reading Kant*, Oxford, 1989.
Wolff, R. P. (ed.), *Kant: A Collection of Critical Essays*, New York, 1967.

General Studies of the Critique of Pure Reason

Allison, H. E., *Kant's Transcendental Idealism*, New Haven, 1983.

Beck, L. W., *Studies in the Philosophy of Kant*, Indianapolis, 1965.

Bennett, J., *Kant's Analytic*, Cambridge, 1966; *Kant's Dialectic*, Cambridge, 1974. Strawson and Bennett discuss each other in *Philosophical Review*, 1968.

Bird, G., *Kant's Theory of Knowledge*, London, 1962.

Buchdahl, G., *Kant and the Dynamics of Reason*, Oxford, 1992.

De Vleeschauer, H. J., *The Development of Kantian Thought*, London, 1962.

Ewing, A. C., *Idealism. A Critical Survey*, London, 1934. Ch. III, 'Kantian Idealism'.

Findlay, J. N., *Kant and the Transcendental Object: A Hermeneutic Study*, Oxford, 1981.

Friedman, M., *Kant and the Exact Sciences*, Cambr., Mass., 1992.

Heidegger, M., *Kant and the Problem of Metaphysics*, trans. J. S. Churchill, Bloomington, 1962.

Martin, G., *Kant's Metaphysics and Theory of Science*, Manchester, 1955.

Powell, C. T., *Kant's Theory of Self-Consciousness*, Oxford, 1990.

Schwyzer, H., *The Unity of Understanding: A Study in Kantian Problems*, Oxford, 1990.

Strawson, P., *The Bounds of Sense*, London, 1966.

Walsh, W. H., *Kant's Criticism of Metaphysics*, Edinburgh, 1975.

Wolff, R. P., *Kant's Theory of Mental Activity*, Cambr., Mass., 1963.

INDEX

Absolute, 250–1
  see also Unconditioned
Absolute necessity of resolving
    transcendental problems of pure
    reason, 348–52
Accidents, 171
Aesthetic, transcendental, 48–68
  general remarks, 61-8
  see also Sensibility
Affinity see Association
Affirmativeness, in quality of
    judgments, 80
Agreement and opposition, 216, 218
Algebra, 472
Amphiboly of the concepts of
    reflection, 216–20
  remark on, 220–31
Analogies of experience, 155, 165–90
Analytic, transcendental see
    Transcendental analytic
Analytic, logic, 73–5
Analytic of concepts, 77–137
Analytic of principles, 139–233
Analytical knowledge, principle of,
    150
Analytical judgments, 35–7, 149–51
Animality, 261
Anticipations of perception, 155,
    159–64
Antinomies of pure reason, 259,
    307–94
  first conflict of the transcendental
    ideas, 317–22
  second conflict, 322–9
  third conflict, 329–34
  fourth conflict, 334–40
  concluding remarks, 393–4
Antithetic of pure reason, 315–40
Apodeictic judgments, 55, 80
A posteriori knowledge, 30, 61
Appearances (Erscheinungen), 48, 57,
    59, 66, 94, 139, 143, 168

composition, 369–72
  illusory, 66–7, 291
Apperception, 66, 131, 304
  highest principle, 101–3
  reality of, 269
  source of knowledge, 130, 131
  synthetical unity of, 99–101, 111,
    126, 137
  transcendental, 126
Apprehension in intuition, synthesis,
    122
A priori knowledge, 14, 15, 18, 30–2
  determination of, 33–5
  reasons for possibility of
    experience, 120–30
  not all transcendental, 72
  synthetical, 37–9
Architectonic of pure reason, 532–42
Archetypes (Plato), 244
Aristotle, 543
  categories, 85, 86
  logical topic, 220
  and understanding, 244
Arithmetic, 38
Assertorical judgments, 80
Association
  empirical rule, 129
  of representations, 134
Augmentative judgments, 35
Axioms, 480–1
  of intuition, 155, 156–9

Bacon, Francis, 1, 13
Baumgarten, A. G., 49n
Belief
  doctrinal, 529
  moral, 530–1
Berkeley, George, 67, 194–5
Body
  concept of, 35–6
  divisibility of, 79, 97
  weight, 104–5

see also Matter
Brucker, on Plato, 246

Canon of pure reason, 513–32
Categorical judgments, 80
Categories, 85–7, 97, 143–4
  list of, 85
  of Aristotle, 85, 86
  possibility, preliminary
    explanation, 128–30
  pure concepts of the understanding,
    83–90
    application to objects of
      experience, 107–9
    application to objects of the
      senses, 109–13
    deduction, 91–119
    not derived from nature, 116
    result of, 117–19
    schemata, 142–8
Causality
  concept of, 94–5
  and empirical judgment, 36–7, 129
  through freedom in harmony with
    the universal law of natural
    necessity, 379–81
  law of, and succesion in time,
    172–85
  principle of, 20
  schema of, 146
  transcendental law of, 413n
  two modes - nature or freedom,
    376
Causality and dependence, category
  of relation, 85
Censura of reason, 495
Change (*Wechsel*)
  concept of, 55, 171–2, 203
  and the reality of time, 58
Cicero, and idle reason, 459n
Civil laws, principles uninvestigated,
  237
Co-existence, principle of, 284–7
Cogito, ergo sum, 262, 270n
Cognition *see* Knowledge
Community (*Gemeinschaft*)
  category of relation, 85, 88–9, 204
  law of, 185–8
  schema of, 146
Comparison, concepts of, 217
Completeness, absolute, 312
Composition of appearances in the
  universe, 369–70

concepts (*Begriffe*), 69
  derived from categories, 86–7
  empirical or pure, 248
  form of knowledge, 248
  and intuition, 107, 248
  of reason, 243
  and thought, 78–9, 96
Conclusio, knowledge, 254
Conflicts *see* Antinomies of pure
  reason
Connections, concept, 98, 261
Consciousness, 98n, 102, 126–7
  see also Self-consciousness
Contingency, 202–3
  see also Necessity
Contradiction, principle of, 37, 150
Copernicus, Nicolaus, 15, 17n
Cosmical concepts, 308, 536n
Cosmological conflict of reason with
  itself, 359–64
Cosmological dialectic,
  transcendental idealism as key,
  355–9
Cosmological idea of the totality of
  the dependence of appearances,
  390–3
Cosmological idea of the totality of
  the derivation of world events
  from their causes, 376–90
Cosmological idea of freedom in its
  connection with universal natural
  necessity, 381–90
Cosmological ideas
  four only, 312
  empirical use of the regulative
    principle of reason, 368–93
  pure reason as regulative principle,
    364–8
  system of, 308–14
Cosmological proof of God,
  impossibility, 412–21
Cosmological questions, sceptical
  exposition of, 353–5
Cosmology, 255
  rational, as part of metaphysics,
    540
  transition to, from rational
    psychology, 273–5
Cosmotheology, 428
Culture, 468

Deduction of pure concepts of the
  understanding, 91–119, 120–38

Definition, 477–80
Deism, 428, 429
Demonstration, 481
Descartes, René
  idealism, 194, 195
  Cogito, ergo sum, 262, 270n
  ontological argument for the
    existence of God, 412
Determinability, 216, 396–7
Dialectic, transcendental *see*
  Transcendental dialectic
Dialectic logic, 73–5
Dialectical illusion in transcendental
  proofs of the existence of a
  necessary being, 418–21
Dialectical inferences of pure reason,
  258–9
Difference *see* Identity and difference
Discipline, the term, 468n
Discipline of pure reason, 468–513
  in its dogmatic use, 470–83
  in its polemical use, 483–99
  in regard to hypotheses, 499–506
  in regard to its proofs, 506–13
Discursive concepts, 55
Disjunctive judgments, 80
Doctrinal belief, 529
Doctrine of space and time (Leibniz),
  224
Dogmatism, 4, 23–4
  and cosmological ideas, 343–4
  dogmatical certainty, and pure
    reason, 470–83
Duration, mode of time, 169
Dynamical class of categories, 87–8

Empirical concepts, 191
Empirical deduction, 91–2
Empirical doctrine of the soul, 260
Empirical judgments (synthetical),
  35–6
Empirical psychology, 541
Empirical use of the regulative
  principle of reason, 368–93
Empiricism, and cosmological ideas,
  344–8
Ens realissimum, 22, 399, 404, 409,
  413, 414, 509
Epicureanism, versus Platonism, 346
Epicurus, 543
  and exercise of reason, 346n
  prolepsis, 159
Epigenesis of pure reason, 118

Examination, 216
Existence/non-existence, category of
  modality, 85
Experience, 15–16, 30
  A priori reasons for possibility of,
    120–130
  analogies of, 155, 165–90
  and knowledge, 31–2
Explicative judgments (analytical), 35

Faculty of judgment, doctrine of,
  139–40
Faculty of principles, i.e. reason, 236
Faith *see* Belief
Fate, 91
Feeling *see* Sensations
Figurative synthesis, 109
Form, 48
Fortune, 91
Freedom
  causality through, 379–81
  cosmological idea of, 381–90
  metaphysical inquiry, 257n
  and Plato, 246
  a problem of pure reason, 20, 22,
    33
Future life *see* Immortality

Galileo Galilei, 13
Generatio aequivoca, 117
Geometry, 13, 38, 51–2, 92–3, 111n
God, 120
  dialectical illusion in all
    transcendental proofs, 418–21
  metaphysical inquiry, 257n
  a problem of pure reason, 21, 31,
    67
  three modes of proving the
    existence of, 406
    cosmological, 412–21
    ontological, 407–12
    physico–theological, 422–7
Zeno's argument, 361–2

Habit, 97
History of pure reason, 542–5
Hume, David, 487, 544
  on causation, 32, 40, 494–7
  on understanding, 96–7
Hypotheses, and discipline of pure
  reason, 499–506
Hypothetical judgments, 80

Ideal, in general, 394–6
Ideal of pure reason, 259, 394–466
Ideal of the highest good, 517–26
Idealism
  dogmatic, 291–2
  formal and material, 356n
  refutation of material idealism,
    25n, 193–200
Ideality
  of external sense, 65
  of space, 53
  with regard to external relation,
    286–93
Ideas
  concepts formed from notions, 248
  in general, 244–8
Identity and difference, 216, 217–18,
  227
Illusion
  dialectical, in transcendental proofs
    of the existence of a necessary
    being, 418–21
  logical, 139, 235
  transcendental, 233–42
Illusory appearances, 66–7, 291
Image (Bild), 144–5
Imagination (Einbildungskraft)
  and perception, 133n
  and schemata, 144
  source of knowledge, 130, 131
  transcendental synthesis, 84,
    110–11
Immanent principles of
  understanding, 233, 240
Immateriality, concept, 261
Immortality
  metaphysical inquiry, 257n
  principle of, 261
  a problem of pure reason, 21, 22,
    33
Impossible see Possible
Incorruptibility concept, 261
Inertia, principle, 40n
Inference, and reason, 253
Infinite judgments, 80
Inherence, 60
  and subsistence, category of
    relation, 85
Intelligence, as self, 113
Intensive quantity, 160–1
Internal and external, 216, 218

Intuition (Anschauung,) 48–9, 61,
    62–3, 64–5, 66, 95–6, 228
  subject to the categories, 105
  form of knowledge, 248
  and concepts, 69, 107
  empirical, 61, 93–4, 107
  manifold of, 99
  basis of perception, 131
  pure, 61, 69, 107
  of space, 50–1, 52–3, 61, 107
  of time, 55, 56, 61, 107
  and understanding, 78
I think, 259, 262ff

Judgment (Urteil)
  analytical and synthetical, 35–7
  deficiency, 140n
  doctrine of faculty of judgment,
    139–40
Judgments
  and apperception of the concepts,
    104–5
  function of thought in, 79–80
  singular and universal, 80

Knowledge
  A posteriori, 30
  A priori, 15–16, 30–2, 72
  pure and empirical, 30–2
  Leibniz/Wolff view, 62
  as objective perception, 248
  and sensibility, 62

Law of community, and principle of
  co-existence, 185–8
Law of reciprocity, and principle of
  co-existence, 185–8
Leibniz, G. W., 543–4
  on appearances, 217–18, 221
  construction of intellectual system
    of the world, 221–2, 223
  and cosmological proof of existence
    of God, 413ff
  kingdom of grace, 521–2
  and knowledge, 62
Limitation, category of quality, 85
Locke, John, 4, 92, 543
  system of noogony, 221
  on understanding, 96–7
Logic, 11ff, 69–71
  analytic and dialectic, 73–6
  of elements, 70

of illusion, 139
based on understanding, judgment
and reason, 139
transcendental, 69–138
of truth, 139
Logical illusion, 235
Logical place, 220
Logical reflection, 217
Logical topic (Aristotle), 220
Logical use of reason, 238–9

Manifold
affinity of, 139
in appearances, 168
of the internal sense, 143
of pure intuition, 84–5, 105, 122,
143, 147
of representations, 98, 100–1,
126–7
Mathematical class of categories,
87–8
Mathematics, 12–13, 97, 107, 154,
352
and A priori judgment, 32, 33, 34
concepts, 207
and Plato, 246n
and pure reason, 470–6
and synthetical judgments, 37–9
transcendental ideas, 374–6
Matter, 48, 73, 219
and form, 219–20
see also Substance
Mendelssohn, Moses, proof for the
permanence of the soul, 267–71
Metaphysics, 3ff, 14ff, 18ff
defined, 33, 539
divisions of, 537, 539
of ethics, 537
of nature, 537, 539
as a science, 41–2
and synthetical judgments, 39, 40,
41
three ideas of, 257n
whole system, 540
Modality
categories, 85
in judgments, 80, 82–3
principles of, 200–1
Monadology (Leibniz), 223
Monads, 228
Moral belief, 530–1
Motion, 111
concept of, 55

Natural dialectic of human reason,
448–66
Natural necessity, 314
Natural science see Physics
Natural theology, 67
Nature, a totality of appearances,
130, 136, 188–9, 314n
Necessary unity, 104
Necessity/contingence
category of modality, 85
schema of, 146
Negation, category of quality, 85,
145
Negative judgments, 80
Noogony (Locke), 221
Nothing (negation), concept of,
232–3
Notio, pure concept, 248
Noumena, defined, 211
Number see Algebra; Arithmetic

Objections, types, 297–8
Objective deduction, 256
Objective synthesis, 307
Objective unity of self-consciousness,
103
Ontological proof of God,
impossibility, 407–12
Ontology, and metaphysics, 540
Ontotheology, 428
Opinion, knowledge and belief, 6,
526–32
Opposition/Agreement, 216, 218
Organon
and general logic, 74, 75
and pure reason, 42

Paralogisms, 258, 259–306
first (substantiality), 267–7
second (simplicity), 277–83
third (personality), 283–6
fourth (ideality), 286–306
Particularity, in quantity of
judgments, 80
Perception, 192
anticipation of, 131–6, 155,
159–64
as representation with
consciousness, 248
Perfection, 90
see also Ens realissimum
Permanence of substance, principle
of, 168–72

Permanence of the soul,
    Mendelssohn's proof, 266–70
Personality
    concept, 261
    third paralogism, 283–6
Phenomena *see* Appearances
Philosophical knowledge, 470–1
Physico-theological proof of God,
    impossibility, 422–7
Physics, 13–14, 97
    and synthetical judgments, 39, 40n
Physiology
    of pure reason, 539
    rational, 540
Place, logical, 220
Plato, 543
    the word 'idea', 244–5
    and idealism, 34
    reprimand to Zeno of Elea, 361–7
    Republic, 246–7
Platonism and Epicureanism, 346
Plurality, category of quantity, 85
Polemic of pure reason, 483–99
Possibility/impossibility, 231–3
    category of modality, 85
    schema, 146
Possibility of experience, 152–3
Post predicaments (Aristotle), 86
Postulates of empirical thought, 155,
    190–4
Power, 437
Practical logic, as transcendental
    doctrine of method, 467
Predicables, 86–7
Predicaments (Aristotle), 86
Preformation system of pure reason,
    118
Priestley, J. B., 487
Principle, term, 236–7
Principle of all analytical knowledge,
    150
Principle of co-existence, 185–8
Principle of co-existence, 185–8
Principle of contradiction, 37, 150
Principle of the permanence of
    substance, 168–72
Principle of the succession in time,
    172–85
Principles, faculty of, i.e. reason, 236
Probability, 233
Problematical judgments, 80
Productive imagination, 110

Progressus in indefinitum, 366–7
Proofs, and discipline of pure reason,
    506–13
Propaedeutic to system of pure
    reason, 12, 43
Protipon transcendentale see
    Transcendental ideal
Psychological paralogism, 272–3
Psychology, 110, 255
    concepts of pure psychology, 261
    consideration of pure psychology,
        293–306
    first paralogism of, 276–7
    transcendental, 277–93
Pure, defined, 48–9
Pure concept, 191
    as a *notio*, 248
Pure concepts of the understanding
    (categories), 83–90
    deduction, 91–119
    result of, 117–19
    schemata, 142–8
Pure use of reason, 239–42

Qualitative completeness, plurality
    and unity, 90
Quality in judgments, 80–1
Quantities, 472
Quantity
    categories, 85
    in judgments, 80
    schema of, 145, 146

Rational cosmology, and
    metaphysics, 540
Rational doctrine of the soul, 260–1
Rational physiology, and
    metaphysics, 540
Rational psychology, and cosmology,
    273–5
Rational theology, and metaphysics,
    540
Rational unity, 251
Reality
    category of quality, 85, 145
    schema of, 146
    of space, 53
Reason (*Vernunft*), 236–8
    architectonic of pure reason,
        532–42
    canon of pure reason, 513–32
    censura of, 495

constitutive principle of, 421
and cosmological conflict, 341–8,
359–64
cosmological ideas, 354–8
critique of, 5–6, 18
and critique of theology, 427–33
critique of pure reason as special
science, 42–5
dialectical inferences of, 258–9
empirical use of the regulative
principle, 368–83
faculty of inference, 253–4
general problem, 39–42
history of pure reason, 542–5
importance, 33
and pure sciences, 350
regulative employment of the ideas
of pure reason, 421, 433–48
regulative principle, and
cosmology, 364–8
speculative, 455–7
seat of the transcendental illusion,
225–31
ultimate end of the use of pure
reason, 514–17
ultimate purpose of the natural
dialectic of human reason,
448–66
Receptivity, 69
see also Sensibility
Reciprocity, law of, 182–5
see also Community
Recognition, synthesis of, 123–7
Reduction, 17n
Reflection, 188, 217
amphiboly of the concepts of,
215–30
Refutation of idealism, 193–200
Regress in infinitum, 366–7
Regulative principle of pure reason,
and cosmological ideas, 364–8
Relations
categories of, 85
in judgments, 80, 81–2
time and space as, 60
Representations (Vorstellungen), 15,
95, 98–9, 109, 122–4
as genus, 248
Reproductive imagination, 110
synthesis of, 122–4
Restraint, 468

see also Discipline
Right, concept of, 62

Scepticicm of Hume, 494–5
Schemata, transcendental, of pure
concepts, 142–8
Segner: Arithmetic, 38
Self-consciousness, 110, 112–13, 131,
195–7
objective unity of, 103
Sensation (Empfindung), 69
form of perception, 248
Sense, source of knowledge, 130–1
Sensibility (Sinnlichkeit), 45, 52–3,
109
defined, 48, 69
faculty, 62, 66
source of knowledge, 233n
Simplicity, second paralogism, 277–8
Singular judgments, 80
Solution of cosmological ideas
composition of appearances in the
unvierse, 369–70
totality of the dependence of
appearances, 390–3
totality of the derivation of world
events from their causes, 376–90
totality of the division of a whole
given in intuition, 372–6
Solution of the transcendental
dynamical ideas, 374–6
Solution of the transcendental
mathematical ideas, 374–6
Soul
immortality, 81
rational doctrine of the, 260–1
Space, 114n
concept, 49–55, 56, 93
and Leibniz, 224
metaphysical exposition, 49–51
transcendental exposition of, 51–2
Speculative reason, arguments in
proof of the existence of a
supreme being, 402–7
Spirituality, 261
Spontaneity, 69, 99, 109, 110
Stahl, Georg Ernest, 13
Stupidity, 140n
Subsistence see Inherence
Substance
concepts of, 191–2
first paralogism of substantiality,
276–7

principle of permanence of, 168–72
schema of, 146
Subsumption, faculty of, 140, 142
Sulzer, 485
Supreme being (*ens summum*), 400
arguments of speculative reason in proof of the existence of, 402–7
see also God
Supreme principle of all analytical judgments, 149–51
Supreme principle of all synthetical judgments, 151–3
Syllogisms, 239, 240, 254
Synthesis, defined, 17n, 84, 98
Synthesis of apprehension, 114
in intuition, 122
Synthesis of recognition in a concept, 124–8
Synthesis of reproduction in the imagination, 122–4
Synthetical *A priori* judgments, 37–9
possibility, 39–42
Synthetical judgments, 35–7, 151–3
Synthetical unity of apperception, 99–101
highest principle, 101–3
System of all principles of pure understanding, 148–205
System of cosmological ideas, 308–14
System of transcendental ideas, 255–8
Systematic representation of all synthetical principles of the pure understanding, 153–205

Terrasson, Abbé Jean, 8
Thales of Miletus, 13
Theism, 428, 429
Theology, 255
based on speculative principles of reason, 427–33
rational, 540
Thought, 7, 48, 69, 265n
Time, 54–60, 122
appearances in, 188–90
concept of, 93
condition of the manifold of the internal sense, 143
and Leibniz, 224
metaphysical exposition, 44–5
three modi – permanence, succession and co-existence, 165

principle of the succession in time, 172–85
reality of, 57–8
and schemata, 145–7
transcendental exposition, 55
Topic, logical (Aristotle), 220
Torricelli, Evangelista, 13
Totality
category of quantity, 85
as universality, 250
Transcendent principles of understanding, 234
Transcendental aesthetic, 48–68, 281
general remarks, 61–8
Transcendental analytic, 75–6ff, 139–42
Transcendental deduction
principles, 91–7
of the pure concepts of the understanding, 98ff
of employment of the pure concepts of the understanding, 114–19
transition to, 95–7
Transcendental dialectic, 76–7, 139, 233–466
Book I, 233–58
Book II, 258–466
Appendix: the regulative employment of the ideas of pure reason, 433–48
Transcendental doctrine of elements, 47–466
Transcendental doctrine of judgment, 142–233
Transcendental doctrine of method, 467–543
Transcendental dynamical ideas, 371–3
Transcendental employment of reason, 139
Transcendental hypotheses, 501
Transcendental ideal, 396–402
Transcendental idealism, key to the solution of cosmological dialectic, 355–9
Transcendental ideas, 248–54
sceptical exposition of cosmological questions, 353–5
system of, 255–8
Transcendental illusion, 232–5
pure reason as seat of, 225–31
Transcendental logic, 69–138, 139

and judgment, 141
first division, Transcendental
   analytic, 76–233
second division, Transcendental
   didactic, 233–466
Transcendental mathematical ideas,
   solution, 374–6
Transcendental philosophy, 43–4,
   539
Transcendental place, 220, 222
Transcendental problems of pure
   reason, 348–52
Transcendental psychology,
   paralogisms
   second, 277–83
   third, 283–6
   fourth, 286–93
Transcendental reflection, 216, 217
Transcendental schemata *see*
   Schemata
Transcendental synthesis of
   imagination, 110–11
Transcendental topic, 220ff
Truth
   defined, 73–4
   logic of, 139
   and schemata, 147–8

Unconditioned, 17, 249–50, 417
Understanding (*Verstand*), 45, 69, 71,
   98
   concepts of, 86, 101–3
   faculty of judgment, 79
   logical function, 79–83
   logical use, 78–9

relation to objects in general,
   130–7
schemata, 147
system of the principles of the pure
   understanding, 7, 153–205
various accounts, 136
see also Logic
Unity
   category of quantity, 85, 89–90
   of the condition of all objects of
      thought, 256
   of intuition, 105n
   of the manifold, 98–9
   of the series of the conditions, 256
   of the thinking subject, 256
   of the understanding, 252
   of the universe, 188n
   rational, 251
Universal law of natural necessity,
   and causality, 379–81
Universal natural necessity, and
   cosmological idea of freedom,
   381–90
Universality, 249
   in quality of judgments, 80
Universe, ignorance, 398n

Wolff, Christian
   and knowledge, 62
   system of philosophy, 24, 223, 534,
      544

Zeno of Elea, reprimanded by Plato,
   361–2

PHILOSOPHY AND RELIGIOUS WRITING
IN EVERYMAN

SAGAS AND OLD ENGLISH LITERATURE IN EVERYMAN

Egils Saga
translated by Christine Fell
A gripping story of Viking exploits in Iceland, Norway and Britain
£4.99

Edda
SNORRI STURLUSON
The first complete English translation of this important Icelandic text
£5.99

Anglo-Saxon Prose
edited by Michael Swanton
Popular tales of Anglo-Saxon England, written by kings, scribes and saints
£4.99

The Fljotsdale Saga and The Droplaugarsons
translated by Eleanor Howarth *and* Jean Young
A brilliant portrayal of life and times in medieval Iceland
£3.99

Anglo-Saxon Poetry
translated by S. A. J. Bradley
An anthology of prose translations covering most of the surviving poetry of early medieval literature
£6.99

Fergus of Galloway: Knight of King Arthur
GUILLAME LE CLERC
translated by D. D. R. Owen
Essential reading for students of Arthurian romance
£3.99

Three Arthurian Romances from Medieval France
translated and edited by Ross G. Arthur
Caradoc, The Knight with the Sword *and* The Perilous Graveyard – *poems of the Middle Ages for modern readers*
£5.99

All books are available from your local bookshop or direct from:
Littlehampton Book Services Cash Sales, 14 Eldon Way, Lineside Estate,
Littlehampton, West Sussex BN17 7HE (*prices are subject to change*)

To order any of the books, please enclose a cheque (in sterling) made payable to
Littlehampton Book Services, or phone your order through with credit card details (Access,
Visa or Mastercard) on 01903 721596 (24 hour answering service) stating card number
and expiry date. (*Please add £1.25 for package and postage to the total of your order.*)

In the USA, for further information and a complete catalogue call 1-800-526-2778

ESSAYS, CRITICISM AND HISTORY
IN EVERYMAN

Essays and Poems
R. L. STEVENSON
Stevenson's hidden treasures
£4.99

The Rights of Man
THOMAS PAINE
*One of the great masterpieces
of English radicalism*
£4.99

Speeches and Letters
ABRAHAM LINCOLN
*A key document of the American
Civil War*
£5.99

Essays
FRANCIS BACON
*An excellent introduction to
Bacon's incisive wit and moral
outlook*
£4.99

Biographia Literaria
SAMUEL TAYLOR COLERIDGE
*A masterpiece of criticism,
marrying the study of literature
with philosophy*
£4.99

Selected Writings
JOHN RUSKIN
'An excellent selection'
The Guardian
£7.99

**Chesterton on Dickens:
Criticisms and Appreciations**
G. K. CHESTERTON
*A landmark in Dickens criticism,
rarely surpassed*
£4.99

History of His Own Time
BISHOP GILBERT BURNET
*A highly readable contemporary
account of the Glorious Revolution
of 1688*
£7.99

**Memoirs of the Life of Colonel
Hutchinson**
LUCY HUTCHINSON
*Biography by his wife of a man who
signed Charles I's death warrant*
£6.99

**Puritanism and Liberty: Being
the Army Debates (1647-49)
from the Clarke Manuscripts**
edited by A. S. P. Woodhouse
*A fascinating revelation of Puritan
minds in action*
£7.99

**The Embassy to Constantinople
and Other Writings**
LIUDPRAND OF CREMONA
*An insider's view of political
machinations in medieval Europe*
£5.99

POETRY
IN EVERYMAN

Amorous Rites: Elizabethan Erotic Verse
edited by Sandra Clark
Erotic and often comic poems dealing with myths of transformation and erotic interaction between humans and gods
£4.99

Selected Poems
JOHN KEATS
An excellent selection of the poetry of one of the principal figures of the Romantic movement
£6.99

Poems and Prose
CHRISTINA ROSSETTI
A new collection of her writings, poetry and prose, marking the centenary of her death
£5.99

Poems and Prose
P. B. SHELLEY
The essential Shelley in one volume
£5.99

Silver Poets of the Sixteenth Century
edited by Douglas Brooks-Davies
An exciting and comprehensive collection
£6.99

Complete English Poems
JOHN DONNE
The father of metaphysical verse in this highly-acclaimed collection
£6.99

Complete English Poems, Of Education, Areopagitica
JOHN MILTON
An excellent introduction to Milton's poetry and prose
£6.99

Women Romantic Poets 1780–1830: An Anthology
edited by Jennifer Breen
Hidden talent from the Romantic era rediscovered
£5.99

Selected Poems
D. H. LAWRENCE
An authoritative selection spanning the whole of Lawrence's literary career
£4.99

The Poems
W. B. YEATS
Ireland's greatest lyric poet surveyed in this ground-breaking edition
£7.99

CLASSIC FICTION
IN EVERYMAN

**The Impressions of
Theophrastus Such**
GEORGE ELIOT
*An amusing collection of character
sketches, and the only paperback
edition available*
£5.99

Frankenstein
MARY SHELLEY
*A masterpiece of Gothic terror in
its original 1818 version*
£3.99

East Lynne
MRS HENRY WOOD
*A classic tale of melodrama,
murder and mystery*
£7.99

**Holiday Romance and
Other Writings for Children**
CHARLES DICKENS
*Dickens's works for children,
including 'The Life of Our Lord'
and 'A Child's History of England',
with original illustrations*
£5.99

The Ebb-Tide
R. L. STEVENSON
*A compelling study of ordinary
people in extreme circumstances*
£4.99

The Three Impostors
ARTHUR MACHEN
*The only edition available
of this cult thriller*
£4.99

Mister Johnson
JOYCE CARY
*The only edition available of this
amusing but disturbing twentieth-
century tale*
£5.99

The Jungle Book
RUDYARD KIPLING
*The classic adventures of Mowgli
and his friends*
£3.99

Glenarvon
LADY CAROLINE LAMB
*The only edition available of the
novel which throws light on the
greatest scandal of the early nine-
teenth century – the infatuation of
Caroline Lamb with Lord Byron*
£6.99

**Twenty Thousand Leagues
Under the Sea**
JULES VERNE
*Scientific fact combines with
fantasy in this prophetic tale
of underwater adventure*
£4.99

All books are available from your local bookshop or direct from:
Littlehampton Book Services Cash Sales, 14 Eldon Way, Lineside Estate,
Littlehampton, West Sussex BN17 7HE *(prices are subject to change)*

To order any of the books, please enclose a cheque (in sterling) made payable to
Littlehampton Book Services, or phone your order through with credit card details (Access,
Visa or Mastercard) on 01903 721596 (24 hour answering service) stating card number
and expiry date. *(Please add £1.25 for package and postage to the total of your order.)*

In the USA, for further information and a complete catalogue call 1-800-526-2778

MEDIEVAL LITERATURE
IN EVERYMAN

The Canterbury Tales
GEOFFREY CHAUCER
The complete medieval text with translations
£4.99

The Vision of Piers Plowman
WILLIAM LANGLAND
edited by A. V. C. Schmidt
The only complete edition of the B-Text available
£6.99

Sir Gawain and the Green Knight, Pearl, Cleanness, Patience
edited by J. J. Anderson
Four major English medieval poems in one volume
£5.99

Arthurian Romances
CHRÉTIEN DE TROYES
translated by D. D. R. Owen
Classic tales from the father of Arthurian romance
£5.99

Everyman and Medieval Miracle Plays
edited by A. C. Cawley
A fully representative selection from the major play cycles
£4.99

Anglo-Saxon Poetry
edited by S. A. J. Bradley
An anthology of prose translations covering most of the surviving poetry of early medieval literature
£6.99

Six Middle English Romances
edited by Maldwyn Mills
Tales of heroism and piety
£4.99

Ywain and Gawain, Sir Percyvell of Gales, The Anturs of Arther
edited by Maldwyn Mills
Three Middle English romances portraying the adventures of Gawain
£5.99

The Birth of Romance: An Anthology
translated by Judith Weiss
The first-ever English translation of fascinating Anglo-Norman romances
£4.99

The Piers Plowman Tradition
edited by Helen Barr
Four medieval poems of political and religious dissent – available together for the first time
£5.99

All books are available from your local bookshop or direct from:
Littlehampton Book Services Cash Sales, 14 Eldon Way, Lineside Estate,
Littlehampton, West Sussex BN17 7HE (*prices are subject to change*)

To order any of the books, please enclose a cheque (in sterling) made payable to
Littlehampton Book Services, or phone your order through with credit card details (Access,
Visa or Mastercard) on 01903 721596 (24 hour answering service) stating card number
and expiry date. (*Please add £1.25 for package and postage to the total of your order.*)

In the USA, for further information and a complete catalogue call 1-800-526-2778